"For whom did Christ die? This volume makes a fresh and impressively comprehensive case for definite atonement as the answer true to Scripture. It shows convincingly, through multi-authored contributions, (1) that the issues of the extent of the atonement and its nature cannot be separated—penal substitution, at the heart of why Christ had to die, stands or falls with definite atonement; and (2) how definite atonement alone provides for a gospel offer of salvation from sin that is genuinely free. In engaging various opposing views on this much-disputed topic, the editors seek to do so in a constructive and irenic spirit, an effort in which they and the other authors have succeeded admirably."

Richard B. Gaffin, Jr., Professor of Biblical and Systematic Theology, Emeritus, Westminster Theological Seminary

"This book is formidable and persuasive. Those familiar with the terrain will recognize that the editors know exactly the key issues and figures in this debate. And none of the authors who follow disappoint. The tone is calm and courteous, the scholarship rigorous and relentless, the argument clear and compelling. This penetrating discussion takes into account the major modern academic criticisms of definite atonement (Barth, the Torrances, Armstrong, Kendall, and others) as well as more popular critiques (Clifford, Driscoll and Breshears). An impressive team of scholars adorns this subject and aims to help Christians toward a deeper gratitude to God for his grace, a greater assurance of salvation, a sweeter fellowship with Christ, stronger affections in their worship of him, more love for people and superior courage and sacrifice in witness and service, and indeed to propel us into the global work of missions with compassion and confidence."

Ligon Duncan, Chancellor and John E. Richards Professor of Systematic and Historical Theology, Reformed Theological Seminary

"Whether you are sympathetic to or suspicious of definite atonement, this book will surprise you. Here are historical details, exegetical links, theological observations, and pastoral perspectives that are fresh and fascinating, even though there is also plenty that will prove controversial. *From Heaven He Came and Sought Her* offers the fullest and most nuanced treatment of definite atonement I know, and will richly add to the substance and quality of future conversations about the intent of the atonement. Whether you think that you agree or disagree with the authors, wrestling with these essays is well worth your time."

Kelly M. Kapic, Professor of Theological Studies, Covenant College

FROM HEAVEN HE CAME

AND SOUGHT HER

FROM HEAVEN HE CAME *and* SOUGHT HER

DEFINITE ATONEMENT
in HISTORICAL, BIBLICAL,
THEOLOGICAL, *and*
PASTORAL PERSPECTIVE

Edited by DAVID GIBSON & JONATHAN GIBSON

Foreword by J. I. PACKER

WHEATON, ILLINOIS

From Heaven He Came and Sought Her:
Definite Atonement in Historical, Biblical, Theological, and Pastoral Perspective

Copyright © 2013 by David Gibson and Jonathan Gibson

Published by Crossway
      1300 Crescent Street
      Wheaton, Illinois 60187

Cover design: Dual Identity, inc.

Cover image: The Bridgeman Art Library

First printing 2013

Printed in the United States of America

Unless otherwise indicated, Scripture quotations are from the ESV® Bible (*The Holy Bible, English Standard Version®*), copyright © 2001 by Crossway. 2011 Text Edition. Used by permission. All rights reserved.

Scripture references marked NIV are taken from *The Holy Bible, New International Version®*, NIV®. Copyright © 1973, 1978, 1984, 2011 by Biblica, Inc.™ Used by permission. All rights reserved worldwide.

Scripture references marked NRSV are from *The New Revised Standard Version*. Copyright © 1989 by the Division of Christian Education of the National Council of the Churches of Christ in the U.S.A. Published by Thomas Nelson, Inc. Used by permission of the National Council of the Churches of Christ in the U.S.A.

Scripture references marked NKJV are from *The New King James Version*. Copyright © 1982, Thomas Nelson, Inc. Used by permission.

Scripture quotations marked KJV are from the *King James Version* of the Bible.

The Scripture quotation marked HCSB has been taken from *The Holman Christian Standard Bible®*. Copyright © 1999, 2000, 2002, 2003 by Holman Bible Publishers. Used by permission.

The Scripture reference marked NEB is from *The New English Bible* © The Delegates of the Oxford University Press and The Syndics of the Cambridge University Press, 1961, 1970.

Scripture quotations marked AT are the author's translation.

All emphases in Scripture quotations have been added by the authors.

Hardcover ISBN: 978-1-4335-1276-6
PDF ISBN: 978-1-4335-1277-3
Mobipocket ISBN: 978-1-4335-1278-0
ePub ISBN: 978-1-4335-2402-8

Library of Congress Cataloging-in-Publication Data

From heaven he came and sought her : definite atonement in historical, biblical, theological, and pastoral perspective / edited by David Gibson and Jonathan Gibson ; foreword by J.I. Packer.
     pages   cm
    Includes bibliographical references and index.
    ISBN 978-1-4335-1276-6 (hc)
    1. Atonement—Reformed Church. 2. Reformed Church—Doctrines. I. Gibson, David, 1975–
II. Gibson, Jonathan, 1977–
BT267.F76   2013
234'.5—dc23   2013011771

Crossway is a publishing ministry of Good News Publishers.

SH   23 22 21 20 19 18 17 16 15 14
15 14 13 12 11 10 9 8 7 6 5 4 3 2

The church's one foundation
is Jesus Christ her Lord;
she is his new creation
by water and the Word.
From heaven he came and sought her
to be his holy bride;
with his own blood he bought her,
and for her life he died.

Samuel J. Stone (1839–1900)

Contents

Foreword

It has been truly said that if you want to survey the full substance of the church's faith you should go to its hymns, just as to appreciate the fullness of Old Testament faith you must immerse yourself in the Psalter. It is supremely from the hymns that you learn the specifics, not only of the church's doctrinal assertions but also of the intimacy of the Father and of the Son into which the Holy Spirit leads believers. The contributors to this volume evidently agree, and ask in effect that their essays be read as elucidations of what is said about the loving action of the Lord Jesus Christ in the verse of the hymn that they have taken as their epigraph:

> From heaven he came and sought her
> to be his holy bride;
> with his own blood he bought her,
> and for her life he died.

In spelling out the Savior's loving initiative and achievement in these biblically warranted terms, the essayists contend, more or less explicitly, for the book's overall thesis, namely, that as the Reformed faith and its pastoral corollaries is the true intellectual mainstream of Christianity, so the belief in definite, particular, and sovereignly effectual redemption—which the above lines express—is its true intellectual center. Their wide-ranging demonstrations that this is the only genuinely coherent way of integrating all the biblical data about Jesus become increasingly impressive when argued as painstakingly against alternatives as is done here.

I count it an honor to be asked to supply a foreword to this massive product of exact and well-informed scholarship. The purpose of a foreword, as I understand it, is to indicate what readers will find in the book and to tune them in on the appropriate wavelength for appreciating it, and this particular request reminds me forcibly of a similar occasion in the past when I was tasked with a comparable assignment. More than half a century ago, in the days of its youth, the Banner of Truth asked me to compose an introductory essay for a reprint of John Owen's 1648 classic, *Salus Electorum, Sanguis Jesu: Or The Death of Death in the Death of Christ*. I remember feeling this to be a significant request, since, on the one hand, many, I knew, starting with Owen himself, saw this as a landmark composition (in fact, it was the first of several that Owen produced in the course of his ministry), and, on the other hand, it gave me an opportunity to nail my own Reformed colors to the mast, so to speak, and commend Owen's reasoning, as one who had himself benefited greatly from it. The piece I then wrote, explaining and affirming the essence of Owen's position, made an impact that surprised me; I am glad to be able to say at this time that I see nothing in it that needs to be modified or withdrawn in the light of more recent work by myself or others, and I am happy that it should still stand as part of my announced identity in Christ. Since then, to be sure, academic exploration of seventeenth-century Puritan thought has become a busy-bee cottage industry, some of which has contributed to parts of this book. Now the wheel has come full circle, and once more I am asked to introduce a volume on the reconciling death of Christ, which, in my estimation, with God's blessing, may itself have landmark significance in furthering what John Gill, over two centuries ago, called "the cause of God and truth." I am very happy to do this.

The heart of Reformed Christianity is its Trinitarian Christocentrism, expressed manwardly in evangelistic and pastoral proclamation attuned to human need, according to Christ's Great Commission, and Godwardly in the worshipful offering, both corporately and individually, of responsive praise, prayer, thanksgiving, and song. Within this two-way street of communion with God and service of God, the sustained personal presence of the crucified, risen, reigning, and returning Lord with his people, and his constant personal address through Scripture heard, read, and preached, both to those who are his and to those who are not yet his, are integral and indeed central. Since the seventeenth century, the relational bond into which the Father through the Son draws sinners has been labeled the *covenant of grace*, and has been seen as undergirded by a prior plan and bond between the Father and the Son, which has been labeled the *covenant of redemption*. Both are witnessed to widely in Scripture, implicitly as well as explicitly, the fullest account of the covenant of grace (the new and eternal covenant) being found in the letter to the Hebrews, and the key evidence on the covenant of redemption (Christ's mediatorial agenda, set by the Father) being contained in John's Gospel. In this understanding of Christianity, Christ's achievement by his cross of the corporate redemption of the whole church—past, present, and future—as the Holy Three know and love it, and thereby the individual redemption of everyone whom the Father has given to the Son to save, is both the mountaintop of glory, in the primary sense of God putting himself fully on display, and the wellspring of glory, in both the secondary sense of the spur to endless doxology and the tertiary sense of divine action to glorify the redeemed in, with, and through Christ, so that they bear his image and likeness in a full sense. Such is the Christianity that is brought into focus by this fine book.

Unhappily, appreciation of Reformed Christianity in its own terms, at least in the English-speaking world, has long been hindered by a habit, formed in conflict with Arminian revisionism, of calling definite redemption *limited atonement*. This habit seems to have been canonized about a century ago, when the mnemonic TULIP came to be used as a summary of what is supposed to make Reformed Christianity into what it essentially is. In fact, the mnemonic covers the five anti-Arminian theses that the Synod of Dordt affirmed in 1619 to counter the Arminian revisionist agenda. Limited atonement is at the center of TULIP, flanked by Total depravity and Unconditional election on one side, and Irresistible grace and Perseverance of the saints on the other. Now, it is true that definite redemption is central to the Reformed understanding of the gospel and that *atonement*, a word meaning *reconciliation*, is an acceptable alternative for *redemption*; but *limited* is an inappropriate emphasis that actually sounds menacing. It is as if Reformed Christians have a primary concern to announce that there are people whom Christ did not die to save, whom therefore it is pointless to invite to turn from sin and trust him as Savior. Were it so, the logic of Reformed pastoral practice would seem to be: comprehensive evangelistic invitations to ordinary audiences should not be issued indiscriminately. This is not the place to argue that thus to restrict making what is called "the well-meant offer of Christ," in preaching and personal witness and counseling, is false to the biblical Christ, to the apostle Paul, and to the practice of history's most outstanding Reformed evangelists (take George Whitefield, Charles Spurgeon, and Asahel Nettleton, for starters), and thus is simply and sadly wrong; readers of this book will soon see that. But perhaps I may say that in my view it is time to lay TULIP to rest, since its middle item does so much more harm than good.

In sum now, I give this book top marks for its range of solid scholarship, cogency of argument, warmth of style, and zeal for the true glory of God—I recommend it most highly. For it, and for the biblical faith it lays out, to the Son of God, our Redeemer-Lord, with the Father and the Spirit, be hearty adoration and thanks. Amen.

J. I. Packer

Vancouver

Preface

We did not grow up believing in definite atonement. We were privileged to be raised in a devout church tradition that nurtured us in Christ, but our love of the doctrine is not the result of an inherited Reformed hermeneutic that has shaped the only world we have ever known. Nor did we come to believe in definite atonement in the same way. One of us studied theology in three different British universities and has specialized in the history of biblical interpretation; the other studied at Moore Theological College, Sydney, and pursued doctoral research in Hebrew studies at a British university. By separate routes, and at different times, we have come to see in the Scriptures that Christ's death for his people does not contradict his mandate to proclaim the gospel to the world.

This book is offered with the prayer that it will paint a compelling picture of the beauty and power of definite atonement, and so revitalize confidence in this profoundly biblical understanding of the cross of Christ. Definite atonement is beautiful because it tells the story of the Warrior-Son who comes to earth to slay his enemy and rescue his Father's people. He is the Good Shepherd who lays down his life for his sheep, a loving Bridegroom who gives himself for his bride, and a victorious King who lavishes the spoils of his conquest on the citizens of his realm. Definite atonement is powerful because it displays the glory of divine initiative, accomplishment, application, and consummation in the work of salvation. The Father sent the Son, who bore our sins in his body on the tree, and the Spirit has sealed our adoption and guarantees our inheritance in the kingdom of light. The doctrine inhabits the poetic drama and the didactic propositions of Scripture. And not only is definite atonement biblical, it comes to us with a textured history, theological integrity, and pastoral riches.

Yet joyful confidence in definite atonement is often lacking. Even for those committed to Reformed theology, this doctrine can sometimes be regarded as the embarrassing relative included in the household more out of duty than delight. But there is no need for any awkwardness. It belongs at the heart of family life. This volume aims to make this plain by providing a depth and breadth of perspective usually only assembled from many disparate sources.

Some who open these pages will be suspicious of definite atonement and will read either convinced that it is wrong or bewildered why some believe that it is true. The essays are written irenically. Dissenting voices are engaged firmly, but there is no shrillness of tone in our replies. There is no animosity of content in the critique of individuals and the movements associated with them. While we do not refer to our position as "Calvinist" (for reasons we will explain), John Newton's designation should be allowed to stand as a fair criticism of some who represent the theology we wish to defend:

> And I am afraid there are Calvinists, who, while they account it a proof of their humility that they are willing in words to debase the creature, and to give all the glory of salvation to the Lord, yet know not what manner of spirit they are of. Whatever it be that makes us trust in ourselves that we are comparatively wise or good, so as to treat those with contempt who do not subscribe to our doctrines, or follow our party, is a proof and fruit of a self-righteous spirit. Self-righteousness can feed upon doctrines, as well as upon works; and a man may have the heart of a Pharisee, while his head is stored with orthodox notions of the unworthiness of the creature and the riches of free grace. Yea, I would add, the best of men are not wholly free from this leaven; and therefore are too apt to be pleased with such representations as hold up our adversaries to ridicule, and by consequence flatter our own superior judgments. Controversies, for the most part, are so managed as to indulge rather than to repress this wrong disposition; and therefore, generally speaking, they are productive of little good. They provoke those whom they should convince, and puff up those whom they should edify.[1]

Precisely because it is articulating the gospel of God, this volume seeks to do away with all self-righteousness on the part of those who love definite atonement as they teach it for the good of the church. It is an invitation to explore the historical foundations of the doctrine and to think afresh about the vitality of its exegetical, theological, and pastoral expressions. Perhaps it is fair to ask for as much charity on the part of the reader as each writer has offered.

David Gibson, Old Aberdeen
Jonathan Gibson, Cambridge
Epiphany 2013

---

[1] John Newton, "On Controversy," in *The Works of John Newton*, 6 vols. (New York: Williams & Whiting, 1810), 1:245.

Acknowledgments

This book, more than six years in the making, would not have happened without several people who helped cultivate the project from idea to reality. We owe them an incalculable debt of gratitude.

Justin Taylor at Crossway was our first point of contact as we wondered whether the project could work. He honed our multivolume enthusiasm into the much more realistic undertaking you now hold in your hands. We have been indebted to Justin at each step of the way, as well as to Jill Carter and Allan Fisher for their oversight. It was a delight to work with the Crossway team. Our thanks to Angie Cheatham, Amy Kruis, Janni Firestone, Maureen Magnussen, and especially to Bill Deckard for his patience and editorial skills.

Garry Williams agreed to act as a theological reader, then became a contributor, and each essay is the better for his many years of reflection on the atonement in all its aspects. Tom Schreiner encouraged us enormously with his help in the early stages, and we are grateful as well to Raymond Blacketer, Henri Blocher, Jonathan Moore, Lee Gatiss, Michael Horton, Peter Orr, and Ian Hamilton, who each provided essential assistance. Kylie Thomas kindly checked references of seventeenth-century French works in the Cambridge University Library, as well as providing excellent editorial help. Tom McCall and Mark Thompson interacted critically with some of the material in a most gracious manner. Thanks are also due to Aaron Denlinger, Mark Earngey, John Ferguson, Will Lind, Peter Matthess, Richard Muller, Paul Reed, David Schrock, and Edwin Tay.

Closer to home, Peter Dickson at Trinity Church, Aberdeen, has been as fine an example and friend as one could hope for. At various stages he willingly took on more work to allow David time to read and write and edit.

Jonathan is indebted to his mentor and friend, Charles De Kiewit, Pastor of Central Baptist Church in Pretoria, South Africa, for first introducing him to Reformed theology.

Our wives, Angela and Jacqueline, have been a constant source of encouragement. They tolerated our late nights and indulged our frequent conversations, and the completed book is as much due to their patience, grace, and humor as anything else. We are grateful to them beyond words.

We dedicate our labors with this volume to our children—Archie, Ella, Samuel, Lily, and Benjamin, respectively. As we write, they are too little to understand all the glorious depths of Christ's atoning death. But enfolded in covenant promise, they have had its beauty proclaimed to them at their baptisms and our prayer is that they will never remember a day when they did not know the love of the Savior.

> For you, little child, Jesus Christ has come, he has fought, he has suffered. For you he entered the shadow of Gethsemane and the horror of Calvary. For you he uttered the cry, "It is finished!" For you he rose from the dead and ascended into heaven and there he intercedes—for you, little child, even though you do not know it. But in this way the word of the Gospel becomes true. "We love him, because he first loved us."
>
> —French Reformed Baptismal Liturgy

Abbreviations

AACM	*Ad Acta Colloquii Montisbelgardensis Tubingae edita Theodori Bezae responsio, Tubingae edita,* 2 vols. (Geneva: J. le Preuz, 1587–1588)
BAGD	W. Bauer, *A Greek-English Lexicon of the New Testament and Other Early Christian Literature,* ed. W. F. Arndt, F. W. Gingrich, and F. W. Danker (Chicago: University of Chicago, 1979)
BDB	F. Brown, S. R. Driver, and C. A. Briggs, *Hebrew and English Lexicon of the Old Testament* (Oxford: Oxford University Press, 1929)
BECNT	Baker Exegetical Commentary on the New Testament
BSac	*Bibliotheca Sacra*
BTP	Moïse Amyraut, *Brief Traitté de la Predestination et de ses principales dépendances* (Saumur, France: Jean Lesnier & Isaac Debordes, 1634; 2nd ed. revised and corrected, Saumur, France: Isaac Debordes, 1658)
CAH	Brian G. Armstrong, *Calvinism and the Amyraut Heresy: Protestant Scholasticism and Humanism in Seventeenth-Century France* (Madison: University of Wisconsin Press, 1969; repr. Eugene, OR: Wipf & Stock, 2004)
CD	Karl Barth, *Church Dogmatics,* ed. G. W. Bromiley and T. F. Torrance, 14 vols. (Edinburgh: T. & T. Clark, 1956–1975)
CO	*Ioannis Calvini Opera quae supersunt omnia,* ed. J. W. Baum, A. E. Cunitz, and E. Reuss, 59 vols. (Braunschweig, Germany: Schwetschke, 1863–1900)
CNTC	Calvin's New Testament Commentaries, ed. David W. Torrance and Thomas F. Torrance (various translators), 12 vols. (Grand Rapids, MI: Eerdmans, 1959–1972)
CRT	Richard A. Muller, *Calvin and the Reformed Tradition: On the Work of Christ and the Order of Salvation* (Grand Rapids, MI: Baker Academic, 2012)
CTCT	Ian McPhee, "Conserver or Transformer of Calvin's Theology? A Study of the Origins and Development of Theodore Beza's Thought, 1550–1570" (doctoral thesis, University of Cambridge, 1979)
CTJ	*Calvin Theological Journal*
CTS	Calvin Translation Society
EQ	*Evangelical Quarterly*

FRR	Jeffrey Mallinson, *Faith, Reason, and Revelation in Theodore Beza 1519–1605* (Oxford: Oxford University Press, 2003)
ICC	International Critical Commentary
JBL	*Journal of Biblical Literature*
JETS	*Journal of the Evangelical Theological Society*
JTS	*Journal of Theological Studies*
KD	Karl Barth, *Die kirchliche Dogmatik* (Munich: Chr. Kaiser, 1932; and Zürich: Evangelischer Verlag Zürich, 1938–1967)
LXX	Septuagint
MT	Masoretic Text
NICNT	New International Commentary on the New Testament
NICOT	New International Commentary on the Old Testament
NIGTC	New International Greek Testament Commentary
NPNF[1]	*Nicene and Post-Nicene Fathers*, A Select Library of the Christian Church, ed. Philip Schaff, First Series, 14 vols. (repr. Peabody, MA: Hendrickson, 1994)
NPNF[2]	*Nicene and Post-Nicene Fathers*, A Select Library of the Christian Church, ed. Philip Schaff and Henry Wace, Second Series, 14 vols. (repr. Peabody, MA: Hendrickson, 1994)
NSBT	New Studies in Biblical Theology
NTS	*New Testament Studies*
PG	Patrologia graeca, ed. J.-P. Migne et al. (Paris: Centre for Patristic Publications, 1857–1886)
PL	Patrologia latina, ed. J.-P. Migne et al. (Paris: Centre for Patristic Publications, 1878–1890)
PNTC	Pillar New Testament Commentary
PRRD	Richard A. Muller, *Post-Reformation Reformed Dogmatics*, 4 vols., vols. 1–2, 2nd ed. (Grand Rapids, MI: Baker Academic, 2003)
RTR	*Reformed Theological Review*
SBET	*Scottish Bulletin of Evangelical Theology*
SJT	*Scottish Journal of Theology*
TB	*Tyndale Bulletin*
TDNT	*Theological Dictionary of the New Testament*, ed. Gerhard Kittel (Grand Rapids, MI: Eerdmans: 1965)
TOTC	Tyndale Old Testament Commentaries
TT	Theodore Beza, *Tractationes Theologiae*
WBC	Word Biblical Commentary
WCF	Westminster Confession of Faith
WTJ	*Westminster Theological Journal*

Contributors

Raymond A. Blacketer is lead pastor at First Cutlerville Christian Reformed Church, Grand Rapids, Michigan. He wrote his PhD in Historical Theology under the mentorship of Richard A. Muller at Calvin Theological Seminary. He has written articles on John Calvin, William Perkins, and Henry Ainsworth. He is currently working on *The Reformation Commentary on Scripture. Volume 3: Exodus–Deuteronomy* (Downers Grove, IL: InterVarsity Press, forthcoming). His work on Calvin includes "No Escape by Deception: Calvin's Exegesis of Lies and Liars in the Old Testament," *Reformation and Renaissance Review* 10.3 (2008): 267–89, and *The School of God. Pedagogy and Rhetoric in Calvin's Interpretation of Deuteronomy*, Studies in Early Modern Religious Reforms 3 (Dordrecht, Netherlands: Springer, 2006).

Henri A. G. Blocher was Gunter H. Knoedler Professor of Systematic Theology, Wheaton College Graduate School of Biblical and Theological Studies, and is *doyen honoraire* at the Faculté Libre de Théologie Évangélique in Vaux-sur-Seine, France, where he was formerly Professor of Systematic Theology and where he still teaches some courses. He was also President of the Fellowship of European Evangelical Theologians. He has contributed articles to many journals and multiauthor volumes. His books in English include *Original Sin: Illuminating the Riddle* (Leicester, UK: Apollos, 1997); *Evil and the Cross* (Leicester, UK: Apollos, 1994); *In the Beginning: The Opening Chapters of Genesis* (Leicester, UK: Inter-Varsity Press, 1984).

Amar Djaballah is Professor of Biblical Studies and Dean of the Faculté de Théologie Évangélique (affiliated with Acadia University) in Montréal, Canada. Djaballah received his MTh from the Faculté Libre de Théologie Évangélique, Vaux-sur-Seine, and his PhD from l'Université Paris I-Panthéon Sorbonne. He is the author of numerous books and articles in French, including a New Testament Greek grammar. Djaballah has written a book on the parables in French (*Les paraboles aujourd'hui*), which is soon to appear in English (Eerdmans, forthcoming), a short English monograph on Islam, and a forthcoming volume on hermeneutics published by les Éditions Excelsis. He is also the author of "Calvin and the Calvinists: An Examination of Some Recent Views," *Reformation Canada* 5.1 (1982): 7–20.

Sinclair B. Ferguson, formerly Senior Minister of First Presbyterian Church, Columbia, South Carolina, serves as Professor of Systematic Theology at Redeemer Theological Seminary, as well as Distinguished Visiting Professor at Westminster Theological Seminary, Philadelphia. A graduate of the University of Aberdeen, he has contributed to several multiauthor volumes, including *The New Dictionary of Theology* (Leicester, UK: Inter-Varsity Press, 1998) and *The New Bible Commentary* (Leicester, UK: Inter-Varsity Press, 1994). His own works include *By Grace Alone: How the Grace of God Amazes Me* (Lake Mary, FL: Reformation Trust, 2010); *In Christ Alone: Living the Gospel-Centered Life* (Lake Mary, FL: Reformation Trust, 2007); and *The Holy Spirit* (Leicester, UK: Inter-Varsity Press, 1997).

Lee Gatiss is the Director of Church Society, and Adjunct Lecturer in Church History at Wales Evangelical School of Theology. He has studied history and theology at Oxford and Cambridge, and has a ThM in Historical and Systematic Theology from Westminster Theological Seminary, Philadelphia. He trained for ministry at Oak Hill Theological College, London, and has served in several Anglican churches. His most recent publications include a new two-volume annotated edition of *The Sermons of George Whitefield* (Wheaton, IL: Crossway, 2012); *For Us and for Our Salvation: 'Limited Atonement' in the Bible, Doctrine, History, and Ministry* (London: Latimer Trust, 2012); and *The True Profession of the Gospel: Augustus Toplady and Reclaiming Our Reformed Foundations* (London: Latimer Trust, 2010). He is one of the editors of the multivolume critical edition of *The Acts of the Synod of Dordt 1618/19* (Göttingen, Germany: Vandenhoeck & Ruprecht, forthcoming).

David Gibson is ordained in the International Presbyterian Church and a minister of Trinity Church, Aberdeen, Scotland. He studied theology at Nottingham University and King's College London, and completed a doctorate in Historical and Systematic Theology at the University of Aberdeen. He has contributed to *"But My Words Will Never Pass Away": The Enduring Authority of the Christian Scriptures*, ed. D. A. Carson, 2 vols. (Grand Rapids, MI: Eerdmans, forthcoming), is the author of *Reading the Decree: Exegesis, Election and Christology in Calvin and Barth* (London/New York: T. & T. Clark, 2009), and coedited, with Daniel Strange, *Engaging with Barth: Contemporary Evangelical Critiques* (Nottingham, UK: Apollos, 2008; New York: T. & T. Clark, 2009).

Jonathan Gibson is a PhD candidate in Hebrew Studies at Cambridge University. He studied for a Bachelor of Science degree at the University of Ulster, Jordanstown, Northern Ireland, and then worked as a physiotherapist for several years, before completing a Bachelor of Divinity degree at Moore Theological College, Sydney, Australia. He is currently researching inner-biblical exegesis within the Hebrew Bible, with specific reference to the book of Malachi. He is the author of "'Cutting off "Kith and Kin," "Er and Onan"?': Interpreting an Obscure Phrase in Malachi 2:12," *JBL* (forthcoming); "Obadiah" in the *NIV Proclamation Bible* (London: Hodder & Stoughton, 2013); and "Jonathan Edwards: A Missionary?," *Themelios* 36.3 (2011): 380–402.

Matthew S. Harmon is Professor of New Testament Studies at Grace College and Theological Seminary. In addition to a degree in communications from Ohio University, he holds a Master of Divinity from Trinity Evangelical Divinity School and a PhD from Wheaton College in Biblical Theology. He is the author of *She Must and Shall Go Free: Paul's Isaianic Gospel in Galatians* (Berlin: deGruyter, 2010); "Philippians" in the *NIV Proclamation Bible* (London: Hodder & Stoughton, 2013), and *Philippians, A Mentor Commentary* (Ross-shire, UK: Christian Focus, forthcoming). He contributed numerous articles to *The Baker Illustrated Bible Dictionary*, ed. Tremper Longman III (Grand Rapids, MI: Baker, 2013), and is currently working on *Galatians, Biblical Theology for Christian Proclamation* (Nashville: B&H, forthcoming).

Michael A. G. Haykin is Professor of Church History and Biblical Spirituality at The Southern Baptist Theological Seminary. He received his MRel and ThD from the University of Toronto. He is the author and editor of a number of books in Patristics and English Baptist history, including *Rediscovering the Church Fathers: Who They Were and How They Shaped the*

Church (Wheaton, IL: Crossway, 2011); *"At the Pure Fountain of Thy Word":
Andrew Fuller as an Apologist* (Carlisle, UK: Paternoster, 2004); *The Spirit
of God: The Exegesis of 1 and 2 Corinthians in the Pneumatomachian Controversy of the Fourth Century* (Leiden, Netherlands: Brill, 1994); *One Heart
and One Soul: John Sutcliff of Olney, His Friends, and His Times* (Darlington, UK: Evangelical Press, 1994).

Paul Helm is a teaching fellow at Regent College, Vancouver. He studied at
Worcester College, Oxford University. Recent publications include *Calvin
at the Centre* (Oxford: Oxford University Press, 2009); *Calvin: A Guide for
the Perplexed* (London: Continuum, 2008); and *John Calvin's Ideas* (Oxford:
Oxford University Press, 2004).

David S. Hogg is Associate Dean of Academic Affairs and Associate Profes-
sor of History and Doctrine at Beeson Divinity School, Samford University.
He holds degrees from the University of Toronto; Westminster Theological
Seminary, Philadelphia; and the University of St. Andrews. He has contrib-
uted to a number of edited volumes, including *Great Is Thy Faithfulness?
Reading Lamentations as Sacred Scripture* (Eugene, OR: Pickwick, 2011);
The Lord's Supper, Remembering and Proclaiming Christ until He Comes
(Nashville: B&H Academic, 2010); *The Dictionary of Historical Theology*
(Grand Rapids, MI: Eerdmans, 2000). He has written on Anselm of Canter-
bury in numerous places, but most notably in his *Anselm of Canterbury: The
Beauty of Theology* (Aldershot, UK: Ashgate, 2004).

Robert Letham is Director of Research and Senior Lecturer in Systematic and Historical Theology at Wales Evangelical School of Theology, Adjunct Professor at Westminster Theological Seminary, Philadelphia, and a
Presbyterian minister with twenty-five years' pastoral experience. He has
degrees from the University of Exeter, Westminster Theological Seminary,
Philadelphia, and the University of Aberdeen (PhD). He is the author of
A Christian's Pocket Guide to Baptism (Ross-shire, UK: Christian Focus,
2012); *Union with Christ* (Phillipsburg, NJ: P&R, 2011); *The Westminster
Assembly: Reading Its Theology in Historical Context* (Phillipsburg, NJ:
P&R, 2009); *Through Western Eyes* (Ross-shire, UK: Mentor, 2007); *The
Holy Trinity* (Phillipsburg, NJ: P&R, 2004); *The Lord's Supper* (Phillipsburg,
NJ: P&R, 2001); and *The Work of Christ* (Downers Grove, IL: InterVarsity

Press, 1993). He has contributed chapters to a number of books, including *Shapers of Christian Orthodoxy* (Nottingham, UK: Apollos, 2010).

Donald Macleod is an ordained minister of the Free Church of Scotland. Since 1978 he was Professor of Systematic Theology at the Free Church of Scotland, Edinburgh, until his recent retirement. He graduated MA from the University of Glasgow in 1958, and was awarded an honorary DD from Westminster Theological Seminary, Philadelphia, in 2008. His many books include *Jesus Is Lord: Christology, Yesterday and Today* (Ross-shire, UK: Christian Focus, 2000); *A Faith to Live By* (Ross-shire, UK: Christian Focus, 2000); and *The Person of Christ* (Leicester, UK: Inter-Varsity Press, 1998).

J. Alec Motyer is a retired minister of the Church of England, having served in parishes in Wolverhampton, Bristol, London, and Bournemouth. In between pastoral work, he served as Tutor, Vice-Principal and Principal, respectively, of Tyndale Hall, Clifton Theological College, and Trinity College, Bristol. He was educated at Dublin University and Wycliffe Hall, Oxford, and holds the degrees of BA, MA, BD (Dublin), and DD (Lambeth/Oxford). His most recent publications are *Preaching for Simpletons* (Ross-shire, UK: Christian Focus, 2013); and *Isaiah by the Day: A New Devotional Translation* (Ross-shire, UK: Christian Focus, 2011). He is best known for his commentary *The Prophecy of Isaiah* (Leicester, UK: Inter-Varsity Press, 1993), as well as serving as the series editor for the Old Testament commentaries in the Bible Speaks Today series.

John Piper is founder and teacher of desiringGod.org, and Chancellor of Bethlehem College and Seminary, Minneapolis. He received his BA from Wheaton College, BD from Fuller Theological Seminary, and doctorate in Theology (New Testament) from the University of Munich. He served thirty-three years as Senior Pastor of Bethlehem Baptist Church, Minneapolis. His books include *Desiring God* (Colorado Springs: Multnomah, revised and expanded 2011); *What Jesus Demands from the World* (Wheaton, IL: Crossway, 2006); *God Is the Gospel* (Wheaton, IL: Crossway, 2004); and *Don't Waste Your Life* (Wheaton, IL: Crossway, 2003).

Thomas R. Schreiner is a preaching pastor at Clifton Baptist Church and the James Buchanan Harrison Professor of New Testament Interpretation at The

Southern Baptist Theological Seminary. He received his doctorate in New Testament from Fuller Theological Seminary. He is the author of numerous books, including *The King in His Beauty: A Biblical Theology of the Old and New Testaments* (Grand Rapids, MI: Baker, 2013); *Galatians*, Zondervan Exegetical Commentary on the New Testament (Grand Rapids, MI: Zondervan, 2010); and *New Testament Theology: Magnifying God in Christ* (Grand Rapids, MI: Baker, 2008).

Daniel Strange is Academic Vice-Principal and Tutor in Culture, Religion, and Public Theology at Oak Hill Theological College, London. He received both his BA and PhD from the University of Bristol, England. With Gavin D'Costa and Paul Knitter, he is coauthor of *Only One Way? Three Christian Responses to the Uniqueness of Christ in a Pluralistic World* (London: SCM, 2011); coeditor with David Gibson of *Engaging with Barth: Contemporary Evangelical Critiques* (Nottingham, UK: Apollos, 2008; New York: T. & T. Clark, 2009); and author of *The Possibility of Salvation among the Unevangelized: An Analysis of Inclusivism in Recent Evangelical Theology* (Carlisle, UK: Paternoster, 2001).

Carl R. Trueman is Paul Woolley Professor of Church History at Westminster Theological Seminary, Philadelphia, and pastor of Cornerstone Presbyterian Church (OPC), Ambler, Pennsylvania. He has an MA from the University of Cambridge and a PhD from the University of Aberdeen. Recent publications include *The Creedal Imperative* (Wheaton, IL: Crossway, 2012) and *Histories and Fallacies* (Wheaton, IL: Crossway, 2010).

Stephen J. Wellum is Professor of Christian Theology at The Southern Baptist Theological Seminary, and editor of *The Southern Baptist Journal of Theology*. He received his MDiv and PhD in Systematic Theology from Trinity Evangelical Divinity School. He is coauthor with Peter J. Gentry of *Kingdom through Covenant: A Biblical-Theological Understanding of the Covenants* (Wheaton, IL: Crossway, 2012). In addition to various journal articles, he has contributed chapters to a number of books, including *The Church: Jesus' Covenant Community* (Nashville: B&H Academic, 2013); *Whomever He Wills: A Surprising Display of Sovereign Mercy* (Cape Coral, FL: Founders Press, 2012); *The Deity of Christ* (Wheaton, IL: Crossway, 2011); *Faith Comes by Hearing: A Response to Inclusivism* (Downers Grove,

IL: IVP Academic, 2008); *Believer's Baptism: Sign of the New Covenant in Christ* (Nashville: B&H Academic, 2007); *Reclaiming the Center: Confronting Evangelical Accommodation in Postmodern Times* (Wheaton, IL: Crossway, 2004); and *Beyond the Bounds: Open Theism and the Undermining of Biblical Christianity* (Wheaton, IL: Crossway, 2003).

Garry J. Williams is Director of the John Owen Centre for Theological Study at London Theological Seminary, and Visiting Professor of Historical Theology at Westminster Seminary, Philadelphia. He read theology at Oxford University, where he completed a doctorate on Hugo Grotius's understanding of the atonement. He has published on subjects including the history of evangelicalism and the atonement, and is writing a biblical, historical, and systematic exposition of penal substitutionary atonement.

Paul R. Williamson is Lecturer in Old Testament at Moore Theological College, Sydney. He studied theology at the Irish Baptist College, Belfast, and received his doctorate from Queen's University, Belfast. He is coeditor of *Exploring Exodus* (Nottingham, UK: Inter-Varsity Press, 2008), and author of *Sealed with an Oath: Covenant in God's Unfolding Purposes* (Nottingham, UK: Inter-Varsity Press, 2007). He has contributed articles to the *Dictionary of the Old Testament* series (Downers Grove, IL: InterVarsity Press, 2003–2008).

INTRODUCTION

Sacred Theology and the Reading of the Divine Word

MAPPING THE DOCTRINE OF DEFINITE ATONEMENT

David Gibson and Jonathan Gibson

It is very common for persons, when they find a subject much disputed, especially if it is by those whom they account good men, immediately to conclude that it must be a subject of but little consequence, a mere matter of speculation. Upon such persons religious controversies have a very ill effect: for, finding difficulty attending the coming at the truth, and, at the same time, a disposition to neglect it, and to pursue other things; they readily avail themselves of what appears, to them, a plausible excuse, lay aside the inquiry, and sit down and indulge a spirit of scepticism. . . . But, if all disputed subjects are to be reckoned matters of mere speculation, we shall have nothing of any real use left in religion.[1]

Introduction

The doctrine of definite atonement states that, in the death of Jesus Christ, the triune God intended to achieve the redemption of every person given to the Son by the Father in eternity past, and to apply the accomplishments of his sacrifice to each of them by the Spirit. The death of Christ was intended to win the salvation of God's people alone.

---

[1] Andrew Fuller, *Reply to the Observations of Philanthropos*, in *The Complete Works of the Rev. Andrew Fuller* (London: Henry G. Bohn, 1848), 233b. "Philanthropos" was the pseudonym of Daniel Taylor, a General Baptist theologian, with whom Fuller dialogued over the nature of Christ's atonement. We are grateful to Henri Blocher for this reference.

Definite atonement says something essential about Christ's death, but it does not say everything there is to say. There are many aspects of the atonement which need to be affirmed alongside its definite intent and nature: the sufficiency of Christ's death for all; the free and indiscriminate proclamation of the gospel to all; God's love for the non-elect and his salvific stance toward a fallen world; the atonement's implications for the entire cosmos and not simply the church. Definite atonement does not exhaust the meaning of the cross.

Nevertheless, the essays in this book contend that definite atonement is at the heart of the meaning of the cross. Often referred to as "limited atonement" or "particular redemption," this is a doctrine of the Reformed churches which is cherished as a profound explanation of the death of Christ. By revealing the Trinitarian nature of Christ's cross-work, definite atonement advances a rich explanation of how his sacrificial death has an objective and Godward direction. It displays salvation, in all its parts, as the shared intention and accomplishment of Father, Son, and Spirit. It is definite atonement which shows us that our salvation is a divine achievement, rendering redemption fully accomplished by the payment of sin's penalty on our behalf by our Savior. These points combine to suggest that the doctrine is a fitting and necessary corollary of penal substitutionary atonement.

To tie definite atonement to penal substitution immediately exposes the debate which attends the doctrine. Some within evangelicalism would deny that the nature of the atonement is both penal *and* definite. The explanation offered at the start of this chapter views the atonement through the lens of election and therefore as intended to save a specific set of people; it suggests the atonement is complete as a saving act; and it contends that accomplishment is bound together with application in the divine will. From within and without evangelicalism and Reformed theology, each of these aspects of definite atonement has courted controversy.

Many Christians protest that definite atonement simply flies in the face of the clear teaching of the Bible: "For God so loved the world, that he gave his only Son" (John 3:16); "[Jesus Christ] is the propitiation for our sins, and not for ours only but also for the sins of the whole world" (1 John 2:2); "[Christ Jesus] gave himself as a ransom for all" (1 Tim. 2:6). In 1610, when forty-six followers of Jacob Arminius (1559/1560–1609) challenged the Reformed orthodoxy of their day on the doctrine of the atonement—and so set in motion events which would lead to the Synod of Dort and the classic statement of definite atonement—they cited John 3:16 and 1 John 2:2 as proof that "Jesus Christ, the Saviour of the world, died for all men and for every man."[2] More than a century later, John Wesley preached that "the whole tenor of the New Testament" was "flatly contrary" to definite atonement and that the doctrine contained "horrible blasphemies." It presented Christ as "an hypocrite, a deceiver of the people, a man void of common sincerity" and represented God "as more cruel, false, and unjust than the devil!"[3] In the modern era, D. Broughton Knox speaks for many when he claims that definite atonement is very simply "a textless doctrine."[4] No biblical text states that Christ died *only* for his elect, but several texts state that he died for *all*. In vivid terms, "the doctrine of limited atonement truncates the gospel by sawing off the arms of the cross too close to the stake."[5]

Objections also arise beyond the exegetical domain. R. T. Kendall wonders "how many Christians would ever come to the view of limited atonement merely by reading the Bible." This is part of his claim that "the traditional doctrine of limited atonement is arrived at by logic and the need to look for it rather than straightforward reading of the Scriptures."[6] The suggestion is that this doctrine feeds off schemes of analytic precision foreign to the texture of the biblical narrative. For Karl Barth, the "grim doctrine of limited atonement follows logically from Calvin's doctrine of double-predestination,"[7] the implication being of course that what follows is as bleak as what precedes.

Claims about the distorting role of logic in definite atonement are common, but they are made in different ways. In the nineteenth century, John McLeod Campbell, a Church of Scotland minister, was deposed from the ministry on heresy charges for teaching that Christ made a universal

---

[2] Text in Gerald Bray, ed., *Documents of the English Reformation* (Cambridge: James Clarke & Co., 1994), 454. Cf. Philip Schaff, *The Creeds of Christendom. Volume III: The Evangelical Protestant Creeds*, 4th ed., revised and enlarged (1877; repr., Grand Rapids, MI: Baker, 2000), 546.

[3] John Wesley, "Sermon CXXVIII: 'Free Grace' (Rom. viii.32). Preached at Bristol in the year 1740," in *The Works of John Wesley. Volume VII: Second Series of Sermons Concluded. Also Third, Fourth, and Fifth Series* (London: Wesley Conference Office, 1872; repr., Grand Rapids, MI: Zondervan, n. d.), 380–83.

[4] D. Broughton Knox, "Some Aspects of the Atonement," in *The Doctrine of God*, vol. 1 of *D. Broughton Knox, Selected Works* (3 vols.), ed. Tony Payne (Kingsford, NSW: Matthias Media, 2000), 260–66 (263).

[5] Jack McGorman in personal conversation with David L. Allen, "The Atonement: Limited or Universal?," in *Whosoever Will: A Biblical-Theological Critique of Five-Point Calvinism*, ed. David L. Allen and Steve W. Lemke (Nashville: B&H Academic, 2010), 107. For a response to this edited volume, see Matthew M. Barrett and Thomas J. Nettles, eds., *Whomever He Wills: A Surprising Display of Sovereign Mercy* (Cape Coral, FL: Founders Press, 2012), esp. David Schrock, "Jesus Saves, No Asterisk Needed: Why Preaching the Gospel as Good News Requires Definite Atonement" (77–119).

[6] R. T. Kendall, *Calvin and English Calvinism to 1649* (Carlisle, UK: Paternoster, 1997), viii.

[7] Karl Barth, *Church Dogmatics*, ed. G. W. Bromiley and T. F. Torrance, 14 vols. (Edinburgh: T. & T. Clark, 1956–1975), IV/1, 57 (hereafter *CD*).

atonement and that assurance is of the essence of faith and necessary for salvation. In his work *The Nature of the Atonement* (1856), Campbell argued that Reformed theologians like John Owen and Jonathan Edwards wrongly began their thinking about the atonement with theological axioms such as "God is just."[8] By starting there, the coming of Christ into the world is viewed as the revelation of God's justice as Christ dies for the elect only and not the reprobate. The universal proclamation of the gospel to all and the revelation that "God is love" are both jettisoned.

As a result, according to Campbell, definite atonement disfigures the doctrine of God. When Owen and Edwards "set forth justice as a necessary attribute of the divine nature, so that God must deal with *all men* according to its requirements, they represent mercy and love as not necessary, but arbitrary, and what, therefore, may find their expression in the history of only *some men*."[9] God is necessarily just toward all, but only selectively loving toward some. All of this is pastorally disastrous, Campbell claimed, for definite atonement "takes away the warrant which the universality of the atonement gives to every man that hears the gospel to contemplate Christ with the personal appropriation of the words of the apostle, 'who loved me, and gave himself for me.'"[10] The charge here is that definite atonement destroys not just the grounds of appeal to the unconverted but also the grounds of assurance for the believer. Can I really be sure that Christ died for *me*?[11]

Campbell's work has proven influential. J. B. Torrance and T. F. Torrance both draw on his thinking to argue that definite atonement represents the worst kind of logical necessity in theology. J. B. Torrance argues that Christ vicariously took to himself the judgment facing all mankind. To deny this is "a sin against the incarnate love of God" and, for Torrance, parallel to the sin against the Holy Spirit.[12] This reveals the key issue in his objections: in the incarnation, Jesus Christ is united with *all* humanity, not merely the elect, so that everything he achieves in his atonement he necessarily achieves for all. Torrance explicitly develops Campbell's stress on

---

[8] John McLeod Campbell, *The Nature of the Atonement*, with a new introduction by J. B. Torrance (Edinburgh: Handsel, 1856; repr., Grand Rapids, MI: Eerdmans, 1996), 67.

[9] Ibid., 73 (emphasis added).

[10] Ibid., 71.

[11] Bruce L. McCormack, "So That He Might Be Merciful to All: Karl Barth and the Problem of Universalism," in *Karl Barth and American Evangelicalism*, ed. Bruce L. McCormack and Clifford B. Anderson (Grand Rapids, MI: Eerdmans, 2011), 240, comments that if limited atonement were true, then "we would very likely despair of our salvation."

[12] J. B. Torrance, "The Incarnation and 'Limited Atonement,'" *EQ* 55 (1983): 83–94 (85).

God as love in his innermost being: "love and justice are one in God, and they are one in *all* his dealings with his creatures, in creation, providence and redemption."[13]

The opening words of our chapter view the atonement through the lens of election, and for Torrance this would simply confirm our captivity to Aristotelian logic. It makes divine election prior to divine grace, and so incarnation and atonement are formulated simply as "God's way of executing the eternal decrees—thereby 'logically' teaching that Christ died only for the elect, to secure infallibly the salvation of the elect."[14]

It falls to individual writers throughout this book to engage with the substance of these arguments, as well as with other criticisms of definite atonement not outlined above. At this stage, however, we want to reflect on the purpose that such criticisms serve in our articulation of the doctrine.

Toward a Fresh Approach

Some reproaches of definite atonement misunderstand it, and others caricature it, but many are weighty and coherent, arising from a faithful desire to read Scripture wisely and to honor the goodness and love of God. Between them they touch on four interrelated aspects of the doctrine: its controversies and nuances in church history, its presence or absence in the Bible, its theological implications, and its pastoral consequences. This indicates that definite atonement has profound significance and a wide-ranging scope which requires a comprehensive treatment.

But the essays in this volume seek to do more than simply cover four distinct areas in which objections exist. Rather, our aim is to show that history, the Bible, theology, and pastoral practice combine together to provide a framework within which the doctrine of definite atonement is best articulated for today. They are not four separate windows through which we view the doctrine; rather, they are four mezzanine levels of the one house where definite atonement lives. By beginning with church history, we recognize that all contemporary reading of the Bible on the atonement is historically located. We are not hostages to past interpretations, nor do we need to pretend there is such a thing as *tabula rasa* (blank slate) exegesis. By carefully attending

---

[13] Ibid., 92. Torrance had earlier expressed his indebtedness to Campbell on these points in "The Contribution of McLeod Campbell to Scottish Theology," *SJT* 26 (1973): 295–311.

[14] Torrance, "Incarnation," 87. The views of J. B. Torrance and T. F. Torrance are engaged in detail in Robert Letham's chapter in this volume.

to Scripture, we seek to submit ourselves to what God has said. By moving from exegesis to theology, we claim that the diverse biblical parts demand the patient work of synthesis to portray the theological whole. By concluding with pastoral practice, we aim to show the implications of the Bible's teaching for the church's ministry and mission. So while the discipline of doctrinal thinking is never less than the ordering of all that the Bible has to say on a given subject, it is also much more.

We suggest that articulating definite atonement is similar to articulating doctrines like the Trinity or the two natures of Christ. The approach needs to be biblical, but not biblicist. No one text "proves" definite atonement, any more than one text "proves" the Trinity or the communion of attributes in christology. In the case of those doctrines, numerous texts are studied and their implications synthesized and their key terms explored in their biblical contexts and historical usage so that, *taken as a whole*, the doctrines of the Trinity or the two natures describe "a pattern of judgment present *in* the texts."[15] With the unfolding of a coherent pattern, these doctrines emerge as the most compelling ways of naming the Christian God or understanding the person of Christ. Although no one text proves the doctrines, several texts teach their constituent parts.

So it is with definite atonement. It is not merely a "biblical" doctrine per se; nor is it a "systematic" construct based on logical or rationalist premises devoid of biblical moorings. Rather, definite atonement is a *biblico-systematic* doctrine that arises from careful exegesis of atonement texts and synthesis with internally related doctrines such as eschatology, election, union with Christ, christology, Trinitarianism, doxology, covenant, ecclesiology, and sacramentology. When both exegetical and theological "domains of discourse" are respected as such *and* taken together,[16] then reductionist objections to definite atonement lose their force and this reading of the meaning of the death of Christ emerges as profound and faithful. This biblico-systematic approach can be viewed pictorially from two angles.

First, doctrinal construction resembles the production of a *web*. The

---

[15] The phrase is part of David S. Yeago's contention that the Nicene theologians had warrant for their discernment that the Son is of one being with the Father. Cf. "The New Testament and the Nicene Dogma: A Contribution to the Recovery of Theological Exegesis," *Pro Ecclesia* 3.2 (1994): 152–64 (153). Much of Yeago's argument about exegetical and theological method could apply to the formulation of definite atonement.

[16] See D. A. Carson, "The Vindication of Imputation: On Fields of Discourse and Semantic Fields," in *Justification: What's at Stake in the Current Debates*, ed. Mark Husbands and Daniel J. Treier (Downers Grove, IL: Apollos, 2004), 46–80, esp. 47–50, on the importance of respecting "fields of discourse" when discussing theological doctrines such as sanctification, reconciliation, and Christ's imputed righteousness.

doctrine of definite atonement arises from the attempt to hold together each canonical thread related to the atonement and the forming of the threads into a coherent framework of thought which faithfully maintains the parts and enables them to be seen in their truest light when viewed in relation to the whole. In much the same way that each strand of a spider's web is one thing when taken on its own, but another when viewed in its relation to other strands, so the different aspects of the doctrine of the atonement can be integrated to display powerful coherence. Kevin Vanhoozer captures the concept nicely in his suggestion that constructive theologies of the atonement should conceive of it as "triune covenantal mediation."[17] For him, three biblical strands (doctrine of God, covenant theology, christology) combine to form one theological web. This volume, in the sum total of its parts, aims to be just such a web.

Second, by showing the relation of historical, exegetical, theological, and pastoral issues to each other, this volume is a *map* to and through the doctrine of definite atonement. Some of the most enduring theological thinking that the church has produced over the centuries has understood itself to be a doctrinal map produced from the biblical terrain in order to be a guide to the biblical terrain. John Calvin's *Institutes of the Christian Religion* is widely regarded as a kind of theological textbook, or even as a pre-critical systematic theology. But this does not quite capture Calvin's own intention. In an introductory note to the reader of the *Institutes*, Calvin writes,

> It has been my purpose in this labour to prepare and instruct candidates in sacred theology for the reading of the divine Word in order that they may be able both to have easy access to it and to advance in it without stumbling. For I believe I have so embraced the sum of religion in all its parts and have arranged it in such an order, that if anyone rightly grasps it, it will not be difficult for him to determine what he ought especially to seek in Scripture, and to what end he ought to relate its contents. If, after this road has, as it were, been paved, I shall publish any interpretations of Scripture, I shall always condense them, because I shall have no need to undertake long doctrinal discussions, and to digress into commonplaces. In this way the godly reader will be spared great annoyance and boredom, provided he approach Scripture armed with a knowledge of the present work, as a necessary tool.[18]

---

[17] Kevin J. Vanhoozer, "Atonement," in *Mapping Modern Theology: A Thematic and Historical Introduction*, ed. Kelly M. Kapic and Bruce L. McCormack (Grand Rapids, MI: Baker Academic, 2012), 175–202 (201).

[18] John Calvin, "John Calvin to the Reader," in *Institutes of the Christian Religion*, ed. John T. McNeill, trans. Ford Lewis Battles, 2 vols. (Philadelphia: Westminster, 1960), 1:4–5.

It is clear that Calvin proposes his *Institutes* to pave a road through the Scriptures on which others may travel as they read the same Scriptures. Notice Calvin does not say he intends his work to instruct theological candidates in doctrine. The *Institutes* is certainly a doctrinal text. But Calvin intends to instruct theological candidates for their "reading of the divine Word." Mined from the Bible, shaped by the Bible, the *Institutes* is a map for the Bible.[19]

Calvin's work illustrates how theological cartography functions and develops. It is not a conceptually alien guide to the Bible, nor is it meant to be a hermeneutical grid forced on top of the Bible. Where it functions well, a doctrinal map grows organically out of the biblical parts and enables a bird's-eye view of the canonical whole.[20] But it is always constrained by the very thing it plots. Further exegesis is always capable of adjusting the shape of the map. Renewed attention to knotty problems, carefully analyzed in the actual terrain and closely studied on any given map, should always be capable of reconfiguring the map and altering the route one takes for the way ahead.[21] This approach sets up a careful part-whole relationship, one in which the doctrine emerging from the texts is constantly examined against the texts to see if the developing whole is really consistent with the individual parts. Where the move to doctrinal synthesis is made too quickly, distortion occurs.

Take, for example, the issue of what it means for God to love the world (John 3:16). A. W. Pink's treatment of divine sovereignty in salvation goes awry with the suggestion that God's self-giving love for the "world" in John 3:16 refers to his love for the elect.[22] Such an interpretation not only assigns meaning to an individual word clearly different from what the text actually says, but the nature of God's love and the universal offer of Christ to all also warp under the weight of the paradigm. Similarly, Mark Driscoll and Gerry

---

[19] For extended treatments of the organic relationship between the successive editions of the *Institutes* and Calvin's preaching and biblical commentaries, see Stephen Edmondson, "The Biblical Historical Structure of Calvin's *Institutes*," *SJT* 59.1 (2006): 1–13; David Gibson, *Reading the Decree: Exegesis, Election, and Christology in Calvin and Barth* (London/New York: T. & T. Clark/Continuum, 2009), 17–27.

[20] Cf. Gerald Bray, "Scripture and Confession: Doctrine as Hermeneutic," in *A Pathway into the Holy Scripture*, ed. P. E. Satterthwaite and D. F. Wright (Grand Rapids, MI: Eerdmans, 1994), 221–36.

[21] The web and map analogies allow this volume's claims to be heard as provisional, in the proper sense, rather than grandiose. To give one example, Stephen Wellum presents an argument for the priestly nature of Christ's atoning work which reflects new covenant theology understandings of the nature of covenant, election, and ecclesiology. His rich theological thinking leads the reader to see the reality of definite atonement in the Scriptures, but the particular route he takes through the biblical terrain is different from our own classically Reformed understanding of the nature of covenant, election, and ecclesiology. The book maps different routes for the same destination, and not all readers will want to travel each and every path in reaching the same goal. To be used as a tool, it is servant not master.

[22] A. W. Pink, *The Sovereignty of God* (Grand Rapids, MI: Baker, 1983), 204–205, 253–55. For Pink, "the love of God, is a truth for the saints only, and to present it to the enemies of God is to take the children's bread and cast it to the dogs" (200).

Breshears understand definite atonement to entail a limiting of God's love to the elect. Arguing for "unlimited limited atonement, or modified Calvinism," they ask, "If the five-point Calvinist is right and no payment has been made for the non-elect, then how can God genuinely love the world and desire the salvation of all?"[23] For Pink, the effective provision of salvation for the elect requires a limitation of God's love to the elect; for Driscoll and Breshears, the effective payment of sin's penalty for all requires the expansion of God's love identically for all. In neither case are the several *different* ways in which the Bible depicts God's love allowed to stand together in relation to its different objects (his world, his people) and its different expressions (intra-Trinitarian, providential, universal, particular, conditional). For these writers a conception of the atonement either mandates, or is mandated by, a singular conception of God's love.[24]

Such doctrinal maps are misaligned with the biblical texts which create them. The move toward synthesis needs to be more patient and careful, more attentive to diverse strands of the biblical witness. Comprised of four sections, we hope this volume goes some way to meeting the need. The issue of integration is important enough for Henri Blocher's chapter to be devoted to it entirely. Of course, readers will want to turn to specific parts to focus on particular issues of interest, and each essay is a self-contained argument which can be read in this way. The overall effect of the project, however, is intended to be cumulative. Taken together, each essay within each section and then each section within the book offers a webbed framework of theological thinking which maps the study of definite atonement in the Bible.

Definite Atonement in Church History

Richard Muller suggests that a question belonging to the Patristic, medieval, and early modern Reformed church was "the meaning of those biblical passages in which Christ is said to have paid a ransom for all or God is said to will the salvation of all or of the whole world, given the large number of biblical passages that indicate a limitation of salvation to some, namely, to the elect or believers."[25] Not only does this identify the puzzle which the doctrine

---

[23] Mark Driscoll and Gerry Breshears, *Death by Love: Letters from the Cross* (Wheaton, IL: Crossway, 2008), 173.

[24] For a more satisfying approach, see Geerhardus Vos, "The Biblical Doctrine of the Love of God," in *Redemptive History and Biblical Interpretation: The Shorter Writings of Geerhardus Vos*, ed. Richard B. Gaffin (Phillipsburg, NJ: P&R, 1980), 425–57; and D. A. Carson, *The Difficult Doctrine of the Love of God* (Leicester, UK: Inter-Varsity Press, 2000).

[25] See Richard A. Muller, "Was Calvin a Calvinist?," in his *Calvin and the Reformed Tradition: On the Work of Christ and the Order of Salvation* (Grand Rapids, MI: Baker Academic, 2012), 51–69 (60).

of definite atonement seeks to address, but it also shows that historical matters are intimately connected to exegetical ones. As Barth put it, "church history is the history of the exegesis of the Word of God."[26]

The historical essays in this book, then, explore the question in significant moments in church history. They provide a survey of past approaches to definite atonement in the Bible, introduce us to key players in the debate, and send us on our way with awareness of how crucial terms have been defined and understood thus far. These essays create several compass points for the map, three of which can be highlighted here.

First, the competing terminologies of "Calvinist versus Arminian," so prevalent in popular debate about definite atonement, need to be set aside in favor of richer and more sophisticated understandings of the history of the doctrine. Even where the parameters are expanded to include the extra perspectives of, say, universalism and Amyraldianism, the reality is that viewing the subject through the lens of labels derived from prominent personal names in Reformation history soon introduces distortion.

On the one hand, sixteenth- and seventeenth-century debates on the atonement did not produce theological ideas and terminology *de novo* but relied on the tradition and sought to develop and apply it, albeit in contested ways, in the particular contexts of the early modern era. The journey from Patristic and medieval through Reformation and post-Reformation periods plotted in this section reveals that this is so. "Calvinism versus Arminianism" simply lobotomizes history. On the other hand, none of the major -isms ever existed for long as monolithic entities with only a single expression. J. C. Ryle once noted that "the absence of accurate definitions is the very life of religious controversy,"[27] and these essays prompt us to recognize distinct positions and nuances on the intent and scope of the atonement—Universalism, Semi-Pelagianism, Arminianism, Amyraldianism and variant approaches to Hypothetical Universalism—always in the service of disciplined theological thinking.[28]

Second, this careful approach to the history of definite atonement explains why the term "Calvinist" is largely absent from the volume's subse-

---

[26] Barth, *CD* I/2, 681.

[27] J. C. Ryle, *Knots Untied* (1878; repr., Moscow, ID: Charles Nolan, 2000), 1.

[28] Richard A. Muller, "Calvin on Christ's Satisfaction and Its Efficacy: The Issue of 'Limited Atonement,'" in his *Calvin and the Reformed Tradition*, 77 n. 22, argues that, "once the language is suitably parsed, there are at least six distinct patterns of formulation [of Christ's satisfaction] among the early modern Reformed."

quent exegetical, theological, and pastoral treatments of the doctrine. Not only do the issues surrounding definite atonement massively predate the life and thought of John Calvin, there is no little irony involved in calling definite atonement a "Calvinist" doctrine when his own relationship to it—as all sides have to admit—is a matter of debate. More than this, it is now abundantly clear that the term expresses a reliance on the person which was as insulting to Calvin as it is historically misleading because it fails to account for his own location in a developing tradition.[29] Therefore each of the writers in the book works with a preference for the term "Reformed" or "Reformed theology," both for historical description and as the way of locating themselves within the particularist trajectory.[30]

It follows, thirdly, that this volume is not a presentation of "the five points of Calvinism" or a defence of the "TULIP" acronym widely used as a summary of the Canons of Dort and consequently of Reformed theology. It is not that there is no value to such language. But there can be a tendency to use such terminology as the soteriological map *itself*, without realizing that such terms simply feature as historical landmarks *on* the map.[31] The language emerged at particular points in time in particular contexts in response to particular challenges, and it is those underlying causes and perennial questions themselves that the historical essays attempt to probe. In the process, they lend weight to J. I. Packer's insight that, historically, the Reformed faith cannot be reduced to simply five points, while at the same time, theologically, the five points stand or fall together as simply one point: *God saves sinners*.[32]

Definite Atonement in the Bible

If historical debates about the atonement arose from certain biblical texts, so also our own contribution requires the same engagement with Scripture as the *norma normans* (norming norm) of the discussion.

---

[29] Carl R. Trueman, "Calvin and Calvinism," in *The Cambridge Companion to John Calvin*, ed. Donald K. McKim (Cambridge: Cambridge University Press, 2004), 226, suggests that the term "Calvinism" is "of no real use to intellectual history." See Raymond A. Blacketer's chapter in the present volume for some of the literature on this issue.
[30] It is the contention of this book that while, historically, Hypothetical Universalism and Amyraldianism came under the umbrella of the Reformed community in the seventeenth century, these positions are, exegetically and theologically, the awkward cousins in the family. This is not to remove them from Reformed orthodoxy, but it is to apply the Reformational principle of *semper reformanda* to the debate, seeking to allow *sola Scriptura* to act as the final authority.
[31] Cf. Richard A. Muller, "How Many Points?," *CTJ* 28 (1993): 425–33.
[32] J. I. Packer, "Introductory Essay," in John Owen, *The Death of Death in the Death of Christ* (London: Banner of Truth, 1959), 5–6.

There currently exists something of an exegetical impasse over texts which, on the one hand, seem to point to the particularity of the atonement, and texts which, on the other hand, imply a universal atonement. The biblical essays in this volume do not claim to constitute a silver bullet to achieve satisfactory consensus on why all these passages should be put together to affirm definite atonement. Indeed, the chapters simply work inductively through the relevant material and attempt to provide convincing readings of important texts on their own terms. Doubtless debate will still continue.

Nevertheless, the exegetical chapters depict a particular relationship between individual atonement texts and an overall theological framework which we hope may deepen the discussion. We contend that this framework is not imposed on the parts, but rather the parts themselves provide the wide-angle lens through which they invite us to view them appropriately. Two points explain what we mean.

First, we do not begin with contested texts but with the unfolding plot line of redemptive history, so that the progression of the chapters matches the biblical narrative. This is a very simple approach, but by itself already begins to expose the fact that doctrines such as election are not theological categories abstractly connected to theologies of atonement by predetermined Reformed hermeneutical agendas. Rather, election is a redemptive-historical category as much as a dogmatic one. God's choosing of a people to belong to him, so formative in and of the Pentateuch, clearly circumscribes the Bible's unfolding theology of sacrifice and atonement such that election is always an expression of God's grace shaping his covenantal dealings with his people. The exegesis of significant texts which then follows,[33] along with discussion of contested issues (the meanings of "many," "all," and "world"), naturally locates them within this context.

Second, some of the exegetical parts themselves indicate the content of the theological whole. Analysis of Ephesians 1:3–14 and 2 Timothy 1:9–11 reveals that biblical soteriology is painted on an eschatological canvas that consists of four key "moments" of salvation: redemption predestined, redemption accomplished, redemption applied, and redemption consummated. These two texts offer a panoramic view of salvation, and, because of their

---

[33] Isaiah 53; Matthew 20:28; Mark 10:45; Matthew 26:28; Luke 22:20; John 3:16; Romans 5:9–11, 12–21; 6:1–11; 8:1–15, 29–34; 14:15; 1 Corinthians 8:11; 2 Corinthians 5:14–15, 19; Galatians 1:4; 4:4–6; Ephesians 1:3–14; 5:25–27; Colossians 1:20; 1 Timothy 2:4–6; 4:10; 2 Timothy 1:9–11; Titus 2:11–14; 3:3–7; Hebrews 2:9; 2 Peter 2:1; 1 John 2:2; 4:10, 14; Revelation 5:9–10.

scope, they unavoidably point toward overall theological frameworks. They help establish a part-whole hermeneutical dialogue whereby we learn to read each of the different parts of the biblical narrative as enveloped within the Bible's own way of looking at its whole story. Our salvation is eternal in origin and inexorably eschatological in movement; it is predestined, accomplished, applied, and consummated, and several biblical texts shine light on aspects of this spectrum. For example, Titus 3:3–7 unfolds two distinct moments of salvation in history (Christ's appearing, and the Holy Spirit's act of regeneration), along with a further anticipatory moment of salvation in the future (unending life with God). The same can be said of Romans 5:9–11 and 8:29–34, with the addition of another moment of salvation (God's foreknowing and predestining). What becomes clear from all these texts is that eschatology is not merely the "goal" of soteriology, "but also encompasses it, constituting its very substance from the outset."[34]

Definite Atonement in Theological Perspective

John Webster has recently argued that the chief task of Christian soteriology is to explain how God is savingly at work in the affliction of Jesus. A dogmatic account "stretches both backwards and forwards from this central event. It traces the work of salvation back into the will of God, and forward into the life of the many, who by it are made righteous."[35] The exegetical essays in the volume reveal that Webster is correct to identify this bidirectional flow in the biblical texts, and the theological and pastoral essays are taken up with expounding both movements. What more can be said about the "pre-history" of the history of salvation in the purposes of the triune God? What does it mean for our salvation to be the work of Father, Son, and Spirit? What does it mean for Jesus to be crushed Servant and interceding High Priest? What kind of sacrifice and payment for sin did he offer? The theological chapters in this volume coalesce to make four key points, each of which shape the map in different ways.

First, the saving work of God is indivisible. This expresses in a single statement the four moments of salvation outlined above,[36] and it has profound

---

[34] Richard B. Gaffin, *Resurrection and Redemption: A Study in Paul's Soteriology*, 2nd ed. (Phillipsburg, NJ: P&R, 1987), 59.

[35] John B. Webster, "'It Was the Will of the Lord to Bruise Him': Soteriology and the Doctrine of God," in *God of Salvation: Soteriology in Theological Perspective*, ed. Ivor J. Davidson and Murray A. Rae (Farnham, Surrey, UK: Ashgate, 2011), 15–34 (15).

[36] Ibid., 19–20, construes the overall shape of soteriology in three unified moments: "the eternal purpose of the perfect God; the establishment of that purpose in the history which culminates in the ministry of the incarnate Son; and the consummation of that purpose in the Spirit."

theological implications. Each of these four moments is distinct, never collapsed into the others, yet never separated from them either. In moment one, our salvation in Christ has been predestined; in moment two, the whole of our salvation has been procured and secured by Christ, even though his redemption is yet to be experientially applied by his Spirit (moment three) and eschatologically consummated in his presence (moment four). None of the moments of salvation belong to separate theological tracks, as if Christ's redemptive work is somehow disconnected from the election of his people. In God's saving work there is unity in distinction and distinction in unity. God's purposes in Christ are one. Such a perspective helps to avoid the error of collapsing the moments of redemption applied into redemption accomplished (as seen in Karl Barth's theology) or the error of fracturing the bond between these moments (as seen in presentations of universal atonement).

Second, the saving work of God is circumscribed by God's electing grace and purpose. That is, God's redemptive love and divine initiative shape and guide the other moments of salvation. God's love toward his own in election and predestination is the fountainhead from which salvation flows. In this regard, there is an inescapable *ordo* within the divine decree.[37] The argument set forth in this book is that, before time, the triune God planned salvation, such that the Father chose a people for himself from among fallen humankind, a choice that would involve the sending of his Son to purchase them and the sending of his Spirit to regenerate them. In the mind of God, the choice logically preceded the accomplishment and the application of Christ's redemptive work, and so in history it circumscribed them both. Louis Berkhof asks, "Did the Father in sending Christ, and did Christ in coming into the world, to make atonement for sin, *do this with the design or for the purpose of saving only the elect or all men?* That is the question, and that only is the question."[38]

This divine *ordo* within the decree, the biblical basis for which is presented in this volume, calls into question attempts that would render election non-determinative for salvation, or that would place the decree of election after the decree of redemption, or that would subordinate God's electing love for his elect at the expense of his universal love for all humankind—problems that attend Semi-Pelagianism and Arminianism, Amyraldianism, and Hypo-

---

[37] For a helpful overview of the various positions on the order of decrees, see B. B. Warfield's table at the end of Donald Macleod's chapter in this volume.

[38] Louis Berkhof, *Systematic Theology* (Edinburgh: Banner of Truth, 1958), 394 (emphasis original).

thetical Universalism, respectively. In the Scriptures, God's electing love is given the most distributive emphasis—it is no mere "afterthought."[39]

Third, the saving work of God has its center in union with Christ. The personal union between Christ and believers encompasses all four moments of salvation. John Murray succinctly encapsulates the different aspects of this mysterious union with Christ:

> Union with Christ is the central truth of the whole doctrine of salvation. All to which the people of God have been predestined in the eternal election of God, all that has been secured and procured for them in the once-for-all accomplishment of redemption, all of which they become the actual partakers in the application of redemption, and all that by God's grace they will become in the state of consummated bliss is embraced within the compass of union and communion with Christ.[40]

Thus, we may never think of Christ's accomplished redemption in abstraction from the union with his people at the moment of election; nor may we detach Christ's redemptive accomplishment—and his people's dying and rising with him—from the vital union with Christ that occurs through faith, or from the union yet to be experienced when believers are finally in Christ's presence. As Sinclair Ferguson points out,

> If we are united to Christ, then we are united to him at all points of his activity on our behalf. We share in his death (we were baptized into his death), in his burial (we were buried with him in baptism), in his resurrection (we are resurrected with Christ), in his ascension (we have been raised with him), in his heavenly session (we sit with him in heavenly places, so that our life is hidden with Christ in God), and we will share in his promised return (when Christ, who is our life, appears, we also will appear with him in glory).[41]

It follows that if the moments of redemption are bound together as distinct-yet-inseparable acts of God *in Christ*, then certain conceptions of the *nature* and *efficacy* of the atonement begin to emerge.

Within certain schemes of thought, Christ's sacrifice secures the salvation of no one in particular, since its efficacy is contingent upon something outside the atonement, namely, faith—either synergistic faith (as in forms of

---

[39] Vos's critique of Amyraldianism ("Biblical Doctrine of the Love of God," 456).

[40] John Murray, *Redemption Accomplished and Applied* (Grand Rapids, MI: Eerdmans, 1955), 210.

[41] Sinclair B. Ferguson, "The Reformed View," in *Christian Spirituality: Five Views of Sanctification*, ed. Donald L. Alexander (Downers Grove, IL: IVP Academic, 1989), 58.

Semi-Pelagianism and Arminianism)[42] or God-elected, monergistic faith (as in Amyraldian Hypothetical Universalism). These accounts introduce contingency into the atonement, which stands in sharp contrast to the efficacy of the cross, argued for here. The saving power of the cross does not "depend on faith being added to it; its saving power is such that faith flows from it."[43] And precisely because Christ does not win a hypothetical salvation for hypothetical believers, but rather a real salvation for his people, the effectiveness of the atonement flows from its penal substitutionary nature.[44] At issue here is the precise meaning of the cross as *punishment* for sin, and the two complementary essays by Garry Williams offer fresh and rigorous accounts which serve to deepen significantly our understanding of penology. We suggest that the very nature of the atonement is radically redefined when its scope is extended to be for all without exception. Packer states the case exactly:

> if we are going to affirm penal substitution for all without exception we must either infer universal salvation or else, to evade this inference, deny the saving efficacy of the substitution for anyone; and if we are going to affirm penal substitution as an effective saving act of God we must either infer universal salvation or else, to evade this inference, restrict the scope of the substitution, making it a substitution for some, not all.[45]

It is union with Christ which secures the efficacy of Christ's atonement, because his death is an "in-union-with" kind of death. Those for whom Christ died cannot but be affected by his death. Union with Christ also defines the "some" for whom his death is effective. It rescues us from an impoverished view of Christ's death as a mere "instead of" penal substitutionary atonement for all, and instead presents us with a *representative* penal substitutionary atonement: Christ dies as *Someone* for *some* people. He dies as King for his people, as Husband for his bride, as the Head for his body, as Shepherd for his sheep, as Master for his friends, as Firstborn for his brothers and sisters, as

---

[42] This synergistic faith occurs through either (a) equal cooperation between God and man's *free* will (as in Semi-Pelagianism), or (b) equal cooperation between God and man's will which is *already freed* as a result of prevenient grace (as in classic Arminianism). In either case, the human free/freed will can resist God's grace; conversely, man's choice is ultimately decisive for faith. For this important distinction, see Roger E. Olson, *Arminian Theology: Myths and Realities* (Downers Grove, IL: IVP Academic, 2006), 158–78, esp. 164–66.

[43] Packer, "Introductory Essay," 10.

[44] John Owen, *Salus Electorum, Sanguis Jesu: Or The Death of Death in the Death of Christ*, in *The Works of John Owen*, ed. W. H. Goold, 24 vols. (Edinburgh: Johnstone & Hunter, 1850–1853; repr. Edinburgh: Banner of Truth, 1967), 10:235, put it well: "Christ did not die for any upon condition, *if they do believe*; but he died for all God's elect, *that they should believe*, and believing have eternal life."

[45] J. I. Packer, "What Did the Cross Achieve? The Logic of Penal Substitution," in *Celebrating the Saving Work of God: Collected Shorter Writings of J. I. Packer, Volume 1* (Carlisle, UK: Paternoster, 2000), 85–123 (116).

the Second and Last Adam for a new humanity.[46] This is why the particularity of the atonement cannot be introduced at the point of application,[47] for we were united to Christ in his death and resurrection *prior* to appropriating the benefits of his atonement by faith—which means that the scope of redemption accomplished and applied are necessarily coextensive.

Fourth, the saving work of God in Christ is Trinitarian. The efficacious and indivisible work of God centered in union with Christ ensures that Christ died for a definite group of people; the Trinitarian shape of this soteriology allows us to go further and say that that is the very *intention* of his death.

The Trinity orchestrates the symphony of salvation in all its movements: the Father elects and sends, the Son becomes incarnate and dies, the Spirit draws and vivifies. But while their works are distinct they are not independent: the Father elects in Christ, the incarnate Son offers himself on the cross through the eternal Spirit to the Father, and the Spirit is sent by the Father and the Son to draw and seal the elect. Grounded in the mutual indwelling of their persons, the Father, Son, and Spirit together serve the shared goal of our salvation. "The Spirit serves the Son by applying what he accomplished, and the Son serves the Spirit by making his indwelling possible. Both Son and Spirit, together on their twofold mission from the Father, serve the Father and minister to us."[48]

If, however, as some might argue, Christ's atoning work on the cross is intended for everyone without exception, while its application is limited only to those who believe by the power of the Spirit, then, we contend, a fatal disjunction is introduced. The disjunction is not just conceptual; it is also personal. Aspects of the one union with Christ are disconnected, redemption accomplished is separated from redemption applied, and the divine persons are cleaved from each other in their saving intentions. The Son dies for all, yet the Father elects only some and the Spirit seals only some.[49] We suggest, however, that the nature of the Trinitarian operations envelops a definite construal of the atonement as part of the bigger picture of God's glorification of himself:

---

[46] Henri A. G. Blocher, "The Scope of Redemption and Modern Theology," *SBET* 9.2 (1991): 102.

[47] Contra Knox, "Some Aspects of the Atonement," 265.

[48] Fred Sanders, *The Deep Things of God: How the Trinity Changes Everything* (Wheaton, IL: Crossway, 2010), 149.

[49] The disjunctions in a universal atonement are many. "It introduces conflict between the purpose of God, who desires the salvation of all, and the will or power of God, who actually either will not or cannot grant salvation to all. It gives precedence to the person and work of Christ over election and covenant, so that Christ is isolated from these contexts and cannot vicariously atone for his people, since there is no fellowship between him and us. It denigrates the justice of God by saying that he causes forgiveness and life to be acquired for all and then fails to distribute them to all" (Herman Bavinck, *Sin and Salvation in Christ*, vol. 3 of *Reformed Dogmatics*, ed. John Bolt, trans. John Vriend, 4 vols. [Grand Rapids, MI: Baker Academic, 2006], 469–70).

> For when God designed the great and glorious work of recovering fallen man and the saving of sinners, to the praise of the glory of his grace, he appointed, in his infinite wisdom, two great means thereof. The one was *the giving his Son for them*, and the other was *the giving his Spirit unto them*. And hereby was way made for the manifestation of the glory of the whole blessed Trinity; which is the utmost end of all the works of God.[50]

Hypothetical Universalists attempt to avoid the accusation of Trinitarian disharmony by arguing that each person of the Trinity wills both limitation and universalism on different levels, thus eliminating any division between them.[51] Their position, however, is not without problems for Trinitarian theology, since it introduces a division within the will of *each* person as they seek to perform salvation. The position must concede that, at the universal level, the person and work of Christ are divided as he performs atonement for everyone without reference to his person, roles, or offices. He therefore dies on the one hand as a *representative* substitute for his people, yet on the other hand as a *mere* substitute for people whom he knows the Father never elected and for whom he will never send his Spirit to draw to himself. The hypothetical scheme not only suggests that God has two economies of salvation running in tandem, but it inadvertently presents us with a confused Christ. Such a position runs counter to the biblical description of Christ's work and person (and his offices) being interrelated, and his substitutionary death being representatively performed in union with his people.

Setting issues such as the intent, nature, and efficacy of the atonement in a full-orbed Trinitarian context allows us to understand the relationship between them. Just as the efficacy of the atonement flows from its penal nature, so we may say in turn that its nature flows from its divine intent. The Servant is crushed and suffers and is made to be a guilt offering *because* it was the will of the Lord (Isa. 53:10). Intending to save all those given to him by the Father, the Son offers himself through the Spirit as an atoning sacrifice and achieves the salvation of his people (Heb. 9:14).

---

[50] John Owen, Πνευματολογια *or, A Discourse Concerning the Holy Spirit*, in *Works*, 3:23 (emphasis original).

[51] For example, John Davenant, "A Dissertation on the Death of Christ, as to its Extent and special Benefits: containing a short History of Pelagianism, and shewing the Agreement of the Doctrines of the Church of England on general Redemption, Election, and Predestination, with the Primitive Fathers of the Christian Church, and above all, with the Holy Scriptures," in *An Exposition of the Epistle of St. Paul to the Colossians*, trans. Josiah Allport, 2 vols. (London: Hamilton, Adams, 1832 [English trans. of 1650 Latin ed.]), 2:398 and 2:542, argued that the Son had a universal intent that "conformed to the ordination of the Father," and yet, at the same time, Christ affirmed the particular will of God when he died, for how else could Christ have "exhibited himself as conformed to the eternal appointment of his Father, if, in his saving passion, he had not applied his merits in a peculiar manner infallibly to effect and complete the salvation of the elect?"

This helps to explain why the terms "definite atonement" or "particular" or "effectual redemption" are to be preferred above "limited atonement," which is commonly used for the doctrine. Not only is there an innate negativity attached to the language of limitation which obscures what the doctrine consistently includes (such as the sufficiency of Christ's death for all or the cosmic implications of the atonement), it also misleads given that other views of the atonement necessarily "limit" it in some way. John Murray is surely right: "Unless we believe in the final restoration of all mankind, we cannot have an unlimited atonement. On the premise that some perish eternally we are shut up to one of two alternatives—a limited efficacy or a limited extent; there is no such thing as an unlimited atonement."[52] In this book, we commonly adopt the term *"definite* atonement," since the adjective "definite" is able to convey that the atonement is specific in its *intention* (Christ died to save his people) and effective in its *nature* (it really does atone).[53]

Definite Atonement in Pastoral Practice

The aim of any doctrinal map must be to show the glory of God in the face of Jesus Christ as revealed in the pages of Scripture. It is the aim of this volume to show the vital place that a definite atonement occupies in just such an account of God's glory. And it is that overall ambition that grounds our understanding of the connection between definite atonement and pastoral care of God's people. The three chapters that conclude the volume are not themselves essays in pastoral practice; rather, they seek to provide the deep foundations upon which pastoral practice may build and flourish. For if the final end of salvation is "the reiteration of God's majesty and the glorification of God by all creatures,"[54] then our greatest human need is to give God glory in gratitude and praise and to structure our creaturely life by the divine wisdom of the crucified Messiah.

His atoning death and resurrection provide the incarnate Son of God

---

[52] John Murray, *The Atonement* (Philadelphia: P&R, 1962), 27.

[53] Similarly, referring to the "extent" of the atonement is less than ideal given that the word can qualify different aspects of the atonement: its intention, accomplishment, or application. As Robert Letham, *The Work of Christ* (Leicester, UK: Inter-Varsity Press, 1993), 225, argues, "extent" gives the impression that the atonement is being calculated mathematically or spatially. "Translated into debate on the atonement, the focus becomes that of *number*: how many, or what proportion benefit from Christ's death? Did Christ atone for the sins of all or simply for those of the elect? Did he atone for the sins of all in a provisional sense? Or, from quite another direction, is the atonement of limited or unlimited value? If the idea of *intent* is the central theme, however, the principal point at stake becomes that of *purpose* or *design*. In short, the issue crystallises into the place of the atonement in the overall plan of God for human redemption. The spatial and mathematical yields to the teleological."

[54] Webster, "It Was the Will of the Lord," 20.

with the full display of the glory of God (Phil. 2:5–11), and so provide the people of God with the deepest of reasons for the praise of God. A definite understanding of Christ's atonement flows from seeing the successive stages of his humiliation and exaltation as unified parts of a complete accomplishment.[55] The glory Jesus receives as the Son of God in power in his exaltation is his *because* he has *triumphed* over sin and death and hell and has lost none of those whom the Father gave to him (John 17). As our Great High Priest, he is seated *because* he has *opened* a new and living way to God and by his sacrifice "has made perfect forever those who are being made holy" (Heb. 10:14, NIV). The glory of God shines with radiance in the cross of Christ because from his sin-bearing death stems the re-creation of the world and the reconciliation of all things to God (Col. 1:20). The atonement secured salvation, a world made new, and eternal *shalom*.

It is often alleged that in the pastoral domain the weaknesses of definite atonement become most acute. This is not so. We contend that, precisely because it is a definite atonement that gives greatest glory to God, so it is this understanding of the atonement that affords church and world the greatest good. The drama of the Son-King who was promised the nations as his inheritance (Ps. 2:8) adds motivation for the evangelization of the peoples of the world. The Lamb has *purchased* people for God (Rev. 5:9–11). Conversely, the "unevangelized" become an uncomfortable "stone in the shoe" for advocates of a universal atonement: Christ has provided a *de jure* salvation for all but which *de facto* is not accessible to all and, inadvertently, ends up in reality limited in its scope. Definite atonement ensures that what is offered in the proclamation of the gospel is the actual accomplishment of redemption. To herald the gospel is to herald a *Savior* who has by his blood *established* the covenant of grace which all are called to join. Proponents of a general, universal atonement cannot in fact, if being consistent, maintain a belief in the sincere offer of salvation for every person. All that can be offered is the opportunity or the possibility of salvation—and that not even to all in reality.

An atonement symbolized by the Good Shepherd who lays down his life for his sheep provides pastoral riches of motivation, joyful obedience, and

---

[55] Bavinck explains the structure of this unity in *Sin and Salvation in Christ*, 323–482, and beautifully explores its cosmic scope (see esp. 473–74). Interestingly, he includes his discussion of the atonement under the exaltation of Christ, not his humiliation. For Bavinck, when Christ rose from the dead and ascended to heaven "he took with him a treasure of merits that he had acquired by his obedience," chief among them the reconciliation which he won in his atoning death (447). Reconciliation is therefore a gift given by the risen and ascended King to his people (450).

perseverance for pastor and people alike. Atonement which radiates from the union of Christ with his people and which is set within the wider paradigm of the triune operations cannot but give assurance to the believer. If God—Father, Son, and Spirit—has worked indivisibly for us in Christ, who then can be against us? Models of the atonement that make salvation merely possible fail to provide this robust assurance and comfort. Assurance of salvation necessarily becomes detached from the secure source of what Christ has done and lodges itself in the unstable realm of our response. Atonement has been made, yes—but knowledge of it sufficient to calm our fears and assure us of our adoption is grounded in human action, not divine. We are salvation's decisive donors.

If John Piper is correct in his concluding essay, that the death of Christ is the climax of the glory of God's grace, which is the apex of the glory of God, then the issues of the intent and nature of the atonement are not subjects of "little consequence" or "matters of mere speculation"—they touch the very nerve center of the glory of God. He is not glorified when his salvation is reduced to a mere opportunity. He is not glorified when his redemption of lost sinners is abridged to being simply a possibility. God is glorified when he is seen and savored and enjoyed for what he actually bestows: *saving* grace. In this glorification, we his creatures are made whole and healthy, worshiping and happy, and commissioned as his ambassadors in his world—*soli Deo gloria.*

I

DEFINITE ATONEMENT
IN CHURCH HISTORY

2

"We Trust in the Saving Blood"[1]

DEFINITE ATONEMENT IN
THE ANCIENT CHURCH

Michael A. G. Haykin

Introduction

When the eighteenth-century Calvinistic polymath John Gill (1697–1771) decided to publicly defend some of the cardinal doctrines of the Reformed faith, the result was *The Cause of God and Truth* (1735–1738), a monumental work of scholarship devoted to an explication of what were popularly known as "the doctrines of grace." Gill was especially concerned to answer the arguments of the Salisbury clergyman Daniel Whitby (1638–1726), whose *A Discourse on the Five Points* (1710), as it is known, was reprinted in the early 1730s and which caused quite a stir, for it was judged to be an irrefutable critique of these central convictions of English Calvinism.[2] Understandably the Scriptures were central to this debate, but the perspective of the ancient church was also extensively considered. Gill's detailed coverage of the Patristic evidence can be found especially in part 4 of *The Cause of God and Truth*. Gill was indeed aware that discussion of the doctrines of grace did not become explicit until the fifth century when the Pelagian heresy arose, yet, like earlier Reformed authors such as François Turretini (1623–1687)

---

[1] The quote is from Justin Martyr, *Dialogue with Trypho* 24.1.
[2] See John Gill, "Preface" to his *The Cause of God and Truth*, (repr., London: W. H. Collingridge, 1855), iii (originally published in four parts between 1735–1738).

and John Owen (1616–1683),[3] he was convinced that there were significant traces of these doctrines detectable in Patristic authors.[4] His treatment of the Fathers on this subject was based upon a diligent reading of various primary sources and contained his own fresh translation of many of the texts that he cited. Having worked in detail through a few of the texts that Gill discussed, one cannot but be impressed by the depth of his knowledge of the Fathers.

It is noteworthy that the number of Fathers cited by Gill in support of the doctrine of particular redemption was greater than those quoted for any of the other four points. He cites thirty-three Patristic authorities in all, ranging from the first-century Italian Clement of Rome (fl. 96) to the late fourth- and early fifth-century Latin translator Jerome (c. 347–420).[5] Gill purposely left out Augustine of Hippo (354–430), as well as Prosper of Aquitaine (c. 388–c. 455) and Fulgentius of Ruspe (c. 462–c. 527), two of Augustine's most prominent advocates, since it was common knowledge where they stood.[6] This sort of "proof-texting" is out of academic fashion today, primarily because of the danger it holds for failing to observe the context of the original text and thus seriously misconstruing the meaning of the passage under discussion. Yet, given the fact that the doctrine of particular redemption was neither the subject of controversy nor the center of detailed discussion in the Patristic era, nor even in the Pelagian controversy of the fifth century,[7] it seems to this writer that any treatment of this subject in the "ancient church," as Gill terms the Patristic period,[8] must follow the general pattern of the Baptist theologian's examination. In fact, Gill's roster of Patristic testimonies really provides an excellent starting point for any essay on this subject. Hence, in what follows, a number of the texts he cites will be reexamined, with due attention to their contexts, to see if we are warranted to say that there is a witness to this doctrine in the ancient church and what the nature of that witness is.[9]

---

[3] See, for example, the brief discussion of Turretin's citation of Patristic authorities by Raymond A. Blacketer, "Definite Atonement in Historical Perspective," in *The Glory of the Atonement: Biblical, Historical, and Practical Perspectives. Essays in Honor of Roger Nicole*, ed. Charles E. Hill and Frank A. James III (Downers Grove, IL: InterVarsity Press, 2004), 308, and the five-page addendum by John Owen to his magisterial *Salus Electorum, Sanguis Jesu: Or The Death of Death In the Death of Christ* (London: Philemon Stephens, 1648), 322–26.

[4] Gill, *Cause of God and Truth*, 220–22.

[5] Ibid., 241–65.

[6] Ibid., 221–22. See the statement of Owen, *Death of Death*, 325, where, after citing a text of Augustine that reveals his belief in particular redemption, he comments, "his judgement in these things is known to all."

[7] W. H. Goold, "Prefatory Note" to *Salus Electorum, Sanguis Jesu: Or The Death of Death in the Death of Christ*, in *The Works of John Owen*, ed. W. H. Goold, 24 vols. (Edinburgh: Johnstone & Hunter, 1850–1853; repr. Edinburgh: Banner of Truth, 1967), 10:140.

[8] Gill, *Cause of God and Truth*, 241.

[9] A major challenge in using Gill's citations in this regard is that he is consulting sixteenth-century editions of the Fathers, which are no longer easily accessible by twenty-first-century readers.

Texts from five of the authors examined by Gill, still only a small representative sample, have been chosen for extended discussion in this essay: Clement of Rome and Justin Martyr (c. 100–165), both from the earliest period of Christian witness after the apostolic era; and Hilary of Poitiers (310/315–367/368), Ambrose (c. 340–397), and Jerome—three significant theologians from the fourth century. In addition, Augustine and Prosper of Aquitaine will also be briefly examined. By such usage of this section of *The Cause of God and Truth*, this essay does not intend itself to be a study of Gill's thought; rather, Gill's citations are being employed as a springboard into the thought of early Christianity. It goes without saying that discussion of all of the early Christian authors who figure in Gill's *The Cause of God and Truth* would require a monograph. Hopefully, though, this brief study will indicate that such a monograph would be a valuable addition to the scholarship on the doctrines of grace.

Preliminary to this discussion, however, a number of general remarks regarding the doctrine of definite atonement in early Christian thinking need to be made. First, as has already been indicated, this is not a controversial issue in the ancient church, not even in the early fifth-century Pelagian controversy. As such, what can be gleaned about this doctrine in this era is mostly from implied comments rather than direct assertion. But this does not mean that there is no evidence of the doctrine. As Raymond A. Blacketer rightly comments, "There is a trajectory of thought in the Christian tradition running from the Patristic era through the Middle Ages that stresses a specific, particular and defined purpose of God in salvation; but it is a minority position and is frequently ambiguous."[10] Then, at the very beginning of the Patristic era, the Fathers had to deal with the elitism of various Gnostic groups, which led them to stress the universalism of the Christian gospel and, understandably, to downplay the particularity of the cross-work of Christ. Also the need to avoid Greco-Roman fatalism, much of it the result of popular Stoicism, issued in a concern to stress the freedom of the human will, and this, in turn, served to diminish any desire to discuss the extent of the atonement. Finally, this lack of discussion in early Christian thought about the people for whom Christ died should not surprise us given the fact that, while the person of Christ was the subject of "lively" discussion in the Patristic era and ultimately vital dogmatic pronouncements, "the saving work of Christ remained

---

[10] Blacketer, "Definite Atonement in Historical Perspective," 313.

dogmatically undefined."[11] What this does not mean is that the Fathers were uninterested in this overall subject—in fact, the very opposite: meditation on and thought about the atonement were a central feature of the piety, exegesis, and worship of the ancient church.[12]

Clement of Rome

Though few details are known about the life of Clement of Rome, his letter to the church at Corinth may well be the oldest Christian text after the canonical writings of the NT.[13] Written to rectify a schism that had rent the Corinthian community,[14] the main purpose of the letter is well summed up by a series of allusions to 1 Corinthians 13 in *1 Clement* 49.5:

> Love knows nothing of division, love does not foment rebellion, love does everything in harmony; in love all the elect of God are made perfect; without love nothing is pleasing to God. In love the Master received us; because of the love he had towards us, our Lord Jesus Christ gave his blood for us (ὑπὲρ ἡμῶν) in accord with the will of God: his flesh for the sake of our flesh, his life for our lives (τὴν ψυχὴν ὑπὲρ τῶν ψυχῶν ἡμῶν).[15]

The Corinthian believers are admonished to act in love because this is the way that their Lord has dealt with them—in love. Not surprisingly for a Chris-

---

[11] Jaroslav Pelikan, *The Christian Tradition. A History of the Development of Doctrine. Volume 1: The Emergence of the Catholic Tradition (100–600)* (Chicago: University of Chicago Press, 1971), 141.

[12] Pelikan, *Emergence of the Catholic Tradition*, 142–43. See also the comments of Sinclair B. Ferguson, "Christus Victor et Propitiator: The Death of Christ, Substitute and Conqueror," in *For the Fame of God's Name: Essays in Honor of John Piper*, ed. Sam Storms and Justin Taylor (Wheaton, IL: Crossway, 2010), 173–74. Brian Daley has made a persuasive case that the Fathers' soteriology was ultimately concerned with the implications of the union of God and humanity in Christ and that the death of Jesus was only part of this larger picture. See his "'He Himself Is Our Peace' (Ephesians 2:14): Early Christian Views of Redemption in Christ," in *The Redemption: An Interdisciplinary Symposium on Christ as Redeemer*, ed. Stephen T. Davis, Daniel Kendall, and Gerald O'Collins (Oxford: Oxford University Press, 2004), 149–76.

[13] For a study of his identity, see Peter Lampe, *From Paul to Valentinus: Christians at Rome in the First Two Centuries*, ed. Marshall D. Johnson, trans. Michael Steinhauser (Minneapolis: Fortress, 2003), 206–17. For the date of *1 Clement*, see Andrew Louth, "Clement of Rome," in *Early Christian Writings: The Apostolic Fathers*, trans. Maxwell Staniforth (1968 repr., Harmondsworth, Middlesex: Penguin Books, 1987), 20; Michael W. Holmes, "First Clement," in *The Apostolic Fathers: Greek Texts and English Translations*, ed. and trans. Michael W. Holmes, 3rd ed. (Grand Rapids, MI: Baker, 2007), 35–36; Andreas Lindemann, "The First Epistle of Clement," in *The Apostolic Fathers: An Introduction*, ed. Wilhelm Pratscher (Waco, TX: Baylor University Press, 2010), 65. *Pace* Thomas J. Herron, who has argued for an earlier date around 70 AD. See his "The Most Probable Date of the First Epistle of Clement to the Corinthians," in *Studia Patristica*, ed. Elizabeth A. Livingston (Leuven, Belgium: Peeters, 1989), 21:106–21. For a helpful overview of the letter and select bibliography, see Hubertus R. Drobner, *The Fathers of the Church: A Comprehensive Introduction*, trans. Siegfried S. Schatzmann and William Harmless (Peabody, MA: Hendrickson, 2007), 47–49.

[14] See, for example, *1 Clement* 1.1; 3.1–4; 46.5. For a discussion of this schism, see especially Andrew Gregory, "*1 Clement*: An Introduction," in *The Writings of the Apostolic Fathers*, ed. Paul Foster (London/New York: T. & T. Clark, 2007), 24–28; and A. Lindemann, "First Epistle of Clement," in *Apostolic Fathers: An Introduction*, 59–62. See also Davorin Peterlin, "Clement's Answer to the Corinthian Conflict in AD 96," *JETS* 39 (1996): 57–69.

[15] Trans. Michael A. G. Haykin. Unless indicated, translations are my own. For Gill's discussion of this text, see *Cause of God and Truth*, 241.

tian author, Clement employs Christ's dying "for us"—which he amplifies as Christ's shedding his blood for us, sacrificing his body for ours and his soul/ life for ours—as an example of what constitutes true love and how it acts unselfishly. The contextual equation of "the elect of God" with the "us" for whom Christ died, an equation that Gill suggests, seems entirely justifiable.[16] This equation is strengthened by an earlier typological reading in the letter of the scarlet cord hung by Rahab from her window (see Joshua 2:15–21): it was a "sign" (σημεῖον) that "through the blood of the Lord there will be redemption for all who believe and hope in God."[17] The shedding of Christ's blood brings about redemption not for all and sundry, but, Clement specifies, for "all who believe and hope in God." In line with this understanding of the death of Christ, Clement later prays that "the Creator of all things may keep intact the specified number of his elect in the whole world,"[18] a passage that echoes the prayer of Jesus specifically for those whom the Father has given to him (John 17:9).

Near the beginning of his letter, however, Clement makes a comment that has been taken as an affirmation of a general redemption. In *1 Clement* 7.4, he urges his readers to "gaze intently at the blood of Christ and understand how precious it is to his Father, because, having been poured out for the sake of our salvation, it made available/won [ὑπήνεγκεν] the grace of repentance for the whole world."[19] In what follows this statement, Clement notes that

---

[16] See also a similar train of argument in *1 Clement* 50.3–7. Charles Merritt Nielsen, "Clement of Rome and Moralism," *Church History* 31 (1962): 135, has noted that the term "elect" was a favorite of Clement.

[17] Clement, *1 Clement* 12.7. See the similar interpretation of this biblical text by Justin Martyr, *Dialogue with Trypho* 111.4.

[18] Clement, *1 Clement* 59.2, trans. Holmes, *Apostolic Fathers: Greek Texts and English Translations*, 123.

[19] Clement, *1 Clement* 7.4. For the translation of ὑπήνεγκεν as "made available," see Frederick William Danker, rev. and ed., *A Greek-English Lexicon of the New Testament and Other Early Christian Literature*, 3rd ed. (Chicago: University of Chicago Press, 2000), 1042–43. For the translation "won," see J. B. Lightfoot, ed. and trans., *The Apostolic Fathers: Clement, Ignatius, and Polycarp* (1889–1890; repr., Grand Rapids, MI: Baker, 1981), 1/2:37; and Holmes, *Apostolic Fathers: Greek Texts and English Translations*, 55.

A good number of English editions of *1 Clement* read the Greek term ὑπήνεγκεν, as above. See Lightfoot, *Apostolic Fathers: Clement, Ignatius, and Polycarp*, 1/2:36–37; Holmes, *Apostolic Fathers: Greek Texts and English Translations*, 54; Bart D. Ehrman, ed. and trans., *The Apostolic Fathers*, 2 vols. The Loeb Classical Library (Cambridge, MA: Harvard University Press, 2003), 1:46. But there is actually a variant at this point, ἐπήνεγκεν, which should be translated as "it granted" or "it gave" (Danker, *A Greek-English Lexicon*, 386), and which is followed by recent French and German editions. See Annie Jaubert, ed. and trans., *Clément de Rome: Épître aux Corinthiens*, Sources chrétiennes 167 (Paris: Les Éditions du Cerf, 1971), 110; Gerhard Schneider, trans. and introduction, *Clemens von Rom: Brief an die Korinther*, Fontes Christiani 15 (Freiburg: Herder, 1994), 80. Though, see Horacio E. Lona, trans. and annotated, *Der erste Clemensbrief*, Kommentar zu den Apostolischen Vätern, 2 vols. (Göttingen, Germany: Vandenhoeck & Ruprecht, 1998), 2:177, who accepts ὑπήνεγκεν as the proper reading.

There are two key Greek manuscripts of *1 Clement*: Codex Alexandrinus (A) from the fifth century, which also contains almost the entire Greek Bible, and Codex Hierosolymitanus graecus 54 (H), dated from 1056. There is also a Latin translation copied in the eleventh century, Codex Latinus (L), which has a version of the text that appears to be a translation made in the second or third century. As such, Codex Latinus is sometimes more reliable than either of the two Greek manuscripts. Two Coptic (Co) manuscripts and one in Syriac (S) also exist. For the textual

the grace of repentance was made available by God—the sovereign ruler of history, or δεσπότης, as he calls him (7.5)—to those past generations that heard the preaching of Noah and then Jonah (7.6–7). Given this context and in the light of the overall concern of the letter to bring the Corinthian church to repentance over the sin of schism, *1 Clement* 7.4 must be seen as emphasizing that the scope of this grace has been broadened in the new covenant, established as it is by the shed blood of Christ, to encompass the whole world.[20] In other words, Clement is stressing that there is abundant grace available to lead the Corinthians to repentance. Now, the means Clement urges the Corinthians to employ in order to come to repentance is by fixing their eyes upon the shed blood of Christ, which may well stand for the death of Christ.[21] Through meditation upon Christ's sacrifice and its worth in the eyes of God the Father, both of which contribute to its universal significance, Clement hopes his first readers will be led to renounce their sin.

A number of students of this letter point out that soteriology is not one of its prime subjects.[22] Undoubtedly this is true. These passages from *1 Clement* that we have examined, though, provide glimpses of soteriological perspectives, one of which seems to be clearly in line with NT emphases on Christ's death being for the elect.

Justin Martyr

The North African theologian Tertullian (fl. 190–220) remembered Justin Martyr as a "philosopher and martyr,"[23] and, as Paul Parvis has recently noted, these two epithets "reflect in different ways the two most enduring aspects of his legacy," though Parvis also rightly points out that there is far more to Justin than what is encapsulated by these terms.[24] Sara Parvis

---

sources of *1 Clement*, see Schneider, *Clemens von Rom: Brief an die Korinther*, 56–61. The reading ὑπήνεγκεν is found in A with support from S and Co, while ἐπήνεγκεν is the reading of H, which is supported by L.

[20] Odd Magne Bakke, *"Concord and Peace": A Rhetorical Analysis of the First Letter of Clement with an Emphasis on the Language of Unity and Sedition* (Tübingen: Mohr [Paul Siebeck], 2001), 332. See the insightful comment of Adolf von Harnack, "The universalism of God's mercy first of all became a fact through the death of Christ" (my translation), in *Einführung in die alte Kirchengeschichte. Das Schreiben der römischen Kirche an die korinthische aus der Zeit Domitians (I. Clemensbrief)*, ed. Adolf von Harnack (Leipzig: J. C. Hinrichs, 1929), 78.

[21] There is no mention of the word "cross" (σταυρός) in the letter. For other references to the "blood of Christ," see *1 Clement* 12.7; 21.6; and 49.6. See also Schneider, *Clemens von Rom: Brief an die Korinther*, 46. Edmund W. Fisher, "'Let Us Look upon the Blood-of-Christ' (1 Clement 7:4)," *Vigiliae Christianae* 34 (1980): 218–36, unconvincingly argues that this verse is a reference to the Lord's Supper.

[22] See, for example, Lona, *Der erste Clemensbrief*, 177 n. 6.

[23] Tertullian, *Against the Valentinians* 5.

[24] Paul Parvis, "Justin Martyr," in *Early Christian Thinkers: The Lives and Legacies of Twelve Key Figures*, ed. Paul Foster (Downers Grove, IL: InterVarsity Press, 2010), 1. This is an extremely helpful introduction to the life and significance of Justin. See also Drobner, *Fathers of the Church*, 77–82.

has argued that it was Justin Martyr who "forged the genre of Christian apologetic."[25] In what follows, we look at some aspects of Justin, the theologian of the cross.

L. W. Barnard has observed that more than any other second-century apologist, Justin "states repeatedly that Christ saves us by his death on the Cross and by his resurrection."[26] In his *First Apology*, for example, Justin cited the messianic prophecy of Genesis 49:10–11 and interpreted the phrase "washing his robe in the blood of the grape" as heralding "beforehand the suffering he [that is, Christ] was going to endure, cleansing through his blood those who believed in him."[27] Justin specified that the term "robe" referred to "the human beings who believe" in Christ. In other words, the cleansing work of the Christ is specifically directed at believers. Justin gives the same interpretation in the *Dialogue with Trypho*, where he stated that Genesis 49:11 was prophetic of the fact that Christ "will cleanse in his own blood those who believe in him. For the Holy Spirit called his robe those who receive forgiveness of sins from him, in whom he is always present in power and among whom he will be visibly present at his second coming."[28]

The *Dialogue with Trypho* is filled with references to the crucified Christ. Through the crucified Christ men and women turn to God.[29] Those who repent of their sins are purified "by faith through the blood of Christ and his death."[30] For all who approach the Father through Christ's sufferings there is healing.[31] Christ endured his sufferings at the cross "for the sake [ὑπὲρ] of those human beings who are cleansing their souls from all sin."[32] By his crucifixion Christ has "ransomed [ἐλυτρώσατο] us, who were immersed under the weightiest of sins [βεβαπτισμένους ταῖς βαρυτάταις ἁμαρτίαις]" and "made us a house of prayer and adoration."[33] Salvation from the sting of Satan has come through the cross and refuge in the One who sent his Son

[25] Sara Parvis, "Justin Martyr and the Apologetic Tradition," in *Justin Martyr and His Worlds*, ed. Sara Parvis and Paul Foster (Minneapolis: Fortress, 2007), 117. See her entire article for her persuasive argument (115–27).
[26] Barnard, *Justin Martyr*, 124. Peter Ensor, "Justin Martyr and Penal Substitutionary Atonement," *EQ* 83 (2011): 220, makes a similar comment with specific reference to Justin's *Dialogue with Trypho*: it is "saturated with references to the cross."
[27] Justin, *First Apology* 32.1, 5, 7, in *Justin, Philosopher and Martyr*, 171.
[28] Justin, *Dialogue with Trypho* 54.1. Cf. also 76.2 and the similar interpretation by, among other Patristic authors, Irenaeus, *Demonstration of the Apostolic Preaching* 57; and Amphilochius of Iconium, *Homily 6: In Illud: Pater si possibile est*, in *Amphilochii Iconiensis Opera*, ed. Carnelis Datema, Corpus Christianorum, Series Graeca, 72 vols. (Turnhout: Brepols/Leuven: University Press, 1978), 3:150–51.
[29] Justin, *Dialogue with Trypho* 11.4, 5.
[30] Ibid., 13.1.
[31] Ibid., 17.1. See also *Second Apology* 13.4.
[32] Justin, *Dialogue with Trypho* 41.1.
[33] Ibid., 86.6.

into the world to be crucified.[34] In a word, the blood of Christ has saved "from all nations those who were once sexually immoral and wicked—they have received forgiveness of their sins and no longer live in sin."[35] All of these references imply a specificity in the extent of the atonement.[36]

In one text, though, Justin appears to speak more generally about the atoning death of Christ. Trypho expressed his incredulity that the Messiah whom he and his people were expecting was Jesus of Nazareth, since he had been crucified and thus experienced so "shameful and dishonourable [αἰσχρῶς καὶ ἀτίμως]" a death that the law specifically named it as cursed.[37] Trypho is clearly thinking of Deuteronomy 21:22–23.[38] In his answer, Justin first rehearsed what he considered to be a number of OT predictions that the Messiah would be crucified.[39] He then specified that while men who die by crucifixion are indeed, according to the law, accursed, Christ himself had done nothing to deserve the curse of God.[40] If the truth be told, Justin continued, the entire human race, apart from Jesus, is under God's curse: no Jew has ever kept the law entirely, and as for the Gentiles, they are clearly accursed for they are idolatrous, sexual corrupters of the young, and doers of all manner of evil.[41] "If therefore the Father of the universe determined that his own Christ, for the sake of human beings from every race, was to take responsibility [ἀναδέξασθαι] for the curses of all," Justin reasoned, "why do you indict him as one accursed who endured this suffering in accord with the will of the Father and not rather bewail yourselves?"[42] Christ suffered, not for sins he had done, but "in the stead of the human race [ὑπὲρ τοῦ ἀνθρωπείου γένους]"—their cursedness he took upon himself and in this sense died in the manner of one accursed.[43] As Steve Jeffery, Michael Ovey, and Andrew Sach rightly comment, this "amounts to a clear statement of penal substitution."[44] Firm support for their judgment is found in the flow of Justin's argument

---

[34] Ibid., 91.4.
[35] Ibid., 111.4.
[36] Here I concur with the opinion of Gill, *Cause of God and Truth*, 242.
[37] Justin, *Dialogue with Trypho* 89.1–2; 90.1. See also 32.1.
[38] Steve Jeffery, Michael Ovey, and Andrew Sach, *Pierced for Our Transgressions: Rediscovering the Glory of Penal Substitution* (Wheaton, IL: Crossway, 2007), 164–65. Justin quotes this passage from Deuteronomy in *Dialogue with Trypho* 96.1.
[39] Ibid., 90–91 and 94. Among these is one Christ himself refers to, namely, the bronze serpent that Moses was instructed to place upon a pole (Numbers 21:6–9). See John 3:14–15.
[40] Justin, *Dialogue with Trypho* 94.5.
[41] Ibid., 95.1.
[42] Ibid., 95.2.
[43] Ibid.
[44] Jeffery, Ovey, Sach, *Pierced for Our Transgressions*, 166.

and his use of the verb ἀναδέχομαι in relation to the death of Christ.[45] In the Greek papyri the verb ἀναδέχομαι is often used with a legal meaning, namely "to become surety for," and G. W. H. Lampe has listed its usage with this meaning in Patristic literature dealing with the atonement.[46]

These texts from the *Dialogue with Trypho* 89–96 are the most extensive discussion of the cross in Justin's writings, but they do not provide an unambiguous statement regarding the extent of the atonement. Justin ended up affirming that Christ died for "the human race," though a little earlier in the text he had stated that he died for "human beings from every race." If these passages are lined up with Justin's other statements about the cross, then they may well be interpreted as affirming a particularity in the extent of the atonement. On the other hand, Justin's basic philosophical position, which, among other things, highlighted the freedom of choice of human beings with regard to the salvation offered in the Christian gospel[47]—an explicit rejection of the fatalism regnant in many quarters of Greco-Roman culture—would have caused strain with a view that regarded Christ's death as one for the elect of God. It is noteworthy that both Barnard and Henry Chadwick have noted an overall tension between Justin's philosophical convictions and his affirmations about the redemptive work of Christ. They have argued that his statements about the cross represent a fundamental part of the "traditional faith of the church" that was current in his day. Justin wholeheartedly accepted this faith though it did not always fit well with his philosophical perspectives.[48]

Hilary of Poitiers

Hilary, a leading champion of biblical Trinitarianism at the height of the fourth-century Arian controversy and a "theological bridge" between the Latin West and the Greek East, was born between 310 and 315 into a non-Christian home in Poitiers (Latin: Pictavis) in Aquitainia Secunda, and died

---

[45] Ensor, "Justin Martyr and penal substitutionary atonement," 222–25. For recent debate about this text, see Derek Flood, "Substitutionary Atonement and the Church Fathers: A Reply to the Authors of *Pierced for Our Transgressions*," *EQ* 82.2 (2010): 142–59 (144–45), and Garry J. Williams's response, "Penal Substitutionary Atonement in the Church Fathers," *EQ* 83.3 (2011): 195–216 (196–99).

[46] H. G. Meecham, *The Epistle to Diognetus* (Manchester, UK: Manchester University Press, 1949), 129; G. W. H. Lampe, *A Patristic Greek Lexicon* (Oxford: Clarendon, 1961), 101.

[47] See, for example, Justin, *First Apology* 43–44.

[48] Barnard, *Justin Martyr*, 124–25; Henry Chadwick, "Justin Martyr's Defence of Christianity," *The Bulletin of the John Rylands Library* 47 (1965): 293. On Justin's view of the atonement as representative of the church of his day, see also Ensor, "Justin Martyr and Penal Substitutionary Atonement," 231–32.

there in either 367 or 368.[49] He probably became a Christian in his early twenties.[50]

As Hilary read the NT he understood the purpose behind the coming of the Lord Jesus Christ into this world and specifically what he had achieved by his death:

> . . . he received the flesh of sin that by assuming our flesh he might forgive our sin, but, while he takes our flesh, he does not share in our sin. By his death he destroyed the sentence of death in order that, by creating our race anew in his person, he might abolish the sentence of the former decree. He allows himself to be nailed to the cross in order that by the curse of the cross all the curses of our earthly condemnation might be nailed to it and obliterated. Finally, he suffers as man in order to shame the powers. While God, according to the Scriptures, is to die, he would triumph with the confidence in himself of a conqueror. While he, the immortal One, would not be overcome by death, he would die for the eternal life of us mortals.
>
> These deeds of God, therefore, are beyond the understanding of our human nature and do not fit in with our natural process of thought, because the work of Infinite Eternity demands an infinite faculty of appraisal.[51]

Hilary is well aware that human reason cannot ultimately comprehend such "deeds of God" as the incarnation and the atonement. Such affirmations as "God became man," "the Immortal dies," and "the Eternal is buried" must be embraced by faith—"the obedience of faith carries us beyond the natural power of [mere human] comprehension," as he noted later in this treatise.[52] Now, immediately before this passage Hilary had cited Colossians 2:8–13, and this delineation of what Christ accomplished by his death is shaped by that Pauline passage. Christ's death, the crucifixion of One without sin, is the means by which mortal humans receive the forgiveness of sins. The mechanics of how this occurs is hinted at in the clause drawn from Colossians 2:14: Christ was nailed to the accursed cross so that the curses that should have fallen on us were taken by him on the cross, which bespeaks an understanding

---

[49] For the life and works of Hilary and select bibliography, see Drobner, *Fathers of the Church*, 253–61. The quoted phrase is from George Morrel, "Hilary of Poitiers: A Theological Bridge between Christian East and Christian West," *The Anglican Theological Review* 44 (1962): 313–16.

[50] For more on the life of Hilary, see my book, *The Empire of the Holy Spirit: Reflecting on Biblical and Historical Patterns of Life in the Spirit* (Mountain Home, AR: BorderStone, 2010), 63–65.

[51] Hilary, *On the Trinity* 1.13, in *Saint Hilary of Poitiers: The Trinity*, trans. Stephen McKenna (New York: Fathers of the Church, Inc., 1954), 14–15, altered. For the Latin of this passage, see *Sancti Hilarii Pictaviensis Episcopi: De Trinitate: Praefatio, Libri I–VII*, ed. Pierre Smulders, Corpus Christianorum Series Latina 62 (Turnhout, Belgium: Brepols, 1979), 14–15.

[52] Hilary, *On the Trinity* 1.37, in *Saint Hilary of Poitiers: The Trinity*, 34.

of Christ's death as a vicarious atonement. Then, his death opens the doorway to eternal life for those who are mortal. Finally, his death is a victory over the powers of evil—the familiar *Christus Victor* theme of the ancient church. This text is a good example of the fact that any analysis of the Patristic doctrine of the atonement cannot pigeonhole the Fathers into simply holding one, and only one, view of the atonement.[53] Here, Hilary enunciated both a view of the cross as a triumph over the powers of evil—*Christus Victor*—and of his death as a vicarious suffering for sinners—*Christus Vicarius*.[54]

In another text, Hilary's commentary on the Old Latin text of Psalm 130,[55] there is a meditation on the necessity of Christ's atoning work because of human sin. Reflecting on the statement "because there is forgiveness [*propitatio*] with you" in Psalm 130:4, Hilary noted that ultimately the reason the psalmist can say this is because

> The only-begotten Son of God, God the Word, is our redemption, our peace, in whose blood we are reconciled to God. He came to remove [*tollere*] the sins of the world, and by fastening the handwriting of the law to his cross [*cruci suae chirographum legis adfigens*], he abolished the edict of long-standing condemnation. . . . "Because there is forgiveness with you": because the Son is in the Father according to the [very] likeness of his glory and the Son himself is the forgiveness of, redemption from and supplication for our sins [*pro peccatis nostris et propitatio et redemption et deprecatio*], therefore he does not remember our iniquities because he himself is their forgiveness.[56]

Hilary again used Colossians 2:14 to explicate how Christ redeems men and women, establishes peace between them and God, and grants them forgiveness of their sins. He removes their sins, which condemn them before a just God, by being fastened to the cross for those very sins. In this way, Christ himself becomes their forgiveness. And the Father can forgive because the Son is in him, and he in the Son, the crucified Son being thus his forgiveness. In so arguing, Hilary implicitly presupposed a penal substitutionary model of the atonement, as do other texts from his commentary on the Psalms.[57]

---

[53] Williams, "Penal Substitutionary Atonement," 215.

[54] See also Hilary's similar exegesis of Colossians 2:14 in *On the Trinity* 9.10, in *Saint Hilary of Poitiers: The Trinity*, 330–31.

[55] Psalm 129 in the Old Latin Bible.

[56] Hilary, *On Psalm* 129.9. For the Latin text, see *Sancti Hilarii Pictaviensis Episcopi: Tractatus super Psalmos: In Psalmos CXIX–CL*, ed. Jean Doignon and R. Demeulenaere, Corpus Christianorum Series Latina 61B (Turnhout, Belgium: Brepols, 2009), 105.

[57] For other texts in his commentary on the Psalms that contain a penal substitutionary view of the atonement, see Hilary, *On Psalm* 53.13; 54.13; 69.9; 135.15: "he redeemed us, when he gave himself for our sins, he redeemed us by his blood, by his suffering, by his death, by his resurrection: these are the great price of our life" (*Tractatus*

Hilary's frequent use of the first-person plural pronoun with regard to the atonement in these texts is indicative that the concept of a particular redemption is not outside the purview of Hilary's thought. In fact, in some remarks Hilary made about Psalm 55[56], he provided a clear statement about particular redemption. He has mentioned the fact that "all flesh has been redeemed by Christ that it might rise again and it is necessary for all to appear before his judgment seat; yet in this resurrection not all have a common glory and honor." As Hilary explained, some will indeed rise again but to divine wrath and punishment. Such, however, is not the future for believers:

> From which wrath the Apostle promises that we shall be rescued, saying, "Because if, when we were still sinners, Christ died for us, much more we, who have been justified by his blood, shall be saved from wrath by him" (Romans 5:8–9). Therefore, he died for sinners that they might have the salvation of the resurrection [*salutem resurrectionis*], but he will save from wrath those who have been sanctified by his blood [*sanctificatos in sanguine suo saluabit ab ira*].[58]

Hilary made a distinction here between "sinners," who will be resurrected to face the wrath of God, and "those who have been sanctified" by the blood of Christ, who will be delivered from divine judgment. Hilary's use of the term *salus* to refer to the resurrection of the wicked is somewhat confusing, and he has clearly misread Romans 5:8–9. He has distinguished between two groups of human beings on the basis of this Pauline passage—sinners and those "who have been justified by his blood"—though a more straightforward reading of this text would read these two as the same. Be this as it may, this text does provide an indication that in Hilary's mind Christ's death has a special import for believers.

Hilary's abiding concern, though, has more to do with the person of the Son than with his work. In his commentary on Psalm 130 cited above, Hilary's tying of the Son's cross-work to the perichoretic relationship of the Son and the Father reveals a major concern that surfaces again and again in

---

super *Psalmos*, 170). For a discussion of Hilary's teaching on penal substitution in his commentary on Psalm 53 (54), see Jeffery, Ovey, and Sach, *Pierced for Our Transgressions*, 167–69.
[58] Hilary, *On Psalm* 55.7. For the Latin text, see *Sancti Hilarii Pictaviensis Episcopi: Tractatus super Psalmos: Instructio Psalmorum, In Psalmos I–XCI*, ed. Jean Doignon, Corpus Christianorum Series Latina 61A (Turnhout, Belgium: Brepols, 1997), 157–58. Gill, *Cause of God and Truth*, 253, cites this text as "a remarkable passage," in which Hilary "distinguishes the salvation of some from others, by virtue of Christ's redemption."

Hilary's exegesis, namely, his concern to demonstrate the full deity of the Son. A good example is *On the Trinity* 10, which is the second longest book in Hilary's magnum opus and which is entirely devoted to a discussion of texts that are central to the Gospel account of the suffering and death of Christ: Matthew 26:38–39, Christ's confession of soul sorrow and plea that the cup of suffering might pass from him; Matthew 27:46, the cry of dereliction; and Luke 23:46, Christ's final act of faith as he dies. Hilary says very little in this entire discussion that can be used to delineate his understanding of the dynamics of the atonement. His resolute focus is the demonstration that these texts do not imply that the Son is at all inferior to the Father.[59] Given the crisis that the church of his day faced with the Arian onslaught, this concern is quite understandable. And from his perspective this was above all a soteriological issue: if the Son is not fully equal to the Father, he cannot be our Savior.[60] So Hilary exhorted his readers, "Hold fast to Christ the God who accomplished the works of our salvation when he was dying!"[61]

The Latin Patristic Tradition after Hilary

The doctrine of the atonement as it was developed by Western thinkers after Hilary was a critical part of the background of Protestant reflection on definite atonement at the time of the Reformation and beyond.[62]

AMBROSE

Key among these Western thinkers was Ambrose, whose role in the formation of Latin Christianity was both "remarkable and complex."[63] A provincial governor before being appointed Bishop of Milan in 374, and thus used to the exercise of power, Ambrose did not find it easy to adjust to his new role. His relationships with those like the Arian empress Justina (d. 388) or the decidedly orthodox Theodosius I (347–395), who made Nicene Trinitarianism

---

[59] See Mark Weedman, *The Trinitarian Theology of Hilary of Poitiers*, Supplements to Vigiliae Christianae 89 (Leiden/Boston: Brill, 2007), 166–73.

[60] Weedman, *Trinitarian Theology of Hilary of Poitiers*, 174.

[61] Hilary, *On the Trinity* 9.10. For the Latin text, see *Sancti Hilarii Pictaviensis Episcopi: De Trinitate: Libri VIII–XII*, ed. Pierre Smulders, Corpus Christianorum Series Latina 62A (Turnhout, Belgium: Brepols, 1980), 381.

[62] Gill references a number of the Latin Fathers after the time of Hilary, including Marius Victorinus, Ambrose, Rufinus of Aquileia, and Jerome (*Cause of God and Truth*, 254–65).

[63] Ivor Davidson, "Ambrose," in *The Early Christian World*, ed. Philip F. Esler, 2 vols. (London/New York: Routledge, 2000), 2:1175. On the life and thought of Ambrose, see Neil B. McLynn, *Ambrose of Milan: Church and Court in a Christian Capital* (Berkeley: University of California Press, 1994); and Daniel H. Williams, *Ambrose of Milan and the End of the Nicene-Arian Conflicts* (Oxford: Clarendon/New York: Oxford University Press, 1995). For selections of his writings, see Boniface Ramsey, *Ambrose* (London/New York: Routledge, 1997). The classic study is F. Holmes Dudden, *The Life and Times of St. Ambrose*, 2 vols. (Oxford: Clarendon, 1935).

the official religion of the Roman Empire, illustrate the dangers faced by influential church leaders in a society now committed to the Christian faith.

Close analysis of Ambrose's statements about the cross reveals the seeds of certain textual explanations and theological arguments that would later be employed in defending definite atonement in the late sixteenth and seventeenth century. For example, Ambrose employs the "double jeopardy" argument so often associated with seventeenth-century Puritans such as John Owen in defense of definite atonement. In his treatise *Jacob and the Blessed Life*, Ambrose argued, "Can he damn you, whom he has redeemed from death [*quem redemit a morte*], for whom he offered himself, whose life he knows is the reward of his own death?"[64]

JEROME

Another of the most influential occidental theologians is Jerome, best remembered for his translation of the Bible into Latin, known today as the Vulgate. He is of interest to us in this chapter because of a comment he made on Christ's words in Matthew 20:28 ("and to give his life as a ransom for many"): "This took place when he took the form of a slave that he might pour out his blood for the world. And he did not say "to give his life as a redemption for all," but "for many," that is, for those who wanted to believe" [*pro omnibus, sed pro multis, id est pro his qui credere voluerunt*]."[65] Here Jerome defines the "many" as "those who wanted to believe." While there may be some ambiguity here in Jerome's statement, the words at least hint that Jerome saw Christ's death to be for a particular group of people—believers.

AUGUSTINE

With the coming of the Pelagian controversy, new issues on the soteriological landscape now came to dominate the horizon. Responding to Pelagius's (fl. 400) denial of original sin and bold assertion that human nature at its core is good and able to do all that God commands it to do, Augustine insisted upon the priority of the grace of God at every stage in the Christian life, from

---

[64] Ambrose, *Jacob and the Blessed Life* 1.6.26, in *Ambroise de Milan: Jacob et la view heureuse*, Sources chrétiennes 534 (Paris: Les Éditions du Cerf, 2010), 386. The translation here is based on that of Gill, *Cause of God and Truth*, 260.

[65] Jerome, *Commentary on Matthew* 3.20, in *St. Jerome: Commentary on Matthew*, trans. Thomas P. Scheck, The Fathers of the Church, 125 vols. (Washington, DC: Catholic University of America Press, 2008), 117:228–29. On Jerome, see especially J. N. D. Kelly, *Jerome: His Life, Writings, and Controversies* (San Francisco: Harper & Row, 1975).

its beginning to its end. As he meditated upon Scripture, and especially the book of Romans, he came to the conviction that human beings do not possess the necessary power or freedom to take any step at all toward salvation. Far from possessing any such "freedom of the will," humans had a will that was corrupted and tainted by sin, one that bent them toward evil and away from God. Only the grace of God could counteract this inbuilt bias toward sin. Augustine's response to Pelagius thus stressed the bondage of the human will and the need for God's radical intervention in grace to save lost sinners:

> Free will is capable only of sinning, if the way of truth remains hidden. And when what we should do and the goal we should strive for begins to be clear, unless we find delight in it and love it, we do not act, do not begin, do not live good lives. But so that we may love it, "the love of God" is poured out "in our hearts," not by free will which comes from ourselves, but "by the Holy Spirit who has been given to us" (Romans 5:5).[66]

For Augustine, then, redemption is possible only as a divine gift. It is the living God who initiates the process of salvation, not men or women.

This monergistic view of salvation logically entailed particular redemption, and there are a good number of passages in the Augustinian corpus that imply this view of the atoning work of Christ.[67] A few examples from his commentaries on John's Gospel and the first Johannine epistle will suffice to make the point. In discussing the term "sheep" in John 10:26, Augustine noted that those who are Christ's sheep "enjoy eternal life," but Christ describes those he is speaking to as not being among them. Why was that? Well, Augustine went on to explain that "he saw that they were predestined to eternal destruction, not secured for eternal life by the price of his blood [*ad sempiternum interitum praedestinatos, non ad vitam aeternam sui sanguinis pretio comparatos*]."[68] As Blacketer rightly notes, Augustine's comment clearly implies that Christ's blood was the price paid for those predestined to eternal life.[69] Then, commenting on the "many dwelling places" of John 14:2, Augustine argues that on the last day, "those whom he [Christ] redeemed by

---

[66] Augustine, *The Spirit and the Letter* 3.5, in *Augustine: Answer to the Pelagians*, trans. Roland J. Teske, The Works of Saint Augustine: A Translation for the 21st Century (Hyde Park, NY: New City Press, 1997), 1/23:152, altered.

[67] For a few of them, see Blacketer, "Definite Atonement in Historical Perspective," 308–10.

[68] Augustine, *Tractatus in Ioannis Evangelium* 48.4 (*PL* 35:1742; *NPNF*[1] 7:267). This work is to be dated from around 406–420s, thus concurrent with Augustine's battles with Pelagianism. For similar statements, see also Augustine, *On the Trinity* 4.3.17; 13.5.19.

[69] Blacketer, "Definite Atonement in Historical Perspective," 308–309.

his blood he will hand over also to his Father."[70] In other words, it is specifically those for whom Christ died who will be saved.

Augustine's particularistic bent in relation to Christ's atoning work is probably most clearly seen in his discussion of 1 John 2:2: "He is the propitiation for our sins, and not for ours only but also for the sins of the whole world." If Augustine had believed in a universal atonement, here was his opportunity to declare such. However, he does not interpret the phrase "whole world" as "all without exception," but rather as the "church of all nations" and the "church throughout the whole world."[71] Moreover, after 418, he rejects the universalistic interpretation of 1 Timothy 2:4 favored by the Pelagians, that God "desires all people to be saved and to come to the knowledge of the truth." Rather, this Pauline text is to be understood to mean "that no man is saved unless he [God] wishes him saved." The import of the text is not that "there is no man whose salvation God does not wish, but that no man is saved unless he wills it."[72] For Augustine, nobody is saved apart from the purposeful will of God, and since not all are saved, he cannot have determined to save all.

PROSPER OF AQUITAINE

What are strong hints of a definite atonement in Augustine become even clearer in the early writings of his younger contemporary, Prosper of Aquitaine. In his early Christian career, Prosper was an ardent disciple of Augustine. In debating with the Pelagians, Prosper admitted that Christ may be said to have died "for all" because he took on the human nature that all humanity shares and because of the "greatness and value" of his redeeming death. Yet, at the same time, Prosper argues that Christ "was crucified only for those who were to profit by his death," that is, only the elect.[73] In a letter to

---

[70] Augustine, *Tractate on the Gospel of John* 68.2, in *St. Augustine: Tractate on the Gospel of John 55–111*, trans. John W. Rettig, Fathers of the Church, 125 vols. (Washington, DC: Catholic University of America Press, 1994), 90:64.

[71] Augustine, *Tractate on the First Epistle of John* 1.8, in *St. Augustine: Tractates on the Gospel of John 112–24; Tractates on the First Epistle of John*, trans. John W. Rettig, Fathers of the Church, 125 vols. (Washington, DC: Catholic University of America Press, 1995), 92:132.

[72] Augustine, *Enchiridion* 27.103, in *Saint Augustine: Christian Instruction; Admonition and Grace; The Christian Combat; Faith, Hope and Charity*, trans. Bernard M. Peebles (New York: CIMA Publishing Co., 1947), 456. This text was written around 421, in the middle of the Pelagian controversy. Augustine cited 1 Timothy 2:4 some twelve times in his corpus. In the five passages that occur in writings after 418, he interprets it in the way noted above. See Roland J. Teske and Dorothea Weber, eds., *Prosper: De vocatione omnium Gentium*, Corpus Scriptorum Ecclesiasticorum Latinorum, 99 vols. (Vienna: Verlag der Österreichischen Akademie der Wissenschaften, 2009), 97:11 n. 5.

[73] Prosper, *Prosper of Aquitaine: Defense of St. Augustine*, trans. P. De Letter, Ancient Christian Writers, 66 vols. (New York: Newman, 1963), 32:149–51. For Prosper's fascinating career, see Alexander Y. Hwang, *Intrepid Lover*

Augustine, he also challenged the view of the so-called Semi-Pelagians that "the propitiation which is found in the mystery of the blood of Christ was offered for all men without exception."[74] From the letter it is clear that Prosper does not agree with this statement, and Augustine does not refute Prosper in his reply. In his later career, Prosper appears to have either softened this commitment to definite atonement,[75] or even rejected it in favor of an advocacy of the universal salvific will of God based on his reading of 1 Timothy 2:4.[76] Nevertheless, thus it was, at the close of the era of the ancient church and through the response of Augustine and his followers to the errors of Pelagianism and Semi-Pelagianism, that definite atonement came within the realm of theological investigation.

Conclusion

In closing, I return to the context of John Gill's impressive marshaling of material from the ancient church in which he was responding to Daniel Whitby's *A Discourse on the Five Points*. Whitby had claimed, "Certainly I do not find one in the first eight ages of Christianity that has said absolutely, and in terms, as is commonly said that Christ died only for the elect."[77] Gill, however, was confident that "some might say it, in other terms and words equivalent, of the same signification, and which amounted to the same sense" and that "the ancients often describe the persons for whom Christ died by such characters as cannot agree with all men."[78] The foregoing discussion has demonstrated that Gill's statement carries significant weight in the light of all the evidence.

The passages from the ancient church that Whitby, and others like the French Huguenot scholar Jean Daillé (1590–1674), employed as proof of a "general redemption," Gill answered by explaining that their language simply reflects the language of "all/world" in Scripture without necessarily meaning every single person in the world. Gill presented various interpretations by the

---

of Perfect Grace: The Life and Thought of Prosper of Aquitaine (Washington, DC: Catholic University of America Press, 2009).

[74] Prosper, *Letter* 225.3, in *Saint Augustine: Four Anti-Pelagian Writings*, trans. John A. Mourant and William J. Collinge, The Fathers of the Church: A New Translation, 125 vols. (Washington, DC: The Catholic University of America, 1992), 86:201. See also Prosper, *Letter* 225.6.

[75] Francis X. Gumerlock, "The 'Romanization' of Prosper of Aquitaine's Doctrine of Grace" (unpublished paper presented at the Annual Meeting of the North American Patristics Society, 2001; available at http://francisgumerlock .com/wp-content/uploads/Romanization-of-Prospers-Doctrine-of-Grace-NAPS-paper.pdf), accessed 4 May 2013.

[76] Teske and Weber, eds., *Prosper: De vocatione omnium Gentium*.

[77] Cited by Gill, *Cause of God and Truth*, 241.

[78] Ibid., 241.

church fathers for these texts, arguing that the meaning intended is possibly: (1) all sorts, ranks, and degrees;[79] (2) Jews and Gentiles;[80] (3) the sufficiency of Christ's death for all;[81] (4) God's will to save all;[82] (5) the world of the elect/saved/believing;[83] or (6) the general benefit for all, such as the resurrection of the dead which Christ's death and resurrection secures for everyone, as distinguished from eternal life for believers[84]—none of which mitigate against definite atonement.

While the fathers of the ancient church did not espouse a full-orbed doctrine of definite atonement, the analysis in this chapter has demonstrated that there was still a "particular and defined purpose of God in salvation"[85] present in their writings. Moreover, some of the key arguments used by late sixteenth- and seventeenth-century Reformers in defense of definite atonement are clearly present in seed form in the ancient church. Whether it be the interpretation of "all" as "all *kinds* of people," the "world" as referring in some cases to the "church" or the "whole church throughout the world," the employment of "double jeopardy" logic in relation to Christ's death and final punishment, particularistic statements about those for whom Christ died, and language about the definite nature of the atonement—all prepared the ground for later and more mature presentations of the doctrine of definite atonement in the history of the church.[86]

---

[79] Justin Martyr (ibid., 243); Irenaeus (ibid., 244); Ambrose (ibid., 258); Jerome (ibid., 265).

[80] Eusebius (ibid., 250); Cyril of Jerusalem (ibid., 256); John Chrysostom (ibid., 262).

[81] Athanasius (ibid., 252); Basil of Caesarea (ibid., 254); Ambrose (ibid., 260); John Chrysostom (ibid., 261); Jerome (ibid., 263).

[82] Hilary the Deacon (ibid., 258).

[83] Eusebius (ibid., 250); Cyril of Jerusalem (ibid., 255–56).

[84] Hilary of Poitiers (ibid., 253).

[85] Blacketer, "Definite Atonement in Historical Perspective," 313.

[86] For help with regard to certain elements of this essay, I am indebted to my research assistants, Ian Clary and Joe Harrod, and also to Paul Smythe, a student at The Southern Baptist Theological Seminary.

3

"Sufficient for All, Efficient for Some"

DEFINITE ATONEMENT IN THE MEDIEVAL CHURCH

David S. Hogg

Introduction

It has often been assumed that the expression and defense of definite atonement lacked clarity or support until the sixteenth and seventeenth centuries. With respect to the medieval church, such an assumption is inaccurate and misleading. To be sure, there were theologians in medieval Europe who disagreed with the idea that Christ died only for the elect who were predestined from before the foundation of the world. Nevertheless, for the most part, medieval theologians, including such giants as Peter Lombard and Thomas Aquinas, wrote about predestination, divine foreknowledge, free will, and the atoning death of Christ in a manner that is not only consistent with later Reformation expressions of definite atonement, but preparatory and foundational for this doctrine.[1]

---

[1] Raymond A. Blacketer, "Definite Atonement in Historical Perspective," in *The Glory of the Atonement: Biblical, Historical and Practical Perspectives: Essays in Honor of Roger Nicole*, ed. Charles E. Hill and Frank A. James III (Downers Grove, IL: InterVarsity Press, 2004), 304–23 (313), argues for a version of this position, stating that, "There is a trajectory of thought in the Christian tradition running from the Patristic era through the Middle Ages that stresses a specific, particular and defined purpose of God in salvation; but it is a minority position and is frequently ambiguous."

To this end, Guido Stucco has shown that there was continuity between theologians of the early medieval period and Augustinian thought. Drawing on the works of Fulgentius of Ruspe (early sixth century), Pope Gregory the Great (late sixth century) and Isidore of Seville (early seventh century), as well as marshaling evidence from early Sacramentaries, Stucco has demonstrated that ideas and theological developments consistent with what would later become defined as definite atonement were very much a part of the early medieval theological tapestry.[2] Additionally, Francis Gumerlock has persuasively argued a similar case with respect to theological discourse in the eighth century in particular.[3] This certainly helps explain how questions of definite atonement and predestination became a topic of heated exchange during the Carolingian period (mid-eighth to late tenth century) in the teaching and writing of Gottschalk of Orbais (ninth century). The details of the dispute that began between Gottschalk and Rabanus Maurus, archbishop of Mainz, in the mid-ninth century are well documented, so we need not linger over them, especially since the locus of attention for the doctrine of definite atonement needs to be on Peter Lombard. Even so, the Carolingian debates do highlight the ongoing vibrancy of a commitment to predestination and definite atonement on the part of prominent theologians and church leaders.[4]

Gottschalk of Orbais (808–867)

Although Gottschalk was the main protagonist in this dispute, it is important to recognize that he was not alone in publishing and preaching his convictions. His allies in the matter included such intellectuals and notables as Ratramnus of Corbie, Florus of Lyons, Prudentius, Bishop of Troyes, who was a member of the court of Emperor Louis the Pious, and Servatus Lupus, abbot of Ferrières.[5] Together, these and lesser-known protagonists of strict Augustinian predestination argued that Christ died for the elect. Granted, none of these men used the terms now commonly employed, such as limited or definite atonement, but the idea that Christ's blood was shed for those

---

[2] Guido Stucco, *The Colors of Grace: Medieval Kaleidoscopic Views of Grace and Predestination* (Bloomington, IN: Xlibris, 2008).

[3] Francis X. Gumerlock, "Predestination in the Century before Gottschalk (Part 1)," *EQ* 81.3 (2009): 195–209. Also, idem, "Predestination in the Century before Gottschalk (Part 2)," *EQ* 81.4 (2009): 319–37.

[4] For more on this debate, see Jaroslav Pelikan, *The Christian Tradition: A History and Development of Doctrine, Volume 3: The Growth of Medieval Theology (600–1300)* (Chicago: University of Chicago Press, 1978). A more technical though helpful resource may be found in G. R. Evans, "The Grammar of Predestination in the Ninth Century," in *JTS* (1982) 33:134–45.

[5] Pelikan, *Growth of Medieval Theology*, 81.

chosen and predestined by God from before the foundation of the world is clearly present.[6]

When we come to the specifics of Gottschalk's position, we must bear in mind that no comprehensive account remains among the works left to us.[7] With this in mind, it appears that the essence of the dispute lay in the relative weight placed on the operation of grace and free will. Gottschalk believed that he was following Augustine by teaching that human will does not possess the ability to choose righteousness apart from grace. Hincmar, Bishop of Reims and among the most forceful of Gottschalk's opponents, believed that such a position was problematic because it ran afoul of free will. This, said Gottschalk, was to give nature priority over grace.[8] Now as much as these two men and their respective companions disagreed over this issue, the more serious problem for Hincmar was that Gottschalk went where Augustine was reluctant to go, to double predestination. Gottschalk contended that both the elect and the reprobate had been chosen and appointed by God to their respective ends before creation. This singular act of predestination, which was applied in two ways, was solely a matter of God's own will.

In his *Shorter Confession*, Gottschalk states that God has predestined "the holy angels and elect human beings to eternal life" and has equally predestined "the devil himself, the head of all the demons, with all of his apostate angels and also with all reprobate human beings, namely, his members, to rightly eternal death."[9] Gottschalk repeats this very same idea in numerous other places as well, such as in his *Reply to Rabanus Maurus*, the *Larger Confession*, his *On Predestination*, and *Another Treatise on Predestination*.[10] For Gottschalk, predestination cannot be applied to just one part of creation (those who receive eternal life); otherwise God would be inconsistent in the manner in which he deals with all creation. Thus, the way in which predestination is applied to the elect cannot be held in distinction from the way in which predestination is applied to the reprobate. The act of election or

---

[6] Jonathan H. Rainbow, *The Will of God and the Cross: An Historical and Theological Study of John Calvin's Doctrine of Limited Redemption* (Allison Park, PA: Pickwick, 1990), 30.
[7] Victor Genke and Francis X. Gumerlock, eds. and trans., *Gottschalk and a Medieval Predestination Controversy: Texts Translated from the Latin* (Milwaukee, WI: Marquette University Press, 2010), 54.
[8] Pelikan, *Growth of Medieval Theology*, 82–83.
[9] Genke and Gumerlock, *Gottschalk*, 54.
[10] Genke and Gumerlock, *Gottschalk*.

predestination (the terms appear to be synonymous for Gottschalk) is one act which is applied in a twofold manner. In his *Longer Confession*, Gottschalk, citing and commenting on Isidore in support of this argument, says that, "'Predestination is twofold, either of the elect to rest or of the reprobate to death.' For he does not say that there are two predestinations, because there are not."[11] The point is that God does not provide direction to one part of creation and leave the other part to chance, since that would bring his sovereignty and providential care into question. This raises the obvious question of how the reprobate can be justly condemned if God predestined their final state in the first place.

Gottschalk's answer to this is inconsistent. As Francis Gumerlock points out, it appears that Gottschalk initially believed that God based his predestination of some to damnation on his foreknowledge of the rebellion and disobedience they would commit in the future.[12] It was only later that he changed his view and believed that God's predestination of the reprobate was as unrelated to their own decisions, actions, and works, as the election of the elect was to theirs.[13] Gumerlock admits, however, that because no firm chronology of Gottschalk's works can be determined, a definitive understanding of Gottschalk's position remains somewhat elusive. Even so, it is worth noting that the majority of what Gottschalk wrote either points to the simple fact that the reprobate are predestined to damnation with no explanation of the basis for God's decision, or he draws his readers' attention to Ephesians 1:11, where God's choice is grounded in his good will. Whichever way Gottschalk would have finally expressed himself, it should be evident that predestination and election were formative aspects of his soteriology. Indeed, this becomes all the more evident when we turn to his treatment of specific biblical texts.

GOTTSCHALK THE EXEGETE

In the 840s Gottschalk was called upon to defend his theology of double predestination by Rabanus Maurus, one of the foremost theologians of the day. In his defense, Gottschalk turned to 1 Timothy 2:4, which says that God wills that all men be saved and come to a knowledge of the truth. From the outset, however, Gottschalk makes it clear that the "all" to which Paul is referring

---

[11] Ibid., 55.

[12] In his *Shorter Confession*, Gottschalk states that all who are reprobate were predestined to eternal death, "on account of their own future, most certainly foreknown merits" (ibid., 56).

[13] Ibid., 58.

is all the elect and not all people. In summary, he says, "They therefore are all saved—all whom he wills to be saved."[14] Here Gottschalk's doctrine of predestination is lurking in the background. It is because God has predestined who will be saved from before the foundation of the world that Paul cannot mean that God wills every single person be saved. Predestination forms the lens through which Gottschalk understands God's saving will. The implication for the atonement, which is made explicit by the end of Gottschalk's letter to Rabanus Maurus, is that, "God, the creator and maker of all creatures, has deigned to be the gratuitous repairer and restorer of all the elect alone, but willed to be the Savior of none of the perpetually reprobate, the redeemer of none, and glorifier of none."[15]

In numerous other places, Gottschalk affirms his position that Christ died for the elect alone. In his collocation of biblical texts that speak about predestination and election (*On Predestination*), Gottschalk states unequivocally that, "We of course correctly believe, rightly hope and trust that the body and blood of Christ were handed over and shed for the church of Christ alone."[16] A little further on he emphasizes that, "[the psalmist] declares that the reprobate were neither redeemed nor set free by God through the blood of Christ's cross."[17]

Against this, one might cite 2 Peter 2:1, where heretics are referred to as those who have been bought by the Lord. Gottschalk was obviously aware of this text and probably had it brought to his attention more than once, which could explain why we discover it cited and interpreted in a number of different places. In each instance, Gottschalk argues that the buying in that passage refers to baptism and not to what Christ accomplished on the cross.[18] He further contends that baptism is effective for forgiving past sins, but not for forgiving future sins.[19] Disappointingly, Gottschalk never elaborated on what he means by this, but it most likely has to do with the popular idea that baptism removes both original sin and original guilt, yet is not a sign of guaranteed salvation. Thus, at the point of baptism, there is nothing in the baptized that would impede that person from entering into God's presence

---

[14] Ibid., 66.
[15] Ibid., 67.
[16] Ibid., 59 (cf. also 127–31, 134–40). Gottschalk also made explicit statements that Christ did not suffer for the reprobate or for all (see 69–70, 131, 181).
[17] Ibid.
[18] Gottschalk says in his *Tome to Gislemar*, for example, "For he bought them by the sacrament of baptism, but did not suffer the cross, undergo death, or shed his blood for them" (ibid., 70).
[19] Cf. Gottschalk's brief treatise, *On Different Ways of Speaking about Redemption* (ibid., 156).

should they die at that moment. If, however, they live to sin and eventually to deny the very one in whose name they were baptized, they would be accountable for rejecting Christ and thus would not be saved.

Some might wish to take exception to Gottschalk's interpretation of Paul and Peter, but my purpose here is not to dissect his exegesis but to point out that he held a position that is consistent with our contemporary notion of definite atonement, that he did so by marshaling evidence from Scripture and theology, and that he was not alone in the convictions he held. It is also worth pointing out that he did not believe his position was new or unusual, but very much rooted in the Augustinian tradition.

The debate was never properly resolved during the Carolingian period. Granted the Council of Quiercy condemned Gottschalk's views in 849, but that had more to do with the fact that the council was under the strong direction and control of his enemy, Hincmar, than with the veracity of his theological claims. In the years that followed, a flurry of literary activity erupted in which defenders of both sides presented their positions and attacked their opponents. Eventually, the Emperor Lothair called a council at Valence in 855 which condemned the condemnation of Quiercy![20]

Understandably, the debate over predestination and definite atonement entered a quiet period once the Vikings started wreaking havoc throughout Europe. Still, this matter did not disappear from the theological scene. As we move forward toward a much more stable period of time, when formal educational structures were beginning to develop in earnest once again, we discover that the idea of definite atonement is taken up once more, but this time without vehement debate and disagreement. Instead, we find that definite atonement was presented to theological students as the dominant view. This situation is best exemplified in Peter Lombard's magisterial work, *The Four Books of Sentences* (*Libri Quatuor Sententiarum*).

Peter Lombard (1100–1160)

Peter Lombard was a twelfth-century canon in the cathedral of Notre Dame, in Paris, whose most significant contribution to theological discourse was his systematic theology known as the *Sentences*.[21] It is because Peter's *Sentences*

---

[20] For a more complete account, see Stucco, *Colors of Grace*, 239–42.
[21] For a thorough biography and account of Peter's theology, see Marcia Colish, *Peter Lombard* (New York: Brill, 1994).

has fallen out of almost every canon of required reading among Protestants in general and evangelicals in particular that he has either been neglected or misrepresented in recent evangelical scholarship, despite being a seminal influence in theological development throughout the Middle Ages and beyond.

The Heart of the Matter

In debates over the extent of the atonement it is not uncommon to hear someone say that they believe that Christ's death was "sufficient for all, efficient for some." This statement is often associated with Amyraldianism and Hypothetical Universalism, but it in fact derives from Peter Lombard. In his third book, *On the Incarnation of the Word*, Peter makes the statement that,

> [Christ] offered himself on the altar of the cross not to the devil, but to the triune God, and he did so for all with regard to the sufficiency of the price, but only for the elect with regard to its efficacy, because he brought about salvation only for the predestined.[22]

What Peter says regarding the extent of the atonement is very much in line with Augustinian theology. Christ died for the predestined. Some, however, have queried whether Peter went far enough. Jonathan Rainbow, for instance, contends that while Peter does provide space for Augustinian theology, he is not strictly Augustinian. The possibility of who constitutes the predestined is left ill defined.[23] Is it possible, for example, that the predestined are those God foreknew would choose to believe? Such was certainly the position of Gottschalk's opponents, for example. In this case, definite atonement is not very limited. It is open for all who believe, and those who believe do so by an exercise of their free will, not by the power of God's grace decreed before the foundation of the world. But is that Peter's position? Does he leave the matter somewhat ambiguous or at least insufficiently defined so as to allow for the possibility of a diminished emphasis on the necessity of grace? While a myopic view of his maxim could be construed as ambiguous, the context of

---

[22] Peter Lombard, *The Sentences, Book 3: On the Incarnation of the Word*, trans. Giulio Silano (Toronto: Pontifical Institute of Mediaeval Studies, 2008), 86 (3.20.5). The remark in the opening sentence about Christ not offering himself to the Devil is a reference to a debate in the Middle Ages over the one to whom the ransom of the Lamb of God was paid (compare, for example, Mark 10:45). One answer, most likely made popular by Origen, was that Jesus was offering himself as a ransom to the Devil in exchange for the release of souls held in his bondage. Anselm of Canterbury roundly rejected this particular perspective on the atonement in the late eleventh and early twelfth century.

[23] Rainbow, *Will of God and the Cross*, 34. Blacketer, "Definite Atonement in Historical Perspective," 311, follows the same line of thought in his chapter: "This distinction, while a significant move toward the concept of definite atonement, still leaves room for ambiguity."

his broader treatment of the atonement, as we will see, mitigates against any ambiguity. For Peter, Christ died for the elect, and the elect are determined by the free will of God apart from the exercise of human will.

UNDERSTANDING THE CONTEXT

Consistent with his way of thinking and writing, Peter does not dive right into the question of what limits may or may not be applied to the extent of Christ's atoning work. In fact, the discussion that informs the previously cited statement from book 3 is found in book 1 on the Trinity. There, in the midst of a discussion on the nature and character of God, Peter turns to consider the wisdom of God with respect to the future. This in itself is a curious notion. How often has the debate over definite atonement, predestination, or similar subjects been couched in terms of God's wisdom? Though only a hint at this stage, the foundation of Peter's thinking on the atonement is very much rooted in God's nature as revealed in Scripture. Consequently, when he comes to define the relevant terms, he asserts clearly that, "predestination concerns all who are to be saved, as well as the good things by which these are freed in this life and will be crowned in the future. For God, from all eternity, predestined men to good things by electing [them], and he predestined by preparing good things for them."[24] Immediately following this contention, Peter quotes a number of biblical passages that he believes support his position.[25]

This statement makes it fairly clear that Peter believes that specific people have been predestined to salvation by God. Notice that it is not enough simply to state that those who are saved were predestined; it must also be affirmed that God has also predestined the manner in which the predestined will be saved. In other words, the circumstances—"good things"—as well as the outcome are the two necessary parts of predestination. But, some may yet insist, could not the "good things" by which the predestined are saved not include free will? That is to say, one of God's good gifts is the ability to choose salvation. To answer this rebuttal, let us turn with Peter to the question of God's foreknowledge.

---

[24] Peter Lombard, *The Sentences, Book 1: The Mystery of the Trinity*, trans. Giulio Silano (Toronto: Pontifical Institute of Medieval Studies, 2007), 194 (1.35.2). All further citations from Peter's *Sentences* will be taken from this translation.
[25] Ibid.: Romans 8:29: "He predestined those whom he foreknew would become molded into the image of his Son"; Ephesians 1:4: "He elected us before the foundation of the world to be saints and spotless"; Isaiah 64:4: "The eye has not seen, O God, apart from you, what you have prepared for those who love, or who wait for, you."

Divine Foreknowledge and Free Will

Could it be that Peter believes that God's predestination is based on what he foreknows people will choose? To begin with, such an interpretation would not be consistent with Peter's insistence that knowledge of the future be grounded in God's wisdom. Here is a rare but significant theological move. Peter grounds God's foreknowledge in God's wisdom. It is not so much that God knows what will happen in the sense that he sees all things or knows all possible contingencies or has planned every moment of every day, but that through his ineffable wisdom he knows what will happen. This puts the debate over foreknowledge on a completely different footing. Foreknowledge is not about knowledge on its own, but about knowledge in the context of wisdom. God is neither orchestrating every event, nor watching to see what happens in a sea of possibilities; rather, by his wisdom he knows and foreknows. This is not wisdom based on observation, but wisdom that is squarely grounded in God himself. Just as true wisdom through the fear of the Lord as presented in Proverbs is contrasted with false wisdom based on observation and creation at large in Ecclesiastes, so Peter is eager to situate God's foreknowledge within God's wisdom in a way that affects the creation, but is not affected by it.

I may add to this, that, just a couple of chapters later, Peter argues that God's "knowledge or wisdom" is of all things temporal and eternal so that, "from eternity, God knew eternity and all that was going to be, and he knew it immutably."[26] On its own, this certainly does not seal the door on the possibility that God predestined someone to salvation whom he knew would choose to believe; but as part of the larger context and argument Peter is making, it does close the gap insofar as God's knowledge of what will happen cannot but take place exactly as he knows it will happen.

Talk of God's wisdom and immutable knowledge is all well and good, but how can either we or God be so sure his knowledge matches future events precisely? The most direct answer Peter gives is to cite Augustine's *Enarrationes in Psalmos* that with God there is neither past nor future. All things are present to God. This is so by "a certain ineffable cognition of God's wisdom."[27] In other words, Peter is eager to continue to affirm God's omniscience, yet equally eager to guard against making God look like a tyrant who

---

[26] Peter, *Sentences, Book 1*, 196 (1.35.8).
[27] Ibid., 197 (1.35.9).

has predetermined all events. Trying to situate himself between the horns of this dilemma is what led Peter to ask the question that has been lingering in the background for several chapters; namely, is God's foreknowledge the cause of events, or are future events the cause of God's foreknowledge? In the light of what I have already noted about God's wisdom, Peter demonstrates his theological consistency by confirming his conviction that God's foreknowledge is the cause of events since what God does not foreknow cannot come to pass. What is more, it is impossible that something foreknown by God could fail to come to pass, since such would mean God's foreknowledge is fallible.[28]

While this line of argumentation may be helpful in contending that nothing takes place outside of God's will or knowledge or wisdom, it does raise a problematic issue. If nothing can come to pass without God's foreknowledge, indeed, if things can come to pass only because of God's foreknowledge, then is God the author of evil? Despite the somewhat lengthy answer Peter gives, his answer is a clear no: God is not the author of evil. How so?

Divine Foreknowledge and Evil

God is not the author of evil, because there is a difference between God's foreknowledge as awareness and God's foreknowledge as "good pleasure or disposition."[29] Here we see Peter modifying or further explaining his position on the relationship between foreknowledge and causality. When God foreknows something as a matter of good pleasure or disposition, then God's foreknowledge is causative; however, when God's foreknowledge is simple awareness of what will happen, there is no causal link between what God knows and the action that takes place. In this way, God still knows all things, but he is not the cause of all things.

It may prove helpful here to explain Peter's distinction in terms more familiar to our contemporary discussion. The first point that must be borne in mind is, once again, the context. Peter is not arguing in a generic or general fashion for the nature and content of God's foreknowledge. This is not an argument in a vacuum. His argument has very specifically to do with God's creating and re-creating our salvation. We might say that Peter's distinction is between particular providence and general providence. Particular provi-

---

[28] Ibid., 213 (1.38.1).
[29] Ibid., 215 (1.38.1).

dence addresses God's direct involvement in caring for his creation, whereas general providence speaks to the fact that God provides the boundaries or space wherein his creation can flourish, but does not directly affect every event within that space.

Take, for example, the shoes that I chose to wear this morning. According to Peter, did God foreknow that I would choose to wear my brown shoes instead of my black shoes? Yes, God did foreknow what color shoes I would wear, but such awareness was not causative. God did not make me choose my brown shoes; I chose them freely. God certainly created the boundaries and space within which I could flourish and succeed to the point where I had a choice between two pairs of shoes. He did not, however, guide and direct my life in all its minutiae so that wearing brown shoes today was directly caused by God. This is general providence. When thinking about general providence, it is vital that we not neglect to recall Peter's insistence that knowledge and foreknowledge operate in the context of, and in concert with, God's wisdom. It is because God is wise that he knows what I will choose freely. Truly, such wisdom is inscrutable.

The point of this discussion as it relates to Peter's argument on definite atonement is that God's foreknowledge can be causative, but need not always be causative. In matters of importance, of which salvation surely is one, God's foreknowledge is causative because humanity, left to its own devices, could never be saved. In matters of lesser importance, of which my choice of shoes is surely one, or in matters involving evil and sin, God's foreknowledge is not causative, but it is still correct and complete. To say, therefore, that God's elective purposes in predestination are causative and thus bring about salvation in particular people is not only to say that God accomplishes what he decrees in foreknowledge; it is also to imply, if not to state plainly, that Christ died for the elect. "From this, it is given to be understood that God conversely foreknows good things as his own, as those things which he will do, so that in foreknowing them his awareness and good pleasure of authorship have joined together."[30]

Is God Fair?

A common response to an argument for particular election and atonement, both in our own day as well as in Peter's day, is that God is acting unfairly.

---

[30] Ibid., 216 (1.38.1).

To phrase the challenge along the lines raised in Peter's own argument: is the number of the redeemed fixed? In other words, could someone who was not predestined from the foundation of the world choose to believe and thus enter the kingdom of God?[31] After canvassing some of the different sides of this debate, Peter, in a moment that is both comical and humble, says that he would, "prefer to hear others than to teach"![32] Nevertheless, in spite of himself, he presses on.[33]

Peter's response is straightforward. God made up his mind, so to speak, from before the creation of the world, and what he has determined will happen, will happen. In other words, what takes place at any given moment or series of moments in time will not undo what was determined from eternity past. In ending this part of the discussion, Peter reinforces his point by asserting that "when we deal with God's foreknowledge or predestination, its possibility or impossibility is referred to the power of God, which was and is ever the same, because predestination, foreknowledge, power is one thing in God."[34] Here we see not only that it is the doctrine of God that constitutes the foundation of Peter's theology, but also that it is the doctrine of the simplicity of God that guides his theological method. The doctrine of the simplicity of God states that God is all that he is in every way and at all times. Such a definition applies solely to God. If, for example, my arm were examined in great detail, as much as might be learned about me from my arm, that is not all of who I am. There are not only other parts to my body, but there are other characteristics to my being. All that I am is not contained in my arm. I am, in this sense, a complex being because I am made up of many parts. God, however, is not complex, but simple. Were it possible to examine just a part of God, and not all of him at once, that part would be all that God is. To put this in more concrete terms, even though we can never comprehend all that

---

[31] Ibid., 221 (1.40.1).

[32] Ibid., 222 (1.40.1).

[33] One might wonder how such a question even arose. While we cannot be entirely certain what debates or discussions may have prompted Peter to include this consideration in his argument, it does seem entirely plausible that this is a continuation of a popular medieval conversation about perfection as it relates to the population of the eschatological city of God. By Peter's time, the topic had been discussed for centuries, but the most famous account of it comes in Anselm of Canterbury's *Cur Deus Homo*. In book 1, chapters 16–18, Anselm is pressed by his interlocutor, Boso, to explain whether or not the number of the redeemed will make up the number of fallen angels or if the number of the redeemed will bring to completion a number greater than the number of angels created. The outcome of the matter, in Anselm's opinion, is that the number of the redeemed will not merely equal the number of the fallen angels but will exceed the total number of angels to a predetermined perfect amount. In this respect, Lombard is continuing in the same vein of thought by arguing that the number of the redeemed is fixed in accord with the predetermined plan of God. Anselm's work may be found in *Anselm of Canterbury: The Major Works*, ed. Brian Davies and G. R. Evans, Oxford World's Classics (Oxford: Oxford University Press, 1998).

[34] Lombard, *Sentences, Book 1*, 222 (1.40.1).

God is, even what little we do know is sufficient to warrant trust and belief, because God is not different in some other part of his being that we have not yet encountered. We will not, for example, discover one day that God has an evil side to him that we could not have predicted.

Returning to Peter's theology of the atonement, predestination, and foreknowledge, this means that he considers it not just improper, but theologically dubious at best and wrong at worst, to separate questions of God's foreknowledge both from his power to save and from his will to choose. God is all that he is always. He does not predestine someone to salvation and then fail to bring it about, because that would be both a denial of his sovereign omnipotence and a denial that all of who he is always works in harmony and without division or separation. Although Peter never uses the term *irresistible grace*, he is definitely thinking along those lines. What God has purposed to do, he cannot fail to accomplish, and he has purposed that some among fallen humanity be saved while others are left to reprobation. All the while, Peter is careful to maintain that God did not cause sin or the fall, even though he foreknew it, and thus he does not bear any blame for those who perish. It is on this ground that Peter is inching ever closer to the statement with which we began, namely, Christ died for the elect whom God had predestined unto salvation.

One aspect of Peter's thoughts that deserves further attention is the equanimity with which he seeks to apply God's actions toward humanity, whether for salvation or for reprobation. As we would expect from someone following Augustine's theology so closely, Peter makes clear that grace is never deserved. There is no work either past, present, or future upon which the extension or reception of grace depends. After all, grace is no longer grace if it is deserved or earned.[35] This grace is applied as a result of God's foreknowledge and predestination according to his divine will. Similarly, however, in those who are reprobate, there are no actions on their part which effected or caused God's foreknowledge and predestination, working as it did in accord with his divine will. Once again, what matters to Peter is that God's choosing and acting is exercised freely.[36] God acts freely to *apply* the salvific grace made possible by the Son's death and resurrection to men and women who are undeserving of it. Equally, God acts freely to *withhold* the

---

[35] Ibid., 224 (1.41.1).
[36] Ibid., 225 (1.41.1).

salvific grace made possible by the Son's death and resurrection to men and women who are undeserving of it.

In this way, Peter seeks to take the sting of unfairness away from counter-arguments, for if there is any unfairness in this, it cannot be rooted in humanity, since both believer and unbeliever are undeserving. The unfairness must be in God, but that cannot be. Not only do we believe that God is fair, that he shows no partiality; we also believe that God is simple, and that he must always and in every instance be just and righteous. This brings us back to where Peter began this discussion in book 1 of his *Sentences*. He contended very early on that the question of predestination and the concomitant doctrines that follow from it—definite atonement, for instance—are rooted in the wisdom of God. This is why Peter lands squarely on the shoulders of the apostle Paul in Romans 11 and claims that he does not have all the answers.[37]

BEGINNING AT THE END

At the beginning of my examination of what Peter Lombard had to say about definite atonement, I highlighted his now famous line that although Christ's death was sufficient for all, it was only efficient for the elect. While, on the strength of this statement alone, one could argue that the elect comprises all who choose to believe, the foregoing assessment of Peter's theology, as clearly outlined in the rest of his *Sentences*, makes it clear that election is determined by God according to his ineffable wisdom. The elect are certainly those who believe, but they are not exercising free will at random; rather, they are responding to divine grace brought to bear on their lives by the power of God in accord with his foreknowledge and predestination.

Peter has considerably narrowed the possibility of unlimited atonement by asserting that Christ died for the elect and that, because the elect were specifically numbered from before the foundation of the world, the application of his atoning work was intended for them. As Peter argues toward the end of book 1 of his *Sentences*, the will of God cannot be thwarted, and thus whatever God seeks to accomplish as an act of his will, is inevitably accomplished in time.[38] Not only did Christ die for the elect, but each one of those elect was known apart from any choice or action of their own, and God's will and power work in concert with his foreknowledge and predetermining pur-

---

[37] Ibid., 224 (1.40.2).
[38] Ibid., 255–58 (1.47.1–3).

poses to bring about salvation through his Son for those he has chosen. When considered as a whole, Peter's theology is consistent with later articulations of definite atonement despite the fact that the technical terms and language used to express definite atonement theology lay in the future.

What is important to understand in all of this, particularly in the contemporary evangelical community, is that definite atonement was not a minority view in the medieval church. Peter's *Sentences* was not just another of a long string of systematic theologies being churned out during the development of cathedral schools in the eleventh century; rather, his was the work that was adopted as the best and most effective. For centuries, Peter's *Sentences* were the required reading of all theology students. Thus, Peter not only synthesized and summarized the popular positions of theology in the centuries leading up to his lifetime, but he became an astoundingly effective purveyor of those views for generations to follow. When, therefore, we arrive at the latter part of the Reformation and its theological aftermath, we witness a continuity between the ages. Reformation theology on this topic did not resurrect what had been lost but was carrying on what had been passed down to them through Peter, among others. To be sure, there were those who took issue with Peter's theology of the atonement, but given that every student for hundreds of years read the *Sentences*, and that countless theologians commented on this great work for an equally long time, and that no other theological text save the *Glossa Ordinaria* can claim the kind of longevity and pervasiveness that is true of the *Sentences*, and that his work was not replaced as standard reading until long after the Reformation, we should take care to realize that, far from being removed from theological discussion during the Middle Ages, the seeds of the doctrine of definite atonement were present in the schools and churches.[39]

Thomas Aquinas (1225–1274)

Evidence of the continuity of thought from Peter Lombard's days in the twelfth century through to the middle and late thirteenth century is best exemplified in the works of Thomas Aquinas. Reading through Aquinas's two

---

[39] Cf. Alister E. McGrath, *Iustitia Dei: A History of the Christian Doctrine of Justification*, 3rd ed. (Cambridge: Cambridge University Press, 2005), 164–65. While McGrath's purpose in this book is not to address the extent of the atonement per se, he does note that the majority of theologians who followed Peter Lombard, including those belonging to High Scholasticism and the early Dominicans, argued for predestination and divine foreknowledge in the manner that I have outlined here in the *Sentences*. Once again, we are faced with the fact that the tenor of medieval theology prepared the ground for what would later become articulations of the doctrine of definite atonement.

most famous works, his *Summa Theologiae* and his *Summa Contra Gentiles*, it is evident that while he was clearly influenced by Aristotle, he was no less inspired and affected by Peter's magnum opus.

SUFFICIENT FOR ALL, EFFICIENT FOR MANY

Notably, Aquinas does not directly address the question of for whom Christ died in the way and to the extent that Peter did. Nevertheless, there are a number of places where Aquinas speaks about the extent of the atonement, and when these are juxtaposed with one another we see a pattern that follows a trajectory leading in the direction of the doctrine of definite atonement. An initial perusal of Aquinas's theology, however, could lead to some doubt about such compatibility, let alone consistency, between his theology and definite atonement. Take Aquinas's comments on the efficacy of Christ's passion, for example. Aquinas defends the point that Christ's suffering and death were indeed a sufficient atonement for the sins of humanity. Here he quotes 1 John 2:2, that Jesus is the propitiation for the sins of the whole world.[40] From this, it would appear that Aquinas disagrees with Peter and supports the view that Christ's atoning death was for all people. This assessment could be further supported by what Aquinas goes on to say just a few pages later when he reiterates that, "Christ's passion was sufficient and superabundant satisfaction for the sins of the whole human race."[41]

Such a conclusion would be premature, however, since Aquinas returns to the subject of the extent of the atonement a little further on when he turns to the question of the appropriateness of the words of consecration for the wine in celebrating the Eucharist.[42] As he probes the various parts of this proclamation, he cites an objection that the statement that the blood of Christ is "for you and for many" could be improved by saying, "for all and for many." The reason for this is that the death of Christ is sufficient for all, "while as to its efficiency it was profitable for many."[43] Aquinas's response was to uphold the formula of consecration as it stood ("for you and for many"), while endorsing the idea that the blood of Christ was shed for the

[40] Thomas Aquinas, *Summa Theologiae*, trans. Fathers of the English Dominican Province, 5 vols. (Notre Dame, IN: Ave Maria, 1948), 3.48.2.
[41] Ibid., 3.49.3.
[42] The words of consecration, as cited by Aquinas, are, "This is the chalice of My blood, of the New and Eternal Testament, the Mystery of Faith, which shall be shed for you and for many unto the forgiveness of sins" (ibid., 3.78.3).
[43] Ibid.

elect alone. He argued that the distinction between "for you" and "for many" (reflecting the different readings in the Gospels) is drawn in order to call attention to the different audiences or, more precisely, the different groups to whom Christ's blood is applied. In other words, Jesus was saying that his blood would be shed for elect Jews ("for you") as well as for elect Gentiles ("for many").[44] Aquinas's position may not be as forceful or neat as those of later proponents of definite atonement would be, but he does profess that Christ's blood was shed to cover the sins of an elect group.

In addition to this brief foray into the relationship between election and atonement, Aquinas discusses subjects such as the nature of the will, the ability to choose, the sovereignty of God in predestination, and on what divine foreknowledge was based (do, for example, one's own goodness or choices affect divine foreknowledge?)—subjects that will further illumine our appreciation of his doctrine of the atonement.

FROM WILL TO PREDESTINATION

In his *Summa Theologiae*, Aquinas arrives at predestination very early on. The reason for this is quite simply that Aquinas begins with God, and the proper context for the doctrine of predestination in his day was within the doctrine of God. In other words, Aquinas does not view predestination as tied primarily to soteriology or theological anthropology. More specifically, Aquinas ties predestination most closely to God's providence. This is why, immediately prior to introducing his discussion of predestination, Aquinas entertains the question of whether divine providence imposes any necessity on what is foreseen.[45] If providence entails the imposition of necessity, then that has significant implications for broader soteriological concerns. Initially, the arguments appear to be in favor of God imposing necessity on what he foreknows. If, for example, something is foreknown by God to happen, and what God foreknows cannot fail to happen, then it seems reasonable that God imposes his power in order to fulfill his providential purposes.

Aquinas takes exception to this, however. He argues that necessity certainly applies to some things, but not to all. In typical fashion, Aquinas is careful to draw distinctions. There are things that God brings about by necessity, that is, by force of his power and will, but there are also things that "may

---

[44] Ibid.
[45] Ibid., 1.22.4.

happen by contingency, according to the nature of their proximate causes."[46] This means that God can accomplish his purposes either directly by the use of his power or indirectly by factors that surround an event or decision such that they bring about a desired end. If we compare this statement with what Aquinas says in his *Summa Contra Gentiles*, we discover that Aquinas is always very keen to uphold both the sovereign providential purposes of God as well as the freedom of human will. Aquinas writes that, "the operation of providence, whereby God works in things, does not exclude secondary causes, but, rather, is fulfilled by them, in so far as they act by God's power."[47] God may not cause things to happen directly, but that does not mean God has no control over their occurrence.

There are, clearly, a lot of ways in which we could take this line of thought, but as it pertains to definite atonement, we should note that Aquinas is keen to apply this most especially to human free will. If God's providence does not necessitate that everything he foreknows will happen as a result of his direct power, then human will remains free. This is entirely fitting because it is "proper to divine providence to use things according to their own mode."[48] If the nature of human will is that it has the power to pursue multiple outcomes, then for God to limit those outcomes to one option alone would be to act contrary to the mode of operation of human will as he created it. Moreover, Aquinas believes it axiomatic that being created in the image of God entails free will, since God's will is free (though in a superior way to ours).[49] But is not the corollary of this that salvation comes by the exercise of free human will, which means that Aquinas, at least implicitly, developed his theology along a line of thought that is inconsistent with definite atonement? In a word, no.

Returning to the *Summa Theologiae*, Aquinas moves from providence to predestination where he states plainly and emphatically that, "it is fitting that God should predestine men. For all things are subject to his providence, as was shown above."[50] Aquinas further elaborates that the attainment of eternal life is beyond the capacity of all people and must therefore be directed by God. In addition, the basis upon which predestination is made is entirely within

---

[46] Ibid.

[47] Thomas Aquinas, *Summa Contra Gentiles*, trans. Vernon J. Bourke (Notre Dame, IN: University of Notre Dame Press, 1975), 3a.72.2.

[48] Ibid., 3.1.73.3.

[49] Ibid., 3a.73.4.

[50] Aquinas, *Summa Theologiae*, 1.23.1. The reference to what "was shown above" is to the previous section, where he addressed divine providence as I have outlined it.

God himself, in his providential purposes, and not in anything inherent in humanity.[51] As Aquinas replies to different objections to this, he argues that predestination requires preparation in the individual. This preparation is of the passions, "in the thing prepared."[52] God does not cause an individual to make a particular decision, but he does prepare the "passions" of the individual.

In the *Summa Contra Gentiles*, Aquinas asks whether certain texts of Scripture require us to believe that God forces the predestined to choose faith. John 6:44, for example, speaks of none coming to the Father except those whom he draws. Romans 8:14 states that all who are led by the Spirit of God are sons of God. Second Corinthians 5:14 says that the love of Christ controls us.[53] Aquinas contends that these passages are best understood not as taking away our free will but as working with it, yet not in such a way that we become merely passive recipients without an active role. He says that "the first cause causes the operation of the secondary cause according to the measure of the latter."[54] This is very much in line with what he said about the passions being prepared within the predestined. God works in us in such a way that our passions and the ability to choose what is virtuous is chosen by us, so that the decision we exercise by our own will is still fully our own choice. As Aquinas says elsewhere, it is impossible that anyone should believe on his own, apart from the preparatory activity of God's Spirit which enables one to choose salvation freely.[55] In fact, in the matter of the necessity of divine prevenient grace being at work in order for salvation to be made possible, Aquinas takes the further step of arguing that humanity in the pre-fall state as well as in our current sinful state requires divine aid. "[I]n both states, man needs Divine help, that he may be moved to act well."[56] In a further affirmation of his position, Aquinas continues to argue that we are unable to prepare ourselves for grace apart from the external aid of grace applied by God's power; he says, "it is clear that man cannot prepare himself to receive the light of grace except by the gratuitous help of God moving him inwardly."[57] This is why Aquinas affirms with conviction that those God predestines to salvation cannot fail to come to faith.[58]

---

[51] Aquinas, *Summa Theologiae*, 1.23.2.
[52] Ibid.
[53] Aquinas, *Summa Contra Gentiles*, 3b.148.1.
[54] Ibid., 3b.148.3.
[55] On the question of sin affecting the will and intellect, see Aquinas, *Summa Theologiae*, 2a.83–86.
[56] Ibid., 2a.109.2.
[57] Ibid., 2b.109.6.
[58] Ibid., 1.23.6.

But could it be that the door of free will has been left ajar? What if the predestined are predestined according to their choice? Such a position is utterly foreign to Aquinas's thinking. First, he argues clearly and forcefully for the fact that nothing in humanity warrants God's predestination. Second, Aquinas assumes the same position as Peter Lombard, that the number of the predestined has been fixed from before the foundation of the world.[59] Third, and most persuasively, Aquinas takes up the question of the predestination of Christ toward the end of his *Summa Theologiae*, and there he makes two significant assertions. The first is that the exercise of divine grace and providence by which Christ was predestined is the selfsame act by which the elect were predestined. In other words, the predestination of Christ and his church can be understood as one act. Predestination can, however, also be viewed as a double action from the vantage point of time. There was a predestination in eternity past which is applied in the unfolding of human history. In this sense, says Aquinas, predestination comes to fruition through Christ's redemptive act.[60]

1 TIMOTHY 2:4

As we saw with Gottschalk and Peter, so now we see with Aquinas, that there are certain passages of Scripture that do not appear to fit so neatly with his theology. Among the most common passages of Scripture to be cited is 1 Timothy 2:4, where Paul states that God wills that all people be saved. In response, Aquinas identifies three important considerations.[61] First, what God wills, he cannot fail to accomplish. As with so many other medieval theologians, Aquinas's first move is to defend God's character. God is not weak; he does not fail. Second, no one is saved apart from God's will. Putting this together with the first point, Aquinas's argument is that all who are saved are saved because God wills that they all be saved. This leads into his third

---

[59] Ibid., 1.23.7. Here some may contend that Hypothetical Universalism, as identified within an Amyraldian theology, mitigates against drawing a corollary between definite election based on grace and definite atonement. Such a notion is not only anachronistic, but fails to appreciate that Aquinas's view of election is the same as Peter's and neither come close to entertaining the idea of Hypothetical Universalism as is clear from the next point below, that the predestination of Christ and of the elect are the same act.

[60] Ibid., 3.24.4: "I answer that, if we consider predestination on the part of the very act of predestinating, then Christ's predestination is not the cause of ours: because by one and the same act God predestined both Christ and us. But if we consider predestination on the part of its term, thus Christ's predestination is the cause of ours: for God, by predestinating from eternity, so decreed our salvation, that it should be achieved through Jesus Christ. For eternal predestination covers not only that which is to be accomplished in time, but also the mode and order in which it is to be accomplished in time."

[61] Ibid., 1.19.6.

consideration, that the "all" in this passage is referring to all kinds or types of people. God wills that all kinds of people, people from every category of humanity, be saved. This line of thinking leads Aquinas to affirm that God's will is not generic or indiscriminate, but takes qualifications and circumstances into account. This means that when God wills that all be saved, his willing accords with his foreknowledge and predestination as much as it accords with his knowledge that all have sinned and as such are children of wrath. An unqualified divine will that leads to an unqualified "all" in 1 Timothy 2:4 does not take sufficient account of God's nature, let alone the rest of revelation.

Putting It All Together

From the above discussion, it should be evident that Aquinas's theology is in keeping with the doctrine of definite atonement. In this, Aquinas was following a long and established tradition in the church at large, and in the medieval church in particular, even though he clearly develops issues related to definite atonement in his own distinctive way.

What mattered most to medieval theologians wrestling with the efficacy of Christ's death, was locating predestination, election, and foreknowledge in the doctrine of God, because they rely and draw on so many of his attributes: wisdom, providential sovereignty, power, grace, mercy, and love, to name a few. Seen in this light, salvation is not just about the individual but about God acting in a manner true to his nature. Understanding medieval soteriology from this perspective helps us to appreciate why Peter Lombard, Thomas Aquinas, and especially Gottschalk, conceived the extent of the atonement in such particular terms. God's plan is to redeem a particular people for himself, a people numbered from before creation for whom the Son of God would die. Time and again, medieval theologians emphasized that God's wisdom and providential purposes, while expansive and difficult to comprehend, are neither random nor reliant on human action or choice. It is true that these theologians did not define a comprehensive articulation of definite atonement, but it is also true that when the late-sixteenth- and seventeenth-century Reformers did, they were not breaking new ground but continuing to water seeds that had been planted long before them.

4

Calvin, Indefinite Language, and Definite Atonement

Paul Helm

The presence in John Calvin's writings of indefinite or indiscriminate language with respect to the scope and efficacy of the atonement is often taken to provide strong evidence that he denied definite atonement.[1] In what follows I shall argue that this is not so, but that Calvin held a view about such language which is thoroughly consistent with being committed to definite atonement, and which cannot be used as convincing evidence that he denied it.

First I shall underscore a distinction that I made some time ago, and that I still regard as important in this debate about whether or not Calvin committed himself to a definite view of the atonement. Writers such as Charles Bell, Brian Armstrong, and R. T. Kendall argue for the indefinite view,[2] while

---

[1] Although the choice of "indefinite" is my own, Raymond Blacketer has pointed out to me that Theodore Beza used "indefinite." For example, "*Q. But surely the calling is universal, as well as the promise.* A. Understand it as indefinite [*indefinatam*], (and in view of certain things I have discussed, with respect to circumstances), and you will have a better sense of it" (Theodore Beza, *Quaestionum et responsionum Christianarum libellus, in quo praecipua Christianae religionis capita* κατά ἐπιτομήν *proponuntur* [Geneva, 1570; London: H. Bynneman, 1571]). This book is now translated as *A Booke of Christian Questions and Answers*, trans. Arthur Golding (London: Wm. How, 1578), retranslated by Raymond Blacketer (unpublished).

[2] Charles M. Bell, "Calvin and the Extent of the Atonement," *EQ* 55.2 (1983): 115–23; Brian G. Armstrong, *Calvinism and the Amyraut Heresy: Protestant Scholasticism and Humanism in the Seventeenth-Century France* (Madison: University of Wisconsin Press, 1969); R. T. Kendall, *Calvin and English Calvinism to 1649*, Studies in Christian History and Thought (New York: Oxford University Press, 1979). Others include: Paul M. van Buren, *Christ in Our Place: The Substitutionary Character of Calvin's Doctrine of Reconciliation* (Edinburgh: Oliver Boyd, 1957); Basil Hall, "Calvin against the Calvinists," in *John Calvin*, ed. G. E. Duffield (Grand Rapids, MI: Eerdmans, 1966), 19–37; James W. Anderson, *"The Grace of God and the Non–Elect in Calvin's Commentaries and Sermons"* (PhD diss., New Orleans Baptist Theological Seminary, 1976); Alan C. Clifford, *Calvinus: Authentic Calvinism, A Clarification* (Norwich, UK: Charenton Reformed, 1996); idem, *Atonement and Justification* (Oxford: Oxford University Press, 1990); Kevin D. Kennedy, *Union with Christ and the Extent of the Atonement in Calvin* (New York: Peter Lang, 2002).

others such as Jonathan H. Rainbow and Roger R. Nicole argue for Calvin's avowal of definite atonement.[3] My own view is that while Calvin did not *commit himself* to any version of the doctrine of definite atonement, his thought is consistent with that doctrine; that is, he did not deny it in express terms, but by other things that he most definitely did hold to, he may be said to be *committed to* that doctrine. The distinction is an important one in order to avoid the charge of anachronism. Calvin lived earlier than those debates that led to the explicit formulation of the doctrine of definite atonement in Reformed theology, and the same applies to Amyraldianism.[4] He did not avow it in express terms, but neither did he deny it. Note that such a conclusion is not equivalent to an affirmative answer to the question, Had Calvin been present at the Synod of Dordt, would he have given his assent to the doctrine of definite atonement? A yes to this begs the question of whether, in the interval between Calvin's last published word and the early years of the seventeenth century, his doctrinal commitments may have changed.[5] That may or may not be a reasonable assumption to make.

I made this distinction in *Calvin and the Calvinists*, published thirty years ago,[6] and the present chapter may be regarded as further work on this theme. After citing data from Calvin supporting penal substitution, from such places as *Institutes*, 2.16.2.3.5 and 3.22.7.10, on the definite scope of the atonement, the distinction was made between Calvin's *being committed to* definite atonement and *committing himself* to that view.[7] A word or two more explaining this distinction may be helpful.

A person may be committed to a doctrine without committing himself to it. How so? It is because the proposition or propositions that a person believes, may have logical consequences that that person does not realize

---

[3] Jonathan H. Rainbow, *The Will of God and the Cross: An Historical and Theological Study of John Calvin's Doctrine of Limited Redemption* (Allison Park, PA: Pickwick, 1990); Roger R. Nicole, "John Calvin's View of the Extent of the Atonement," *WTJ* 47 (1985): 197–225. See also: Fredrick S. Leahy, "Calvin and the Extent of the Atonement," *Reformed Theological Journal* 8 (1992): 54–64.

[4] Not even Rainbow, who argues that definite atonement was the default medieval view of the atonement with which Calvin concurred, ever points to Calvin's use of the doctrine in debate. Had Calvin *committed himself* to definite atonement (as Rainbow claims), then that would almost certainly have emerged in various polemical contexts, for example, in his debates with Sebastian Castellio.

[5] For example, more could be said about those views of Calvin that cohere with the idea of definite atonement, even though Calvin does not avow that idea. In his writing against Sebastian Castellio, *The Secret Providence of God*, published in 1558, we see Calvin's hostile attitude toward Castellio's rejection of his understanding of the two wills doctrine, to the unconditionality of divine foreknowledge, and to the idea of divine bare permission. Rejecting these doctrines became part of the Arminian outlook. See John Calvin, *The Secret Providence of God*, ed. Paul Helm, trans. Keith Goad (Wheaton, IL: Crossway, 2010), 30–31.

[6] Paul Helm, *Calvin and the Calvinists* (Edinburgh: Banner of Truth, 1982).

[7] Ibid., 18.

(even though such consequences may, to later students, be as plain as a pike-staff). None of us knows all the logical implications of what we believe. Why so? Basically, because of our finitude, expressed, perhaps, through a simple failure of logical perception, by not noticing that p and q entail r, or that accepting that the truth of p and q raise the probability of r to a high degree. Or perhaps because the logical consequences had not been brought to our attention. Whatever the explanation, to use the language of philosophers, belief is not closed under entailment: I may have the true belief that p entails q, and p and q may entail r, but it does not follow that I believe that p and q entail r.

One result of controversy may be that those engaged in it, and bystanders too, come to have their noses rubbed in some of the logical consequences of the positions being argued over. Think of the connection Christ drew between "God is the living God" and "Abraham, having died, nevertheless lives on and will be resurrected" (see Matt. 22:29–32). Or consider early Christological debates and the role that they played in refining understanding of the person and natures of Jesus Christ.[8]

Seeing that p entails q might make a person affirm q or it might provide a reason for him to deny p. The question of whether Calvin was committed to definite atonement may lead us to ask another question: Is it plausible to believe that, had the fully developed doctrine of definite atonement been available to Calvin, he would have embraced it? Or would he have back-pedaled to a more vague or even contrary view? But in asking and attempting to answer such counterfactual questions, the mists and fogs of anachronism begin to descend.[9]

It is possible to assemble a collection of sentences where Calvin writes in universal terms about Christ's being the Savior of the world, and of his dying for all men and women, and a second collection of sentences which go the other way, which stress the particularistic, focused scope of Christ's atonement.[10] Each of these collections may then be used as "proof texts" by those

---

[8] Kennedy, *Union with Christ*, 74, claims that the distinction between committing oneself to p and being committed to p is a "mystery," while P. L. Rouwendal, "Calvin's Forgotten Classical Position on the Extent of the Atonement: About Sufficiency, Efficiency and Anachronism," *WTJ* 70 (2008): 33, regards it as a "weak conclusion." I leave readers to form a judgment of these verdicts on a distinction that is obviously valid.

[9] Note that Richard A. Muller, "A Tale of Two Wills?," *CTJ* 44.2 (2009): 212, refrains from using the term "atonement" in connection with our topic because it is "highly anachronistic." I shall use the term, but Muller's caution still stands.

[10] For expressions of Calvin's universal language, see appendix 1 of the new edition of R. T. Kendall, *Calvin and English Calvinism to 1649* (Carlisle, UK: Paternoster, 1997). For examples of Calvin's non-universalistic language, see his exegesis of 1 John 2:2 in *Commentaries on the Catholic Epistles*, Calvin's Commentaries, vol. 22, ed. and trans. John Owen (Grand Rapids, MI: Baker, 1979; repr. of the CTS translations of the commentaries). All subsequent references to Calvin's commentaries are to this CTS edition.

holding one position or another. But it is impossible to settle what Calvin's view was from his own somewhat underdeveloped language over the precise question of the extent of the atonement, or indeed to make much progress, without undertaking a wider examination of Calvin's thought.[11]

Calvin's indefinite or universalistic language is widely noticed by participants in this game of evidential ping-pong, for they bat the data to and fro across the table much like the little white ball is batted. As much as I enjoy a game of Ping-Pong, I disavow such "proof texting," or any other forms of it.[12] It is not an appropriate tool for the accumulation and assessment of evidence for Calvin's position, one way or the other. For proof texting of this kind abstracts from Calvin's deeper theological outlook.

Those who claim that Calvin held to indefinite atonement are by no means agreed about its consequences. G. Michael Thomas refers to a "dilemma" in Calvin's theology, the existence of "stress points," rendering Calvin's overall position "inherently unstable."[13] R. T. Kendall holds that while Calvin had an unlimited view of the atonement, Christ's intercessions were definite, on behalf of the elect alone.[14] Kevin D. Kennedy claims that, according to Calvin, while atonement is universal, union with Christ is particular.[15] The difficulty with the last two views, which tend in the direction of post-redemptionism, or Amyraldianism, is that they imperil the unity of the divine decree, and the divine operations *ad extra* that Calvin emphasized. The purpose of the Son to make a universal atonement is different in scope from his purpose in interceding, or different from that of the Spirit who brings a particular set of men and women into union with Christ. This is a serious weakness, for Calvin takes great pains to stress both the unity of the divine will, and its singularity, that it is one will.[16]

We are better not to seek an answer to the question of whether Calvin committed himself to definite atonement by trying to provide a decisive "proof text" one way or the other. Instead, we must ask the question posed

---

[11] The game of pitting definite against indefinite language seems about to peter out, only for the same data to be revisited once more. See, for example, Paul Hartog, *A Word for the World: Calvin on the Extent of the Atonement* (Schaumburg, IL: Regular Baptist Press, 2009).

[12] For the ping-pong analogy, see Basil Mitchell, *How to Play Theological Ping Pong: Collected Essays on Faith and Reason*, ed. William J. Abraham and Robert W. Prevost (London: Hodder & Stoughton, 1990).

[13] G. Michael Thomas, *The Extent of the Atonement: A Dilemma for Reformed Theology from Calvin to the Consensus* (Carlisle, UK: Paternoster, 1997), 34.

[14] Kendall, *Calvin and English Calvinism to 1649*, 17–21.

[15] Kennedy, *Union with Christ*.

[16] Kennedy's proposal carries the additional problem that it has to discount Calvin's opinion that union with Christ is grounded in God's eternal election (*Commentary on Ephesians*, 197–98, on 1:4).

by Roger Nicole, namely, whether definite atonement fits better than universal grace into the total pattern of Calvin's teaching.[17] This chapter may be thought of as an attempt to further strengthen an affirmative answer to such a question by drawing attention to features of Calvin's overall outlook, particularly his anthropology, which as far as I am able to tell have not so far been treated in this connection.

So the reader should not expect what follows to be a rehearsal of the entire case for holding that Calvin was committed to definite atonement. Nor am I going to argue that Calvin's substitutionary view of the atonement, his view that the divine operations accomplishing and applying redemption are highly unified, and the importance he attached to logical consistency, are all relevant to establishing that he was committed to definite atonement, even though I happen to believe that they are. Rather, the additional arguments to be presented are an attempt to offer a further strengthening of the conclusions of such dogmatic arguments offered by others. In the remainder of this chapter, I shall concentrate on what those who deny that Calvin's view is consistent with definite atonement frequently focus on, namely, Calvin's *indefinite language*, but I shall draw different conclusions from theirs.

What follows are three arguments to support the view that Calvin (or anyone else) may (and perhaps must) consistently use indefinite, universalistic language about the scope of Christ's atonement even if being committed to definite atonement. The arguments concern providence and the future in relation to aspirational prayer, and the indiscriminate terms in which the gospel may be offered. In concentrating on Calvin's theology, combatants over the question of Calvin's attitude toward the extent of the atonement have rather strangely neglected his anthropology. So the overall case, while avoiding ping-pong, must keep closely to the contours of Calvin's thought as expressed in various contexts. If this strategy succeeds, then it will follow that there is no need for proponents of the view that Calvin is committed to definite atonement to attempt the unappealing task of gerrymandering his universalistic language. Its presence need not give rise to awkwardness or embarrassment. The strength of the case rests on the seriousness with which it treats Calvin's language *as it is*.

Offering an appreciation of such language will be our chief concern, and considering it, I shall argue, will add strength to the conclusion that

---

[17] Nicole, "John Calvin's View of the Extent of the Atonement."

Calvin *is committed to* definite atonement, a trajectory already established by his use of definite language, his notion of substitutionary atonement, the unity of the divine decree, his rejection of the idea that reference to God's two wills is a reference to two decrees, the denial of bare divine foreknowledge, and so on.

(1) Providence and the Future

The first strand of evidence is general in character and so may seem to be rather distant from debates about the extent of the atonement. It is well known that Calvin has a strongly decretal view of divine providence: he claims that all events, down to the most minute, are ordained by God, upheld by his will, and governed by him according to his good pleasure. But he is anxious that if we believe this, as he holds that Scripture urges us to, we should not become fatalistic in our attitudes toward the future. He therefore believes that it is important not only to distinguish the doctrine of Christian providence from Stoic fate, but also to distinguish properly Christian attitudes to that doctrine from fatalistic attitudes to it. He is keen to promote exactly the opposite temper: not *Que sera, sera*, but a view of providence that does not enervate believers but energizes them.

How does he argue for this? For one thing, he stresses the close connection between means and ends. The providential order is not blindly fatalistic, but it is intelligently purposive, the will of the all-wise Creator and Redeemer, and there is a close connection between the ends that God has chosen for his people and the means that they are to take to gain those ends. Thus,

> For he who has fixed the boundaries of our life, has at the same time entrusted us with the care of it, provided us with the means of preserving it, forewarned us of the dangers to which we are exposed, and supplied cautions and remedies, that we may not be overwhelmed unawares. Now, our duty is clear, namely, since the Lord has committed to us the defence of our life—to defend it; since he offers assistance—to use it; since he forewarns us of danger—not to rush on heedless; since he supplies remedies—not to neglect them. But it is said, a danger that is not fatal will not hurt us, and one that is fatal cannot be resisted by any precautions. But what if dangers are not fatal, merely because the Lord has furnished you with the means of warding them off, and surmounting them? See how far your reasoning accords with the order of divine procedure. You infer that danger is not to be guarded against, because, if it is not fatal, you shall escape without

precaution; whereas the Lord enjoins you to guard against it, just because he wills it not to be fatal.[18]

So in order to be intelligent and wise members of God's providential order, we ought to take the precautions and adopt the policies that, as far as we can tell, match means to ends.

But it is a further aspect of this anti-fatalistic attitude that I wish to emphasize. For rather surprisingly Calvin says, or seems to say, that in carrying out our own plans, and while carrying in the back of our minds the knowledge that *all things are decreed by God*, we should face the future *as if God had not decreed it*. We should regard the future as epistemically open, even if, from a metaphysical point of view, from the point of view of God's eternal purposes, the future is closed, closed by virtue of what God has infallibly decreed. Do we then have to believe what is not true, that God has not decreed what is future, when Scripture teaches that he has? Not exactly, for since (by and large) the future is closed to us, to suppose that it is decreed by God in either one way or another is operationally equivalent to its not being decreed at all. For either God has decreed that I will live till I am ninety, or he has decreed that I not live until then. Which of these is the future is unknown to us, and perhaps unknowable, and therefore it would not be reasonable to believe one rather than the other in attempting to guide our lives. We ought not to believe what is false, but to suspend our judgment respecting the shape of the future:

> Hence as to future time, because the issue of all things is hidden from us, each ought so to apply himself to his office, *as though nothing were determined about any part*. Or, to speak more properly, he ought so to hope for the success that issues from the command of God in all things, as to reconcile in himself the contingency of unknown things and the certain providence of God.[19]

There is a parallel passage in the *Institutes*:

> But since our sluggish minds rest far beneath the height of divine providence, we must have recourse to a distinction which may assist them in rising. I say then, that though all things are ordered by the counsel and certain arrangement of God, to us, however, they are fortuitous,—not because we imagine

---

[18] John Calvin, *Institutes of the Christian Religion*, trans. Henry Beveridge (Peabody, MA: Hendrickson, 2008), 1.17.4. Unless otherwise indicated, the Henry Beveridge translation (various editions) is used throughout.
[19] John Calvin, *Concerning the Eternal Predestination of God*, trans. J. K. S. Reid (1552; repr., London: James Clarke, 1961), 171 (emphasis added).

that fortune rules the world and mankind, and turns all things upside down at random, (far be such a heartless thought from every Christian breast); but as the order, method, end, and necessity of events, are, for the most part, hidden in the counsel of God, though it is certain that they are produced by the will of God, they have the appearance of being fortuitous, such being the form under which they present themselves to us, whether considered in their own nature, or estimated according to our knowledge and judgment.[20]

Here we find Calvin referring to two wills in God, but with a somewhat different twist. This is not the routine distinction between the secret will and the revealed will, but the will we are commanded to follow as against the apparently fortuitous will of God that we cannot will to follow. So it is appropriate to act in ignorance of what God has decreed for the future.

(2) The Language of Aspiration

The second argument concerns Calvin's understanding of what I shall call the "language of aspiration." The following seems to be a regular feature of his thought: *that a person may properly hope for something, irrespective of whether or not what is wished for or aspired to is decreed by God, and even if it could be known not to be decreed by God. Not knowing whether or not it is decreed by God does not make the wish or aspiration immoral or unspiritual or in any other way defective.* I offer three examples of this, two from Calvin's comments on the attitude of the apostle Paul, and one from his understanding of Christ's prayer in Gethsemane.

First, in relation to Christ's prayer: "My Father, if it be possible, let this cup pass from me; nevertheless, not as I will, but as you will" (Matt. 26:39). Here Calvin makes the following comments on the propriety of Christ's prayer that the cup may pass from him:

> I answer, there would be no absurdity in supposing that Christ, agreeably to the custom of the godly, leaving out of view the divine purpose, committed to the bosom of the Father his desire which troubled him. For believers, in pouring out their prayers, do not always ascend to the contemplation of the secrets of God, or deliberately inquire what is possible to be done, but are sometimes carried away hastily by the earnestness of their wishes. Thus Moses prays that he may be *blotted out of the book of life* (Ex. 32:32); thus Paul *wished to be made an anathema* (Rom. 9:3). . . . In short, there is no

---

[20] Calvin, *Institutes*, 1.16.9.

impropriety, if in prayer we do not always direct our immediate attention to everything, so as to preserve a distinct order.

Calvin goes on:

> Though it be true rectitude to regulate all our feelings by the good pleasure of God, yet there is a certain kind of indirect disagreement with it which is not faulty, and is not reckoned as sin; if, for example, a person desire to see the Church in a calm and flourishing condition, if he wish that the children of God were delivered from afflictions, that all superstitions were removed out of the world, and that the rage of wicked men were so restrained as to do no injury. These things, being in themselves right, may properly be desired by believers, though it may please God to order a different state of matters: for he chooses that his Son should reign among enemies; that his people should be trained under the cross; and that the triumph of faith and of the Gospel should be rendered more illustrious by the opposing machinations of Satan. We see how these prayers are holy, which appear to be contrary to the will of God; for God does not desire us to be always exact or scrupulous in inquiring what he has appointed, but allows us to ask what is desirable according to the capacity of our senses.[21]

Notice a few things about this. It is allowable to ask God for what is desirable "according to the capacity of our senses," that is, according to our present epistemic position. Secondly, Calvin's words "leaving out of view the divine purpose" clearly refers to the intersecting of the secret will and the revealed will of God. Thirdly, we should note Calvin's reference to "indirectness." What does he mean? He means that there may be a prima facie conflict between what is desired and what may be decreed, and the need to relate all that we do to the good pleasure of God. But such indirectness is "not faulty." There is, fourthly, a "custom of the godly" to say certain things, even to pray for certain matters, while leaving the divine decree out of view, or out of consideration. Though they may be carried away by their earnest wishes, Calvin does not fault them for this. And there can be no fault attaching to such a prayer uttered by the immaculately holy Christ. So Christ is warranted in leaving out of view the divine purpose, not ascending to the secrets of God, but remaining preoccupied with his immediate concerns. There is no impropriety about this.[22]

---

[21] John Calvin, *Harmony of the Gospels*, 3:230–32.

[22] What does Calvin mean by leaving the decree "out of view"? Presumably, he means that in certain circumstances it is reasonable not to try to take into account, in our actions, what the outcome of the decree may be. We may take

The second passage is Acts 26:29: "I would to God that not only you but also all who hear me this day, might become such as I am—except for these chains." Calvin comments,

> This answer doth testify with what zeal, to spread abroad the glory of Christ, this holy man's breast was inflamed, when as he doth patiently suffer those bonds wherewith the governor had bound him, and doth desire that he might escape the deadly snares of Satan, and to have both him and also his partners to be partakers with him of the same grace, being in the mean season content with his troublesome and reproachful condition. We must note that he doth not wish it simply, but from God, as it is he withdraweth us unto his Son; because, unless he teach us inwardly by his Spirit, the outward doctrine shall always wax cold.[23]

Here Calvin makes the same point about desire as before, but in this instance (he believes) the desire is explicitly qualified by reference to the divine will ("I would to God," i.e., "I desire this if it is in accord with the will of God, and I hope that it is").

Coupled with this is the third example, his comment on Romans 9:3, "For I could wish that I myself were accursed and cut off from Christ for the sake of my brothers":

> It was then a proof of the most ardent love, that Paul hesitated not to wish for himself that condemnation which he was impending over the Jews, in order that he might deliver them. It is no objection that he knew that his salvation was based on the election of God, which could by no means fail; for as those ardent feelings hurry us on impetuously, so they see and regard nothing but the object in view. So Paul did not connect God's election with his wish, but the remembrance of that being passed by, he was wholly intent on the salvation of the Jews.[24]

Once again Calvin draws attention to the presence of deep feelings which focus on the object that is immediately in view, disregarding everything else. Of course Paul's desire is focused on his fellow Jews, and it is in that sense definite, but he expresses that desire for the entire class of Jews, and without reference to the decree of God:

---

into account *that* there is a decree, but not *what* it is. For an account of Calvin's overall understanding of prayer, see Oliver D. Crisp, "John Calvin and Petitioning God," in *Engaging with Calvin: Aspects of the Reformer's Legacy for Today*, ed. Mark D. Thompson (Nottingham, UK: Apollos, 2009), 136–57.

[23] John Calvin, *Commentary on the Acts of the Apostles*, 2:390.

[24] John Calvin, *Commentary on Romans*, 335.

> Since we do not know who belongs to the number of the predestined, and
> who does not, it befits us so to feel as to wish that all be saved. So it will
> come about that, whoever we come across, we shall study to make him a
> sharer of peace.[25]

Here, in a work on predestination against Pighius, Calvin formalizes the position that the deeply aspirational attitude expresses. The presence of such an
attitude is regarded by him as a mark of godliness, both on the part of Christ
and of Paul. But behind the attitude that we have identified lies a more general
point that Calvin expresses: because of our ignorance of who is and who is
not predestined, and a desire for the good of anyone who is our neighbor, we
may wish all to be saved.[26] In certain circumstances a person, even the person
of the Mediator, may be distracted from the revealed will of God and instead
express his immediate aspiration for the salvation of those who may or may
not be elected to salvation.

This is supported by a broader theological point. For in his sermon on
1 Timothy 2:4 Calvin sees the words of Paul as part of the theological pattern that Paul articulates in Romans and Galatians. God chose all those who
descended from Abraham as children of the promise, the circumcised, the
children of Abraham. Yet "was there not a special grace for some of that
people? . . . Not all they that came of the race of Abraham after the flesh are
true Israelites." So though the promise to Abraham's promised seed was indefinite, its implementation was definite. "Behold therefore this will of God
which was toward the people of Israel, shows itself at this day toward us."[27]

In a similar way, human beings, eminent and godly human beings such
as the apostle Paul, even the God-man himself, may have aspirations for
themselves or for others that are perfectly legitimate even though they are
formed in ignorance of what God has decreed in respect of them, or even,
in the heat of the moment, without any thought of God's decree—though
in the case of Christ, of course, there was no such ignorance, since the will
of his Father regarding his death was fully revealed to him. Sometimes, in

---

[25] Calvin, *Concerning the Eternal Predestination of God*, 138.

[26] From time to time Calvin himself used universal language in his prayers. So in his sermons on Genesis in John
Calvin, *Sermons on Genesis Chapters 1–11*, trans. Rob Roy McGregor (Edinburgh: Banner of Truth, 2009), for
example, 72, 88, 124, Calvin routinely ends his prayers after the sermon with the aspiration, "May he grant that
grace [renewal "in the image of his Son, our Lord Jesus Christ"] not only to us, but to all peoples and nations of
the earth" (72).

[27] John Calvin, *John Calvin's Sermons on Timothy and Titus*, trans. I.T., facsimile ed. (Edinburgh: Banner of Truth:
1983), 157 col. 1. I have modernized the spelling of the original translation and retained the word order.

expressing their aspirations, believers may explicitly defer to the will of God, but sometimes not.

Calvin expresses this viewpoint in general terms in a number of places, for example, in the following passage:

> As then we flee to God, whenever necessity urges us, so also we remind him, like a son who unburdens all his feelings in the bosom of his father. Thus in prayer the faithful reason and expostulate with God, and bring forward all those things by which he may be pacified towards them; in short, they deal with him after the manner of men, as though they would persuade him concerning that which yet has been decreed before the creation of the world: but as the eternal counsel of God is hid from us, we ought in this respect to act wisely and according to the measure of our faith.[28]

So, summarizing, there is here an important strand of Calvin's thought about the human condition, about the condition of the incarnate Christ, and that of the godly apostle Paul, which stresses the legitimacy of an expansive aspiration for the eternal good of everyone, expressed in situations of human ignorance as to what God's will is. This second epistemic constraint is a part of the human condition and so it is shared by ministers of the gospel and by evangelists, who out of the fullness of their hearts and in fulfillment of their calling may call men and women to Christ having no reason not to, and with an ardor for their salvation, while all the while remaining ignorant of what God's purposes are with respect to these men and women.

(3) Universal Preaching

Bearing in mind the conclusions of our first two arguments, we finally come to consider the indefinite language of the preacher, the language of universal or indiscriminate invitation. Here are some representative quotations from Calvin about preaching:

> Some object that God would be inconsistent with himself, in inviting all without distinction while he elects only a few. Thus, according to them, the universality of the promise destroys the distinction of special grace. . . . The mode in which Scripture reconciles the two things, viz., that by external preaching all are called to faith and repentance, and that yet the Spirit of faith and repentance is not given to all, I have already explained, and will

---

[28] See John Calvin, *Commentary on Jeremiah and Lamentations*, commenting on Jeremiah 14:22 (1:244). I am grateful to Jon Balserak for this reference.

again shortly repeat. . . . But it is by Isaiah he more clearly demonstrates how he destines the promises of salvation specially to the elect (Isa. 8:16); for he declares that his disciples would consist of them only, and not indiscriminately of the whole human race. Whence it is evident that the doctrine of salvation, which is said to be set apart for the sons of the Church only, is abused when it is represented as effectually available to all. For the present let it suffice to observe, that though the word of the gospel is addressed generally to all, yet the gift of faith is rare. Isaiah assigns the cause when he says that the arm of the Lord is not revealed to all (Isa. 53:1).[29]

Calvin's concern is to establish that the external call to believe and repent, and the restriction of the true faith and repentance only to the elect, are not conflicting courses of action. A universal call does not imply a call that is "effectually available to all."[30]

The expression of our Saviour, "Many are called, but few are chosen" (Matt. 22:14), is also very improperly interpreted.[31] There will be no ambiguity in it, if we attend to what our former remarks ought to have made clear, viz., that there are two species of calling: for there is an universal call, by which God, through the external preaching of the word, invites all men alike, even those for whom he designs the call to be a savor of death, and the ground of a severer condemnation. Besides this there is a special call which, for the most part, God bestows on believers only, when by the internal illumination of the Spirit he causes the word preached to take deep root in their hearts.[32]

There are two gospel calls, each with a distinct purpose and effect:

But if it is so, (you will say), little faith can be put in the Gospel promises, which, in testifying concerning the will of God, declare that he wills what is contrary to his inviolable decree. Not at all; for however universal the promises of salvation may be, there is no discrepancy between them and the predestination of the reprobate, provided we attend to their effect. We know that the promises are effectual only when we receive them in faith, but, on the contrary, when faith is made void, the promise is of no effect. If this is the nature of the promises, let us now see whether there be any inconsistency between the two things, viz., that God, by an eternal decree, fixed the number of those whom he is pleased to embrace in love, and on whom he

---

[29] Calvin, *Institutes*, 3.22.10.
[30] Battles translates this as, "Hence it is clear that the doctrine of salvation, which is said to be reserved solely and individually for the sons of the church, is falsely debased when presented as effectually profitable to all" (Calvin, *Institutes*, 3.22.10).
[31] See *Institutes*, 3.2.11.1.
[32] Ibid., 3.24.8.

is pleased to display his wrath, and that he offers salvation indiscriminately to all. I hold that they are perfectly consistent, for all that is meant by the promise is, just that his mercy is offered to all who desire and implore it, and this none do, save those whom he has enlightened. Moreover, he enlightens those whom he has predestinated to salvation. Thus the truth of the promises remains firm and unshaken, so that it cannot be said there is any disagreement between the eternal election of God and the testimony of his grace which he offers to believers. But why does he mention all men? Namely that the consciences of the righteous may rest the more secure when they understand that there is no difference between sinners, provided they have faith, and that the ungodly may not be able to allege that they have not an asylum to which they may retake themselves from the bondage of sin, while they ungratefully reject the offer which is made to them. Therefore, since by the Gospel the mercy of God is offered to both, it is faith, in other words, the illumination of God, which distinguishes between the righteous and the wicked, the former feeling the efficacy of the Gospel, the latter obtaining no benefit from it. Illumination itself has eternal election for its rule.[33]

The scope of the call, to "all men" or "the world," does not determine the extent of God's salvific intentions. As we are seeing, Calvin takes some trouble to argue that the universality of the invitation is consistent with the particularity or exclusivity of the salvific intentions.

As noted earlier, some scholars have been inclined to see in the indefinite language of preaching that Calvin endorses some version or other of post-redemptionism; that is, they have seen the language as referring to the first of two different steps or stages in the divine application of redemption, two distinct divine willings. The first phase, the indefinite phase, depicts God as willing or wishing or desiring the salvation of all people, or of the world, or of men and women indiscriminately. And then there is a second phase, a second eternal divine willing, which is interpreted as a response to the divine foreknowledge of the failure of the universalistic intent to bear fruit. Note that the decreeing of these phases is not to be understood as temporal events, but as logical distinctions in the divine mind. The second phase is the decreeing of the definite application of an atonement which had (initially, in its first phase) a universal scope. This second phase is ushered in by the intercession of Christ (Kendall) or by the provision of union with Christ (Kennedy).

An objection to my argument from this quarter might be taken from Kevin

---

[33] Ibid., 3.24.17.

D. Kennedy.[34] Kennedy maintains that when dealing with "all" and "many" as used in the NT to characterize the scope of the work of Christ, Calvin employs two hermeneutical "rules" for their interpretation. First, according to Kennedy, in those passages in Scripture which state that Christ came to give his life as a ransom for "many," Calvin understands such passages to mean that Christ died for all people rather than for some. The second rule is that "all" does not always mean "all without exception," or "each and every one." Kennedy's claim has a rather paradoxical appearance: "many" may often mean "all," and "all" may often mean "not all." He thus continues to hold that Calvin was not a Calvinist with respect to the extent of the atonement.

While I have argued for a weaker version of the "continuity" thesis than some, namely, that Calvin was committed to definite atonement without committing himself to the view, the defense of this weaker claim requires that I deny that Calvin operates with two such rules. The first line of such a defense is that there is no evidence to show Calvin formulating or adopting such rules. Moreover, Kennedy recognizes that Calvin's actual practice is often at variance with such rules, as Kennedy's use of quotation marks around "rules" may indicate. Kennedy also thinks that there is significance in the fact that in some of this data drawn from Calvin "all" refers to the scope of salvation rather than the scope of election. Neither election nor salvation have to do in explicit terms with the atonement. We have noted that Calvin has a variety of possible ways of justifying the NT writers' use of indiscriminate language. Such language may refer to the scope of Christ's work as embracing Gentile as well as Jew, or to the world as a whole rather than to every individual in the world, or it may be the justifiable language of aspiration, and spoken in necessary human ignorance of the outcome of God's ways.

The upshot of the first part of my argument, if it is sound, is that post-redemptionist hypotheses offered as ways of understanding the nature of Calvin's theology are unnecessary, besides being anachronistic. I shall use two case studies to establish the point.

Case Study (a): Ezekiel 18:23

An interesting test case for Calvin's position is his attitude toward the knowledge and will of God in Ezekiel 18:23. We have evidence of Amyraut's

---

[34] Kevin D. Kennedy, "Hermeneutical Discontinuity between Calvin and Later Calvinism," *SJT* 64.3 (2011): 299–312.

attitude toward the same text, where he expresses his belief that he could co-opt Calvin as an ally. In a fascinating article, "A Tale of Two Wills?," Richard Muller shows that Amyraut approaches the text in terms of positing two wills in God, a first will according to which God wills salvation universally on the basis of covenant obedience; and, that, since the purpose to save would have been frustrated had God not also willed absolutely to save the elect, a second, efficacious decree to save an elect number was made. Amyraut believes that he has an ally in Calvin himself, given his understanding of Calvin's own remarks on this verse. Calvin's treatment of the text in his *Lectures on Eze-kiel* is noteworthy, according to Muller, because it is one of the few places in which Calvin discusses the universality of the offer of the gospel explicitly in the light of the eternal decree.

While on Amyraut's view the prophet speaks of mercy that is universal in its scope but implicitly or tacitly conditional, Muller argues that this is not Calvin's view. Rather, according to Muller, Calvin holds that

> The prophet's words of universal promise do not refer to the eternal coun-sel of God, nor do they set the universal promise of the gospel against the eternal counsel as a different will. Rather, God always wills the same thing, presumably, the salvation of the elect, albeit in different ways, namely in his eternal counsel and through the preaching of the gospel.[35]

Muller quotes Calvin's words: "If any one again objects that in this way God acts in two ways, the answer is ready, that God always wishes the same thing, though by different ways, and in a manner inscrutable to us."[36] Calvin thinks that there is one divine decree but various means of bringing it to pass. Some of these ways involve the actions of those who flout the revealed will of God, such as the actions of those who crucified Christ, while others involve the upholding of the revealed will, his commands. So there are not two separate wills, but only one will. The distinction is between the secret and the revealed will, the revealed will being subordinate to the secret will, not between an antecedent and a consequent divine will.[37]

So here is Calvin taking a "non-Amyraldian" line, one that is consistent with his other writings, while not, of course, being aware of the Amyraldian developments to come, and despite Amyraut's attempt to have him on his team.

---

[35] Muller, "A Tale of Two Wills?," 218.
[36] Ibid., citing Calvin on Ezekiel 18:23, in John Calvin, *Commentaries on Ezekiel*, 2:247.
[37] Ibid., 2:222, citing Ezekiel 18:5–9.

On Calvin's view there are not two wills in God, but different elements of the one will, operating through various phases. These are not (in this case) the much-discussed covenantal or redemptive-historical phases, but periods in which both those elected and those reprobated live through different epistemic stages in which certain outcomes must first be hidden from those about to enjoy them, if they are to receive them with understanding, and then, later on, revealed or made plain to them. Discriminate grace, but indiscriminate preaching.

In Calvin's remarks on Ezekiel 18:23 there are also these words:

> But again they argue foolishly, since God does not wish all to be converted, he is himself deceptive, and nothing can be certainly stated concerning his paternal benevolence. But this knot is easily untied; for he does not leave us in suspense when he says, that he wishes all to be saved. Why so? For if no one repents without finding God propitious, then this sentence is filled up [fulfilled]. But we must remark that God puts on a twofold character: for here he wishes to be taken at his word. As I have already said, the Prophet does not here dispute with subtlety about his incomprehensible plans, but wishes to keep our attention close to God's word. Now, what are the contents of this word? The law, the prophets, and the gospel. Now all are called to repentance, and the hope of salvation is promised to them when they repent; this is true, since God rejects no returning sinner: he pardons all without exception.[38]

Why on Calvin's view does God choose to bring his grace to sinners by means of an announcement that anyone who turns from his sin will be received, or by saying that Christ died for the world?[39] Partly, Calvin says, because the believer may be humbled and the wicked may be without excuse.[40] And partly, of course, because it is true! Whoever wills may come. God does welcome the return of any penitent sinner. Calvin emphasizes in the passage above that the invitations of the gospel, the calls to all to repent, are sincere. They are not deceptive or duplicitous. But more than this, our epistemic condition requires such invitations in order to highlight the graciousness of the gospel.

Case Study (b): 1 Timothy 2:4

The indefinite invitation of the gospel comes out vividly in Calvin's lengthy sermon on 1 Timothy 2:4. Why may preachers of the gospel make indefinite

---

[38] Calvin, *Commentaries on Ezekiel*, 2:248.
[39] He "offers salvation to all. . . . All are equally called to penitence and faith; the same mediator is set forth for all to reconcile them to the Father" (Calvin, *Secret Providence*, 103).
[40] Ibid., 71.

or universal statements regarding the death of Christ? Because of the epistemic situation of both hearers and preachers. For among the reasons that Calvin offers for such universalistic language is that Paul's wording here is a sign or token of God's love to the Gentiles, and draws attention to our ignorance otherwise:

> For we cannot guess and surmise what God's will is, unless he shew it to us, and give us some sign or token, whereby we may have some perseverance in it. It is too high a matter for us, to know what God's counsel is, but so far forth as he sheweth it by effect, so far do we comprehend it.[41]

> When it is said that God will receive sinners to mercy, such as come to him to ask forgiveness, and that in Christ's name. Is this doctrine for two or three? No, no, it is a general doctrine. So then it is said that God will have all men to be saved, not having respect to what we devise or imagine, that is to say so far forth as our wits are able to comprehend it, for this is that measure that we must always come to.[42]

Calvin is here adopting the point of view of the hearers of gospel preaching, but this is easily transposed to preachers and teachers.

Consider this illustration: one way in which a bank may show its sincerity in stating that it will meet all of its obligations to depositors is by honoring them in fact. Another way is sincerely to make the declaration but to be prevented from keeping it, but this failure is still compatible with its sincerity. According to Calvin, God shows his sincerity in offering grace to sinners by receiving any and all who respond.[43] He honors all who come to him.

Here is Calvin making this point in a less formally theological, more pastoral vein:

> So likewise, when it is said in the holy scripture that this is a true and undoubted saying, that God hath sent his only begotten son, to save all miserable sinners: we must include it within this same rank, I say, that everyone of us apply this same particularly to himself: when as we hear this general sentence, that God is merciful. Have we heard this? Then may we boldly call upon him, and even say, although I am a miserable and forlorn creature, since it is said that God is merciful to those which have offended him: I will run unto him and to his mercy, beseeching him that he will make me

---

[41] Calvin, *Sermons on Timothy and Titus*, 155 col. 1. The original has been slightly modernized.
[42] Ibid.
[43] See also Calvin, *Secret Providence*, 100.

to feel it. And since it is said, *That God so loved the world, that he spared not his only begotten son: but delivered him up to death for us*, it is meet I should look to that. For it is very needful, that Jesus Christ should pluck me from that condemnation, wherein I am since it is so, that the love and goodness of God is declared unto the world in that that [*sic*] his son Jesus Christ hath suffered death, I must appropriate the same to myself, that I may know that it is to me, that God hath spoken, that he would that I should take possession of such a grace, and therein to rejoice me.[44]

Let us suppose for a moment that there was no such phase of ignorance, but instead a preaching economy that was conducted in all its stages under uniform epistemic conditions, either in terms knowingly and uniformly directed to the elect, or in terms knowingly and uniformly directed to the reprobate. If this happened (as it has tended to be made to happen in some hyper-Calvinist settings), the hearers could not be invited to come to Christ, but first (by the terms of the preaching) they would each be forced to ask, Which am I? Am I among the elect, or among the reprobate? Do I fulfill the requirements or conditions or states of being among the former or among the latter? In these circumstances there could be no full, free invitation. The gospel could not be received "by invitation only," but only through the fulfillment of some prior state or condition together with the assurance that such a condition had been fulfilled.

In other words, under such terms "gospel preaching" would have the effect not of turning men and women to receive the good news of a Christ who invites freely and graciously, but of turning hearers in upon themselves in a search for sure signs of election or reprobation. And such a turning in on oneself is but a very short step from a person being concerned about whether he is qualified to come to Christ, in which case there is the prospect of despair over what would be taken to be the marks of retribution, or presumption as to election. Either way, instead of facing Christ who has outstretched arms, a person would introspect. At such a point the "grace" of Calvin's gospel of free justification would become legalistic by the need for the fulfillment of certain preconditions.

So I suggest that what Calvin is identifying in his use of indiscriminate,

---

[44] John Calvin, *John Calvin's Sermons on the Hundred and Nineteenth Psalm* (Audubon, NJ: Old Paths, 1996), 133–34. I am grateful to Jon Balserak for this reference. An interesting feature is that Calvin couches his argument in terms of a practical syllogism. The argument is: God is merciful to those who have offended him; (the "general sentence") "I have offended him"; (the "particular application") "therefore, I will call upon him for mercy."

universalistic language is a necessary feature of the preaching of God's free grace in Christ as he understood this. This is a pastoral necessity, and perhaps even a logical necessity. There is a strong pastoral rationale for maintaining this indiscriminateness, as well as, of course, important dogmatic grounds for holding to it.

In closing this discussion I wish to note three further matters. One is that, when given the opportunity to make the scope of Christ's work universal in intent, Calvin does not take it, as his exegesis of 2 Corinthians 5:14 shows.[45] Christ is also portrayed as the "only Saviour of all his people."[46] The presence of particularistic language can hardly be denied. The context is a discussion of the relation between election and assurance. It is also interesting to compare Calvin here with his comments on 1 John 2:2. Here he is happy with the scholastic sufficient–efficient distinction applied to Christ's suffering, yet believes it is not applicable to this text "for the design of John was no other than to make this benefit common to the whole Church. Then under the word all or whole, he does not include the reprobate, but designates those who should believe as well as those who were then scattered in various parts of the world."[47] So if through his use of indefinite language Calvin presupposes a universal atonement (as some proponents suggest), why, when he comes to the standard passages for "universal atonement," such as 1 John 2.2, does he not take the opportunity to state unequivocally that he is a proponent of universal atonement?

Secondly, in the universalistic language that Calvin endorses, God commands men and women to come to Christ, and he commands with the same divine authority as when he says, "Thou shalt not steal." To use Paul's words, "he commands all people everywhere to repent" (Acts 17:30). The language of command draws attention to the scope of human obligation or responsibility. But it is the universality of the command which, in an "ineffable" way, actually serves the fulfillment of God's decree, his particular purposes. For in responding to it, men and women will come to Christ as he is freely offered in the gospel. In this way God's decree of election will be fulfilled. By contrast, his commands may be flouted and his invitations spurned. Men and women may not in fact repent and believe the gospel, though invited to do so. This is an application of Calvin's teaching about providence more generally, that

---

[45] John Calvin, *Commentary on 2 Corinthians*, 230–31.
[46] Calvin, *Institutes*, 3.24.6
[47] John Calvin, *Commentary on 1 John*, 173.

it is (as we noted earlier), a means-ends order: in the case of election, among the means of being assured that one is chosen are invitations that are univer-salistic or indiscriminate in their logic, an indiscriminate invitation to come to Christ. In the case of some, the invitation will be accepted in penitence and faith, a ground for the assurance of being one of the Lord's chosen.

The question may be raised, would such indiscriminate language war-rant a preacher asserting to all and sundry that "Christ died for you"? Only if the formulation were taken as an inference drawn from "Christ died for all" or "Christ died for the world," but not if from "Christ died for everyone in particular." The first premise, Calvin would hold, is true, while the second is false. That is, a distinction must be made between the world as comprised of classes of individuals, and the world as comprised of individuals of a class. Taken in the first way, the language would not be warranted, but in the second sense, the language is clearly warranted. Christ died for the world.[48]

Thirdly, such universal or indiscriminate preaching may be understood as a working out of Calvin's well-known teaching that Christ is the mirror of election. He raises this question: If God's grace is decreed only for the elect, and hearers of the gospel may know that, how will a person who is told this come to know whether he is among those to whom God's grace comes ef-fectively? His answer is, Christ is the mirror of election. We cannot know of our election in Christ by some direct appeal to God himself to intimate the fact that we are eternally elect, but only as this is reflected to us (by inference) through our communion with Christ:

> But if we are elected in him, we cannot find the certainty of our election in ourselves; and not even in God the Father, if we look at him apart from the Son. Christ, then, is the mirror in which we ought, and in which, without deception, we may contemplate our election. For since it is into his body that the Father has decreed to ingraft those whom from eternity he wished to be his, that he may regard as sons all whom he acknowledges to be his members, if we are in communion with Christ, we have proof sufficiently clear and strong that we are written in the Book of Life.

---

[48] In remarks on 1 Timothy 2:4, Martin Foord calls into question the view that Calvin simply follows Augustine's view that the verse teaches nothing more than that God wills all *kinds* of people to be saved ("God Wills All People to Be Saved—Or Does He? Calvin's Reading of 1 Timothy 2:4," in *Engaging with Calvin*, 179–203). Calvin certainly refers to all orders of men and women. It was Augustine's view that this is God's decreed will that (some of) all orders of men and women be saved. But the claim that Foord next makes, that Calvin is in fact referring to *all* people of all kinds (a claim absent from Augustine), is less obvious. It makes equal if not more sense for Calvin to be understood as interpreting the text as being indefinite with respect to individuals but definite with respect to all classes and all nations: some men and women of all nations. Space does not allow a more detailed treatment of Foord's interesting paper.

He continues:

> The practical influence of this doctrine ought also to be exhibited in our
> prayers. For though a belief of our election animates us to involve God, yet
> when we frame our prayers, it were preposterous to obtrude it upon God, or
> to stipulate in this way, "O Lord, if I am elected, hear me." He would have
> us rest satisfied with the promises, and not to inquire elsewhere whether
> or not he is disposed to hear us. We shall thus be disentangled from many
> snares, if we know how to make a right use of what is rightly written, but
> let us not inconsiderately wrest it to purposes different from that to which
> it ought to be confined.[49]

Note here that, once again, Calvin clearly links this entire matter to human
ignorance. But here our ignorance is not of our future, but of God's secret
will. We cannot know directly that we are elect, or that we are not. But we can
know God's promise, and trusting that, and thus being in communion with
Christ, we shall make a right use of what is rightly written.

Conclusion

So Calvin has a vivid appreciation of three factors about the human condition,
each of which has to do with human ignorance. One is our limited knowledge
of the future, and so our ignorance of God's eternal decree respecting the future.
He advises that, while trusting in God's meticulous providence, we should live
as if the future were not decreed, and in a parallel way, that we should seek our
assurance of election through our awareness of communion with Christ. A second is Calvin's justification of the use of indiscriminate or universal language
in aspirational praying, even when those who pray, in the heat of the moment,
neglect to refer to God's decree. Calvin thinks that such an attitude is excusable,
even commendable. The third is the universal terms of preaching, adopted due
to the preachers' and the hearers' ignorance, notwithstanding God's unconditional election and his provision of effectual grace to those whom he chose. In
addition, Calvin holds that without this element in gospel preaching, hearers
of it are inclined to turn inward rather looking to Christ alone.

---

[49] Calvin, *Institutes*, 3.24.5. Compare Calvin's language in his sermon on 1 Timothy 2:4, referred to earlier: "We
are ingrafted as it were into the body of our Lord Jesus Christ. And this is the true earnest penny of our adoption:
this is the pledge which is given us, to put us out of all doubt that God taketh us and holdeth us for his, when we
are made one by faith with Jesus Christ, who is the only begotten son, unto whom belongeth the inheritance of life.
Seeing then that God giveth us such a sure certificate of his will, see how he putteth us out of doubt of our election,
which we know not of, neither can perceive it, and it is as much, as if he should draw out a copy of his will, and
give it to us" (Calvin, *Sermons on Timothy and Titus*, 253 col. 2).

Summarizing the argument, we may say that as far as Calvin is concerned belief in meticulous providence is consistent with planning for the future as if the future were open. There is nothing inconsistent in holding to the definiteness of providence and acting as if the future were indefinite. Similarly, in the case of aspirational prayer, the one who prays, knowing that there is a divine decree of election, is, according to Calvin, nonetheless warranted by his ignorance of whom exactly God has elected and the love he shows to his neighbor, to pray for the salvation of men and women the world over. Finally, because of the preacher's ignorance of who is and who is not elected, and his desire to see the kingdom of God enlarged in accordance with the terms of the Great Commission, a preacher may call men and women to Christ in universal or unrestricted terms. These three instances show that in appropriate circumstances, definiteness in belief can be allied with indefiniteness of expression.

If so, then we have established that definite beliefs can exist consistently with certain kinds of indefiniteness. May we not conclude, then, that the use of indefinite language is not only consistent with definite providence and definite election but that it is also consistent with being committed to the doctrine of definite atonement? Even though, as I have argued, Calvin does not commit himself to that belief. The use of indefinite language cannot therefore be used as an argument against such a commitment.

The case for Calvin's being committed to definite atonement is a cumulative one, embracing his unitary, singular view of the divine decree; his beliefs in substitutionary atonement, unconditional election, and effectual grace; and his denial of bare foreknowledge, as well as his explicit statements regarding the definite scope of the atonement. It has been widely held, however, that his use of indefinite language presents an insuperable obstacle to the completion of this trajectory. In this chapter it has been argued that Calvin's attitude toward indefinite language, which might be thought to favor a rejection of definite atonement, is in fact perfectly consistent with a commitment to it, and may be integrated with it. This further strengthens the overall case that Calvin was committed to definite atonement. Correspondingly, the case for Calvin's rejection of definite atonement becomes ever weaker.[50]

---

[50] Thanks to Jon Balserak, Oliver Crisp, Richard Muller, and other readers for help of various kinds with an earlier draft of the chapter.

Blaming Beza

THE DEVELOPMENT OF DEFINITE ATONEMENT IN THE REFORMED TRADITION

Raymond A. Blacketer

A Historical Labyrinth

Did John Calvin teach "limited atonement," or did later Reformed thinkers, such as Theodore Beza, concoct this allegedly harsh doctrine by substituting Calvin's restrained biblical exegesis with a deterministic, rationalistic, and deductive system? The fact that scholars have had difficulty answering this question arises out of the fact that the question itself is flawed on a number of levels. Studies of this issue are often plagued with wrong turns and false starts, depositing students of the question into a methodological labyrinth, to use one of Calvin's favorite terms.

First, the phrase "limited atonement" is misleading,[1] derived from the ill-fitting and infelicitous TULIP acronym that originated at the turn of the twentieth century to summarize the teachings of the Canons of Dordt.[2] In addition,

---

[1] "The terms 'universal atonement' and 'limited atonement' do not represent the sixteenth- and seventeenth-century Reformed view—or, for that matter, the view of its opponents" (Richard A. Muller, *After Calvin: Studies in the Development of a Theological Tradition* [New York: Oxford University Press, 2003], 14). See also Muller's *Dictionary of Latin and Greek Theological Terms* (Grand Rapids, MI: Baker, 1985), s.v. *satisfactio*; and cf. the discussion in Roger R. Nicole, "Particular Redemption," in *Our Savior God: Man, Christ, and the Atonement*, ed. James Montgomery Boice (Grand Rapids, MI: Baker, 1980), 165–78.

[2] See Richard A. Muller, "Was Calvin a Calvinist?," in his *Calvin and the Reformed Tradition: On the Work of Christ and the Order of Salvation* (Grand Rapids, MI: Baker Academic, 2012), 51–69, hereafter cited as *CRT*; and Kenneth J. Stewart, "The Five Points of Calvinism: Retrospect and Prospect," *SBET* 26.2 (2008): 187–203. The

the English term *atonement* does not correspond directly to the terms that continental theologians employed; and one would be hard pressed to find any Reformed thinker in the early seventeenth century who would limit the value or sufficiency of Christ's satisfaction, or, for that matter, any thinker in Christendom at that time who would not limit its efficacy to believers.[3]

Attempts to determine whether Calvin taught "limited atonement," perhaps more aptly termed "definite redemption,"[4] anachronistically ignore the fact that this question received increasing clarification and definition in the decades following Calvin's death.[5] The Synod of Dordrecht (or Dordt, 1618–1619) formulated the doctrinal boundaries of Reformed thought on the subject but left considerable room for variation in doctrinal formulation.[6] Thus, while the Reformed churches excluded the views of Jacob Arminius and Simon Episcopius at Dordt, later synods only scolded the Hypothetical Universalism of Moïse Amyraut. Thus there was no such thing as "the Amyraut heresy."[7]

While there are clearly identifiable precedents throughout the Christian tradition for this teaching, one must be cautious about reading the results of later debates back into Calvin's thought.[8] Calvin turned over the detailed expo-

---

TULIP acronym seems to have originated in a c. 1905 lecture by a Presbyterian pastor from New York, Cleland Boyd McAfee, reported by William H. Vail, "The Five Points of Calvinism Historically Considered," in the New York City weekly *The New Outlook* 104 (1913): 394.

[3] The views of Johannes Piscator and later Herman Witsius were exceptions, and the Canons of Dordt can be seen as a "quiet rebuttal" of Piscator's views in particular, as Muller observes, *CRT*, chapter 3 nn. 22 and 49.

[4] The phrase "definite redemption" might more accurately reflect the teachings of the Canons, heading 2, rejection of errors 1, with the caveat that *redemptio* can be used both in an objective indefinite sense and in a definite sense as applied to the elect. Cf. Muller, *CRT*, chapter 3 n. 66.

[5] For an overview, see Raymond A. Blacketer, "The Doctrine of Limited Atonement in Historical Perspective," in *The Glory of the Atonement: Biblical, Theological, and Practical Perspectives: Essays in Honor of Roger Nicole*, ed. Charles Hill and Frank A. James III (Downers Grove, IL: InterVarsity Press, 2004), 304–23. On the terminology used to refer to the Reformed theological tradition, see Richard A. Muller, "Was Calvin a Calvinist?" cited above. On the diversity within the Reformed tradition, see the essays in Michael A. G. Haykin and Mark Jones, eds., *Drawn into Controversie: Reformed Theological Diversity and Debates within Seventeenth-Century British Puritanism* (Göttingen, Germany: Vandenhoeck & Ruprecht, 2011).

[6] See Muller, *CRT*, chapter 3 n. 22. On the Synod, see Donald W. Sinnema, "The Issue of Reprobation at the Synod of Dordt (1618–1619) in Light of the History of This Doctrine" (PhD diss., University of St Michael's College, Toronto, 1985); W. Robert Godfrey, "Tensions within International Calvinism: The Debate on the Atonement at the Synod of Dort, 1618–1619" (PhD diss., Stanford University, 1974); and idem, "Reformed Thought on the Extent of the Atonement to 1618," *WTJ* 37 (1975–1976): 133–71. See also Sinnema, "The Canons of Dordt: From Judgment on Arminianism to Confessional Standard," in *Revisiting the Synod of Dordt (1618–1619)*, ed. Aza Goudriaan and Fred A. van Lieburg (Leiden, Netherlands: Brill, 2011), 313–33.

[7] Contra Brian G. Armstrong, *Calvinism and the Amyraut Heresy: Protestant Scholasticism and Humanism in Seventeenth-Century France* (Madison: University of Wisconsin Press, 1969), hereafter cited as *CAH*. See Richard A. Muller, *Post-Reformation Reformed Dogmatics*, 4 vols., 2nd ed. (Grand Rapids, MI: Baker Academic, 2003), 1:76–77; hereafter cited as *PRRD*.

[8] Those who contend that Calvin held to a universal redemption include: Paul M. van Buren, *Christ in Our Place: The Substitutionary Character of Calvin's Doctrine of Reconciliation* (Edinburgh: Oliver Boyd, 1957); Basil Hall, "Calvin against the Calvinists," in *John Calvin*, ed. G. E. Duffield (Grand Rapids, MI: Eerdmans, 1966), 19–37; Charles M. Bell, "Calvin and the Extent of the Atonement," *EQ* 55.2 (1983): 115–23; Alan C. Clifford, *Calvinus: Authentic Calvinism* (Norwich, UK: Charenton Reformed, 1996). Proponents of definite redemption in Calvin include Jonathan H. Rainbow, *The Will of God and the Cross: An Historical and Theological Study of John Calvin's*

sition and defense of the Reformed doctrine of predestination to his successor, Theodore Beza, whom scholars in the mid-twentieth century tended to indict as the one who allegedly distorted Calvin's views.[9] This is an extremely unlikely scenario, given Calvin's high regard for Beza and the fact that, during Calvin's lifetime, Beza commented more explicitly than did Calvin on the limits of the intention and application of Christ's satisfaction. Rather than a radical departure from Calvin's teaching, Beza's comments on the matter represent a refinement and development of what was already present, not only in Calvin's writings but in a considerable number of other thinkers throughout the Christian exegetical and theological tradition. Beza makes his own original contributions to the development of Reformed thought on this matter, but his contributions are completely in line with earlier Reformed patterns of exegesis, which continued to be reflected as the doctrine received confessional codification.[10]

Some scholars have failed to critically evaluate statements by the seventeenth-century theologian Moïse Amyraut, who attempted to drive a wedge between Calvin and Beza in order to defend his own particular doctrinal formulations.[11] Calvin scholarship in the twentieth century was particularly plagued by a tendency to read Calvin through the filter of neoorthodoxy,[12]

Doctrine of Limited Redemption (Allison Park, PA: Pickwick, 1990); and Roger R. Nicole, "John Calvin's View of the Extent of the Atonement," *WTJ* 47.2 (1985): 197–225. Cf. the balanced treatment in Hans Boersma, "Calvin and the Extent of the Atonement," *EQ* 64.4 (1992): 333–55, though he fails to distinguish the terms *universal* and *indiscriminate*. P. L. Rouwendal somewhat oversimplifies the problem in his "Calvin's Forgotten Classical Position on the Extent of the Atonement: About Sufficiency, Efficiency, and Anachronism," *WTJ* 70.2 (2008): 317–35. Muller takes up the question in detail in *CRT*, 66–101. For precedents, see, for example, Rainbow, *Will of God and the Cross*, 8–22; and Blacketer, "Definite Atonement," 307–13.

[9] In addition to Armstrong, *CAH*, see Johannes Dantine, "Das christologische Problem in Rahmen der Prädestinationslehre von Theodore Beza," *Zeitschrift für Kirchengeschichte* 77 (1966): 81–96; idem, "Les Tabelles sur la doctrine de la prédestination par Théodore de Bèze," *Revu de théologie et de philosophie* 16 (1996): 365–67; Walter Kickel, *Vernunft und Offenbarung bei Theodor Beza: Zum Problem der Verhältnisses von Theologie, Philosophie und Staat* (Neukirchen, Germany: Neukirchener Verlag, 1967); and John S. Bray, *Theodore Beza's Doctrine of Predestination* (Nieuwkoop, Netherlands: DeGraaf, 1975), 111–18.

[10] On Beza's development of this doctrine, see Paul Archbald, "A Comparative Study of John Calvin and Theodore Beza on the Doctrine of the Extent of the Atonement" (PhD diss., Westminster Theological Seminary, 1998).

[11] See, for example, the works of Alan C. Clifford, who makes no attempt to distinguish his own theological agenda from his analysis of the historical record in *Atonement and Justification: English Evangelical Theology 1640–1790—An Evaluation* (Oxford: Oxford University Press, 1990), and the essentially self-published *Amyraut Affirmed: Or, "Owenism, a Caricature of Calvinism"* (Norwich, UK: Charenton Reformed, 2004). Note the refutations of Clifford's arguments by Richard A. Muller, "A Tale of Two Wills? Calvin and Amyraut on Ezekiel 18:23," *CTJ* 44.2 (2009): 211–25, and Carl R. Trueman, *The Claims of Truth: John Owen's Trinitarian Theology* (Carlisle, UK: Paternoster, 1998), 233–40.

[12] On this confessional bias, see, for example, Jeffrey Mallinson's well-documented study *Faith, Reason, and Revelation in Theodore Beza 1519–1605* (Oxford: Oxford University Press, 2003), 6–10, hereafter cited as *FRR*; Muller, *PRRD*, 2:17–18. This bias continues to appear in Calvin scholarship; see the recent *Cambridge Companion to John Calvin*, ed. Donald K. McKim (Cambridge, 2004), where one author anachronistically claims that Calvin "never confused the gospel content—the Christ—with the words of Scripture" (258). This modern distinction makes no sense before the Enlightenment and reflects the unacknowledged influence of Barth. It does not and could not possibly reflect Calvin's actual teaching. Theologians of the sixteenth and seventeenth centuries universally assumed that their thought was centered on Christ, despite the anachronistic Barthian criticism that some lacked a "christocentric" methodology.

but other Reformed parties have also claimed Calvin as a proponent of their distinctly modern concerns.[13]

Another methodological cul-de-sac to be avoided is the cliché of opposing the biblical and humanistic Calvin to the later, not-so-biblical, "scholastic," and (therefore) rationalistic Reformed tradition, represented by the likes of Beza and the theologians of Dordt.[14] According to this historiographical mythology, Calvin alone represents the pristine purity of the Reformed tradition,[15] and any development in Reformed thought is considered a distortion.[16] The foundations of this myth have crumbled with more contextual research into the phenomena of humanism and scholasticism.[17] Scholasticism can no longer be caricatured as a speculative enterprise with a rationalistic deductive content, often associated with a regrettable addiction to Aristotelian philosophy.[18] In the sixteenth century, reform-minded scholars could use the term "scholastic" as a pejorative epithet to be launched against one's enemies, indicating an overreliance on reason or a benightedness with respect

---

[13] See, for example, Keith C. Sewell, "Theodore Beza—The Man Next to John Calvin: A Review Essay," *Pro Rege* 33.3 (2005): 15–19. Because of his overpowering allegiance to so-called "Reformational" philosophy, Sewell is unable to see scholasticism primarily as a method, and continues to maintain the historical mythology that Beza and the later Reformed tradition, albeit perhaps unwittingly, betrayed Calvin's foundational ideas.

[14] See, for example, Armstrong's often cited definition of scholasticism (*CAH*, 32); and cf. the caricature in Edward A. Dowey, *The Knowledge of God in Calvin's Theology*, 3rd ed. (Grand Rapids, MI: Eerdmans, 1994), 218.

[15] Note the telling title of R. T. Kendall's "The Puritan Modification of Calvin's Theology," in *John Calvin: His Influence in the Western World*, ed. W. Stanford Reid (Grand Rapids, MI: Zondervan, 1982), 197–214; cf. his *Calvin and English Calvinism to 1649* (New York: Oxford University Press, 1979). This "great thinker" approach is observable in works such as Hall, "Calvin against the Calvinists," 19–37; Armstrong, *CAH*; and Holmes Rolston III, *John Calvin versus the Westminster Confession* (Richmond, VA: John Knox, 1972). On the concept of historiographical mythologies, see Quentin Skinner, "Meaning and Understanding in the History of Ideas," *History and Theory* 8.1 (1969): 3–53.

[16] See, for example, J. B. Torrance, "The Incarnation and 'Limited Atonement,'" *EQ* 55 (1983): 83–94; idem, "The Concept of Federal Theology—Was Calvin a Federal Theologian?," in *Calvinus Sacrae Scripturae Professor*, Fourth International Congress on Calvin Research, 1990, ed. Wilhelm H. Neuser (Grand Rapids, MI: Eerdmans, 1994): 15–40. J. Todd Billings demonstrates that such isolation of Calvin from the confessional tradition is more a scholarly self-projection than a reality ("The Catholic Calvin," *Pro Ecclesia* 20.2 [2011]: 120–34).

[17] See the essays in Carl R. Trueman and R. Scott Clark, eds., *Protestant Scholasticism: Essays in Reassessment* (Carlisle, UK: Paternoster, 1999). Richard A. Muller's work in this area is pioneering; in addition to his *PRRD*, see, for example, "The Myth of 'Decretal Theology,'" *CTJ* 30.1 (1995): 159–67, and "Calvin and the 'Calvinists': Assessing Continuities and Discontinuities between the Reformation and Orthodoxy," parts I and II, in *CTJ* 30.2 (1995): 345–75 and 31.1 (1996): 125–60, later published in *After Calvin*, chapters 4–5. Numerous scholars have come to similar conclusions, for example, Martin I. Klauber, "The Context and Development of the Views of Jean-Alphonse Turrettini (1671–1737) on Religious Authority" (PhD diss., University of Wisconsin-Madison, 1987); Paul Helm, *Calvin and the Calvinists* (Edinburgh: Banner of Truth, 1982); Willem J. van Asselt and P. L. Rouwendal, eds., *Inleiding in de Gereformeerde Scholastiek* (Zoetermeer: Boekencentrum, 1998); and cf. the traditional view of Beza represented in the first edition of David C. Steinmetz, *Reformers in the* Wings (Philadelphia: Fortress, 1971), 162–71, with the substantially revised perspective in the 2nd edition (Oxford: Oxford University Press, 2001), 114–20.

[18] Note Armstrong's often-cited definition of scholasticism (*CAH*, 32); and cf. the disparaging remarks in Edward A. Dowey, *The Knowledge of God in Calvin's Theology*, 3rd ed. (Grand Rapids, MI: Eerdmans, 1994), 218. This viewpoint is represented by H. E. Weber, *Reformation, Orthodoxie, und Rationalismus*, 2 vols. in 3 (Gütersloh, C. Bertelsmann 1937–1951); and Ernst Bizer, *Frühorthodoxie und Rationalismus*, Theologische Studien 71 (Zürich: EVZ-Verlag, 1963). See the discussion in Muller, *PRRD*, 1:135–46; 2:382–86, and note Richard A. Muller, "Found (No Thanks to Theodore Beza): One 'Decretal' Theology," *CTJ* 32.1 (1997): 145–53. The discovered decretal theology is that of Pierre Poiret (1646–1719), whose rationalist system is derived not from Aristotle but Descartes.

to newer forms of thought. Calvin himself made use of scholastic (and Aristotelian) terminology, distinctions, and methods,[19] while at the same time he could employ the term pejoratively, as he often did when referring to the Paris theologians, the *Sorbonnistes*.[20]

The final dead end is to abstract thinkers in the Reformed tradition from their intellectual context. Many thinkers, not just Calvin, contributed to the formation of a clearly identifiable yet internally diverse theological tradition. As other chapters in this volume demonstrate, there is a clearly identifiable trajectory of thought in the Christian tradition that can be described as particularist, that is, a line of thinking that identifies those to whom God intends to bestow the benefits of Christ's satisfaction as the elect alone.

Calvin's views on election and God's sovereignty in salvation extend this particularist trajectory of thought, and exclude a universal, indefinite satisfaction and redemption obtained in some manner by Christ which would be potentially (not simply hypothetically) available to each human individual. Rather than an unfortunate rupture between Calvin and the later Reformed, the evidence instead supports a continuing development of doctrine within a clearly identifiable yet increasingly diverse trajectory of reflection on predestination and the extent of Christ's redemption.

Beza in Context, or The Man in the Black Hat

A 1597 portrait of Theodore Beza depicts Calvin's personally chosen successor in his later years: his beard is long and grey, and he is wearing a black hat.[21] Curiously, historical theologians of the modern era have portrayed Beza as the primary villain in the history of Reformed thought, quickly distorting the dynamic christocentrism of Calvin into the static, rigid forms of rationalistic, scholastic Reformed orthodoxy.[22] Armstrong claims that "one may lay much of the blame for scholasticism at his feet."[23] The result is a twisted caricature

---

[19] See David C. Steinmetz, "The Scholastic Calvin," in idem, *Calvin in Context*, 2nd ed. (New York: Oxford, 2010), 247–61, who notes, for example, Calvin's treatment of necessity and contingency in his *Institutes*, 1.16.9; cf. Richard A. Muller, "Scholasticism, Reformation, Orthodoxy, and the Persistence of Christian Aristotelianism," *Trinity Journal* 19.1 (1998): 81–96.

[20] See Richard A. Muller, "Scholasticism in Calvin: A Question of Relation and Disjunction," in *The Unaccommodated Calvin: Studies in the Foundation of a Theological Tradition* (New York: Oxford, 2000), 39–61.

[21] This portrait is owned by La Société de l'Histoire du Protestantisme Français and can be viewed online, http://www.museeprotestant.org, accessible at date of publication.

[22] Reformed orthodoxy did not replace christology with predestination as the *principium cognoscendi* (although a certain christology might function as such in modern neoorthodoxy); rather, Scripture provided the foundation of theological thought, contra Kickel, *Vernunft und Offenbarung*, 167–69; cf. Muller, *PRRD*, 1:126.

[23] Armstrong, *CAH*, 38. Amyraut's method was just as scholastic as any theologian of the era, and his claims to simply reproduce Calvin do not bear scrutiny. See his *Defense de la Doctrine de Calvin sur le suiet d'election et de*

of the humanist, pastor, philologist, exegete, political advisor and diplomat, as well as the theologian and intellectual leader of the Reformation who was Theodore Beza.[24] It also leads to a distorted picture of the development of the concept of definite redemption.

In fact, the humanist-turned-Reformer from Vézelay was at least as accomplished with respect to French humanism as was Calvin, indeed, probably more so.[25] They shared much of the same academic pedigree, studying at Orléans, obtaining degrees in law, and learning Greek from Melchior Wolmar. Beza put his humanistic training to use, writing a rather successful collection of love poems (which later caused him some embarrassment), and subsequently composing theological treatises, biting satire, a dramatic tragedy based on Abraham's near-sacrifice of Isaac, and Psalms for congregational singing. Like Erasmus, he produced annotated editions of the Greek NT, and helped to preserve an important Greek codex that bears his name.[26] He published sermons and meditations on the Christian life. Above all, Beza was a pastor, preacher, and provider of pastoral care for his congregations in Lausanne and Geneva.[27] Even in his *Tabula Praedestinationis*, which older scholarship tended to misconstrue as a rationalistic deductive system, Beza's aim was to demonstrate that predestination was a practical doctrine that pastors should preach from the pulpit, as long as they did so in the correct manner.[28]

---

la reprobation (Saumur, France: Isaac Desbordes, 1644), and cf. Armstrong, *CAH*, 158–60, and Bray, *Predestination*, 17. Bray's study (12–17) follows Armstrong's prejudicial view of later Calvinism. On Amyraut's misreading of Calvin, see Richard A. Muller, "A Tale of Two Wills?" The nadir of anti-Beza scholarship is represented by Philip C. Holtrop, *The Bolsec Controversy on Predestination, from 1551 to 1555*, 2 vols. (Lewiston, NY: Edwin Mellon, 1993), esp. 830–78. Note the devastating review by Brian G. Armstrong (himself no admirer of Beza) in *The Sixteenth Century Journal* 25.3 (1994): 747–50; and Muller's review in *CTJ* 29.2 (1994): 581–89.

[24] Richard A. Muller, *Scholasticism and Orthodoxy in the Reformed Tradition: An Attempt at Definition*. inaugural address as P. J. Zondervan Professor of Historical Theology, September 7, 1995 (Grand Rapids, MI: Calvin Theological Seminary, 1995), 29.

[25] See Jill Raitt, *The Eucharistic Theology of Theodore Beza: Development of the Reformed Doctrine* (Chambersburg, PA: American Academy of Religion, 1972); Scott M. Manetsch, "Psalms before Sonnets: Theodore Beza and the *Studia Humanitatis*," in *Continuity and Change: The Harvest of Late Medieval and Reformation History* (*Festschrift for Heiko A. Oberman*), ed. Robert J. Bast and Andrew C. Gow (Leiden, Netherlands: Brill, 2000), 400–416; Ian McPhee, "Conserver or Transformer of Calvin's Theology? A Study of the Origins and Development of Theodore Beza's Thought, 1550–1570," (doctoral thesis, University of Cambridge, 1979), v–xiii, hereafter cited as CTCT; Mallinson, *FRR*.

[26] On Beza's NT scholarship, see Irena Backus, *The Reformed Roots of the English New Testament: The Influence of Theodore Beza on the English New Testament* (Pittsburgh: Pickwick, 1980); Jan Krans, *Beyond What Is Written: Erasmus and Beza as Conjectural Critics of the New Testament* (Leiden and Boston: Brill, 2006).

[27] A leading Beza scholar refers to him as a "shepherd of souls concerned for their growth in Christ" (Jill Raitt, "Beza, Guide for the Faithful Life," *STJ* 39.1 [1986]: 83–107 [here 83]; see also Shawn D. Wright, *Our Sovereign Refuge: The Pastoral Theology of Theodore Beza* [Carlisle, UK: Paternoster, 2004]).

[28] Theodore Beza, *Tabula praedestinationis. Summa totius christianismi, sive descriptio et distributio causarum salutis electorum. . . .* (Geneva, 1555), reprinted in idem, *Volumen tractationum theologicarum*, 3 vols., 2nd ed. (Geneva: E. Vignon, 1570–1582), hereafter cited as *TT,* 1:170–205. On the *Tabula* and the older scholarship's caricature thereof, see Muller, "The Use and Abuse of a Document: Beza's *Tabula Praedestinationis*," in *Protestant*

Like Calvin, Philip Melanchthon, and other humanist scholars, Beza was concerned about proper method in his work. His rhetorical and dialectical precision in no respect constitutes rationalism.[29] Ironically, Beza's attitude toward the "scholastics," in the pejorative rhetorical sense, is, if anything, even more scathing than the same use of the term by Calvin. Both had in mind primarily the doctors of the Sorbonne.[30] Beza even resorts to scatological terms to refer to traditional academic theology. In typical French humanist fashion, Beza compares Gratian's *Decretals* to a latrine.[31]

Beza's insistence upon conceptual coherence was nothing out of the ordinary.[32] All of the Reformers (including Luther, despite his penchant for paradox) sought to deploy coherent rational arguments for their views and against their opponents. Beza's reflections on predestination and the extent of Christ's redemption are based not on speculation (a fault which he finds, rather, in his opponents), but on his exegesis of biblical texts.[33] One may challenge Beza's exegesis, but the charge of rationalism is unfounded. In fact, a critical and selective appropriation of Aristotle was characteristic of sixteenth-century French humanism.[34]

Beza was a "scholastic" in the sense that he was engaged in academic training of pastors and the ongoing defense and academic development and refinement of Reformed thought in the face of polemical attacks, without which the Reformed thought of the sixteenth century could not survive. It

---

Scholasticism, 33–61. Even Karl Barth disagreed with those who claimed Beza made predestination into a "central dogma" that became a kind of "speculative key . . . from which they could deduce all other dogmas" (*Church Dogmatics*, ed. G. W. Bromiley and T. F. Torrance, 14 vols. [Edinburgh: T. & T. Clark, 1956–1975], II/2, 77–78).

[29] The common accusation is that Beza's addiction to Aristotelian reason led him away from Calvin's alleged biblicism; see, for example, Armstrong, *CAH*, 32, 38.

[30] See Muller, *Unaccommodated Calvin*, 50–52.

[31] As Mallinson observes, *FRR*, 43–44; Beza throws the whole theological library at St. Victor into the same toilet.

[32] Bray, *Predestination*, 81 n. 71, confuses an insistence on coherence with rationalism. Calvin and others in the Reformed tradition argued that Luther's view of the *communicatio idiomatum* was not only contrary to the orthodox councils and creeds but also incoherent; Beza makes the same point against Andreae's view of universal atonement. Since at least Beza's time, the Lutheran tendency toward dialectical paradox has been subject to the Reformed criticism that it is a cover for incoherence. The Reformed view has been typically misunderstood and misrepresented by more confessionally driven Lutheran theologians, for example, David P. Scaer, "The Nature and Extent of the Atonement in Lutheran Theology," *Bulletin of the Evangelical Theological Society* 10.4 (1967): 179–87.

[33] Thus, for example, Beza charges Sebastian Castellio with being speculative and warns about the limits of human knowledge of God's purposes, while at the same time pointing out the logical absurdities of Castellio's position. Originally titled *Ad sycophantarum quorundam calumnias . . . responsio* (Geneva: C. Badius, 1558), Beza later identifies the sycophant in question as Castellio: *Responsio ad defensiones et reprehensiones Sebastiani Castellionis*, in *TT*, 1:337–424 (here 340).

[34] "If one should point to the fact that Beza had a generally Aristotelian view of the world, this does little to distinguish him from the majority of sixteenth-century men" (Mallinson, *FRR*, 55, cf. 57; see also Eugene F. Rice, "Humanist Aristotelianism in France: Jacques Lefèvre d'Étaples and His Circle," in *Humanism in France at the End of the Middle Ages and in the Early Renaissance*, ed. A. H. T. Levi [Manchester, UK: University of Manchester, 1970], 132–49). Muller, "Persistence of Christian Aristotelianism," 90–91, puts into context Luther's early attacks on Aristotle, which are best understood in terms of Luther's rejection of an ethically based view of salvation, such as advocated by late medieval Semi-Pelagian theology.

is a mistake to identify this refinement as a corruption of a pure aborigi-
nal revelation, and to dismiss those who refined and developed Reformed
thought as either fools or knaves. The "scholastic" label is useless as a
descriptor of doctrinal content. The term "scholasticism" describes an academic approach that employed careful conceptual distinctions and focused
on proper method. To put it as simply as possible, "scholastic" simply meant
"academic," with all of the latter's various positive, neutral, or pejorative
implications.[35]

Augustinian Exegesis

Typical of the older scholarship, John Bray claims that Beza abandoned
the "cautious restraint" that Calvin exhibited in adhering strictly to God's
revealed and accommodated knowledge of himself. Beza "deviated from
Calvin" by inventing the doctrine of "limited atonement."[36] A comparison
of their respective exegesis of certain passages, Bray argues, will make this
obvious.

On the contrary, Beza's thoughts on the extent of Christ's redemption
prove to be rather close to those of Calvin, and of Augustine before him. In
his commentary on 1 Timothy 2:4, Calvin mocks as a childish hallucination
the idea that the apostle's reference to the universal will of God for all to
be saved contradicts the doctrine of predestination. Paul, Calvin argues, is
not referring to individual persons (*de singulis hominibus*), and the passage
has nothing to do with predestination. Rather, it refers both to the fact that
God calls persons from every people and rank, as well as to the obligation
to preach the gospel to all people indiscriminately. Calvin repeats that this
passage is about classes of people, not every individual[37]—a point that makes
manifest sense in the context. Calvin concludes by noting the duty of Christians to pray for the salvation of all people, since God calls people of every
rank and nation.[38]

This is the typical exegetical strategy that Augustine employed when he
encountered universalizing texts. "All" means all classes and nationalities,

---

[35] See Muller, *Scholasticism and Orthodoxy*; cf. *PRRD*, 1:34–37.
[36] Bray, *Predestination*, 111–12. Bray bases his assertion that Beza is to blame for "limited atonement" primarily on secondary sources including Armstrong and Hall (Armstrong, *CAH*, 41).
[37] "At de hominum generibus, non singulis personis, sermo est" (John Calvin, *Ioannis Calvini Opera quae supersunt omnia*, ed. J. W. Baum, A. E. Cunitz, and E. Reuss, 59 vols. [Braunschweig, Germany: Schwetschke, 1863–1900], hereafter cited as *CO*, 52:268). Translations of the commentaries are from the Calvin Translation Society (Edin-burgh, 1844–1856), revised by the author, and cited as CTS.
[38] "tam ordinibus quam nationibus" (*CO*, 52:269).

not every individual.[39] Calvin uses this hermeneutic frequently, as does Beza. In fact, while Beza treats this passage at greater length in his annotations on the NT (which were published during Calvin's lifetime), his comments maintain substantial continuity with those of Calvin.

Beza begins his comments on this text by noting that God gathers his church from every sort (*genus*) of people. To make this clearer, Beza chooses to translate πάντας as *quosvis* rather than *omnes*, preferring "indefinite" over "universal." The duty of the Christian, then, is to pray for all, and not "to judge whoever has not yet come into the church as forsaken by God."[40] This is a rather magnanimous interpretation for a man accused of being coldly rationalistic. A similar sentiment, that one can never judge a person to be reprobate, occurs in his *Tabula Praedestinationis*.[41] Beza argues, with an intentional lack of originality, that the text refers to sorts or classes of people, not every individual. Nor is this passage referring to the cause of our faith: that rests in the gratuitous display to us of Christ alone, received through the gratuitous gift of faith.[42] So much for Beza's alleged lack of a Christ-centered focus. Nor does the passage speak of the cause of condemnation, which is not God's decree of reprobation but, importantly, human corruption and the fruits thereof.

Beza then expands on something Calvin had merely mentioned in passing: the distinction between God's secret decree and its visible effects. Calvin had noted that while the "external signs" of God's secret judgment may not be a perfect indicator of his eternal will, this does not mean that God has not determined the destiny of each individual.[43] Beza extends this discussion into a *locus communis* on predestination and free will. In his usual fashion, he speaks of ascending from the effects of God's decree to the decree itself, which is a means by which an individual can be assured that one is elect.[44]

---

[39] See, for example, *Enchiridion* 3, in J. P. Migne, ed., *Patrologia Cursus Completus*, series Latina, 217 vols. (Paris, 1844–1855), hereafter cited as *PL*, 40:280–281; *De civ. Dei*, 22.2.2, *PL* 41:753; *Tract. in Ev. Joan.*, 52.11, *PL* 35:1773; *De Corr. et Grat.*, 44, *PL* 44:943.

[40] ". . . qui Ecclesiam suam ex quorumvis hominum genere congregat. Nostrum est igitur pro quibusvis precari, non autem iudicare abjectos a Deo quicunque nondum ad Ecclesiam accesserunt" (Theodore Beza, *Novum D. N. Iesu Christi Testamentum. A Theodoro Beza versum . . . cum eiusdem annotationibus. . . .* [Basel: Johan Oporinus; Geneva: Nicolas Barbier and Thomas Courteau, 1559]: 697, hereafter cited as *Annotations*).

[41] Beza, Cap. 7, *TT* 1:198. Ministers "ab extrema illa sententia abstineant, cui nulla addita sit conditio. Nam haec jurisdictio ad unum Deum pertinet."

[42] "Non agimus de salutis causa: illam enim constat uno Christo niti gratuito nobis exhibito, et per gratuitum fidei donum apprehenso" (*Annotations*, 698).

[43] "Nam etsi Dei voluntas non ex occultis ipsius iudiciis aestimanda est, ubi externis signis eam nobis patefacit: non tamen propterea sequitur quin constitutum intus habeat quid de singulis hominibus fieri velit" (*CO*, 52:268).

[44] "Quia huc usque nos subvehit Spiritus sanctus, nempe quoties ita facere necesse est, ab inhaerentibus causis ad ipsum usque Dei propositum conscendens, tum in electis, tum in reprobis" (*Annotations*, 698). On the continuity between Calvin and Beza on this point, see Muller, "Use and Abuse," 47–49.

Moreover, Beza denies that this line of reasoning is speculative. Indeed, to make such a claim is blasphemous, because the Holy Spirit has revealed these things in Scripture. In fact, without the sure foundation of election our faith would be undermined and "justification by faith would be preached in vain."[45] Beza continues to elaborate on issues of human free choice, and to refute Pelagianism and Semi-Pelagianism and the late-medieval idea of an initial grace (*gratia prima*) that would enable persons to take a decisive role in their own salvation. None of this discussion differs substantially from Calvin's thought on these matters, nor does it constitute the invention of particular redemption beyond the exegetical moves Augustine had already made numerous times before.

Luther himself had interpreted this text in a similar, Augustinian vein: "For these verses must always be understood as pertaining to the elect only, as the apostle says in 2 Tim. 2:10 'everything for the sake of the elect.' For in an absolute sense Christ did not die for all, because He says: 'This is My blood which is poured out for you' and 'for many'—He does not say: for all—'for the forgiveness of sins.'"[46] Calvin had made much the same connection between election and the purpose of Christ shedding his blood in a retort to the Lutheran Tilemann Heshusius: "I should like to know how the wicked can eat the flesh of Christ which was not crucified for them? And how they can drink the blood which was not shed to expiate their sins?"[47] The comments of both Reformers are reminiscent of Augustine's explanation of Jesus's words to the Pharisees in John 10:26: "He saw them predestined to everlasting destruction, not won to eternal life by the price of His own blood."[48]

Bray alleges that Beza was "pushed beyond the limits of Calvin's theology by the compelling logical force latent within his doctrine of predestina-

---

[45] Apertae vero blasphemae fuerit existimare curiosas, spinosas, inutiles quaestiones a Spiritu sancto nobis explicari, quia frustra praedicatur iustificatio ex fide, nisi fidei substernatur electio certa et constans" (*Annotations*, 698).

[46] "Quia haec dicta intelliguntur de electis tantum, ut ait Apostolus 2. Tim.: 'Omnia propter electos.' Non enim absolute pro omnibus mortuus est Christus, quia dicit, 'Hic est sanguis, qui effundetur pro vobis' et 'pro multis'—non ait: pro omnibus—in remissionem peccatorum'" (Martin Luther, *Scholia in Romans* 8.2, in *Werke*, Weimarer Ausgabe [Weimar: Böhlau, 1883–2009] 56:385; *Luther's Works*, ed. H. T. Lehmann et al., 55 vols. [St. Louis: Concordia, 1955–1986], 25:376). On Luther's sometimes inconsistent statements about universality and particularity in salvation, see Archbald, "Extent of the Atonement," 40–43.

[47] "Et quando tam mordicus verbis adhaeret, scire velim quomodo Christi carnem edant impii, pro quibus non est crucifixa, et quomodo sanguinem bibant, qui expiandis eorum peccatis non est effusus" (*CO*, 9:484; English translation in *Tracts and Treatises*, trans. Henry Beveridge [Edinburgh: Calvin Translation Society, 1849], 2:527). See Muller's discussion of this crucial text, *CRT*, 91–93.

[48] "Quia videbat eos ad sempiternum interitum praedestinatos, non ad vitam aeternam sui sanguinis pretio comparatos" (*Tract. in Ev. Joan.*, 48.4, *PL* 35:1742).

tion," evidenced by a comparison of his exegesis of 2 Peter 3:9 with that of Calvin. But this is also misleading. Calvin specifically states that this text is not referring to "the hidden purpose of God, according to which the reprobate are doomed to their own ruin, but only of his will as made known to us in the gospel." The invitation of the gospel is indiscriminate, yet God "lays hold only of those, to lead them to himself, whom he has chosen before the foundation of the world."[49] Beza's exegesis agrees with this, but goes into more detail to refute those who oppose the doctrine of predestination. A number of interpreters, Beza notes, distort this passage in order to remove the distinction between eternal election and reprobation, not realizing in the meantime that they get themselves caught by Charybdis while seeking to flee Scylla. For if that is the case, people would perish contrary to God's will. A permission that is indifferent and separate from the decree is more Epicurean than Christian.[50] Those, on the other hand, who would assert that in reality the will of God can be changed utter an even greater impiety than Epicurus.[51] Thus, while Beza elaborates on election, he does not suddenly invent any new doctrine of definite redemption.

Turning the Table

Scholars have particularly identified Beza's doctrine of predestination, especially as presented in his *Tabula Praedestinationis*,[52] as a turn toward a rationally deductive system, detached from exegesis and pastoral concerns. But this work was the product of a polemical task that Calvin himself delegated to Beza with a view to answering Jerome Bolsec.[53] If it constituted a substantial deviation from Calvin's own sentiments, and not an intellectual refinement of them, one would expect some corrective response from Calvin, who, along with Bullinger and Vermigli and others, was in correspondence

---

[49] CTS *Catholic Epistles*, 419–20. The editor, John Owen, notes that Calvin holds the same view as the Roman Catholic Willem Hessels van Est (Estius), Johnannes Piscator, and Beza!

[50] Compare Calvin's remarks in his sermon on 1 Timothy 2:3–5, cited below, n. 85.

[51] "Hunc etiam locum nonnulli depravant, ut aeternae electionis et reprobationis discrimen tollant: nec interim considerant sese in Charybdin incidere, dum Syllam volunt effugere. Nam si ita res est, ut ipsi volunt, certe invito Deo perimus. adeo ut eum omnipotentem esse negent. Nam permissio otiosa et separata a decreto, Epicureorum est potius quam Christianorum. Mutari autem revera Dei voluntatem qui dixerit, magis etiam impie de Deo loquatur quam Epicurus" (*Annotations*, 802).

[52] See, for example, the entry on Beza in the *Oxford Dictionary of the Christian Church*, 3rd ed. (Oxford: Oxford University Press, 2005), 199.

[53] In contrast to the studies of Kickel and Bray, see Joel R. Beeke, "The Order of the Divine Decrees at the Genevan Academy: From Bezan Supralapsarianism to Turretinian Infralapsarianism," in *The Identity of Geneva: The Christian Commonwealth, 1564–1864*, ed. John B. Roney and Martin I. Klauber (Westport, CT: Greenwood, 1998), 57–75.

with Beza over the project. On the contrary, Calvin recommended to Castellio that he read Beza's *Tabula*.[54]

Despite the grandiose subtitle, *Summa Totius Christianismi*, this short treatise deals only with the chain of salvation, and not the full range of Christian doctrine.[55] It is the "sum total" of Christianity in the same way that John 3:16 might be said to be the sum total of the faith. It represents the complete causes of salvation, from divine decree to the execution of that decree in history—and even then, only in outline.[56] It is Beza's first, not his fullest, treatment of the doctrine of predestination; Beza continued to defend this doctrine as he perceived it to have been taught by his colleague Calvin, while also bolstering, refining, and developing it in response to attacks by their opponents.[57]

Beza's *Tabula Praedestinationis* does not contain an explicit doctrine of definite redemption; one would have to deduce it from chapter 4, which, importantly, pertains to the execution of the decree. This distinction between the decree and its execution was crucial to understanding both Calvin and Beza's teaching regarding predestination.[58] Though it is clear that Beza views Christ's work as particular in effect ("with Christ's one sacrifice and offering of himself he will sanctify all the elect"[59]), Beza does not explicitly ask in the *Tabula* the question that William Ames would later pose: *An mors Christi omnibus intendatur?* (Is the death of Christ intended for all?)[60] And even then, Ames's question could conceivably be parsed and interpreted

---

[54] McPhee, CTCT, 78–81; Muller, "Use and Abuse," 37; Donnelly, *Calvinism and Scholasticism*, 134–35; Archbald, "Extent of the Atonement," 88 n. 37.

[55] See Bray, *Predestination*, 75.

[56] Contrast McPhee, CTCT, 301, and Donald W. Sinnema, "God's Eternal Decree and Its Temporal Execution: The Role of This Distinction in Theodore Beza's Theology," in *Adaptations of Calvinism in Reformation Europe: Essays in Honour of Brian G. Armstrong*, ed. Mack P. Holt (Aldershot, UK: Ashgate, 2007), 55–78 (60 n. 15). Beza's work is in no sense a *Summa Theologiae* nor is there a "broad theological character" to this narrowly focused treatise. Cf. Muller, "Use and Abuse," 34; Bray, *Predestination*, 72.

[57] On Beza's writings see Frédéric Gardy and Alain Dufour, *Bibliographie des oeuvres théologiques, littéraires, historiques et juridiques de Théodore de Bèze*, Travaux d'Humanisme et Renaissance 41 (Geneva: Librairie Droz, 1960). Beza's other works on or including predestination include *Quaestionum et responsionum Christianarum libellus, in quo praecipua Christianae religionis capita* κατὰ ἐπιτομήν *proponuntur* (Geneva, 1570; London: H. Bynneman, 1571); English trans. Arthur Golding, *A Booke of Christian Questions and Answers* (London: W. How, 1578); *De Praedestinationis doctrinae et vero usu tractatio absolutissima. Ex Th. Bezae praelectionibus in nonum Epistolae ad Romanos*, etc., 2nd ed. (Geneva: E. Vignon, 1583). On the latter work, see Bray's extremely negative characterization, *Predestination*, 73.

[58] Cf. Donald W. Sinnema, "Beza's Doctrine of Predestination in Historical Perspective," in *Théodore de Bèze (1519–1605): Actes du Colloque de Genève (Septembre 2005)*, Travaux d'Humanisme et Renaissance 424, ed. Irena Backus (Geneva: Librairie Droz, 2007), 219–39.

[59] "Denique ut una sui ipsius oblatione eligendos omnes sanctificaret . . ." (Beza, *Tabula* 4.5, in *TT*, 1:181).

[60] William Ames, *De Arminii Sententia qua electionem omnem particularem, fidei praevisae docet inniti, Disceptatio Scholastica. . . .* (Amsterdam: J. Janssonius, 1613), 1, cited in Godfrey, "Reformed Thought," 163. Ames concluded that the scope of God's intention, application, and accomplishment are in complete harmony; thus God intended Christ's redemption or satisfaction only for the elect.

in different ways. The question of divine intention would become a more focused and explicit question in the context of theological controversy, and even more so after Beza's time as a leading Reformed thinker. While some minor development can perhaps be seen in Beza's sparring with Lutheran polemicist Jacobus Andreae at the 1586 Montbéliard Colloquy,[61] the debate over the extent of Christ's redemption would become clearer and more refined in the later Remonstrant controversy.

Defense and Development

In the same way that Reformed assemblies would circumscribe Reformed teaching on definite redemption in response to the challenge of Remonstrant theology, so Beza's own clarification and development of the concept came in response to polemical attacks, particularly those of Andreae at the Montbéliard Colloquy. The conference was called on behalf of refugee Huguenots in the city who resisted conformity to Lutheran doctrines and practices. The topics of dispute were to be christology and Christ's presence in the Lord's Supper. Predestination was not even on the agenda, but Beza, under pressure, reluctantly agreed at the last minute to debate the matter.[62] The colloquy achieved little agreement and served only to highlight the animosity between the principal opponents. It is doubtful whether Andreae, having already fought for a universally acceptable Lutheran confession, had any real intention of finding common ground with Beza. The theology of Geneva provided a unifying common enemy; and Beza's thought was far too akin to that of Flacius Illyricus, which the Lutheran compromise rejected. Moreover, by now the battle was one of church-political dominance, and Montbéliard represented one more territory to be gained or lost. The days when Melanchthon could write a poem to honor his cobelligerent Beza were now but a distant memory.[63]

Beza's published editions of the Montbéliard Colloquy demonstrate, even in polemics, a method that derives its arguments primarily from scriptural

---

[61] See the substantial article on Andreae by Robert Kolb in *The Oxford Encyclopedia of the Reformation*, 4 vols. (Oxford: Oxford University Press, 1996), 1:36–38.

[62] See Jill Raitt, *The Colloquy of Montbéliard: Religion and Politics in the Sixteenth Century* (New York: Oxford University Press, 1993), 134. In his single-volume French rejoinder, *Response de M. Th. De Beze aux Actes de la Conference de Mombelliard Imprimes à Tubingue* (Geneva: Jean Le Preux, 1587), Beza limits his discussion of predestination primarily to the preface and in appending excerpts from Luther's *De Servo Arbitrio*.

[63] Etienne Trocmé, "L'Ascension de Théodore de Bèze (1549–1561), au miroir de sa correspondance," *Journal des savants* 4 (1965): 607–24 (613); text in Gardy, *Bibliographie*, 80–81. On the synergistic controversy, see Kolb, *Bound Choice, Election, and Wittenberg Theological Method: From Martin Luther to the Formula of Concord* (Grand Rapids, MI: Eerdmans, 2005), 109–69.

exegesis, the ancient creeds, and writings of the church fathers, despite the fact that Andreae accused him of arguing solely from reason and ignoring Scripture.[64] The rhetoric in the debate was intense. Andreae claimed that Beza's views constituted a new religion; Beza claimed that the Lutherans distorted Luther. Beza was concerned to counter what he considered extreme statements that jeopardized the doctrine of election, particularly assertions by later Lutherans that Christ died for every individual, that his death removes original sin, and that the only sin for which one can be condemned is that of unbelief. He contended that the sacramental christology of Andreae and Johannes Brenz was contrary to Scripture, the Athanasian creed, and the early fathers, and that it represented a new form of Eutychianism and other ancient christological heresies; Beza even turned the Lutheran accusation of Reformed Nestorianism back on his accusers.[65] Infuriating to Andreae was Beza's stinging employment of a strategy that pitted Luther against the Lutherans, citing, for example, the Reformer's *The Bondage of the Will*.[66] The compromise Lutheran position embodied in the 1580 *Book of Concord,* compiled by Andreae and Martin Chemnitz, asserted election but not reprobation, and gave a more substantial role to human free will in salvation than the Reformed. Beza saw this development as a departure from Luther's teaching; for him it compromised a key Reformation insight, namely, that salvation is solely a gift of God's grace. Beza went so far as to lampoon this compilation of Lutheran confessions as "The Book of Discord."[67]

For Beza, Luther's argument about human inability to will what is good or to embrace God or the gospel was a key factor for the Reformation understanding of Christ's work. To make salvation merely available or potential would have no effect on bound wills, nor can Beza abide any alleged universal grace that would enable, but not bring about, the human choice to believe. For Beza, this would undercut the whole biblical teaching of God's unconditional election and make human choice the tipping point for an individual's

---

[64] Beza's response to the *Acta* published in Tübingen was quickly countered by Andreae, *Kurtzer Begriff des Mümpelgartischen Colloquii oder Gesprächs . . . sampt angehenckter gründtlicher Widerlegung der Antwort D. Bezae auff die Acta gedachtes Colloquii . . .* (Tübingen: G. Gruppenbach, 1588), 72. Cf. also folio):( ):(iii v° and 153, where Andreae demonstrates his extreme antipathy toward Beza and the Reformed position by refusing to offer Beza the *"Hand auff Bruderschafff"* at the colloquy, because he considered Beza an enemy of the Christian faith. For Andreae's side of the dispute over predestination and God's intentions in Christ's satisfaction (*genug machen*), see 128–40, 143–46.

[65] Beza, *Response de M. Th. De Beze aux Actes*, 225.

[66] Later Lutherans would contend that Luther altered his views on this topic later in life. On Lutheran developments in this area, see Kolb, *Bound Choice*.

[67] Beza, *Response de M. Th. De Beze aux Actes*, 177. Rudolf Hospinian would later make a similar comparison in his *Concordia Discors: De origine et progressu Formulae Concordiae Bergensis* (Zurich: Wolph, 1607).

salvation. The Reformed, he argued, were better Lutherans than the latter-day Lutherans who now overemphasized the role of human choice in salvation. Andreae, for his part, worried that Beza's predestinarian views would undermine the assurance of persons who might worry that they were not elect.

While Beza and Andreae may have spoken past each other in the disputation, one thing became clear for Beza, if it was not clear already. Peter Lombard's old distinction between efficient and sufficient had become neither.[68] In his commentary on 1 John 2:2, Calvin had dismissed the "dotages of the fanatics" and the "monstrous" argument that this passage somehow offers salvation to the reprobate. Calvin makes reference to Lombard's distinction, and while he accepts its validity, he does not think that it applies to the present passage. Rather, the intention of John was to make this benefit, the atoning sacrifice (ἱλασμός) of Christ, "common to the whole Church." This is strong evidence that Calvin did not teach a universal redemption that included every individual, but one that was particular to the elect. The "whole world" here "does not include the reprobate, but indicates those who would believe as well as those who were scattered throughout various regions of the world."[69]

But while others like Zacharias Ursinus would use the distinction to teach early forms of definite redemption, Beza judged it no longer adequate to the current debate.[70] Andreae, on the basis of 1 John 2:2, had argued that Christ died to propitiate God for the sins of the entire world, namely, every individual. Beza replied that "the benefit of the propitiation necessarily applies to the elect alone, and, because they are elect, to believers." Moreover, the whole world in that passage means all nations, in fulfillment of the promise to Abraham in Genesis 12, and must be interpreted as the elect from the whole world, as Augustine (and indeed, Calvin) had argued.[71]

Beza did not entirely reject Lombard's distinction, if properly understood; yet he thought it an uncultivated expression that did not get to the heart

---

[68] Contrast Rouwendal, "Calvin's Forgotten Classical Position." Peter Lombard's distinction is as follows: "Christus ergo est sacerdos, idemque et hostia pretium nostrae reconciliationis; qui se in ara cruces non diabolo, sed Trinitati obtulit pro omnibus, quantum ad pretii sufficientiam; sed pro electis tantum quantum ad efficaciam, quia praedestinatis tantum salutem effecit" (*Sententiae in IV Libris Distinctae*, 3.20.3, in *PL*, 192:799).

[69] "Ergo sub omnibus, reprobos non comprehendit: sed eos designat, qui simul credituri erant, et qui per varias mundi plagas dispersi erant" (*CO*, 55:310).

[70] Zacharias Ursinus, *Explicationum Catecheticarum* etc., ed., David Pareus (Neustadt, Germany: Mattheus Harnisch, 1595), 2:33–39. Pareus (33) notes that Ursinus did not originally deal with the question in that place, but he has collected Ursinus's thoughts on the matter due to recent controversies—a fact omitted by the nineteenth-century translator G. W. Willard.

[71] Theodore Beza, *Ad Acta Colloquii Montisbelgardensis Tubingae edita Theodori Bezae responsio*, *Tubingae edita*, 2 vols. (Geneva: J. le Preuz, 1587–1588), 2:215–16, hereafter cited as *AACM*. Beza refers to Augustine, *Contra Julian*, 6.24.80.

of the matter in dispute.[72] In the context of Andreae's attack on the doctrine of predestination as taught in Geneva, Beza found the distinction too ambiguous to be useful, and for this French humanist, it was also rhetorically abominable.[73] Moreover, Beza also observed that the word "for" is ambiguous when one claims that Christ's death is sufficient for all sinners. Does this refer to God's intention and purpose in Christ's suffering, or to the effect of Christ's passion, or to both? In any case, Beza contends, it can refer only to the elect.[74] Surely, Beza conceded, the value of Christ's offering of himself would be enough "to make satisfaction for an infinite number of worlds, if there were multiple worlds, and if all the inhabitants of these worlds were given faith in Christ, let alone for every individual person of one world, without exception, if God willed to have mercy on them all."[75] Beza does not explore whether such sufficiency would be inherent in Christ's death, as Reformed thinkers like Zacharias Ursinus argued,[76] or whether it was an "ordained sufficiency," as Hypothetical Universalists would later propose.[77] In any case, the divine intention is coextensive with the effect.

Beza adduces biblical evidence for the doctrine that God elects and reprobates from eternity, and that God intends to save the elect, and not the reprobate. To claim that God wills to save the reprobate would be incoherent. He appeals to John 17:9, where Jesus prays not for the world, but only for the disciples, whom the Father gave to him. Christ would not offer himself for those for whom he did not intercede. Calvin had made remarkably similar observations on this text, asserting that Christ prayed for the elect, not the reprobate. Christians must pray for all indiscriminately, because they cannot, unlike God himself, distinguish between the elect and reprobate in this life; but their intention, according to Calvin, is still to pray for whomever happens to be elect.[78]

---

[72] "Distinctionem autem illam inter SVFFICIENTER & EFFICIENTER, quam sane recte intellectam non nego, duris & ambiguis verbiis conceptam esse, nec ad quaestionem quae inter nos agitata est proximè praecedente responsione ostendi" (*AACM*, 2:221).

[73] "Illud enim, *Christus mortuus est pro omnium hominum peccatis Sufficienter, sed non Efficienter,* et si recto sensu verum est, dure tamen admodem et ambigue non minus quam barbare dicitur" (*AACM*, 2:217).

[74] "Illud enim PRO, vel consilium Patris ex quo passus est Christus, vel ipsius passionis effectum, vel potius utrumque declarat, quorum neutrum ad alios quam ad electos spectat . . ." (*AACM*, 2:217, cf. 221).

[75] "quamvis negandum non sit tanti esse hanc oblationem ut potuerit etiam pro infinitis mundis satisfacere, si plures essent mundi, et mundani omnes fide in Christum donarentur, nedum pro singulis unius mundi, nullo excepto, hominibus, si Deus eorum omnium vellet misereri" (*AACM*, 2:217).

[76] See Rainbow, *Will of God and the Cross*, 133 and n. 1.

[77] See Jonathan D. Moore, "The Extent of the Atonement: English Hypothetical Universalism versus Particular Redemption," in *Drawn into Controversie*, 147–48.

[78] *CO*, 47:380–81. Note especially the following: "Respondeo, preces, quas pro omnibus concipimus, restringi tamen ad Dei electos. Hunc et illum et singulos optare debemus salvos esse, atque ita complecti totum humanum genus, quia nondum distinguere licet electos a reprobis: interea tamen adventum regni Dei optando simul precamur, ut hostes suos perdat" (380).

Beza deflects Andreae's use of Lombard's distinction as nothing but an evasive maneuver (*tergiversatio*) and a strategic dissimulation. Their entire debate over predestination is not about whether only believers will be saved; only the diabolical Origenists doubt that. Rather, the real argument, Beza contends, centers around two points: first, whether God really decrees to elect and reprobate persons from eternity (which Beza affirms and Andreae denies); and secondly, whether God intends to save every individual (which Andreae affirms and Beza denies).[79] What Beza finds reprehensible is Andreae's contention that "Christ suffered for the damned, and was crucified and died and made satisfaction for their sins, no less than for the sins of Peter, Paul, and all the saints."[80] Beza does not deny the sufficiency of Christ's redemption, or its (ordained or inherent) value, but only its efficacy for the reprobate. Like Calvin, Beza denies that God effectively wills the salvation of the reprobate; such a concept would be incoherent.

In addition, Beza expresses outrage at Andreae's contention that persons are condemned only for not believing in Christ, when in fact people are condemned—not because they are reprobate—but because of their sin, and not exclusively for unbelief. For Beza, this is an abominable, monstrous, and novel doctrine that Andreae has impudently dared to introduce into the church.[81]

Beza had previously touched on this issue in his 1570 *Book of Questions and Answers*. There (as in his exegesis of 1 Timothy 2:4) he made the notable distinction that the external call of the gospel is not *universal*, but rather, *indefinite*.[82] There are many who never hear the gospel; the call does not reach them. Nor can God's revelation in nature be construed as a universal call, since some persons die in infancy before they are capable of rational reflection on created reality. To claim that "all are called universally under the condition that they believe" is true up to a point (*aliquatenus*), yet it can be misleading. Not only does the call not reach every individual: "the decree does not depend on the condition, but rather the condition upon the decree, seeing that it precedes all subordinate causes." Nor is it entirely correct that

---

[79] *AACM*, 2:217–18.

[80] "hoc etiam ausus totidem verbis (proh scelus) scribere, et aeternum ac immutabilem veritatem vocare, quod Christus NON MINUS pro DAMNATIS SIT PASSUS, crucifixus et mortuus et pro ipsorum peccatis satisfecerit, quam pro Petri, Pauli, et omnium Sanctorum peccatis" (*AACM*, 2:218).

[81] *AACM*, 2:218–19.

[82] "Qu. *At certe universalis est vocatio, et promissio.* Re. Indefinitam intellige, (et quidam certarum, de quibus diximus, circumstantiarum respectu), et rectius senseris" (Beza, *Quaestionum et Responsionum*, 122).

"this vocation is not universally efficacious, not on account of God, but on account of the stubbornness of unbelievers who spurn the good that is set before them." Here Beza may be anticipating an argument like Andreae's, that persons are condemned only for rejecting Christ. On the contrary, Beza insists that for some, "there is no stubbornness against the offered gospel to be found, but merely original corruption, which, nonetheless, indeed suffices by itself for the condemnation of the reprobate."[83]

Beza's comments substantially reflect the teachings of Calvin on these points, as one can demonstrate by comparing them to Calvin's sermon on 1 Timothy 2:3–5. Here Calvin makes the point—repeatedly—that God does not will the salvation of every individual, but of people from every nation and class, Jew and Gentile, both great and small.[84] God presents himself to all the world, but this does not undermine election and reprobation, or imply that God's will is indifferent.[85] Nor does God will that the gospel come to every person.[86] Moreover, God does not provide a universal grace that he extends randomly; God's grace is only for those whom he has chosen.[87] The church is to present the promise of the gospel to all, but only because human beings cannot determine who is elect and who is reprobate. This does not imply two wills in God (which would violate the doctrine of divine simplicity); rather, because of limited human capacity one must speak of two ways of considering God's will.[88] As far as the preaching of the gospel is concerned, God wills the salvation of all, which simply means, one cannot discriminate in the preaching of the gospel.[89] Calvin is referring to what theologians distinguished as the *voluntas praecepti*, the will of the precept, which indicates

---

[83] Ibid., 123–24.

[84] "Cependant notons que sainct Paul ne parle point ici de chacun en particulier, mais de tous estats et de tous peuples. . . . Pourtant sainct Paul n'entend pas que Dieu vueille sauver chacun homme, mais il dit que les promesses qui avoyent esté donnees à un seul peuple, ont maintenant leur estendue par tout" (*CO*, 53:148). Calvin denies that it follows from Paul's statement that it is in the power of each individual's free choice to be saved, ". . . que sainct Paul ne parle point ici de chacune personne (comme nous avons declaré), mais il parle de tous peuples, et des estats . . ." (*CO*, 53:150). We are to pray for all generally, "car sainct Paul nous monstre comme Dieu veut que tous soyent sauvez, c'est à dire de tous peuples et nations" (*CO*, 53:159).

[85] ". . . Dieu se presente à tout le monde . . . Car voilà qu'ils disent, Si Dieu veut que tous soyent sauvez, il s'ensuit qu'il n'a point eleu certain nombre du genre humain, et qu'il n'a point reprouvé le reste, mais que sa volonté est indifferente" (*CO*, 53:149–50).

[86] "Et mesmes encores depuis l'Evangile il n'a pas voulu que du premier coup tous cognussent l'Evangile" (*CO*, 53:151).

[87] "Et puis tant souvent il nous est monstré que Dieu ne iette point comme à l'abandon sa grace, mais qu'elle est seulement pour ceux qu'il a eleus, et pour ceux qui sont du corps de son Eglise et de son troupeau" (*CO*, 53:154–55). Cf. Calvin's *Institutes*, 3.22.10).

[88] ". . . l'Escriture saincte nous parle de la volonté de Dieu en deux sortes: non point que ceste volonté-là soit double, mais c'est pour s'accommoder à nostre foiblesse, d'autant que nous avons l'esprit grossier et pesant" (*CO*, 53:151–52, cf. 155, 156).

[89] "Mais nous disons ce que chacun voit, c'est que selon nostre regard Dieu veut que nous soyons tous sauvez, toutesfois et quantes qu'il ordonne que son Evangile nous soit presché" (*CO*, 53:155).

human obligation but not divine decree.[90] But with respect to God's eternal counsel, God does not will all to be saved and does not grant saving knowledge to every individual.[91] Calvin, moreover, here grounds assurance not in Christ himself, or some experience of Christ, but in the doctrine of election, in which the Father gives the elect to Christ.[92]

For both Beza and Calvin, it was crucial to maintain a doctrine of salvation that was ultimately dependent on divine grace, not human choice or a combination thereof. While Andreae was anxious that fear of being reprobate might hinder faith in the weak, Beza was concerned that the church would slide back into a pre-Reformation view of salvation that made human choice pivotal. In his judgment, developments among Lutheran theologians, rather ironically, endangered salvation by grace alone.

The Extent of Christ's Satisfaction as an Emerging Question

Beza's views on this matter were not exceptional. Peter Martyr Vermigli (1499–1562), a former Augustinian monk turned reformer, asserted that "God decreed to give his own Son up to death, and indeed a shameful death, in order to rid his elect of sin."[93] Vermigli was mentor to another Augustinian monk, Jerome Zanchi (1516–1590), who posed the question in his Ephesians commentary: for whom did Christ offer himself? Zanchi answered: "For us, the elect, who are nonetheless sinners." Zanchi affirmed that Christ's sacrifice is efficacious for the salvation of the elect, though it would be completely sufficient for the redemption of the whole world.[94] Similar formulations are

---

[90] See Muller, *Dictionary*, 331–33.

[91] Contrast Martin Foord, "God Wills All People to Be Saved—Or Does He? Calvin's Reading of 1 Timothy 2:4," in *Engaging with Calvin: Aspects of the Reformer's Legacy for Today*, ed. Mark D. Thompson (Nottingham, UK: Apollos, 2009), 179–203. Foord claims, unconvincingly, that Calvin produces "his own unique formulation" and that Calvin is closer to the medieval Semi-Pelagian Robert Holkot (202) in emphasizing the revealed will of God. Foord's claim that Calvin teaches that God wills the salvation of "all from all kinds" is incoherent, perhaps based on his misreading of *tous peuples* as "all people" rather than "all nations" (198). He makes Calvin choose the revealed will as an alternative to the hidden will, when in fact Calvin, unremarkably, implies both distinctions in turn. Calvin obviously and clearly limits the use of the term "all" by restricting it to classes with respect to God's *voluntas beneplaciti*, and by referring "all" to the revealed will of God, not his secret will. This is hardly "unique." Foord's work retains a residue of the problematic older tendencies, including a desire to set Calvin apart from "scholastics" and their "slavish" renditions of particular schools of thought, as he prejudicially alleges against Vermigli (whose use of the *voluntas signi* he misidentifies and whom he blames for being unoriginal, despite the fact that early modern theologians considered novelty to be characteristic of heterodoxy). He also sets Calvin's (undefined) "humanism" against "small hints of scholastic influence," despite the fact that Foord's own analysis of Calvin relies entirely on scholastic distinctions regarding the divine will (203). For a clear and precise analysis, see Muller, *CRT*, chapter 3.

[92] "Ainsi nous voyons combien ceste doctrine de l'election nous est utile. . . . Et n'est-ce point aussi le vray fondement sur lequel toute la certitude de nostre salut s'appuye?" (*CO*, 53:152–53).

[93] ". . . decreverit Filium suum dare in mortem, et quidem ignominiosam, ut a suis electis peccatum depelleret" (Peter Martyr Vermigli, *Loci Communes* [London: Thomas Vautrollerius, 1583], 607).

[94] "Pro quibus obtulerit: Pro nobis, electis, scilicet, sed peccatoribus. Efficaciter enim pro Electorum tantum salute oblatum esse hoc sacrificium: quanquam ad totius mundi redemptionem sufficientissimum sit" (Jerome Zanchi,

to be found in Wolfgang Musculus, and the Heidelberg theologians Ursinus, Caspar Olevianus, and the lesser-known Jacob Kimedoncius, who wrote a treatise on the subject that was translated into English.[95] Kimedoncius was not moving far beyond Calvin or Beza, or even Luther or Augustine, when he claimed that "redemption is peculiar to the church, and yet universal, after that sort as we confess the church to be universal."[96] Kimedoncius could even claim that Christ died for all, but not effectually for all.[97]

Ultimately, the historiographical mythology that Beza distorted Calvin's teaching on the extent of Christ's redemption cannot be maintained. In fact, neither Calvin nor Beza provide a fully elaborated doctrine of the extent of Christ's redemption, though they share a discernible tendency toward particularism. Beza's teachings are clearer and more refined than those of Calvin, not because he invented the doctrine of definite redemption but because he—along with many others—developed and refined their teachings in the context of attacks on predestination from the likes of Castellio and Andreae. As the extent of Christ's satisfaction became the center of further controversy, and thus a discrete doctrine, later Reformed thinkers would continue to develop the concept. Others would eventually propose alternative formulations, such as Amyraut's multiple decrees, or the Hypothetical Universalism of certain English theologians, designed to demonstrate some sort of universal salvific intention on God's part without transgressing into Semi-Pelagian or Remonstrant territory.

By the time of Dordt, the traditional distinction between the sufficiency and efficiency of Christ's sacrifice could no longer bear the weight of the controversies that developed in the latter sixteenth century, at least not without considerable clarification. Already in Calvin's day this tool was no longer adequate for the job. Thus the majority of Reformed thinkers made increasingly explicit what was latent in the particularist strand of Christian thought, that the divine intention in the sacrifice of Christ was to provide satisfaction specifically for the elect. Historical study can map out the development

---

Commentarius in Epistolam Sancti Pauli ad Ephesios, ed. A. H. De Hartog, 2 vols. [1594; repr., Amsterdam: J. A. Wormser, 1888], 2:266).

[95] See Roger R. Nicole, "The Doctrine of Definite Atonement in the Heidelberg Catechism," *Gordon Review* 3 (1964): 138–45. Kimedoncius's major work on the subject (among others) was *De redemptione generis humani Libri tres* (Heidelberg: Abraham Smesmannus, 1592); *The Redemption of Mankind in Three Bookes*, trans. Hugh Ince (London: Felix Kingston, 1598). On Kimedoncius, see Jonathan D. Moore, *English Hypothetical Universalism: John Preston and the Softening of Reformed Theology* (Grand Rapids, MI: Eerdmans 2007), 67–68.

[96] *De redemptione*, 324; *Redemption of Mankind*, 180.

[97] *De redemptione*, 323; *Redemption of Mankind*, 179. This represents a form of non-Amyraldian, nonspeculative Hypothetical Universalism similar to that of Pierre du Moulin; see Muller, *CRT*, chapter 5.

of thought and variations on this topic, but cannot make value judgments about the validity of such developments. Much less can it spin a credible tale of one nefarious individual who was seduced by the dark side of scholastic rationalism. Rather, there is a pattern of continuity with variations in an emerging Reformed tradition that refined its theological conceptions in an apologetic and polemical context and, through its confessions, defined its doctrinal boundaries in a way that privileged particularism, yet left breathing room for minority positions.[98]

---

[98] For example, the English Hypothetical Universalist delegates such as John Davenant and Samuel Ward could subscribe to the Canons of Dordt because of the inclusion of the term *efficaciter* applied to Christ's death in 2.8. See Moore, "The Extent of the Atonement"; and idem, *English Hypothetical Universalism*. While Hypothetical Universalists might prefer to see their formulation as a "softening" of Reformed theology, those opposed to this view would hardly concede that their views were rigid or in need of mitigation.

The Synod of Dort and Definite Atonement

Lee Gatiss

Definite atonement achieved confessional status at the Synod of Dort. This first ecumenical synod of Reformed churches met between November 1618 and May 1619 in the Dutch town of Dordrecht (also known as Dordt or Dort). It comprised the cream of Dutch Reformed theologians, representatives from Great Britain (including the bishop of Llandaff in Wales, and a Scot), several important German cities, and separate delegations representing Geneva and the rest of Switzerland. Invitations also went out to the newly combined state of Brandenburg-Prussia, though for various reasons they were not able to attend. A row of empty chairs was set up in honor of delegates from the Reformed churches of France, who were prohibited from attending by the (Roman Catholic) French government. The importance of this international gathering of Reformed theologians cannot be underestimated, since it is here that the so-called "five points of Calvinism" were first carefully defined.

Several studies in the last few decades have looked in depth at the Synod's debates and deliverances on the subject of the atonement.[1] Since the British delegates were particularly involved on this issue, studies of their

[1] For example, W. Robert Godfrey, "Tensions within International Calvinism: The Debate on the Atonement at the Synod of Dort" (PhD diss., Stanford University, 1974); Stephen Strehle, "The Extent of the Atonement and the Synod of Dort," *WTJ* 51.1 (1989): 1–23; Michael Thomas, *The Extent of the Atonement: A Dilemma for Reformed Theology* (Carlisle, UK: Paternoster, 1997).

role are also especially useful.[2] My aim in this chapter is not necessarily to repeat what they have said, or even to give a full exposition of the Synod's deliberations.[3] To avoid treating the Canons of Dort in merely an abstract fashion, I will put the Synod into historical context and note some of the diversity among the delegates. Its longer-term impact, however, was felt not just through its doctrinal Canons but also, and perhaps more deeply, through the Bible translation and commentary it commissioned. Since these have been unduly neglected in the scholarship to date I will therefore look at the biblical annotations alongside their dialogue partners and rivals to understand better what Dort's legacy has been in terms of making clear the Bible's teaching. I will focus particularly on the classic sufficient–efficient distinction as it was employed at Dort, to show that this was carefully nuanced and clarified in a particular direction as a result of the clash with Arminianism. Yet I will also note that although there was widespread agreement among the Reformed, there was no monolithic homogeneity but a degree of diversity in their responses to the theological threat.

I. Historical Context

The United Provinces of the Netherlands were famously tolerant of a certain degree of religious diversity. Having liberated themselves from Spanish Roman Catholic rule, they came together in the Union of Utrecht in 1579, which agreed that "nobody shall be persecuted or examined for religious reasons."[4] Nearly a century later, one foreign observer wrote about "how many religions there are in this country, which have complete freedom to celebrate their mysteries and to serve God as they please," including Lutherans, Arminians, Anabaptists, Socinians, and even Jews and Turks (Muslims), since "the Estates give an unlimited freedom to all kinds of religions; in Holland you will find more Sects, open and recognised, than in the rest of Europe."[5] One Swiss

---

[2] Nicholas Tyacke, *Anti-Calvinists: The Rise of English Arminianism* (Oxford: Clarendon, 1987); Peter White, *Predestination, Policy, and Polemic* (Cambridge: Cambridge University Press, 1992); Anthony Milton, *The British Delegation and the Synod of Dort* (Woodbridge, UK: Boydell, 2005).

[3] Sympathetic commentaries include Homer Hoeksema, *The Voice of Our Fathers: An Exposition of the Canons of Dordrecht* (Grand Rapids, MI: Kregel, 1980); Cornelis Venema, *But for the Grace of God: An Exposition of the Canons of Dort* (Grand Rapids, MI: Reformed Fellowship, 1994); Peter Feenstra, *Unspeakable Comfort: A Commentary on the Canons of Dort* (Winnipeg: Premier Publishing, 1997); and Cornelis Pronk, *Expository Sermons on the Canons of Dort* (St. Thomas, ON: Free Reformed, 1999); Matthew Barrett, *The Grace of Godliness: An Introduction to Doctrine and Piety in the Canons of Dort* (Kitchener, ON: Joshua, 2013).

[4] C. Berkvens-Stevelinck, J. Israel, and G. H. M. Posthumus Meyjes, eds., *The Emergence of Tolerance in the Dutch Republic* (Leiden, Netherlands: Brill, 1997), 41.

[5] Jean-Baptiste Stouppe, *La Religion des Hollandois* (Cologne, 1673), 32, 79. Translations of non-English texts are my own unless stated otherwise.

delegate to Dort had the unusual experience of staying with a family where the mother and daughter were Reformed, the father and son Roman Catholic, the grandmother a Mennonite, and an uncle a Jesuit.[6]

Yet this pluriform religious culture existed under a Reformed Protestant umbrella; the politically dominant church of the Republic subscribed to the Reformed standards of the Belgic Confession and Heidelberg Catechism. Roman Catholicism, too closely associated with Spanish rule and the Inquisition, was outlawed. This officially Reformed, confessional state was, however, more likely to encourage a conniving containment of religious dissent than either strict enforcement or libertarian laxity. By the end of the seventeenth century this resulted in what Jonathan Israel describes as "an ambivalent semi-tolerance . . . seething with tension, theological and political."[7] It is important to recognize that this is the backdrop for the Synod of Dort and also, in part, its legacy.

The union between Holland and Zeeland in 1575 included an agreement to maintain "the practice of the Reformed evangelical religion."[8] What this religion actually was, however, became the subject of dispute when Jacobus Arminius had his first clash with the authorities in 1592.[9] After preaching an unorthodox view of Romans 7, he was ordered to consign to oblivion the dispute he had with another preacher over this and not to let it spread beyond their congregations in Amsterdam.[10] Yet the Arminian controversy was destined to cause great trouble for many years, and became part of a political tussle between the republic's patrician oligarchs, represented by the Advocate of Holland, Johan van Oldenbarnevelt, and the popular, militarily successful Maurice, Stadtholder of various provinces and son of the William of Orange who had led the revolt against Spain. For a time, they shared power in a complex and strained relationship. Political and religious passions ran especially high when Oldenbarnevelt attempted in 1607 to persuade Reformed leaders to allow a national synod, which would amend their doctrinal standards and make the public church theologically broader.

---

[6] See J. Pollmann, "The Bond of Christian Piety," in *Calvinism and Religious Toleration in the Dutch Golden Age*, ed. R. Po-Chia Hsia and Henk van Nierop (Cambridge: Cambridge University Press, 2002), 56.

[7] Jonathan Israel, *The Dutch Republic: Its Rise, Greatness, and Fall* (Oxford: Clarendon, 1998), 676. Cf. J. Spaans, "Religious Policies in the Seventeenth-Century Dutch Republic," in *Calvinism and Religious Toleration*, 72–86.

[8] Israel, *Dutch Republic*, 362.

[9] There is a debate among historians about whether Arminius's theology can be regarded as generally Reformed but idiosyncratic, or as something fundamentally different. Carl Bangs, *Arminius: A Study in the Dutch Reformation* (Nashville: Abingdon, 1971), as a representative of the former position, is outgunned by Richard A. Muller, "Arminius and the Reformed Tradition," *WTJ* 70.1 (2008): 19–48, who advocates the second position. Cf. Keith D. Stanglin and Thomas H. McCall, *Jacob Arminius: Theologian of Grace* (Oxford: Oxford University Press, 2012), 201–204.

[10] Bangs, *Arminius*, 140–46.

Reformed leaders insisted that the Belgic Confession should not be altered. Under the leadership of Johannes Uytenbogaert, those who had been inspired by Arminius (who died in 1609) issued a vigorous protest or "Remonstrance" in 1610 in which they detailed their objections to official Reformed doctrine.[11] This document, according to one Dutch theologian, set the pace for "liberalism" more generally,[12] and made five classic doctrinal points concerning predestination, the extent of the atonement, free will, resistible grace, and Christian perseverance. They asserted that God decreed to save those who by his grace believe and persevere in obedience to the end, and

> That in agreement with this, Jesus Christ the Saviour of the world died for all people, every individual, so that he merited reconciliation and forgiveness of sins for all through the death of the cross; yet so that no-one actually enjoys this forgiveness of sins except those who believe.[13]

John 3:16 and 1 John 2:2 were cited in defense of this.

A year later, at the Hague Conference between leaders on both sides, the Reformed issued a "Counter Remonstrance."[14] They complained that the Remonstrance was deliberately ambiguous and dishonest.[15] They insisted that God decreed the end first, then the means:

> That to this end [to save his elect] he has first of all presented and given to them his only-begotten Son Jesus Christ, whom he delivered up to the death of the cross in order to save his elect, so that, although the suffering of Christ as that of the only-begotten and unique Son of God is sufficient unto the atonement of the sins of all men, nevertheless the same, according to the counsel and decree of God, has its efficacy unto reconciliation and forgiveness of sins only in the elect and true believer.[16]

---

[11] The Remonstrance was in harmony with Arminius's teaching, although not inspired by him alone, and Arminian theology developed further once he died. On Arminius, see Theodoor van Leeuwen, Keith Stanglin, and Marijke Tolsma, eds., *Arminius, Arminianism, and Europe: Jacobus Arminius* (Leiden, Netherlands: Brill, 2009); and William den Boer, *God's Twofold Love: The Theology of Jacob Arminius* (Göttingen, Germany: Vandenhoeck & Ruprecht, 2010), esp. 185–86.

[12] L. Van Holk, "From Arminius to Arminianism in Dutch Theology," in *Man's Faith and Freedom: The Theological Influence of Jacobus Arminius*, ed. Gerald McCulloh (Eugene, OR: Wipf & Stock, 2006), 41.

[13] Philip Schaff, The *Creeds of Christendom. Volume III: The Evangelical Protestant Creeds* (New York: Harper & Brothers, 1877), 546 (my translation).

[14] Rival accounts were published by Henricus Brandus, *Collatio Scripto Habita Hagae Comitis* (Middelburg, 1615), and by Petrus Bertius, *Scripta Adversaria Collationis Hagiensis* (Leiden, 1615). See Milton, *British Delegation*, 62 n. 40, 218 n. 110.

[15] Cf. the assessment of Jan Rohls, "Calvinism, Arminianism, and Socinianism in the Netherlands until the Synod of Dort," in *Socinianism and Arminianism: Antitrinitarians, Calvinists, and Cultural Exchange in Seventeenth-Century Europe*, ed. Martin Mulsow and Jan Rohls (Leiden, Netherlands: Brill, 2005), 19.

[16] Peter Y. De Jong, *Crisis in the Reformed Churches: Essays in Commemoration of the Great Synod of Dort* (Grand Rapids, MI: Reformed Fellowship, 1968), 247–50.

As William den Boer points out, "for the Remonstrants, sufficiency presupposes actual procurement, as well as the will on God's part to extend to all what is sufficient for all."[17] For the Contra-Remonstrants, the will, decree, and counsel of God was focused on the efficacy rather than the sufficiency of redemption. So the meeting broke up without agreement. When Maurice eventually came out on top of the political wrangling, however, it allowed the Reformed to call for a synod to clarify the ecclesiastical situation. As a national synod, it would boost the national unification process involving regions and states that up until then had remained relatively independent. But others from outside the Netherlands would also be invited to participate. The scene was set for the biggest ever international gathering of Reformed theologians.

II. The Canons of Dort on the Death of Christ

We can learn a great deal about the manner and method of the Synod from its official and unofficial papers and contemporary accounts of its everyday workings. Often cited in this regard are the letters of John Hales, chaplain to the British Ambassador to the Netherlands.[18] Each delegation prepared its own position paper on the five doctrines chosen by the Arminians for dispute, which were then read in the gathered Synod. After discussion of these papers, later collected and published,[19] the Canons or judgments of the Synod were drawn up.[20] The British played a full part in this discussion, Walter Balcanquhall at one point speaking for more than an hour on the subject of the death of Christ to the assembled divines,[21] and the delegation resisted certain aspects of the draft Canons on this point.[22] Their position was, as we shall see, different from the majority but had some significant influence on the final wording.

The Remonstrants themselves spoke several times at the Synod and were repeatedly asked to give an account of their disagreements with the officially accepted doctrine. They had challenged the Belgic Confession and sought to

---

[17] Den Boer, *God's Twofold Love*, 234. Cf. James Arminius, *The Works of James Arminius*, trans. James Nichols and William Nichols, 3 vols. (London, 1825; repr. Grand Rapids, MI: Baker, 1956), 3:345–46.

[18] I am editing the relevant correspondence of Hales and Balcanquhall for a multivolume critical edition of the Synod's documents, due to be published on its 400th anniversary in 2018. See Anthony Milton, "A Distorting Mirror: The Hales and Balcanquhall Letters and the Synod of Dordt," in *Revisiting the Synod of Dort*, ed. Aza Goudriaan and Fred van Lieburg (Leiden, Netherlands: Brill, 2011), 135–61, on the particular care needed in using Hales, and not overplaying British involvement. See also Donald Sinnema, "The Drafting of the Canons of Dordt: A Preliminary Survey of Early Drafts and Related Documents," in the same volume, on extant documents.

[19] *Acta Synodi Nationalis* (Leiden, 1620), 1.78–126; 3.88–153.

[20] On the acrimonious debate over drafting procedure, see Milton, *British Delegation*, 295–97, and John Hales, *Golden Remains of the Ever Memorable Mr. John Hales of Eton College, &c* (London, 1673), ii.146–50.

[21] *Acta*, 1.195; Hales, *Golden Remains*, ii.93.

[22] Ibid., ii.144–45; Sinnema, "Drafting," 299–307.

amend it for many years, but rather than accept the opportunity to defend their case they engaged in political posturing and obstructive maneuvering. Due to what Balcanquhall called their "incredible obstinacy,"[23] they were eventually discharged in January 1619. One commentator asserts that this "proves that the whole of the proceedings against the Arminian party were those of a faction, contending for pre-eminence without regard to justice."[24] Balcanquhall did at times complain about their treatment at the hands of some delegates.[25] Their opinions were, however, very well known and a matter of public record, being plainly set out in the *Remonstrance*, the extensive records of the Hague Conference, the *Sententia Remonstrantium* officially presented at two sessions in December 1618,[26] and the published works of their leaders such as Simon Episcopius. These were given a fair hearing,[27] by a far from homogenous international gathering which cannot fairly be said to represent a mere "faction" within the Dutch church. Those who wrote and subscribed to the Canons of Dort were very well informed about Remonstrant teaching, and the official record celebrates the "diversity in smaller matters" (*in minutioribus diversitas*) which could be seen among them, as indicating the liberty of speech and judgment they exercised while remaining solidly anti-Arminian.[28]

When it finally came to deal with the doctrinal issues, the Synod did not deal with the points in the order we might expect. It is true that the acronym TULIP was later invented as a mnemonic for the five areas in dispute at Dort.[29] However, the central petal, the "L" of so-called "limited atonement," was actually the *second* head of doctrine covered by the Synod, mirroring its place in the Arminian *Remonstrance*.[30] As Alan Sell warns us, the nature of "the five points" as responses should "caution us against thinking that they represent the *sum* of Calvinism,"[31] or even its core. Reformed theology was also committed to

---

[23] Hales, *Golden Remains*, ii.73; Tyacke, *Anti-Calvinists*, 95.

[24] Frederick Calder, *Memoirs of Simon Episcopius* (New York, 1837), 327.

[25] Mark Ellis, *The Arminian Confession of 1621* (Eugene, OR: Pickwick, 2005), xii–xiii n. 36, collects some of his statements.

[26] *Acta*, 1.113, 116–18.

[27] Several Synod sessions were spent reading pages out. See, for example, Hales, *Golden Remains*, ii.108, 113. Delegates had detailed knowledge of Arminian writings, according to Goudriaan, "The Synod of Dort on Arminian Anthropology," in *Revisiting the Synod of Dort*, 84–86.

[28] See the end of "Præfatio ad Ecclesias," *Acta*, 1.

[29] William Aglionby, *The Present State of the United Provinces* (London, 1669), 283, speaks of a time when "the fancy for tulips did reign over all the Low Countries." So it is not an entirely inappropriate flower to be associated with a Dutch Synod!

[30] Definite atonement did not go by the name "limited atonement" in the sixteenth, seventeenth, or eighteenth centuries, although the word "limited" was sometimes used, as in William Troughton, *Scripture Redemption, Restrayned and Limited* (London, 1652).

[31] Alan Sell, *The Great Debate: Calvinism, Arminianism, and Salvation* (Eugene, OR: Wipf & Stock, 1998), 14; Richard A. Muller, "How Many Points?," *CTJ* 28 (1993): 425–33.

Reformation doctrines such as salvation *sola fide* and *sola gratia* to distinguish it from Roman Catholicism, for example, as well as a sacramentology which distinguished it from Lutheranism and a Trinitarianism which distinguished it from Socinianism—all of which, some may argue, are of greater significance than limited atonement. That is not to say these five points are unimportant, however, since they were church-defining issues at a pivotal moment.

THE SUFFICIENCY OF THE CROSS

I turn to look now at the Synod's debates on the sufficiency and efficacy of the atonement, and the diversity of Reformed responses to the Arminian use of this formula. The first point made by the Canons on the second head of doctrine, however, concerns the actual need for atonement. God's supreme justice, they say, requires that our sins deserve temporal and eternal punishments (*temporalibus [et] æternis pœnis*). We are unable to do anything about this ourselves, and yet "God, in his infinite mercy, has given us as a Surety his only begotten Son, who, to make satisfaction for us, was made sin and became a curse on the cross, for us and in our place" (*pro nobis seu vice nostra*).[32] This is a classic description of the need for and accomplishment of penal substitutionary atonement.[33]

The Arminian position at Dort continued to be that

> The price of the redemption which Christ offered to God his Father is not only in itself and by itself sufficient to redeem the whole human race (*toti generi humano*) but was also paid for all people, every individual (*pro omnibus et singulis hominibus*),[34] according to the decree, will, and grace of God the Father.[35]

This takes the first part of the Lombardian formula ("sufficient for all, effective for the elect") but pushes it further. Not only was the cross sufficient but it was actually effective in paying for each and every person, and indeed was designed by God to do so. As they had said at the Hague Conference,

---

[32] Articles II.1–II.2. Translations are from the Latin in *Acta*, 1.241–71. My translation of all the Articles and Rejectio Errorum (rejection of errors) on this head can be found in Lee Gatiss, *For Us and for Our Salvation: "Limited Atonement" in the Bible, Doctrine, History, and Ministry* (London: Latimer Trust, 2012).
[33] Cf. Heidelberg Catechism, Q. 10–13.
[34] I am reading the *et* here as epexegetical.
[35] *Acta*, 1.116. The Heidelberg Catechism, Q. 37, speaks of Christ bearing "the wrath of God against the sin of the entire human race" (*peccatum universi generis humani*), although Gisbertus Voetius argued that this was not a reference to the extent of the *atonement*. See Roger R. Nicole, "Moyse Amyraut (1596–1664) and the Controversy on Universal Grace, First Phase (1634–1637)" (PhD diss., Harvard University, 1966), 142; Pronk, *Expository Sermons*, 126.

Christ died not just for the elect or for those who will finally be saved, but he obtained reconciliation for everyone, and this by the counsel and decree of God.[36] Thus the Arminian position on the atonement made an explicit claim not just about its extent but also about its purpose and intention in God's will.

In response to this, the delegates at Dort separated out the two issues of sufficiency and intentionality. As the representatives from Groningen and Omlands said in their submission, the question was not really about the sufficiency of Christ's death at all, for they had no doubts that his sacrifice had such power and value that it was abundantly sufficient to expiate the sins of everyone. There was no defect or insufficiency in the cross which could be blamed for the loss of the reprobate. Rather, they said, the question was about the *intention* (singular) of God the Father and God the Son, and whether together they designed the death of Christ to actually obtain forgiveness and reconciliation for more than just the elect.[37] Others, from the Palatinate, Hesse, Belgium, and Utrecht, for example, also linked Christ's sufficiency to his two natures and perfect obedience.[38]

The Genevan delegation did not, however, utilize the concept of sufficiency. They wrote only of the infinite value of Christ's death, to which is added an efficacious intention for the elect.[39] In this they were following Theodore Beza, who considered the Lombardian distinction to be potentially ambiguous and confusing.[40] Those from North Holland were somewhat ambivalent about sufficiency,[41] and the ministers of Emden considered the issue using the term *adæquate* rather than *sufficienter*.[42] The final approved statement, however, made the following points:

> This death of the Son of God is the only and most perfect sacrifice and satisfaction for sins, and is of infinite value and worth, abundantly sufficient to expiate the sins of the whole world.

> This death, therefore, is of such great value and worth because the person who submitted to it was not only truly man and perfectly holy, but also the only-begotten Son of God, of the same eternal and infinite being with the Father and the Holy Spirit, which it was necessary for our Saviour to be.[43]

---

[36] *Collatio Scripto Habita Hagae Comitis*, 139.
[37] *Acta*, 3.139.
[38] *Acta*, 2.86, 89; 3.88, 117; Heidelberg Catechism, Q. 14–18.
[39] *Acta*, 2.101.
[40] W. Robert Godfrey, "Reformed Thought on the Extent of the Atonement to 1618," *WTJ* 37.2 (1975): 142.
[41] *Acta*, 3.107–108.
[42] Ibid., 2.120. Cf. *adæquate* in *Acta*, 2.100.
[43] Article II.3–4.

Medieval scholastics debated whether the merit of Christ in his life and death was infinite, because of his divine nature, or finite because merited through his human nature.[44] The Canons of Dort ground Christ's infinite merit in both his divine nature and his perfect human obedience.[45] In distinction from medieval thinkers, seventeenth-century Reformed theologians considered Christ to have acted as a mediator in both of his natures rather than just in his human nature,[46] and it may be that this lies behind their connections here. Naturally, however, the early, medieval, and Reformed churches were agreed that Christ could not *be* mediator unless he were both God and man,[47] which is why Article IV adds ". . . which it was necessary for our Saviour to be."

The British delegation did not use the sufficient–efficient distinction because they could not agree on it among themselves.[48] They did however link Christ's "ransom for the sins of the whole world" to the sincere, universal proclamation of the gospel.[49] Others were happier to base indiscriminate preaching on what Michael Thomas calls "ministerial inability to distinguish elect from reprobate."[50] Thomas also reads two of the delegations as foreshadowing "Hyper-Calvinism," backing away from the idea that there is a strict obligation to evangelize everyone. Yet the finally agreed Article V asserts rather strongly that,

> Moreover, the promise of the gospel is that whoever believes in Christ crucified shall not perish, but have eternal life. This promise ought to be declared and published promiscuously and without distinction, to all nations and people to whom God according to his good pleasure sends the gospel, together with the command to repent and believe.

The linking word at the start of this article is not *ergo* ("therefore") or *proinde* ("accordingly/consequently"), which would have made the same connection as the British. The Latin is *cæterum*, which simply means "moreover, furthermore, in addition."[51] That is, the Canons place the abundant sufficiency of Christ's sacrifice side by side with the necessity for indiscriminate

---

[44] See Richard A. Muller, *Dictionary of Latin and Greek Theological Terms* (Grand Rapids, MI: Baker, 1985), 190–91.
[45] The British spoke of Christ's *thesaurus meritorum*, "treasury of merits" (*Acta*, 2.79), which sounds positively medieval, but is an alternative way of discussing sufficiency.
[46] Lombard, *Sentences*, 3.19.6–7; Aquinas, *Summa Theologiae*, 3.26.2; Westminster Confession, 8.7; John Owen, Χριστολογία (London, 1679), 312–13.
[47] Cf. Augustine, *Enchiridion*, 108; Lombard, *Sentences*, 3.2.3.2.
[48] See Milton, *British Delegation*, 215; Hales, *Golden Remains*, ii.130–31.
[49] *Acta*, 2.78–79. The latter was based on (*fundatur*) the merits of the former.
[50] Thomas, *Extent of Atonement*, 149.
[51] Cf. Articles I.15, III.11.

evangelism, but without explicitly making a logical connection between them. This allowed the British (and those like them) to join the dots themselves if they wished, but did not spell it out for the sake of those who ground universal proclamation another way (e.g., simple obedience to Matthew 28:18–20). All this lends credence to Godfrey's assertion, and my thesis here, that "the history of the Synod when viewed in detail reveals that the Calvinism at Dort was neither irrelevant, monolithic nor uncompromising."[52]

One thing was clear, however: if anyone failed to believe and therefore did not inherit the promise of eternal life through Christ, the finger of blame could not be pointed at Jesus on the cross. Their loss, warns Article II.6, is "not because of any defect in the sacrifice offered by Christ upon the cross, or indeed any insufficiency in it" (as those from Groningen had put it), "but is their own particular fault" (*propria ipsorum culpa*).[53]

THE INTENTIONAL EFFICACY OF THE CROSS

On that sobering note, the Canons turn to discuss the other side of the classic distinction: the effectiveness of the cross for the elect. The efficacy of Christ's work to actually save those given to him by the Father (John 10:25–30) is intimately linked in the Canons to the divine will. What Christ's work effected is what God designed, purposed, and intended it to do. The Remonstrants had affirmed not only universal sufficiency but also that the price of redemption was "paid for all people, every individual, *according to the decree, will, and grace of God the Father*" (emphasis added). This meant that no one was excluded from a share in Christ's death by an antecedent decree of God, but only by their own unbelieving abuse of God's gifts.[54] The Reformed, however, refused to allow God's eternal will to save whomsoever he wished to be thwarted by supposed human freedom. He decreed to elect certain people by his unconditional grace, and consequently sent Christ to save those people, even giving them the faith they needed to appropriate this salvation.[55] As Richard Muller neatly summarizes it,

> Whereas the Reformed doctrine of the will of God tends to resolve all distinctions into a single, simple, eternal will of God to actualize certain possibilities and not others, the Arminian doctrine tends to emphasize the

---

[52] Godfrey, "Tensions," 268.
[53] Cf. Articles I.5, III/IV.9.
[54] *Acta*, 1.113–14, 116.
[55] Rejectio Errorum 2.3.

distinctions for the sake of arguing interaction between God and genuinely free or contingent events.[56]

Hence, the Arminians stressed contingency and conditions where the Reformed saw sovereignty and certainty. The latter acknowledged the free offer of the gospel to all; as Article II.7 puts it, "as many as truly believe . . . are by the death of Christ freed and saved from sin and destruction," not just potentially, but actually. For them the atonement *did* something, rather than simply making something possible. Yet alongside this temporal, human-level proclamation, the Reformed discerned (in Scripture) the revelation of an eternal divine purpose. Many are called but few are chosen. Salvation history, they said, has been divinely ordered from the start to achieve God's ultimate goal, which could not be uncertain or in doubt without undermining God's sovereignty.

Article VIII, the longest of the positive articles on this head, expounds the particular design of God:

> For this was the most free purpose and most gracious will and intention of God the Father, that the life-giving and saving efficacy of the most precious death of his Son should extend to all the elect, for bestowing upon them alone justifying faith, thereby to bring them unfailingly to salvation; that is, God willed that Christ through the blood of the cross (by which he confirmed the new covenant) should effectually redeem out of every people, tribe, nation, and language, all those, and those only, who were from eternity chosen for salvation and given to him by the Father; that he should bestow upon them faith (which, together with all the other saving gifts of the Holy Spirit, he acquired for them by his death); that he should purify them by his blood from all sins, both original and actual, whether committed after or before believing; and having faithfully protected them even to the end, should finally establish them glorious before him, free from every spot and blemish.

As far as Dort is concerned, therefore, Lombard's sufficient–efficient distinction needed to be clarified in the light of the Arminian error. Even Arminians could affirm that the cross was ultimately only "efficient for some."[57] But in doing so they made each individual's human will the decisive factor, rather

---

[56] Richard A. Muller, *God, Creation, and Providence in the Thought of Jacob Arminius* (Grand Rapids, MI: Baker, 1991), 189.

[57] Raymond A. Blacketer, "Definite Atonement in Historical Perspective," in *The Glory of the Atonement: Biblical, Historical, and Practical Perspectives: Essays in Honor of Roger Nicole*, ed. Charles E. Hill and Frank A. James (Downers Grove, IL: InterVarsity Press, 2004), 311.

than God's will. So the Synod said, more carefully, that the cross was some-how sufficient for all, but only *intended* to be efficacious for the elect. By focusing on the divine purpose and design behind the coming of Christ (he came not to make us redeemable but to redeem), the Reformed put human decisions into what they saw as the proper biblical perspective. Hence they rejected the view of those

> Who teach: That God the Father has ordained his Son to the death of the cross without a certain and definite purpose to save anyone in particular, so that the necessity, profitableness, and worth of what Christ obtained by his death might remain in good repair, perfect in all its parts, complete and intact, even if the obtained redemption had never in fact been applied to any individual. For this assertion is insulting to the wisdom of God the Father and the merits of Jesus Christ, and is contrary to Scripture.[58]

There was almost unanimous agreement among the delegations about God's will being behind the efficacy of the cross for the elect. There was also wide-spread agreement on the coextensive link between Christ's purchase of re-demption and its application, which the Remonstrants denied by making the purchase wider than the application.[59] Those from Nassau-Wetteravia, for example, spoke of Christ being given up "by the will and intention of the Father" to both acquire and apply salvation to those who were given to him, and that they would be given the Spirit of regeneration simultaneously along with forgiveness.[60] So in this Trinitarian view, the Father gives the elect to the Son, who dies for them, and then gives them the Spirit and faith.

Reformed Variations

Two delegations were divided among themselves on these issues. Those from Britain and Bremen gave minority reports to the Synod, and aroused some very strong passions. The British delegation had to write home for help in reconciling their internal divisions, but John Davenant claimed he would rather have his right hand cut off than change his mind, so some compromise was inevitable.[61] When Matthias Martinius from Bremen in-

---

[58] Rejectio Errorum 2.1.

[59] See Rejectio Errorum 2.6 on the Arminian use of this distinction as introducing "the pernicious poison of Pela-gianism." Contra White, *Predestination*, 192, the Synod did not condemn the distinction itself as Pelagian, only its usurpation.

[60] *Acta*, 2.96–97. Others also linked Christ's sacrifice and intercession, excluding the reprobate from both, using John 17:9.

[61] Hales, *Golden Remains*, ii.101, 182.

delicately expressed some of his more Arminianizing opinions on this subject, Franciscus Gomarus was so incensed that he threw down the gauntlet and challenged him to a duel! The Synod president tried to calm things down, but after prayers Gomarus renewed his request for combat.[62] The two would fight again (verbally) in the Synod, in an undignified manner which did not impress the other foreign delegates, and though others in the Bremen delegation did not agree with Martinius, they nearly left because of this incivility.[63]

Why the fuss? Martinius inclined toward Remonstrant views, particularly on the atonement,[64] and was not afraid to say so or strongly to criticize both sides. Davenant, however, was stubbornly devoted to the cause of moderation, and to finding a middle way on this doctrine. Having been tasked with not upsetting relations with the Lutheran churches (particularly offended by Contra-Remonstrant views here), with not being overly precise, and with taking the Anglican formularies into account,[65] he and Samuel Ward managed to use their positions in the British delegation to air their minority opinion. This eventually triumphed over the other British delegates. Davenant held to a sophisticated form of what is now known as Hypothetical Universalism,[66] and this made an impact on the British submission. To begin with, this clearly affirmed that "Christ died for the elect out of a special love and intention of both God the Father and Christ, that he might truly obtain and infallibly confer on them forgiveness of sins and eternal salvation." To make this effectual, God also gives faith and perseverance to those elect; they are saved not "if they are willing" (*si velint*) but "because God wills it" (*quia Deus vult*).[67] So far, so anti-Arminian.[68]

On top of this, however, the British paper posited a second intention in the cross: Christ also

---

[62] The request was never granted. Hales, preaching at the Hague about dueling, inveighed against "an over-promptness in many young men, who desire to be counted men of valour and resolution, upon every sleight occasion to raise a quarrel, and admit of no other means of composing and ending it, but by sword and single combat" (ibid., i.71).

[63] Ibid., ii.109. See also G. Brandt, *History of the Reformation in the Low-Countries* (London, 1722), 3.7–8, on Gomarus's first run-in with the Bremenese.

[64] Hales, *Golden Remains*, ii.131; *Acta*, 2.103–108. British delegate Samuel Ward spoke about the cross making all people "redeemable," thus changing the nature of the atonement from definite to indefinite, following Martinius's lead. See Milton, *British Delegation*, 201–203.

[65] Milton, 216–22.

[66] See his *Dissertationes Duæ: Prima de Morte Christi* (Cambridge, 1650), and Jonathan D. Moore, *English Hypothetical Universalism: John Preston and the Softening of Reformed Theology* (Cambridge: Eerdmans, 2007), 187–213.

[67] *Acta*, 2.78.

[68] The first of three "theses heterodoxæ" rejected by the British also refutes the idea that God's sole intention in sending Christ was "suspended on the contingent act of man's faith."

died for all, that all and every one by means of faith might obtain remission of sins, and eternal life by virtue of that ransom.[69] But Christ so died for the elect, that by the merit of his death in special manner . . . they might infallibly obtain both faith and eternal life.[70]

So as well as dying efficaciously for the elect, Christ also intended to die conditionally for all. As Davenant later explained, "the Divine Will or Intention sometimes denotes merely the appointment of means to an end, although there is no determinate will in God of producing that end by those means."[71] This appears to marry the Reformed insistence on a single, simple will of God with Arminian distinctions concerning contingency, and is in outline the same via media construction suggested by Anglican bishop John Overall in an influential paper, where he also spoke of a second "conditional intention" of God as being behind the general grace of the gospel promise.[72]

Further, as a letter from the British divines to the Archbishop of Canterbury explained, there are "some fruits of Christ's death, not comprised in the decree of Election, but afforded more generally, yet confined to the Visible Church (as viz. true and spiritual Graces accompanying the Gospel, and conferred upon some *non-electi*)."[73] That is, there are spiritual benefits short of conversion (such as those spoken of in Hebrews 6:4–5) which are merited by the cross and dispensed to the non-elect.[74] Yet, it should be noted, these are available only "in the Church" (the visible church), according to the British.[75] Word and Spirit are inseparably joined together in the ministry of the Word, they claimed, so when the gospel is proclaimed, there the Spirit is at work, even among the non-elect. The Word "insinuates itselfe into the secretest closets of the soule" to awaken believers or eventually harden the stubborn.[76]

Many have seen the British as having a major role in softening the Canons of Dort on this head, especially on sufficiency and the gospel call.[77] Evidently their views were greatly respected,[78] and they played a helpful role

---

[69] *The Collegiat Suffrage of the Divines of Great Britaine* (London, 1629), 47, adds "paid once for all mankind."
[70] *Acta*, 2.79.
[71] Milton, *British Delegation*, 399.
[72] Cambridge University Library, MS Gg/1/29, fo. 6v. Oldenbarnevelt had recommended Overall, known to favor the Remonstrants, to be a delegate at the Synod (Milton, *British Delegation*, xxviii–xxxi).
[73] Hales, *Golden Remains*, ii.185.
[74] Ibid., ii.187.
[75] *Acta*, 2.79.
[76] *Collegiat Suffrage*, 52. This view seems to be reflected in Dort's Article III/IV.9, where it is said that "various gifts" are conferred by God on those who are called by the ministry of the Word but do not come to Christ.
[77] White, *Predestination*, 191; Godfrey, "Tensions," 263–64; Moore, *English Hypothetical Universalism*, 213.
[78] The British view is always placed first in the foreign position papers in the *Acta*, which indicates a certain primacy of honor.

in mediating many disputes personally. Yet the final Synodical statements, about sufficiency at least, can be adequately explained as reflecting the majority view of the Synod, without supposing a British counterweight was necessary to balance Genevan dislike of the concept. The British did not use the standard sufficient–efficient distinction in their submission in any case. It is possible that the *Rejectio Errorum* may have included a rejection of "ordained sufficiency" or "conditional intentionality" if Davenant had not espoused the latter idea, but this is merely conjecture. The British were divided among themselves on whether the universal language in verses such as 1 John 2:2 (partly echoed in their Prayer Book) should be restricted to the elect only.[79] Perhaps this too was left undefined in the Articles as a result of British concerns, but again this is speculation.[80]

British concerns probably did lie behind the statement of the gospel promise in Article II.5. This does not, however, enlarge grace beyond the elect per se, as Davenant would have wished, or put forward an unconditional new covenant for the elect alongside a conditional gospel covenant for all,[81] or even connect theoretical sufficiency with universal proclamation. However, what Davenant wanted to protect by means of his twofold-intention theory was the idea that if people are not saved, "it arises from themselves alone, and the hardness of their heart repelling the means of salvation."[82] The Canons, as with several delegations, made exactly this point in Article II.6, without needing to posit contingency or conditionality in God's eternal will. Article II.8 affirmed that God "willed that Christ . . . should *effectually* (*efficaciter*) redeem . . . all those, and those only, who were from eternity chosen," but this left a back door open for Davenant and others by not technically denying an ultimately *ineffectual* universal redemption in addition to this.[83] Other Reformed statements on the subject were phrased in such a way as to exclude this view, but Dort refrained from doing so.[84] Without the British pressing the Synod on these points the Canons may perhaps not have been so carefully stated.

---

[79] Hales, *Golden Remains*, ii.101, 130–31; Milton, *British Delegation*, 215.

[80] Tyacke, *Anti-Calvinists*, 98. We await a definitive study by Sinnema and Milton of the scattered documents relating to the formation of the Canons, which will shed light on these issues.

[81] Davenant's covenant schema, as seen in Milton, *British Delegation*, 398–99.

[82] Ibid., 397, 401.

[83] Jonathan D. Moore, "The Extent of the Atonement," in *Drawn into Controversie: Reformed Theological Diversity and Debates within Seventeenth-Century British Puritanism*, ed. Michael A. G. Haykin and Mark Jones, (Göttingen, Germany: Vandenhoeck & Ruprecht, 2011), 145–46.

[84] *Synopsis Purioris Theologiae* (Leiden, 1625), XXIX.xxix, says, "the end, object, and 'for whom' (ᾧ or *cui*) of satisfaction is only Elect and true believers."

Genevan delegate Giovanni Diodati complained that the English were "so scrupulous and speculative" on these matters and had so many difficulties that it caused a great deal of time and trouble to find "the centre point."[85] Yet he did not see their Hypothetical Universalism as a grave threat to Reformed unity.[86] Balcanquhall reported to the British Ambassador, at the end of all the wrangling, that regarding the atonement,

> there was not altogether so uniform a consent both in regard of phrases and forms of speaking, and in regard of some propositions, as was in the first Article: yet certainly there was very great [agreement], more than could well have been expected from so great a number of learned men in so hard and controverted an Article.[87]

III. After the Synod

In the immediate wake of the Synod, around two hundred Remonstrants were deprived of their right to preach by the authorities. A fifth of these subsequently conformed and were reinstated, while approximately seventy agreed not to preach or teach but to live quiet lives as private citizens. The remainder who refused to follow either of these courses, were banished from the United Provinces, which could ill afford internal strife or potential civil war as the Twelve Year Truce with Spain came to an end and Europe geared up for what became the Thirty Years War.[88] To complete his consolidation of power in the fragmented Provinces, the Prince of Orange ensured that his rival (and patron of the Arminians) van Oldenbarnevelt was executed before that bloody religious conflict could begin. Hugo Grotius was imprisoned, but soon made a famous escape to Roman Catholic France where leading Arminians Uytenbogaert and Episcopius also fled.[89] Foreign delegations urged mildness and peace upon the Dutch as they departed and, indeed, the Remonstrant Brotherhood was openly tolerated within a few years, though no longer within the pale of the official national church.

The French Reformed church, whose delegates had been kept away from the Synod, adopted the Canons for themselves as binding on churches and

---

[85] MS Lullin 53, fols. 55^r–55^v.

[86] Nicolas Fornerod, "A Reappraisal of the Genevan Delegation," in *Revisiting the Synod of Dort*, 211.

[87] Hales, *Golden Remains*, ii.132.

[88] Israel, *Dutch Republic*, 462–63; Spaans, "Religious Policies," 78; Archibald Harrison, *Beginnings of Arminianism to the Synod of Dort* (London: University of London Press, 1926), 287–88.

[89] Several hundred patrician Remonstrants had converted to Roman Catholicism by 1625, according to R. Po-Chia Hsia, *The World of Catholic Renewal, 1540–1770* (Cambridge: Cambridge University Press, 1998), 85.

universities.[90] There were also attempts in England, as Arminianism began to rise there, to bring peace to the church by officially adopting the Canons alongside the *Thirty-nine Articles*, but these were ultimately unsuccessful.[91] In 1646, however, the Westminster Assembly debated the issue of the extent of the atonement, and Dortian divisions cast their shadow over proceedings, with a range of Reformed opinions again being acknowledged.[92] The Canons of Dort have since been accepted as part of the confessional makeup of many denominations and institutions around the world and, given their origin in such an honored assembly, are often considered a touchstone of Reformed orthodoxy.

THE DUTCH ANNOTATIONS

The Synod spent a week in November 1618 discussing a plan for a new Dutch translation of the Bible.[93] The British explained how work on the King James Version (1611) had been organized, and it was noted that this quite deliberately had no marginal annotations, unlike the Geneva Bible (1560). The Synod, however, decided that their authorized version would have notes to clarify difficult passages, but supposedly would not be too doctrinal.[94] This laborious work was finally completed by members of the Synod and others in 1637. At the urging of Archbishop Ussher and the Westminster Assembly, it was also published in English as *The Dutch Annotations*.[95] Around the same time, the *Pious Annotations* of Geneva's delegate to Dort, Italian-born Giovanni Diodati, were also published in English,[96] as well as the so-called *English Annotations* commissioned by Parliament and associated with several members of the Westminster Assembly.[97] These may be profitably compared with contemporary works out of the Arminian stable by Hugo Grotius and Henry Hammond.[98]

It may be surprising for some to realize that the theologically sophisticated

---

[90] *Articles Agreed On in the Nationall Synode of the Reformed Churches of France, Held at Charenton* (Oxford, 1624).

[91] Milton, *British Delegation*, 383. Tyacke, *Anti-Calvinists*, 152, 170, 176–77.

[92] Lee Gatiss, "'Shades of Opinion within a Generic Calvinism': The Particular Redemption Debate at the Westminster Assembly," *RTR* 69.2 (2010): 101–18; and "A Deceptive Clarity? Particular Redemption in the Westminster Standards," *RTR* 69.3 (2010): 180–96.

[93] *Acta*, 1.21–27.

[94] Ibid., 1.23; Milton, *British Delegation*, 135.

[95] Theodore Haak, *The Dutch Annotations upon the Whole Bible . . . Ordered and Appointed by the Synod of Dort* (London, 1657).

[96] Giovanni Diodati, *Pious Annotations upon the Holy Bible* (London, 1643).

[97] *Annotations upon All the Books of the Old and New Testament* (London, 1645). See Richard A. Muller and Rowland S. Ward, *Scripture and Worship: Biblical Interpretation and the Directory for Public Worship* (Phillipsburg, NJ: P&R, 2007), 4–5.

[98] Grotius's commentaries were first published in Amsterdam and Paris (1641–1650); Hammond, *A Paraphrase and Annotations upon all the Books of the New Testament* (London, 1659).

Canons of Dort were put together by a body which was not merely interested in polemics or "systematics," but keenly concerned with the Bible and its proper exegesis.[99] The Synod's authorized annotations give us insight into how Dort's biblical scholars understood certain verses which were important in the atonement debate. Alongside other Reformed annotations they also illustrate the variety of responses to Arminian exegesis within the recognizably Reformed family. I will look briefly at four key texts to illustrate this, noting that the *Dutch Annotations*, while not un-theological, often stick closer to the text than others.

FOUR KEY TEXTS

We see the variety in Reformed commentary on Isaiah 53:10–12. Diodati stressed that the purpose of the suffering Servant's work was to execute "Gods eternall decree concerning the salvation of the Elect." The *English Annotations* spoke more of the salvation of "us," "the church," than of the elect in this chapter. The *Dutch Annotations* were generally more subtle theologically. Echoing the Heidelberg Catechism, they said that Christ suffered "when the heavy wrath of God for the sins of mankind lay upon him," and that he "suffered so much for mankind."[100] Yet verse 10 spoke of Christ both "purchasing and procuring for them pardon for sin" in order to "deliver his elect." A confessional reading was thus nuanced in the light of Dort's judgment against the Arminian distinction between purchase and procurement.

John 3:16 was cited by the Remonstrants as supporting their view of atonement. Hammond's Arminian commentary paraphrased Christ in John 3:17 saying, "For this my mission from God my Father was designed . . . on purpose that all men might be rescued from punishment."[101] An unlimited design and purpose seems to have been squeezed in here. Similarly, Grotius wrote on this verse that God had a covenant not just with the Jews but had covered the sins of everyone in the human race,[102] although the verse itself says nothing of covenant or covering. The *Dutch Annotations*, however, interpreted God's love for the world as being for "not onely the Jews, but also the Gentiles, scattered throughout the whole world" picking up themes from the Gospel itself. This

---

[99] See also W. Robert Godfrey, "Popular and Catholic: The *Modus Docendi* of the Canons of Dordt," in *Revisiting the Synod of Dort*, 243–60, on the pastoral presentation of the Canons.

[100] That is, mankind as a race, not angel-kind, animal-kind, or elf-kind.

[101] Hammond, *Paraphrase*, 274. See his similar comments on John 3:16 about "design," and on John 1:29 and 1 John 2:2 about the conditional "obtaining" of salvation.

[102] Hugo Grotius, *Annotationes in Novum Testamentum*, 9 vols. (Groningen, 1826–1834), 4:44.

was close to the *English Annotations*, which interpreted verse 16 as referring to "mankind" but particularly believers. Diodati said God's love is for "man-kinde in its generality, though with a distinction of his elect." So among the Reformed, the *Dutch Annotations* adhered somewhat closer to the text, while not being as doctrinally expansive or specific as they could have been.

The Remonstrants also used 1 John 2:2 in their case for indefinite atonement. Grotius spoke here generally of the propitiation offered by Christ as a benefit that will be furnished to all those who will choose to follow Christ,[103] assuming a universal atonement procured for all just waiting to be appropriated by whoever wants it. The *Dutch Annotations* argued, however, that Christ was the propitiation for our sins and not for ours only, "namely, the Apostles and other believers who now live," but also for the sins "of all men in the whole world out of all Nations, who shall yet believe in him." In support of this reading they cited John 11:52 and Revelation 5:9, which were both thought to be by the same apostle John who wrote the epistle, with the implication that Christ did not die for every single person but only for some "out of" (ἐκ) all nations. They went on to explain, further, that the alternative Arminian reading could not be correct, "For that he doth not reconcile all and every man in the whole world unto God, appears both by experience, and also this, that he prayed not to the Father for all and every one, Joh. 17.9, but only for them who shall believe in him, Joh. 17.20." Diodati was similar, while the *English Annotations* added a possible Jew-Gentile contrast here as well, though on John 17:9 they simply commented that Christ prayed "not for reprobates." Again, the *Dutch Annotations* looked closer at the verse in its immediate and Johannine context, to arrive at their conclusion.

Finally, 1 Timothy 2 refers to God's desire for all to be saved and to Christ giving himself as "a ransom for all." On this text, Grotius said God's desire to save all is his preceding will (*voluntas præcedens*), which comes before any limitation of salvation to the elect.[104] He conceived of God as sending Jesus with the plan and purpose to save all. The ransom of the cross brought general benefits to the entire human race (*ad totius humani generis*).[105] The *Dutch Annotations*, on the other hand, were keen to stress that "all" means "all sorts" of people, as it does in verses 1–2, since if God willed all people to be saved, they would be saved, "for God doth whatsoever he will." They were at pains

---

[103] Ibid., 8:156.
[104] Ibid., 7:221.
[105] Ibid., 222.

to refute synergism, adding, "If any man should say that God wills this if men do will it also, that is to hang salvation partly on Gods will, partly on mans will, which is contrary to what the Apostle teacheth." The *English Annotations* made the same point about "all" referring to every class of individuals (*pro generibus singulorum*), "excluding none by name neither nation nor condition." They added that Christ "hath purchased his Church by his blood," and then qualified the ransom for all as being for all those who believe, citing a string of passages linking atonement to faith. This closely followed Diodati's approach,[106] but the Genevan annotations made it clear that although Paul was here discussing the revealed will of God, "his secret will do make a distinction of his elect" (citing Acts 13:48 among other passages).

It seems, then, that there was careful exegetical work standing behind the doctrinal formulations of the Synod. Their annotations summarized this long-standing interpretative tradition and gave biblical mandate to Dort's conception of definite, intentional atonement, while attempting to demonstrate the flimsy exegetical basis of Arminian interpretations. The annotations were clear, contextually sensitive, and interpreted Scripture with Scripture but did not, as perhaps Diodati or Grotius might be accused of, push doctrinal and polemical issues to the fore.[107] It simply will not do, therefore, to imagine that the theologians at Dort never attempted to wrestle with the fullness of Scripture, that they were interested only in abstract theorizing or logical consistency at the expense of the Bible itself, or that they more than others imposed a systematic grid upon the Word of God. Again, however, we also see from the differences between the English, Dutch, and Genevan annotations that there were a variety of responses to Arminian interpretations, within a recognizable family of Reformed biblical studies.

Tiptoeing through TULIP

The fact that the Canons of Dort carefully left certain questions undecided and were framed to enable subscription by Davenant and Ward is significant. It has been suggested that Davenant held to an Amyraldian view of the order of God's decrees, before Amyraut. There is no real evidence for this,[108] but

---

[106] There were accusations that the *English Annotations* had plagiarized large swathes of Diodati (Muller and Ward, *Scripture and Worship*, 17–19, 66–69).

[107] Marten H. Woudstra, "The Synod and Bible Translation," in *Crisis in the Reformed Churches*, 141, is too positive, however, to claim that there was *no* bias in the "universalist" passages. That may be so in terms of the *translation*, but it is not accurate with regard to the *annotations*.

[108] Moore, *English Hypothetical Universalism*, 188 n. 74, against Thomas, *Extent of Atonement*, 151, 165.

it is clear that Davenant did espouse a variety of Reformed Hypothetical Universalism. It is not true that the Overall-Davenant position (shared to a large extent by others such as Archbishop Ussher) was the definitive Church of England word on the subject, as Peter White claims.[109] The other British delegates did not think so, and neither did the Archbishop of Canterbury.[110] There were many fights still to come over what the official Anglican view was.[111] Yet for tactical, political, or other reasons, Reformed Hypothetical Universalism was allowed to prevail among the British delegation, and to exert some influence on the Synod.

Those who have since held to Reformed varieties of Hypothetical Universalism have sometimes referred to themselves as "four or four-and-a-half point Calvinists." This, however, may well be technically inaccurate for some. Despite disagreements with other delegations, Davenant and Ward happily subscribed to the original pristine statement of "five-point Calvinism." Perhaps, then, others who take a less "strict," non-Genevan view on this issue may also lay claim, historically speaking, to all five petals of the TULIP (though not in the oversimplified way in which this is sometimes defined). Richard Baxter certainly considered himself to be in accord with Dort, despite his famous disagreement with John Owen on the issue.[112] Indeed, he stated that "the meer *Doctrinal Decrees* of the Synod of *Dort* are so moderate and healing, that where Violence hath been forborn, and Reason used, many have been pacified by them."[113] The question, however, must be whether he or Hypothetical Universalists today are as careful to avoid the slippery slope of Arminianism as the British at Dort were, and whether the Reformed are as willing now as they were at Dort to tolerate a certain amount of diversity within their robust internal debates.[114]

---

[109] White, *Predestination*, 191.

[110] Milton, *British Delegation*, 215. George Carleton was aware of some bishops holding to a more Arminian view on the atonement but confessed, "I never thought that their Opinions were the Doctrine of the Church of England" (Hales, *Golden Remains*, ii.180).

[111] See Henry Hickman, *Historia Quinq-Articularis Exarticulata* (London, 1673). From the next century, Augustus Toplady, *Historic Proof of the Doctrinal Calvinism of the Church of England* (London, 1774) is a classic defense of Anglican Reformed credentials on this and other points.

[112] In *Richard Baxter's Confession of his Faith* (London, 1655), 25, Baxter writes, "in the article of the extent of redemption, wherein I am most suspected and accused . . . I do subscribe to the Synod of Dort, without any exception, limitation, or exposition of any word as doubtful and obscure." See Hans Boersma, *A Hot Pepper Corn: Richard Baxter's Doctrine of Justification in Its Seventeenth-Century Context of Controversy* (Vancouver: Regent College Publishing, 1993), 209–19.

[113] Richard Baxter, *The True History of Councils* (London, 1682), 184. Cf. Baxter's views on Dort in *Catholick Theologie* (London, 1675), I.i.124–26; ii.51–54; iii.67–69; II.57–59, 61, and *Universal Redemption of Mankind* (London, 1694).

[114] I wish especially to thank Raymond Blacketer, Martin Foord, Jonathan Moore, and Anthony Milton for commenting on drafts of this chapter.

Controversy on Universal Grace

A HISTORICAL SURVEY OF MOÏSE AMYRAUT'S *BRIEF TRAITTÉ DE LA PREDESTINATION*

Amar Djaballah

Introduction

In 1634, Moïse Amyraut published a book titled *Brief Traitté de la Predestination et de ses principales dependances*.[1] Eighteen months later, in 1636, he defended his main thesis in *Six Sermons* and *Eschantillon de la Doctrine de Calvin Touchant la Predestination*, the latter being an argument for his faithfulness to John Calvin.[2] Amyraut's works courted much controversy, becoming the central topic for a number of national synods in the Reformed Churches of France. While initially avoiding the charge of heresy, Amyraut's teachings were eventually rejected by the Swiss Reformed Churches

---

[1] Moïse Amyraut, *Brief Traitté de la Predestination et de ses principales dependances* (Saumur, France: Jean Lesnier & Isaac Debordes, 1634; 2nd ed., revised and corrected; Saumur, France: Isaac Debordes, 1658). Hereafter the work will be referred to as *BTP*.

[2] Moïse Amyraut, *Six Sermons: De la natvre, estendve, necessité, dispensation, et efficace de l'Euangile* (Saumur, France: Claude Girard & Daniel de Lerpiniere, 1636); published with *Eschantillon de la Doctrine de Calvin Touchant la Predestination*. Amyraut's *Six Sermons* were republished in a volume containing several sermons by him in 1653: *Sermons svr divers textes de la Sainte Ecritvre prononcés en diuers lieux* (Saumur, France: Isaac Desbordes, 1653). *Eschantillon* was republished, with very few changes, along with the second edition of *BTP* in 1658. N.B.: In quoting from Amyraut and other old texts, I have kept the spelling and grammatical peculiarities as found in the sources, without seeking to bring them to uniformity or to conformity with contemporary usage. Though references to the secondary literature on the subject will be made, this article concentrates on the relevant primary documents.

in the *Formula Consensus Helvetica* (1675) but continued to exert influence in Europe and further afield.[3] Debates surrounding Amyraut's presentation of predestination and its relation to Christ's atonement—now known as "Amyraldianism"—have continued to the present day.[4] Indeed, it would not be untrue to say that evangelicals at large have been impacted by the discussion: knowingly or unknowingly, a form of Amyraldianism (Hypothetical or Conditional Universalism) is sometimes the default position on the atonement for most evangelicals with Reformed leanings.[5] Nevertheless, even among those who hold to "Amyraldian" positions on predestination and the atonement, many are unfamiliar with Amyraut's theses on the doctrines. This is due mainly to the fact that his main thesis, *Brief Traitté*, and its concomitant works were written in seventeenth-century French and have not been translated into English.

The purpose of this chapter is not to provide a comprehensive critique of

---

[3] Amyraut's theological contribution, especially in relation to the doctrines of predestination and atonement, was studied quite regularly, it would seem, in the eighteenth and nineteenth centuries, as shown by the number of theses at Protestant schools and not a few books. See Charles Edmond Saigey, "Moïse Amyraut. Sa vie et ses écrits" (Faculté de théologie protestante de Strasbourg, 1849); Ernest Brette, "Du système de Moïse Amyraut, désigné sous le nom d'universalisme hypothétique" (Faculté de théologie protestante de Montauban, 1855); André Sabatier, "Etude historique sur l'universalisme hypothétique de Moïse Amyraut" (Faculté de théologie protestante de Montauban, 1867); Théodore-Ernest Roehrich, "La doctrine de la prédestination et l'école de Saumur" (Faculté de théologie protestante de Strasbourg, 1867); and Marc Fraissinet, "Essai sur la morale d'Amyraut" (Faculté de théologie protestante de Montauban, 1889).

[4] It has been quite thoroughly investigated in the twentieth century in some major contributions: Jürgen Moltmann, "Gnadenbund und Gnadenwahl: Die Prädestinationslehre des Moyse Amyraut, dargestellt im Zusammenhang der heilsgeschichtlich-foederal theologischen Tradition der Akademie von Saumur" (doctoral thesis, University of Göttingen, 1951); idem, "Prädestination und Heilsgeschichte bei Moyse Amyraut," *Zeitschrift für Kirchengeschichte* 65 (1953–1954): 270–303; Lawrence Proctor, "The Theology of Moïse Amyraut Considered as a Reaction against Seventeenth-Century Calvinism" (doctoral thesis, University of Leeds, 1952); François Laplanche, *Orthodoxie et prédication: L'œuvre d'Amyraut et la querelle de la grâce universelle* (Paris: PUF, 1965; revised version of a doctoral thesis, University of Angers, 1954); Roger R. Nicole, "Moyse Amyraut (1596–1664) and the Controversy on Universal Grace. First Phase (1634–1637)" (PhD diss., Harvard University, 1966; hereafter cited as "Moyse Amyraut"); the work contains a very full bibliography that was updated in *Moyse Amyraut: A Bibliography: With Special Reference to the Controversy on Universal Grace*, Garland Reference Library of the Humanities, vol. 258 (New York and London: Garland, 1981); Brian G. Armstrong, *Calvinism and the Amyraut Heresy: Protestant Scholasticism and Humanism in Seventeenth-Century France* (Madison: University of Wisconsin Press, 1969), hereafter cited as *CAH*; the work also contains an important bibliography, and appendices where the author interacts with the most important works published at the time; Frans P. van Stam, *The Controversy over the Theology of Saumur, 1635–1650: Disrupting Debates among the Huguenots in Complicated Circumstances* (Amsterdam and Maarsen: APA-Holland University, 1988). More recent presentations include G. Michael Thomas, *The Extent of the Atonement* (Carlisle, UK: Paternoster, 1997); Alan C. Clifford, *Atonement and Justification: English Evangelical Theology, 1640–1790. An Evaluation* (Oxford: Clarendon, 1990); idem, *Amyraut Affirmed* (Norwich, UK: Charenton Reformed, 2004). Richard A. Muller, recognized specialist of post-Reformation Reformed theology, has contributed a number of writings in the field; they will be mentioned below.

[5] While sharing various similarities with British Hypothetical Universalism, the difference between the two positions centers mainly on the order of decrees. As will be shown, Amyraut believed that, logically speaking, the decree of election comes after the decree of redemption. Hypothetical Universalists of the British mold affirmed Christ's universal atonement for all on the condition of faith, but did not necessarily place election after redemption in the order of decrees. On British Hypothetical Universalism, see Jonathan D. Moore, *English Hypothetical Universalism: John Preston and the Softening of Reformed Theology* (Grand Rapids, MI: Eerdmans, 2007); idem, "The Extent of the Atonement: English Hypothetical Universalism versus Particular Redemption," in *Drawn into Controversie: Reformed Theological Diversity and Debates within Seventeenth-Century British Puritanism*, ed. Michael A. G. Haykin and Mark Jones (Göttingen, Germany: Vandenhoeck & Ruprecht, 2011), 124–61.

Amyraut's teaching on predestination and the atonement but rather to present a historical survey of Amyraut and his writings and the controversy that ensued as a result of their publication. To date, there is no detailed, published presentation of Amyraut's main theses in the English language, and so this chapter aims to provide just that.[6] Those who wish to engage with Amyraut and Amyraldianism from historical, biblical, theological, or pastoral perspectives will have to look elsewhere.[7] This chapter aims to be a helpful resource for engaging with Amyraut's position while avoiding hagiography on the one side and caricature and misrepresentation on the other.

Method

I propose to present the doctrine of "Hypothetical Universalism" as expounded by Amyraut in the *Brief Traitté*. It has been said that the doctrine proposed by Amyraut was the most serious discussion that agitated the Protestant churches in France in the first half of the seventeenth century.[8] Since Amyraut's works have provoked a number of heated debates, then and more recently, it seems prudent to adopt the following methodological perspective: (I) understand Amyraut himself: his background and upbringing, his education and theological training; (II–III) present the main tenets of Amyraut's thesis on predestination as contained in *Brief Traitté*; (IV) trace the subsequent historical controversy over grace in France and beyond; and finally, (V) provide some brief examples of Amyraldianism in evangelical theology in the last century.

In all this, we should remember that Amyraut wrote as a professor of theology in a confessional Reformed academy and that he was cleared of accusations of heresy by a national synod and allowed to teach theology until his death. Hence, notwithstanding the *Wirkungsgeschichte* (reception history) of his theses in the history of Reformed thought, he should be studied as a member of the Reformed theological community, with whom one may differ,

---

[6] Nicole, "Moyse Amyraut," 37–66, does contain a very useful summary of Amyraut's work, but it has not been published. Armstrong's *CAH* stops short of providing an outline of the tenets of Amyraut's main theses: "For this reason I shall not give a systematic analysis of the *Brief Traitté*, but shall utilize its contents by relating them to the more complete presentation of his thought found in the various answers Amyraut gave to the critics of his *Brief Traitté*" (171). Two other works have sought to summarize the *Brief Traitté*, but these have been written in German and French (Alexander Schweizer, *Die Protestantischen Centraldogmen in ihrer Entwicklung innerhalb der reformierten Kirche*, 2 vols. [Zurich, 1854–1856], 2:279–97; and Laplanche, *Orthodoxie et prédication*, 87–108).

[7] For a short general critique, see Roger R. Nicole, "Brief Survey of the Controversy on Universal Grace (1634–1661)," *Standing Forth: Collected Writings of Roger Nicole* (Ross-shire, UK: Mentor, 2002), 313–30 (322–25). See also, Donald Macleod, "Definite Atonement and the Divine Decree," chapter 15 in this volume.

[8] The debated questions have been set in context, with unequal success, in the various publications referred to in n. 4.

not as an adversary to reduce to silence.[9] This assumption is at the basis of the following presentation.

I. Biography of Moïse Amyraut (1596–1664)[10]

Moïse Amyraut, as he is known in French[11] (Moses Amyraldus, in English), was born in 1596 at Bourgueil, in Touraine, in the same year and region as René Descartes, an interesting coincidence in the light of the charge of rationalism brought against Amyraut.[12] He first undertook law studies and succeeded in obtaining his Licentiate within one year (1616), by studying fourteen hours a day. Thereafter, under the influence of a compatriot Reformed minister from Saumur, Samuel Bouchereau, who was impressed by his great intellectual gifts, Amyraut was brought to consider an ecclesiastical vocation and thus to undertake theological studies. The reading of Calvin's *Institution de la religion chrétienne* convinced him to take that route. Initially, he experienced opposition from his father, who was preparing him to succeed his uncle in the charges of seneschal but later agreed to his son's request to abandon law for the study of theology. Amyraut transferred to the Reformed Academy of Saumur, founded by a national synod of French Reformed Churches in 1598 (though the school began its operations only in 1604), under the influence of Philippe Duplessis-Mornay (1549–1623), a Protestant leader and governor of Saumur.

At Saumur, Amyraut studied under the influential John Cameron (1579–1625) from Scotland, star theologian at the time, of whom he became a disciple.[13] Amyraut declared that, second to the Holy Scriptures, he learned

---

[9] See Richard A. Muller, "Diversity in the Reformed Tradition: A Historiographical Introduction," in *Drawn into Controversie*, 11–30; and Carl R. Trueman, *John Owen: Reformed Catholic, Renaissance Man* (Aldershot, UK: Ashgate, 2007), 29–31.

[10] See Pierre Bayle, "Amyraut (Moïse)," in *Dictionnaire historique et critique de Pierre Bayle*, new augmented ed. (Paris: Désoer, Libraire, 1820[1679]), 507–19, the source of much that is contained in this paragraph. See also the biographical entry devoted to him in John Quick, "Amyraut," in *Icones sacrae Gallicanae*, 2 vols. (MS transcript, Dr Williams's Library, London, 1700), 1:958–1028. This text was written around 1695; a handwritten copy was made in 1863, according to Nicole, *Moyse Amyraut, A Bibliography*, 178. Both original manuscript and handwritten copy are available in Dr. Williams's Library, Gordon Square, London.

[11] Several spellings of the name are found: Amyraut, Amiraut, Amyrault, Amyraud, Amyrauld. I have kept the one used by Amyraut himself, who always signed his writings "Amyraut."

[12] Armstrong, *CAH*, 177–82, and appendix 1: "A Note on Amyraut's Rationalism," 273–75.

[13] On John Cameron, see the standard article by Eugène Haag and Emile Haag, *La France protestante* (Paris and Geneva: Cherbuliez, 1852), 3:174–78. The major works on Amyraut in general devote a section to Cameron: hence Laplanche, *Orthodoxie et prédication*, 50–57; Nicole, "Moyse Amyraut," 29–32; Armstrong, *CAH*, 42–70; Thomas, *Extent of Atonement*, 162–86; see also the recent contribution to the debate by Richard A. Muller, "Divine Covenants, Absolute and Conditional: John Cameron and the Early Orthodox Development of Reformed Covenant Theology," *Mid-American Journal of Theology* 17 (2006): 11–56; vast bibliographies are found therein. Born and educated in Glasgow, Cameron went to France in 1600, where he taught Latin and Greek at the Protestant Collège de Bergerac. After teaching philosophy at the Academy of Sedan, serving in a pastorate in Bordeaux, and undertaking

everything worthwhile in theology from Cameron.[14] John Cameron thought that Reformed theology itself needed to be reformed (a desire clearly in line with the *semper reformanda* principle) and did not hesitate to denounce what he perceived in it as narrowness, intolerance, and despotism. Though he wrote very little himself,[15] he intended to train bright young minds who would bring about the desired reformation in the future. Of his extensive influence on Amyraut, mention must be made of his novel doctrine of three covenants, which would deeply impact his pupil.[16]

On the question of particular redemption, Cameron left four letters where he answered objections raised from an Arminian perspective, and they shed some light on his position.[17] He clearly rejects Arminianism; presents, in connection with the death of Christ, the distinction "sufficient for all, efficient for the elect"; and, on the basis of his *foedus hypotheticum*, upholds the proposition that Christ died for all men, but not equally.[18] He illustrates his view with a comparison with the sun: though it shines on all, not all benefit from its light (some may be asleep, while others close their eyes, etc.). "Now, this is not because of any deficiency in the sun; rather it is the fault of the one who makes no use of this benefit. Accordingly, Christ died for all, but his death makes blessed only those who lay hold of him by faith."[19] Nicole opines that Cameron

must have developed his views very considerably in the direction of an emphasis on the universal saving will of God. Otherwise it would be difficult to

---

further studies in Paris, Geneva, and Heidelberg between 1608 and 1618, Cameron was called to occupy the chair of theology at the Academy of Saumur for three years (1618–1621) before being constrained to leave France. Upon returning to his native Scotland, he was appointed divinity principal of the College of Glasgow, where he remained for two years before returning to France in 1623, where he briefly resumed his teaching at Saumur, finishing his theological career as theology professor at the Academy of Montauban.

[14] ". . . tout ce peu que ie puis en l'explication de la saincte Theologie, ie le dois apres la lecture de l'Escriture, aux ouuertures que ce grand homme m'y a données" (Amyraut, "Réplique à Monsieur de L. M.," in *BTP*, 2nd ed., 302). Almost all studies of Cameron (Moltmann, Laplanche, Nicole, Armstrong, Thomas) underscore his influence on Amyraut and consider him "the originator of most of the distinctive elements in the theology of Amyraut" (Thomas, *Extent of Atonement*, 163), though obviously it is Amyraut who gave them the impetus and development that will be debated in the history of theology. For Moltmann, "Gnadenbund," 285, Amyraut's covenant theology is an "*absolut treue Kopie*" of Cameron's.

[15] A large number of Cameron's works have been conveniently gathered in *Ioannis Cameronis Scoto-Britanni Theologi eximij [τὰ Σψξοηέυα], siue Opera partim ab auctore ipso edita, partim post eius obitum vulgata, partim musquam hactenus publicata, vel è Gallico idiomate nunc primum in Latinam linguam translata. In unum collecta, & variis indicibus instructa*, ed. Friedrich Spanheim (Genève: Chouet, 1642, and again in 1659).

[16] See Armstrong, *CAH*, 47–59, and the literature there cited: ". . . it needs to be emphasized that in this explanation of the covenants we find many of the distinctive features of the Salmurian theology" (47–48). The doctrines of different expressions of God's love (for humanity as a whole and for the elect) and the *foedus hypotheticum* (hypothetical covenant) are found in Cameron's writings.

[17] The letters referred to, written between 1610 and 1612, can be found in the edition of Cameron's works already cited in n. 15.

[18] Convenient summary in Armstrong, *CAH*, 47–59.

[19] Letter written in December 1611, as translated in ibid., 59.

understand how several of his students who acknowledged being beholden
to him in this respect should have concurred precisely on this issue.[20]

Yet, for Muller, Cameron's theological work "did not stand in opposition to
the trends in early Reformed orthodoxy but is in fact quite representative of
that development."[21] Muller's assertion here is consistent with his thesis of a
diversity and fluidity of Reformed theology in the sixteenth and seventeenth
centuries.

After spending a few years in the pastorate, first in Saint-Aignan, and,
from 1626 on, in Saumur, where he succeeded John Daillé, Amyraut was
called to occupy the chair of theology at the Academy of Saumur in 1633, at
the same time as two close and capable friends of his: Louis Cappel (1585–
1658) and Josué de la Place (1596–1655). His inaugural thesis for his in-
stallation as professor of theology, articulated in his *Theses theologicae de
sacerdotio Christi*,[22] was much appreciated by his examiners and those who
heard it.[23] In spite of the difficulties he encountered in the following years,
due mostly to his views on predestination and atonement, Amyraut remained
professor at Saumur until his death in 1664, serving as principal of the Academy from 1641 onward. He exercised a deep influence on generations of
theological students there and elsewhere.

It is worth narrating a few episodes of Amyraut's life, before we focus
on our precise topic. During his pastorate at Saumur, Amyraut was commissioned by the National Synod of Charenton in 1631 to present a list of
complaints and grievances at the violation of the Edict of Nantes to the king
of France. He proposed to appear before the king without kneeling, as the
Protestants were obliged to do at the time. Though at first the king refused
his request, Amyraut's patience (it took him fifteen days) and arguments won
him the sympathy of the very powerful Cardinal Richelieu, who convinced
the king to grant the Reformed theologian audience according to the normal
ecclesiastical procedure, and not on his knees. It might also be of interest to
recall that Amyraut was the first preacher to quote Calvin in the pulpit and

---

[20] Nicole, "Moyse Amyraut," 32. Among Cameron's students, Nicole refers to Amyraut, Daillé, La Milletière,
La Place, and Testard. Testard wrote a treaty very similar to Amyraut's *BTP*, though it did not exercise a similar
historical influence. In his response to Cameron's views, André Rivet did not find in them clear formulations of a
universal intent of Christ's death (*contra* Testard and Amyraut). Rightly, Nicole maintains that on this point Cameron's former students (who were quite close to him) must have been better informed of their teacher's theology
than Rivet ("Moyse Amyraut," 104).
[21] Muller, "Divine Covenants, Absolute and Conditional," 13.
[22] Amyraut, *Theses theologicae de sacerdotio Christi* (Saumur, France: Jean Lesnier & Isaac Desbordes, 1633).
[23] Bayle, "Amyraut," 508.

that he was reproached for the practice.[24] Though it may have been at times self-serving, on the one hand, it shows that despite his heavy reliance on Cameron and his known distaste for Beza, Amyraut wanted to be perceived as faithful to Calvin; on the other hand, it shows that for the "orthodox" (well represented at the time by Pierre Du Moulin, who criticized the practice), it was Holy Scripture that was decisive, well ahead of Calvin himself.

Some commentators have highlighted Amyraut's "irenicism" and "ecumenism." They point out his tolerance and support for theological views divergent from his own, exemplified by an episode narrated in Bayle's and Aymon's articles on Amyraut. At the National Reformed Synod of Charenton in 1644–1645, La Place's views on original sin—he denied the doctrine of direct imputation of Adam's sin[25]—came under deserved criticism; though Amyraut claimed not to share his colleague's views, he defended his right to uphold them.[26] The second characteristic, ecumenism (Richard Stauffer referred to Amyraut as a "precursor of ecumenism"[27]), has been documented in Amyraut's expressed desire for and efforts at a rapprochement and unity of the Reformed Church and the Augsburg Communion, as he did not see any irreconcilable differences between them. As he put it, though there were some important differences between the two churches, which he sought to delineate, "Calvinists" and Lutherans were in agreement on "the fundamental points of veritable religion."[28] On the other hand, he considered the differences with the Roman Catholic Church to be such that no reconciliation could be envisaged: ecumenism has its limits, determined by doctrinal and church practices. Yet Amyraut was more than open to converse with individual Roman Catholics

---

[24] What Pierre Du Moulin found exasperating was perhaps not so much the simple referring from the pulpit to Calvin per se as the magnitude and the self-serving aim of the practice. See Pierre Du Moulin, *Esclaircissement Des Controuerses Salmvriennes: Ou Defense de la Doctrine des Eglises Reformees svr l'immutabilité des Decrets de Dieu, l'efficace de la Mort de Christ, la grace universelle, l'impuissance à se convertir: et sur d'autres matieres* (Genève: Imprimerie de Pierre Aubert, 1649), 197, where he complains that Amyraut cites passages from Calvin in his sermons "iusqu'à en reciter cinq pages d'vne halaine" ("reciting up to five pages in one breath"). Du Moulin complains not only that Amyraut quotes Calvin very copiously (many pages at a time) but also that he refers to him in too adulatory terms (198). Amyraut refers to Calvin as "incomparable, excellent, great"; his name is said to be a "benediction"; his words are worthy of "immortality" (see Amyraut, *Sermons svr divers textes de la Sainte Ecritvre prononcés en diuers lieux*, already in the preface, x, and then 15, 19, 20, 24, 49, 60, 69, 74, 76, 79, 90, 94, 101, 153, 207, 242).

[25] La Place promoted the idea that Adam's sin was not imputed to his descendants; however, because of his sin, they are born corrupt, and incur God's displeasure and condemnation because of their corruption.

[26] Bayle, "Amyraut," 509; Jean Aymon, *Actes ecclésiastiques et civils de tous les synodes nationaux des Eglises réformées de France*, 2 vols (The Hague: Charles Delo, 1710), 2:663.

[27] Richard Stauffer, *Moïse Amyraut: un précurseur français de l'œcuménisme* (Paris: Librairie protestante, 1962); cf. also his "Amyraut, Advocate of Reconciliation between Reformed and Lutherans," in Richard Stauffer, *The Quest for Church Unity: From John Calvin to Isaac d'Huisseau* (Allison Park, PA: Pickwick, 1986), 25–51.

[28] Amyraut, *Eirenikon sine de rationepace in religionis negation inter Evangelicos constutuendae consilium* (Saumur, France: Isaac Desbordes, 1662), 1:32–33, 40; 2:341; as quoted in Stauffer, *Quest for Church Unity*, 29.

on theological issues: as we shall see, the *Brief Traitté* is a kind of *apologia*, written as a result of a conversation with a Roman Catholic parishioner.

The circumstances behind the publication of the *Brief Traitté* are told by Amyraut in the "Preface to the Reader" of *Eschantillon de la Doctrine de Calvin Touchant la Predestination*, published shortly after the *Brief Traitté*. During a meeting with a Roman Catholic nobleman ("homme de qualité"[29]) at the home of the Roman Catholic bishop of Chartres, Calvin's doctrine of predestination was attacked as harsh, narrow, and unworthy of God. For Amyraut, such a misunderstanding was quite widespread and could hinder people's desire to embrace the Reformed faith. After a long and cordial discussion with the bishop of Chartres and a meeting with the Roman Catholic gentleman the next day, in which Amyraut expressed his understanding of the doctrine of predestination, in order to alleviate the perceived stumbling blocks, the Salmurian theologian undertook to compose a treatise on the subject.[30] Feeling that that sentiment was no doubt shared by other potential converts to the Reformed faith, Roman Catholics or Arminians, Amyraut undertook to write a treatise that would persuade him and others of the acceptability of a doctrine that was both Calvin's and the Bible's.[31] In his writings of this period, Amyraut gives the strong impression that he views the doctrines he expresses not only as consonant with Scripture but also as faithful to Calvin and the first generation of Reformers, and indeed as compatible with the Canons of Dort. Yet, the influence of his former teacher and mentor, Cameron, is evident in the treatise; in fact, Pierre Bayle comments that, therein, Amyraut "explained the mystery of predestination and of grace according to the hypotheses of Cameron."[32]

II. Main Tenets of Amyraut's *Brief Traitté* (1634; 2nd ed., 1658)

I shall now present the main theses contained in Amyraut's *Brief Traitté* in the order in which they appear in his book.

---

[29] Bayle, *Dictionnaire critique*, 512.

[30] *BTP*, 1st ed., "Au Lecteur," 1: "Mon intention a seulement esté de rendre ceste doctrine qu'on estime communément si difficile & espineuse, capable d'estre comprise de tous . . ." ("My intention has only been to make this doctrine, which is commonly thought so difficult and thorny, capable of being understood by all . . ."). This, very likely, explains Amyraut's choice to write in French, not in Latin, and to treat the subject in non-technical fashion.

[31] Nicole, "Brief Survey," 313–14, mentions Amyraut's desire to offset the charge that the Reformed faith presented "God as arbitrary, unjust, and insincere; creating the reprobates for sin and then punishing them for sinning; offering in the gospel a salvation which he had no intention to convey," thus removing a cause that may have prompted the Reformed to convert to Roman Catholicism. The treatise may also have been written to provide an acceptable basis for the union he desired with the Lutherans.

[32] Bayle, *Dictionnaire critique*, 508.

CHAPTER 1: WHAT IS THE PREDESTINATION IN QUESTION[33]

Before defining "predestination," Amyraut sets forth the theological setting in which to do so: God does not produce his actions without order and purpose; and since man is his highest creature, he took special care to create him with a purpose. In this context, the word "predestination," defined generally, refers to God's providence, "the care that God the Creator of the universe, in his wisdom, shows for the conservation and the conduct of all the things that are and those that are done in the world" (Ps. 115:3; Eph. 1:11; Acts 4:28).[34] More precisely, as Paul makes clear, the word refers to God's ordaining his creation and creatures to the specific purpose he set for them (Rom. 8:29–30; Eph. 1:11, 5).[35] The chapter ends on a discordant note: between the act of creation and God's purpose to make believers conform to the image of Christ, sin entered the world and radically altered the situation, with dramatic consequences; Adam's sin "seems not only to have changed the whole face of the universe but even the whole purpose of his first creation and, if one ought to say so, induced God to make new counsels."[36]

CHAPTER 2: WHY GOD CREATED THE WORLD[37]

To answer the question of the title, Amyraut underscores both God's wisdom ("sapience") and his goodness ("bonté"), on one hand, and the perfect order of his creation, on the other.[38] If it were to act on the intelligence God gave it, creation would respond to the Creator by glorifying him.[39] For God created the world to display his glory and manifest therein his goodness and infinite power. Within creation, man has been singled out by being endowed with a reasonable soul, a ray of God's intelligence, and an integrity that allowed him, from the start, to contemplate the Creator in his creation. This is the principle of virtue in man, which should allow him to live according to God's holiness and goodness. In creating man, God intended that the practice of these virtues

---

[33] *BTP*, 1–9/1–8 (page numbers for first and second editions, respectively): "Que c'est que la Predestination dont il s'agist." N.B.: There are a number of variations in spelling between the two editions of the *Brief Traité*; I have taken quotations from the 1634 edition and kept the spelling as found in this source.

[34] Ibid., 7/6: "[L]e soin que Dieu Createur de l'Vniuers prend en sa sapience & de la conduite de toutes les choses qui sont & qui se font au monde." Scriptures reference in that order; and hereafter.

[35] Ibid., 8/7: The word *predestination* "a esté appliqué a denoter non pas seulement ceste prouidence . . . , mais celle particulierement selon laquelle Dieu les a ordonnés à leur but."

[36] Ibid., 9/8: Adam's sin "semble auoir changé non seulement toute la face de l'vniuers, mais mesmes tout le dessein de sa premiere creation, & s'il faut ainsi parler, induit Dieu à prendre de nouueaux conseils."

[37] Ibid., 10–22/9–19: "*Pourquoy Dieu a creé le monde.*"

[38] Ibid., 10–12/9–10.

[39] Ibid., 11–12/10.

would insure his happiness ("félicité"). This connects with Amyraut's idea on how God manifests his glory: it is not so much the direct display of his glory that is the first aim of creation, "as the exercise of his virtues, from which . . . his glory results."[40] Chief among God's virtues is his goodness, as all of God's creation, intelligent and otherwise, would declare (Ps. 145:9).[41] God's goodness, by its nature, is displayed in *giving* to other than God, with no other reason than itself. In fact, from God's perspective, his glory should not be considered as the primary end of creation; God freely displays his goodness to his creatures, without, as it were, expecting returns for himself.[42] As one can see, ambiguities remain in Amyraut's presentation: if God's glory is presented as the chief end of creation, a strong emphasis is maintained on his goodness, a preeminent attribute set above his power and wisdom.[43]

CHAPTER 3: WHY IN PARTICULAR GOD CREATED MAN[44]

Man was created in a most singular fashion; he was granted privileges none of the other creatures received: a body and feelings, a will and, above all, a reason or understanding ("intelligence" and "entendement") that made him fit to know and glorify his Creator in a unique way. God sought to be glorified by a creature whom he endowed with holiness and reason, and who would thus understand that his happiness lay in seeing God's imprint in the whole of creation. Amyraut, once more, emphasizes God's goodness as seen particularly in the unique prerogative he granted humanity by creating it in his own image.[45] God's image in man is especially seen in the understanding he gave him, as a ray of God's own intelligence.[46] In God, there are two distinct and conjoint qualities ("choses"): his extreme goodness and holiness, on the one hand; his happiness and blessedness, on the other. In creating man in his image, he granted him what was necessary for both qualities: holiness and virtue, and the proper conditions for happiness (Psalm 8; 45:6–7). For man

---

[40] Ibid., 17/15: ". . . la principale fin à laquelle Dieu aura visé en la creation du monde, à la considerer ainsi precisément, n'aura pas tant esté sa propre gloire, comme l'exercice de ses vertus, desquelles comme nous auons dit cy dessus, resulte necessairement la gloire."

[41] Ibid., 17–18/15–16.

[42] Ibid., 21–22/18: "La fin donc à laquelle Dieu a principalement visé en la creation de l'Vniuers, est qu'il a voulu estre bon & en sa nature & en ses effects, en faisant que les choses qui n'estoyent point fussent, & fussent en vn estat extrememement conuenable & heureux, autant comme chacune d'elles pouuoit desirer de bon-heur selon sa nature."

[43] Ibid., 22/19: ". . . est la gloire de celuy qui en leur creation a desployé vne puissance infinie, vne sapience incomprehensible, & vne bonté qui semble encore ici ne sçay comment les surpasser & l'vne & l'autre."

[44] Ibid., 22–30/19–26: *"Pourquoy particulierement Dieu à creé l'homme."*

[45] Ibid., 24–26/21–22.

[46] Ibid., 25–26/22: ". . . mais luy auoit donné en ceste excellente faculté par laquelle il est homme, vn rayon de son intelligence, & par ce moyen le principe des vertus qui le representent."

to be his image, both of these aspects were demanded by God's goodness and wisdom. As holiness and bliss are conjoined and inseparable in God, so must they be in man. Thus, man could not experience God's felicity without being holy: neither God's justice nor his wisdom would suffer such a state of affairs. Man's revolt against his Creator brought about his fall and misery, proportional to the gravity of a fault committed against God's infinite glory and majesty.[47]

CHAPTER 4: WHY GOD PERMITTED THAT THE FIRST MAN WOULD SIN[48]

The question heading chapter 4 follows logically from the previous chapter. If Scripture and our experience clearly show that man has fallen from his created state of blessedness, a difficult question ensues: Why did God, who showed such a superior goodness in creating man, allow Satan to tempt successfully the latter, and to provoke a situation in which man turned away from God in sin and revolt, and fell into the miserable state that is presently his? If God could have stopped him from doing so, why did he not take such an action? If he could not, how could he be said to be all-powerful?[49] Alternatively, how is it possible that the all-powerful Creator allowed the created humanity and Satan, also a created being, to resist and overcome his will? Amyraut rejects a first facile answer: explaining man's sin by his freedom. Appealing to God's counsel, Amyraut justly remarks that man's free decisions were not excluded from God's foreknowledge.[50] Moreover, God could have created man in such a way that, without violating his will, man would have accomplished perfectly God's will.[51] Having rejected this motive, Amyraut considers the role played by man's understanding ("entendement"): it must have presented to the will, which is submissive to it, reasons to suggest that the proposed evil acts are useful and advantageous (e.g., the fruit was good for eating, was desirable to the eye, and would grant him a science that would make him equal to God; Gen. 3:6). Sin is thus due to a vicious debilitation of man's understanding that resulted in his being deceived by Satan (cf. 2 Cor. 11:3). Man's will is

---

[47] Ibid., 29–30/24–26.

[48] Ibid., 31–47/26–39: "*Pourquoy Dieu a permis que le premier homme pechast.*"

[49] Ibid., 32/27. In Amyraut's formulation of the question, one can recognize Leibniz's future formulation of the problem of evil (see Gottfried W. Leibniz, *Theodicy: Essays on the Goodness of God, the Freedom of Man, and the Origin of Evil*, 1710).

[50] *BTP*, 33/28.

[51] Ibid., 33/28: ". . . il ait sçeu trouuer le moyen de leur donner des facultez qu'il peust regir & gouuerner, pour executer au monde tout ce qu'il luy plaist sans leur faire aucune contrainte & sans les despoüiller des conditions & des inclinations qu'il leur a dónnees . . ."

not to blame, for it followed the lead of a defective reason. But in the end, that too was allowed by God. Other possibilities are evoked: God could have illuminated man's understanding without violating his freedom; Adam would have uncovered the deceitfulness of Satan, thus maintaining the knowledge of truth, the fundamental and most excellent function of his mind. Or, would it not have been better for God not to have given man such a freedom (or to have removed it after it was given), than to have allowed him to use it for his perdition? One can see that man's freedom was defective in some sense, since it provoked evil decisions against the will of God and was detrimental to man's happiness.[52] One should not go beyond these attempted explanations: due to debilitating deficiencies of his understanding and perversions of his will, man has sinned; and God allowed it. Scripture does not allow us to probe this mystery beyond the realization of its reality; proper human humility should incline us to realize that our finite minds will not be able to comprehend this mystery.[53] God's providential dealings narrated in Scripture show that God not only allows evil to occur but uses it for his glory: Joseph being sold by his brothers; the evil Pharaoh of Egypt rising to power, Eli's sons' reprehensible sins, Judas's betrayal of his Lord; none of these detracts from God's sovereign governance—he displays his rule also in hardening the heart of sinners.[54] There is no explanation beyond this; the Spirit thus intimates to us that there is an abyssal mystery that we cannot solve.

Nevertheless, in view of the strong biblical assertion of God's love and goodness, Amyraut feels constrained to return to his fundamental question: Why did God not maintain Adam, created in his image, in a condition of blessedness? He advances a plausible (and perhaps rationalist) explanation: Adam's created perfection was *natural* and his blessedness was hence also *natural*. God had decreed to create man in a condition *as perfect as his nature would allow*, a step necessary *en route* to a supernatural state that God had destined for him. Creating him directly with supernatural capabilities would have been against his wisdom.[55]

---

[52] Ibid., 35/29–30.
[53] Ibid., 37–38/32: "Comme si expressement le S. Esprit auoit voulu tirer le rideau dessus, & nous apprendre qu'il y a là dedans des abysmes qu'il est impossible que l'on sonde."
[54] Ibid., 36–37/31–32.
[55] Ibid., 43–44/37: "[La nature a] touiours cela de defectueux qu'elle est muable. . . . Si donc Dieu eust creé l'hóme tel qu'il eust esté impossible qu'il pechast, il ne l'eust pas mis en l'estat de la nature, mais en vne condition surnaturelle. [. . . Faire passer Adam] du non estre, dont il auoit esté tiré, a vn estat surnaturel, sans esprouuer le milieu de la condition de la nature, n'eust pas esté chose conuenable a ceste intelligence qui conduit tout auec vne si merueilleuse sapience." This distinction is important to Amyraut, for he returns to it in later chapters: ibid., 62/53, and 68–69/58.

CHAPTER 5: WHAT ARE THE CONSEQUENCES
OF THE SIN OF THE FIRST MAN[56]

This chapter deals with the double consequences of man's fall: his inability to self-recover his original state (due to the darkening of his understanding and a self-love he developed in his state of sin), and the transmission of corruption and misery to all his descendants, a transmission as unavoidable as that of life itself, that affects body and soul.[57] Man's sinful condition is so corrupt that Scripture calls it being "slaves" to sin (Rom. 6:16–17). Clearly, Amyraut teaches a universal depravity of man, and this recognition shows, on his part, "a decided cleavage from the Arminian line of thinking."[58] Yet his understanding of Adam's transmitted sin mainly in terms of inherited corruption may have prepared the way for Josué de la Place's views of mediate imputation that would be condemned at the Synod of Charenton in 1644–1645. The Synod explicitly "condemned the said doctrine in that it restrained the nature of original sin only to the hereditary corruption of Adam's posterity, without imputing to it the first sin by which Adam fell."[59]

CHAPTER 6: WHAT WAS GOD'S PURPOSE FOR
SENDING HIS SON TO THE WORLD[60]

This chapter's locus, expressed in its title, is fundamental to our subject. Radical and radically evil though it is, the sinful condition of humanity did

---

The distinction supports a weighty argument of Amyraut; his commentators have related it to his *heilsgeschichtlich* theology and the doctrine of the three covenants which he partly inherited from Cameron. Nicole, "Moyse Amyraut," 42, comments on this feature: "the distinction between an order or covenant of nature implied in original creation, and a supernatural order or covenant to which man is to graduate according to God's design," is an outlook that related to Amyraut's doctrine of the three covenants. For Moltmann, "Prädestination und Heilsgeschichte bei Moyse Amyraut," 275, this doctrine signaled affinities between Amyraut's theology and Federal theology. Moreover, one may discern here rationalistic elements perceived by Armstrong and others: as if, in spite of his denegation, Amyraut could not resist the urge to explain what cannot be explained: How was sin possible?

[56] *BTP*, 47–61/ 40–51: "*Quelles sont les suites du peché du premier homme.*"
[57] Ibid., 47/40: "*L'vne que de soy-mesme il ne s'en pourroit releuer: L'autre, qu'en ceste condamnation il enueloperoit toute sa race.*" On the state of sin, Amyraut writes: "*. . . le premier effect du peché est de laisser de si espaisses tenebres en l'entendement, que desormais il ne puisse estre esclairci que par vne lumiere surnaturelle*" (48/41). Toward the end of this chapter, he reiterates the gravity of man's corruption and sinful condition (58–59/49–50). In 1647, he develops fully his understanding in *De libero Hominis Arbitrio Disputatio* (Saumur, France: Lesnier, 1647). Amyraut's emphasis on the preeminence of understanding over the will and emotions, and his explanation of the fall mainly in terms of man's understanding being utterly darkened (*BTP*, 48/40–41), have been interpreted as evidence of rationalism in his thought, perhaps to counter Roman Catholic fideism. See David W. Sabean, "The Theological Rationalism of Moïse Amyraut," *Archiv für Reformationsgeschichte* 55 (1964): 204–16, and especially Armstrong, *CAH*, 101–102, 179–80, 273–75. Nicole, "Moyse Amyraut," 44, deemed this approach "very congenial to Cartesian philosophy which was to exercise a considerable sway in Saumur," an ironic situation in view of the accusation of rationalism that Armstrong levels frequently at Amyraut's adversaries.
[58] Nicole, "Moyse Amyraut," 44.
[59] Aymon, *Tous les Synodes*, 2:680 (chapter 14, article 1). Laplanche, *Orthodoxie et prédication*, 108, goes so far as to say, ". . . on the problem of the transmission of original sin, Amyraut adopts the doctrine of his colleague and friend Josué de la Place."
[60] *BTP*, 61–77/52–65: "*Quel a esté le dessein de Dieu en l'enuoy de son Fils au monde.*"

not escape God's sovereign control. From all eternity, he foresaw that Adam would not resist Satan's temptation; he foreknew and, permissively, willed that mankind would revolt against him, fall into sin, and be in danger of his judgment.[61] However, if God's justice required that humanity and the world be left to perish, his compassion sought their salvation.[62] In fact, God resolved to put man in a better, supernatural condition, superior to the first one, wherein he could not fail his Creator. But man's offense was committed against an infinite God: only an infinite price could pay for it, and man himself was and is totally unable to satisfy such a demand. Resolving to restore man's nature to its integrity and to restore his blessedness by sparing him from the just judgment his sin deserved, God ordained that his Son would take our human nature: hence the incarnation of the Son of God. The Lord had two purposes in view: the first was to suffer death for our sins and disobedience, in order to satisfy God's infinite justice as our Guarantor and Surety.[63] The Son, being the eternally blessed God, was able, by the "infinite value" of his sufferings, to satisfy God's infinite justice.[64] Satisfaction is predicated on the basis of substitution, and substitution itself was possible on the fulfillment of three conditions: the Son had taken our human nature, the Father explicitly ordered the redemptive action contemplated, and Christ willingly submitted to his Father's will. For whom did Christ's death satisfy God's justice?

In this chapter, Amyraut is not very explicit: if the incarnation enabled the Son "to procure salvation for *mankind* [du genre humain]," his sufferings are for "*our* offenses [pour nos offenses]."[65] The second aim of Christ's incarnation and sufferings was to provide him with "the right and honor to accomplish himself the work of their salvation and to be their model" in holy living, in relationship to the Father, in the life in the Spirit, in union with him, in this life and the life to come.[66] Scripture's promise is that believers will be united with Christ, and will be conformed to his "glorious body [corps glorieux]."[67] Our salvation will be brought to its fulfillment with our resurrection from the dead, as the Lord promised (John 6:39–40; 1:12), and the

---

[61] Ibid., 64/54.
[62] Ibid., 65/55.
[63] Ibid., 72/61: "en se constituant nostre pleige."
[64] Ibid., 73/61–62: "Et en ce qu'il estoit Dieu benit eternellement, il estoit capable de faire que ceste sienne souffrance en qualité de peine pour nos offences, equipollast à leur demerite, & par ce moyen satisfist par sa valeur infinie à la iustice diuine."
[65] Ibid., 73/61, emphasis added. Amyraut had already referred, earlier in the paragraph, to Christ accomplishing the "redemption of others" ("la redemption des autres").
[66] Ibid., 73/62: "il eust le droit & l'honneur d'accomplir luy mesme l'oeuure de leur salut & d'en estre le modele."
[67] Ibid., 74/62.

apostles confirmed in different ways (2 Pet. 1:4; 1 John 3:9; 4:7; Rom. 8:16–17).[68] Amyraut subsumes all these graces under the labels of "adoption," for it is a grace of redemption with no contribution from human nature; and "adoption in Christ," for we have them by his merits and mediation.[69] In this chapter, Amyraut maintains strongly a penal and substitutionary atonement: in willingly accepting God's plan to suffer vicariously for sinners, Jesus took their place; he took upon his person crimes he himself did not commit; their sins have been transferred upon him.[70] Moreover, rich blessings accrue for them from his redemptive work. Nonetheless, the question remains: What is the intent and extent of Christ's redemptive work?

CHAPTER 7: WHAT IS THE NATURE OF THE DECREE BY WHICH GOD HAS ORDAINED TO ACCOMPLISH THIS PURPOSE, EITHER FOR ITS EXTENT OR FOR THE CONDITION ON WHICH IT DEPENDS[71]

This chapter is central to Amyraut's treatise. In setting forth his view on the intent and extent of the atonement procured by Christ, he seeks to answer his basic question: how can one conciliate in God a universal intent of salvation and the decree of predestination as expressed in Reformed theology? The question of formulation being vital, I shall quote Amyraut's text at length:

> The misery of men being equal and universal [equal omitted], and the desire that God had to deliver them from it through the means of such a great Redeemer proceeding from the compassion he had upon them, as upon his creatures fallen into such great misery, and since they are equally [indifferently] his creatures, the grace of redemption he offered to them and obtained for them must have been equal and universal [equal omitted], on the condition that they find themselves equally [all] ready to receive it. And thus far [And in this and thus far], there is no difference between them. The Redeemer has been taken from their race and made a participant of the same flesh and blood as all of them, to wit of the same human nature conjoined in him to the divine in a unity of person. The sacrifice he offered for the propitiation of their offenses, has been equally for all [equally omitted]; and

---

[68] Scriptures cited in this order (ibid., 75–76/64).

[69] Ibid., 76–77/64–65.

[70] The point is emphasized by Armstrong, *CAH*, 174: "Amyraut taught that the sufferings and death of Jesus were vicarious in that Jesus took the place of sinners, that their guilt and punishment were transferred to him."

[71] *BTP*, 77–90/65–76: "*Quelle est la nature du decret [conseil ou de la volonté] par lequel Dieu a ordonné d'accomplir ce dessein, soit pour son estenduë, soit pour la condition dont il depend [qui y est annexée: which is annexed to it].*" In this section, I indicate within brackets the changes introduced in the 1658 edition of the *Traitté*. These changes should be taken into consideration, whether they were constrained only by the need to satisfy the demands of the authorities of the time (specially the Synod of Alençon), to remove language offensive to the strict "Calvinists" of the day, or/and (one wonders) if they represent Amyraut's convictions.

the salvation that he received from his Father in order to communicate it to men through the sanctification of the Spirit, and the glorification of the body, is intended equally for all [equally omitted], provided I say, that the necessary disposition to receive it is also equal [in all].[72]

Amyraut affirms clearly the universality of salvation on condition of faith. He establishes this conviction on the basis of three propositions: (1) Men, who are equal in creation, partook equally of the misery of sin. (Amyraut has shown previously the universal reality of sin, corruption, and suffering.) (2) God's compassion to deliver humanity from the bonds of sin must be the same: universal. (3) In the incarnation, the Son of God partook of human nature as such; hence the sacrifice he offered must be equally for all. The conclusion follows: the salvation the Son received from his Father to communicate to sinners is intended for all, provided that they receive it by faith. (There are no Scriptures quoted in this long paragraph.)

Thereafter, Amyraut introduces a brief salvation history narrative to show that God's promises to triumph over evil have been fulfilled through his promises to and covenants with Abraham and Israel: the limitations of the manifestation of God's saving grace in the OT were both temporary (the NT economy put an end to it) and the means by which Christ becomes the Savior of the world (through Abraham's posterity, salvation is extended from the Jews to the Gentiles).[73]

It is possible that at this point a major objection was raised in Amyraut's own mind by his asserted universalism. In fact, Nicole surmises that Amyraut must have been

> singularly impressed by the force of the objection that was raised to his view of universal saving intent: "If God desired to save all men, why did He not see to it that all men were confronted with the Gospel call?" The

---

[72] Ibid., 77–78/65–66: "La misere des hommes estant egale & vniuerselle [egale omitted], & le desir que Dieu a eu de les en deliurer par le moyen d'vn si grand Redempteur, procedant de la compassion qu'il a euë d'eux, comme de ses creatures tombées en vne si grande ruine, puis qu'ils sont ses creatures egalement [egalement replaced by indifferemment], la grace de la redemption qu'il leur a offerte & procurée a deu estre egale & vniuerselle [egale omitted], pourueu qu'aussi ils se trouuassent egalement [changed to tous] disposés à la receuoir. Et iusques là il n'y a nulle [Et en cela, ny iusques là, il n'y a point de] difference entr'eux. Le Redempteur a esté pris de leur race, & fait participant de mesme chair & de mesme sang auec eux tous, c'est à dire, d'vne mesme nature humaine coniointe en luy auec la diuine en vnité de personne. Le sacrifice qu'il a offert pour la propitiation de leurs offenses, a esté egalement [omitted] pour tous; & le salut qu'il a receu de son Pere pour le communiquer aux hommes en la sanctification de l'Esprit & en la glorification du corps, est destiné egalement [omitted] à tous, pourueu, di-je, que la disposition necessaire pour le receuoir soit egale [egale replaced by en tous] de mesme." In the above quotation in the second edition, five instances of the words "equal" or "equally" have been removed, and two have been changed but not removed (and many more elsewhere in the *Brief Traitté*). In each case, they do not alter substantially Amyraut's views.
[73] Ibid., 79–80/67–68, with quotations from Romans 1:14 and Acts 10:34–35; 13:46–47.

manifest limitations of the external call demand a particular rather than a universal saving will.[74]

For the simple fact is that there are peoples and nations who have never heard the gospel. How then can one maintain the universality of God's saving intention? Amyraut's response to this objection is his view of two modes of preaching, with two kinds of faith that may respond to them. In principle, there are two possible ways of salvation: the preaching of the gospel, that gives rise to faith in the context of saving knowledge of Christ; and natural revelation, that is sufficient to bring people to Christ on the condition that they are ready to accept the testimonies God gives of his mercy.[75] None are in principle excluded, not even those nations and individuals that never heard of Christ nor had access to any revealed knowledge of God; his patience and temporal blessings constitute a "sufficient preaching, if they would take heed of it";[76] they would then understand that there is salvation upon repentance and faith.[77] Amyraut goes so far as to assert that even if such "a person did know not distinctly the name of Christ, and knew nothing of the manner in which he obtained for us redemption, he would, nonetheless, be participant in the remission of his sins, in the sanctification of his spirit, and the glorious immortality."[78] Amyraut cites here 1 John 2:2, 1 Timothy 2:4–5 (cited wrongly as 4:4–5), and Titus 2:11.[79]

In this context Amyraut writes a long digression on John 3:16.[80] Though, on the surface, this text seems to limit God's salvation to those who believe, it is in fact coherent, according to Amyraut, with the proposals he has just made. He develops a theory of two different faiths, which respond to two different sorts of preaching. The apostolic preaching of the Word issues in faith based on knowledge; the other is dependent solely on God's providence and his patience; but, if it were not for men's blindness, this providential preaching,

[74] Nicole, "Moyse Amyraut," 51.
[75] *BTP*, 80–81/68: "Et bien qu'il y ait plusieurs nations vers lesquelles peut-estre la claire predication de l'Euangile n'est point encore paruenuë par la bouche des Apostres, ni de leurs descendans, & qui n'ont aucune distincte cognoissance du Sauueur du monde, il ne faut pas penser pourtant qu'il y ait ni aucun peuple, ni mesmes aucun homme exclus par la volonté de Dieu, du salut qu'il a acquis au genre humain, pourueu qu'il face son profit des tesmoignages de misericorde que Dieu luy donne."
[76] Ibid., 81/68: "vne predicatió suffisante, s'ils y estoyent attentifs."
[77] Ibid., 80–82/68–69. See remarks on Amyraut's *Six Sermons* below (sermon 2).
[78] *BTP*, 82/69: ". . . qu'il ne cognust pas distinctement le nom de Christ, & qu'il n'eust rien appris de la maniere en laquelle il nous a obtenu la redemption, il ne laisseroit pas pourtant d'en estre participant en la remission de ses pechez, en la sanctification de son esprit, & en l'immortalité glorieuse."
[79] Ibid., 82–83/70.
[80] Ibid., 83/70.

though destitute of the distinct knowledge of the Redeemer preached in the gospel, would nonetheless be sufficient to allow men to enjoy the salvation of which he is the author.[81]

Amyraut's apologetic concern is paramount here, for he wants to avoid a conception wherein God could be conceived as unjust; hence his desire to show that there can be neither nations nor individuals who may *a priori* think of themselves as excluded from salvation by God. Not only does God not exclude anyone from salvation, but he invites the whole world and wishes ("il serait bien aise"; literally, "he would be delighted") that the world would turn to him for salvation.[82] Propitiation is for all, salvation is presented to all, if they would believe. It thus, on the surface of things, depends on man's decision to accept the offered salvation: "All that depends on this condition, that they prove not to be unworthy of it."[83] God wants the salvation of all, provided that they do not refuse it, but believe. This is a key part of Amyraut's position on the atonement.

For Amyraut, God's mercy and the hope of salvation are possible because God's justice has been satisfied at the cross: sin has been dealt with, on the condition that men do not show themselves to be unworthy of it.[84] Before the Redeemer could accomplish salvation in us, it was necessary for men to receive him and come to him (John 3:14–16; 1 John 5:9–10). God's grace in providing salvation by sending his Son into the world—and all that he suffered—is universal and presented to all.[85] But the condition of believing in his Son means that, however great God's love toward humanity, he still offers salvation to men on the condition that they do not refuse it: ". . . these words, *God wants the salvation of all men*, necessarily receive this limitation, *as long as they believe*. If they do not believe, he does not want it."[86]

---

[81] Ibid., 84–85/71: This preaching is "par l'entremise de la prouidence de Dieu seulement, qui conserue le monde nonobstant son iniquité, & l'inuite à repentance par sa longue patience, laquelle, si les hommes n'estoyent point naturellement aueugles & obstinez en leur aueuglement, seroit capable d'engendrer en eux vne foy en [persuasion de] la misericorde de Dieu, destituee à la verité de la distincte cognoissance de ce Redempteur que l'Euangile nous presche, neantmoins suffisante pour rendre les hommes iouyssans du salut duquel il est autheur."

[82] Ibid., 83/70: "[I]l seroit bien aise que tout le monde s'en approchast, voire il y conuie tout le monde, comme estant vne grace laquelle il a destinee à tout le genre humain, s'il ne s'en monstre point indigne [if they prove not to be unworthy of it]" (reference to Titus 2:11: "for which reason St. Paul calls it a *saving grace for all men* [*grace salutaire à tous hommes*]"; emphasis original).

[83] Ibid., 85/72: "Mais tout cela depend de ceste condition, qu'ils ne s'en monstrent pas indignes."

[84] Ibid., 85/72: "s'ils ne s'en móstrent point indignes."

[85] Ibid., 89/75–76.

[86] Ibid., 89–90/76: ". . . ces paroles, *Dieu veut le salut de tous les hommes*, reçoiuent necessairement ceste limitation, *pourueu qu'ils croyent*. S'ils ne croyent point, il ne le veut pas."

In sum, the affirmation of a double will of God constrains the Salmurian theologian to conclude that God's marvelous charity ("merveilleuse charité") by itself is incapable of bringing salvation; it is effectively limited by man's decision and action to believe or refuse to do so: "This will to render the grace of salvation universal and common to all human beings is so conditional that without the fulfilment of the condition it is entirely inefficacious."[87] Which brings Amyraut to the next consideration.

CHAPTER 8: WHAT IS, AFTER SIN, MAN'S INABILITY
FOR THE ACCOMPLISHING OF THIS CONDITION[88]

This chapter is devoted to an exposition of the radical depravity of man, a doctrine that is treated in a classical Reformed understanding, and that also plays an important role in Amyraut's particular scheme. Man's total depravity does not allow him to receive the free gift of redemption offered by God: his darkened mind provokes a spiritual blindness that refuses God's grace; both experience and Scripture show that man's heart is corrupted (Rom. 6:20; 8:7; Ezek. 36:26; Eph. 2:2); he is a willing slave to sin, refuses to see the light of God's testimony, is dead in his sins, incapable of receiving God's salvation wrought by Christ; this refusal itself is a sin that exacerbates man's guilt before God.[89] God's universal redemption accomplished by Christ on the cross cannot become effective because man will not fulfill the conditions of salvation: to believe. This unbelief is "ordinary" and universal. For if some do believe, their faith is due to God's efficient grace in them: only he can draw them to himself (e.g., John 6:44).[90] Man's inability to believe is rooted deeply in him, not in some outside constraint; hence, he is guilty of his inability to turn to God in faith. Man's culpability is aggravated by the realization that it is due neither to a difficulty in the message nor to the absence in him of adequate faculties to receive the message: it is due solely to his sin.[91] Here, Amyraut is in line with the teaching of Scripture, Calvin, and the Canons of Dort.

---

[87] Ibid., 90/76: "Ceste volonté de rendre la grace du salut vniuerselle & cómune à tous les humains estant tellement conditionnelle, que sans l'accomplissement de la condition, elle est entierement inefficacieuse."
[88] Ibid., 90–102/77–86: "*Quelle est depuis le peché l'impuissance de l'homme pour l'accomplissement de ceste condition.*"
[89] Ibid., 93–98/80–83.
[90] Ibid., 95–96/81–82.
[91] Ibid., 100–101/85–86. The universal character of the covenant of grace, which plays a paramount role elsewhere in Amyraut's writings, is not mentioned here.

CHAPTER 9: WHAT IS THE ELECTION AND PREDESTINATION OF GOD
BY WHICH HE ORDAINED TO ACCOMPLISH THIS CONDITION IN SOME
AND TO LEAVE THE OTHERS TO THEMSELVES, AND WHAT IS ITS CAUSE[92]

Amyraut begins chapter 9 as follows: "The nature of humanity was such that
if God, in sending his Son into the world, had only determined to offer him
as Redeemer equally [omitted] and universally to all . . . the sufferings of
his Son [would have been] entirely in vain."[93] Amyraut then expounds the
solution to man's plight: moved by his mercy, God determined to bestow
his Spirit on some among fallen humanity; out of his mercy, God elects
some to believe. In them, he vanquishes all resistance to the manifestation
of his truth, conquers the corruption of their will, and brings them to faith
willingly, abandoning others to their corruption and their ensuing perdition.[94]
In so doing, God remains just: if he creates in some the condition necessary to salvation (faith), he does not cause unbelief in the rest: the cause is
their blindness and perverted heart.[95] A question remains, however: men are
equally miserable in their perdition and guilty in their corruption; there is
no difference in them, nothing in their nature or behavior that would bring
favor to some and not to others; therefore, on what basis did God choose
some to faith and salvation, leaving the rest to eternal perdition? Scripture
does not answer, except to say that "it depends absolutely on God using his
mercy with a complete freedom, to which we can ascribe no other cause but
his will."[96] God's decree and ensuing action are due solely to his will and
good pleasure.[97] Yet, God's dealings are not arbitrary: here, as everywhere
else, God acts according to his wisdom. This chapter ends on a beautiful
doxology: those who believe should recognize that they owe their salvation
entirely to God's mercy; unbelievers should lay responsibility on the hardness of their own heart; rather than enquiring about the cause of the faith of
some and the unbelief of others, let us worship God who is sovereign and
free in the dispensation of his graces.[98]

---

[92] Ibid., 102–119/87–100: "*Quelle est l'Eslection & predestination de Dieu par laquelle il a ordonné d'accomplir
en quelques-uns ceste condition, & laisser les autres à eux mesmes, & quelle en est la cause.*"
[93] Ibid., 102–103/87: "La nature de l'homme estant telle, si Dieu n'eust pris autre conseil en ordonnant d'enuoyer
son Fils au monde, que de le proposer pour Redempteur egalement [omitted] & vniuersellement à tous . . . les
souffrances de son Fils [eussent été] entierement frustratoires."
[94] Ibid., 103–104/88.
[95] Ibid., 109/93.
[96] Ibid., 111–12/94–95, for the question asked, and for the answer: "la chose depend absolument de ce que Dieu vse
de sa mercy auec vne liberté toute entiere, & dont nous ne pouuons fonder autre cause que sa volonté" (117/99).
[97] Ibid., 118/100.
[98] Ibid., 118–19/100.

CHAPTER 10: THAT ACCORDING TO THIS DOCTRINE GOD CANNOT
BE ACCUSED OF RESPECT OF PERSONS, NEITHER OF BEING THE
AUTHOR OF SIN, NOR THE CAUSE OF MEN'S PERDITION[99]

The thesis of this chapter is conveniently expressed in its title. Amyraut revisits the basic reason he wrote the treatise: to counter accusations that the Reformed doctrine of predestination implies that God shows favoritism, is the author or sin, and cruelly glorifies himself in men's eternal suffering. In fact, God is no respecter of persons in regard to aspects of wealth, power, or beauty and similar things. He always acts in total conformity to his justice and what is right. In his dealing with humanity, God does injustice to no one. He has created all men; they have all equally fallen into sin and corruption; and they are equally guilty before him as the righteous Judge.[100] But God found "in his wisdom the means to manifest his clemency without harming his justice. Hence, he offers grace equally to all these criminals; demands of them only that they refuse it not, and not show themselves to be unworthy of it."[101] This is God's general decree: Yet "all refuse it with an equal stubbornness and trample it contemptuously under foot."[102] The faith of the one group does not diminish the other's incredulity and guilt. God's granting faith to some does not put others in a position to complain about his decision.[103]

In predestination, as in his providential control of creation and humanity, God shows his goodness and never contributes, directly or otherwise, to man's sin and corruption: he is not the author of sin; humans are responsible for their unbelief and perdition. Amyraut's double apologetic purpose requires this development to persuade his readers of the justice of a God who predestines some to faith and salvation, but also to continue setting the framework for his thesis of a double decree and what becomes a hypothetical universal gift of grace.

---

[99] Ibid., 119–31/101–11: "*Que selon ceste doctrine Dieu ne peut estre accusé d'acception de personnes, ni d'estre autheur de peché, ni cause de la perdition des hommes.*"
[100] Ibid., 121–22/102–103.
[101] Ibid., 123/104: "Mais Dieu . . . a trouué en sa sapience le moyen de faire voye à sa clemence sans endommager la iustice. Il offre donc la grace à tous ces criminels egalement; requiert seulement d'eux qu'il [*sic*.] ne la refusent pas & ne s'en monstrent pas indignes."
[102] Ibid., 123/104: "Ils la refusent tous auec vne egale obstination, & la foulent aux pieds auec outrage." Without referring to it explicitly, Amyraut may be alluding here to Hebrews 10:29. If so, he misreads the passage by applying it to the universal refusal of God's universal grace.
[103] Ibid., 123–24/105. Elsewhere: "Car s'il ne leur donne pas d'y croire, ce n'est pas à dire pour cela qu'il leur donne de n'y croire pas. Si, di-je, il n'engendre pas la foy en eux, il ne s'ensuit pas qu'il y engendre le côtraire" (126/107).

CHAPTER 11: OF THE MEANS BY WHICH GOD ACCOMPLISHES
THIS CONDITION OF FAITH IN HIS ELECT, AND RENDERS HIS
PREDESTINATION OF AN EVENT CERTAIN AND INFALLIBLE,
AND OF THE KNOWLEDGE WE CAN HAVE OF IT[104]

In presenting God's means of conversion, Amyraut introduces his theory of two decrees ("conseils absolus") in God. The one is conditional and depends for its execution or the lack thereof on the condition set by God: Adam maintaining a perfect integrity before his fall, Israel's obedience to the law in order to enjoy God's blessings in Canaan, and salvation granted to all in Christ's death on condition of faith.[105] The other decree, uncondi- tional or absolute, refers to what God determined by his pure will and for his good pleasure: ". . . God, moved by his pure will, resolved to do something without consideration of any condition, the event will undoubt- edly happen."[106] Having established this duality to his satisfaction, Amyraut endeavors to explain God's means to bring those whom he predestined ab- solutely to saving faith. Though we are ignorant of the precise mechanisms (the *how*), we can be sure of the efficacy of the action: God's elect do come to faith and salvation.[107] Amyraut thinks, however, that he can pinpoint a double process:[108] one external, related to the preaching of the gospel and the absolute truth for salvation and the life that it brings to those who hear it; and the other internal, related to the work of the Holy Spirit, who il- luminates man's mind ("entendement"), which in turn affects his will and other dispositions to bring him to saving faith.[109] This dual process infal- libly brings those to whom it is applied to faith and hence to salvation; and yet, they believe willingly and not begrudgingly (John 6:45; 1 Cor. 2:4; Eph. 1:17–19; 3:18–19), the will and the affections necessarily following the enlightened mind.[110]

---

[104] Ibid., 131–47/111–24: "*Du moyen par lequel Dieu accomplit ceste condition de la Foy en ses Esleus, & rend sa predestination d'un euenement certain & infallible, & de la cognoissance qu'on en peut auoir.*"

[105] The conditionality of the event does not alter its certain knowledge by God, who knows infallibly the fulfillment or lack thereof of the conditions he set (ibid., 135–36/115). See the summary in Nicole, "Moyse Amyraut," 57.

[106] *BTP*, 134/114: ". . . Dieu meu de sa pure volonté a resolu de faire quelque chose sans auoir égard à condition quelconque, l'euenement en est absolument indubitable."

[107] Ibid., 137–38/116–17.

[108] Vital to this double movement in the process of acquiring saving faith is Amyraut's definition of faith as a persua- sion of truth: "Car croire, comme chacun le peut entendre, n'est rien sinon estre persuadé de la verité de quelque chose. Et pour estre digne de l'excellence de la nature de l'homme, ceste persuasion doit estre accompagnée voire proceder de la cognoissance de la nature de la chose que l'on croit" (ibid., 139/118). This intellectualist understand- ing of faith plays a central role in his doctrine of Hypothetical Universalism.

[109] Ibid., 142–44/120–22.

[110] Ibid., 144–47/122–24.

CHAPTER 12: THAT IN ACTING IN THIS MANNER, GOD
DOES NOT DESTROY THE NATURE OF MAN'S WILL[111]

The question Amyraut addresses in this chapter follows immediately from the
thesis expressed in the previous one: how can God infallibly bring to salvation those whom he predestined? Answer: through the preaching of the gospel. When people hear it, God enlightens their understanding, which causes
them to receive the truth of the gospel. God's saving activity is irresistible:
no one can understand God's truth without receiving it in faith. How does
that cohere with man's freedom of choice? If God's action is irresistible, how
can man be free? If God respects man's freedom, how can election be immutable? Amyraut sees the problem, articulates it, but refuses to try solving
what he considers to be a mystery. He affirms God's sovereign work in his
elect without violating their free agency, illustrating the truth of his affirmation by the examples of angels in heaven and the saved in eternity: neither
commits any evil though they remain free. He does, however, emphasize the
practical importance of being able to receive salvation even in the absence of
a freedom of choice. For of what interest would a freedom be to us if it can
cause us to reject Christ and his salvation? It is far better for the believer to
experience God's efficacious grace in him.[112]

As for faith itself, Amyraut puts forward the thesis that God does not
constrain us but acts by persuasion: "Belief is a persuasion. No one is persuaded by force. Men are induced to receive a given truth by reasons, not
by constraint or violence. . . . Hence we receive the truth of the Gospel in
that we perceive it, and it is natural for man that the mind [entendement]
that perceives clearly and certainly a truth would acquiesce to it."[113] In the
same way, one cannot love someone or something against his will. "Love is
a movement of the will. To love is thus either to want good for that which
we love, or to want good for ourselves by its enjoyment."[114] The operation

---

[111] Ibid., 147–62/125–37: "*Que par ceste maniere d'agir Dieu ne ruine point la nature de la volonté de l'homme.*"
[112] Ibid., 148–49/125–26: "Or n'estime ie pas qu'il fust beaucoup necessaire aux Chrestiens de s'enquerir quelle est la nature de la volonté de l'homme & de sa liberté, pourueu qu'ils sentissent par experience vne telle efficace de la grace de Dieu en eux, que non seulement ils creussent en Christ, mais mesmes qu'il leur fust impossible de ne pas croire. Car quel interest auons nous à la conseruation de ceste liberté, si son office est de nous maintenir en tel estat que nous soyons autant portés a rejetter Iesus Christ comme a le receuoir, à nous priuer nous mesmes de l'esperance du salut, comme a l'embrasser quand l'Euangile le nous presente?"
[113] Ibid., 156–57/132–33: "La croyance est vne persuasion. Et on ne persuade personne par la force. Ce sont les raisons qui induisent les hommes à receuoir quelque verité, non la contrainte & la violence. . . . Ce donc que nous receuons la verité de l'Euangile est que nous l'apperceuons, & qu'il est naturel à l'homme que l'entendement qui apperçoit clairement & certainement vne verité y acquiesce."
[114] Ibid., 156–57/132–33: "Et l'amour est vn mouuement de la volonté. Aimer donc est ou vouloir du bien à ce que nous aimons, ou nous vouloir à nous mesmes du bien par sa iouissance."

of the Holy Spirit in the believer "fits marvellously" ("merveilleusement convenable") with our nature and in consequence with the divine wisdom itself.[115] Amyraut's accent on the preeminency of the mind, which has been already mentioned, should be underscored here: as his mind is illuminated by the Spirit, man understands God's grace shown to him; in the presence of such a revelation, his will and affections follow, in a process that is at the same time necessary and free.[116]

Chapter 13: That this doctrine does not induce a [false] security, and does not extinguish a concern to live well, but the opposite[117]

This chapter seeks to answer a more general objection addressed to the doctrine of predestination; it can be expressed in the words of Laplanche: "If man's destiny is fixed *ab aeterno*, why should one torment himself to live properly?"[118] Here Amyraut emphasizes the distinction between the two sorts of predestination for which he is known. In his words, "we must distinguish carefully between predestination unto salvation and predestination unto faith."[119] The first is conditional, the second absolute. Though Amyraut is aware that his language is neither in harmony with Scripture (Rom. 8:28, for example) nor the language commonly used in Reformed theology, he goes to great lengths, especially in the second edition of the *Traitté*, to justify his peculiar usage:[120]

---

[115] Ibid., 157/133: "conuenablement à leur nature/condition."

[116] See ibid., 157/133, 159/135; and 161/136: "naturellement & necessairement les hommes desirent leur souuerain bien," ("naturally and necessarily men desire their sovereign good") and the gospel offers believers in Christ "vn souuerain bien qui excelle infiniment par dessus tout ce que les Philosophes en ont iamais peu penser" ("a sovereign good which infinitely surpasses all that the Philosophers could ever have conceived"). The summary of Laplanche deserves to be quoted here: "L'action irrésistible de la grâce divine dans la conversion des élus ne fait donc pas violence à la nature humaine, mais au contraire comble ses vœux au-delà de tout ce qu'elle pouvait espérer" ("Thus the irresistible action of divine grace in the conversion of the elect does not do violence to human nature, on the contrary it fulfils its desires beyond all that it could hope for") (*Orthodoxie et prédication*, 102). Nicole, "Moyse Amyraut," 59, suggests an influence of Cameron here, which might have brought Amyraut more in line with the Arminian emphasis on *suasio moralis* (moral suasion), than with the emphasis on the efficacy of God's grace acting through the Holy Spirit. That tendency was condemned in the Canons of Dort (3–4, error 7). Armstrong, *CAH*, 256, dissents with this evaluation, pointing to a greater depth in Amyraut's definition of faith: "The action [of faith embracing the gospel] is so dynamic that it is certainly less than fair to call it a simple moral suasion, and it is certainly much more than a rational persuasion." Though Armstrong emphasizes in particular the internal role of the Holy Spirit in Amyraut's conception to exonerate him from Nicole's charge, I am not persuaded that he succeeds.

[117] *BTP*, 163–82/138–54: "*Que ceste doctrine n'induit point à Securité & n'esteint point le soin de bien vivre, au contraire.*"

[118] Laplanche, *Orthodoxie et prédication*, 102.

[119] *BTP*, 163/138: "[I]l faut soigneusement distinguer la predestination au salut d'auec [l'eslection ou] la predestination à la foy."

[120] Ibid., 163–66/138–41 (164/138–39).

Predestination to salvation being conditional, and having regard to the whole human race equally, and the human race being universally corrupted by sin and incapable of accomplishing this condition upon which salvation depends, it happens necessarily, not through any fault in predestination itself, but through the hardness of the heart and the stubbornness of the human mind that this predestination is in vain for those who do not have a part in the second.[121]

As Laplanche notes, here Amyraut

acknowledges the fragility of the distinction between absolute predestination and conditional predestination, the foundation of his whole theory. He confesses . . . that the universalism of the conditional predestination is completely illusory: there is no real predestination but the particular one, since faith is in fact given only to the elect.[122]

Amyraut is really saying that Holy Scripture ignores the distinction he seeks to promulgate. Election is an absolute decree, and it applies both to the giving of faith and to salvation, without distinction. The rest of the chapter is devoted to answering the question posed in the title: if election robs in no way those who remain in their state of perdition (the consequence of their voluntary refusal of the gospel), believers are not only given faith unto salvation; they are also called to a life of love (1 John 2:10–11) and holiness, for "predestination to salvation is principally predestination to holiness," which God accomplishes in us through enlightening our minds and reforming our wills.[123]

CHAPTER 14: THAT THIS DOCTRINE FILLS THE CONSCIENCE
OF THE FAITHFUL WITH JOY AND CONSOLATION[124]

The last chapter of the book underscores the consolation brought about by the Reformed doctrine of predestination: not speculation, but the action of

---

[121] Ibid., 164–65/138–40. There is considerable variation in the 1658 edition: "[L]a raison de cela [of his peculiar usage] est que la prédestination au salut [la volonté de Dieu qui concerne le salut] estant conditionnelle & regardant tout le genre humain egalement [omitted], & le genre humain estant vniuersellement corrompu de peché & incapable d'accomplir ceste condition dont le salut depend, il arriue necessairement, non par aucun vice de la predestination en elle mesme [de cette volonté de Dieu, à la côsiderer en elle mesme], mais par la dureté du cœur & l'obstination de l'esprit humain, que ceste premiere predestination [volonté de Dieu, que quelques uns, comme i'ay dit, appellent predestination, contre le stile de l'Escriture] est frustratoire [2nd ed., infructueuse; the basic meaning is not affected] pour ceux qui n'ont point de part en la seconde [l'autre]."

[122] Laplanche, *Orthodoxie et prédication*, 103.

[123] *BTP*, 176/149: "Car puis que la predestination au salut est principalement la predestination à la saincteté, comment voulons-nous que Dieu nous amene au but auquel il nous a destinez qu'en nous sanctifiant?" (2nd ed. rephrased: "Car puis que le conseil de Dieu qui concerne le salut, regarde principalement à la saincteté, comment voulons nous que Dieu execute son conseil en nous sinon en nous sanctifiant?")

[124] Ibid., 182–96/155–66: "*Que ceste doctrine remplist la conscience des Fideles de ioye & de consolation.*"

the Holy Spirit in the believer, assures him that God has elected him. The illumination of his mind, the peace of the conscience given by the assurance of sins forgiven, the love for God and fellowmen that are wrought in his will and affections, the hope for the life to come—these are the marks of Christ's life in him.[125] Even here, though, Amyraut's intellectualism is evident as seen in some of his affirmations.[126] This assurance carries with it three vital ingredients: the certain realization that God has produced a radical conversion in the soul of the believer, the assurance of life eternal, and the assurance that the gift of salvation received is immutable: God, who has granted his gift freely, out of love and compassion to undeserving sinners, without taking into consideration their own dispositions, will not turn back on them.[127] The last pages of the treatise are a celebration of God's gracious and sure salvation, freely given to undeserving sinners.[128]

III. Synthesis of Amyraut's Basic Theses on Predestination

Amyraut's *Brief Traitté* reveals his departure from a number of orthodox teachings in the Reformed churches at the time. They are succinctly summarized by Du Moulin in his letter on Amyraut and Testard to the Synod of Alençon. He accuses them of teaching

> that it is not absolutely necessary to Salvation to have a clear Knowledge of *Jesus Christ* . . . that Jesus Christ died equally and indifferently for all People . . . that the Reprobate could be saved if they willed, or that *God* has Counsels & Decrees that will never produce their Effect . . . that *God* has removed the Natural Inability of People to believe, & turn themselves to him . . . that he renders the Efficacy of the regenerating Spirit dependent on a Counsel that might change.[129]

The bifurcation of God's will (revealed and secret) is the key to understanding Amyraut's doctrine of predestination and the atonement. For Amyraut, God's revealed will concerned a universal desire to save all men on the condition that they believe. God willed that his Son should make atonement for all

---

[125] Ibid., 184/156.
[126] Ibid., 184/156–57: ". . . trouuant, dis-je, en soy toutes ces marques de la vie de Christ, il [the believer] raisonnera, que puis qu'il ne la peut auoir d'ailleurs que de la grace de Dieu, comme l'Escriture l'enseigne, . . . il faut necessairement qu'il y ait part, & que Dieu l'ait aimé des auparauant la fondation du monde. Or, n'y a il personne qui ne iuge aisement combien grande consolation ceste consideration est capable de donner a vne bonne ame."
[127] Ibid., 188–89/159–60.
[128] Ibid., 193–94/163–64.
[129] Pierre du Moulin, *Lettre de Monsieur du Moulin*, in Aymon, *Tous les Synodes*, 2:618.

on the condition that they believe. The extent of this salvation was universal because the Redeemer was taken from among the race of men, being of the same flesh and blood. All people are equally fallen; God's compassion to deliver humanity from the bonds of sin must be the same for all; the Son partook of human nature—therefore, the extent of Christ's work must be universal. However, if the condition of faith is not met, then God's universal salvific will is rendered inefficacious. In other words, Christ's procurement remains *in suspenso* until the condition is fulfilled. As Armstrong comments, on Amyraut's scheme,

> there is no necessary cause and effect relationship between salvation as procured by Christ and its application. . . . Strictly speaking, while he maintains repeatedly that no salvation would have been possible without Christ's death and resurrection, in this economic understanding of Christ's work of satisfaction no one can be saved simply through his work.[130]

This, then, is Amyraut's "Hypothetical Universalism": fulfilling God's will for universal salvation, Christ procured atonement for all. But it is hypothetical, for salvation is effectual only *when and if* the condition of faith is fulfilled.[131] However, to save God from being entirely frustrated by a decree that is not realized, in his eternal counsel he ordained another decree (his secret will), whereby he would, out of his mercy, predestine a group of sinners to receive his Spirit and thus be enabled to believe in Christ's atoning work. In this decree there is no condition on man's part, since God elects people to faith and so ensures that the condition is met. If the Son's work is the fulfillment of a universal atonement equally for all, then the Spirit's work is the fulfillment of the application of that atonement for some. The key distinction to note here in Amyraut's theology is the *order of decrees*: the decree of election is posterior to that of redemption, and comes in only to rescue the first one from failure.

IV. Controversy over Universal Grace Generated by Amyraut's Writings

Following studies by François Laplanche and Roger Nicole, we may distinguish three main phases in the controversy generated by Amyraut's

---

[130] Armstrong, *CAH*, 210.
[131] Ibid., 212.

writings on predestination and universal grace: 1634–1637, 1641–1649, and 1655–1661.[132]

The first phase (1634–1637) is rightfully said to start with Amyraut's publication of the *Brief Traitté* (1634)[133] and comes to a first resolution at the National Synod of Alençon (1637). Though Amyraut's *Traitté* received some favorable echoes from some of his colleagues, others immediately objected to its main theses (especially two anonymous books that were deemed malicious by Amyraut and his friends).[134] In part to respond to these accusations, in part to meet objections and misrepresentations from Roman Catholics, Amyraut preached the doctrine expounded in the *Traitté* in six sermons that he published afterwards under the title *Six Sermons: De la nature, estendue, necessité, dispensation, et efficace de l'Euangile*. The *Six Sermons* were preceded by a lengthy (seventy-five pages) *Eschantillon de la Doctrine de Calvin touchant la Predestination*.[135] Though the *Eschantillon* was printed first, the sermons seem to have been preached and written before, the *Eschantillon* serving as it were as a theological and historical preface to the published *Six Sermons*.[136]

Amyraut's published views were defended by some of his colleagues at Saumur and by the pastors of the influential Reformed Church of Charenton, but they were immediately opposed by a number of Reformed theologians who found them fundamentally lacking and unsatisfactory. Though Pierre Bayle's statement—"a civil war among the Reformers"—is an obvious exaggeration, Amyraut's adversaries responded to what they detected as numerous flaws: they averred that some of his theses contravened the statements of the Synod of Dort and in fact constituted a return to Arminian positions. His treatment of Calvin was found insufficient and mistaken. His three main

---

[132] Laplanche, *Orthodoxie et prédication*, ad loc.; and Nicole, "Brief Survey," in *Standing Forth,* 313–20; idem, *Moïse Amyraut: A Bibliography*, 9–21.

[133] Amyraut's publication had been preceded by one on the same subject from the pen of his colleague Paul Testard, a year earlier: *Eirenikon seu Synopsis doctrinae de natura et gratia*. Concerning this work, Pierre Courthial, "The Golden Age of Calvinism in France: 1533–1633," in *John Calvin: His Influence on the Western World,* ed. W. Stanford Reid (Grand Rapids, MI: Zondervan, 1982), 75, wrote: "This was the first work of a theologian of the Reformed churches in France to undermine, in a covert way, the faith of these churches as declared in their Confession of 1559 and the Canons of Dordrecht accepted and ratified by their National Synod at Alès in 1620." On Amyraut's work, Courthial opines that it "leaned even more strongly toward Arminianism."

[134] John Quick, *Synodicon in Gallia Reformata, or, the Acts, Decisions, Decrees, and Canons of those famous National Councils of the Reformed Churches in France*, 2 vols. (London: T. Parkhurst & J. Robinson, 1692), 2:362; on Synod of Alençon, XVI, 11.

[135] See n. 2.

[136] Space precludes any treatment of these, but see summaries in Laplanche, *Orthodoxie et prédication*, 111–17, and especially Nicole, "Moyse Amyraut," 67–84. The sermon texts were Ezekiel 18:23; Romans 1:19–20; 1 Corinthians 1:21; 2 Corinthians 3:6; Romans 11:33; and John 6:45.

opponents were Pierre Du Moulin (1568–1658), a very influential and respected professor of theology then at the somewhat rival Reformed Academy
of Sedan; André Rivet (1572–1651), also a leading theologian at the time,
then in the Netherlands, who had been Amyraut's professor; and Friedrich
Spanheim (1600–1649), professor at Geneva and later at Leiden.[137] These
three theologians, in different ways, intended to show that Amyraut either
misunderstood or misrepresented Calvin, and, more seriously, was not faithful to the biblical teaching on this topic.[138]

The National Synod of Alençon (1637) brought a first and momentary
halt to the debate: the matter was taken very seriously by the Assembly, which
commissioned a special committee to examine and report on the matter. The
writings of Amyraut and his colleague Testard (whose views were similar to
Amyraut's) and those of their critics (the most important were the writings
of Du Moulin and Rivet, but there were other, more strident accusations),
together with letters from Reformed theological faculties, were carefully
examined. The Saumur professors were given ample time and occasion to
respond to their critiques. Both Testard's and Amyraut's responses show that
they maintained their basic position on universal grace (reflecting Cameron's):

> . . . explaining their opinions about the Universal Goal of Christ's Death,
> they declared, that Jesus Christ Died for all Men sufficiently, but that he
> Died Effectually for the Elect only: and that consequentially his Intention
> was to die for all Men in respect of the Sufficiency of his Satisfaction, but
> for the Elect only in respect of its Quickening and Saving Virtue and Ef-
> ficacy; that is to say, that the Will of Jesus Christ was that the Sacrifice of
> the Cross should be of an Infinite Value and Price, and abundantly sufficient
> to expiate the Sins of the whole World; and that however the Efficacity of
> his Death should belong only to the Elect.[139]

---

[137] Du Moulin was the most outspoken of the three theologians. His answer was first pirated and published without his agreement or knowledge but later he gave his consent to its publication. The title aptly summarizes the
content: *Esclaircissement Des Controuerses Salmvriennes: Ou Defense de la Doctrine des Eglises Reformees svr
l'immutabilité des Decrets de Dieu, l'efficace de la Mort de Christ, la grace universelle, l'impuissance à se convertir
et sur d'autres matieres* ("Clarification of the Salmurian Controversies: Or Defense of the Doctrine of the Reformed
Churches concerning the immutability of God's Decrees, the efficacy of the Death of Christ, universal grace, one's
inability to convert and other matters") (see n. 24). Rivet had himself published a book on the atonement in 1631,
pointing to some universal gains of Christ's death on the cross; Amyraut had hoped to find an ally in him. On this
relationship, see Nicole, "Moyse Amyraut," 96–99. On Spanheim's contribution to the debate, see Roger R. Nicole,
"Friedrich Spanheim (1600–1649)," in *Through Christ's Word. A Festschrift for Philip E. Hughes*, ed. W. Robert
Godfrey and Jesse L. Boyd III (Phillipsburg, NJ: P&R, 1985), 166–79.

[138] For complete references, see Roger R. Nicole, "John Calvin's View of the Extent of the Atonement," *WTJ* 47.2
(1985): 197–225 (reprinted, with additions, in *Standing Forth*, 283–312); Armstrong, *CAH*, 298–317.

[139] Quick, *Synodicon in Gallia Reformata*, 2:353; Aymon, *Tous les Synodes*, 2:572–732: ". . . touchant le But Uni-
versel de la Mort de Jésus-Christ, ils [Amyraut and Testard] declarerent, que Jesus-Christ étoit Mort pour tous
les Hommes sufisamment; mais qu'il étoit Mort Eficacement pour les Elûs seulement: & que par consequent son
Intention étoit de mourir pour tous les Hommes, quant à la Sufisance de sa Satisfaction, mais pour les Elûs seule-

The Assembly was satisfied, and the professors were "honourably dismissed to the Exercise of their respective Charges," with mild condemnation.[140] Moreover, the Synod forbade any further publication or discussion of the subject, which may have been the prudent road to take from a pragmatic perspective, but which hardly helped the cause of truth in the long run. "[I]t implied erroneously," Nicole judiciously points out, "that discussion on these topics was wrong rather than that certain opinions on these issues were false."[141] However, a few remarks must be made: it should be noted that although the Synod cleared Amyraut and Testard of any Arminianism or Pelagianism, it censured the incriminated expressions (explained by Amyraut and Testard either as anthropomorphisms or as accommodations to the language of adversaries of the Reformed faith). In so doing, they may be deemed to have condemned the doctrines expressed by that sort of language. One should notice moreover that Du Moulin and Rivet were neither criticized nor blamed.

Amyraut's and Testard's explanations must be taken with a serious grain of salt. Their protestations to the contrary, later publications (for example, Amyraut's *Specimen Animadversionum*) show that "Their language was undoubtedly an index of their thought."[142] And though their intentions must remain known only to God, future publication and the development of the movement show that either they were not entirely forthright in their presentation, or, more charitably but patronizingly, they did not fully understand the

---

ment quant à sa Vertu & Eficace Vivifiante & Sanctifiante; c'est-à-dire, que la Volonté de Jesus-Christ étoit, que le Sacrifice de la Croix fût d'un Prix & d'une Valeur Infinie, & très abondamment sufisant pour expier les Péchés de tout le Monde; que cependant l'Eficace de sa Mort apartient seulement aux Elûs."

[140] Quick, *Synodicon in Gallia Reformata*, 2:357; the record of the proceedings is found in 2:352–57; 397–411; see also, Aymon, *Tous les Synodes*, 2:576. The Synod required of Amyraut and Testard that they abstain from speaking of Christ's death "equally" for all, drop expressions such as "conditional, frustratory or revocable decree," avoid anthropomorphisms, and avoid calling knowledge, derived from general revelation, faith. The synod's dealings and decisions are treated by Nicole, "Moyse Amyraut," 106–18; idem, "Brief Survey," 314–16; Armstrong, *CAH*, 93–96. Amyraut's agreement with Cameron's views may have prompted the Synod to be very lenient on the two Salmurian professors: it may have seemed unjust to condemn them for views he had espoused, and tarnish the memory of someone who had rendered precious service to the Reformed cause. Note the strange conclusion of Armstrong, derived from the order of examination of Amyraut's theses by the Synod. Though remarking that it followed Du Moulin's discussion in his *Examen*, he concludes that "[T]his order suggests that the Synod agreed Christ was sent for all" (91). Clearly, it shows nothing of the sort.

[141] Nicole, "Moyse Amyraut," 114.

[142] Ibid., 115–16; Armstrong, *CAH*, 95–96, explains the outcome, surprisingly in favor of the Salmurian professors, by prudential reasons (the desire to avoid a possible schism or harmful consequences for the Academy of Saumur) and what he calls the "French Motif": the churches of France united to defend a *French* theologian against attacks coming mostly from outside the French kingdom. It is rather strange to find Armstrong's study often quoted without much critical appraisal. In spite of very serious research behind it (particularly at a time where the works studied were very difficult to access), his presentation of the debate is seriously slanted. For a perceptive critique, see John M. Frame's review of Armstrong's book in *WJT* 34.2 (1972): 186–92, republished in the author's *The Doctrine of God: A Theology of Lordship* (Phillipsburg, NJ: P&R, 2002), 801–806.

implications of their expressed views, or they simply changed their views.[143] At any rate, reading Amyraut's own writings, it is difficult to seriously maintain their conformity with the Canons of Dort to which he subscribed, or that later he conformed to the regulations of Alençon.[144]

The second phase of the controversy (1641–1649) was provoked by the publication in 1641 of Amyraut's *Doctrinae J. Calvini de Absoluto Reprobationis Decreto Defensio* (with an amplified French translation by the author published in 1644),[145] a work in defense of Calvin's view of reprobation. If the work is fundamentally a response to attacks and misrepresentations of Calvin's views from an Arminian perspective (by an anonymous author), Amyraut seized the occasion to recast his views on predestination. Spanheim, Rivet, and others produced a number of responses to Amyraut, at times at great length, and sometimes in such detail that the main arguments were obscured.[146] The heat and passion of the controversy increased considerably.[147] At the National Synod of Charenton (1644–1645), Amyraut was accused of heresy again, but later was acquitted. The intervention of a Protestant prince, Henri-Charles de la Trémouille, put an end to this second round: in 1649, he gathered the main protagonists of the dispute (Amyraut, Guillaume Rivet, and others)[148] in a private meeting in his domains and requested of them that they desist from any public polemics on this matter and abstain from writing about it. An agreement, known as the "Acte de Thouars," was signed on 16 October, 1649. If this political move succeeded in cooling public expressions of the polemic (in 1655, there was a personal reconciliation even between Amyraut and Du Moulin), it did not resolve the theological debate.

The third phase of the controversy (1655–1661)[149] did not directly involve Amyraut himself; it was led by David Blondel (1590–1665) and Jean Daillé

---

[143] Nicole, "Moyse Amyraut," 117.

[144] It is almost amusing to note that Armstrong, who defends Amyraut so vigorously, has to concede here that the incriminated writings (*Defensio* and *Dissertationes*) "probably did violate these [the Synod's] regulations" (Armstrong, *CAH*, 104). Laplanche, *Orthodoxie et prédication*, 163, attributes the success of Amyraut and Testard to "the skilfulness of their explanations [and] the support of the Parisian ministers."

[145] Moïse Amyraut, *Defense de la Doctrine de Calvin svr le Sviet de l'Election et de la Reprobation* (Saumur, France: Isaac Desbordes, 1644).

[146] Nicole, "Brief Survey," 316–19. A detailed account of this second stage of the controversy can be found in Laplanche, *Orthodoxie et prédication*, 211–34.

[147] Ibid., 211–29; Armstrong, *CAH*, 113–15, on the possibility of a schism in the Church of France that the controversy over universal grace could have provoked; hence the intervention of the prince.

[148] André Rivet joined in the agreement later; Spanheim had passed away that year.

[149] Summary in Nicole, "Brief Survey," 319–20.

(1594–1670) defending his Amyraut's theses, with Samuel Demarest (1599–1673) upholding the orthodox confession; there were a number of written contributions by a younger generation of pastors and theologians (sons of both Pierre Du Moulin and Friedrich Spanheim participated in the debate). Officially, this phase ended with the National Synod of Loudun in 1659, where Daillé was elected moderator, and the orthodoxy of Amyraut and Daillé was recognized. As Nicole concluded, "it was apparent that the spirit of Saumur was gaining ground."[150]

And afterwards (1661–1675 and after) If Amyraut's doctrine was at first only tolerated in French Reformed churches, it gained steady influence in the last part of the seventeenth century: a growing number of Saumur graduates, a seeming disinterest in the debate on the part of the orthodox, the fear of provoking a schism, and the "French factor" may have contributed to this influence. Be that as it may, Amyraut's ideas "slowly undermined respect for the confessional standards and disrupted internal unity and cohesion."[151] Perhaps the best example of this can be seen in the teaching of Claude Pajon, a successor to Amyraut at Saumur, who taught that neither the work of the Holy Spirit nor special grace was required in the process of conversion: the simple intellectual persuasion was sufficient to enlighten the mind in matters of faith as in other matters.

The church in Switzerland was perhaps the most alert in resisting the movement, both by warnings, encouraging those in France to keep to orthodox convictions, and by ensuring that ministers influenced by Amyraldianism were not accepted into the ministry in Switzerland. In 1675, a number of theologians from Zurich and Geneva, including Johan Heinrich Heidegger and François Turretini, drew up a statement of faith that sought to halt the Salmurian views: the *Formula Consensus Ecclesiarum Helveticarum* (the majority of its articles are directed against Amyraut's doctrine of universal grace and some of La Place's doctrines). In spite of the Formula, the new ideas gained ground, and the Formula was later abrogated as a test of faith, under the influence of, among others, J. A. Turretini, the son of François Turretini, one of its main architects!

---

[150] Nicole, *Moyse Amyraut: A Bibliography*, 16; "Brief Survey," 320. Armstrong, *CAH*, 115–19, is very sympathetic to these developments.

[151] Nicole, "Brief Survey," 326: "The doctrine of hypothetical universalism acted as a corrosive factor in the French Reformed Church. . . . The advantages [of the doctrine] that Amyraut had envisioned failed to materialize, and the dangers against which his opponents had warned did in fact eventuate." Laplanche, *Orthodoxie et prédication*, 308, sees in Amyraut a "precursor of liberal theology."

The Netherlands, where the Canons of Dort were framed, was, at first, able to resist the Amyraldian influences. Some of the main critics of the new ideas—Du Moulin, André Rivet, and Spanheim—resided and exercised their ministry there. Yet, after the Revocation of the Edict of Nantes (1685), an influx of French refugees imported their Salmurian views. Moreover, freedom of press gave adherents of universal grace the opportunity to publish and disseminate their views.

More difficult is tracing Amyraut's influence in Germany, since views with considerable similarity were already held by some in Bremen (Crocius, Martinius), Hesse, and Nassau.[152]

In the British Isles, Amyraut's teaching did not exert direct influence, since his works were never translated into English. The views of prominent Hypothetical Universalists, such as John Davenant in England and James Ussher in Ireland, while exhibiting some conceptual similarities with Amyraut's position, should not be simplistically equated with it, not least because these men wrote prior to Amyraut.[153] Moreover, there were variant approaches to Hypothetical Universalism across the British Isles and Europe. The main difference between the Hypothetical Universalist approaches of Davenant and Ussher (and Du Moulin in France) on the one hand, and Amyraut on the other, was in the order of decrees: whereas Amyraut placed the decree of election after the decree of redemption, Davenant and Du Moulin, for example, defended their Hypothetical Universalist schemes while still maintaining an infralapsarian position on the order of decrees.[154] These men also differed with Amyraut in his presentation of universal grace.

V. Amyraut *Redivivus?* Amyraldianism Today

In evangelical circles today, self-consciously affirmed Amyraldianism is not frequently observed. The one exception is in Britain, where it is represented by Alan Clifford and the Amyraldian Association which he founded. Clifford defends Amyraut's theology as a faithful expression of Calvinian and

---

[152] Nicole, "Brief Survey," 328.

[153] For example, Richard Baxter connected John Davenant's views with those of James Ussher, Archbishop of Armagh, both of which provided antecedents to his own position on the extent of Christ's satisfaction. In Baxter's assessment, Davenant and Ussher's views were distinct from Amyraut's. See Richard Baxter, *Certain Disputations of Right to the Sacraments, and the True Nature of Visible Christianity* (London: William Du Gard, 1657), fol. b2 verso.

[154] See, for example, John Davenant, *Animadversions written by the Right Reverend Father in God John, Lord Bishop of Salisbury, upon a Treatise in titled Gods love to Mankind* (Cambridge: Roger Daniel, 1641). For a helpful overview of Davenant's views on the order of decrees and the extent of the atonement, see Moore, *English Hypothetical Universalism*, 187–214.

198 DEFINITE ATONEMENT IN CHURCH HISTORY

genuine Reformed theology, biblically sound, pastorally useful, answering the extremes of Arminianism on the one hand and rigid Calvinistic orthodoxy on the other.[155] Clifford has been involved in debates with some "classical Calvinists" (J. I. Packer, Iain Murray, Paul Helm) who defend definite atonement as the proper teaching of Scripture.

Among evangelicals with Reformed leanings, however, a form of Amyraldianism may be the default position on the atonement, even though the French theologian is not often explicitly acknowledged or directly responsible for the influence.[156] Bruce Demarest's *The Cross and Salvation* may serve as an example. Though the author claims to present a thesis that is an improvement on Arminianism and Calvinism, he defends in fact a thesis that is indistinguishable from classical Amyraldianism:[157]

> We choose to ask the question, *For whom did Christ intend to provide atonement through his suffering and death?* Accordingly we will divide the question in two parts. We inquire, first, into the *provision* Christ made via his death on the cross. And we explore, second, the *application* of the benefits gained by Calvary to sinners.[158]

With the issue established, Demarest provides this solution:

> In sum, regarding the question, For whom did Christ die? We find biblical warrant for dividing the question into God's purpose regarding the *provision* of the Atonement and his purpose concerning the *application* thereof. . . . Christ died to provide salvation for all. The *provision* side of the Atonement is part of the general will of God that must be preached to all. . . . The *application* side of the Atonement is part of the special will of God shared with those who come to faith. This conclusion—that Christ died to make atonement for all to the end that its benefits would be applied to the elect—coheres with the perspective of Sublapsarian Calvinism.[159]

---

[155] See n. 4.

[156] See, for example, D. Broughton Knox, "Some Aspects of the Atonement," in *The Doctrine of God*, vol. 1 of *D. Broughton Knox, Selected Works* (3 vols.), ed. Tony Payne (Kingsford, NSW: Matthias Media, 2000), 265: "the decree of election is logically after the decree of atonement, where also, in fact, it belongs in the working out of the application of salvation." (Knox was more of a Hypothetical Universalist on the nature of the atonement, but on this point he was in agreement with Amyraut.) Lewis Sperry Chafer, *Systematic Theology, Volume III* (Dallas: Dallas Seminary Press, 1948), 187: "The highway of divine election is quite apart from the highway of redemption." A. H. Strong, *Systematic Theology* (London: Pickering & Inglis, Limited, 1907), 771: "Not the *atonement* therefore is limited, but the *application* through the work of the Holy Spirit."

[157] Bruce Demarest, *The Cross and Salvation: The Doctrine of Salvation*, Foundations of Evangelical Theology (Wheaton, IL: Crossway, 1997), 189–95.

[158] Ibid., 189 (emphasis original).

[159] Ibid., 193.

Demarest presents nothing new or particularly innovative here, not least because in calling it "Sublapsarian Calvinism" he is placing the decree of election after the decree of redemption—exactly what Amyraut did. *Mutatis mutandis*, a similar thesis is defended by Stephen Lewis (who distinguishes between provision and application)[160] and P. L. Rouwendall (who offers it as a solution to the vexing question of Calvin's belief on the matter).[161]

Conclusion

This chapter has expounded Amyraut's views on predestination and the atonement as contained within his *Brief Traitté* and has reported on the historical controversy that followed in its wake. My aim has been to inform more than to pursue an argument, since Amyraut's views are so rarely understood from the primary sources. Further research on Amyraut would benefit from closely comparing *Eschantillon* and *Six Sermons* with the *Brief Traitté* and then assessing his continuity or discontinuity with Calvin.[162] It is hoped that this chapter provides a firm foundation and clear basis for future critical work on Amyraut. I leave the biblical, theological, and pastoral implications of his thought to such work and to the other chapters in this volume.

---

[160] Stephen Lewis, "Moise Amyraut 1596–1664: Predestination and the Atonement Debate," *Chafer Theological Seminary Journal* 1.3 (1995): 5–11.

[161] P. L. Rouwendall, " Calvin's Forgotten Classical Position on the Extent of the Atonement: About Sufficiency, Efficiency, and Anachronism," *WTJ* 70 (2008): 317–35.

[162] In this regard, Richard A. Muller has already made an excellent start in his meticulous comparative analysis of Calvin's and Amyraut's understandings of the divine will ("A Tale of Two Wills? Calvin and Amyraut on Ezekiel 18:23," *CTJ* 44.2 [2009]: 211–25). Muller's article is a model of text study.

Atonement and the Covenant of Redemption

JOHN OWEN ON THE NATURE OF CHRIST'S SATISFACTION

Carl R. Trueman

Introduction

While it is clear that any understanding of atonement which purports to be Christian must ultimately stand or fall by its conformity or lack thereof to the teaching of Scripture, historical theological studies also have their part to play in this discussion. History serves numerous pedagogical purposes in the church, not least allowing those in the present to understand how the church has moved from the text of Scripture to doctrinal and creedal syntheses over the years and, therefore, why the church thinks and speaks the way she does in the present. This in turn leads to a further point which is often forgotten: historical theological studies also allow us to explore the complexity of doctrinal formulation and the interconnectedness of one doctrinal locus to another. One obvious example would be the connection of our understanding of the incarnation to that of the Trinity. One cannot ultimately understand the Chalcedonian Formula of 451 without having a grasp of the Niceno-Constantinopolitan Creed of 381, along with its associated debates and discussions.[1]

---

[1] See Carl R. Trueman, *The Creedal Imperative* (Wheaton, IL: Crossway, 2012), esp. chapter 3.

The same is true for the issue of "limited atonement." In fact, the very term is problematic because it supposes the abstraction of one aspect of Christ's work as Mediator (his death) from his overall work as Savior. Competent proponents of this unfortunately named "limited atonement" do not generally argue for the position on the basis of a few isolated passages or proof texts in the Bible. Rather it is based on the implications of a series of strands of biblical teaching, from the foundations of redemption in the intra-Trinitarian relationship of Father, Son, and Holy Spirit to biblical teaching on the efficacy of Christ's death and the nature of representative headship.[2]

Given such, the term "limited atonement" is unfortunate, and that not simply because of its lopsided emphasis on Christ's death. It also places the language of restriction and limitation at the center of the discussion, rather than soteriological efficacy and sufficiency. As such, it is to be hoped that it can be replaced in due course in common Reformed theological parlance with a more appropriate term such as definite atonement, particular redemption, or perhaps effectual redemption.[3]

It is with this in mind that I approach the work of John Owen on atonement. Historically, his 1647 treatise, *The Death of Death in the Death of Christ*, is often considered by friend and foe to be the definitive statement of so-called "limited atonement."[4] Certainly, it represents a very thorough exposition of the nature of Christ's work of redemption, the product of seven years of hard study, as Owen himself claims in his note to the reader.[5] Nevertheless, to approach the book through the lens of "limited atonement" is problematic for the reasons noted above and because it consequently lends itself to refutations which are simply too narrowly focused to do justice to the arguments it contains.

Thus, while J. I. Packer famously characterized Owen's treatise as a definitive treatment, its critics have not been convinced. Yet critical responses have too easily reverted to refutations based upon single lines of reasoning

---

[2] The recent works by Lee Gatiss and Jarvis J. Williams are good examples of this approach: Lee Gatiss, *For Us and for Our Salvation: "Limited Atonement" in the Bible, Doctrine, History, and Ministry* (London: Latimer Trust, 2012); Jarvis J. Williams, *For Whom Did Christ Die? The Extent of the Atonement in Paul's Theology* (Milton Keynes, UK: Paternoster, 2012).

[3] For the purposes of this volume, I will generally use "definite atonement."

[4] Thus, J. I. Packer regards it as the treatise by which the doctrine of definite atonement stands or falls: see his "Introductory Essay" to John Owen, *The Death of Death in the Death of Christ* (London: Banner of Truth, 1959).

[5] John Owen, *Salus Electorum, Sanguis Jesu: Or The Death of Death in the Death of Christ*, in *The Works of John Owen*, ed. W. H. Goold, 24 vols. (Edinburgh: Johnstone & Hunter, 1850–1855; repr. Edinburgh: Banner of Truth, 1967), 10:149. The Banner of Truth reprint edition omits volume 17. Thus, references in this essay to volume 17 and 19 will be to the nineteenth-century edition of the same series.

focused on the aspect of limited salvific intention and efficacy. For example, Alan Clifford refutes Owen on the basis of his alleged use of Aristotelian teleology, which he regards as distorting Owen's understanding of the biblical material and therefore preventing him from appreciating the biblical teaching on the wider bounds of God's mercy.[6] In this, Clifford has been followed by Hans Boersma in his major study of Richard Baxter's doctrine of justification.[7] More recently, Tim Cooper, an authority on seventeenth-century theology in its social and political context, argued that Owen's position was erroneous because it failed to be faithful to Scripture at key moments and also warped the reading of certain universalist texts to suit Owen's systematic convictions.[8]

In this chapter, I do not intend to revisit these specific criticisms of Owen at any great length. Instead, I want to tease out the way in which Owen's treatise indicates the interconnections that exist between various soteriological points. To do this I want to use as my entry point a question that perhaps seems somewhat abstruse today but which proved highly contentious in Owen's own time and provided the pretext for the most significant challenge to his understanding of redemption, that mounted by his contemporary and lifelong rival, Richard Baxter. The question as Owen faced it was this: if Christ on the cross suffers the very punishment due to our sins, and if that punishment provides a full and efficacious satisfaction precisely for the sins of the elect, then why are the elect not justified at that moment, or even in eternity?[9] Further, does the moment that the individual comes to faith in Christ have any real significance, or is it simply a moment of spiritual enlightenment, whereby the person comes to realize that he has always been justified? These were points raised against Owen's work by Richard Baxter who, in an appendix to his 1649 work, *Aphorismes of Justification*, lambasted Owen's position on redemption as undergirding a clear antinomianism and thus as laying the ground for a potentially very dangerous theology, both socially and politically.

This specific issue might well seem remote and of little but antiquarian

---

[6] Alan C. Clifford, *Atonement and Justification: English Evangelical Theology, 1640–1790: An Evaluation* (Oxford: Clarendon, 1990). I disagree with Clifford's thesis and deal with his arguments at length in Carl R. Trueman, *The Claims of Truth: John Owen's Trinitarian Theology* (Carlisle, UK: Paternoster, 1998).

[7] Hans Boersma, *A Hot Peppercorn: Richard Baxter's Doctrine of Justification in Its Seventeenth-Century Context of Controversy* (Zoetermeer: Boekencentrum, 1993).

[8] Tim Cooper, *John Owen, Richard Baxter, and the Formation of Nonconformity* (Aldershot, UK: Ashgate, 2011), 67, 72.

[9] Owen defines the concept of satisfaction as "a term borrowed from the law, applied properly to things, thence translated and accommodated unto persons; and it is *a full compensation of the creditor from the debtor*" (*Death of Death*, in *Works*, 10:265; emphasis original). He then proceeds to distinguish it into two kinds: the payment of the very thing in the obligation; and the payment of an equivalent in another kind.

interest today, but Baxter's challenge to Owen forced him to reflect upon and elaborate the conceptual foundations of his view of redemption in a manner that remains instructive at the very least for the insight it gives into the elegant nature of Christian doctrinal construction.

The Historical Context

In order to understand the reason for Baxter's critical response to Owen's work, it is necessary to know something of the immediate background, historical and theological, to the discussion. The 1640s were a time of remarkable social and political turmoil in England. War between the Crown and Parliament had wreaked havoc on the countryside. The rise of the New Model Army under Thomas Fairfax and Oliver Cromwell had brought to prominence the power of religious sects. There was significant concern among more conservative Reformed churchmen that the rise of Independency as a political force was going to lead to social anarchy. Indeed, the Presbyterian Thomas Edwards, in his work *Gangraena* (London, 1646), outlined the outlandish practices of various sects, both real and very probably imagined.[10] The fear of antinomianism also stalked the nightmares of various Protestants and even impacted discussions at the Westminster Assembly.[11]

Richard Baxter had firsthand experience of such sectarianism during his time as military chaplain, and his ministry from the mid-1640s onward was to be marked by an ever-present fear of anything which even hinted at antinomianism. In fact, this concern would lead him to a reformulation of the doctrine of justification which has remained a source of controversy to the present day concerning its orthodoxy and its relationship to the earlier Reformation.[12] Indeed, it was in the context of discussing justification that Baxter launched his salvo against John Owen on atonement.

Baxter's central point was based upon a rather arcane distinction, that be-

---

[10] On Edwards and the political function of his work, see Ann Hughes, *Gangraena and the Struggle for the English Revolution* (New York: Oxford University Press, 2004).

[11] On antinomianism in early seventeenth-century England, see Theodore Dwight Bozeman, *The Precisianist Strain: Disciplinary Religion and Antinomian Backlash in Puritanism to 1638* (Chapel Hill: University of North Carolina Press, 2004); David R. Como, *Blown by the Spirit: Puritanism and the Emergence of an Antinomian Underground in Pre–Civil-War England* (Stanford, CA: Stanford University Press, 2004). On antinomianism and the Westminster Assembly, particularly as it impacted the debate on justification, see Robert Letham, *The Westminster Assembly: Reading Its Theology in Historical Context* (Phillipsburg, NJ: P&R, 2009), 251–76.

[12] On Baxter's theology, see J. I. Packer, *The Redemption and Restoration of Man in the Thought of Richard Baxter* (Vancouver: Regent College Publishing, 2003); Clifford, *Atonement and Justification*; Boersma, *A Hot Peppercorn*. On Baxter and antinomianism, see Tim Cooper, *Fear and Polemic in Seventeenth-Century England: Richard Baxter and Antinomianism* (Aldershot, UK: Ashgate, 2001).

tween equivalent payment (*solutio tantidem*) and identical payment (*solutio eiusdem*), which originated in Roman law but had come in the seventeenth century to be applied to the work of Christ on the cross. We will discuss this distinction in the context of Baxter and Owen later; first, it is important to understand the origins and significance of this distinction in the nature of payment and thus to understand something of the European theological background against which Baxter and Owen were operating.

In the late sixteenth century, the most significant theological challenges to Reformed orthodoxy had not come from either the Catholics or the Lutherans; rather, it was from a radical Reformed group known as the Socinians. The Socinians were the followers of a pair of Italian theologians, Laelius and Faustus Socinius who, as uncle and nephew, became the most notorious heretical family in Europe. Of the two men, Faustus was undoubtedly the more brilliant and influential. In his *De Jesu Christo Servatore* (*On Jesus Christ Savior*) he launched what remains the most significant attack on the doctrine of what is today known as the penal substitutionary view of the atonement.[13]

At the heart of Faustus Socinus's critique was a deceptively simple point: the notions of forgiveness and penal satisfaction are fundamentally antithetical to each other. If God forgives sin, then there is surely no need for him to punish it. Indeed, for him to punish sin would render the whole notion of forgiveness entirely equivocal. After all, if an earthly father forgives his child for misbehaving but still spanks him for the same transgression, one might well ask if "forgiveness" means anything at all in such a context.[14]

The Socinian challenge to orthodoxy was powerful and one that was taken very seriously by all major Protestant theologians. In fact, Socinianism, as embodied in its primary confessional document, the Racovian Catechism, represented a radical reconstruction of the whole of Christian theology, advocating as it did the rejection of the doctrine of the Trinity, the reconstruction of christology along adoptionist lines, and the transformation of salvation into something essentially pedagogical.[15]

---

[13] Socinus wrote the work in Basel in 1578, but it was not published until 1594 in Poland. On Socinianism, see Alan W. Gomes, "*De Jesu Christo Servatore*: Faustus Socinus on the Satisfaction of Christ," *WTJ* 55 (1993): 209–31. On Socinianism in the English context, the work of H. J. McLachlan is dated but still useful: *Socinianism in Seventeenth-Century England* (Oxford: Oxford University Press, 1951). A more recent study which examines the function of Socinian writings in shaping seventeenth-century theological debates is that by Sarah Mortimer, *Reason and Religion in the English Revolution: The Challenge of Socinianism* (Cambridge: Cambridge University Press, 2010).

[14] For a full exposition, see Gomes, "*De Jesu Christo Servatore*."

[15] The Racovian Catechism was published in Cracow, Poland, 1594, where Reformed Protestantism had always had a radical edge and thus proved fertile soil for deviations from Reformed orthodoxy. This work was translated into English in the seventeenth century by the English Socinian John Biddle, against whom John Owen was

Perhaps the most significant response to the Socinian critique of the atonement came from the Dutch Remonstrant theologian and legal theorist Hugo Grotius (1583–1645). In his 1617 work, *A Defence of the Catholic Faith*, Grotius adopted the *solutio tantidem/solutio eiusdem* distinction from Roman law and applied it to the atonement. In response to the Socinian claim that Christ's paying the penalty for sin would render any notion of forgiveness incoherent, Grotius argued that Christ paid the equivalent, not identical, penalty for our sins. On this basis, he was then able to argue that a further action of God—that of graciously accepting the equivalent as payment—was necessary. For him, this allowed a place for gracious forgiveness and thus answered the Socinian objection.[16]

An analogy might make this point clearer. Person A owes person B $500 cash. If A gives B a literal $500 (an identical payment: *solutio eiusdem*), then the debt is immediately paid as an act of justice, pure and simple. Indeed, B cannot refuse the payment because it is exactly what is owed, in form and value, and thus B shows no mercy in accepting the money and releasing the debt. He is legally obliged so to do. If, however, A offers B a car which is worth $500 in lieu of the money (an equivalent payment: *solutio tantidem*), then B still has to agree to accept the car as an equivalent payment. Once he has done so, the debt is released; but crucially, B has to agree to the deal. That he does so is an act of mercy toward A. Thus, both mercy and justice are held together. To make the analogy even closer to that of Grotius, if person A has done something to subvert the government of a ruler, he may take the punishment himself or the ruler may agree to take something else as its equivalent. Again, the key is that a separate act, an act of the king's will, is required to accept as equivalent to the appropriate penalty that which is not in itself identical with it.[17]

If the distinction helped Grotius answer the Socinian challenge on relating justice and mercy, in the hands of Baxter it became a means of avoiding any hint of antinomianism or eternal justification. After all, if Christ actually has A's sins imputed to him on the cross, and if A's sins are punished there,

---

commissioned to write by a parliamentary committee in the 1650s. See John Owen, *Vindiciae Evangelicae: Or, the Mystery of the Gospel Vindicated*, in *Works*, 12:1–590. This work is a refutation both of Biddle's own catechetical writings and of the Racovian Catechism.

[16] Hugo Grotius, *Opera omnia theologica* (Amsterdam, 1679), 3:319.

[17] For further discussion of Grotius and the atonement, see Garry J. Williams, "Punishment God Cannot Twice Inflict: The Double Payment Argument *Redivivus*," chapter 18 in this volume. Of particular note is his analysis of Owen's view of satisfaction as containing both commercial and judicial elements.

A is then immediately justified from that moment on, however he behaves. The first moment A exerts faith is thus the first moment he consciously realizes what he has actually been all along: justified.

The point may well seem somewhat abstruse, if not irrelevant, to modern discussions of the extent of the atonement, but an exploration of Owen's arguments on this point and his response to Baxter's critique actually helps in an understanding both of the nature of Reformed orthodox views of the atonement in the seventeenth century, and also of the perennial problems associated with the isolation of one aspect of Christ's work as Mediator from the other aspects of his work. Indeed, the problematic term "limited atonement" is itself a function of such questions, isolating as it does the death of Christ from his life, resurrection, and intercession. Further, while the Grotian language might now seem archaic, it is clear from Paul's own teaching that a close connection exists in the NT between the blood of Christ and the divine act of justification of the ungodly (e.g., Rom. 3:21–26). This is a point which must therefore be reflected in the systematic structure of theology as it connects atonement to justification.[18]

John Owen and the Two Kinds of *Solutio*

Owen grapples with the distinction between the two kinds of *solutio* in book 3, chapter 7 of his *Death of Death*.[19] Citing Grotius as the principal architect of the distinction, he also notes that Grotius's denial of the *solutio eiusdem* is based on two objections. First, that such a *solutio* brings with it "actual freedom from the obligation," where he uses the term "actual" to mean "real and immediate." In other words, Grotius sees the *solutio eiusdem* as placing those whose sin has been so punished immediately into a state of grace. Second, that such a *solutio* removes any need for forgiveness or pardon.[20] We might summarize the two objections by saying that Grotius regards *solutio eiusdem* as giving the elect sinner an instant legal right to an immediate state of grace which God has a legal obligation to grant.

Owen's response is twofold. To the first objection, he draws an analogy between the status of a sinner whose sin Christ has paid for on the cross and that of a man languishing in prison in a foreign country. A friend might well

---

[18] For example, see Williams, *For Whom Did Christ Die?*, 202–205.
[19] Owen, *Death of Death*, in *Works*, 10:265–73.
[20] Ibid., 10:268.

pay the ransom for such a man, but until the messenger arrives at the prison with the relevant legal papers, the prisoner has neither knowledge of his forgiveness nor actual freedom.[21]

As to the second, that of a *solutio eiusdem* eliminating the need or even the possibility of any notion of grace or mercy or forgiveness in God's act of salvation, Owen responds by setting the death of Christ within the context of the plan of redemption as a whole. First, he points to the act of imputation of sins to Christ as being a free, gracious decision which God himself made without any coercion or necessity of so doing. Second, he points to the imputation of Christ's righteousness to the believer as also an act of grace and mercy. In short, the grace and mercy of God are not opposed to the merits of Christ; they are opposed to the merits of fallen human beings.[22]

Underlying Owen's concern here are two further points, one exegetical and one systematic. As to the exegetical point, Owen sees the *solutio eiusdem* as a good and necessary consequence of the Bible's teaching on the objective efficacy of Christ's death. Both immediately before and after the discussion of the two forms of *solutio*, Owen affirms that Christ's death has an objective efficacy and supports this claim with an arsenal of biblical texts.[23] If Christ's death *in itself* had efficacy, as these texts teach, then the positing of a further act or decision on the part of God is unnecessary and, indeed, theologically speculative.[24]

Second, Owen's response to Grotius also depends upon a further point which is central to his whole understanding of Christ's office as Mediator: the individual acts of Christ's mediation must ultimately be understood as parts of a unity. This unity is grounded in the concept of the covenant of redemption, to which we shall return after noting Richard Baxter's criticism.

Richard Baxter on Owen, Atonement, and Antinomianism

Although he was a year older than Owen, Baxter was certainly his junior in terms of ecclesiastical and theological stature in the late 1640s. Baxter was also something of a theological enigma. Unusual for a seventeenth-century

---

[21] Ibid.

[22] Ibid., 10:268–69.

[23] 1 Peter 2:24; Isaiah 53:5, 10, 11, 12; Ephesians 5:2; Hebrews 9:13, 14; Leviticus 5:1; 7:2; 1 John 2:2; Job 19:25; 2 Corinthians 5:21; Romans 3:25, 26; 8:3 (Owen, *Death of Death*, in *Works*, 10:266–67, 269).

[24] The objective efficacy of Christ's atonement is the perennial center of arguments for inferring the limitation of intention behind his death; see J. I. Packer, "What Did the Cross Achieve? The Logic of Penal Substitution," in *Celebrating the Saving Work of God: The Collected Shorter Writings of J. I. Packer, Volume 1* (Carlisle, UK: Paternoster, 1998), 85–123.

scholastic, Baxter was not university educated and thus his theology had all of the mercurial brilliance one might expect from a sharp intellect with a voracious appetite for books combined with the idiosyncracies of the autodidact.

As noted earlier, Baxter was driven by a particular set of concerns. He was worried about the proliferating sectarianism of the 1640s; and, above all, he was worried about the antinomianism which seemed to be a hallmark of much of this. These twin fears made him ecumenical in ambition, in that he was always trying to find a bridge or middle position between two extremes, and earnest in his commitment to formulating his understanding of salvation in a way that accented the moral imperatives of the Christian life.

As Baxter read Owen's *Death of Death*, he became convinced that Owen's arguments about the atonement played straight into antinomian hands. Indeed, by advocating the *solutio eiusdem*, Owen's theology seemed to him to push toward a doctrine of eternal justification or, if not that, at least justification which took place at the cross and whose objectivity and effectiveness thus stood independent of any need for individual repentance, faith, and a disciplined Christian life.

For this reason, Baxter engaged Owen in the appendix to his *Aphorismes of Justification* (1649). Baxter's opening concern with Owen is that, in asserting the *solutio eiusdem*, he proposes a situation whereby the sacrifice cannot be refused by God the Father and that it is therefore vulnerable to the Socinian critique that mercy and justice are opposed to each other. Baxter objects to this point on various grounds, but one of his main concerns is the fact that it pushes toward a doctrine of eternal justification. Given the fact that the objective efficacy of Christ's death is a staple of arguments for definite atonement, the challenge which Baxter poses has contemporary significance.[25]

Two aspects of Baxter's response are of particular interest. First, he presses the point that a *solutio eiusdem* must by definition be a non-refusable payment and is therefore vulnerable to the Socinian critique. Further, it is vulnerable to the accusation that no further conditions may be attached to it. This has obvious implications for conceiving of salvation in an antinomian way: if the sinner's debt is paid in full, God can demand nothing further from said sinner.[26]

Second, Baxter focuses in particular on Owen's analogy of the prisoner who is pardoned by the payment of a ransom yet who remains in prison until

---

[25] On eternal justification, see Trueman, *Claims of Truth*, 207–209.
[26] Richard Baxter, *Aphorismes of Justification* (London, 1649), 149–51.

such time as the messenger arrives at the jail to provide the certificate that allows him to be released. He raises a series of objections against this analogy. First, he argues that the distinction between being delivered and actually being released from prison is specious. If one is not actually released at the moment of deliverance, what exactly does deliverance mean? Second, he points out that coming to a knowledge of one's status is a comparatively small thing. Third, and consequently, faith is reduced to a mere epistemological point, not the moment of transition from wrath to grace. Fourth, it would seem odd that God denies us for so long in actuality that which we have a right to from the moment of Christ's death.[27]

Despite Baxter's relatively unknown standing at this point, his work clearly irritated Owen, who responded with a treatise written during his sojourn in Ireland as Cromwell's chaplain: *Of the Death of Christ* (1650).[28] While *Death of Death* is Owen's most famous treatise on redemption, this second work is itself highly instructive from a systematic theological perspective. It makes very clear that the problem Baxter perceives with the distinction between the two types of *solutio* is in large part a function of the isolation of Christ's death from his priesthood and mediatorial office as a whole. This is something which the unfortunate term "limited atonement" has canonized, abstracting as it does the events of the cross from the life of Christ as a whole, and generating a raft of questions and logical problems in its wake.

Person and Penalty

One of the distinctions Owen made in *Death of Death* and which Baxter subsequently seized hold of in his *Aphorismes* was his claim that, in Christ's atonement, the penalty was relaxed in terms of the person suffering but not in terms of the penalty suffered.[29] One of Baxter's objections to Owen's affirmation of the *solutio eiusdem* was that it was incoherent on the grounds that Christ did not suffer eternally but only for a finite period. On the Grotian scheme, Baxter could argue that Christ's death was taken as an equivalent; Owen, he argued, had no such luxury.[30]

---

[27] Ibid., 155–57.
[28] John Owen, *Of the Death of Christ, the Price He Paid, and the Purchase He Made*, in *Works*, 10:430–79. (Not to be confused with his other work entitled *Of the Death of Christ, and of Justification*; see below.)
[29] Owen, *Of the Death of Christ*, in *Works*, 10:442.
[30] Baxter, *Aphorismes*, 144–46.

In *Death of Death*, Owen spoke of God relaxing the law by allowing another to stand in place of those who were the real debtors.[31] This was thus nothing to do with any lowering of the standard required by God. Then, when responding to Baxter in *Of the Death of Christ*, Owen makes the point that the penalty required for sin was death.[32] This is an important point: there is a danger when thinking of Christ's atonement in terms of satisfaction for debt that one can be led astray into thinking in crudely quantitative terms: sin has accumulated x amount of debt; so the penalty is to be paid in terms of x, where x is analogous to money or property. That is not the model with which Owen is operating: the penalty is not quantitative in such a way; rather, it is perhaps better described as qualitative. It is not that Christ has to pile up a heap of suffering to match the offense human beings have given to God; it is that he has to die. Death is the penalty. Thus, Owen is able to maintain the *solutio eiusdem*: Jesus Christ dies and thus pays precisely the same penalty that is required of a sinner. There are rich and obvious implications here for the connection between atonement and incarnation.

The Prisoner Analogy Revisited

Owen also responds to Baxter's criticism of his use of the prisoner analogy. It is important here to set his original use of this in *Death of Death* in context. Immediately prior to its introduction, he writes,

> By death he did deliver us from death, and that actually, so far as that the elect are said to die and rise with him. He did actually, or *ipso facto*, deliver us from the curse, by being made a curse for us; and the hand-writing that was against us, even the whole obligation, was taken out of the way and nailed to his cross. It is true, all for whom he did this do not instantly actually apprehend and perceive it, which is impossible; but yet that hinders not but that they have all the fruits of his death in actual right, though not in actual possession, which last they cannot have until at least it be made known to them.[33]

It is Owen's use of the term *ipso facto* here to which Baxter objects, apparently because he sees it as demanding the immediate temporal pardon of the sinner whose debt is paid.[34] Owen concedes in his response to Baxter in *Of*

---

[31] Owen, *Death of Death*, in *Works*, 10:270.
[32] Owen, *Of the Death of Christ*, in *Works*, 10:443.
[33] Owen, *Death of Death*, in *Works*, 10:268
[34] E.g., Baxter, *Aphorismes*, 140, 150.

the Death of Christ that he could have spoken more clearly on this point.[35] Nevertheless, he offers a series of clarifications which make the context of the analogy somewhat clearer. First, he denies that he believes in justification prior to faith.[36] Second, he explains that he used the term *ipso facto* specifically to repudiate Grotius's argument that Christ's atonement is of benefit only to individuals on the basis of the performance of a further condition. In other words, not only does the atonement pay the price for sin, it also procures the conditions necessary for the application of Christ's death to the believer in time. As Owen expresses it,

> That the Lord Jesus, by the satisfaction and merit of his death and oblation, made for all and only his elect, hath actually and absolutely purchased and procured for them all their spiritual blessings of grace and glory; to be made unto them, and bestowed upon them, in God's ways and time, without out dependence on any condition to be by them performed, not absolutely procured for them thereby; whereby they become to have a right unto the good things by him purchased, to be in due time possessed, according to God's way, method, and appointment.[37]

To use language of causality, Christ's death is the meritorious cause of the individual's salvation; thus, his use of the term *ipso facto* should be seen as referring to causality, not chronology. What changes at Calvary is not the *state* of the unbelieving elect but their *right*: as elect, they are not immediately justified;[38] but they do immediately have the full right to enjoy all the benefits of Christ's death when they are united to him at the time he has appointed.[39] This, in turn, points toward the causal ground of the economy of redemption in the intra-Trinitarian establishment of Christ as Mediator by way of the covenant of redemption.

The Ground of Redemption: The Covenant of Redemption

The burden of Owen's response to Baxter lies in his assertion of the covenant of redemption (*pactum salutis*). The covenant of redemption emerged as a separate terminological concept c. 1645, though its roots lie in Reformation and post-Reformation discussions of the Protestant claim (and Roman Catho-

---

[35] Owen, *Of the Death of Christ*, in *Works*, 10:450.
[36] Ibid., 10:449.
[37] Ibid., 10:450.
[38] Ibid., 10:456–57.
[39] Ibid., 10:465–67.

lic denial) that Jesus Christ is Mediator according to both natures.[40] Hints of the notion can be found in the collection of Dutch disputations known as the *Synopsis Purioris Theologiae* and also in the work of Jacob Arminius.[41] However, while its origins lie in specific theological debates about the hypostatic union and the nature of the incarnate Son's subordination to the Father, by the 1630s and 1640s the issue of the Son's appointment as Mediator had taken on significance for discussing the merit or efficacy of his work.

The first time covenantal language appears in the context of discussing voluntary intra-Trinitarian relations relative to salvation occurs at the General Assembly of the Church of Scotland in 1638 in David Dickson's speech concerning the evils of Arminianism.[42] What is historically interesting is that the language of covenant in this context does not appear to catch the general theological imagination until about 1645, when suddenly it starts to proliferate in works of divinity both in the British Isles and on the continent.[43]

Owen himself bears witness in his own writings to the terminological innovations of the 1640s: in his earliest work, *A Display of Arminianism*, he does not use covenantal language to describe the relationship between Father and Son in redemption, but by 1647 he is quite happy to do so. The theology of the two works is consistent; what the new language does is bring a conceptual clarity to the whole that was absent before.[44]

The Purpose of the Covenant of Redemption

The theological purpose of covenant of redemption language is to ground the historical economy of Christ's work in the inner life of the Trinity. I have argued elsewhere that Owen's theology as a whole represents an extended reflection upon how to integrate a Trinitarian understanding of God with an

---

[40] Carl R. Trueman, *John Owen: Reformed Catholic, Renaissance Man* (Aldershot, UK: Ashgate, 2007), 80–81; also idem, "The Harvest of Reformation Mythology? Patrick Gillespie and the Covenant of Redemption," in *Scholasticism Reformed: Essays in Honour of Willem J. van Asselt*, ed. Maarten Wisse, Marcel Sarot, and Willemien Otten (Leiden, Netherlands: Brill, 2010), 196–214. See also, Carol A. William, "The Decree of Redemption Is in Effect a Covenant" (PhD diss., Calvin Theological Seminary, 2005).

[41] Herman Bavinck, ed., *Synopsis Purioris Theologiae* (Leiden, Netherlands: Donner, 1881), XXVI.xvi; Jacob Arminius, *Private Disputation 33*, in *Disputationes Publicae et Privatae* (Leiden, 1614), 76–78.

[42] Alexander Peterkin, ed., *Records of the Kirk of Scotland, Containing the Acts and Proceedings of the General Assemblies, From the Year 1638 Downwards* (Edinburgh: Peter Brown, 1843), 159.

[43] See, for example, Edward Fisher, *The Marrow of Modern Divinity* (London, 1645); Peter Bulkeley, *The Gospel-Covenant; or The Covenant of Grace Opened* (London, 1646). Willem J. Van Asselt offers a discussion of the development of the concept and terminology on the continent; see his *The Federal Theology of Johannes Cocceius* (Leiden, Netherlands: Brill, 2001), 227–47.

[44] For example, Owen, *Death of Death*, in *Works*, 10:168.

orthodox christology and an anti-Pelagian soteriology.[45] Central to this is the covenant of redemption.

In brief compass, the covenant of redemption is that which establishes Christ as Mediator, defines the nature of his mediation, and assigns specific roles to each member of the Godhead. The Father appoints the Son as Mediator for the elect and sets the terms of his mediation. The Son voluntarily accepts the role of Mediator and the execution of the task in history. The Spirit agrees to be the agent of conception in the incarnation and to support Christ in the successful execution of his mediatorial role.

What is important to understand at this point is that it is the covenant of redemption and not any other theological consideration that determines the nature and significance of any act that Christ performs as Mediator. For example, this is directly relevant to any discussion of the value of Christ's atonement. To take an earlier classic treatment of atonement, that of Anselm in *Cur Deus Homo*, the value or potency of Christ's death is a function of his existence as the God-man. God is infinite and therefore, because Christ is God, his death has infinite value. A similar point is made in the Canons of Dort:

> This death is of such infinite value and dignity because the person who submitted to it was not only the begotten Son of God, of the same eternal and infinite essence with the Father and the Holy Spirit, which qualifications were necessary to constitute Him a Saviour for us; and, moreover, because it was attended with a sense of the wrath and curse of God due to us for sin. (Article II.4)[46]

Discussions of the value of Christ's atonement in isolation from his whole work as Mediator, however, are problematic and somewhat speculative, and by the time Owen was writing in the 1640s, the difficulties with such terminology were obvious: how does the language of universal sufficiency connect to notions of divine intention in the constitution of Christ as Mediator? What does it mean for the death to be sufficient for all, if its meaning is rooted in the divine intention to establish Christ as Mediator relative to the whole economy of salvation?[47] For Owen, arguments for universal suf-

---

[45] See Trueman, *Claims of Truth*, passim.

[46] In Philip Schaff, The *Creeds of Christendom. Volume III: The Evangelical Protestant Creeds* (New York: Harper & Brothers, 1877), 586.

[47] For interesting discussion of the increasing complexity of debates about atonement and particularism in the early seventeenth century, see Jonathan D. Moore, *English Hypothetical Universalism: John Preston and the Softening of Reformed Theology* (Grand Rapids, MI: Eerdmans, 2007).

ficiency based on the Son's ontology are of very limited value and are likely to provoke the obvious commonsense response of "So what?" He certainly allows that there is nothing in the death of Christ, considered in isolation, to prevent its being sufficient for all; the question is whether such sufficiency has any real meaning in the actual economy of salvation. This is clear in his reflections on the Lombardian notion of universal sufficiency/particular efficacy:

> "That the blood of Christ was sufficient to have been made a price for all" . . . is most true, as was before declared: for its being a price for all or some doth not arise from its own sufficiency, worth, or dignity, but from the intention of God and Christ using it to that purpose, as was declared; and, therefore, it is denied that the blood of Christ was a sufficient price and ransom for all and every one, not because it was not sufficient, but because it was not a ransom.[48]

This point is extremely important: for Owen, abstract discussions of universal sufficiency are just that: abstract and irrelevant. It is not a question of whether the death of the Son of God could be sufficient for all; it is a question of what that death was intended to accomplish. That intention was determined by God in the establishment of the covenant of redemption.[49]

The Covenant of Redemption and the Nature of Merit

Underlying Owen's position is the notion that merit is covenantally determined. Connecting finite creatures to an infinite God had been a perennial concern of Christian theology, and discussions of merit had long roots back into the medieval period. In the Middle Ages, for example, theologians had argued that Adam in the garden had enjoyed a "superadded gift" (*donum*

---

[48] Owen, *Death of Death*, in *Works*, 10:296. Cf. Francis Turretin, *Institutes of Elenctic Theology*, ed. James T. Dennison, Jr., trans. George Musgrave Giger, 3 vols. (Phillipsburg, NJ: P&R, 1993), 2:458–59: "It is not asked with respect to the value and sufficiency of the death of Christ—whether it was in itself sufficient for the salvation of all men. For it is confessed by all that since its value is infinite, it would have been entirely sufficient for the redemption of each and every one, if God had seen fit to extend it to the whole world. . . . But the question properly concerns the purpose of the Father in delivering up his own Son and the intention of Christ in dying."

[49] Owen is quite clear that the constitution of Christ and the suffering which he endured would be quite sufficient for the redemption of all: "Now, such as was the sacrifice and offering of Christ in itself, such was it intended by his Father it should be. It was, then, the purpose and intention of God that his Son should offer a sacrifice of infinite worth, value, and dignity, sufficient in itself for the redeeming of all and every man, if it had pleased the Lord to employ it to that purpose; yea, and of other worlds also, if the Lord should freely make them, and would redeem them. Sufficient we say, then, was the sacrifice of Christ for the redemption of the whole world, and for the expiation of all the sins of all and every man in the world. This sufficiency of his sacrifice hath a twofold rise:—First, The dignity of the person that did offer and was offered. Secondly, The greatness of the pain he endured, by which he was able to bear, and did undergo, the whole curse of the law and wrath of God due to sin" (*Death of Death*, in *Works*, 10:295–96).

superadditum) of grace which had enabled him to perform works of real merit.[50] While later Protestants repudiated the Roman Catholic notion of grace, they nevertheless had to wrestle with precisely the issue of how infinite and finite can connect and, indeed, of how the finite can come to merit eternal rewards. Reformed theology from the late sixteenth century onward typically articulated this in terms of pre-fall Adam by use of the concept of the covenant of works: subsequent to creation, God entered into a covenant with Adam (as representative of his posterity) whereby he would reward Adam's obedience by giving him eternal life and punish his disobedience by death. The key point is that the value of Adam's obedience, as far as meriting eternal life goes, was not intrinsic but was the result of the extrinsic determination of God.[51] Thus, in his massive Latin work, *Theologoumena Pantodapa*, Owen pointed out that it was only the freely constituted covenant of works which provided the framework by which Adam, a mere creature, could have achieved a supernatural end. God condescended to establish a covenant with Adam; and then Adam was able to claim a debt from God, but only by virtue of the divinely initiated and determined covenant.[52]

The covenant of works concept has not been without subsequent critics within the Reformed tradition, most notably John Murray, partly because the language of covenant is absent from the Genesis account.[53] From a historical perspective, such criticism misses an important historical point: the covenant of works was not developed simply by exegeting Genesis 1 and 2; it arose more out of reflection on the Pauline epistles than on the creation account, still less the linguistically ambiguous Hosea 6:7.[54] This is

---

[50] For example, Thomas Aquinas, *Summa Theologiae*, 1a.95.1.

[51] On the origins and development of the covenant of works in Reformed theology, see Lyle D. Bierma, *German Calvinism in the Confessional Age* (Grand Rapids, MI: Baker, 1996); R. Scott Clark, *Caspar Olevian and the Substance of the Covenant* (Edinburgh: Rutherford, 2005); Robert Letham, "The *Foedus Operum*: Some Factors Accounting for Its Development," *Sixteenth Century Journal* 14 (1983): 457–67; Richard A. Muller, "The Covenant of Works and the Stability of Divine Law in Seventeenth-Century Reformed Orthodoxy: A Study in the Theology of Herman Witsius and Wilhelmus A Brakel," in idem, *After Calvin: Studies in the Development of a Theological Tradition* (New York: Oxford University Press, 2003); Willem Van Asselt, *The Federal Theology of Johannes Cocceius (1603–1669)*, Monographs of the Peshitta Institute Leiden (Leiden, Netherlands: Brill, 2001), 254–87.

[52] John Owen, *Theologoumena Pantodapa*, in *Works*, 17:40. Turretin, *Institutes*, 1:578, makes a nice distinction between types of debt with reference to Adam and the first covenant: "Therefore, there was no debt (properly so called) from which man could derive a right, but only a debt of fidelity, arising out of the promise by which God demonstrated his infallible and immutable constancy and truth."

[53] For example, John Murray, "The Theology of the Westminster Confession of Faith," in *Collected Writings of John Murray. Volume 4: Studies in Theology* (Carlisle, PA: Banner of Truth, 1982), 261–62.

[54] Cf. the comment of Richard Muller: "Of interest here is that all of these writers [pre-Westminster Assembly divines] understood the primary ground of the covenant of works, apart from Genesis 2:17, as Pauline and as found in Romans and Galatians. None of these writers looked to Hosea 6:7, although they surely knew of its long tradition of covenantal interpretation" (Richard A. Muller and Rowland S. Ward, *Scripture and Worship: Biblical Interpretation and the Directory for Worship* [Phillipsburg, NJ: P&R, 2007], 71–72).

important because it points to the close connection in Reformed dogmatics between the covenant with Adam and the work of Christ. Representative headship is covenantally grounded and determined, and discussion of such headship must therefore be rooted in discussion of the nature and terms of the covenant.

One could engage in an illuminating thought experiment at this point: for Owen, it would have been possible for the Logos to become incarnate, to live a sinless life, to die on the cross, to be resurrected from the dead, and to ascend to the right hand of the Father—and for the whole process to have no salvific value whatsoever. The mere ontological constitution of Christ as the God-man would have had no wider significance had he not been appointed as the federal representative of his people under terms of a covenant. The efficacy, the value, the very nature, of Christ's mediation is entirely determined by the terms of the covenantal structure of salvation.

The Covenant of Redemption and the Unity of the Office of Mediator

The importance of the covenant of redemption in determining the merit of Christ's death is a significant point because it highlights a point of major divergence between Baxter and Owen: in his desire to defend a universal salvific will in God, Baxter needs to separate out discussion of Christ's death or satisfaction from any discussion of prior particularity in the will of God to save. On this point, he stands in continuity with Hypothetical Universalist/Amyraldian thinking. For Owen, however, this prior particularity is crucial, not because of some simplistic logic whereby God elects only some and Christ can therefore only be said to die for some; Owen's case is more elaborate than that. Rather, the very causal ground of Christ becoming incarnate and taking the role of Mediator must be understood at the outset as being driven by God's desire to save, and that particularly. This means that Owen must insist that Christ's actions as Mediator must not be understood in isolation from each other. They are separate acts but derive their meaning from his one office as Mediator, an office which is defined by the covenant of redemption. This covenant not only appoints him to die but determines the value or significance of that death and undergirds the entirety of his role as Mediator, from conception to intercession at the right hand of the Father.

Thus, in *Death of Death*, Owen's response to the Grotian idea that *solutio eiusdem* precludes any notion of the freedom of God in forgiveness is answered by an implicit appeal to the terms of the covenant of redemption:

> *First*, The will of God freely appointing this satisfaction of Christ, John iii. 16; Rom. v. 8; 1 John iv. 9. *Secondly*, In a gracious acceptation of that decreed satisfaction in our steads; for so many, no more. *Thirdly*, In a free application of the death of Christ unto us.[55]

In short, Owen would answer the Socinian objection that Christ's penal death precludes any notion of the mercy of forgiveness by pointing to the prior decision of God as Trinity to establish the economy of salvation, and to the fact that such a decision was free and uncoerced. It is not that grace is introduced at the moment the Father accepts the Son's sacrifice as atonement for his people; grace is found in the divine act in eternity whereby the Father appoints the Son as Mediator and the Son voluntarily accepts the role. God did not have to establish Christ as Mediator any more than he had to establish a covenant of works with Adam in the garden; and as Adam's reward would have been both merited and the result of divine condescension, so salvation in Christ is both merited by Christ but established by an act of God's mercy.

Owen returns to this theme repeatedly in *Of the Death of Christ*. As noted above, one of Baxter's major concerns was the fact that a *solutio eiusdem* is a non-refusable payment and thus precludes mercy. In other words, God the Father cannot refuse the offering of the Son and therefore, according to Baxter, the Socinian objection about the conflict between justice and mercy stands.

Such an objection is problematic in a number of ways. For a start, it seems to posit an almost adversarial relationship between Father and Son and surely misses the point that Father and Son are at one in their salvific intentions. After all, to say that the offering is refusable does not simply imply something about the nature of the offering; it logically implies something about the Father as well, that he might hypothetically wish to refuse the offering that his Son is making. In other words, the Son might offer an atonement to the Father that the Father could refuse, thereby placing himself in conflict with his Son. That is surely problematic from the perspective of orthodox Trinitarian theology, with its adherence to the *homoousian*. If Father and Son are of the same substance, both equally God and one God,

---

[55] Owen, *Death of Death*, in *Works*, 10:269.

then such a potential conflict between them is impossible even at the hypo-thetical level.[56]

In addition to the ontological problems that refusability would create, there is the connected issue of the terms of the compact or covenant:

> Nothing can possibly tend to the procurement and compassing of any end, by the way of payment, with the Lord, but what is built upon some free compact, promise, or obligation of his own. But now consider it as an issue flowing from divine constitution making it a payment, and so it was no way refusable as to the compassing of the end appointed.[57]

The payment cannot be refused because God has already in eternity stipulated that it is a payment which will be accepted. While Owen does not point out the Trinitarian underpinnings of this, it should also be clear that the concept of the covenant of redemption itself reflects the commonality of will that exists between the consubstantial persons and is an attempt to conceptualize God's plan for salvation in a manner that respects the nature of God as Trinity. One might turn the argument back against Baxter at this point: if the payment is refusable, then it is necessary either that God the Father is able to break a prior compact which he has made; or one must allow that Father and Son might be set in opposition to each other relative to salvation. Neither option seems consistent with a biblical, Trinitarian doctrine of God.

Elsewhere in the treatise, Owen presses this back to the covenant of redemption by distinguishing between Christ's suffering as conceived in the abstract and as conceived relative to the covenant. In the abstract, Christ's suffering cannot be considered a refusable payment for the simple reason that it is not actually a payment at all, refusable or otherwise. It can only be considered a payment if one presupposes the existence of the covenant establishing it as such.[58] With reference to this covenant, however, Christ's suffering is constituted as a payment which is not refusable because of "the wisdom, truth, justice and suitable purpose of God being engaged to the contrary."[59] The covenant as an act of the triune God cannot create adversarial relationships between the members of the Godhead.

---

[56] One might respond by saying that the Father will accept the offering even though he can do otherwise; but if conflict is even possible within the Godhead, the implications for the doctrine of the Trinity are surely catastrophic.
[57] Owen, *Of the Death of Christ*, in *Works*, 10:441.
[58] Ibid., 10:458.
[59] Ibid.

Further, because the covenant determines the value and meaning of Christ's death, it is also the determining factor in how, when, and under what conditions the benefits of the death will be applied to the individual.[60] It is hard not to see here the fruit of the kind of discussion that had taken place from the Middle Ages onward concerning the dialectic of God's absolute and ordained power, which essentially guarded God's freedom while also guaranteeing the stability of the actual world he chose to establish.[61]

To Baxter's objection that adherence to *solutio eiusdem* requires that elect sinners be justified prior to believing (and thus as opening the way to antinomianism), Owen responds by making distinctions among different types of causes and by once again pointing to the need to see Christ's act of redemption as a whole.

According to Owen, Christ's death is the meritorious cause of salvation. As a meritorious cause, it does not require the immediate chronological existence of the effect to which it is determined. Thus, it is not like the floor which supports the chair upon which I am sitting: the existence of the floor here and now is the immediate cause of the fact that I am not at this moment plunging toward the earth's center. Christ's death is of a different kind of causality: it is the reason why individuals are forgiven at that time and under those conditions which God has chosen to establish via the covenant. The effects of a moral cause are mediated via the legal or covenantal framework which establishes their causality; and as a moral cause, the effects of Christ's death are determined by the covenant of redemption.[62] This in turn leads to Owen's second point: the death of Christ is that which not only pays the price for sin but which also provides the causal basis for all of

---

[60] "Hence it is that the discharge of the debtor doth not immediately follow the payment of the debt by Christ; not because that payment is refusable, but because in that very covenant and compact from whence it is that the death of Christ is a payment, God reserveth to himself this right and liberty to discharge the debtor when and how he pleaseth" (ibid.).

[61] The dialectic of God's absolute power and his ordained power was a distinction made in the Middle Ages. In brief, it was argued that God, being omnipotent, could do anything according to his absolute power, subject only to the law of noncontradiction (for example, he could not will A to exist and not exist at one and the same time). According to his ordained power, however, God had decided to realize a world which contained only a subset of the possibilities available to him in terms of his absolute power. Having realized this subset, however, he was committed to maintaining it in the manner in which he had willed. The created order was thus finite and contingent, but nonetheless stable and reliable. It was essentially an epistemological distinction which came increasingly into play in the late Middle Ages as a means of circumscribing the competence of human logic to predict how God must act. In this context, it would seem that Owen is making the point that the logical problems which seem to arise out of holding to the *solutio eiusdem* do not hold because they fail to take into account that God can transcend the limits that human logic might care to place upon him. On this distinction, see Heiko A. Oberman, *The Harvest of Medieval Theology: Gabriel Biel and Late Medieval Nominalism* (Durham, NC: Labyrinth, 1983), 42–47.

[62] Owen, *Of the Death of Christ*, in *Works*, 10:459–60.

the conditions attached to salvation for the elect. Indeed, while faith is the condition of receiving the benefits of Christ's death, it is itself procured by the death of Christ.[63]

One further aspect of Owen's articulation of effective redemption is the crucial unity that he sees between the sacrifice and the intercession of Christ. This is also vital because once again it highlights the systematic theological problems generated by trying to separate out the death of Christ and deal with it in isolation. If one were to look for a single theme that preoccupied Owen throughout his career, one could probably not do better than to point to Christ's priestly office.[64] It dominates his commentary on, and, indeed, presumably influenced his choice of the book of Hebrews, which occupied much of his scholarly energy in the later years of his life. Yet it was also central to the argument of his earliest work, *A Display of Arminianism*. Here, for example, is a comment on how to construe the relationship between the death and intercession of Jesus Christ:

> His intercession in heaven is nothing but a continued oblation of himself. So that whatsoever Christ impetrated, merited, or obtained by his death and passion, must be infallibly applied unto and bestowed upon them for whom he intended to obtain it; or else his intercession is vain, he is not heard in the prayers of his mediatorship.[65]

We must bear in mind that, in 1642, Owen does not yet have in hand the conceptually precise terminology of the covenant of redemption. Even so, his words here clearly indicate his belief that Christ's priestly office must be seen as a unity, grounded in the particular will to save which established him as Mediator. It is impossible, Owen argues, to claim that Christ intercedes for those for whom he died but who are not ultimately saved. To be explicit, that would create an adversarial relationship between Father and Son, and, indeed, play directly to the kind of caricatures of penal substitution which imagine a merciful Son cajoling an otherwise angry and reluctant Father into

---

[63] Ibid., 10:464. In another work responding to Baxter, *Of the Death of Christ, and of Justification*, published as an appendix to his 1655 work against the Socinians, *Vindiciae Evangelicae*, Owen sharpens his understanding of the timing of justification by connecting it to union with Christ by faith, and also by underscoring the fact that this faith which forges the union is itself an effect of the death and intercession of Christ. In this work it is clear that Owen regards the kind of logical problems Baxter lodged against his position as themselves being the result of a speculative isolation of one aspect of Christ's priestly office from all others (in *Works*, 12:606–608).

[64] This makes the virtual silence of Clifford on this matter in his *Atonement and Justification* very surprising, given that the focus of his study of Owen is atonement, a doctrine which cannot be appropriately assessed without setting it in the context of Christ's priesthood.

[65] Owen, *Death of Death*, in *Works*, 10:90.

being merciful toward sinners. Again, the implications for orthodox Trinitarianism would be catastrophic.[66]

Essentially the same position is articulated at greater length toward the end of Owen's life in his commentary on Hebrews. In the preliminary dissertation on the priesthood of Christ, Owen stresses the inseparability of Christ's death on the cross and his entry into the Holy of Holies before God to plead the cause of his people.[67] Then, in addressing the key text of Hebrews 7:25, he refers the whole action to the covenant of redemption both as its causal ground and as that which strictly defines and circumscribes the scope of Christ's priesthood as a whole.[68] This precludes the kind of distinction between the universality of intention behind Christ's death and the particularity of application in the intercession. Both death and intercession are two sides of the same coin, a coin whose purpose and value is determined by the covenant of redemption.

In the light of this, it has to be conceded that Owen's original analogy of the prisoner who is ransomed but not immediately released does have its dramatic shortcomings, as Baxter does not hesitate to point out. Yet that is surely a problem with all analogies. It is a truism that any analogy must by definition lack identity with, and thus possess only similarity to, that which it is designed to elucidate. Similarity supposes difference, difference which may be greater or lesser depending on the case in point. The truth of the doctrine, however, does not stand or fall with the appropriateness of the analogy. Clearly, the prisoner analogy does not really help to elucidate the crucial connection between Christ's death and his heavenly intercession; nor does it offer any insights into the grounding of the whole in a prior covenant. Indeed, it falls short as well because Christ is not, strictly speaking, offering ransom to a hostile foreign power but rather is carrying out the will of his Father, the one to whom the offering is to be made. Yet when set in context, Owen never intended the analogy as anything more than an illustration of his previous point about meritorious causality, a point which is itself quite coherent.

Concluding Thoughts

The clash between Owen and Baxter on the issue of atonement is instructive for a number of reasons. First, it highlights the fact that the limitation of the

---

[66] Owen also draws out the obvious implication of the non-effectual nature of universal atonement for notions of substitution: "[T]hough the Arminians pretend, very speciously, that Christ died for all men, yet, in effect, they make him die for no man at all" (ibid., 10:93).
[67] John Owen, *An Exposition of the Epistle to the Hebrews*, in *Works*, 19:194–97.
[68] Ibid., 19:524.

atonement is not the only issue that has proved controversial in this matter over the years. The connection between atonement and justification, touching as it does upon issues of the nature of imputation, of Christ's suffering, and of God the Father's disposition, is also a key part of the debate. In this, it reflects at a systematic level the connections the apostle Paul makes between Christ's blood and justification in the NT.

Secondly, the debate highlights the way in which questions about Christ's death cannot be separated from larger questions about his role as Mediator and, therefore, from questions about the Trinitarian economy of salvation. A formulation of atonement needs to respect catholic teaching on the nature of God as Trinity, particularly the consubstantiality of the Father and the Son. Any formulation of atonement which places Father and Son in adversarial roles (or even hypothetically allows for such) transgresses doctrinal boundaries that go far beyond Calvary and into the very being of God himself.

Thirdly, the debate provides some good examples of how the isolation of the death of Christ from its context in the broader economy of salvation can generate questions and logical problems which can take on a life of their own and which can only be resolved by refusing such isolation and insisting that Christ's mediatorial work be set within its larger contexts: the biblical context of sacrifice and intercession rooted in the OT; and the theological context of the Trinitarian economy of salvation. The blunt question, For whom did Christ die?, is perfectly legitimate, but the answer arises out of a host of interconnected biblical and theological themes.

Finally, we should note that this is far from an abstract discussion for Owen. In *Death of Death* he notes six natural consequences that flow from his commitment to *solutio eiusdem*, all of which have significant practical, existential implications for the believer: the full debt of the sinner has been paid; God cancels all suits and actions against the sinner; the payment was not for this or that sin but for all sins of those for whom Christ died; God can demand no further payment; God has obliged himself to grant pardon to those whose debts he has himself paid; the law is silenced, because in Christ it has been fulfilled in a full and final manner.[69] That is indeed good news, and good news worth proclaiming.

---

[69] Owen, *Death of Death*, in *Works*, 10:273.

II

DEFINITE ATONEMENT
IN THE BIBLE

"Because He Loved Your Forefathers"

ELECTION, ATONEMENT, AND INTERCESSION IN THE PENTATEUCH

Paul R. Williamson

Introduction

One must readily admit that the Pentateuch may seem infertile soil to yield the doctrine of definite atonement. After all, atonement does not seem to play a significant role in Genesis, and there is little explicit connection between sacrifice and atonement until the ritual legislation at the start of Leviticus.[1] Moreover, the Day of Atonement (Leviticus 16) encompasses the entire community, as do similar provisions such as Aaron's censer of incense (Numbers 16), the water of cleansing (Numbers 19), and the bronze snake (Numbers 21). Indeed, even the Passover sacrifice (Exodus 12) and the intercession of Moses (Exodus 32–34) seem to have a general rather than a particular focus,

---

[1] In Genesis the key verb (Piel כפר) is used only in relation to Jacob's intention to "appease" Esau with his gifts of livestock (32:20); in Exodus the verb is used in relation to "atonement" associated with the ordination and consecration of the priests (29:33, 36–37), the annual atonement of the altar of incense (30:10), the atonement associated with the census tax (30:15–16), and Moses's offer to atone in some way for Israel's apostasy during the golden calf incident (32:30). Space does not allow a detailed investigation into the meaning of this important term. While the Qal conveys the idea of "to cover" (cf. Gen. 6:14), the Piel seems to connote either "to ransom" (cf. Ex. 30:11–16; Num. 35:29–34) or "to wipe clean" (i.e., "to purge"; cf. Jer. 18:23, where it is used in parallel with "to blot out"). For a detailed discussion, see Richard E. Averbeck, "כפר," in *New International Dictionary of Old Testament Theology and Exegesis*, ed. Willem A. VanGemeren, 5 vols. (Grand Rapids, MI: Zondervan, 1997), 2:689–710.

in that these benefit the Israelite community as a whole rather than some subgroup within it (such as an elect remnant).

Having said this, however, a closer look at this biblical corpus, including the specific texts mentioned above, will demonstrate that while definite atonement is nowhere explicitly mentioned, there are certainly hints of the concept embedded within this body of literature. Rather than suggesting some kind of general atonement, the relevant texts all point toward a more definite focus—either in terms of Israel as God's chosen people, or in terms of individuals whose actions set them apart from the community as a whole.

Before looking more closely at particular texts relating to atonement and priestly intercession, it is important to set all these within their biblical-theological context. After all, it was not just any nation that enjoyed the special privileges and blessings depicted here, but the people of Israel, the national embodiment of God's promise to Abraham. Thus any consideration of Israel's experiences must take on board Israel's unique status as the elect people of God. God's special dealings with Israel, to which the Pentateuch repeatedly attests, are firmly premised on the idea of Israel's divine election. It is within this larger theological construct that any OT theology of atonement must be understood.

Israel's Status as God's Elect

Israel's unique status as the nation whom God had personally chosen is underscored explicitly on several occasions in the Pentateuch, most notably in Deuteronomy (cf. 4:37; 7:6–7; 10:15; 14:2). As the first of these texts highlights, Israel's redemption from Egypt and subsequent blessings flowed out from the love that Yahweh had for Israel's ancestors: "Because he loved your ancestors and chose their descendants after them, he brought you out of Egypt by his Presence and his great strength" (Deut. 4:37, NIV). Now admittedly—as is evident from a comparison of various English translations—there is no consensus over where the protasis ends and the apodosis begins. Consequently, some translations begin the latter after the first clause: "Because He loved your fathers, He chose their descendants after them and brought you out of Egypt by His presence and great power" (HCSB). In view of the string of infinitive constructs in verse 38, the ESV begins the apodosis clause with the switch to the *weqatal* at the start of verse 39:[2]

---

[2] The MT of verse 37 has a series of *wayyiqtol* clauses after the opening, unspecific X-*qatal* clause ותחת כי אהב ("on account of that he [Yahweh] loved"). While any of these *wayyiqtols* could constitute the apodosis clause, it seems

‏. . . וּיֹוצִאֲךָ . . . וּיִּבְחַר . . . וַתַּחַת כִּי אָהַב‏	extended protasis
‏. . . וּיֹדֵעַת‏	apodosis

Whatever understanding is correct, verse 37 assumes a logical sequence of events: viz., Israel's experience of deliverance ultimately derives from the fact that Yahweh had loved their ancestors. Indeed, Yahweh's love was also an expression of divine election (Gen. 18:19; cf. Neh. 9:7). It is on this basis, and this alone, that Israel is the recipient of God's mercy and the beneficiary of God's saving acts (cf. Deut. 7:7–8; 9:4–6). While the benefits may certainly encompass others—as clearly they sometimes do (cf. Ex. 12:38; Num. 11:4)—God's saving actions in the Pentateuch are primarily focused on his chosen people, the nation he has chosen from all others to be his "treasured possession" (Ex. 19:5; Deut. 7:6). Thus understood, any atonement that encompasses the entire community of Israel cannot really be interpreted in a general or universal sense; rather, it must be seen to have a definite or particular focus. The community it encompasses is a special community—the object of God's love and special favor, a people evidently distinguished from all others (cf. Deut. 4:32–35; 32:8–9).[3] Thus it would be inappropriate to infer some kind of general atonement from *Israel's* corporate experience of atonement. Any such atonement is accomplished and applied on the basis of Israel's divine election—the latter is the spring from which the former flows; atonement is made for Israel *as* God's elect people.[4]

This does not imply, however, that each individual Israelite was thus equally atoned for and thus "eternally forgiven." Such was evidently not so, as is clear from the judgments experienced by both renegade individuals and apostate generations.[5] National atonement provided for the purification and survival of the nation as *a nation*; apparently it did not secure the permanent purification and survival of each individual or generation it embodied.

---

more likely that each of these expands on the initial X-*qatal* clause to form a protracted protasis, with the apodosis introduced by the *weqatal* clause and renominalized subject (Yahweh) of verse 39. Such a reading would also tie in better with the theological rhetoric of the pericope (vv. 35–39), which emphasizes the uniqueness of Israel's God.

[3] While these texts present significant exegetical challenges, there is no doubt that they serve to illustrate and emphasize the fact of Israel's uniqueness vis-à-vis the nations.

[4] Moreover, contrary to what some have suggested, election here clearly circumscribes atonement, not vice versa. Admittedly, those who have suggested otherwise have generally had in view the logical order of the eternal decrees of God rather than their outworking in history; nevertheless, it is surely significant that in Israel's experience (and thus within the redemptive-historical plot line of the Bible), election precedes atonement and is its theological prerequisite. As later essays in this volume will demonstrate, the same is true of all those who were chosen in Christ "before the foundation of the world" (Eph. 1:4).

[5] Of course, such "temporal" judgment may not necessarily imply eternal judgment. However, it is difficult to imagine otherwise in cases where Israelites are "cut off" (by whatever means) as a consequence of high-handed sin.

Rather, personal transgressions had still to be atoned for, so as not to evoke God's judgment on either the individual or the community as a whole. It is clear, therefore, that any atonement Israel experienced and appropriated at a national or corporate level must be carefully distinguished from that experienced and appropriated at a more personal or individual level. In other words, when discussing atonement in the OT, the covenant–elect distinction must be borne in mind. While all Israelites might outwardly enjoy the benefits secured for the covenant community through national atonement, ultimately such benefits belonged exclusively to the remnant—those Israelites whose circumcision was more than an outward ritual and whose covenantal status was more than merely physical.[6]

Sacrifice and Atonement in Genesis

While the concept of substitutionary sacrifice has sometimes been inferred from Genesis 3:21,[7] this is probably reading more into the text than is exegetically warranted. As John H. Walton observes, "the institution of sacrifice is far too significant an occurrence to leave it entirely to inference."[8] Moreover, the primary point here seems to relate to the inadequacy of the garments Adam and Eve produced, rather than the necessity of violent death (which again must be inferred) for the provision of suitable coverings. Thus, whatever its potential as an illustration of definite atonement, the link between this text and substitutionary sacrifice seems tenuous at best.

In the following narrative, individual offerings provide the setting for Cain's killing of Abel; however, once again nothing is said in terms of any substitutionary or atoning significance (Genesis 4). In the subsequent flood story, Noah's postdiluvian sacrifices certainly do have atoning significance, the "soothing aroma" precipitating God's merciful response to innate human sinfulness (Gen. 8:20–21). It is reasonable to infer some kind of intentional theological association from the use of such language with respect to Levitical offerings (cf. Lev. 1:9; 2:2; 3:5; 4:31).[9] Moreover, one could argue that these atoning sacrifices in Genesis had a very definite focus—substituting

---

[6] For example, all Israel was redeemed out of Egypt, but Korah, Dathan, and Abiram died under God's wrath (Numbers 16; cf. 2 Tim. 2:19).

[7] So Bruce K. Waltke, *Genesis: A Commentary* (Grand Rapids, MI: Zondervan, 2001), 95.

[8] John H. Walton, *Genesis*, New International Version Application Commentary (Grand Rapids, MI: Zondervan, 2001), 229.

[9] So Gordon J. Wenham, "The Theology of Old Testament Sacrifice," in *Sacrifice in the Bible*, ed. Roger T. Beckwith and Martin J. Selman (Carlisle, UK: Paternoster, 1995), 80–81; also Christopher J. H. Wright, "Atonement in the Old Testament," in *The Atonement Debate*, ed. Derek Tidball et al. (Grand Rapids, MI: Zondervan, 2008), 76.

for those who had just escaped the deluge of the flood and constituted the nucleus of the new humanity.

The concept of substitution is first explicitly introduced in the account of the near slaying of Isaac, where the ram in the thicket plays a significant substitutionary role (Gen. 22:13). While there is no explicit suggestion here of an atonement for sin, Gordon Wenham is surely correct in his conclusion "that Genesis 22, like many stories in Genesis, is also paradigmatic and elucidates the OT understanding of sacrifice in general."[10] In any case, it can be extrapolated from this incident that at least some OT sacrifices involved a substitutionary element and had a very specific focus (in this case, Isaac is the primary beneficiary, although Abraham and Sarah also benefited in some measure).

Aside from these few examples, Genesis has little that explicates the theology of either sacrifice or atonement. Moreover, what there is requires significant unpacking in the light of subsequent teaching in the Pentateuch and beyond. The book of Exodus, however, seems much more promising, with its focus on the Passover ritual.

The Passover Ritual (Exodus 12–13)

The Passover ritual, the first example of community sacrifice in the Pentateuch, is not expressly associated with either sin or atonement.[11] Thus its relevance to the present discussion could arguably be called into question. However, the fact that the Passover is described here as a "sacrifice," that it averts God's judgment from the Israelite households,[12] and that it is explicitly linked to the death of Jesus in the NT (e.g., John 19:36; 1 Cor. 5:7; 1 Pet. 1:19),[13] certainly makes it germane. Given its clear typological significance, its peculiar features demand close examination and reflection.

The following aspects immediately stand out. The amount of flock

---

[10] Wenham, "Theology of Old Testament Sacrifice," 80.

[11] If this were the author's main point, the connection between the blood of the Passover animal and Israel's sin would arguably have been spelled out in the book of Exodus. The book, however, does not primarily portray the Israelites in Egypt as transgressors in need of reconciliation, but rather as slaves in need of emancipation. Thus, while the former is certainly true and should not be denied (see below), it does not seem to be the major focus in the book of Exodus prior to Israel's experience at Sinai.

[12] While judgment is explicitly mentioned only in relation to "all the gods of Egypt" (Ex. 12:12), it is clear that the death of Egypt's firstborn primarily constituted judgment on Pharaoh and the Egyptian populace, not only for their foolish reliance on such deities that were unable to protect, but also for their refusal to comply with Yahweh's demands (4:23; 11:1; cf. 5:3) and their abuse of Abraham's descendants (cf. Gen. 12:3; 15:14). This same judgment would befall any Israelite household not covered by blood.

[13] See also the allusions in the narratives of the Last Supper.

animal consumed was to be directly proportionate to the number in each household (Ex. 12:4), suggesting that each animal slain provided for only a limited number of individuals.[14] Its apotropaic effects were thus restricted to a carefully qualified group of people within each household. Each lamb served a specific body of people and redeemed a prescribed household. Moreover, only those who actually participated in the Passover meal could find refuge behind the blood-smeared door frames (12:7–13, 21–23).[15] There is thus no idea here of an all-embracing sacrifice, but rather one that served a specific goal for a specific group. While the text explicitly mentions only the Egyptians, presumably the same judgment was visited on every household in Egypt that evening which was not protected by Passover blood (12:13). The same disaster would apparently have befallen the Israelite households as well, had they not followed Yahweh's instructions with respect to the Passover ritual (12:21–28).[16] The Passover cannot therefore be conceived as some kind of general sacrifice that made provision for all and sundry; rather, it is clearly portrayed as having a definite goal and a particular focus. As noted earlier, that particular focus derives from God's election of Israel. In Exodus, the reason God will deliver his people is because of the covenant that he made with their forefathers whom he had chosen (2:24; 3:10; 6:1–8).

Such is further underscored by the various regulations for its subsequent commemoration. "Outsiders" were excluded. Only those who had actually become part of the Israelite community (i.e., via circumcision) were permitted to eat the Passover (12:43–45, 48–49). Moreover, only the firstborn of every womb *among the Israelites* belonged to Yahweh (13:2) and, as such, were to be handed over to Yahweh unless redeemed (13:12–13). Significantly, when Yahweh later substituted the Levites in place of Israel's firstborn sons (cf. Num. 3:40–51; 8:5–19), rather precise calculations were involved, with a redemption price required for each of the 273 surplus Israelite firstborn (Num. 3:46–50). Thus the primary beneficiaries of the Passover were

---

[14] For the translation of שֶׂה as "flock animal" rather than the traditional "lamb," see John I. Durham, *Exodus*, WBC (Waco, TX: Word, 1987), 151. As Douglas K. Stuart, *Exodus*, New American Commentary (Nashville: B&H, 2006), 273 n. 15, observes, the convention of translating the word "lamb" reflected in most modern English translations is simply due to the fact that a more accurate rendition such as "lamb or goat kid" would be literally awkward to employ on a regular basis.

[15] A close reading of the text suggests that once the animal's blood had been smeared on the doorframe, everyone had to remain inside the house until after the destructive plague had passed by.

[16] With T. Desmond Alexander, "The Passover Sacrifice," in *Sacrifice in the Bible*, ed. Roger T. Beckwith and Martin J. Selman (Carlisle, UK: Paternoster, 1995), 17, one can reasonably infer from this that the Israelite firstborn were no different from those of their Egyptian overlords, and thus were atoned for by the blood of the Passover sacrifice.

apparently the Israelite community in general, and the Israelite firstborn in particular.[17] Consequently, it is the Israelites who are portrayed as Yahweh's redeemed people (cf. Ex. 15:13), and, not surprisingly, it is this same community that is the focus of Moses's intercession after they had jeopardized their future in the episode involving the golden calf.

Priestly Intercession for Israel (Exodus 32)

The seriousness of Israel's apostasy in Exodus 32 cannot be overstated. Yahweh was angry enough to annihilate Israel and begin afresh with Moses (v. 10). While such immediate disaster was averted only because this would be misconstrued by others (v. 12) and undermine the covenant promises of Yahweh himself (v. 13), the bleak consequences of Israel's "great sin" are vividly underscored: they had broken Yahweh's covenant (v. 19), and even the summary executions carried out by the Levites (vv. 25–29) had not placated God's wrath (vv. 30–35). Their only hope was in the mercy of God, and it was on those grounds that Moses pleaded to Yahweh on their behalf.[18] After his initial efforts to secure forgiveness failed, Moses continued to implore Yahweh's favor until, finally, his petitions were answered and Yahweh's covenant with Israel was restored.

While this section of Exodus contains a number of exegetical challenges,[19] one thing is clear: throughout this divine-human exchange the primary focus of Moses's concern was Israel; Moses begged that this nation as God's chosen though undeserving people might remain the object of his grace and mercy. It was the people of God for whom he interceded, and it was as the people of God that Israel experienced Yahweh's mercy and was brought back into covenant relationship with him. Moses's priestly intercession was focused on Israel as God's elect. Not surprisingly, a similarly narrow focus is reflected in the nation's annual purification ritual on the Day of Atonement.

---

[17] Whereas the former (all Israel) foreshadows the corporate redemption of God's elect, the latter (Israel's firstborn) foreshadows their individual redemption.

[18] While it has sometimes been suggested that Moses was offering his own life in exchange for Israel's (v. 30), this interpretation seems rather unlikely. The immediate context has Yahweh threatening to annihilate Israel and realize the ancestral promise through Moses (v. 10). In such a setting, Moses's words are best understood as an explicit dismissal of such an option: if Yahweh is not prepared to spare Israel, then Moses is willing to share Israel's fate. A similar sentiment seems to be expressed in Numbers 11:15.

[19] These are discussed in the standard commentaries. None is particularly relevant for the present discussion.

The Day of Atonement (Leviticus 16)

However obscure some of the details may remain,[20] the key elements of this ritual are fairly clear. On this significant day in Israel's religious calendar, the high priest "made atonement for himself and for his house and for all the assembly of Israel" (v. 17). This is explained in terms of purifying the Most Holy Place, the tent of meeting, and the altar (v. 20) from the polluting effects of Israel's sin (v. 16), as well as cleansing the entire Israelite community from all their sins (v. 30; cf. vv. 33–34). The latter is symbolically portrayed by the transfer of "all the iniquities of the people of Israel, and all their transgressions, all their sins" onto the live goat, which then carries them to the remote place where it is released (vv. 21–22).[21] Hence, by means of this special ritual, purification from all the polluting effects of sin was eloquently proclaimed.

A particular focus (i.e., Israelite) of the Day of Atonement is in one sense unquestionable.[22] However, a more general concept of atonement has been extrapolated from the fact that this particular ritual encompassed all Israelites, both elect and non-elect.[23] Two responses are necessary.

First, it is a non sequitur to argue from an atonement for a "mixed" Israel to a general, universal atonement for everyone, because even atonement in the OT was bound by covenant and election. Israel's status as God's chosen nation must not be overlooked here. It was exclusively for Israel, God's elect nation, that the high priest secured this annual ritual purification. No such purification or forgiveness of sins accrued for the surrounding (non-Israelite) nations. The Day of Atonement benefited only those who physically belonged to the Israelite community—the nation with whom God had established a unique covenant relationship. It was this covenant community—"the people

---

[20] For example, the precise meaning and significance of עֲזָאזֵל is unclear. The ancient versions interpreted it as "scapegoat," a compound of עֵז ("goat") and אָזַל ("to go away"), hence "the goat that departs." Others take it to refer to the goat's destination, identifying this as either a physical location (e.g., "a rocky precipice" or "rough ground"), or some kind of spiritual entity (a demon or the Devil himself). The parallels between לַעֲזָאזֵל ("for/to ʿazāʾzēl") and לַיהוה ("for/to Yahweh") in Leviticus 16:8–10 may lend support to the latter interpretation. Thus understood, the ritual signified the removal of Israel's sins to their source, but certainly not the payment of a ransom to a "goat demon" (cf. Lev. 17:7) or any other malevolent spiritual being. The second goat is never said to be sacrificed.

[21] As will be argued later, the high priest's placing of *both* hands on the goat (v. 21) reflects the fact that both his own sins and the sins of the community are being transferred to this condemned goat.

[22] In some respects this day was all-inclusive (i.e., everyone in the Israelite camp, whether native-born or foreigner residing in their midst, had to participate in some manner; v. 29); however, in the most significant respect it was strictly exclusive (only the sins of the Israelites are said to be atoned for; v. 34). Moreover, given the way that foreigners residing in Israel are included in Israel's worship regulations elsewhere (e.g., 22:18), they are most probably conceived here as those who have been fully incorporated into Israel. Such is apparently confirmed by the penalty imposed in Leviticus 23:29.

[23] For example, see Mark Driscoll and Gerry Breshears, *Death by Love: Letters from the Cross* (Wheaton, IL: Crossway, 2008), 179.

of Israel" (vv. 16, 17, 19, 21, 24, 33, 34)—that was the focus of both the atonement ritual and the priestly intercession that was carried out on this annual basis.[24] Thus atonement and intercession had a particular focus and definite effect for national Israel. Covenant and election circumscribed atonement. So a particular atonement may still be maintained for a "mixed" covenant community.

Secondly, this leaves unexplained how OT atonement operates in relation to the Israelite community, comprised of elect and non-elect individuals. Given that only the former were ultimately redeemed, in some sense the measure of purification obtained and forgiveness experienced by the individuals within this covenant community must be differentiated. Moreover, how an atonement for "mixed" Israel relates to Christ's atonement in the NT requires explanation. This brings us to the area of typology. The issue is a complex one, but at the risk of oversimplification, two main approaches may be discerned from those who defend definite atonement.

THE DAY OF ATONEMENT AND COVENANTAL FRAMEWORKS

New Covenant Theology Approach

In regard to the typology of OT sacrifice, Barnes has argued that "the atoning sacrifices and the redeeming acts of Yahweh in the Old Testament are only typological. . . . when it comes to the forgiveness of sin and eternal salvation, it was always only the remnant, a smaller group within Israel, who was in view."[25] While this discounts the wider purview of ritual purification and temporal forgiveness that does seem to have been experienced by the entire community (see above), Barnes differentiates between God's purpose for Israel as a nation and his purpose for the believing remnant (part of the true Israel of which Paul speaks) within that nation. For Barnes, while atonement for the entire Israelite community *typified* what Christ would ultimately accomplish through the cross and resurrection (i.e., the purification of all *true* Israel), only the remnant within OT Israel actually *experienced* the saving benefits (i.e., cleansing and forgiveness) of Christ's work, foreshadowed in the OT rituals of sacrifice and atonement. Thus, as he concludes,

---

[24] Significantly, the intercession of the high priest was coextensive with the atonement secured for all Israel. Like its NT antitype (Christ's high-priestly intercession on behalf of his elect), there is no thought here of intercession (or atonement) extending beyond the people of God.

[25] Tom Barnes, *Atonement Matters: A Call to Declare the Biblical View of the Atonement* (Darlington, UK: Evangelical Press, 2008), 78.

> When we read of the elective or the effective particular atoning and re-
> demptive acts of God on behalf of all Israel (larger than the remnant) we
> must remember that it was typological in order to set a backdrop for how
> salvation would be accomplished through Jesus Christ. The breadth of this
> typological work with the entire nation was never meant to define the extent
> of the atonement through Jesus Christ. As Paul clarifies in Romans 4 and
> 9 the purpose of God when it comes to his sovereign gracious salvation of
> individuals was always more particular than the typological purpose ac-
> complished throughout [sic] all Israel.[26]

In sum, while the entire community experienced *ritual* purification on the
Day of Atonement, this falls far short of the ultimate reality that such annual
purification and forgiveness merely foreshadowed: spiritual cleansing and
eternal forgiveness.[27] This ultimate reality could not be secured "by the blood
of goats and calves" (whether on the Day of Atonement or at any other time),
but only through "the blood of Christ" (cf. Heb. 9:11–28). Thus those who
have construed a general focus in the Day of Atonement ritual have inadvertently confused the symbolism with the spiritual reality.

Reformed Covenantal Approach

While agreeing in part with new covenant theology, theologians of a Reformed
covenantal persuasion may well find some of Barnes's approach problematic.
There is agreement that the atonement in the OT offered through animal sacrifices cannot properly atone for sin. The One to whom these sacrifices pointed
is alone the sufficient grounds for the forgiveness of OT believers (Rom.
3:25–26). However, differences surface at the level of typology. For Barnes,

> God was working on two levels in the Old Testament. On one level he was
> working with all the Israelites, the whole nation . . . in order to provide the
> concrete, visual lesson for how salvation takes place. . . . On the second
> level he was truly saving individuals—those who trusted him for salvation,
> the remnant (Gen. 15:6; Ps. 32:1–2; Rom. 9:6–13).[28]

On this reading, the atonement for *national* Israel is *only* typological.[29] This
gives the impression that there were no benefits for Israel as a nation in the

---

[26] Ibid., 82.
[27] The same may be said of circumcision, an outward sign placed on all Israel, but the inward reality only experienced by the true Israel, the elect remnant.
[28] Barnes, *Atonement Matters*, 66.
[29] Ibid., 78: "the atoning sacrifices and the redeeming acts of Yahweh in the Old Testament are only typological."

OT or that the non-elect Israelites did not benefit in some ways from the national atonement, whether physically as a nation (in the exodus), or even in the sense of temporal forgiveness, whether it be national or individual (Day of Atonement or personal sacrifices). Redemption from Egypt secured a real freedom from slavery for Israel as a nation, as Barnes himself notes,[30] but it also culminated in a covenantal relationship with Yahweh, one that incorporated temporal forgiveness of sins on a yearly basis through the Day of Atonement, as Reformed covenantal theologians point out. Barnes appears to discount the latter: ritual purification and temporal forgiveness were applied to *all* Israel, both elect and non-elect, through the annual atonement for Israel's sins and also through the sacrifices offered by individuals for their own sins (elect and non-elect alike). Reformed covenant theologians would concur with Barnes that the national sacrifice—either in the Passover or in the Day of Atonement—is a type of Christ's sacrifice for his elect: Christ is our Passover Lamb (1 Cor. 5:7), whose legs were not broken (John 19:36; cf. Ex. 12:46), as he bled for those whom the Father had given him (John 17); Christ is the final, perfect Yom Kippur sacrifice, offered once and for all for the sins of all his people (Heb. 2:17; 9:11–14, 23–28; 10:1–14).

However, traditional covenant theology assumes that the OT typology of atonement is more complex than Barnes allows, discerning a covenant–elect distinction that works itself out in relation to the atonement in the OT and NT. Observing the Israel-within-Israel distinction means that benefits of atonement for national Israel (atonement made for Israel *as a whole*) may accrue to non-elect Israelites by virtue of their association with the covenant. But this does not mean that all individuals were full partakers *of* the atonement and thus *true* members of the covenant.[31] What was outward and ritual for all was inward and spiritual for only some, as it was with circumcision. The former benefit from the national atonement temporarily and show all the signs of partaking of it, but in time they turn away from the faith and become apostate (e.g., Korah, Dathan, and Abiram in Numbers 16); they are not true members of the covenant for whom the reality becomes internal. Atonement

---

[30] Ibid., 65–66.

[31] Reformed covenant theologians argue for a distinction between members *in* the covenant and members *of* the covenant. See, for example, Louis Berkhof, *Systematic Theology* (Edinburgh: Banner of Truth, 1958), 284–90. Whatever one thinks of such a distinction, the main point—that some benefits of redemption/atonement extended to non-elect Israelites—does not depend on it.

and provision in the OT was thus for true Israel, but non-elect Israelites enjoyed some benefits, albeit temporally.

According to the Reformed covenantal approach, the same is true in the NT: Christ's atonement is for his church (Eph. 5:25), the elect, but, as with Israel, a distinction must be made between the visible (mixed) and invisible (true) church. On this view, the visible church is synonymous with the new covenant community, whereas the invisible (true) church constitutes the elect, for whose sins Christ's death made full atonement. Even the former, however, may experience certain benefits of Christ's death for a time. There are thus places in the NT where Christ is said to have died for non-elect members of the covenant community. These visible members of the church are said to be part of "the church," which Christ "obtained with his own blood" (Acts 20:28–30),[32] but they are those who are "denying the Master who bought them" (2 Pet. 2:1). They are described as those who have "tasted of the heavenly gift" (Heb. 6:4), who have "trampled underfoot the Son of God" and "profaned the blood of the covenant" (Heb. 10:29); they are those who have "escaped the defilements of the world through the knowledge of our Lord and Savior Jesus Christ" (2 Pet. 2:20). In short, according to Reformed covenantal theologians, while these non-elect members of the covenant community experience benefits of the atonement,[33] over time they are shown not to be lasting beneficiaries or part of the church in the fullest sense.

Summary

The issue of a "mixed" Israel/church/new covenant community and its relations to the atonement impinges upon larger issues that are outside the scope of this chapter, namely, the differences between new covenant theology and Reformed covenant theology, and readers will have to form their own judgments on which approach is best suited to the biblical material in both Testaments.[34] Suffice it to say, what is seen on either reading is that to deduce a general, universal atonement in the NT from an atonement for a "mixed" Israel in the OT is a non sequitur. Atonement in the OT is circumscribed by covenant and election, and is therefore necessarily particular.

---

[32] Note how Paul says that some of the false teachers will arise from within the church itself.

[33] See John Murray's comments in his essay, "The Atonement and the Free Offer of the Gospel," in *Collected Writings of John Murray. Volume 1: The Claims of Truth* (Edinburgh: Banner of Truth, 1976), 62–65.

[34] Space also forbids a full assessment of the typology of atonement in the OT and the relation between type and antitype in the NT.

Other Examples of Corporate Cleansing or Atonement in the Pentateuch

In addition to those already considered, there are at least five other instances in the Pentateuch in which corporate cleansing or atonement is involved.

ATONEMENT FOR UNINTENTIONAL SINS (NUM. 15:22–31; CF. LEV. 4:13–21)

Once again, the "atonement" secured here appears to involve the Israelite community as a whole.[35] The unintentional sin—failure to keep any of Yahweh's commands—is a corporate oversight,[36] through which "all the congregation of the people of Israel" incurs guilt and stands in need of atonement and forgiveness (v. 25).[37] Moreover, the atonement and forgiveness procured by the priestly sin offering encompasses "all the congregation of the people of Israel, . . . and the stranger who sojourns among them" (v. 26).

Admittedly, in this instance the distinction made between "all the congregation of the people of Israel" and "the stranger who sojourns among them" is more difficult to reconcile with the idea of a corporate Israel that includes the entire community, whether native-born or foreigner. This might be less of a problem if "congregation" (עדה) here is interpreted more narrowly, in terms of the Israelite community's legal representatives—whether conceived of as tribal elders or as able-bodied males over twenty (cf. 14:29). However, what the passage appears to be stressing is the application of the same law to all and sundry; there is not one rule for the native-born Israelite and a different rule for the foreign resident in their midst (cf. 15:29). Thus, the emphasis is not on the foreigner as a non-Israelite (i.e., excluded from Israel as the people of God), but rather on his status as a non-native Israelite. Whether native-born or a foreign immigrant, unintentional sin must be atoned for lest the community suffer.

Particularly interesting in this case is the distinction between the unintentional sin (and subsequent atonement) of the community and that of the individual (vv. 27–31). Each is held to be culpable, whether as a community

---

[35] Whether "congregation" here encompasses the entire nation (as v. 26 suggests; cf. Num. 20:1–2) or refers only to the adult males (so Wenham, *Numbers*, TOTC [Downers Grove, IL: InterVarsity Press, 1981], 102 n. 2), it is this body that is held accountable and must therefore be atoned for and forgiven.

[36] "if you [plural] sin unintentionally and do not observe all these commandments that the LORD has spoken . . ." (v. 22).

[37] The elders are representative of the entire community; thus they alone are required to identify with the sacrificial victim through placing their hands on its head (cf. Lev. 4:15).

or as an individual. The atonement for one apparently did not suffice for the other; each case had to be dealt with according to its particular circumstances. Corporate atonement did not work for the individual, and something more than individual atonement was required for the community as a whole.

Perhaps even more significant is the fact that atonement for unintentional sin did not secure forgiveness for any intentional sin. Rather, for this the defiant sinner—whether foreigner or native-born—paid the ultimate price (vv. 30–31). Thus, however efficacious atonement for unintentional sin(s) was for either an individual or the community, there were certain sins (and hence, certain sinners) that were expressly not atoned for by the sacrifices and offerings of the OT cult.[38] This at least begs the question as to whether the same is true of the NT antitype: were there certain sins and/or certain sinners for whom the sacrifice of Jesus was also ineffectual—in the sense that it was not intended to cover such?[39]

Aaron's Censer (Num. 16:41–50)

The context of this incident, like the later one in Numbers 25, is an outbreak of God's wrath in the form of a devastating plague. This divine judgment resulted from community disquiet over the deaths of the 250 men who had attempted to usurp Aaron's role by offering incense to God (cf. vv. 35–40). Ironically, it is through offering authorized incense to God that Aaron is able to make atonement for the people and thus halt the spread of the killer plague (vv. 46–50).

Clearly in this episode, like that of chapter 25, the scope of atonement was restricted to some extent—there is a sharp distinction between those who fell victim to God's wrath (i.e., the 14,700 people who died from the plague) and those who were delivered from punishment through Aaron's incense-burning in the midst of the camp. Only the latter were strictly atoned for, the others having paid the fateful consequences for their own sinful behavior.

The Water of Cleansing (Numbers 19)

From the peculiar ritual involved in the manufacture of this special water, some form of substitutionary sacrifice is most likely to be inferred.[40] In any

---

[38] Eli's sons offer an OT example of such (1 Sam. 2:22–34); their cultic and moral transgressions were not atoned for by the OT cult, over which they themselves officiated.

[39] This is not to imply that the sacrifice of Jesus was incapable of atoning for such (i.e., that it was somehow deficient or ineffective), but rather that it never had such a design or purpose.

[40] Whatever the significance of the cedar wood, hyssop, and scarlet wool, the slaughter of the red heifer and sprinkling of its blood fits the imagery of other such sacrifices that had an atoning effect.

case, it is the ashes of this burned purification offering that gives the resultant concoction its properties of ritual cleansing (v. 17). While such "purification in a bottle" may initially seem to be a somewhat general remedy, the following prescriptions suggest otherwise. Unless these are merely exemplary in nature, it seems that this "emergency" provision had a very limited application: it was prescribed for the purification of those who had become unclean through direct contact with death (vv. 11–22). Significantly, its cleansing properties were efficacious only in the case of those who actually applied it in the prescribed manner; once again, failure to do so invoked the death penalty (vv. 13, 20). Thus, while a gracious provision for anyone in need of such purification, this means of cleansing was never intended for those who willfully despised Yahweh's laws and defiled his sanctuary.

THE BRONZE SNAKE (NUM. 21:4–9)

Once again, the provision made by Moses here appears to encompass the entire Israelite community—rebellious sinners as well as any righteous remnant. However, since the people's rebellion had precipitated this outbreak of venomous snakes, the provision of a remedy must be prefaced by community repentance (v. 7). From this it may be inferred that the bronze snake had a particular rather than a general focus; it was designed for the benefit of penitent Israelites, not impenitent rebels. Moreover, the actual beneficiaries were only those who actually looked to the bronze snake and thus exercised faith in Yahweh's promise of healing (vv. 8–9). Now, while it could be argued that this is therefore a general provision qualified only by personal faith (i.e., the bronze snake was sufficient for all, but efficient for some—those who believed), it is better—in view of the way this incident is picked up and applied by Jesus in the NT—to conclude that the provision was made specifically and intended exclusively for those who *would* believe. Jesus restricts the intended beneficiaries of the "lifting up" of the "Son of Man" to "whoever believes" (John 3:14–15), and this is also implicit in the fact that the "all people" mentioned in John 12:32 are in fact drawn to Jesus. Indeed, the protasis–apodosis construction of John 12:32 makes it clear that Jesus's death is the *cause* of his effectual drawing of all people to himself: "And I, when I am lifted up from the earth, will draw all people to myself." Thus Numbers 21 should not be used in an isolated fashion to substantiate the idea of a general atonement, but must be read in conjunction with the NT texts which allude to it and elucidate its typological significance.

Phinehas's Action at Baal Peor (Numbers 25)

This incident is particularly significant since it has actually been employed to discredit the notion of penal substitution upon which definite atonement so heavily depends.[41] The setting for Phinehas's action was Israel's physical and spiritual seduction by the Moabites.[42] This evoked God's wrath against the nation—manifested by another devastating plague in the camp (vv. 8b–9, 18; cf. Ps. 106:29)—which would be appeased only by the summary execution of the nation's leaders (Num. 25:3–4).[43] It is difficult to ascertain whether the execution of actual offenders subsequently commanded by Moses (v. 5) was in keeping with the spirit of Yahweh's instruction (cf. the explicit link between the offenders and leaders in vv. 14–15) or was some kind of "compromise solution" (as others have argued).[44] In any case, the only execution explicitly recorded is the one carried out by Phinehas, which proved effective in placating God's wrath and halting the plague (v. 7–9).[45] Presumably it was this plague that had evoked the community lament alluded to in verse 6 ("the whole congregation of the people of Israel . . . weeping in the entrance of the tent of meeting"). Given these circumstances, the brazen behavior of Zimri and Cozbi was all the more outrageous,[46] provoking Phinehas to act as he did (vv. 7–8) and thus "make atonement for" and "turn God's anger back from" the people of Israel (see vv. 11, 13). Despite the contrary suggestion of Campbell, it was not merely the zeal of Phinehas that accounts for this atonement, but the punishment (by death) of these two individuals. Indeed, arguably Campbell has misunderstood the significance of the plague itself—this was the penalty for sin being borne by the community so long as those held accountable remained unpunished; only the death of those responsible for this intolerable situation, as represented by Zimri and Cozbi, would turn God's anger away from the community as a whole. Therefore the death of Zimri and

---

[41] John McLeod Campbell, *The Nature of the Atonement and Its Relation to Remission of Sins and Eternal Life*, 1st ed. (Cambridge: Macmillan, 1856), 118–20. While Campbell's immediate concern is with penal substitution, definite atonement is something he finds equally offensive.

[42] Balaam was the primary architect of this seduction, as is revealed subsequently (cf. Num. 31:16).

[43] It is not quite clear why only the "chiefs" are singled out: either they were in some sense culpable, having failed to restrain or rebuke the actual offenders, or as leaders they had some kind of representative role. Ancient and modern attempts to identify the "chiefs" of verse 4 with the actual offenders of verse 5 are probably misplaced.

[44] For example, Gordon J. Wenham, *Numbers: An Introduction and Commentary*, TOTC (Downers Grove, IL: InterVarsity Press, 1981), 186; Roland K. Harrison, *Numbers: An Exegetical Commentary* (Grand Rapids, MI: Baker, 1992), 337; and Timothy R. Ashley, *The Book of Numbers*, NICOT (Grand Rapids, MI: Eerdmans, 1993), 519.

[45] Some argue that the plague began only after the actions recorded in verse 5, but this seems unlikely, given its close association with God's wrath both here and elsewhere. In any case, the plague persisted until the decisive action of Phinehas (v. 7).

[46] While the precise nature of their offensive behavior is debatable, it is obviously depicted as a "high-handed sin" justly punishable by death.

Cozbi expressed God's judgment on the guilty parties, while simultaneously turning away God's wrath from a penitent Israelite community. Moreover, while the Israelites were atoned for through this action of Phinehas, not all were quite so fortunate (e.g., Zimri). A similar inference could also be drawn from the instructions to make atonement in verses 4 and 5, where the death of some was also deemed necessary to secure atonement for the community as a whole.

Up to now the focus has been largely on passages that relate to the Israelite community as a whole. However, as well as dealing with the purification of the community as a whole, the Pentateuch also deals with the purification of individuals. The latter is particularly significant for our understanding of atonement in the Pentateuch, as the following discussion will briefly demonstrate.

Individual Atonement in the Pentateuch

A number of texts indicate that atonement was required, not only for the Israelite community as a whole but also for individuals within the community (cf. Num. 5:7–8). While such is implicit for any of the non-capital personal offenses mentioned in Israel's law-codes,[47] it becomes explicit in the regulations governing the making of *personal* sacrifices. One of the most notable features of the latter is the requirement of personal identification with the sacrificial victim. As was the case for the consecration of the priests (Ex. 29:10, 15, 19), regular cultic worship involving animal sacrifice (Lev. 1:4; 3:2, 8, 13; 4:4, 24, 29, 33) required identification of the worshiper with the victim: anyone being atoned for had to identify with the victim by placing a hand on its head before the animal was slain. As noted above, a similar requirement (the placing of hands on the sacrificial victim's head) was also involved in the Day of Atonement ritual (Lev. 16:21), where this action was expressly associated with the confession of Israel's corporate sins. Admittedly, such a confession of sins is not explicitly noted in these other cases. However, it seems reasonable to infer that a similar symbolic transfer of guilt was intended by the individual worshiper placing a hand on the intended victim.[48] Understood thus, the guilt

---

[47] Relatively few such offenses are actually discussed; the majority are transgressions for which the offender is to be "cut off" from the community.

[48] Contra Notker Füglister, "Sühne durch Blut—Zur Bedeutung von Leviticus 17.11," in *Studien zum Pentateuch*, ed. Georg Braulik (Wien: Herder, 1977), 146. Füglister's interpretation—that laying on one hand simply marked

of the worshiper was figuratively transferred to the sacrificial animal through the laying on of hands. Such a symbolic act implies a close identification of the worshiper with the victim, and thus an atoning sacrifice that had a quite definite focus (i.e., the sins of that particular worshiper and none other). The slain victim atoned and thus secured forgiveness for one person in particular.[49]

This is further illustrated by the fact that when more than one person was incorporated in such a symbolic act, more than one hand had to be laid on the victim. Thus, in the case of an unintentional sin by the community, the elders, representing the community, collectively laid hands on the sacrificial victim (Lev. 4:15). Likewise, on the Day of Atonement, on which the sins of both priest and people were symbolically expiated by the second goat, the high priest laid both hands (one representing himself, the other representing the community) on the condemned animal (Lev. 16:21). Thus the necessity for such a close identification between the worshiper(s) and the sacrificial victim correlates well with the concept of a definite atonement (i.e., an atonement designed for a particular individual or, as in these other cases, a particular community or group).

Such may also be implied from the distinction that is made in the Pentateuch between communal and individual atonement (cf. Lev. 4:3–35). Clearly atonement for the whole community did not suffice for the sins of an individual, nor did atonement for the individual suffice for those of the community. Each of these serves as a distinctive type. The former is a type of Christ's purification of the whole people of God (the elect) understood organically, whereas the latter is a type of such purification for the individual believer. As noted previously, it would be a mistake to collapse one of these types into the other, or to overplay one at the expense of the other.

Conclusion

The above discussion has argued that the idea of definite atonement, although not fully developed, is present in the Pentateuch in a number of ways. Most

---

personal ownership of the offering—can be rejected on the grounds that, as Emil Nicole, "Atonement in the Pentateuch," in *The Glory of the Atonement: Biblical, Historical and Practical Perspectives*, ed. Charles E. Hill and Frank A. James III (Downers Grove, IL: InterVarsity Press, 2004), 44, insists, such ownership would have been beyond doubt even without such a hand-laying ritual. Somewhat cautiously, Nicole concludes that "by this gesture the animal was presented as a substitute for the human being who offered it." Likewise, Wenham, "Theology of Old Testament Sacrifice," 79. But even if this were all there was to it, the "identification" ritual still points to a definite atonement: the sacrifice was for a specific individual.

[49] In view of Hebrews 10:1–4 it is more accurate to say that such atonement and forgiveness was not actually secured by "the blood of bulls and goats" but by the death of Jesus, which the former simply anticipated and foreshadowed.

significantly, election is the crucial theological prerequisite for atonement. Israel's experience of atonement rested squarely on Yahweh's choice of them and their ancestors as his chosen people. Atonement and intercession were made only for the people of Israel, representative of God's elect. Numerous examples of sacrifice and atonement in the Pentateuch have a specific rather than a general focus. The Passover victim made provision for only a certain number of individuals within each household. Some sins (and therefore, some sinners) were not atoned for at all in the OT sacrificial system. Provision for cleansing, recovery, or forgiveness did not necessarily become an internal reality for everyone in Israel, but rather for a subsection of the community, the believing remnant. Personal identification with the sacrificial victim through the laying on of hands implies a particular as opposed to a general atonement. The fact that corporate and individual atonement had to be secured suggests that one was in some respect insufficient for the other, and that both serve as distinctive types of the sacrificial work of Jesus Christ: corporate atonement symbolized Christ's propitiation for the elect as an organic whole, while individual atonement symbolized his propitiation for the individual believer.

The foregoing discussion has also noted that atonement in the OT is bound by covenant and election, and thus, even though it covered a "mixed" group of elect and non-elect within the covenant, it is a false hermeneutical move to deduce a general, universal atonement from this. The most that can be argued is that atonement in the OT and Christ's death in the NT may sometimes be said to encompass those who are non-elect, but who are nevertheless visible, professing members of the church and/or covenant community. Those wishing to affirm more discontinuity between old and new covenants prefer to speak of such texts as phenomenological language,[50] whereas those stressing covenantal continuity sharply distinguish between the covenant community and the elect. But in neither case can a general, universal atonement be deduced.

While these arguments for finding definite atonement in the first major corpus in the Bible may prove persuasive only for those already convinced, the above discussion should certainly prompt readers to reflect carefully on the relevant biblical texts—not only those within the Pentateuch but also those which later chapters of this volume will pick up and explore in depth.

---

[50] Barnes, *Atonement Matters*, 221.

"Stricken for the Transgression of My People"

THE ATONING WORK OF ISAIAH'S SUFFERING SERVANT

J. Alec Motyer

Presuppositions

The wise word of Aslan is that we are never told what would have happened, but, with all due respect to the Great Lion, sometimes we cannot help wondering. Just suppose that the nineteenth-century founding fathers of what is thought of as modern, scientific OT study had been bitten with the bug of biblical harmonization—and a holistic vision—instead of a passion for fragmentation, multiple authorship, editorial tinkerings . . . suppose . . . just suppose . . . ! In the case of Isaiah, Bernhard Duhm would have exercised his huge talents to show how the "Servant Songs" belong exactly where they are, and we would see the Isaiah literature as an ordered, well-planned book—and what blessed bunnies we would all be! Sadly things are very different, but if only we could persuade ourselves that it is sound method to see Isaiah as an author who wrote a book—not a magnet attracting disparate fragments—then the real thrust of, for example, Isaiah 40–55, would begin to emerge.

It is right to declare one's presuppositions, and these few sentences clarify where this chapter is coming from and whither it is tending. What follows

is an inductive exploration of Isaiah 53[1] in its literary context, with a view to
the resources it supplies for the doctrine of definite atonement.

Context of Isaiah 53

In order to understand Isaiah 53 aright we need to set it in its context, captur-
ing the whole sweep of Isaiah's thought, at least since 40:1.

INCLUSION OF THE GENTILES INTO YAHWEH'S WORLDWIDE SALVATION

Was it the dire forecast of the people of God being absorbed into the dominant Gentile superpower (39:6) that made Isaiah, wrestling with the future
for Israel, wrestle equally with the future for the Gentile worlds? Perhaps. In
any case, we find that the more Isaiah exalts the greatness of Yahweh as the
only God, the more he affirms the security of Israel in such a mighty God,
and the more he faces the question whether this Creator has any plan for the
major part of his creation. The tension between these two themes dominates
Isaiah 40–41, culminating in the prophet's awareness of a huge Gentile need
waiting to be met (41:21–29).

THE GENTILE WORLD AND THE SERVANT'S WORK[2]

The linking together of Isaiah 41:29 and 42:1 by the repetition of "Behold"
(הֵן) highlights the relationship between the Servant's work and the Gentile
nations. Spiritually speaking, the Gentile world is void of significance—
they are deluded (אָוֶן), incapable of achievement, their efforts (מַעֲשֵׂיהֶם) get
nowhere (אֶפֶס), and their spiritual resources are vacuous (רוּחַ; 41:29). Onto
this stage steps "my Servant" (עַבְדִּי; 42:1), equipped for the task of establishing מִשְׁפָּט on earth in all its truth (42:4) and of bringing מִשְׁפָּט to the nations
(42:12). Our understanding of the Servant's task turns, then, on the meaning
we give to מִשְׁפָּט.

Its majority meaning, "justice," chimes in with the present-day enthusiasm for "freedom," social equality, and fairness, but misses by a wide margin
what Isaiah sees the world to need. It needs to share in the revealed truth of
God hitherto given only to Israel. This, of course, is the fundamental OT
significance of מִשְׁפָּט. Rooted in the notion of an authority figure making

---

[1] Strictly speaking, Isaiah 52:13–53:12. Quotations of Scripture in this chapter are the author's translation.
[2] What can only be sketched here is worked out in detail in J. Alec Motyer, *The Prophecy of Isaiah* (Leicester, UK: Inter-Varsity Press, 1993), 25–30.

an authoritative decision (√שׁפט),[3] settling issues by "giving a judgment," מִשְׁפָּט is the resulting "judgment," an authoritative directive for thought and conduct (cf. Deut. 5:1). This is what the world needs, and what the Servant comes to provide.

WHAT SERVANT?

As one reads Isaiah 40 and following, the question arises as to just who this Servant is who will usher in God's cosmic purposes. In 41:8, Israel is named as "my Servant," and we must carry this forward to 42:1, for it is the corporate destiny of the Lord's people to be the light of the world. But as Isaiah develops his argument, 42:18–25 quickly disabuses us of any thought that, nationally considered, Israel, as Isaiah knew it, is either fit or able for the task. This line of thought continues until it climaxes in the almost strident condemnations of 48:1–22. A people of such flagrant apostasy, who have refused the Lord's way of peace, can no longer, with credibility, claim even the name of "Israel" (48:1). There is, therefore, both joy and sorrow in the forecast of the return home from Babylon. The "voice of loud shouting" (קוֹל רִנָּה) over this veritable redemption is suddenly stilled by the realization that a change of address is not a change of heart, and that "there is no peace . . . for the wicked" (48:20–22).

A NEW JOB DESCRIPTION

It is onto this reordered stage that the Servant now steps with a new job description. The world-task of 42:1–4 is, by itself, insufficient; he is also the restorer of fallen Israel, for the nation has forfeited the right to the honored name (48:1), and it is now the Servant alone who is "Israel" (49:3). Does this then mean that the Servant must be understood as a "corporate" entity?

CORPORATE BODY OR INDIVIDUAL?

The testimony of the third Servant Song is decisive (49:1–50:11). Throughout, the delineation of the Servant is cast in terms of an individual. The birth-vocabulary and the arrow imagery of 49:1–2 are strongly individualistic but, awaiting further light, must be held in tension with the fact that the Servant bears the name "Israel" (49:3). The prophet, however, successfully

---

[3] √ refers to the root of the verb.

turns us away from seeing the Servant as either Israel as a national whole or Israel considered in its true identity as a believing, God-fearing remnant. First, in contrast to the despondency (49:14) and unresponsiveness (50:1–3) of Zion—here symbolizing the actual Israel in its foreseen ruination—there is the obedience of the Servant, and his buoyant faith in the midst of awesome suffering (50:4–9). He is not, therefore, national Israel, but stands out over against the mass of the nation (cf. 42:18–25). Second, the concluding comment on the third Song (50:10–11) sets up the Servant as the Example to follow (cf. 50:4–9), distancing him from the remnant as a corporate body. His are to be the distinguishing marks of the believing remnant within professing Israel. The Servant is "for" the remnant in this fundamental way.

The Servant and the Saving "Arm of Yahweh"

This "Servant/remnant" distinction and relationship controls the prophet's thinking as he moves toward his intended climax in 52:13–55:13. In 51:1–52:12, three "Listen to me" "calls" (שִׁמְעוּ אֵלַי; 51:1, 4, 7) are balanced by the three "Awake . . . awake . . . Awake . . . awake . . . Depart . . . depart" "calls" (הִתְעוֹרְרִי הִתְעוֹרְרִי . . . עוּרִי עוּרִי . . . סֻרוּ סֻרוּ; 51:17; 52:1, 11), while the center ground is occupied mainly by a summons to the "arm of Yahweh" (זְרוֹעַ יְהוָה) to act redemptively as at the exodus (51:9–11).

The initial invitation goes out to those "who follow after righteousness, who seek Yahweh" (רֹדְפֵי צֶדֶק מְבַקְשֵׁי יְהוָה; 51:1)—in a word, to the believing remnant. It is they who are the seed of Abraham (51:2), the ones who will enjoy the comforted Zion (51:3). It is this Jerusalem/Zion that is summoned to enjoy peace with God (51:17, 22), holiness (52:1), and separation (52:11), the true Zion as it was meant to be, the city of the remnant whose membership consists of those who pursue righteousness and seek the Lord (51:1), "my people . . . my nation" (עַמִּי וּלְאוּמִּי; 51:4), and those who have God's law in their hearts (51:7). It is they who are called to "Behold!" (הִנֵּה; 52:13), for the coming salvation is for them.

How this salvation would be accomplished we are not yet told, save that it is foreseen as an act of the "arm of Yahweh" (זְרוֹעַ יְהוָה) operating as at the exodus (51:9–11). The "arm" (זְרוֹעַ) as such is used in the OT as the symbol of personal strength. Coupled with "hand" (יָד), symbolizing personal intervention, it is a pervasive Exodus image (Ex. 6:6; 15:6), and particularly the "strong hand and outstretched arm" (וּבְיָד חֲזָקָה וּבִזְרוֹעַ נְטוּיָה)

of Deuteronomy (e.g., 4:34). In Isaiah, the "arm of Yahweh" (40:10–11) is the way the Lord himself acts in power (cf. 51:5), but in 51:9–10 Isaiah transforms metaphor into personification, and the "arm" becomes Yahweh himself, who comes in person to effect his people's deliverance and redemption as at the exodus. He continues in this mode in 52:10: with typical Isaianic vividness, messengers arrive at Zion, and watchmen welcome them and join in proclaiming that the Lord has done his royal, redemptive, restorative work, not through any agency[4] but in his own person: "Yahweh has made bare his holy arm" (חָשַׂף יְהוָה אֶת־זְרוֹעַ)—or, as we might say, "has rolled up his sleeves," the act of someone directly and personally undertaking a task. The "arm of Yahweh," then, is no mere metaphor or literary flourish; it is Yahweh's alter ego.

In the context of these frequent occurrences of the "arm of Yahweh," the Servant reenters the scene: "Behold! My Servant shall succeed!" (הִנֵּה יַשְׂכִּיל עַבְדִּי; 52:13). It is the Servant who achieves the universal salvation of 51:1–8 and the individual and corporate realities of 51:17–52:12. Here is the Servant of the Lord as he really is: to the outward eye, a man among men (53:2–3), impressive only in rejection and sadness, but to the supernaturally opened eye, the "arm of Yahweh," the Lord of 51:9–10 and 53:10, the divine Yahweh himself come to save.

The Servant's Success

The Servant is truly human and truly divine, and as such, in what he undertakes he will "succeed" (יַשְׂכִּיל).[5] In a word, Isaiah's "Behold! My Servant will succeed!" matches the great cry, "It is finished" (τετέλεσται) at Calvary (John 19:30) and forces us, at the start of our study of Isaiah 53, to enquire what "finished" means in John and what "succeed" means in Isaiah. On any "open-ended" view of the atonement—that is, that the work of Christ only made salvation possible rather than actually secured salvation—"finished" only means "started" and "succeed" only means "maybe, at some future date, and contingent on the contribution of others." "Finished" is no longer "finished" and "success" is no longer a guaranteed result. This is far from both the impression and the actual terms of Isaiah's forecast, as we shall see.

---

[4] As through Moses in Egypt (cf. 63:12).

[5] √שׂכל in Qal, "to behave wisely" (cf. 1 Sam. 18:30), but, contextually, "to succeed in battle"; the Hiphil blends acting with prudence with acting effectively/successfully (e.g., Josh. 1:7–8). √שׂכל in 52:13 is balanced with "by his knowledge" in 53:11. The Servant knows exactly what to do, does it, and succeeds in what he undertakes.

The Servant's Great Accomplishment: The Dimensions of Salvation

(1) THE GOAL: WORLDWIDE, TRIUMPHANT SALVATION

At its outset (52:13–15) the Song picks up and gives poetical expression to the universal salvation heralded in the foregoing promissory section (51:4–5). This theme is, in fact, the inclusio of the whole Song, being reiterated and developed at the end (53:12). "Many nations" (גּוֹיִם רַבִּים; 52:15) is matched, and more closely defined, by "the many" (הָרַבִּים; 53:12); the "kings" (מְלָכִים; 52:15) are revisited as "the strong" (עֲצוּמִים; 53:12), and their subservient "silence" (יִקְפְּצוּ מְלָכִים פִּיהֶם; 52:15) becomes the more emphatic metaphor of defeat and spoliation (יְחַלֵּק שָׁלָל; 53:12).

(2) THE MEANS: THE SERVANT'S DEATH

Central to Isaiah's portrayal is that this submission is produced by the Servant's suffering, and this too forms an inclusio. The opening stanza (52:14) notes the extremity of the Servant's suffering: a mutilation of his physical form exceeding that inflicted on any other, and, then, mental, psychological, and spiritual torment such that those who saw the result were compelled to ask, "Is this even human?" Yet, as 53:12 develops the theme, the mutilation and dehumanization were not caused by the wear and tear of a stressful life but exclusively by the nature of his death, the self-imposed outpouring of his soul.

In summary, the Song begins as it intends to go on, and ends by confirming the same truths that it stressed throughout:

(1) A universal task is going to be accomplished successfully (52:13).
(2) It will be achieved by suffering, and the suffering and its result will exactly match each other. As the structure of Isaiah 52:14 displays:

> "According as many were appalled over you (כַּאֲשֶׁר שָׁמְמוּ עָלֶיךָ רַבִּים)—
> to such an extent was his appearance mutilated more than any
> individual (כֵּן־מִשְׁחַת מֵאִישׁ מַרְאֵהוּ),
> and his bodily form beyond anything human (וְתֹאֲרוֹ מִבְּנֵי אָדָם)
> —exactly so he will sprinkle[6] many nations (כֵּן יַזֶּה גּוֹיִם רַבִּים)."

---

[6] Should it read "sprinkle" (√יזה) or "startle" (from Arabic cognate)? Given its use in the OT with the meaning of "sprinkle" (twenty-two times), albeit with a different syntax, the balance of probability is overwhelmingly on the side of "sprinkle." See Motyer, *Prophecy of Isaiah*, 425–26.

The verse equates those who are appalled by the Servant's suffering with those who become the beneficiaries of his shed blood, and thus the verse introduces us to the concept of the Servant's substitutionary atonement.

(a) A Perfect Substitutionary Atonement

Isaiah is content to make the principle of substitution the centerpiece of his portrait of the Servant's work, and in Isaiah 53 we find all four of the essentials of the perfect substitute.

i. Identified with us in our condemnation. Translators are strangely satisfied to tell us that the Servant of Yahweh was "wounded 'for' [מִן] our transgression ... bruised 'for' [מִן] our iniquities" (53:5).[7] The Hebrew preposition מִן is basically the preposition of cause and effect. Thus, "he was wounded *because of* our transgressions, crushed *because of* our iniquities." There was a cause and there was an effect: on the one hand, our sins; on the other, his death-stroke, for here, as throughout Isaiah 53, the sufferings he endured refer not in a general way to the sorrows of life but to the infliction of death, so that we can speak pointedly and say that our sin *caused* his death. A possible—indeed preferable—rendering of 53:8 makes the same point in a very precise way: "he was cut down from the land of the living *because of* [מִן] the rebellion of my people to whom the blow belonged!"

ii. Without stain of our sin. Beginning with Exodus 12:5, the demand runs throughout the Levitical system that "your lamb must be perfect." Even though it does not seem to be directly stated, the reason for this requirement is not hard to find: only the perfect can accept and discharge the spiritual/religious obligations of another; an imperfection incurs personal obligation and disqualifies the imperfect from the gracious task of substitution.

Isaiah has his own brief but penetrating way of bringing the Servant of the Lord within this category of the perfect. He tells us that "he had done no violence, nor was any deceit in his mouth" (53:9). This verse uses the Hebrew idiom of "totality expressed by means of contrast." Thus action ("done"; עָשָׂה) contrasts with speech ("mouth"; פֶּה); outer ("violence"; חָמָס)

---

[7] BDB, 577–83, devotes twelve and a half columns to a comprehensive discussion of the ambience of מִן but does not include the vague meaning "for." For the causative use, see BDB, 580, 2f (e.g., Isa. 6:4; 28:7).

with inner ("deceit"; מִרְמָה); action toward others ("violence"; חָמָס)[8] with mastery of himself ("mouth"; פֶּה). But the bare statement of 53:9 does not stand alone; we are led to it step by step. The perfection of the Servant was far from being a "fugitive and cloistered virtue." Rather it was tested and tried from many directions: he was subjected to persecution but held his tongue, even when the persecution was imminently to end at the gallows (53:7); he endured illegality and perversion of due process of law (מֵעֹצֶר וּמִמִּשְׁפָּט לֻקָּח),[9] and died bereft of contemporary understanding (53:8; cf. 1 Pet. 2:21–25). His virtues were tested to destruction yet he remained without sin (cf. Heb. 4:15).

iii. Perfectly acceptable to the offended God. This third requirement of a perfect substitution brings us to the heart of the matter. There can be no salvation unless God is satisfied. Within human experience, sin is a regrettable, uncomfortable, and damaging fact. It soils our ideals, diminishes our moral accomplishments, corrupts our practices, threatens and often destroys our relationships, and foils our hopes. In other words, it is a pity! But what makes sin an issue—an eternal crisis—is the nature of God. Were God morally indifferent, we would still regret sin but, in an ultimate sense, it would not matter. God, however, is holy; holiness is his essential state; everything about him is "holy." His name is holy; his love is holy.[10] In the Bible, holiness is the constitutive fact of God. Very well, then, until that holiness is satisfied there can be no salvation for the sinner.

How does Isaiah's teaching in chapter 53 measure up to this requirement? Verse 6 tells the whole story: something true of all ("all we"; כֻּלָּנוּ), something true of each ("every one"; אִישׁ), and finally something true of the Lord ("and Yahweh"; וַיהוָה). In the Hebrew the final sentence accentuates divine agency: "And Yahweh—yes, Yahweh!—laid on him . . ." (וַיהוָה הִפְגִּיעַ בּוֹ). As a translation, that would deserve no prizes; as a representation of Isaiah's emphasis, ten out of ten! Behind whatever agencies hounded the Servant to his death (53:7–9), there was a divine management: Yahweh himself acting as his own High Priest to satisfy his own holiness (cf. Lev. 16:21); literally, "Yahweh caused to meet on him the iniquity of us all" (53:6).[11] Drama indeed! The death of the Servant is the intersection point of all space and all time. From

---

[8] חָמָס specifically means socially disruptive behavior; hurt done to the other person (e.g., Gen. 6:11; Isa. 59:6; Obad. 10).

[9] "Taken from prison and from judgment" (NKJV) or "taken off without restraint and without justice."

[10] The adjective "holy" is used of the name of God more often than all other instances of its use put together.

[11] Hiphil of √פגע, "to cause to meet upon, interpose."

north, south, east, and west, from past, present, and future, the divine hand gathers in the sins of all the sinners he proposes to save, and personally conducts them to a solemn and holy spot—the head of his Servant.

We meet "Yahweh" as an emphatic agent again in 53:10, where we read (with the same emphasis), "And Yahweh—yes, Yahweh!—was delighted to crush him" (וַיהוָה חָפֵץ דַּכְּאוֹ); "he made him sick" (הֶחֱלִי).[12] The reference to "sickness," of course, looks back to 53:4, where "griefs" (חֳלִי) equals "sicknesses," i.e., metaphorical of the personal, debilitating effects of sin. It is easy for the words "Yahweh delighted" to be misunderstood and misused, but Scripture insists that the Father sent the Son to be the Savior of the world, and that the Father loves the Son because he laid down his life (John 10:17; 1 John 4:14). No doubt Isaiah uses strong words; and, no doubt too, he was inspired to enter into sacred ground where we can but dimly follow him. But take, for example, a human father who delights that his son is obedient to God's call into full-time ministry, and that he has not shunned a sacrificial, demanding, even dangerous role. Such a father could well say that he was delighted with what his son is undertaking. Human that we are, however, there might well come a point in sacrifice where "delighted" would be beyond our ability—but, says Isaiah, not beyond the Lord's. So intense was his determination to deal savingly with sinners and their sin, that even the sacrifice was his delight. It is not for us to blunder with clumsy steps into such territory but to fall down in wonder, love, and worship. This is our God, and this is the heart-stopping extent to which what his Servant did is acceptable to him.

iv. Voluntarily accepting the role of a substitute. The quadrilateral of substitution is now complete. From earliest times the principle of substitution was known and practiced, and, we believe, was a matter of divine revelation. The Passover regulations vividly stressed equivalence between the lamb that was to die and the Israelites who entered the blood-stained houses. Their number ("according to the number") and their needs ("according to each man's need") were taken into careful reckoning in the choice of the lamb, and the requirement that anything that remained be burnt catered for human inadequacy and error in calculation, so that in fact the equivalence was made exact (Ex. 12:4, 10).

---

[12] This reading takes דַּכְּאוֹ in its plain sense as a Piel infinitive construct, "to crush" (√דכא). Some prefer to treat it as the adjective דכא, "crushed" (57:15; Ps. 34:10): "Yahweh delighted in his crushed one." This avoids the felt difficulty of Yahweh delighting in crushing his Servant, but surely Isaiah ruled out this understanding of דַּכְּאוֹ when he added the word of closer definition, הֶחֱלִי: "he made him sick" (Hiphil of √חלל).

Furthermore, when Moses set up the Levitical system, the common requirement in all categories of sacrifice was that the offerer lay his hand on the head of the animal, an act explained in the Day of Atonement ritual as the off-loading of sin from the guilty to the "perfect" (Lev. 1:4; 3:2; 4:4; 16:21–22).

It fell to the towering genius of Isaiah to see and teach that, in the ultimate, only a human could substitute for humans—and to show the reason why in his delineation of the Servant. Isaiah 53:1–3 sets out to show that the divine "Arm of Yahweh" was actually and truly human: his ancestry and growth (v. 2a), his appearance and the reactions he provoked (v. 2b), and the trials he experienced (v. 3). But the key thought is reserved for 53:7–9. The verbs in verse 7 are in the Niphal mode, often used, as here, to express what the grammarians call a "tolerative" sense[13]—"he let himself be brutalized" (נִגַּשׂ):[14] indeed, as far as he was concerned, "he let himself be downtrodden— and he did not open his mouth!" (וְהוּא נַעֲנֶה וְלֹא יִפְתַּח־פִּיו). Nothing altered his silent acquiescence. Yet he was the Arm of Yahweh! We must, therefore, go beyond "acquiescence," and speak of his deliberate, sustained, and willing acceptance of his role. The beasts, through the centuries, knew neither what nor why; nor, if asked, could they answer; nor did they possess a will whereby they might voluntarily accept their role. They could provide a body in place of a human body, their "perfection" in place of human corruption and failure, but the one thing they could not do was represent and stand in for humans at the very center of human sinfulness—the will that flouted the will of God. Their substitution was a true picture, but "the blood of bulls and goats could never take away sin." That task had to await One who could say, "Behold, I have come to do your will, O God" (Heb. 10:4–7).

With the Servant's coming, then, came also a perfect substitutionary atonement.

(b) A Complete Atonement

Our present task is to follow Isaiah as he explains how the Servant of the Lord in his substitutionary work dealt totally and actually with our sin.

i. The multifaceted nature of sin. In Isaiah 53 we find the full OT vocabulary of sin. In verse 12, the word חֵטְא ("sin") focuses on the fact of sin as

---

[13] W. Gesenius, E. Kautzsch, and A. E. Cowley, *Gesenius' Hebrew Grammar* (Oxford: Oxford University Press, 1910), § 51c.

[14] Cf. the tolerative Niphal in verse 12, "he let himself be numbered" (נִמְנָה).

shortcoming. The parent verb, חטא√, "to sin," occurs in Judges 20:16 of not missing a target. In its moral usage, "sin" is the specific matter we find that we have to confess—whether thought, word, or deed, inward imagination or outward act. We have "missed," fallen short, of the Lord's commandment.

In Isaiah 53:5, the word is עָוֹן, "iniquity." The parent verb, עוה√, means "bend, twist" (e.g., Isa. 21:3[15]), making the noun mean "crooked behavior, perversion." In the total vocabulary of sinfulness, it is the "internal" word—strictly, therefore, the warped human nature from which all wrongdoing derives, though in use it reaches out into iniquitous deeds, their consequences, and the resulting guilt.

Thirdly, there is the menacing word פֶּשַׁע, "rebellion" (53:5, 8). Why "menacing"? Because it is the killer-word. No matter how much we make an excuse for the fallen nature which prompts and effectuates actual sin, the fact remains that, in cases too numerous to recall, a choice was presented to us and we chose the path of deliberate, conscious, willful rebellion. We sinned because we wanted to.[16]

ii. Sin completely dealt with. By the vocabulary he chose, then, Isaiah showed that the Servant dealt with sin in all its totality. No debt was left unpaid, or fault without covering. He is equally comprehensive in respect of sin's consequences. Isaiah presents us with three major areas of the ill effect of sin that the Servant's work touches on: the inward, the Godward, and the manward.

Inward (a): "he carried our sorrows." Isaiah diagnoses the state in which we find ourselves under the words "sicknesses" and "sadnesses" (חֳלִי), "griefs" and "sorrows" (מַכְאֹב). Sin is a malady, debilitating the sinner, spreading like a malignant infection, increasing its grip on the vital functions of the soul like some pitiless disease, its appetite unsatisfied until it has destroyed every function and brought the sinner down to death. Sin is also a blight, touching and diminishing every longed-for brightness in life, making every hope fall short of its fulfillment, and making our happinesses turn to ashes. When Isaiah speaks of the Servant as a "man of sorrows" (v. 3), he uses the same word (מַכְאֹב).[17] The Servant entered into the full

---

[15] NKJV: "distressed"; NIV: "staggered," someone "bent double" under disaster.

[16] Second Kings 3:7; 8:20 illustrate the idea (cf. Isa. 1:3; Jer. 3:13, for religious rebellion).

[17] From כאב√, "to be in pain" (e.g., Gen. 34:25; Job 14:22, of bodily pain; but also of mental pain, Prov. 14:13; Ezek. 13:22).

reality of the human lot as we experience it (cf. Heb. 4:15). But in particular he "took away" from us (נשׂא√)[18] and "made his own" (סבל√)[19] the full weight, in malady and blight, of our sin. The former word is the "lifting up" of the burden, the latter is the "shouldering" of the burden—first "acceptance" then "endurance." Isaiah is using the imagery of the "scapegoat" in Leviticus 16 (cf. vv. 21–22), where all the main words of the sin-vocabulary occur, including נשׂא√.

Inward (β): "he provided righteousness for many." The surplus of sin includes the fact that every sinful act, outward or inward, "kicks back" at the sinner. We are defiled and debased by our actions, thoughts, and words. This too has been dealt with by the Servant's death. To see this, however, we need to come closer to the Hebrew of 53:11 than the traditional "justify many" (NJKV; NIV), or "make many to be accounted righteous" (ESV). The Hebrew here is יַצְדִּיק צַדִּיק עַבְדִּי לָרַבִּים. It contains a feature not found elsewhere in the OT,[20] giving the meaning "to provide righteousness for." It is a strong statement. The Servant "knows" the need that is to be met and how to meet it; what he has actually done is to share himself with (literally) "the many": he is "that righteous One, my Servant" and he "provides righteousness"—his righteousness, as we can say in the light of the whole Bible,[21] imputed to us in our need.

Godward (α): "the chastisement for our peace." The words in v. 5 teach us that the Godward effects of our sin were also dealt with in the death of the Servant. Both the verb (יסר√) and its noun (מוּסָר) move within the semantic range of "discipline, chastening, correction, admonition," with the context determining the meaning in each case. In the present case, we are helped by comparing the words "the chastisement of our peace" (מוּסַר שְׁלוֹמֵנוּ; v. 5) with "the covenant of my peace" (בְּרִית שְׁלוֹמִי; 54:10). The latter means "my covenant legally pledging peace," hence, 53:5, "the legal penalty which secures peace."[22] This satisfies the penal stress that animates these verses as well as the equally pervasive "concreteness" of the benefit secured.

---

[18] "He bore" (NKJV; ESV; NRSV); "took up" (NIV).

[19] "Carried" (NKJV; ESV; NRSV; NIV).

[20] The Hiphil of צדק√, "to be righteous," is usually followed by a direct object as in Deuteronomy 25:1; 2 Samuel 15:4. Only here is it followed by an indirect object with prefixed ל.

[21] For example, Genesis 15:6; Isaiah 54:17; etc.

[22] "Peace" (שָׁלוֹם) derives from שלם√, "to be whole, entire," and is used throughout the OT, as a concordance reveals, of the establishment of an all-embracing wholeness, a totality of well-being in our relationship with God, with people, and, within our own personalities. In Isaiah 40–55, "peace" could even be thought of as one of the strands of the golden cord which unites the chapters—the peace that was lost, and why (48:18), the peace which cannot be

What was thus, by deserving and culpability, "ours," was in fact "upon him." A heart-stopping equivalence if ever there was one—substitution and legal transference!

Godward (β): from straying sheep to family members. A second Godward aspect of our sin that Isaiah deals with is our alienation from God. That the Servant should come among us and we fail to notice him is evidence of how far the fallen human mind is from the mind of God. Further proof of mental alienation comes when onlookers see his sufferings but not their true explanation (v. 8), applying only the "light" of misleading human logic (v. 4). No wonder, then, that verse 6 says that we have all strayed. But when "Yahweh laid on him the iniquity of us all" (וַיהוָה הִפְגִּיעַ בּוֹ אֵת עֲוֺן כֻּלָּנוּ) a genuine miracle happened: those who strayed as sheep are brought home as sons, for, "when you make his soul an offering for sin, he shall see his seed" (אִם־תָּשִׂים אָשָׁם נַפְשׁוֹ יִרְאֶה זֶרַע; v. 10). The protasis–apodosis construction reveals that the travail of his soul creates family members, eliminating forever any previous estrangement.

Manward: the guilt of hurting others. Isaiah shows how the Servant of the Lord has made provision for the damage inflicted inwardly on ourselves, the offense given to the Lord, and, finally, the hurt caused to other people.

Isaiah 53:10 uses the important word אָשָׁם.[23] The primary meaning of the root is "guiltiness," the act that incurs guilt, the condition of guilt, and the penalty/restitution which guilt requires. Among the offerings, the regulations for the אָשָׁם include the making recompense for hurt inflicted on the other person. There are three possible translations of line 3 in verse 10 (אִם־תָּשִׂים אָשָׁם נַפְשׁוֹ), each with its own element of the truth:

(a) "When you (Lord) appoint him/his soul as a trespass offering . . ."
(b) "When he/his soul makes a trespass offering . . ."
(c) "When you (the individual) offer/make him/his soul a trespass offering . . ."

Isaiah, the supreme wordsmith, must have been aware of the multiple possibilities in what he wrote, and surely intended that we should for fullness

---

(48:22), coming peace proclaimed (52:7), accomplished (53:5), secured by covenant (54:10), and enjoyed in the fruition of what the exodus foreshadowed (55:12).

[23] NKJV: "offering for sin"; NIV: "guilt offering." Cf. Leviticus 5–6, "trespass offering."

embrace all three: (a) the Lord was the "real" Agent behind the death of the Servant, as in verse 6, and therefore we can be sure of both the effectiveness and acceptability of the offering; (b) the Servant himself voluntarily offered himself, as in verses 7–9, as the trespass offering, therefore providing a complete substitution for the sinner; (c) the individual response is sought—as Isaac Watts put it in his fine hymn "Not All the Blood of Beasts":

> My faith would lay her hand
> On that dear head of Thine,
> While as a penitent I stand
> And there confess my sin.

But, whichever rendering we choose, the notion of the אָשָׁם remains the same, that the effects of our sin reach out like ripples, affecting our fellow humans. Sin is wider and more far-reaching than the act itself. The Lord, making his Servant the אָשָׁם, knows the full extent of all such rippling, and, laying our sin on his Servant, lays it in full (v. 6). The Servant, willingly offering himself, likewise has such knowledge (בְּדַעְתּוֹ; v. 11), and accepts the full penalty for the full reality of our sin. We who come making his soul our אָשָׁם know our sin only in a very minute part, but, laying our hands on his head, acknowledging him as our substitute, we act in faith: all our sin in its full extent was borne by the Servant in his death, without remainder, balance, or surplus.

In sum, Isaiah has given us a comprehensive picture of the Servant's work—it is a complete atonement encompassing all aspects of sin—but what of its effectiveness, its actuality? The Servant's death may have accomplished redemption in full, but what of its application? And what of the connection between the two?

(3) The Result: Atonement Accomplished and Applied

(a) An Effective Atonement

Isaiah does not use the big words like salvation, redemption, or reconciliation in his portrait of the Servant, but, without using the word, he draws on the vocabulary of atonement, and both by direct statement and by implication declares that the full atoning work lies in the past, achieved and completed by the Servant's death.

Isaiah, however, also speaks for those who have been given eyes to see. The "we," who once looked at the Lord's Servant and saw nothing to make them look twice (53:2b–3), have somehow become the "we" who have a report to make, a revelation to share (53:1), the "our," "we," and "my" who have been made confidently aware of the nature, meaning, and effect of his death (53:4–9). It is a matter of considerable importance to trace the sequence of 53:4–6:

> Verse 4 describes our initial state of blindness. The Servant died, and his death had in it, objectively, all the fullness of its inherent substitutionary significance, but, subjectively, it was met by misunderstanding and misinterpretation.

> No explanation is offered in verse 5, but blindness has been replaced by testimony to the objective reality of substitution, and the subjective reality of healing (i.e., from the "malady" of sin)—an OT equivalent to "Once I was blind, now I can see" (John 9:25).

> Verse 6 develops the new self-awareness of what is true of the whole company embraced by "we," and of individual culpability, and a correct realization of the Lord's place and action in the Servant's death—a corrective inclusio to the misinterpretation of verse 4b.

Clearly, personal conversion has taken place, yet nothing is said about hearing and responding to the truth; there is no reference to personal decision, commitment, or faith. It is totally a story of needy sinners in the hand of God. It is the secret history of every conversion, the real story, the OT counterpart of "you did not choose me, but I chose you" (John 15:16). It is also the death knell to any open-ended understanding of the atonement, which seeks to posit a disjunction between redemption accomplished and applied. It matters not how the question is asked. Could any whose iniquities the Lord laid on his Servant fail to be saved? Could that laying-on prove ineffectual? Were any iniquities laid on the Servant save with the divine purpose of eternal salvation? Since universalism is ruled out by Isaiah's insistence on "the many" (see below), 53:4–6 commits the unprejudiced interpreter to an effective, particularistic understanding of the atonement. The heart of the matter is boldly put: the "we" of these crucial verses were locked into a failure to grasp what the Servant was all about, but our iniquities were laid by Yahweh on his Servant; and *this* is what led to our "seeing." The theological implications are profound: the atonement *itself*, and not something outside of the atonement, is the cause for any conversion. The resources for conversion are found in the Servant's death; they flow from it. Thus, it is the atonement that activates conversion, not vice versa (cf. Titus 3:3–5).

This element of definiteness, of effected and effectual atonement, which is the kernel of 53:4–6, is also the leading thought of the last section of the Song (53:10–12). The relationship between the first and last stanzas of this final Servant Song (52:13–15; 53:10–12) is that of enigma and explanation. The enigma is the exact matching between the Servant's suffering and the response of astonishment and submission it elicits, and how all this bears on the unique exaltation that awaits the Servant.[24] In 53:10–12, we find the same relationship between suffering and result,[25] but now all is explained. The astonishing fruits of suffering arose from the fact that the Lord himself is at work: he is the Agent behind the bruising (53:10), and the Guarantor and Apportioner of the results (53:12), not in any artificial or fictional way but by making sure that the Servant is rewarded as he deserves. Moreover, the Servant's reward arises not from his righteousness nor even from his shocking suffering, but solely from his sin-bearing death: in 53:10, his life ("soul") is a recompense offering (אָשָׁם); in 53:11, he provides righteousness for the many (יַצְדִּיק צַדִּיק עַבְדִּי לָרַבִּים) by bearing their iniquities (וַעֲוֹנֹתָם הוּא יִסְבֹּל), and in 53:12, his gaining of "the many" as his prize (אֲחַלֶּק־לוֹ בָרַבִּים) and his despoiling of the strong (וְאֶת־עֲצוּמִים יְחַלֵּק שָׁלָל) follow exactly from (תַּחַת אֲשֶׁר) pouring out his life ("soul") to death (הֶעֱרָה לַמָּוֶת נַפְשׁוֹ), his voluntary self-enumeration with the rebels (וְאֶת־פֹּשְׁעִים נִמְנָה), bearing their sin (וְהוּא חֵטְא־רַבִּים נָשָׂא), and interposing for transgressors (וְלַפֹּשְׁעִים יַפְגִּיעַ)[26]—in a word, his death, that and nothing else, ensures the results of redemption applied.

(b) The Servant Administrator

The Servant is not just the Procurer of the results of his death; he is also the Administrator of them. According to 53:7–9, the Servant of the Lord voluntarily submitted himself to injustice and death—even though the burial itself

---

[24] The exaltation is threefold: "exalted . . . extolled . . . very high" (NKJV); more accurately, NIV: "raised . . . lifted up . . . highly exalted"—foreshadowing Jesus's resurrection, ascension, and heavenly session.

[25] The bracketing stanzas match each other exactly. "My Servant" (עַבְדִּי; 52:13) is balanced by "the righteous one, my Servant" (צַדִּיק עַבְדִּי; 53:11), and the suffering of 52:14–15 is matched by the bruising of 53:10. Just as 52:14–15 expressed the relationship between cause and effect by "just as . . . so" (כֵּן . . . כַּאֲשֶׁר), so 53:12 uses the preposition of causative exactitude: "precisely because" (תַּחַת אֲשֶׁר).

[26] √פגע in the Qal (simple active), "to meet, reach, arrive at." In the Hiphil (causative active), "to cause to meet upon, interpose" (53:6); but also (possibly with the sense of causing two parties to meet together), "to interpose, mediate" (cf. 59:16); "made intercession" (NKJV; NIV).

mysteriously contradicted the expectations of his executioners.[27] But now Isaiah reveals the Servant alive after his passion. He is not, however, like others who died, experiencing the half-life of Sheol; he is active, dominant, with prolonged days, bestowing the blessings for which he died, and enjoying the fruits of his voluntary and victorious death. Isaiah did not use the word "resurrection," but he might as well have done so.

Isaiah ties the Servant's "post-resurrection" administration to Yahweh's will by bracketing the verb "pleased" (חָפֵץ) and its noun "pleasure" (חֵפֶץ) in 53:10. Yahweh's pleasure/will prompted and was fulfilled in the work of atonement, but it also continues through the Servant, who lives to administer the atonement he accomplished by his death. The Servant's hand—the organ of personal intervention and action—now dispenses the atonement, applying it to whom he wills. The Servant is not engaged in further self-offering; he is administering the fruits of a past, historical act. The decision to bestow is his; there is no other hand or agency that can save.[28] We need to bear this in mind when we recall that one possible meaning of 53:10b is "when you make his soul a guilt-offering." This truly personal decision and response is not a contributory element in the work of salvation; it is embraced in the administrative function of the Servant's dispensing hand.

In summary, then, two truths stand out in this final section of the Song. The first is that the atonement was achieved in totality by the Servant's death, and is applied by the Servant himself, who actively distributes and applies the saving largesse of what Hebrews will call "one sacrifice for sins forever" (Heb. 10:12). Secondly, the pleasure of the Lord, which prompted the saving death, includes also his pleasure concerning the enjoyment of its benefits. It is the "hand" of the Servant that brings the benefits of atonement to those whom the Lord wills. The Lord thus wills the work and the reception of salvation, and the Servant willingly ensures both. The will of God to save, the Servant's atoning work, and his subsequent administration of that work, all belong to the same theological "track." Isaiah allows for no disjunction or discord among any of these three elements: all synchronize in perfect harmony, producing a complete and effective salvation—redemption accomplished *and* applied.

---

[27] More "mysteriously" than the translators allow, too, for the Hebrew writes of "wicked men" (רְשָׁעִים) (plural) and "a rich man" (עָשִׁיר) (singular). As with the threefold exaltation of 52:13, the circumstances of the burial of the Servant constitute an Isaianic clue, which will, in its time, identify the Servant (Matt. 27:38, 57).

[28] It is also important to revert to 53:1, which teaches that the Servant can be recognized only as a result of divine revelation. The "Arm of Yahweh" has to be revealed, else he will continue to be seen in merely human terms.

One final aspect of the Servant's work needs to be given attention: For whom was this effective and applied atonement intended?

The Intended Recipients of the Servant's Salvation

The beginning and end of the Song are linked by references to "many" or "the many": "many" (רַבִּים) were appalled/horrified (52:14); "many nations" (גּוֹיִם רַבִּים) benefited from the sprinkling (52:15); the Servant "provided righteousness for the many" (לָרַבִּים; 53:11); "I will apportion to him the many"/"give him the many as his portion" (בָּרַבִּים; 53:12);[29] "he himself lifted up the sin of many" (רַבִּים; 53:12). How are we to understand this obviously significant word?

Its general use in the OT does not help. For the most part, it is used in a nonspecific way—"many" (1 Sam. 14:6) contrasts with "few" (Num. 13:18)—or to express the general idea of "numerousness" (Ex. 5:5). A handful of cases exemplify the plural adjective with the definite article, as in 53:11 (cf. 8:7; Jer. 1:15; Dan. 11:33, 39; 12:3), but do not give the guidance we need. It is best, therefore, to look at the verses individually.

In 52:14–15, in the light of the promised universal salvation that the Servant is to achieve (42:1–4; 49:6–9; 51:4–5), the "many nations" to be "sprinkled" must refer to the numerous company involved worldwide; that is, many nations in contrast to the one nation which had, so far, enjoyed divine revelation.

The references to "many" and to "the many" in Isaiah 53:11–12 raise a whole different set of questions, simply because they pose the effectiveness of the Servant's saving death for individuals. In verse 11, "the many" are those whose iniquities the Servant has shouldered and to whom the blessings of his atoning death have actually come in the gift of righteousness. In verse 12a, the subject is the reward from the Lord that the Servant has merited. He has "earned" (לָכֵן אֲחַלֶּק־לוֹ) "the many" as his allotted portion (cf. John 6:37). Isaiah 53:12b returns again to how the Servant has come by this reward—"in exact return for" (תַּחַת אֲשֶׁר), pouring out his soul to death, letting himself be numbered with rebels, and carrying the sin of "many."

How is all this to be understood? In 52:15, "many" is implicitly all nations outside Israel, now brought within the circle of salvation, a numerous-

---

[29] The prefixed preposition is here the *beth essentiae*: "I will give him his portion in terms of the many."

ness that extends to all. This does not, however, commit us to universalism ("all without exception"), for the analogy requires that the nations will be saved as Israel is saved, and we know that, in the OT as in the NT, "they are not all Israel who are of Israel" (Rom. 9:6), so that even when "many" seems to imply "all," it still effectively applies only on the individual level—to some in contrast to all.

Shall we then say that "many" in 53:11–12 simply assures us of numerousness, and leave the matter at that? In one way this has to be true, for only the passage of time actually brings to light the spreading dimensions of the worldwide assembly resulting from the once-for-all atonement (45:14–25; 51:4–5). But if we take this to mean that the atoning death goes no further than making salvation possible for "many," and needs the contribution of individual faith to complete what the Servant's death only started, we have strayed from what Isaiah teaches. The Song is very precise in linking 53:10–12 back to 53:4–6. The climax of verses 4–6 is strikingly emphatic: "And Yahweh" (וַיהוָה); this is where verses 10–12 begin (וַיהוָה). In the hands of such a skilled wordmaster as Isaiah, such a strong coincidence of wording must be deliberate. Further, the two sets of three verses each have seven significant words in common, all bearing on the nature and meaning of the Servant's death, sharing the imagery of sickness, sin-bearing (Day of Atonement), and mediation.[30] Moreover, in each set there is the same blending of the agency of the Servant and the agency of Yahweh. The implication of this is that "the many," who are the object of both the saving work of the Servant and its application in verses 10–12, are the straying sheep of verse 6 whose iniquities Yahweh laid upon the Servant, and who are converted (miraculously!) by his death. "Many," then, has a certain specificity to it, while also retaining its inherent numerousness: it refers to those for whom the Servant made atonement and to whom he applies that same atonement (cf. Rev. 7:9).

Other terms Isaiah uses coextensively with "the many" support this point. "My people" (עַמִּי; 53:8), and the Servant's "seed" (זֶרַע; 53:10),[31] are the product of the Yahweh's will and pleasure, and of the Servant's saving and administering office; they are consequent upon his life being a guilt-

---

[30] In each case, the first line involves √חלל, "to be sick," and the last line √פגע (in the Hiphil), "to cause to meet upon, interpose"; the sin-bearing verbs √נשא, "to lift up, bear, carry," and √סבל, "to shoulder"; the verb of suffering √דכא, "to crush," is common to both sets, as are the "sin" words עָוֹן, "iniquity," and פֶּשַׁע, "rebellion."

[31] Thus, accurately, NKJV. NIV and ESV "offspring" is, of course, correct but sadly obscures what is a specially key word in salvation history.

offering; it was for them he endured "the travail of his soul." The intended recipients and the actual beneficiaries of the Servant's atoning death are one and the same group.

Combining all these elements together, we may conclude that the referent of רַבִּים: is an innumerable family from every nation, including Israel, which constitutes God's elect people, for whom redemption is both accomplished *and* applied.

In closing, lest we seek to draw our own "logical" conclusions that such a "particularistic" edge of the Servant's work must necessarily negate universal proclamation of Yahweh's salvation and invitation to the whosoever, the wider universe of Isaiah 53 prohibits us (cf. 54:1–55:13). The completeness and efficaciousness of the Servant's death, intended for his innumerable elect from every nation, does not inhibit the universal proclamation and invitation to receive God's salvation, as Isaiah 55 reveals; rather, if anything, the Servant's definite atonement forms the basis for the proclamation and invitation.

For the Glory of the Father and the Salvation of His People

DEFINITE ATONEMENT IN THE SYNOPTICS AND JOHANNINE LITERATURE

Matthew S. Harmon

Without question the death and resurrection of Jesus is the central emphasis of the Gospels. But the Gospels are not content merely to describe the events surrounding Jesus's death and resurrection; they also explain the significance of those events. As part of that significance these biblical books directly and indirectly address the purpose of Christ's atonement. Indeed, there are few corpora in Scripture that have more to say on this subject than the Synoptic Gospels and Johannine Literature.[1]

In surveying this material, I shall argue three things. First, Jesus died to display the glory of the Father. Second, Jesus died to accomplish the salvation of his people. Third, Jesus died for the sins of the world. I will then conclude by summarizing my findings and offering some final reflections. Holding together all three of these truths is essential in constructing a biblical understanding of the purpose of Christ's atonement.

---

[1] There is so much material that this chapter will be unable to deal with every passage that is relevant to the subject.

I. Jesus Died to Display the Glory of the Father

Before determining for whom Christ died, it is necessary first to establish the ultimate purpose of his death.[2] Doing so provides a starting point for evaluating other purposes and benefits of Christ's death as stated in Scripture. According to the Synoptics and Johannine Literature, the ultimate purpose of Christ's death is to display the glory of God definitively. The Son glorifies the Father by doing the work of the Father, which is to accomplish effectively the salvation of those whom the Father gave him.

THE ULTIMATE PURPOSE OF THE ATONEMENT: THE GLORY OF THE FATHER

The Gospels repeatedly emphasize that everything Christ does is for the glory of the Father. According to John 1:14, a result of the incarnation is that "we have seen his glory, glory as of the only Son from the Father, full of grace and truth."[3] By alluding to Exodus 33–34, John asserts that the same glory displayed to Moses is now visible in the incarnate Word.[4] Just a few verses later John further explains that this same Word in the flesh "has made him [God] known" (1:18). The Greek verb used here (ἐξηγέομαι) means "to provide detailed information in a systematic manner—'to inform, to relate, to tell fully.'"[5] The stunning point that John makes is that, as the Word-made-flesh, Jesus Christ is the fullest revelation of God. As such, John intends the reader to see that everything that Jesus says and does is a manifestation of God's glory.

Thus it is no surprise when Jesus's miraculous signs are framed as a display of his glory. After Jesus turns water into wine during the wedding at Cana, John explains: "This, the first of his signs, Jesus did at Cana in Galilee, and manifested his glory. And his disciples believed in him" (2:11). This statement is more than chronological; it indicates that in some sense this first sign is paradigmatic for all of Jesus's miracles.[6] Repeatedly in the Gospels, people respond to Jesus's miracles (Luke 5:25–26; 7:16; 13:13, 17; 17:15,

---

[2] Even some who hold to "universal atonement" recognize that this is the central issue. For example, Robert P. Lightner, *The Death Christ Died: A Case for Unlimited Atonement* (Des Plaines: Regular Baptist Press, 1967), 33: "There is no question about it; the issue between limited and universal atonement centers in the design or purpose of the redemptive work of Christ."

[3] Compare Luke 2:14, where the angels proclaim, "Glory to God in the highest!" to announce the birth of Jesus to the shepherds in the field.

[4] See D. A. Carson, *The Gospel According to John*, PNTC (Grand Rapids, MI: Eerdmans, 1991), 129.

[5] Johannes E. Louw and Eugene A. Nida, *Greek-English Lexicon of the New Testament: Based on Semantic Domains* (New York: United Bible Societies, 1989), 1:410.

[6] Compare the conclusion of Carson, *John*, 175: "it is just possible that John is saying this *first* sign is also *primary*, because it points to the new dispensation of grace and fulfillment that Jesus is inaugurating."

18; 18:43; 19:38) and even his teaching (Luke 4:15) by glorifying God. Yet despite the number of signs Jesus performed, many refused to believe in him (John 12:37–40). So even though Jesus Christ was the definitive expression of God's glory, most did not believe in him because of their hardness of heart.

The clearest display of God's glory is the death, resurrection, and ascension of Christ.[7] Throughout the Gospels, God's glory is especially tied to these distinct events in Jesus's life. The transfiguration is presented as an advanced preview of the glory that Jesus will have once his exodus is fulfilled in Jerusalem (Luke 9:28–36). In his Gospel, John frequently uses the verb "to glorify" (δοξάζω) as a shorthand for the death and resurrection of Jesus (7:39; 12:16, 23, 28; 13:31–32; 17:1, 4–5). Two clear texts stand out. In John 12, in response to some Greeks who wanted to see him, Jesus answers, "The hour has come for the Son of Man to be glorified" (12:23). The context makes it clear that Jesus has his death and resurrection in view. First, the analogy of the wheat falling into the earth, dying, and bearing fruit pictures his death and resurrection (12:24). Second, in 12:28, Jesus asks the Father to, "Glorify your name." The Father responds, "I have glorified it, and I will glorify it again." Several verses later Jesus asserts, "I, when I am lifted up from the earth, will draw all people to myself" (12:32). John explains that Jesus "said this to show by what kind of death he was going to die" (12:33). Jesus makes a similar connection between the hour coming and God being glorified, in John 13:31–32. Once Judas leaves to betray him, Jesus says to his remaining disciples, "Now is the Son of Man glorified, and God is glorified in him. If God is glorified in him, God will also glorify him in himself, and glorify him at once." By sending the betrayer off, Jesus sets in motion the chain of events that will lead to the ultimate expression of God's glory—his sacrificial death and triumphant resurrection. Thus the ultimate sign that displays God's glory is the death, resurrection, and ascension of Christ.

THE MEANS OF GLORIFYING THE FATHER: DOING THE WORK OF THE FATHER

Scripture does more than simply present the death of Jesus as glorifying the Father—it sets his death within the larger framework of the Son glorifying

---

[7] Although the crucifixion, resurrection, and ascension of Jesus are distinct events, they together comprise one (albeit complex) redemptive act of Christ on our behalf. So while Scripture does sometimes attribute a certain benefit to one of these events, that specific event would lack its true significance if divorced from the other two (see further Michael S. Horton, *The Christian Faith: A Systematic Theology for Pilgrims on the Way* [Grand Rapids, MI: Zondervan, 2010], 521–47).

the Father by accomplishing the work that the Father gave him to do before he ever took on flesh. The Son agrees to display the glory of the Father by redeeming the people that the Father gave to him.[8] As a result, these redeemed people will participate in the intra-Trinitarian communion shared by the Father and the Son from all eternity. Several passages in the Johannine literature describe this agreement, but three are particularly important.

The first is in the Bread of Life Discourse (John 6:22–58), where Jesus explains the work that the Father gave him to do. After identifying himself as the Bread of Life, Jesus asserts,

> All that the Father gives me will come to me, and whoever comes to me I will never cast out. For I have come down from heaven, not to do my own will but the will of him who sent me. And this is the will of him who sent me, that I should lose nothing of all that he has given me, but raise it up on the last day. For this is the will of my Father, that everyone who looks on the Son and believes in him should have eternal life, and I will raise him up on the last day. . . . No one can come to me unless the Father who sent me draws him. And I will raise him up on the last day. (6:37–40, 44)

Several times in this section Jesus emphasizes that he has come down from heaven to accomplish the will of the Father. From this passage, the plan established by the Father and the Son may be summarized as follows: (1) the Father gives a specific group of people to the Son; (2) the Son comes down from heaven to do the Father's will; (3) the Father's will is for the Son to lose none of them but raise them on the last day; (4) these people come to the Son by looking on him and believing; (5) the Son gives them eternal life; (6) the Son will raise them on the last day; and (7) no one can come to the Son unless the Father who sent the Son draws them. Thus it is the Father's election of a specific group of people that defines who comes to the Son and is raised on the last day.[9]

---

[8] This agreement is sometimes referred to as the covenant of redemption, or the *pactum salutis*. For helpful treatments, see the following: Louis Berkhof, *Systematic Theology* (Grand Rapids, MI: Eerdmans, 1996), 265–71; Richard A. Muller, "Toward the *Pactum Salutis*: Locating the Origins of a Concept," *Mid-American Journal of Theology* 18 (2007): 11–65; Herman Bavinck, *Sin and Salvation in Christ*, vol. 3 of *Reformed Dogmatics*, ed. John Bolt, trans. John Vriend, 4 vols. (Grand Rapids, MI: Baker, 2011), 212–16; John B. Webster, "'It Was the Will of the Lord to Bruise Him': Soteriology and the Doctrine of God," in *God of Salvation: Soteriology in Theological Perspective*, ed. Ivor J. Davidson and Murray Rae (Farnham, Surrey, UK: Ashgate, 2011), 15–34. Even if one is uncomfortable with the expression "covenant of redemption," there can be no doubt that Scripture speaks of an agreement in eternity past between the Father and the Son that lays out the plan of redemptive history.

[9] Note that later in the same chapter Jesus returns to the same theme when, after observing that some do not believe, he states, "This is why I told you that no one can come to me unless it is granted him by the Father" (6:65). This helps explain how Judas was part of the Twelve and yet betrayed Jesus (6:70–71).

This progression seriously undermines the contention that "the decree of election is logically after the decree of atonement, where also, in fact, it belongs in the working out of the application of salvation. That is to say, the atonement is general, its application particular."[10] According to John 6:37–44, the Father does not plan to send the Son to save everyone, and then only elect some, knowing that apart from such an election none would believe. Such a contention suggests that redemption circumscribes election; in other words, God's general beneficence to all of mankind ultimately drives the atonement, and election is necessary only because without it none would believe. But John 6 indicates that the Father gives a specific group of people to the Son for whom he *then* comes to die in order to give them eternal life. Particularism attends the planning and the making of the atonement, not just its application.[11] Thus it is election that circumscribes the atonement, not the other way around.

The second key passage is the High Priestly Prayer (John 17:1–26), which makes it even clearer that the Son glorifies the Father by accomplishing the work that the Father gave him to do. After announcing that the hour has come, Jesus prays, "glorify your Son that the Son may glorify you" (17:1). The combination of "hour" (ὥρα) and "glorify" (δόξασόν) recalls 12:23–24, where Jesus spoke of his death and resurrection. That connection clarifies what Jesus means when he prays, "I have brought you glory on earth by finishing [τελειώσας] the work [τὸ ἔργον] you gave me to do" (17:4, NIV). That he refers to his impending death and resurrection is further confirmed by John's use of the verb τελειόω ("to finish"),[12] which is similar to the verb τελέω in 19:30, where Jesus cries out, "It is finished [τετέλεσται]," immediately before his death.[13] The participle in 17:4, τελειώσας ("by finishing"), indicates that the completion of the work is the means by which Jesus glorifies the Father.[14] Thus the connection is clear: the Son glorifies the Father by finishing the work the Father gave him to do, which involves his dying and rising.

---

[10] D. Broughton Knox, "Some Aspects of the Atonement," in *The Doctrine of God*, vol. 1 of *D. Broughton Knox, Selected Works* (3 vols.), ed. Tony Payne (Kingsford, NSW: Matthias Media, 2000), 265.

[11] Contra Knox, ibid.

[12] For a similar conclusion, see, for example, Andreas J. Köstenberger, *John*, BECNT (Grand Rapids, MI: Baker, 2004), 489; and Carson, *John*, 556–57.

[13] Twice before this, John uses the verb τελειόω with the noun ἔργον ("work") to denote the totality of Jesus's ministry (4:34; 5:36). But whereas in these two previous occurrences ἔργον is plural, here in 17:4 it is singular, which likely emphasizes the totality of Jesus's work (Köstenberger, *John*, 489).

[14] So also J. Ramsey Michaels, *The Gospel of John*, NICNT (Grand Rapids, MI: Eerdmans, 2010), 860.

But while the focus of "the work" (τὸ ἔργον) in view is clearly the cross, the larger context of John 17 indicates that more is in view. Jesus asserts that he has manifested the Father's name "to the people whom you gave [ἔδωκάς[15]] me out of the world" (17:6). He gave them the words that the Father gave to him (17:8, 14), and kept them in the Father's name (17:12). The glory that he had with the Father he has now given to his disciples (17:22). So now he prays for the Father to protect them (17:11, 15), unify them (17:11, 20–23), fulfill their joy (17:13), sanctify them (17:17–19), and allow them to see and share in the Son's glory (17:22–24). In the meantime, he sends them into the world just as the Father sent him (17:17–19). Thus "the work" (τὸ ἔργον) that Jesus accomplishes in order to glorify the Father, while certainly focused on the cross, encompasses everything that Jesus does to ensure that the people whom the Father gave to him will be with the Son and participate in the glory that they share (17:20–26).

It is the totality of this work that Christ asserts he has finished—atoning for the sins of those whom the Father gave him *and* praying for them as their High Priest in order to bring them to glory. And it is the totality of this work (atonement *and* intercession) that is applied to those whom the Father gave to the Son; indeed, it is on the basis of the Son's work that the Father will draw them (cf. 12:32). To claim that Christ atones for the sins of everyone but then applies that atonement only to the elect runs contrary to the totality of the work that Christ performs in order to glorify the Father. Such a claim also presents the persons of the Trinity working at cross-purposes with each other: the Father intends the atonement to cover the sins of elect; the Son atones for everyone but then applies it only to the elect by the Spirit. By contrast, John 17 emphasizes not only the totality of the work that Christ effectively accomplished to glorify the Father, but also the Trinitarian harmony in planning, accomplishing, and applying that work to the elect.[16]

The third key passage is the Throne Room vision of Revelation 4:1–5:14. John provides a further picture of Christ glorifying the Father by accomplishing the work that the Father gave him to do. As "the Lion of the tribe of Judah" (5:5) and the "Lamb standing, as though it had been slain"

---

[15] This is the same verb used in 6:37.
[16] Another example of Trinitarian harmony is that the Father and Son both do the drawing of people to the Son (6:44; 12:32, respectively). Indeed, it is the Son's being lifted up on a cross that surfaces as the *basis* for the drawing of people to himself (12:32; note the protasis–apodosis construction). Contributing to this harmony is the fact that Jesus gives his Spirit to those who believe, his elect, after he is glorified through his death (7:39; 14:16–17; 16:7–11; 20:19–23).

(5:6), Christ alone is worthy to take the "scroll written within and on the back, sealed with seven seals" (5:1, 7). Although debated, it seems best to understand this unusual scroll as a "heavenly tablet containing the purpose and end of redemptive history."[17] As the Lion and the Lamb, the Son is worthy to open this scroll because only he has the authority to execute the divine plan of redemption.[18] This authority is confirmed by the elders' song of praise:

> Worthy are you to take the scroll
>> and to open its seals,
> for you were slain, and by your blood you ransomed people for God
>> from every tribe and language and people and nation,
> and you have made them a kingdom and priests to our God,
>> and they shall reign on the earth. (Rev. 5:9–10)

Two particular features of this song are noteworthy. First, Christ's sacrificial death is the focal point of what the Lamb has done to accomplish God's redemptive plan;[19] as such it is the means by which the Son brings glory to the Father. Second, his death ransomed people *for God* (τῷ θεῷ); in other words, their salvation was first and foremost to further his own purposes—the main purpose being, that because of Christ's death he is now worthy to share in the unique glory and praise that belongs to God alone. This is initially realized as myriads of angels (5:11–12) and all of creation (5:13–14) join in ascribing worth to the Lamb who was slain, but it awaits the consummation for its final fulfillment.

From this passage a rough sketch of God's redemptive plan emerges. (1) The Father determines to display his glory. (2) The Son executes this plan by giving his life to ransom for the Father people from every tribe and language and people and nation. (3) The Son makes these ransomed people into a kingdom and priests to God who reign on the earth. (4) The result is that all creation extols the glory of the Father and the Son. This is the goal toward which God is directing all of redemptive history. Once again it is clear that the Son glorifies the Father by accomplishing the work that the Father gave him to do.

---

[17] Grant R. Osborne, *Revelation*, BECNT (Grand Rapids, MI: Baker, 2002), 249.
[18] G. K. Beale, *The Book of Revelation: A Commentary on the Greek Text*, NIGTC (Grand Rapids, MI: Eerdmans, 1999), 340.
[19] This point is further reinforced if indeed the scroll (5:1) is pictured as a Roman will that required the death of the testator in order for the inheritance to be executed. On this possibility, see Beale, *Revelation*, 344–46.

SUMMARY

Other texts (John 10:18; 12:49–50; 14:30–31) testify to the redemptive agreement between the Father and the Son. But the texts considered above are sufficient to show not only that such an agreement exists, but also that it is the overarching framework in which the incarnation, life, ministry, death, resurrection, and ascension must be understood.[20] The ultimate goal of this agreement was to display the glory of the Father to all of creation so that he would be worshiped. The Son executes this plan by redeeming those whom the Father has given to him through his life, death, resurrection, and ascension. Because the Son accomplishes all the work that the Father sent him to do, his people will be one with the Father and the Son, seeing the glory that they share. As a result, both the Father and the Son receive unceasing praise in heaven now in anticipation of the day when all creation will acknowledge the glory of God displayed in the redemption of his people dwelling in a transformed cosmos.

When understood against this backdrop, it becomes clear that the display of God's glory depends on the Son effectively accomplishing everything necessary for the redemption of his people. Jesus clearly states, "And I, when I am lifted up from the earth, *will* draw all people to myself" (John 12:32). The protasis–apodosis construction shows that there is a necessary link between the event of redemption and its application. Thus when it comes to salvation "we are not in the realm of the fleeting or conditional, but the realm of history under the faithful promise of God to himself and therefore to us."[21] If even one of those whom the Father gave to the Son is lost, then God does not receive all the glory that he deserves, because the display of his glory depends on the elect being one with the Father and Son in future glory. But since the Son does effectively accomplish everything necessary, God is glorified as the source, agent, and goal of our salvation.

Thus to frame the issue of the purpose of the atonement as a difference between the intention to save all people (Arminian) or the elect (Reformed) misses the larger point.[22] As John Webster notes,

> The salvation of creatures is a great affair, but not the greatest, which is God's majesty and its promulgation. . . . Salvation occurs as part of the

---

[20] For a similar conclusion, see especially Webster, "It Was the Will of the Lord," 15–34.
[21] Ibid., 30.
[22] See, for example, Lightner, *Death Christ Died*, 33–56.

divine self-exposition; its final end is the reiteration of God's majesty and the glorification of God by all creatures. Soteriology therefore has its place within the theology of the *mysterium trinitatis*, that is, God's inherent and communicated richness of life as Father, Son and Holy Spirit.[23]

So when Scripture speaks of God's purpose in the atonement in terms of saving people from sin or demonstrating his love for the world, these statements must be evaluated in the light of God's ultimate purpose of displaying his glory. Put another way, the salvation of mankind was not the primary purpose of the atonement, but rather the essential means by which the ultimate goal of glorifying the Father was accomplished.

II. Jesus Died to Accomplish the Salvation of His People

Complementary to the first point, there are many texts that specify that Jesus died for a particular group of people who are described in various ways.

Synoptics and Acts

Matthew indicates from the very beginning of his Gospel that the work of Jesus is for his people. The angel of the Lord tells Joseph that Mary "will bear a son, and you shall call his name Jesus, for he will save his people from their sins" (1:21). More than simply explaining the etymology of Jesus's name, the angelic announcement indicates that the salvation which Jesus will accomplish is specifically for his people. The remainder of Matthew fleshes out the identity of "his people," often with surprising results.[24] Two passages in particular are crucial for determining the referent of "his people."

(1) Matthew 20:28

Shortly before his final entry into Jerusalem, Jesus responds to the request of James and John for special places of honor in the Messianic kingdom (20:20–28). In contrasting greatness in the kingdom with greatness in this age,

---

[23] Webster, "It Was the Will of the Lord," 20.

[24] D. A. Carson, "Matthew," in *The Expositor's Bible Commentary*, ed. Frank E. Gaebelein (Grand Rapids, MI: Zondervan, 1994), 77, comments, "Though to Joseph 'his people' would be the Jews, even Joseph would understand from the OT that some Jews fell under God's judgment, while others became a godly remnant. In any event, it is not long before Matthew says that both John the Baptist (3:9) and Jesus (8:11) picture Gentiles joining with the godly remnant to become disciples of the Messiah and members of 'his people' (see on 16:18; cf. Gen. 49:10; Titus 2:13–14; Rev. 14:4). The words 'his people' are therefore full of meaning that is progressively unpacked as the Gospel unfolds. They refer to 'Messiah's people.'" R. T. France, *The Gospel of Matthew*, NICNT (Grand Rapids, MI: Eerdmans, 2007), 53, notes that it is also possible to see a connection between "his people" and "my church" in 16:28.

Jesus points to his own example when he states that "the Son of Man came not to be served but to serve, and to give his life as a ransom for many [ἀντὶ πολλῶν]" (20:28). Although it is possible to take "many" as synonymous with "all,"[25] there are reasons to see a narrower reference. First, Jesus likely echoes the language of Isaiah 52:13–53:12, where the Servant dies on behalf of the many.[26] Within that passage, "the many" (הָרַבִּים [MT]/οἱ πολλοί [LXX]) refers to those to whom the saving work of the Servant is *actually* applied, including not only Jews but "many nations" (52:15) as well.[27] Second, the language of ransom (λύτρον) indicates the payment of a specific price (Jesus's life) for the release of a specific people (many).[28] His life is given in exchange for (ἀντί) that of the many, not for all without exception.

(2) Matthew 26:28

During the Last Supper (26:26–29), Jesus offers the cup to his disciples and explains, "This is my blood of the covenant, which is poured out for many for the forgiveness of sins" (26:28). Just as the sprinkling of blood sealed a particular people in the old covenant (Ex. 24:1–8), so here the inauguration of the new covenant requires Jesus to shed his blood for a particular people. That particular people is the "many" for whom Jesus gives his life as a ransom (Matt. 20:28). The combination of "many" and "forgiveness of sins" here in 26:28 forges a link back to the angelic announcement in 1:21 that Jesus "will save his people from their sins." Furthermore, this combination likely alludes again to the work of the Suffering Servant of Isaiah 53.[29]

---

[25] Perhaps the most influential example is Joachim Jeremias, "πολλοί," *TDNT* 6:543–45, who argues that πολλοί is used inclusively (= "all") based on the OT evidence. But although Jeremias discusses Isaiah 52:13–53:12, he does not take into account that the work of the Servant for the many is actually *applied* to the many (see J. Alec Motyer, "'Stricken for the Transgressions of My People': The Atoning Work of Isaiah's Suffering Servant," chapter 10 in this volume). Furthermore, Jeremias's assertion that, with the exception of Matthew 24:12 and 2 Corinthians 2:17, πολλοί always means "all" is quite overstated; for a whole series of Pauline texts where πολλοί means "many" or "most" but not "all," see Douglas J. Moo, *The Epistle to the Romans*, NICNT (Grand Rapids, MI: Eerdmans, 1996), 336 n. 100.

[26] For the connections between Mark 10:45//Matthew 20:28 and Isaiah 53, see especially Rikki E. Watts, *Isaiah's New Exodus in Mark*, Biblical Studies Library (Grand Rapids, MI: Baker, 2000), 257–90.

[27] There is also evidence that at Qumran the term "the many" (הָרַבִּים) at times refers to the elect community in contrast to those who are not yet fully initiated into the community (1QS 6:11–27) (Hanns Walter Huppenbauer, "Rb, rwb, rbym in der Sektenregel," *Theologische Zeitschrift* 13 [1957]: 136–37, and Ralph Marcus, "*Mebaqqer* and *rabbim* in the Manual of Discipline 6:11–13," *JBL* 75 [1956]: 298–302). While the Qumran interpretation does not *prove* "many" is equivalent to "the elect" in Isaiah 53, it does demonstrate clear precedence for this interpretation.

[28] The payment of a price to secure release is fundamental to this word group (Leon Morris, *The Apostolic Preaching of the Cross*, 3rd ed. [Grand Rapids, MI: Eerdmans, 1965], 12–13). In addition to referring to purchasing freedom for slaves or prisoners of war, this word group could also refer to sacrifices made to pay for sins against the gods (Adela Yarbro Collins, "The Signification of Mark 10:45 among Gentile Christians," *Harvard Theological Review* 90 [1997]: 371–82).

[29] On the allusion to Isaiah 53 here, see Douglas J. Moo, *The Old Testament in the Gospel Passion Narratives* (Sheffield, UK: Almond, 1983), 127–32.

Thus "his people" in Matthew 1:21 is further clarified by the "many" in 20:28 and 26:28 for whom Jesus dies to forgive their sins. As the fulfillment of the OT hope, Jesus seals the new covenant by ransoming a particular people from their bondage to sin through his death and resurrection.

These texts emphasize Jesus dying for a particular group of people rather than for humanity in general. Regardless of whether the term used is "many" or "his people," the point remains the same: Jesus gave his life as a ransom for the eschatological people of God, composed of Jews and Gentiles who believe in him.

Johannine Literature

We find the same kind of particularist statements in the Johannine literature. But unlike the Synoptics, John also includes numerous statements about God's election of a particular people to receive the benefits of Jesus's death. In addition to John 6, which was treated above, the following passages are particularly significant.

In John 10:11–18, Jesus presents himself as the Good Shepherd who lays down his life for his sheep (10:11). Jesus further describes these sheep as "my own," who know him "just as the Father knows me and I know the Father" (10:15). But who are these sheep? They are the eschatological people of God, drawn from Jew and Gentile alike (10:16). The religious leaders do not believe because they are not part of Jesus's flock (10:26). By contrast, Jesus's sheep hear his voice, follow him, and are given eternal life (10:27–28). They are his sheep because the Father gave them to the Son (10:29). Notice that Jesus does not say that the religious leaders are not part of his flock because they do not believe. Rather, Jesus makes it clear that the unbelief of the religious leaders is an outworking of the fact that they are not his sheep. From this passage we see that Jesus's sheep are a particular set of people that exist before they exercise faith in him, and that those who are not part of that divinely selected group do not believe (cf. 8:47). As the Good Shepherd, Jesus lays down his life for a particular group of people (his sheep) in distinction from others (those who are not his sheep).[30]

---

[30] It simply will not do to assert that a text like this does not explicitly "say that Christ died *only* for the Church or that He did not die for the non-elect," as does David L. Allen, "The Atonement: Limited or Universal?," in *Whosoever Will: A Biblical-Theological Critique of Five-Point Calvinism*, ed. David L. Allen and Steve W. Lemke (Nashville: B&H Academic, 2010), 79. True, the claim that Jesus laid down his life for his sheep does not *logically demand* that he died *only* for the elect. But it must be stressed that this claim does not exist in a vacuum; it is part of a larger matrix of ideas in this passage that describes the purpose of Christ coming into the world, the means of

John even describes Jesus's enemies as testifying that his death was directed toward a particular group of people. In the wake of Jesus raising Lazarus from the dead, the Sanhedrin meets in an emergency session to discuss what to do about Jesus (11:47–53). The high priest Caiaphas argues that "it is better for you that one man should die for the people, not that the whole nation should perish" (11:50). John goes on to explain that Caiaphas was unwittingly prophesying "that Jesus would die for the nation, and not for the nation only, but also to gather into one the children of God who are scattered abroad" (11:51–52). Whereas Caiaphas clearly means that the death of Jesus would spare the Jewish people from trouble with Rome, John sees the theological significance of the statement. Jesus's death is for "the nation" (i.e., the Jewish people) as well as others who must be gathered into the united children of God.[31] Following on the heels of the discussion of Jesus's sheep in chapter 10, we should understand this as a reiteration of the idea that the true people of God, composed of Jew and Gentile alike, are the people for whom Jesus dies.

As Jesus prepares his disciples for his impending death, he once again stresses that it is for a particular group of people. After commanding his disciples to love one another as he has loved them (15:12), Jesus describes the nature of his love: "Greater love has no one than this, that someone lay down his life for his friends" (15:13).[32] Just as the Good Shepherd lays down his life for the sheep, so here Jesus lays down his life for his friends out of love for them. This particular love for his friends is grounded in divine election: "You did not choose me, but I chose you" (15:16).[33]

Although not a major emphasis in the Johannine epistles, there are a couple

---

accomplishing that purpose, and the specific distinction between his sheep and those who are not his sheep. Thus "to take the formula 'laying down his life for' out of the relationship in which it occurs and apply it to those who finally perish is to make a distinction that Jesus' own teaching forbids" (John Murray, "The Atonement and the Free Offer of the Gospel," in *Collected Writings of John Murray. Volume 1: The Claims of Truth* [Carlisle, PA: Banner of Truth, 1976], 76).

[31] Notice that this group of people ("children of God") exists before they believe in Jesus, another indication of their divine election.

[32] It is common to speak of God's love in a way that obliterates any distinctions in how the Bible speaks of it. But, following Carson, it is possible to identify at least five different ways that the Bible speaks of God's love: (1) The special love between the Father and the Son; (2) God's providential love for his creation; (3) God's salvific stance toward his fallen world; (4) God's particular, effective, selecting love toward his elect; and (5) God's provisional or conditional love for his people (D. A. Carson, *The Difficult Doctrine of the Love of God* [Wheaton, IL: Crossway, 2000], 16–24; and also Murray, "Atonement and the Free Offer of the Gospel," 69–74). Geerhardus Vos, "The Biblical Doctrine of the Love of God," in *Redemptive History and Biblical Interpretation: The Shorter Writings of Geerhardus Vos*, ed. Richard B. Gaffin (Phillipsburg, NJ: P&R, 1980), 456, is correct to point out that (4) is given the most distributive emphasis in Scripture. In other words, God's love for the elect is no mere "afterthought," as it must be in the Amyraldian scheme. This approach is far more faithful to Scripture than simply asserting, "The crux of the matter is, 'Does God love all men or does He not?'" (Lightner, *Death Christ Died*, 111).

[33] Here I would remind the reader of the inseparable link between those for whom the Son dies and those for whom he intercedes, as described in John 17 (see discussion above).

of texts that refer to the work of the Son as specifically directed toward his people (1 John 3:16; 4:10). But Revelation 5:9–10 is particularly significant because it clearly combines the ultimate goal of God's glory, the death of Christ, and the redemption of a particular people. The heavenly creatures sing that by his blood the Lamb ransomed a particular people, not the whole world. They are purchased *out of* (ἐκ) "every tribe and language and people and nation." The text does not say that Christ ransomed every tribe and language and people and nation, but rather people *from* every tribe and language and people and nation. So Beale is correct in noting that, "This is not a redemption of all peoples without exception but of all without distinction (people *from* all races), as 14:3–4, 6 makes clear."[34] The allusion to Exodus 19:5–6 makes it clear that it is these particular people who are made into a kingdom and priests to God.

SUMMARY

This collection of texts, drawn primarily from the Johannine writings and supported by texts in the Synoptic Gospels as well, demonstrates that when Jesus lived, died, rose, ascended, and interceded, he did so for a particular group of people. This group is variously referred to as his people, the church, the many, his sheep, the children of God, and his friends. They are the ones whom the Father has given to the Son before he came to earth, and whom the Father draws so that they come to the Son, who then grants them eternal life. Drawn from every tribe and language and people and nation, they are the sheep for whom the Good Shepherd lays down his life and who will share in the intra-Trinitarian love and glory.

III. Jesus Died for the Sins of the World

Alongside the numerous texts noted so far, there are others that stress the universal scope of the work of Christ. These "universalistic" texts emphasize that those whom the Father has given to the Son are not limited to one particular ethnic group, but rather are drawn from all of humanity.

SYNOPTICS AND ACTS

There are several texts in the Synoptics and Acts where the offer of forgiveness through the gospel is made to all (e.g., Matt. 11:28; 24:14; 28:18–20;

---

[34] Beale, *Revelation*, 359.

Luke 2:30–32; Acts 1:8). Advocates of universal atonement claim that these texts rule out definite atonement. For example, Norman Douty asks,

> [H]ow can God authorize His servants to offer pardon to the non-elect if Christ did not purchase it for them? . . . The advocates of Limited Atonement attribute the problem to *God*, Who, they say, has told them in His Word that Christ died only for the elect, and that they are to offer salvation to all. They honor Him by meekly believing both, without any attempt at reconciling them.[35]

That the gospel is to be preached to all indiscriminately is clear and undeniable. However, these texts have nothing directly to say about the extent of the atonement. They simply emphasize the necessity of preaching the gospel to any and all who will hear. There is no contradiction, biblical or logical, in saying that Christ died for a particular group of people while at the same time affirming that this good news is to be preached to all without distinction. What Douty and others fail to appreciate is that God has ordained that the means by which the elect will believe in Christ is the indiscriminate preaching of the gospel (Rom. 8:29–30; 10:14–17). Since no one but God knows who the elect are before their conversion, the gospel is preached to all without distinction in the confidence that Jesus's sheep will hear his voice and believe (John 10:27).[36]

Furthermore, in many of these texts there are indications in the context that the emphasis is on the offer of the gospel to all irrespective of ethnicity. That is clearly the emphasis in Matthew 24:14 and 28:18–20, where the phrase "all nations" (πάντα τὰ ἔθνη) is explicitly used. The same is true with respect to Luke 2:30–32 and Acts 1:8. The point in these texts is that the gospel is not to be limited to the Jewish people but is to be proclaimed to all peoples of the earth.

Additionally, Matthew 11:28 and its surrounding context weave together particularity and the indiscriminate offer of the gospel. Right before inviting all who are weary to come to him (11:28), Jesus says, "All things have been handed over to me by my Father, and no one knows the Son except the Father, and no one knows the Father except the Son and anyone to whom

---

[35] Norman F. Douty, *The Death of Christ: A Treatise Which Answers the Question: "Did Christ Die Only for the Elect?"* (Swengel, PA: Reiner, 1972), 41.

[36] This is more satisfactory than claiming that "a universal atonement truly honors God's grace and frees God from the charge that he is responsible, through election, for excluding some from his kingdom" (Donald M. Lake, "He Died for All: The Universal Dimensions of the Atonement," in *Grace Unlimited*, ed. Clark H. Pinnock [Minneapolis: Bethany Fellowship, 1975], 43). For a helpful treatment of this issue, see Roger R. Nicole, "Covenant, Universal Call, and Definite Atonement," *JETS* 38 (1995): 405–411.

the Son chooses to reveal him" (11:27). That this revelation is not given to all is evident from verse 25, where Jesus praises the Father "that you have hidden these things from the wise and understanding and revealed them to little children." Particularism and universalism are complementary realities, not contradictory ones.

JOHANNINE LITERATURE

In arguing that the extent of the atonement is "universal," frequent appeal is made to the Johannine literature. This is quite understandable as there are a number of texts that emphasize the universal scope of God's redemptive work through Christ. However, when understood within the larger context of John's writings, these texts are best understood as emphasizing that the atonement extends beyond the Jews to include people from every tribe and tongue.

Central to the discussion is the use of the word κόσμος ("world"). Of the 186 occurrences in the NT, 105 are in the Johannine Literature.[37] As one should expect, κόσμος is used in several different ways, and only the context can determine which sense it has in a particular verse. One common way of categorizing the uses is to divide them into occurrences with positive, neutral, or negative overtones.[38] But this approach has only a limited value, because (1) there are no unambiguous positive occurrences,[39] and (2) even when an occurrence might be classified as neutral there is very often a negative occurrence close by.[40] Indeed, Carson is correct when he notes that

> although a handful of passages preserve a neutral emphasis the vast majority are decidedly negative. The "world," or frequently "this world" (*e.g.* 8:23; 9:39; 11:9; 18:36), is not the universe, but the created order (especially of human beings and human affairs) in rebellion against its Maker (*e.g.* 1:10; 7:7; 14:17, 22, 27, 30; 15:18–19; 16:8, 20, 33; 17:6, 9, 14).[41]

To organize our discussion, we will look at three different categories of usage for κόσμος in the Johannine literature. But in doing so we must

---

[37] The breakdown is as follows: Gospel of John (78×); 1 John (23×); 2 John (1×); Revelation (3×).

[38] See, for example, N. H. Cassem, "Grammatical and Contextual Inventory of the Use of *kosmos* in the Johannine Corpus with Some Implications for a Johannine Cosmic Theology," *NTS* 19 (1972): 81–91.

[39] Some attempt to place texts such as John 1:29 and 3:16 here, but, as I will argue below, the context suggests otherwise.

[40] Even those who advocate this method of categorization acknowledge the frequent blurring that takes place; see, for example, Stanley B. Marrow, "*Kosmos* in John," *CBQ* 64 (2002): 96.

[41] Carson, *John*, 122–23; see similarly, Bill Salier, "What's in a World? *Kosmos* in the Prologue of John's Gospel," *RTR* 56 (1997): 106–107.

remember that some examples could fit into more than one category; as a result, we must be careful not to view these categories as mutually exclusive.

The first category is those places where κόσμος refers to the world as the stage of God's redemptive work through Christ. Christ is introduced as the true light who comes into the world (John 1:9–10; cf. 9:5). He is the one "whom the Father consecrated and sent into the world" (10:36), and as his final Passover approached he "knew that his hour had come to depart out of this world to the Father, having loved his own who were in the world" (13:1; cf. 16:28). Several more texts could be listed,[42] but the point is sufficiently clear—the world is the stage where God accomplishes his redemptive purposes in and through Christ. Yet it must be noted that even in these passages, where κόσμος appears to have a neutral sense, the negative overtones are never completely absent. For example, even the seemingly "neutral" sense of κόσμος in John 1:9–10 introduces the rejection that the Word experiences. As a result, "When [John] says of the κόσμος that it does not know the Son of God, that it does not know God, that it does not believe, that it hates, the κόσμος is in some sense personified as the great opponent of the Redeemer in salvation history."[43] Or, as Marrow puts it, "κόσμος will stand as the opposing power to the revelation, the sum of everyone and everything that sets its face adamantly against it and becomes, in consequence, the object of judgment."[44]

The second category is more germane to our subject. In the Johannine literature κόσμος is frequently used to emphasize the scope of God's redemptive work. In other words, the emphasis falls on Christ's work as encompassing all people without distinction, not just the Jewish people.[45] Sometimes this emphasis is clear in the immediate context, whereas other times it is not. But in each of the following texts John draws attention to the truth that Christ's redemption transcends ethnic boundaries to include not simply Jews but Gentiles as well.

The first example is John 1:9–13.[46] After stating that the "the world did not know" the Word, John distinguishes between "his own people" (i.e., the

---

[42] See, for example, John 6:14; 8:26; 9:39; 11:27; 12:46; 16:21, 28; 18:37; 1 John 4:1, 3, 9, 17; 2 John 1:7; Revelation 11:15; 13:8; 17:8.

[43] Hermann Sasse, "κοσμέω, κόσμος, κόσμιος, κοσμικός," *TDNT*, 3:894.

[44] Marrow, "*Kosmos* in John," 98.

[45] The view argued for here is to be distinguished from the claim that κόσμος actually means "elect" in these contexts. The point rather is that God's saving love is not limited to one particular ethnicity but extends to all human beings without distinction.

[46] For a helpful treatment of κόσμος in this text, see Salier, "What's in a World?," 110–14.

Jews) who did not receive him and those who did (1:11–12). This distinction paves the way for John to stress that all, whether Jew or Gentile, who did receive Jesus are children of God (τέκνα θεοῦ). Thus John connects κόσμος to a distinction between Jews and non-Jews as a means of stressing the universal scope of Christ's redemptive work.

John 4:42 should be understood in a similar way. After Jesus converses with the Samaritan woman (4:7–26), her testimony to her fellow Samaritans leads many to believe in him (4:39). But after they speak with Jesus themselves, what they hear leads them to conclude, "this is indeed the Savior of the world" (4:42). In other words, they believe that Jesus is not merely the Savior of the Jewish people, but rather of the whole world, even Samaritans. They recognize that his salvation transcends even the sharp divide between Jew and Samaritan to encompass all who believe without distinction.[47]

The scope of Christ's redemption extends not just to Samaritans, but even to Greeks.[48] In response to some Greeks who wish to see Jesus (John 12:20–21),[49] Jesus asserts, "I, when I am lifted up from the earth, will draw all people [πάντας] to myself" (12:32). It is against this background that Jesus's statement in 12:47 should be understood—"I did not come to judge the world [οὐ γὰρ ἦλθον ἵνα κρίνω τὸν κόσμον] but to save the world [ἀλλ᾽ ἵνα σώσω τὸν κόσμον]." Coming as it does at the end of the Book of Signs, this emphasis on the universal scope of Christ's redemptive work is all the more significant.

These examples shed light on other texts where κόσμος occurs without explicit clarification in the immediate context. In John 1:29, John the Baptist identifies Jesus as "the Lamb of God, who takes away the sin of the world [τὴν ἁμαρτίαν τοῦ κόσμου]!" While it is true that there is nothing in the immediate context to indicate what κόσμος means here, the numerous other "restricted" uses must be brought to bear. As such it is slightly misleading to claim that there is nothing in the context to indicate this distinction;[50] the relevant context is how κόσμος is used elsewhere in John. Thus the point of this statement is not that Jesus will take away the sin of every single person

---

[47] Indeed, the order of the material suggests this: in chapter 3, Jesus offers salvation to a religious Jewish man; in chapter 4, he offers it to an immoral Samaritan woman.
[48] While some have argued that the Greeks in view here are actually Greek-speaking Jews, it makes far more sense in the context to regard them as Gentiles (Carson, *John*, 435–36).
[49] Note that this incident immediately follows the statement of the Pharisees that "the whole world" has gone after Jesus (John 12:19).
[50] So Lightner, *Death Christ Died*, 68.

in the world without exception, but rather that his death would redeem all without distinction, not merely Israel. This conclusion is confirmed by the fact that the Lamb of God *actually* takes away sin rather than merely *potentially* doing so.

A similar dynamic is present in John 3:16. As further explanation of Jesus's conversation with Nicodemus ("a ruler of the Jews"; 3:1), John states, "For God so loved the world, that he gave his only Son, that whoever believes in him should not perish but have eternal life."[51] In contrast to the Jewish particularism that characterized many within Israel at the time,[52] Jesus stresses that the scope of God's redemptive purposes extends beyond the Jewish people to incorporate the entire world.[53] This conclusion is reinforced by the larger context. In fact, the next time κόσμος is used after 3:16–19 is in 4:42, where it clearly emphasizes the scope of Jesus's work (see above). So Jesus is emphasizing to this *Jewish* ruler that *whoever* believes, whether Jew or Gentile, has eternal life. This in no way diminishes the stunning nature of God's love described here. As Carson notes, "God's love is to be admired not because the world is so big and includes so many people, but because the world is so bad: that is the customary connotation of *kosmos*."[54] Despite the world's rebellion against its Maker, God gives his Son so that all who believe may have eternal life.[55]

This larger backdrop sheds light on 1 John 2:2. After referring to Christ as our Advocate, John says that Christ "is the propitiation for our sins, and not for ours only but also for the sins of the whole world." The broader context of the letter must be kept in view here. John writes to believers who are dealing with false teachers who claim to be so spiritual that they do not sin (1:6–10),

---

[51] Whether these are Jesus's words or John's is not germane to our topic; the point made here stands either way.

[52] On this point, see Adolf von Schlatter, *Der Evangelist Johannes*, 2nd ed. (Stuttgart: Calwer, 1948), 48–49; and Köstenberger, *John*, 67–68.

[53] Further confirmation that this understanding of κόσμος is correct is found in how the word is used in John 3:17. If it is insisted that κόσμος in 3:16 must be understood as all without exception, then the same must be true of 3:17, which results in universalism (Murray, "Atonement and the Free Offer of the Gospel," 80). In arguing that κόσμος must refer to all without exception, Laurence M. Vance, *The Other Side of Calvinism*, rev. ed. (Pensacola, FL: Vance, 1999), 435–36, makes much of the reference to Numbers 21:6–9 in John 3:14–15. He fails to realize, however, that Jesus uses this example as a point of contact from Nicodemus's Jewish framework to make a larger point about the salvation of Jew and Gentile alike. The point, then, is that just as the serpent being lifted up was the means of salvation for the Israelites in the wilderness, so too the lifting up of the Son of Man is the means of salvation for Jew and Gentile alike.

[54] Carson, *John*, 205.

[55] Passages such as John 6:35, 51; 8:12; 9:5; 12:46 should be understood this way also. With respect to John 3:16, the comments of John Murray are worth quoting: "There is, after all, nothing in this text to support what it is frequently supposed to affirm, namely, universal atonement. What it actually says is akin to definite atonement. Something is made infallibly certain and secure—all believers will have eternal life" ("Atonement and the Free Offer of the Gospel," 80).

despite their obvious disobedience to God's commandments (2:3–6, 9–11). Although they were originally part of the community, the fact that they left demonstrates that they were not truly part of the community (2:19–27). "They are from the world; therefore they speak from the world, and the world listens to them" (4:5). So in the face of opponents who viewed themselves as a spiritual notch above everyone else, John responds by emphasizing that when Christ died "it was not for the sake of, say, the Jews only or, now, of some group, gnostic or otherwise, that sets itself up as intrinsically superior. Far from it. It was not for our sins only, but also for the sins of the whole world."[56] This conclusion is confirmed by the close parallel with John 11:50–52, where John uses similar language to emphasize that Jesus's death applies to all "the children of God who are scattered abroad":

John 11:52:   . . . καὶ **οὐχ** ὑπὲρ τοῦ ἔθνους **μόνον ἀλλ᾽** ἵνα **καὶ** τὰ τέκνα τοῦ θεοῦ τὰ διεσκορπισμένα συναγάγῃ εἰς ἕν.

. . . and **not** for the nation **only, but also** to gather into one the children of God who are scattered abroad.

1 John 2:2:   καὶ αὐτὸς ἱλασμός ἐστιν περὶ τῶν ἁμαρτιῶν ἡμῶν, **οὐ** περὶ τῶν ἡμετέρων δὲ **μόνον ἀλλὰ καὶ** περὶ ὅλου τοῦ κόσμου.

He is the propitiation for our sins, and **not** for ours **only but also** for the sins of the whole world.

John Calvin nicely summarizes the point when he states, "the design of John was no other than to make this benefit common to the whole Church. Then under the word *all* or whole, he does not include the reprobate, but designates those who should believe as well as those who were then scattered through various parts of the world."[57] The point, then, is that the death of Christ—portrayed here as an *actual* propitiation for the sins of the world, not a *potential* one[58]—is for all without distinction, not all without exception.[59]

This emphasis on the universal scope of the atonement appears again in

---

[56] Carson, *Difficult Doctrine of the Love of God*, 76.

[57] John Calvin, *Commentaries on the Catholic Epistles*, Calvin's Commentaries 22, ed. and trans. John Owen (Grand Rapids, MI: Baker, 1996; repr. of the CTS translations of the commentaries), 173.

[58] See Henri Blocher's helpful comments on the sloppy logic of "potentiality" language in regards to the atonement ("Jesus Christ *the* Man: Toward a Systematic Theology of Definite Atonement," chapter 20 in this volume).

[59] For other possible ways of understanding how κόσμος is used here in 1 John 2:2, see Roger R. Nicole, "Particular Redemption," in *Our Savior God: Man, Christ, and the Atonement*, ed. James Montgomery Boice (Grand Rapids, MI: Baker, 1980), 176–77; and George M. Smeaton, *The Apostles' Doctrine of the Atonement; with Historical Appendix* (Grand Rapids, MI: Zondervan, 1957 [1870]), 459–60: John intimates that Christ's propitiation "was not for him and those to whom he wrote alone, but for the redeemed of every period, place, and people—that is, prospectively and retrospectively" (460).

1 John 4:7–14. The ultimate expression of God's love is that he "sent his Son to be the propitiation for our sins" (4:10). God's love for his people is the reason believers should love each other (4:11), and by doing so they demonstrate that God abides in them by his Spirit (4:12–13). As a result, believers "testify that the Father has sent his Son to be the Savior of the world [σωτῆρα τοῦ κόσμου]" (4:14). Again, we see the universal scope of the atonement stated alongside the particular love that God has for his people.

The third category of John's use of κόσμος consists of places where a sharp distinction is made between God's people and the world.[60] Although there are numerous texts that draw this distinction, our focus will be John 14–17. At several points in these chapters Jesus distinguishes things that are true of his followers but not the world. Whereas believers receive the Spirit of truth, the world cannot (14:16–17). Soon the world will no longer see Jesus, but his disciples will (14:18–24). They should expect hatred from the world because they are not of the world but rather have been chosen out of the world (15:18–19). Although the disciples will weep when Jesus dies, the world will rejoice (16:20).

This contrast is most prominent in John 17. After describing what he has done for those whom the Father has given him (17:6–8), Jesus says, "I am praying for them. I am not praying for the world but for those whom you have given me, for they are yours" (17:9). Because Jesus will no longer be in the world but his people will be, he prays for the Father to watch over them (17:10–13). The world will hate his people because they are not of the world, just as Jesus is not of this world (17:14–16). But just as Jesus was set apart and sent into the world, so too are his people (17:17–19). Jesus continues by praying for those who will believe through the testimony of his people, that their unity may demonstrate to the world that the Father sent the Son (17:20–23). Whereas the world does not know the Father, the Son and his people do (17:25).

Thus in all of these texts (and others, such as 1 John 2:15–17; 3:1, 13; 4:4–5; 5:4–5, 19), there is a sharp distinction drawn between those whom the Father has given the Son and the world. By explicitly praying for his people and not the world, Jesus makes it clear that his redemptive work—including his incarnation, life, ministry, death, resurrection, and exaltation—is done par-

---

[60] This distinction, of course, is rooted in the fact that Jesus often contrasts himself, his ways, his kingdom, etc., with the world; see, for example, John 7:7; 8:23; 18:36; 1 John 3:1; 4:4.

ticularly for his people in contrast to the world. Jesus's sheep experience the benefits of his work in a way that the world does not (indeed, cannot) receive.

So in the light of our brief survey of how κόσμος is used in the Johannine writings, it simply will not do to assert, as some advocates of "universal atonement" do, that "world means world" as if it were self-evident that κόσμος refers to all without exception rather than all without distinction.[61] When the Pharisees exclaim, "You see that you are gaining nothing. Look, the world has gone after him!" (John 12:19), they certainly do not mean every single person without exception went after Jesus. Or when Jesus says to the high priest, "I have spoken openly to the world" (John 18:20), he clearly does not mean that he has spoken to every single person without exception. As a result, when texts such as John 1:29 speak of Jesus as "the Lamb of God who takes away the sin of the world," it does not follow that this must and can only mean that Jesus makes atonement possible for every single person. Only the context can determine what κόσμος means, not *a priori* assumptions.

SUMMARY

The repeated insistence that Christ's death is not merely for the Jewish people but extends to all people without distinction is a glorious truth. Jesus is not merely the Jewish Messiah, but ultimately the "Savior of the world" (John 4:42). Because of this, the gospel can be freely and indiscriminately offered to all in the confidence that those whom the Father has given to the Son are taken from Jew and Gentile alike, and that the Father will draw them to Christ.

CONCLUSION

When the Father sent the Son into the world, his ultimate purpose was to display the glory of God. The means chosen to glorify the Father was the death of the Son for the people whom the Father gave to him in advance. These elect are drawn from every tribe and tongue and language and people to constitute the one people of God. The Son also intercedes for his people to ensure that they will indeed experience all that God intends for them. This conclusion does not exclude non-salvific benefits that the non-elect experience as a result of the death of Christ. Nor does it deny that God loves his

---

[61] See, for example, Terry L. Miethe, "The Universal Power of the Atonement," in *The Grace of God and the Will of Man*, ed. Clark H. Pinnock (Minneapolis: Bethany, 1995), 80.

fallen creation. Nor does it invalidate the genuine offer of the gospel to all the nations. It simply affirms that the ultimate purpose of the atonement is God-centered rather than man-centered: *the Son came down from heaven in order to glorify his Father by doing his will, which was to save those whom the Father had given him.* The only appropriate response on our part is worship, a reality that is captured in these stanzas of Matthew Bridges's hymn, "Crown Him with Many Crowns":

Crown Him with many crowns, the Lamb upon His throne.
Hark! How the heavenly anthem drowns all music but its own.
Awake, my soul, and sing of Him who died for thee,
And hail Him as thy matchless King through all eternity.

Crown Him the Lord of life, who triumphed o'er the grave,
And rose victorious in the strife for those He came to save.
His glories now we sing, who died, and rose on high,
Who died eternal life to bring, and lives that death may die.

For Whom
Did Christ Die?

PARTICULARISM AND
UNIVERSALISM IN THE
PAULINE EPISTLES[1]

Jonathan Gibson

Introduction

It is obvious enough that the apostle Paul does not directly address the question "For whom did Christ die?" His epistles are occasional letters written to various churches in Asia Minor in the latter half of the first century AD. The issue, however, does arise when one tries to hold together various texts in the Pauline corpus that relate to his atonement theology. For example, in Paul's atonement theology there is a tension between particularism and universalism. On the one hand, Christ is said to have died for "me" (Gal. 2:20), for the "church" (Acts 20:28;[2] Eph. 5:25), for "his people" (Titus 2:14), for "us" believers (Rom. 5:8; 8:32; 1 Cor. 5:7; Gal. 3:13; Eph. 5:2; 1 Thess. 5:10; Titus 2:14). On the other hand, Christ is said to have died for "many" (Rom. 5:15, 19), for "all" (2 Cor. 5:14–15; 1 Tim. 2:6), for the "world" (2 Cor. 5:19); God will have mercy on "all" (Rom. 11:32); he desires "all" to come to a knowledge of the truth (1 Tim. 2:4); he is the Savior of "all" (1 Tim. 4:10);

---

[1] I am grateful to Dirk Jongkind and Peter Orr for their helpful comments on an earlier draft of this chapter.
[2] Included here, since Luke records that Paul spoke these words to the Ephesian elders.

God's salvation appeared to "all people" (Titus 2:11); through Christ God intends to reconcile "all things" to himself by "making peace through the blood of his cross" (Col. 1:20). In addition to these strong universalistic elements, Paul speaks of Christ's death for people who are deemed false teachers (Acts 20:28–30) or who may finally perish (Rom. 14:15; 1 Cor. 8:11). Thus, the question "For whom did Christ die?" naturally arises when one reads Paul synchronically. This brief survey of texts reveals that there exists in Paul's atonement theology, prima facie, a tension between particularism and universalism.

These, however, are not the only texts that relate to Paul's atonement theology; there are other texts in the wider sphere of his soteriology that directly impinge upon his atonement theology.[3] I call these "doctrinal loci" texts. They concern various doctrines—such as eschatology, election, union with Christ, christology, Trinitarianism, doxology, covenant, ecclesiology, and sacramentology—which are like interconnected threads in the web of Paul's soteriology, providing significant and important influence on the intent and nature of the atonement.

In sum, at the risk of oversimplification, I understand Paul's atonement theology to be comprised of at least four groups of texts (with some overlap between them): (1) particularistic texts that concern Christ's death for a particular group ("me," "church," "his people," "us"); (2) universalistic texts that concern Christ's death for an undefined, ambiguous group ("many," "all," "world"); (3) "perishing" texts (for want of a better term) that concern Christ's death for people who may finally perish, either because they are exposed as false teachers or because they stumble into sin through a weak conscience; and (4) "doctrinal loci" texts that concern important doctrines which directly impinge upon the intent and nature of the atonement (such as eschatology, election, union with Christ, christology, Trinitarianism, doxology, covenant, ecclesiology, and sacramentology).[4] These four groups of

---

[3] I am aware that there are competing definitions of the word "soteriology." For example, E. D. Morris, "Soteriology," in *Encyclopedia of Religious Knowledge (Schaff–Herzog)*, 13 vols. (London/New York: Funk & Wagnalls, 1908), 11:9b, restricts the term to "the work of the Savior," and excludes "on the one side, the elective purpose and love of the Father, or, on the other, the interior ministry of the Spirit in the application of saving grace." He later distinguishes between objective soteriology (the work of the Savior) and subjective soteriology (regeneration and sanctification by the Spirit) (11:11a). Louis Berkhof, *Systematic Theology* (Grand Rapids, MI: Eerdmans, 1941), 415, in contrast, restricts the term to the application of the work of redemption. For the purposes of this chapter and the next, soteriology consists of God's saving acts, which are commenced in eternity past by God the Father, revealed in Jesus Christ, and applied by the Spirit. It therefore encompasses everything from election and predestination to final glorification.

[4] The list is not intended to be exhaustive.

texts constitute important components of a unified theological lens through which the intent and nature of the atonement may be viewed.

This chapter analyzes in close detail the first three groups of texts; the next chapter will present the fourth group of texts, where I propose a new approach to the issue of definite atonement in Paul. In that chapter, I will argue that discussions over the intent and nature of the atonement often produce a textual *quid pro quo*, which then results in an impasse. However, while a new approach is required—one which understands Paul's doctrine of the atonement through the wider lens of his soteriology—exegesis of particularistic, universalistic, and "perishing" texts is still necessary, since these texts are themselves important constituent parts of that lens.

In this chapter, I will analyze in Paul's epistles (1) particularistic texts; (2) universalistic texts; (3) "perishing" texts; (4) important qualifications in the interpretation of the terms "all" and "world"; and (5) the practical relationship between his atonement theology and evangelism. In doing so, I will demonstrate that the universalistic elements in Paul's atonement theology complement rather than compromise the possibility of interpreting Christ's death as a definite atonement.

I. Particularistic Texts: Christ Died for "Me," for the "Church," for "His People," for "Us"
ACTS 20:28; ROMANS 5:8; 8:32; GALATIANS 2:20;
EPHESIANS 5:25; TITUS 2:14

Throughout his epistles, Paul describes the atonement in particularistic terms: Christ died for his "church" (ἐκκλησία; Acts 20:28; Eph. 5:25), "for me" (ὑπὲρ ἐμοῦ; Gal. 2:20), for "a people" (λαόν; Titus 2:14), "for us" (ὑπὲρ ἡμῶν) (Rom. 5:8; 8:32; cf. 8:34; Gal. 3:13; Eph. 5:2; 1 Thess. 5:10; Titus 2:14). The particularistic texts in Paul require little discussion in many ways, since Semi-Pelagians and Arminians, Amyraldians and Hypothetical Universalists all acknowledge their existence. For these proponents, the reality of Christ's death for a group more particular than the world is generally resolved at the level of application: Christ died universally for everyone, but this is applied only to those who believe; or it is resolved at the level of twin intentions: Christ provided atonement for everyone contingent upon their faith, but he only secured actual atonement for his elect. In this respect, the particularistic texts can be affirmed by all sides.

The argument put to the proponents of definite atonement, however, is that the particularistic texts do not *in themselves* rule out Christ making atonement for the non-elect.[5] To infer such is to commit the negative inference fallacy. The fact that Paul can say "the Son of God who loved me and gave himself for me" (Gal. 2:20) does not militate against Paul also affirming Christ's death for the church (Acts 20:28; Eph. 5:25). In turn, Paul's affirmation of Christ's death for the church does not cancel out statements regarding Christ's death for "many," for "all," or for the "world" (e.g., Rom. 5:15; 1 Tim. 2:6; 2 Cor. 5:19, respectively). Scripture nowhere states that Christ died for the elect *alone* or for them *only*.[6] This kind of argumentation is, prima facie, entirely fair.[7]

Nevertheless, upon closer examination the argument is too simplistic to carry much weight for a few reasons. First, to deduce universal atonement from this argument is a non sequitur. Just because the word "only" or "alone" does not appear in texts referring to Christ's death for a particular people, that does not in itself mean that his death therefore also had reference to those outside the particular group that is mentioned. To illustrate: the word "alone" does not appear in the promises God gave to Abraham, but this does not mean that those promises are somehow also applicable to people outside the family of Abraham. Context makes it clear that only Abraham and his descendants were the recipients of such promises, even though the word "only" or "alone" is absent. The same holds true for the particularistic texts in Paul. As Francis Turretin commented, "All the [particularistic] passages adduced, if not explicitly yet implicitly include an exclusion in the description of those for whom Christ died (which cannot pertain to others)."[8] So, for example, in Ephesians 5:25, Paul's description of Christ as the Head and Husband of his body and bride, the church,

---

[5] For example, see Robert P. Lightner, *The Death Christ Died: A Biblical Case for Unlimited Atonement*, 2nd ed. (Grand Rapids, MI: Kregel, 1998), 62; D. Broughton Knox, "Some Aspects of the Atonement," in *The Doctrine of God*, vol. 1 of *D. Broughton Knox, Selected Works* (3 vols.), ed. Tony Payne (Kingsford, NSW: Matthias Media, 2000), 263; and Terry L. Miethe, "The Universal Power of the Atonement," in *The Grace of God and the Will of Man*, ed. Clark H. Pinnock (Minneapolis: Bethany, 1995), 73.

[6] So Knox, "Some Aspects of the Atonement," 263: "The Bible certainly affirms that Christ laid down his life for his sheep, and that he purchased his church with his own blood; but nowhere is the sentiment expressed negatively, i.e., that he died for his sheep only, or that redemption is to be spoken of the elect only . . ."

[7] The argument is based on Aristotelian logic: if all S is P, then it may be inferred that some S is P; conversely, it cannot be inferred from the fact that if some S is P, then the remainder of S is not P (this observation is pointed out by Robert L. Reymond, *A New Systematic Theology of the Christian Faith* [Nashville: Thomas Nelson, 1997], 674). Ironically, one of the accusations often leveled at the proponents of definite atonement is the unwarranted use of Aristotelian logic. I have no issue with it here.

[8] Francis Turretin, *Institutes of Elenctic Theology*, ed. James T. Dennison, Jr., trans. George Musgrave Giger, 3 vols. (Phillipsburg, NJ: P&R, 1993), 2:460.

assumes an organic union, such that when he dies, he dies united to his body and bride in a way that necessarily rules out other people or another organic entity—unless one wishes to entertain the thought of polygamy.[9] Moreover, the purpose of Christ's sacrificial self-giving is for the sanctification and final salvation of the church, something that does not belong to the non-elect. "And since he delivered himself up for none except this end, he can be said to have delivered himself up for no one who will not obtain that end."[10] As for Galatians 2:20, Paul is not speaking of "a privilege peculiar to himself, but as one common to himself and other elect or believing persons to whom he sets himself forth as an example that they might predicate the same thing concerning themselves in the same state."[11]

Secondly, if Paul wanted to be unambiguous regarding the universality of the atonement, he had the mechanism to do so through the use of absolute negatives, something he employs elsewhere in his writing. Paul emphasizes the universality of sin by the use of absolute negatives: "as it is written: 'None is righteous, no, not one [οὐδὲ εἷς]; . . . no one does good, not even one [(οὐκ ἔστιν) ἕως ἑνός]'" (Rom. 3:10–12). The language is indisputably unambiguous,[12] and could easily have been employed by Paul when he came to speak of Christ's atonement if he had wanted to stress that it was intended for every single person: "there was not one for whom Christ did not die."[13] Yet when it comes to Paul "universalizing" the target audience of Christ's atonement, he employs deliberately *ambiguous* language: "many," "all," and "world," may mean "all without exception," but the terms may equally mean "all without distinction." Context must determine the meaning in each particular case.[14]

Finally, while the Reformed do need to explain the universalistic texts, arguably the onus lies with proponents of a universal atonement to explain why Paul would employ limited or definite language, if there really was no limitation in the intended object of the atonement.[15] If God's love is displayed

---

[9] "An exclusion is intimated with sufficient plainness by the words themselves and the nature of the thing" (ibid., 462).
[10] Ibid.
[11] Ibid., 460.
[12] An OT example would be 2 Samuel 13:30: "Absalom has struck down all the king's sons, and not one of them is left (וְלֹא־נוֹתַר אֶחָד מֵהֶם)."
[13] I am indebted to Andrew D. Naselli, "John Owen's Argument for Definite Atonement in *The Death of Death in the Death of Christ:* A Brief Summary and Evaluation," *Southern Baptist Journal of Theology* 14.4 (2010): 75–76, for this point.
[14] Interestingly, references to "all" in relation to the cross are as frequent as similar statements of "all" in relation to application and ultimate destiny.
[15] William Cunningham, *Historical Theology: A Review of the Principal Doctrinal Discussions in the Christian Church since the Apostolic Age, Volume 2* (1862; repr., Edinburgh: Banner of Truth, 1960), 340.

at its best and most brilliant in a universal atonement in which Christ dies for all (which is argued in the Semi-Pelagian, Arminian, and Amyraldian Hypothetical Universalist schema), what advantage is achieved by speaking of his death in particularistic terms? To particularize the atonement makes God's love no more intense or precious.

In conclusion, as A. A. Hodge notes,

> Particular and definite expressions must limit the interpretation of the general ones, rather than the reverse. It is plainly far easier to assign plausible reasons why, if Christ died particularly for his elect, they being as yet scattered among all nations and generations, and undistinguishable by us from the mass of fallen humanity to whom the gospel is indiscriminately offered, he should be said in certain connections to have died for the world or for all, than it can be to assign any plausible reason why, if he died to make the salvation of all possible, he should nevertheless be said in any connection to have died for the purpose of certainly saving his elect.[16]

The particularistic texts that I have mentioned above support definite atonement, but there is one Pauline text that usually goes under the radar and which seems further to support a particularistic reference to Christ's death.

ROMANS 3:24–26

> ... and are justified by his grace as a gift, through the redemption that is in Christ Jesus, whom God put forward as a propitiation by his blood, to be received by faith. This was to show God's righteousness, because in his divine forbearance he had passed over former sins. It was to show his righteousness at the present time, so that he might be just and the justifier of the one who has faith in Jesus.

In this passage, Paul spotlights God's justice in presenting Christ as a propitiation (ἱλαστήριον). The propitiatory atonement of Christ vindicates God's justice, retrospectively and prospectively (vv. 25–26). With respect to the past, Paul states that God's punishment of sin at the cross justifies his passing over (πάρεσιν) sins previously committed (τῶν προγεγονότων ἁμαρτημάτων; v. 25). But whose sins? Frédéric Godet argues that it has a universal reference,[17] while for Douglas Moo the referent is to the "sins in

---

[16] A. A. Hodge, *The Atonement* (1867; repr., London: Evangelical Press, 1974), 425.
[17] Frédéric Godet, *Commentary on St. Paul's Epistle to the Romans*, Clark's Foreign Theological Library, 2 vols. (Edinburgh: T. & T. Clark, 1892), 2:263–64.

the Old Covenant."[18] The faith community of the old covenant is surely in view, since Paul goes on to speak of God's justice at the present time (ἐν τῷ νῦν καιρῷ; v. 26) in justifying those who have faith in Jesus—the faith community of the new covenant. Indeed, in Romans 4, to bolster his argument for justification by faith alone, Paul speaks of the forgiveness of Abraham and David on the basis of their faith, both of whose sins were *definitely* passed over until they were punished in Christ. If the "former sins" have a universal reference, then one has to ask what Christ's propitiatory death accomplished for the sins of Pharaoh and the Egyptians, for example. It makes more sense to understand the "former sins" to be those of the OT faith community, and thus, in this regard, the atonement that Christ offered already had a particular focus. It seems reasonable, then, that it would also have a definite reference in the "present time."

II. Universalistic Texts: Christ Died for "Many," for "All," for the "World"

A number of Pauline texts concerning God's saving work in Christ have a universal reference.

ROMANS 5:12–21

> Therefore, just as sin came into the world through one man, and death through sin, and so death spread to all men because all sinned—for sin indeed was in the world before the law was given, but sin is not counted where there is no law. Yet death reigned from Adam to Moses, even over those whose sinning was not like the transgression of Adam, who was a type of the one who was to come.
>
> But the free gift is not like the trespass. For if many died through one man's trespass, much more have the grace of God and the free gift by the grace of that one man Jesus Christ abounded for many. And the free gift is not like the result of that one man's sin. For the judgment following one trespass brought condemnation, but the free gift following many trespasses brought justification. For if, because of one man's trespass, death reigned through that one man, much more will those who receive the abundance of grace and the free gift of righteousness reign in life through the one man Jesus Christ.
>
> Therefore, as one trespass led to condemnation for all men, so one act of righteousness leads to justification and life for all men. For as by the one

---

[18] Douglas J. Moo, *The Epistle to the Romans*, NICNT (Grand Rapids, MI: Eerdmans, 1996), 240.

man's disobedience the many were made sinners, so by the one man's obedience the many will be made righteous. Now the law came in to increase
the trespass, but where sin increased, grace abounded all the more, so that,
as sin reigned in death, grace also might reign through righteousness leading to eternal life through Jesus Christ our Lord.

In this extended paragraph, Paul assumes a union between Adam and all his
descendants and a union between Christ and all his descendants: "there exists
a life-giving union between Christ and his own that is similar to, but more
powerful than, the death-producing union between Adam and his own."[19] The
union is seen by the connection of Adam and Christ to "the many" (οἱ πολλοί;
vv. 15b, c, 19a, b) and the "all" (πάντες; v. 18a, b) throughout this paragraph.
A careful handling of these terms is required to do them justice within their
context but also within the context of wider NT theology.

For a start, the word πολλοί ("many") does not always denote "everyone" or "all" in an inclusive sense.[20] In Paul, the majority of occurrences of
οἱ πολλοί are restrictive, designating "many" or "most" but not "all."[21] Here
in Romans 5 the word πολλοί carries both an inclusive sense and a restrictive
sense: that is, when it is used in relation to those whom Adam's work affects,
it refers inclusively to "all," as in "everyone" (v. 15; cf. v. 12); but when it is
used in relation to those whom Christ's work affects, it refers to those who
receive (λαμβάνοντες) the gift of righteousness (v. 17).

The same goes for Paul's use of πᾶς ("all"); it too needs to be interpreted
within its context.[22] In many Pauline passages it is necessarily limited by the
context (Rom. 8:32; 12:17, 18; 14:2; 16:19). In the particular case of Romans
5:18, where it occurs twice, debate exists as to the proper referent of πάντες,
first in relation to the work of Adam and then in relation to the work of Christ:

---

[19] Moo, *Romans*, 318.
[20] Contra J. Jeremias, "πολλοί," *TDNT* 6:536–41.
[21] For (οἱ) πολλοί, see Romans 16:2; 1 Corinthians 1:26 [2×]; 11:30; 16:9; 2 Corinthians 2:17; 6:10; 11:18; Galatians 3:16; Philippians 3:18; Titus 2:10. For πολύς, see 1 Corinthians 10:5; 15:6; Philippians 1:14 (articular);
2 Corinthians 2:6; 4:15; 6:10. For πάντες, see 1 Corinthians 9:19; 10:1–4 (passim); 15:6; Philippians 1:13. Although
a number of these could be inclusive, Moo, *Romans*, 336 n. 100, rightly counters Jeremias's claim that "οἱ πολλοί
is always used inclusively" in the NT except in Matthew 24:12 and 2 Corinthians 2:17 (*TDNT* 6:540). See Romans
12:5 and 1 Corinthians 10:17 for places where Paul uses οἱ πολλοί inclusively but where the context limits the
group intended.
[22] J. William Johnston, *The Use of Πᾶς in the New Testament*, Studies in Biblical Greek (New York: Peter Lang,
2004), 35, outlines four basic scopes of πᾶς in the NT: (1) "all without exception"; (2) "everything which has just
been the subject of discussion"; (3) "all kinds" or "all without distinction"; (4) "all in the highest or purest sense."
More broadly, Johnston argues that πᾶς suggests quantification either in a summative sense ("all without distinction" or "a set of items taken as a whole") or in a distributive sense ("all without exception" or "each and every
single one in a group").

Ἄρα οὖν ὡς δι᾿ ἑνὸς παραπτώματος εἰς **πάντας** ἀνθρώπους εἰς κατάκριμα,
οὕτως καὶ δι᾿ ἑνὸς δικαιώματος εἰς **πάντας** ἀνθρώπους εἰς δικαίωσιν
ζωῆς·
Therefore, as one trespass led to condemnation for **all** men, so one act of
righteousness leads to justification and life for **all** men.[23]

Based on alleged parallels to Romans 11:32 and 1 Corinthians 15:22, Ernst
Käsemann concludes that the πάντες in Romans 5:18b is of the same extent
as the πάντες in verse 18a: "all-powerful grace is unthinkable without eschatological universalism."[24] Bruce L. McCormack believes that the parallel
with 1 Corinthians 15:22 does not fit,[25] but he nevertheless, on other grounds,
argues similarly to Käsemann on Romans 5:18: Scripture does not confirm
eschatological universalism as a fact, but it does allow us to hope for it.[26]
Certainly Paul's δικαιο- language is always employed to confer a *status* on
the individual so that it is not merely objective provision that he has in mind,[27]
or "potential" redemption,[28] but actual, real salvation. Both Käsemann and
McCormack, however, miss the point of the text: Paul's interest is to demonstrate "not the numerical extent of those who are justified as identical with
the numerical extent of those condemned but the parallel that obtains between
the way of condemnation and the way of justification. It is the *modus oper-
andi* that is in view."[29] The scope of each πάντες is necessarily constrained
by the scope of each ἑνός and his work.[30] As Moo states, "Paul's point is not
so much that the groups affected by Christ and Adam, respectively, are coextensive, but that Christ affects those who are his just as certainly as Adam
does those who are his."[31] To argue for an exact denotation between the two

---

[23] Romans 5:18 provides the apodosis of the comparison started in 5:12: "Therefore, just as sin came into the world
through one man, and death through sin, and so death spread to all men because all sinned—. . . [Therefore, as one
trespass led to the condemnation for all men,] so one act of righteousness leads to justification and life for all men."
[24] Ernst Käsemann, *Commentary on Romans*, trans. Geoffrey W. Bromiley (Grand Rapids, MI: Eerdmans, 1980), 157.
[25] Bruce L. McCormack, "So That He Might Be Merciful to All: Karl Barth and the Problem of Universalism,"
in *Karl Barth and American Evangelicalism*, ed. Bruce L. McCormack and Clifford B. Anderson (Grand Rapids,
MI: Eerdmans, 2011), 231–32, argues that the wording of 1 Corinthians 15:22 shows that each "all" has a different
reference. The second "all" is restricted to "those who belong to Christ" (v. 23).
[26] Ibid., 238–39.
[27] Contra R. C. H. Lenski, *The Interpretation of St. Paul's Epistle to the Romans* (1936; repr., Minneapolis: Augsburg,
1961), 383: "What Christ obtained for all men, all men do not receive." Cf. also Lightner, *Death Christ Died*, 135–47.
[28] Udo Schnelle, *Apostle Paul: Life and Theology*, trans. M. Eugene Boring (Grand Rapids, MI: Baker Academic,
2005), 579, commenting on 1 Corinthians 15:23.
[29] John Murray, *The Epistle to the Romans*, 2 vols., NICNT (Grand Rapids, MI: Eerdmans, 1959), 1:203. McCormack, "So That He Might Be Merciful to All," 233, seems to concur at one point. Commenting on Romans 5:17
he says, "The contrast here is between the effect of the act of the first man and the effect of the act of the second."
But see below, where McCormack fumbles over the text as well.
[30] Compare also the relation of οἱ πολλοί to ἑνός in verses 15 and 19.
[31] Moo, *Romans*, 343. This is not to press for a *particularism of grace* by the terms "many" or "all"—such a move
would be unwarranted; but it is equally unwarranted to conclude that the terms denote an absolute universalism.

groups related to Adam and Christ is to opt for the position of universalism, which, in the light of other Pauline texts, seems untenable (e.g., Rom. 2:12; 2 Thess. 1:8–9). Indeed, contrary to McCormack's contention, even the immediate context restrains us from travelling down that path. Life does not reign in everyone by the mere fact of Christ's work; rather, life reigns in "those who receive" (οἱ . . . λαμβάνοντες) God's abundant provision of grace (Rom. 5:17).[32] McCormack (and Käsemann) have failed to see the apostle's *unbalanced* comparison in verse 17. As Calvin noted,

> The curse of Adam is overturned by the grace of Christ, and the life which Christ bestows swallows up the death which came from Adam. *The parts of this comparison, however, do not correspond.* Paul ought to have said that the blessing of life reigns and flourishes more and more through the abundance of grace, instead of which he says that *believers* "shall reign." The sense is the same, however, for the kingdom of believers is in life, and the kingdom of life is in believers.[33]

This helps to counter M. Eugene Boring's claim that in Romans 5:12–21 Paul demonstrates that "in Jesus Christ the kingly power of God is asserted, and the final picture is that of God-the-king who has *replaced* the reign of sin and death with the reign of righteousness and life, and has done so *for all human beings.*"[34] Boring fails to see the unbalanced comparison that Calvin does.

---

[32] Contra McCormack, "So That He Might Be Merciful to All," 233, who states that "the literary context [of Romans 5:18] requires that the second 'all' be as universal in its scope as is the first ['all']." But verse 17 demonstrates that the literary context does *not* require such a conclusion. What is puzzling is that McCormack goes on to quote verse 17. The point McCormack makes is incorrect because of the simple fact that the equal *extent* of Christ's work to Adam's work is *not* what makes his work "so much more" effective than Adam's; rather, it is the *effect* of Christ's work that makes it superior to Adam's: not only does Christ reverse Adam's work but he supersedes it by ensuring that there is an *abundance* of grace and that life *reigns* again. Even Ulrich Wilckens, *Römer*, Der Brief an die *Römer (Röm 6–11)*, 3 vols., Evangelisch-Katholischer Kommentar zum Neuen Testament VI/2 Studienausgabe (Neukirchen, Germany: Neukirchener Verlag, 1980), 1:325, admits that οἱ . . . λαμβάνοντες are Christians, though he then wiggles his way out of the specific referent of "all" by suggesting that they are merely representative of the totality of people who are freed by Christ from sin and death ("die Gesamtheit der durch Christus von Sünde und Tod befreiten Menschen"). The argument by M. Eugene Boring, "The Language of Universal Salvation in Paul," *JBL* 105.2 (1986): 287, that the vast majority of Paul's uses of λαμβάνοντες are passive, may help to temper Bultmann's enthusiasm for "the necessity to decide" being read into the text, but it does not militate against the fact that Christ's work reigns only in those who receive it.

[33] Calvin, *Romans and Thessalonians*, CNTC (Grand Rapids, MI: Eerdmans, 1960), 116 (emphasis added).

[34] Boring, "Universal Salvation in Paul," 283–84 (emphasis added on the last phrase). Boring's seminal article presents the view that Paul's "conflicting" soteriological language is due to encompassing images that possess their own inherent logic, but which are not necessarily reconcilable with each other. So, according to Boring, "Just as the encompassing image of God-as-judge has two-group thinking built into it, so one-group thinking is inherent in the image of God-as-king" (280). My contention here is not with Boring's point that Paul works with various images in his soteriology—granted Romans 5:12–21 conveys the kingly image with its use of the "reign" terminology—or that such images have their own "inherent logic"—that much is true—rather, my contention is that Boring has not properly deciphered the inherent logic of the kingly image in 5:12–21: Christ's overthrow of Adam's transgression is not said to be for "all human beings" but for all "those who receive" the abundance of grace (v. 17). While Boring acknowledges the phrase in verse 17, he fails to grasp the "soft implication" (to use his own words) of it: that there are therefore *two* groups and not one *within the kingly image*: those who receive God's free gift and those who do

Christ's work in Romans 5 is related to believers, to those who receive his grace (v. 17); Adam's work relates to all humankind without exception (v. 12). McCormack acknowledges the "receiving" aspect of verse 17 but then follows it up with a rejoinder: "But *how* it is received and *when* are questions left unresolved at this stage of Paul's argument in Romans."[35] This statement is puzzling in the light of the number of times that Paul speaks of the *how* and *when* of receiving God's grace up to this point in Romans. Faith, the mechanism by which people receive God's grace, is mentioned some thirty times up to Romans 5:12,[36] and in each case, either implicitly or explicitly, the faith occurs during the lifetime experience of the person concerned—hardly something "unresolved" at this stage of Paul's argument in Romans.

Of course, McCormack's argument is more nuanced: he simply wants to temper the conclusion that "'receiving' is an act which can only take place within the limits of history."[37] May faith not occur *after* the end of history and time? McCormack asks. For him, this is the "mystery" that Paul speaks about: not the setting aside of the condition of faith, but rather how that faith can be engendered once history has been consummated.[38] He bases such hope on statements that Paul makes in Romans 9–11, especially 11:25b: "a partial hardening has come upon Israel, until the fullness of the Gentiles has come in." For McCormack, "that surely refers to the end, the final act of history."[39] Paul's eschatology underwent a "conspicuous development," according to McCormack, such that God is willing and able to save ethnic, national Israel beyond the limits of history. This does not include just *some* of national Israel, but "all Israel" (11:26), which means "every Jewish individual, living or dead."[40] This explains why Paul opens the aperture even wider in 11:32: "For God has consigned all to disobedience, that he may have mercy on all."

---

not. Moreover, it seems that Paul would see different, encompassing soteriological images as *complementary* (and therefore surely also "reconcilable" and compatible), since the kingly image of 5:12–21 is employed in Paul's wider argument in order to prove his point in 5:1–11, that God is a *Judge* who will save believers on the day of his wrath, the "soft implication" being that there are those who will not be saved. In other words, the kingly image of 5:12–21 serves to support the juridical image of 5:1–11, suggesting a compatible relation between the two rather than an "irreconcilable" one. As Boring himself admits, even 5:12–21 contains juridical terminology (κρίμα, κατάκριμα, κλτ.); and, as Richard H. Bell, a universalist, points out, even in Romans 11 there is justification terminology, creating problems for Boring's kingly image in that chapter ("Rom 5:18–19 and Universal Salvation," *NTS* 48 [2002]: 432 n. 97). (Bell's paper does not progress the debate any further.)

[35] McCormack, "So That He Might Be Merciful to All," 233.
[36] Romans 1:5, 8, 12, 16, 17; 3:22, 25, 26, 27, 28, 30, 31; 4:3, 5, 9, 11 (2×), 12, 13, 14, 16 (2×), 17, 18, 19, 20, 22, 24; 5:1, 2. (Some read διὰ πίστεως Ἰησοῦ Χριστοῦ in 3:22 as a subjective genitive—"through the faithfulness of Jesus Christ"—but this hardly impacts on the statistics.)
[37] McCormack, "So That He Might Be Merciful to All," 233.
[38] Ibid., 236–37.
[39] Ibid., 236.
[40] Ibid., 238.

In short, McCormack's proposal for the hope of universal salvation is that if God will save every Jew beyond the limits of time and history, is it not reasonable to hold out hope that he may do so for everyone else?

CRITIQUE OF MCCORMACK

A number of points may be presented in response. (1) McCormack's proposal that "this mystery" [τὸ μυστήριον τοῦτο] refers to how faith can be engendered once history is consummated is novel among commentators (old and recent). This is not to deny the validity of the argument, but it does raise the question as to what in the context suggests that Paul has the creation of faith beyond the limits of time and history in his purview. The logic of the text points more in the direction that the "mystery" refers to the sequence by which Israel will be saved: "Israel is hardened *until* [ἄχρι] the Gentiles come in, and *in this way* [οὕτως] all Israel being saved."[41] (2) J. William Johnston, in his study of πᾶς in the NT, states that from the syntactical-semantic standpoint, anarthrous geographical (political or racial) nouns modified by πᾶς generally convey a summative sense.[42] "All Israel" (πᾶς Ἰσραήλ, כל־ישראל), was a well-known idiom in OT and Jewish sources,[43] having a corporate significance rather than an "each and every" sense here. Certainly, in context, the picture of the olive tree (11:16–24) is more collective in nature than individualistic. (3) In relation to the "all" of 11:32, McCormack has neglected the distinctive element in Paul's call to gospel ministry: "Apostle to the Gentiles" (see 11:13). Throughout Romans, Paul emphasizes that Jew *and Gentile* are included in God's salvation plan,[44] and that has been his theme here in the preceding verses: that after the fullness of the Gentiles has come in, all Israel as an organic entity (though not necessarily every Jew) will be saved. Attending to this aspect of Paul's theology and mission gives a more reasonable explanation for why he used all-inclusive language in 11:32.[45] (4) It follows

---

[41] Moo, *Romans*, 716. The other proposals for what the "mystery" is are: (1) the hardening that has come upon Israel; (2) the partial and temporary hardening of Israel; (3) all Israel will be saved.

[42] For example, Matthew 2:3; 3:5; Luke 6:17; Acts 1:8. And, even if some of these NT texts have a more geographical reference than populations, there are numerous examples from the LXX (Judg. 3:3; 1 Sam. 18:16; 2 Kings 22:13; 2 Chron. 23:8; Neh. 13:12).

[43] For Jewish sources, see *Jub.* 50:9; *T. Levi* 17:5; *T. Jos.* 20:5; *T. Ben.* 10:11; *Ps. Philo* 22:1; 23:1.

[44] See also Romans 1:5, 7, 13–14, 16; 2:11, 26–29; 3:23, 29–30; 4:9–12, 16–17; 9:24–26, 30; 10:11–13, 20; 11:12, 15, 17, 19–20; 15:9–12; 16:26.

[45] See Thomas R. Schreiner, *Paul: Apostle of God's Glory in Christ* (Downers Grove, IL: Apollos, 2001), 184. See also Johnston, *Use of* Πᾶς *in the New Testament*, 143–48, on the "all" of Romans 11:26 and how it need not be taken in the fully implicative sense of "every individual within national Israel." Johnston rightly states, "All Israel can be saved as a group even if a few individual ethnic Israelites do not share that destiny" (148).

from these three points that the conclusions which McCormack makes from various aspects of Paul's salvation-historical scheme in Romans are absent in Paul's own thinking. Nowhere does Paul draw such conclusions, which even McCormack admits; and had he wanted us to live with such hope, then why not at this crucial point in the epistle, or elsewhere, make such an obvious point? (5) Even if one allows, under the inspiration of the Holy Spirit, for some "development" in Paul's soteriology, what cannot be allowed is the clear incompatibilism that universal salvation presents with the other texts in which Paul speaks of the damnation of the lost, not least even here in Romans 9–11.[46]

In sum, unless one opts for absolute universalism, the use of οἱ πολλοί and πάντες in Romans 5:12–21 must be interpreted in the light of the ἑνός to whom they are connected.

2 CORINTHIANS 5:14–15

> For the love of Christ controls us, because we have concluded this: that one has died for all, therefore all have died; and he died for all, that those who live might no longer live for themselves but for him who for their sake died and was raised.

The controversial issue in this text is the word "all." T. F. Torrance, commenting on the universality of this passage, remarked that it must "be taken with full seriousness and not whittled down."[47] I agree. The main *crux* for interpreters is the referent of each instance of πάντες in verses 14 and 15, and the referent of οἱ ζῶντες in verse 15. Commentators have presented four main interpretations:[48]

(1) "Universalist" reading: the threefold use of πάντες and οἱ ζῶντες refers to all people without exception—the whole of humankind.[49]

(2) "Universal-particular" reading: the three uses of πάντες denote all people without exception, while οἱ ζῶντες describes those "in Christ." On this reading, the death (ἀπέθανον) of all is actual: "When Christ died, all died; what is more, his death involved their death."[50] The

---

[46] For example, Romans 9:3, 6–7, 13, 18, 21–22, 31–33; 10:2–4; 11:7–10, 20–23, 28. Even Boring, "Universal Salvation in Paul," 288, counters McCormack's point: particularism occurs in both early and late Pauline texts.

[47] T. F. Torrance, *The Atonement: The Person and Work of Christ* (Downers Grove, IL: IVP Academic, 2009), 183.

[48] The labels for each interpretation are my own description of the positions.

[49] J. Lambrecht, "'Reconcile yourselves . . .': A Reading of 2 Cor 5,11–21," *Benedictina* 10 (1989): 161–209.

[50] Murray J. Harris, *The Second Epistle to the Corinthians*, NIGTC (Grand Rapids, MI: Eerdmans, 2005), 421–22.

death occurs at the same time as Christ's death (ἀπέθανεν)[51] and "may be the death deservedly theirs because of sin, or an objective 'ethical' death that must be appropriated subjectively by individual faith, or a collective participation in the event of Christ's death by which sin's power was destroyed."[52] But, "while all persons 'died' when Christ died, not all rose to new life when he rose from the dead."[53] Although Murray J. Harris discourages talk of "potential" death for all, as in option (3) below, he nevertheless seems to end up in a similar position when he writes, "There is a universalism in the scope of redemption, since no person is excluded from God's offer of salvation; but there is a particularity in the application of redemption, since not everyone appropriates the benefits afforded by this universally offered salvation."[54]

(3) "Potential-actual" reading: viewing the εἰς-πάντες motif as reminiscent of Romans 5:12 and 5:18, the death of Christ remains potentially inclusive for "all" who are "in Adam," but is actual for those "in Christ" who have appropriated it through faith.[55] Thus the potential-actual distinction is applied to the word πάντες in 2 Corinthians 5:14: Christ potentially died for all (in Adam), but only all (in Christ) actually died: "The 'all' who have died 'in Christ' are not coextensive with the 'all' who sin and die 'in Adam.'"[56]

(4) "All-actual" reading: the threefold referent of πάντες is coextensive with οἱ ζῶντες; and the death of Christ for all and the death of all is viewed as actual.[57] The difference between this interpretation and the "Universalist" reading is that here "all" refers to an undefined group of people, but one which does not equate to all people without exception; in other words, "all" in this context means all people without distinction—not the whole of humankind.

In coming to a decision over the referent of πάντες, a number of points should be kept in mind. First, the allusion back to Romans 5:12, 15–19 through the εἰς-πάντες motif does not necessitate interpreting πάντες as referring to everyone, since in the Romans passage πάντες is circumscribed by

---

[51] Since both verbs appear in the aorist, there is no reason to distinguish the timing of these deaths (ibid., 421).

[52] Ibid., 422.

[53] Ibid., 421.

[54] Ibid., 423.

[55] Paul Barnett, *The Second Epistle to the Corinthians*, NICNT (Grand Rapids, MI: Eerdmans, 1997), 290 n. 10: "Christ's death and resurrection is for all, canceling the effects of sin and death and thus providing the potentiality, objectively and subjectively, of the end of death and the beginning of life for all."

[56] Ibid., 290.

[57] Charles Hodge, *Commentary on the Second Epistle to the Corinthians* (Grand Rapids, MI: Eerdmans, 1953), 135–37: "Christ died for the all who died when he died" (136). Cf. also John Murray, *Redemption Accomplished and Applied* (Edinburgh: Banner of Truth, 1955), 81.

either Adam or Christ: in relation to the former, the whole of mankind is certainly included—all sinned and died because of their union with Adam—but not so in relation to the latter, unless one opts for universalism. This rules out option (1). Indeed, the words Χριστὸς ὑπὲρ ἡμῶν ἀπέθανεν in Romans 5:8 are just as close to 2 Corinthians 5:14 and have believers in mind. Second, most commentators admit that the most sensible reading is to take πάντες in all three occurrences as being coextensive (apart from the potential-actual reading). The definite article (οἱ) before πάντες in verse 14b is anaphoric, pointing back to the πάντες of verse 14a; and, whether one takes καί as epexegetic or conjunctive in verse 15a, the following phrase ὑπὲρ πάντων ἀπέθανεν is identical in sense to verse 14a. Thus it makes sense to take each πάντες to have equal reference. Certainly the context provides no indicators for different scopes.[58] This would suggest option (3) is not worthy of support. Third, an undue focus on the word πάντες can neglect the important conjunctive ἄρα. In many ways the meaning of the verse turns on this one word: Christ died for all, *therefore* all died. The point that Paul wishes to make, inter alia, is that Christ's death *effects* the spiritual death of others, such that (καί) he died for all so that (ἵνα) those who live (having died in Christ) should no longer live for themselves but for him who died for them and rose again (v. 15).[59] In other words, Christ's death is both effective and purposive and reveals there is an implicit union between Christ and those for whom he died, something that Paul makes more explicit in Romans 6:1–11.

While Harris affirms the efficacy of Christ's death in 2 Corinthians 5:14, his explanation of what exactly this death entails is less specific.[60] He

---

[58] Harris, *Second Corinthians*, 421, agrees with this point but takes the referent of "all" to be everyone, before going on to argue that οἱ ζῶντες "suggests that a new, distinct category is being introduced," that is, believers. He suggests that had Paul meant οἱ ζῶντες to be coextensive with πάντες, we would have expected Paul simply to write καὶ ὑπὲρ πάντων ἀπέθανεν ἵνα μηκέτι ἑαυτοῖς ζῶσιν κτλ, or . . . ἵνα ζῶντες μηκέτι κτλ. But this is to put words into Paul's mouth/pen. The introduction of οἱ ζῶντες does not by necessity require the introduction of a new category of people, if we observe that Paul is now speaking of the same group but in a new way: πάντες refers to those who died as a result of Christ's death; οἱ ζῶντες, to all those living (ζῶσιν) for Christ. Thus, the introduction of a new phrase for the same group is entirely appropriate given what Paul goes on to say about them.

[59] Contra people on opposite sides of the atonement debate who suggest that the death of "all" refers to the *state* of people for whom Christ died. See, for example, John Owen, *Salus Electorum, Sanguis Jesu: Or The Death of Death in the Death of Christ*, in *The Works of John Owen*, ed. W. H. Goold, 24 vols. (Edinburgh: Johnstone & Hunter, 1850–1855; repr. Edinburgh: Banner of Truth, 1967), 10:350–51, on the one side; and John F. Walvoord, "Reconciliation," *BSac* 120 (January–March 1963): 10, on the other. But the verb is active, not passive: "all died," not "all were dead (for whom Christ died)." Contra also Norman F. Douty, *The Death of Christ: A Treatise Which Answers the Question: "Did Christ Die Only for the Elect?"* (Swengel, PA: Reiner, 1972), 70: "all for whom He died that Friday afternoon, died *in law* when He expired—not that they ceased to sin. In other words, their death was *legal* in character, not spiritual; it was *objective*, not subjective; it was *judicial*, not moral (or ethical)."

[60] Harris, *Second Corinthians*, 420–21. Barnett, *Second Corinthians*, 290–91, speaks only of what Christ's death was "intended" to procure, and misses this main point on actual efficacy. He affirms the actuality of Christ's death for all, but only once there is a faith-commitment in Christ (290). This implies that the actuality of the atonement is thus contingent on human faith.

proposes a few explanations, but each is unconvincing. The "death deservedly theirs because of sin" makes little sense because Christ dies the death "deservedly theirs" *for* them; the death of "all" is a death that they die to themselves. Harris's second and third options move in the right direction— "an objective 'ethical' death that must be appropriated subjectively by individual faith" or "a collective participation in the event of Christ's death by which sin's power was destroyed"—but in each case he fails to capture some of the consequences of his own interpretation of the verse. If the "objective 'ethical' death" must be appropriated subjectively by faith, he has immediately narrowed the referent of πάντες to *all those who believe*, which is inconsistent with his view that πάντες refers to everyone, and that only in verse 15 is there a narrowing with the introduction of the new category οἱ ζῶντες.

As for his third option, Harris is inconsistent in playing out the implications of "a collective participation in the event of Christ's death by which sin's power was destroyed." If this is true, and sin's power is destroyed—and I think it is: Christ's death for all *effects* the death of all—then all (everyone) would surely die to themselves, thus either making universalism true, if πάντες means everyone, or restricting the scope of πάντες to the same as οἱ ζῶντες. Moreover, as verse 15 goes on to explain, Christ died *and was raised* for believers (τῷ ὑπὲρ αὐτῶν ἀποθανόντι καὶ ἐγερθέντι).[61] If his death for all resulted in the spiritual death of all, then surely by implication his being raised would result in the spiritual resurrection of all, something Paul makes explicit elsewhere (Rom. 6:1–11). In order for Harris to maintain his position, he has to argue that "While all persons died, in one sense [one of the three senses above, presumably], when the Man who represented them died, not all were raised to new life when he rose."[62] But this begs the question why not, since Harris earlier argues that ὑπὲρ αὐτῶν means that Christ represented them,[63] and thus his representation must surely function in *both* his death and his resurrection. There seems to be an inconsistency here on Harris's part. At times he seems to suggest an implicit union with Christ in both phases of Christ's death and resurrection, and at other times he wishes to allow for a disjunction between them: union with Christ in his death but not in his resurrection. But, as Paul says in Romans, "For if we have been united with him in a death like his, we shall certainly be united with

---

[61] Since the single article τῷ modifies both ἀποθανόντι and ἐγερθέντι, it seems that ὑπὲρ αὐτῶν may be construed with both participles.
[62] Harris, *Second Corinthians*, 423.
[63] Ibid., 422.

him in a resurrection like his" (6:5). Note what the apostle argues here: if union with Christ occurred in his death, then union with Christ in his resurrection necessarily follows. There can be no disjunction.

For Paul, redemption accomplished (Christ's death *and* resurrection) *conditions* redemption applied.[64] The redemptive-historical perspective does not merely provide the basis for an analogy to explain what goes on in the believer's existential experience; it is "both dominant and determinative,"[65] such that all those for whom Christ died also died in Christ, and all who died in Christ will also certainly rise again with him, so "that those who live might no longer live for themselves but for him who for their sake died and was raised." All this is so because of the unbreakable bond between Christ and those for whom he died and rose again.

In sum: it seems that the only consistent position to take exegetically and theologically is option (4). Those who wish to argue for "all" being everyone, with verse 15 then introducing a more narrow group (Harris), or with verse 14 denoting potentiality and verse 15 actuality (Barnett), must deal with the consequence of saying that Christ's death effected the "death" of everyone but then failed to bring about their new life (Harris), or that his death did not actually effect the death of everyone in the first place (Barnett).

2 CORINTHIANS 5:19

> . . . that is, in Christ God was reconciling the world to himself, not counting their trespasses against them, and entrusting to us the message of reconciliation.

Understanding the basic theological point in 2 Corinthians 5:14–15 helps when interpreting the referent of "world" (κόσμος) in verse 19. Taking the combination of ὡς ὅτι as epexegetical ("that is"[66]), verse 19 explains and expands the thought of verse 18: "All this is from God, who through Christ reconciled us to himself and gave us the ministry of reconciliation." Debate exists as to the best translation for verse 19, but a number of considerations weight the scales in favor of "God was in Christ, reconciling the world to

---

[64] John Murray, "Definitive Sanctification," *CTJ* 2 (1967): 5–21 (19): "Something occurred in the past historical which makes necessary what is realized and exemplified in the actual life history."

[65] Richard B. Gaffin, *Resurrection and Redemption: A Study in Paul's Soteriology*, 2nd ed. (Phillipsburg, NJ: P&R, 1987), 59.

[66] The other viable but less convincing options are to take the phrase as comparative or causal. See Harris, *Second Corinthians*, 438–40, for assessment of each option.

himself."[67] On this translation, θεὸς ἦν ἐν Χριστῷ does not refer to the incarnation, though it certainly includes it, but rather to the whole of Christ's life, and in particular, given the context (vv. 14–15), to the death of Christ by which God reconciled the world to himself. Thus we have a profound statement of christology in this brief expression: ontologically, God was in Christ and acted through Christ to secure the divine redemption of the world.

This "God in Christ" act of reconciliation has as its focus the κόσμος, a term which may refer to the totality of creation (cf. Rom. 1:20; 1 Cor. 3:22), but more likely, in context, the world of human beings (cf. Rom. 3:6; 5:12–13; 2 Cor. 1:12), as demanded by the pronouns αὐτοῖς and αὐτῶν, and as indicated by παραπτώματα. But who exactly is included in the word κόσμος? Certainly no exegete should doubt the all-encompassing, all-inclusive connotation that κόσμος carries. Its full weight and corporate nature must not be diminished in any way (see below). Nevertheless, as with other uses of the term in Paul (cf. Rom. 11:12, 15), the word does not by default mean "all without exception," or "every single person." Reflection on the immediate context and careful attention to what exactly 2 Corinthians 5:19 states makes one hesitant to draw such a conclusion. For a start, if ὡς ὅτι is rightly taken as epexegetical, then κόσμος explains and expands on the ἡμᾶς of verse 18, who are clearly believers. Moreover, the first of the two succeeding participial clauses (μὴ λογιζόμενος αὐτοῖς τὰ παραπτώματα αὐτῶν) provides constraints on equating the "world" with "everyone."[68] "The world" are those against whom (αὐτοῖς[69]) God does not reckon their sins (τὰ παραπτώματα αὐτῶν).[70] Unless one is willing to adopt universalism, the "world" in verse 19 then simply cannot mean "everyone."[71] The world is forgiven by God, which means it must be a *believing* world that Paul has in mind.[72]

---

[67] See ibid., 440–42, for these. The ESV translation is acceptable too.

[68] Both participial clauses state two implications or consequences of God's act of reconciliation through Christ.

[69] A dative of disadvantage.

[70] The mere use of the present tense participle καταλλάσσων does not mean that this act of reconciliation was ongoing or incomplete. Context ought to determine the meaning here. If, as argued, verse 19 expands on verse 18, then Christ's completed act of reconciliation is in Paul's purview. S. E. Porter, Καταλλάσσω *in Ancient Greek Literature, with Reference to Pauline Writings* (Cordoba: El Amendro, 1994), 138–39, argues on aspectual grounds that verse 19 should be rendered, "God's *act* of reconciliation," with the periphrastic construction used for emphasis.

[71] Commenting on this verse, David L. Allen, "The Atonement: Limited or Universal?," in *Whosoever Will: A Biblical-Theological Critique of Five-Point Calvinism*, ed. David L. Allen and Steve W. Lemke (Nashville: B&H Academic, 2010), 64, writes: "God's plan in the atonement was to provide a punishment and a satisfaction for sin as a basis for salvation for all humanity and to secure the salvation of all who believe in Christ." But nowhere in the text does Paul affirm a split-level intention in the atonement. Allen has to read it into this particular text.

[72] A possible allusion here to Psalm 32:2 supports this view, that those who make up the "world" are believers. The phrase μὴ λογιζόμενος most likely recalls David's words in LXX Psalm 32:2: "μακάριος ἀνήρ, οὗ οὐ μὴ λογίσηται κύριος ἁμαρτίαν" (cf. Jer. 31:34).

It seems best, then, to view "world" in 2 Corinthians 5:19 as a reference to people in a general sense ("all without distinction"), as opposed to a distributive and inclusive sense ("all without exception"). When Paul uses the term, he has in mind Jews and Gentiles.[73] "God's grace embraces a whole cosmos in its organic capacity, including the Gentiles; not one branch, but the whole tree of the human race is the object of His reconciling act."[74]

Colossians 1:20

> ... and through him to reconcile to himself all things, whether on earth or in heaven, making peace by the blood of his cross.

In 2 Corinthians 5:19 the word "world" denotes humanity. Christ will save the world in the sense that he will save a new humanity: Jew and Gentile united as one man (Eph. 2:15). There are, however, other Pauline texts, such as Colossians 1:20, that demonstrate that Christ's death will impact "the universe," the whole created order. Paul states clearly that through Christ (δι' αὐτοῦ) God will reconcile (ἀποκαταλλάξαι) to himself all things (τὰ πάντα), by making peace (εἰρηνοποιήσας[75]) through the blood of his cross (διὰ τοῦ αἵματος τοῦ σταυροῦ αὐτοῦ). On the basis of the universal impact of Christ's death, some have argued retrospectively for a universal atonement: Surely if Christ's death leads to the reconciliation of all things on earth and in heaven, he must have died for everyone? So Shultz argues: "In order for Christ to reconcile all things to the Father, He had to pay for all sin, including the sins of the nonelect. Otherwise some sin would be outside His atoning work and thus outside His cosmic triumph."[76] In the discussion below, this will be shown to be a wrong deduction. The universal repercussions for the created order are premised, in fact, on a definite atonement, not a universal one.

Since the time of Origen, some interpreters have employed Colossians 1:20 as an argument for universal salvation. The rare verb ἀποκαταλλάξαι occurs only twice in the NT (here and Eph. 2:16), but its base form καταλλάσω is found more frequently in Paul (Rom. 5:10 [2×]; 1 Cor. 7:11; 2 Cor. 5:18, 19, 20), as is its cognate noun (Rom. 5:11; 11:15; 2 Cor. 5:18, 19). In each

---

[73] Stanley E. Porter, "Reconciliation as the Heart of Paul's Missionary Theology," in *Paul as Missionary: Identity, Activity, Theology, and Practice*, ed. Trevor J. Burke and Brian S. Rosner, Library of New Testament Studies 420 (London: T. & T. Clark, 2011), 175.

[74] Geerhardus Vos, "The Biblical Doctrine of the Love of God," in *Redemptive History and Biblical Interpretation: The Shorter Writings of Geerhardus Vos*, ed. Richard B. Gaffin (Phillipsburg, NJ: P&R, 1980), 450.

[75] A participle of means.

[76] Gary L. Shultz, Jr., "God's Purposes in the Atonement for the Nonelect," *BSac* 165 (April–June, 2008): 157.

of these cases (with 1 Cor. 7:11 as an exception), "reconcile/reconciliation" refers to "the restoration of fellowship between God and sinners."[77] But the object of ἀποκαταλλάξαι, here τὰ πάντα, suggests that the scope of this "reconciliation" is wider than humanity. The phrase τὰ πάντα occurs five times in the context (cf. esp. Col. 1:16), and each time it refers to the created universe. Paul even specifies τὰ πάντα as things on earth (τὰ ἐπὶ τῆς γῆς) and things in heaven (τὰ ἐν τοῖς οὐρανοῖς; v. 20). In 2:15, he speaks of "rulers and authorities" (τὰς ἀρχὰς καὶ τὰς ἐξουσίας) being disarmed through the cross. Thus, what is "reconciled" to God is not just humanity but the whole created cosmos. And this should not surprise us, since from a biblical-theological point of view, the plot line of the Bible reveals an integral relationship between redemption and creation: "God does not create the world of redemption without regard to the antecedent world of nature";[78] and since the creation encompasses everything—"the heavens and the earth"—it is understandable that Christ's redemptive work will have a *universal* restorative impact. Christ's blood will penetrate every nook and cranny of this whole created universe.

The issue, however, becomes what exactly is meant by the term "reconcile" (ἀποκαταλλάξαι). Of the various possibilities,[79] evangelicals have presented two main proposals.

1. "Reconcile" Means "Pacify"

F. F. Bruce and Peter T. O'Brien propose that, in context, ἀποκαταλλάξαι means "pacification."[80] That is, earth and heaven have been restored to their divinely created and determined order, the universe is again under its rightful Head, and cosmic peace reigns.[81] Through his death on the cross (διὰ τοῦ αἵματος τοῦ σταυροῦ αὐτοῦ), Christ has wrought this peace (εἰρηνοποιήσας) for the universe, a peace that was the eschatological hope of the OT prophets (Isa. 52:6–10; Jer. 29:11; Ezek. 34:25; Mic. 5:5; Hag. 2:9; Zech. 9:10). It is not that all human beings are hereby brought into a *loving* relationship with God in which they submit willingly to his rule over their lives; rather,

---

[77] Douglas J. Moo, *The Letters to the Colossians and to Philemon*, PNTC (Nottingham, UK: Apollos, 2008), 134.

[78] Geerhardus Vos, *Biblical Theology: Old and New Testaments* (Edinburgh: Banner of Truth, 1948), 21.

[79] For which, see Peter T. O'Brien's helpful overview (*Colossians, Philemon*, WBC 44 [Waco, TX: Word, 1982], 54–55); and Robert A. Peterson, "To Reconcile to Himself All Things: Colossians 1:20," *Presbyterion* 36.1 (Spring 2010): 37–46.

[80] F. F. Bruce, *Commentary on the Epistles to the Ephesians and Colossians*, NICNT (Grand Rapids, MI: Eerdmans, 1957), 210; O'Brien, *Colossians, Philemon*, 55–56.

[81] To paraphrase Eduard Lohse, *Colossians and Philemon*, trans. W. R. Poehlmann and R. J. Karris from the 14th German ed. (Philadelphia: Fortress, 1971), 59.

the peace wrought by Christ may be "freely accepted, or . . . compulsorily imposed" (Phil. 2:10–11).[82] But there is nevertheless a reordering, a restoration and renewal of the previously fractured universe.[83] Moo concurs: what is in Paul's purview here is not cosmic salvation or redemption, but rather cosmic restoration.[84]

2. "Reconcile" Means "Peace with God"

I. Howard Marshall proposes that ἀποκαταλλάξαι "has the sense of the actual restoration of good relations," but that the thought in Colossians 1:20 is simply of God's "provision of reconciliation for the world."[85] The realization of this reconciliation is dependent on acceptance of the gospel and faith, and "therefore," for Marshall, "it is most improbable that any kind of universal salvation of all creation is taught here."[86] Paul's stress is not so much on the *fact* of the reconciliation of "all things," which Marshall takes to be the rulers and authorities in verse 16, as on their own *need* for reconciliation. This interpretation avoids "desperate attempts to give 'reconcile' a sense other than it usually bears."[87]

John Piper argues similarly. Taking his cue from the language of "peace" in Ephesians 2:14–15, he argues that ἀποκαταλλάξαι cannot carry the meaning of pacification.[88] Piper's interlocutors are Bruce Ware and Mark Driscoll, who argue that people in hell are "reconciled" to God; they too comprise τὰ πάντα. In order to refrain from what he believes is an unbiblical position, Piper necessarily restricts the meaning of τὰ πάντα to "all things in the new heaven and the new earth."[89] He thinks that such a perspective explains why Paul perhaps omits the term καταχθονίων ("under the earth"; cf. Phil. 2:10) when he says that Christ will "reconcile to himself all things, whether on earth or in heaven" (Col. 1:20). For Piper, there will be an "outside darkness,"

---

[82] Bruce, *Ephesians and Colossians*, 210. See also Henri A. G. Blocher, "Everlasting Punishment and the Problem of Evil," in *Universalism and the Doctrine of Hell*, ed. Nigel M. de S. Cameron (Grand Rapids, MI: Baker, 1992), 282–312, who argues for the cessation of sin but an eternal remorse for that sin.

[83] Herman Bavinck, *Sin and Salvation in Christ*, vol. 3 of *Reformed Dogmatics*, ed. John Bolt, trans. John Vriend, 4 vols. (Grand Rapids, MI: Baker Academic, 2006), 472, understands this to mean that the demons and the wicked will be sent to hell but the whole creation with its inhabitants will be restored in the new heaven and the new earth.

[84] Moo, *Colossians and Philemon*, 136.

[85] I. Howard Marshall, "The Meaning of 'Reconciliation,'" in *Unity and Diversity in New Testament Theology: Essays in Honor of George E. Ladd*, ed. Robert A. Guelich (Grand Rapids, MI: Eerdmans, 1978), 126.

[86] Ibid.

[87] Ibid.

[88] John Piper, "'My Glory I Will Not Give to Another': Preaching the Fullness of Definite Atonement to the Glory of God," chapter 23 in this volume.

[89] He is influenced on this point by H. A. W. Meyer, *Critical and Exegetical Hand-Book to the Epistles to the Philippians and Colossians, and to Philemon* (1883; repr., Winona Lake, IN: Alpha, 1980), 241–42.

an "under the earth" that is unreconciled to God. "In the new reality all things are reconciled to Christ by his blood."[90]

Colossians 1:20 and Definite Atonement

Marshall and Piper's position carries some weight, though one wonders if they are guilty of an unwarranted restriction of the semantic field of ἀποκαταλλάξαι. However, whatever interpretation one adopts of this verse, the text is of no consequence to the doctrine of definite atonement. The universal impact of the death of Christ is not synonymous with a universal atonement. The distinction is an important one. In this text, Paul is no more arguing that Christ propitiated God's wrath for every human being than he is arguing that Christ propitiated God's wrath for rocks and birds and stars, or even fallen angels. Rather, Paul is simply stating that one of the eschatological consequences of Christ's death is a universal peace among all things on earth and in heaven. Through his death, Jesus is the *Christus Victor* who brings everything in the universe back into its rightful place and order. The scope of redemption accomplished is not in Paul's peripheral vision here; his focus is the eschatological impact of Christ's cross, not the substitutionary extent of it. To argue retrospectively from the eschatological effects of Christ's death back to a universal atonement is a false deduction. Indeed, the parallel passage, Romans 8:19–23, shows that what lies behind the *cosmic* renewal is not a universal provision made by Christ's atonement but a consummated redemption of a *particular* group of people—"the sons of God."

Definite Atonement and Creation's Restoration (Romans 8:19–23)

Careful analysis of Romans 8:19–23 reveals that in Paul's soteriology there is an integral connection between physical human believers, "the sons of God," and the physical created universe. The creation (ἡ κτίσις) waits (ἀπεκδέχεται) with eager longing (ἀποκαραδοκία) for the revealing (τὴν ἀποκάλυψιν) of the sons of God (τῶν υἱῶν τοῦ θεοῦ; v. 19); the creation itself will be set free (ἐλευθερωθήσεται) from its bondage to corruption (ἀπὸ τῆς δουλείας τῆς φθορᾶς) to obtain the freedom of the glory of the children of God (τὴν ἐλευθερίαν τῆς δόξης τῶν τέκνων τοῦ θεοῦ; v. 21); the whole creation (πᾶσα ἡ κτίσις) groans together (συστενάζει), as we do, waiting for the adoption

---

[90] Piper, "'My Glory I Will Not Give to Another,'" chapter 23 in this volume.

as sons (υἱοθεσίαν), the redemption (τὴν ἀπολύτρωσιν) of our bodies (τοῦ σώματος ἡμῶν; vv. 22–23).

God has subjected (ὑπετάγη) the creation to futility (τῇ ματαιότητι; v. 20) because of human sin (cf. Gen. 3:17–19), but it was subjected "in hope" (ἐφ᾽ ἐλπίδι; Rom. 8:20), the hope that it would one day be renewed. What anticipates and inaugurates the renewal of this created world is the consummated redemption of a particular group of people, "the sons of God." There is an integral relationship between the two: the former is dependent on the latter: that is, "it is only with and because of the glory of God's children that creation experiences its own full and final deliverance."[91] Thus, contrary to some arguments, it is not a *universal, potential* atonement that brings about a universal re-creation, but rather a *particular, realized* redemption of God's children—definite atonement. Thus, when the principle of *analogia fidei* is applied, and Colossians 1:20 and Romans 8:19–23 are read together, definite atonement and not universal atonement emerges as the best explanation for the cause of cosmic renewal.

1 TIMOTHY 2:4–6

... who desires all people to be saved and to come to the knowledge of the truth. For there is one God, and there is one mediator between God and men, the man Christ Jesus, who gave himself as a ransom for all, which is the testimony given at the proper time.

This passage is commonly employed in the arsenal of opponents of definite atonement.[92] Nevertheless, I wish to show that a close reading of 1 Timothy 2:4–6 is compatible with the doctrine of definite atonement. A number of points will help to elucidate the text.

First, from a mirror reading of 1 Timothy, most commentators acknowledge that Paul wrote to Timothy in an ecclesiological context of false teaching, aspects of which included an exclusivism/elitism influenced by esotericism (myths, genealogies; 1:4–6), Jewish law (1:7), and asceticism (abstention from marriage and certain foods, etc.; 4:3). In this regard, one of Paul's major concerns in the epistle is a refocusing of the universal scope of

---

[91] Moo, *Romans*, 517.
[92] So, for example, I. Howard Marshall, "Universal Grace and Atonement in the Pastoral Epistles," in *Grace of God and the Will of Man*, 61–63. Bruce Demarest, *The Cross and Salvation: The Doctrine of Salvation*, Foundations of Evangelical Theology (Wheaton, IL: Crossway, 1997), 191, argues that "Paul's citation in v. 4 that God 'wants all men to be saved' indicates that every last person is in view" in verse 6: "and gave himself a ransom for all men."

312 DEFINITE ATONEMENT IN THE BIBLE

the gospel over against this heretical exclusivism and narrowness. The "all" (2:2, 4, 6; 4:10) and "world" (3:16) statements thus make good sense when read against this background. Interestingly, the "all" statements of chapter 2 come after references to the heretical elitism (1:4–7), and likewise, the "all" of 4:10 comes after the references to the abstention teaching (4:1–8). As Philip Towner concludes,

> the reason behind Paul's justification of this universal mission is almost certainly the false teaching, with its Torah-centered approach to life that included either an exclusivist bent or a downplaying of the Gentile mission. . . . Paul's focus is on building a people of God who incorporate all people regardless of ethnic, social, or economic backgrounds . . .[93]

Secondly, the literary context demonstrates that Paul's references to "all" should be understood in terms of categories or subgroups of people. So, in 2:1, Paul requests prayers "for all people" (ὑπὲρ πάντων ἀνθρώπων)—hardly an achievable task if he means "every single person on earth." In verse 2, the repetition of ὑπέρ, alongside further specification of the subgroup of kings and civil rulers (βασιλέων καὶ πάντων τῶν ἐν ὑπεροχῇ ὄντων), adds support to the view that "all people" means "all kinds of people"; that is, "individuals from all kinds of diverse groups." In verse 4, God's desire for "all people" (πάντας ἀνθρώπους) to be saved is grounded in the truth of monotheism ("For there is one God"; Εἷς γὰρ θεός), and in the exclusive mediatorial work of Christ ("and one mediator between God and men"; εἷς καὶ μεσίτης θεοῦ καὶ ἀνθρώπων; v. 5)—something that grounds the availability of the gospel for both Jew and Gentile elsewhere in Paul (Rom. 3:21–31). Moreover, the witness of Christ's "ransom for all" (ἀντίλυτρον ὑπὲρ πάντων)—both in the event itself and in the subsequent preaching of it—has now been revealed (1 Tim. 2:6), which supports the idea of "all" referring to salvation being offered to the Gentiles as well as the Jews at this point in history. The "all" is therefore redemptive-historical: Christ's death is *now* all-inclusive: it is for Jew and Gentile. This reading is supported in verse 7: "For this purpose [that is, for the purpose of bearing testimony to the all-inclusive redemptive work of Christ] I was appointed a herald and an apostle . . . and a teacher of the true faith to the *Gentiles*" (AT).[94]

---

[93] Philip H. Towner, *The Letters to Timothy and Titus*, NICNT (Grand Rapids, MI: Eerdmans, 2006), 177.
[94] In 1 Timothy 3:16, Paul's use of "world" is clearly a reference to "Jews and Gentiles" but not everyone, unless one adopts a universalist position.

In the light of the immediate literary context, it seems entirely reasonable to view the reading of "all" in verses 4 and 6 as meaning "all kinds of people": individuals from diverse ethnicities (Jew and Gentile), from different classes of society normally deemed outside the pale of salvation (kings and civil authority), and even from different moral backgrounds (chief of sinners, as Paul was; 1:15). This position is also strengthened by the absence of any reference to the individual. Nowhere in the text does Paul write as if he were arguing at the level of the individual, thus making the position that "all" refers to "every single person" less plausible.

Thirdly, alongside the ecclesiological and immediate literary contexts, the wider context of Paul's call to the ministry points us in the direction of reading "all" as "all without distinction."[95] In Acts 22:15, Paul states that God's call on him to the ministry related to his being a witness to "all people"—again supporting the idea of Jew and Gentile.

Fourthly, Paul's theology supports this reading. Elsewhere in the NT, Paul uses monotheism and Christ's death as a basis for salvation being "all-inclusive": available for both Jew and Gentile (Rom. 3:21–31).

Fifthly, attending to inner-biblical connections between 1 Timothy 2:6 on the one hand, and Matthew 20:28 and Mark 10:45 on the other, strengthens my reading of 1 Timothy 2:6. The phrase "gave himself as a ransom for all" echoes the Matthean and Marcan phrase "The Son of Man came . . . to give his life as a ransom for many":[96]

> 1 Timothy 2:6: . . . ὁ **δοὺς** ἑαυτὸν **ἀντίλυτρον ὑπὲρ πάντων** . . .
> . . . who **gave** himself as **a ransom for all** . . .

> Matthew 20:28: . . . ὥσπερ ὁ υἱὸς τοῦ ἀνθρώπου οὐκ ἦλθεν
> διακονηθῆναι ἀλλὰ διακονῆσαι καὶ **δοῦναι** τὴν ψυχὴν
> αὐτοῦ **λύτρον ἀντὶ πολλῶν**.
> . . . even as the Son of Man came not to be served but to serve, and to **give** his life as **a ransom for many**.

---

[95] For example, Paul's use of "all" elsewhere includes different named categories of humankind (Gal. 3:8; Col. 3:11).
[96] F. Buschel, "ἀντίλυτρον," *TDNT* 4:349, says that 1 Timothy 2:6 "is plainly based on Mark 10:45." In agreement: James R. Edwards, *The Gospel according to Mark*, PNTC (Leicester, UK: Apollos, 2002), 327 n. 65; and George W. Knight III, *The Pastoral Epistles: A Commentary on the Greek Text*, NIGTC (Grand Rapids, MI: Eerdmans, 1992), 123: "[Paul's] words here are as identical to the Gospel accounts as a restated objectification of a personal statement can be." Marshall, "Universal Grace and Atonement in the Pastoral Epistles," 59, argues that Paul's use of "all" is an appropriate paraphrase of the Synoptic texts: "It is the natural word to use in moving from a crassly literal rendering of the Hebrew ["many"] to more idiomatic Greek." The apostle alternates the terms "many" and "all" in Romans 5:12–21.

Mark 10:45: καὶ γὰρ ὁ υἱὸς τοῦ ἀνθρώπου οὐκ ἦλθεν διακονηθῆναι ἀλλὰ διακονῆσαι καὶ **δοῦναι** τὴν ψυχὴν αὐτοῦ **λύτρον ἀντὶ πολλῶν.**
For even the Son of Man came not to be served but to serve, and to **give** his life as **a ransom for many**.

Most commentators agree that the two Gospel texts carry with them an allusion to Isaiah 53,[97] and thus 1 Timothy 2:6 may have within it a latent echo of Isaiah 53. Certainly, this would be in accord with Paul's explicit use of Isaiah 52:13–53:12 elsewhere, always in the context of the free offer of the gospel to all people.[98] If this inner-biblical connection is valid, then the observation restricts the meaning of "all" in 1 Timothy 2:6 to those who are finally saved, since in Isaiah 53 "the many" are not only those for whom the Servant makes atonement, but they are coextensive with "the many" who are justified by the Servant (v. 12).

This is not to argue that by "many" Isaiah meant "many believers" or that by "all" Paul means "all believers." In both cases, tautologies would be created: why would the Servant need to justify "many believers," and why would God want "all believers" to be saved and to come to a knowledge of the truth?[99] In both texts, the target group of the saving work are sinners in need of salvation. Thus I am not arguing here for a direct correlation in the meaning of "many" and "all" with "believers." What I am arguing is that "many" and "all" in both texts are restricted by their contexts and therefore cannot mean "everyone." Beyond that, the terms are left deliberately undefined and ambiguous.

Other factors in the text support the idea of a definite atonement for "all": (1) the hapax ἀντίλυτρον points to an "actual" ransom, not a "potential" one.[100] Of the two possible meanings for ἀντίλυτρον—"payment" or "delivery from bondage"—the latter is to be preferred (cf. Titus 2:14).

---

[97] Apart from the connecting word πολύς ("many"), the allusion works mainly at the conceptual level more than the linguistic level (so most commentators on Matthew and Mark, contra Morna D. Hooker, *Jesus and the Servant* [London: SPCK, 1959]). For a detailed argument in response to Hooker, see Rikki E. Watts, "Jesus' Death, Isaiah 53, and Mark 10:45," in *Jesus and the Suffering Servant: Isaiah 53 and Christian Origins*, ed. William H. Bellinger, Jr., and William R. Farmer (Harrisburg, PA: Trinity Press International, 1998), 125–51. Cf. also, O. Betz, "Jesus and Isaiah 53," 70–87, in the same volume.

[98] See Romans 15:14–21; cf. verses 16, 20, 21 with Isaiah 52:13; Romans 10:11–20; cf. verse 11 with Isaiah 28:16, and verse 16 with Isaiah 53:1 (Knight, *Pastoral Epistles*, 123).

[99] The tautologies would be avoided if one substitutes "potential believers" or "the elect," but even then, my argument is that neither Isaiah nor Paul has "the elect" in mind; they simply have in mind a large number of sinners of all different kinds, but not all sinners without remainder.

[100] Leon Morris, *The Apostolic Preaching of the Cross*, 3rd ed. (Grand Rapids, MI: Eerdmans, 1965), 51, renders it "substitute-ransom."

Moreover, the way in which the *lutr–* word group is used in the NT (e.g., Matt. 20:28; Mark 10:45) gives no example of a "potentiality" to Christ's ransom. (2) The phrase "gave himself up" (ὁ δοὺς ἑαυτόν) is a typically Pauline way of referring to Christ's definite self-sacrifice on the cross (Rom. 8:32; Gal. 1:4; 2:20; Eph. 5:2; Titus 2:14). Interestingly, these texts speak of Christ "giving himself up for *us*," that is, believers who have already been saved through faith in the self-giving "ransom" of Christ. Why then does Paul use the word "all" in 1 Timothy 2:6 instead of "us"? This is easily explained by recourse to the historical context, where he addresses an exclusivist and elitist heresy in Ephesus. At times, Paul speaks of Christ's death with strict particularism (for "me"; for the "church"; for "his people"; for "us"); at other times, with open universalism (for "all"). The reason for his switch is always contextual.

Taken together, the points above demonstrate that the "all" of 1 Timothy 2:4–6 is best understood as "all without distinction" rather than "all without exception." This understanding best suits the ecclesiological, literary, redemptive-historical, theological, and inner-biblical contexts.

1 TIMOTHY 4:10

> For to this end we toil and strive, because we have our hope set on the living God, who is the Savior of all people, especially of those who believe.

Alongside 1 Timothy 2:6, proponents of a universal atonement often employ 1 Timothy 4:10 as one of the most impressive texts in defending Christ's death for everyone.[101] For some, this text serves as justification for a twofold purpose in Christ's death. So, for example, E. H. Johnson represents many when he writes, "The NT declares with equal distinctness that Christ died for all men, and that he died in a special sense for some men. . . . Both aspects of the case are presented together in 1 Tim. 4:10; the living God . . . is Savior of all men, especially of believers."[102] Of the "problematic texts" for a definite atonement, 1 Timothy 4:10 is certainly one of the more difficult texts, and therefore it deserves careful handling.

---

[101] Miethe, "Universal Power of the Atonement," 80: "Thus, quite obviously, this verse is saying that although Christ died for *all men*—i.e., the free gift was extended to all—it is finally effective only for those who accept it."
[102] E. H. Johnson, *An Outline of Systematic Theology* (Philadelphia, 1895), 239–40. Similarly: Knox, "Some Aspects of the Atonement," 262; and Demarest, *Cross and Salvation*, 191–93.

1 Timothy 4:10 Read in Parallel with 2:4?

Towner is helpful in reminding us to "read this closing statement of the section [1 Tim 4:6–10] with the polemical battle in mind." He provides three reasons: First, the ascetic requirements of 4:4–5 "would conform to the presence of a Judaizing exclusivism at work in the community." Second, "godliness" was affirmed as the authentic life associated with Paul's gospel (2:2 and 4:7–8). Third, this reality and the rejection of the Pauline gospel by the opponents led Paul in 2:7 and 4:10 to insist on the authority of his (universal) mission to the Gentiles. Towner concludes, "This pattern of themes suggests that the potentially confusing statement ('who is the Savior of all people, especially of those who believe') should be read in the light of 2:1–7 and especially 2:4."[103] For Towner, 4:10 "replicates almost perfectly the affirmation of 2:4,"[104] as this parallelism shows:

> 1 Timothy 4:10:   εἰς τοῦτο γὰρ κοπιῶμεν καὶ ἀγωνιζόμεθα, ὅτι ἠλπίκαμεν ἐπὶ θεῷ ζῶντι, **ὃς ἐστιν σωτὴρ πάντων ἀνθρώπων** <u>μάλιστα πιστῶν</u>.
> For to this end we toil and strive, because we have our hope set on the living God, **who is the Savior of all people**, <u>especially of those who believe</u>.

> 1 Timothy 2:4:   . . . **ὃς πάντας ἀνθρώπους θέλει σωθῆναι** καὶ <u>εἰς ἐπίγνωσιν ἀληθείας ἐλθεῖν</u>.
> . . . **who desires all people to be saved** and <u>to come to the knowledge of the truth</u>.

God's universal will/desire in 2:4 (ὃς πάντας ἀνθρώπους θέλει σωθῆναι) is matched in 4:10 by the phrase "who is the Savior of all people" (ὃς ἐστιν σωτὴρ πάντων ἀνθρώπων), while "to come to the knowledge of the truth" (εἰς ἐπίγνωσιν ἀληθείας ἐλθεῖν) corresponds to "especially of those who believe" (μάλιστα πιστῶν). The first part of each text refers to God's salvific stance, while the second part of each text concerns the reality of that salvation in believers. In other words, God's universal will is connected to a response to the gospel. As Towner concludes: "The point made in this way is that God's universal salvific will is realized 'particularly' through proclamation of and belief in the gospel."[105] This interpretation fits well with the immediate

---

[103] Towner, *Timothy and Titus*, 311.
[104] Ibid., 312.
[105] Ibid.

context of extreme exclusivism and asceticism, which was producing elitism within the Ephesian church (4:3–5, 7). Paul wants to remind the church that God is the Savior of all people, not just the ascetically elite.

While I certainly agree with Towner's encouragement to read 1 Timothy 4:10 in its ecclesiological and literary contexts, the one problem with his interpretation is that the parallelism with 2:4 is not as neat as he suggests. In 2:4, there is no sharp distinction between God's universal will and the provisional response to the gospel (on Towner's reading), as there is in 4:10. The conjunctive καί in 2:4 links two infinitives that complement the main verb θέλω: God desires (θέλω) for all people to be saved (σωθῆναι) and (καί) to come (ἐλθεῖν) to a knowledge of the truth. The second infinitival clause does not introduce a new reality different from being "saved," but the same reality expressed in a different way. In other words, the two infinitival clauses cannot be divided to match the two different parts of 4:10—they are both part of the one universal will of God. In this regard, the comparison with 2:4 is weakened.

Μάλιστα *Means "That Is"?*

Acknowledging that σωτήρ means "Savior" in the soteriological sense that it has elsewhere in 1 Timothy and the Pastoral Epistles (1 Tim. 1:1; 2:3; 2 Tim. 1:10; Titus 1:3, 4; 2:10, 13),[106] some scholars aim to sidestep the potential challenge to definite atonement by arguing that μάλιστα means "that is," rather than "especially."[107] In other words, the verse reads "the living God, who is the Savior of all people, that is, those who believe." This interpretation of μάλιστα seems unlikely, however, since the common means of expressing "that is" or "namely" is τοῦτ᾽ ἔστιν, which Paul employs in other places (e.g., Rom. 7:18; 9:8; 10:6, 7, 8; Philem. 12).[108] It begs the question as to why Paul would use μάλιστα for this expression, when μάλιστα has the common meaning of "especially, above all."[109] To do so would be to create a new meaning for the adverb.

---

[106] "The focus on the promise of ζωῆς τῆς νῦν καὶ τῆς μελλούσης, and on a hope set upon θεῷ ζῶντι, demands that understanding of σωτήρ here" in 1 Timothy 4:10 (Knight, *Pastoral Epistles*, 203).
[107] For example, Knight, *Pastoral Epistles*, 203–204. Surprisingly, Marshall, "Universal Grace and Atonement," 55, agrees with the interpretation, while holding to universal atonement. Knight is influenced by T. C. Skeat, "'Especially the Parchments': A Note on 2 Timothy iv. 13," *JTS* 30 (1979): 174. R. A. Campbell, "KAI MALISTA OIKEIWN—A New Look at 1 Timothy 5:8," *NTS* 41 (1995): 157–60, has added support to Skeat's position.
[108] Vern S. Poythress, "The Meaning of μάλιστα in 2 Timothy 4:13 and Related Verses," *JTS* 53 (2002): 523–32, who disputes every one of Skeat's examples, showing that his understanding of the term is flawed in both the Greek papyri and the NT examples. According to Poythress, Skeat's readings are either ambiguous (and therefore not provable) or mistaken.
[109] BAGD.

Σωτήρ Carries Two Senses: Preserver (Physically) and Preserver (Spiritually)

Another option is that σωτήρ carries two senses in the verse: it is first used in the broadest sense of God as "Preserver and Giver of life" to all people (cf. 1 Tim. 6:13; cf. Acts 14:15–17; 17:28, with possible allusion to LXX Ps. 36:6: σῴζω), and then in a spiritual sense for believers.[110] That every other use of σῴζω and its cognate nouns (σωτήρ and σωτήρια) and adjective (σωτήριος) in the Pastoral Epistles is used in a soteriological sense may seem, at first glance, to persuade one away from this interpretation. But Paul does use both the verb σῴζω and the cognate noun σωτηρία in the sense of physical life in Acts 27:31 and 34, respectively, as he urges the soldiers onboard the troubled vessels to save their own lives. The sense of "Preserver and Giver of life" is therefore entirely plausible and not outside the apostle's semantic range for this word group. Indeed, as Henri Blocher comments in this volume, the context of 1 Timothy supports it:

> The immediate context, from verse 7b, introduces the duality: bodily exercise does bring some profit—we could speak of a temporal "salvation"—but the exercise of godliness is fruitful at both levels, earthly and (Paul could have said) μάλιστα heavenly. Paul does not restrict the benefits of godliness to the higher level, since some affect also life in the body. The duality obtains with God the Father's saving work: it secures the goods of present life *for all* (common grace rooted in the cross), and life of the coming age *for believers only*. The adverb μάλιστα cannot signify the difference between potential and actual.[111]

This latter interpretation is certainly plausible and avoids some of the difficulties that accompany the other interpretations.

1 Timothy 4:10 and Definite Atonement

Whatever interpretation one opts for—and I am most sympathetic to the latter one—a closer look at the text reveals that there is in fact no dilemma for the

---

[110] This is an interpretation with a long tradition from early church fathers (Chrysostom, Oecumenius, Primasius and Ambrose) through medieval commentators (Aquinas) to the Reformers (Calvin) and post-Reformation theologians (Turretin). Aquinas interpreted the verse, "who is the Savior of the present and future life because he saves with a bodily salvation as to all, and thus he is called the Savior of all men. He saves by a spiritual salvation also as to the good and is hence said to be the Savior especially of them that believe" (*Angelici Doctoris Divi Thomae . . . Commentaria in Epistolas omnes D. Pauli*, II/V [1856], 34, cited in Turretin, *Institutes*, 2:461); and John Calvin, *2 Corinthians and Timothy, Titus, and Philemon*, CNTC (Grand Rapids, MI: Eerdmans, 1964), 245: "For here σωτήρ is a general term, meaning one who guards and preserves." More recently, W. Foerster, "σωτήρ," *TDNT* 7:1017, interprets the verse as "God being the Benefactor and Preserver of all men in this life and of believers in the life to come."

[111] Henri A. G. Blocher: "Jesus Christ *the* Man: Toward a Theology of Definite Atonement," chapter 20 in this volume. See Blocher's engagement with Thomas R. Schreiner's interpretation in this volume.

Reformed doctrine of definite atonement. Though I disagree with Towner that there is "no need to posit two shades of meaning for the term 'Savior,'" he is right to remark, "There is no division here based on limited and unlimited atonement."[112] He can say this because the text is not explicitly about *Christ's* atoning work. Certainly there are connections, and "Savior" does carry a soteriological sense here for those who believe, but God the *Father* is the referent of θεὸς ζῶντος in 4:10 (cf. 1:1; 2:3) and thus is the referent of σωτήρ—not the Son.[113] The phrase "living God" may well be "a polemical aside aimed at the false veneration of men who were no longer living, yet who were publicly honored as gods and Saviors upon the Ephesian inscriptions."[114] Thus, what Paul may also be stressing here is the uniqueness of God, in that for all individuals of every kind there is only one Savior—God, who preserves the lives of all people now in the present age, and especially of believers in the life to come.

TITUS 2:11–14

> For the grace of God has appeared, bringing salvation for all people, training us to renounce ungodliness and worldly passions, and to live self-controlled, upright, and godly lives in the present age, waiting for our blessed hope, the appearing of the glory of our great God and Savior Jesus Christ, who gave himself for us to redeem us from all lawlessness and to purify for himself a people for his own possession who are zealous for good works.

This passage is similar to 1 Timothy 2:4–6 in presenting a possible challenge to the doctrine of definite atonement. Paul writes that "the grace of God has appeared, bringing salvation for all people" (Ἐπεφάνη γὰρ ἡ χάρις τοῦ θεοῦ σωτήριος πᾶσιν ἀνθρώποις; Titus 2:11). As with the earlier discussion, the question centers on the meaning of "all."

A number of factors suggest that "all without distinction" is the most plausible reading. First, similar to 1 Timothy, a mirror reading of Titus indicates that Paul is critiquing some Jewish teachers who were constructing genealogies in order to exclude some from salvation (Titus 1:10, 14–15; 3:9). Paul's emphasis is therefore that God's saving grace appeared for all people, not just some Jewish elite. Secondly, the "for" (γάρ) of 2:11 shows that the grace of God serves as the basis for Paul's exhortatory material to various

---

[112] Towner, *Timothy and Titus*, 312.
[113] Bruce Demarest, therefore, overstates his case when he comments, "Thus 1 Tim 4:10 teaches that Christ is universal Savior in that he makes redemptive provision for all persons, but he is the effectual Savior of those who believe" (*The Cross and Salvation*, 191).
[114] Steven M. Baugh, "'Savior of All People': 1 Tim 4:10 in Context," *WTJ* 54 (1992): 338.

kinds of Christians: in verses 1–10, Paul addresses older men and women, younger women and men, and slaves. Given the syntactical relationship that γάρ creates between the material of verses 1–10 and verse 11, it makes good sense for πᾶσιν ἀνθρώποις to refer to "all without distinction." Thirdly, that Paul does not intend to mean "all without exception" is made clearer by the purpose clause of verse 14. Christ "gave himself for *us*" (ὃς ἔδωκεν ἑαυτὸν ὑπὲρ ἡμῶν) in order "to redeem *us*" (ἵνα λυτρώσηται ἡμᾶς) "from all lawlessness and to purify *a people* for his own possession" (καὶ καθαρίσῃ ἑαυτῷ λαὸν περιούσιον). As Robert Reymond concludes,

> So in the very context where some would urge a distributive universality for Christ's atoning work, the *particularity* of the intention behind Christ's cross work and the *speciality* of the redeemed community resulting from that cross work receive the emphasis.[115]

Observing the inner-biblical connections between Titus 2:14 and the LXX of Ezekiel 37:23 reinforces the point even more:

> LXX Ezek. 37:23: . . . ἵνα μὴ μιαίνωνται ἔτι ἐν τοῖς εἰδώλοις αὐτῶν. καὶ *ῥύσομαι* αὐτοὺς ἀπὸ **πασῶν** τῶν **ἀνομιῶν** αὐτῶν, ὧν ἥμάρτοσαν ἐν αὐταῖς, καὶ **καθαριῶ** αὐτούς, καὶ ἔσονταί μοι εἰς **λαόν**, καὶ ἐγὼ κύριος ἔσομαι αὐτοῖς εἰς θεόν.
> . . . so that they never again defile themselves with their idols. And *I will rescue* them from **all** their **lawlessness**, in which they have sinned, and **I will purify** them, and they shall be **for me as a people**, and I, the Lord, will be a God for them.[116]

> Titus 2:14: . . . ὃς ἔδωκεν ἑαυτὸν ὑπὲρ ἡμῶν, ἵνα *λυτρώσηται* ἡμᾶς ἀπὸ **πάσης ἀνομίας** καὶ **καθαρίσῃ ἑαυτῷ λαὸν** περιούσιον, ζηλωτὴν καλῶν ἔργων.
> . . . who gave himself for us to *redeem* us from **all lawlessness** and **to purify for himself a people** for his own possession who are zealous for good works.

The similarity in purpose exists not only in (a) *what* God in the OT and Christ in the NT intended to do—to rescue, redeem, and cleanse—but also in (b) *for whom* they intended it. (a) The purpose of God in the new covenant as

---

[115] Reymond, *Systematic Theology*, 694 (emphasis original).
[116] My translation.

presented in Ezekiel, to rescue (ῥύσομαι) people from all their iniquities (ἀπὸ πασῶν τῶν ἀνομιῶν αὐτῶν) and to cleanse them to be a people for himself (καὶ καθαριῶ αὐτούς, καὶ ἔσονταί μοι εἰς λαόν), is presented in Titus as the purpose of the incarnate Son, who gives himself to ransom (λυτρώσηται) people from all their iniquity (ἀπὸ πάσης ἀνομίας) and to cleanse for himself a people for his own possession (καὶ καθαρίσῃ ἑαυτῷ λαὸν περιούσιον). (b) In Ezekiel, God promised to redeem a particular people (a reconstituted Israel); in Titus, the Son's intention is to redeem a particular people for his own possession (the new covenant people of God). In this regard, the will of God in the OT and the will of the Son in the NT are one.

III. "Perishing" Texts: False Teachers "Obtained with His Own Blood"; Destroying the Brother "for Whom Christ Died"

ACTS 20:28–30

> Pay careful attention to yourselves and to all the flock, in which the Holy Spirit has made you overseers, to care for the church of God, which he obtained with his own blood. I know that after my departure fierce wolves will come in among you, not sparing the flock; and from among your own selves will arise men speaking twisted things, to draw away the disciples after them.

ROMANS 14:15 AND 1 CORINTHIANS 8:11

> For if your brother is grieved by what you eat, you are no longer walking in love. By what you eat, do not destroy the one for whom Christ died.

> And so by your knowledge this weak person is destroyed, the brother for whom Christ died.

Besides the commonly known universalistic texts, opponents to definite atonement often see Acts 20:28–30, Romans 14:15, and 1 Corinthians 8:11 as problematic for a limited intent in Christ's atonement. In each text, Christ is said to have died for people who may perish, either because they are later exposed as a false teacher or because, as weak believers with a tender conscience, they stumble into sin. Does this not prove that Christ died for some who are finally lost?

I will answer this question by starting with the last two texts: Romans 14:15 and 1 Corinthians 8:11. The texts share similar contexts: they concern a stronger Christian possibly abusing his freedom in dietary matters in a way that might cause a "weaker" brother (ἀδελφός) to perish. Paul says that it is possible for a Christian to eat in such a way as to cause another brother or sister with a weaker conscience about the foods that are being consumed to stumble and be destroyed (ἀπόλλυμι). In each case, Paul describes the weaker Christian as one "for whom Christ died" (οὗ Χριστὸς ἀπέθανεν; Rom. 14:15; ὃν Χριστὸς ἀπέθανεν; 1 Cor. 8:11). Opponents of definite atonement argue that the texts state that Christ died for some who may finally perish.[117] The argument would appear to turn upon the meaning of ἀπόλλυμι. The term might refer to spiritual grief or self-condemnation,[118] but when Paul uses the verb ἀπόλλυμι with a personal object it most often refers to ultimate spiritual ruin—eternal destruction (Rom. 2:12; 1 Cor. 1:18; 8:11; 15:18; 2 Cor. 2:15; 4:3; 2 Thess. 2:10).[119] If one opts for this interpretation, then it seems that the argument against a definite atonement gains some traction.

However, to follow this line of thought is a false hermeneutical move. Even if one opts for the interpretation of "eternal destruction" in both texts, the argument loses its force when one sees that Paul (and also other NT writers) can refer to those who may finally perish as, for a time, visibly possessing all the descriptions of genuine believers. So, for example, John refers to Judas as one of Jesus's "disciples" (John 12:4), and Peter can speak of false teachers as those who once had "known the way of righteousness" (2 Pet. 2:21) and therefore those who were "bought" by Christ (2 Pet. 2:1). Acts 20:28 presents a comparative example: Paul exhorts the elders in Ephesus to care for the "church of God, which he obtained with his own blood," and then goes on to say that false teachers would arise *from within* that same church (v. 30). That is, at-one-time *visible* members in the covenant community, they are described as those purchased by Christ. But this is not to say that they were necessarily *genuine, elect* members *of* the covenant community; rather, while members *in* the covenant community, they are described with all the full-orbed descriptions of the elect members: in this case, those "obtained by his own blood."

---

[117] For example, Knox, "Some Aspects of the Atonement," 263. Fritz Guy, "The Universality of God's Love," in *Grace of God and the Will of Man*, 49 n. 31, argues that this pair of Pauline statements suggest "that in some sense it is possible for a person to limit the effectiveness of the atonement *for others* by failing to respect their religious convictions."

[118] So Judith M. Gundry-Volf, *Paul and Perseverance: Staying in and Falling Away*, Wissenschaftliche Untersuchungen zum Neuen Testament 2/37 (Tübingen: Mohr, 1990), 1:96. Similarly, John R. W. Stott, *The Message of Romans: God's Good News for the World* (Leicester, UK: Inter-Varsity Press, 1994), 365–66; Robert A. Peterson, *Salvation Accomplished by the Son: The Work of Christ* (Wheaton, IL: Crossway, 2011), 572; and Craig L. Blomberg, *1 Corinthians* (Grand Rapids, MI: Zondervan, 1994), 163.

[119] Three possible exceptions are 1 Corinthians 10:9, 10; 2 Corinthians 4:9. The majority meaning of "spiritual ruin" does not necessitate that meaning here, but, for the sake of argument, let me suppose that this is the best interpretation.

The same would apply here in Romans 14:15 and 1 Corinthians 8:11: if the weaker "brother" was led into sin and perished, then the issue would become whether he was a genuine brother in the first place.[120] But even this is to get ahead of the text. Paul does not say that the brother *will* actually be destroyed; rather, he is using direct language of an eschatological reality that *would* occur *if* the stronger Christian does not change his behavior. The warning is real yet not realized.[121] The warning about a brother for whom Christ died possibly perishing serves as the motivation to the stronger Christian to live sacrificially for him, just as Christ did for him in his death. The foundation for Paul's exhortation is thus in fact the language of a definite atonement: Christ died for *this brother*. Those wishing to allow for the scenario of a brother for whom Christ died finally perishing as proof of universal atonement must reckon with the bigger issue of Paul's teaching on the security of God's people (e.g., Rom. 8:29–39; Phil. 1:6; 2 Tim. 2:13; Jude 24).

IV. Christ Died for "All," for the "World": Important Qualifications and True Optimism

QUALIFICATION ON THE MEANING OF "ALL"

By arguing that "all" in these kinds of texts does not mean "all without exception," I do not want to give the impression that the only other alternative is that the apostle means "all believers" or "all potential believers" or "all the elect." It is not an either-or choice. There is a third category: "all" means "all *sinners* without *distinction*." I agree with Marshall at this point in his comments on 1 Timothy 2:4–6: the text is "not concerned with believers but with those who need both a mediator who will offer himself as a ransom on their behalf and an apostle to proclaim the gospel to them."[122]

Marshall is guilty, however, of caricaturing the definite atonement position when he suggests that the Reformed interpretation therefore necessarily means "all the elect/believers."[123] I have struggled in vain to find a Reformed

---

[120] See Moo, *Romans*, 854–55 n. 28. Moo is incorrect to say that those who believe in limited atonement *must* draw the conclusion that the brother was genuinely regenerate in the first place (see below).

[121] The NT can speak of apostasy (and subsequent eternal destruction) as a real, genuine possibility for believers in order to warn them away from falling into sin (cf. Heb. 6:1–12; 10:26–31). For further comment, see Peter T. O'Brien, *The Letter to the Hebrews*, PNTC (Grand Rapids, MI: Eerdmans, 2010), ad loc. The problem with treating such warnings as hypothetical is that the *reality* of the warning is often *assumed* in the warning. Judas and Demas really did fall away.

[122] Marshall, "Universal Grace and Atonement," 57–58.

[123] Ibid.

exegete of caliber who interprets "all" as Marshall suggests.[124] Calvin is an example of someone who avoids the false dichotomy in the interpretation of the word "all" in verses 4–6. In his commentary, Calvin engages with those who have a "childish illusion" that this passage contradicts predestination. After giving them short shrift, he passes on from the topic of predestination because it is "not relevant to the present context":

> the apostle's meaning here is simply that no nation of the earth and no rank of society is excluded from salvation, since God wills to offer the Gospel to all without exception. Since the preaching of the Gospel brings life, he rightly concludes that God regards all men as being equally worthy to share in salvation. But he is speaking of classes and not of individuals and his only concern is to include princes and foreign nations in this number.[125]

On verses 5 and 6, Calvin writes,

> this Mediator is not given only to one nation, or to a few men of a particular class, but to all, for the benefit of the sacrifice by which He has expiated for our sins, applies to all. Since at that time a great part of the world had alienated itself from God, he explicitly mentions the Mediator through whom those who were far off now draw nigh. The universal term 'all' must always be referred to classes of men but never to individuals. It is as if he had said, 'Not only Jews, but also Greeks, not only people of humble rank but also princes have been redeemed by the death of Christ.' Since therefore He intends the benefit of His death to be common to all, those who hold a view that would exclude any from the hope of salvation do Him an injury.[126]

In short: nowhere does Calvin suggest that "all" refers to "all the elect" or "all believers," but neither does he think that "all" refers to "every single individual." For Calvin, "all" refers to "all categories of people in the alienated world."[127]

---

[124] Even a conservative, Reformed exegete such as William Hendriksen, *1 and 2 Thessalonians, 1 and 2 Timothy and Titus*, New Testament Commentary (1955; repr., Edinburgh: Banner of Truth, 1991), 95–99, who wishes to defend "limited atonement," does not argue in this way.

[125] Calvin, *2 Corinthians and Timothy, Titus and Philemon*, 208–209.

[126] Ibid., 210.

[127] Contra Martin Foord, "God Wills All People to Be Saved—Or Does He? Calvin's Reading of 1 Timothy 2:4," in *Engaging with Calvin: Aspects of the Reformer's Legacy for Today*, ed. Mark D. Thompson (Nottingham, UK: Apollos, 2009), 179–203, who claims that Calvin means that God wills the salvation of "all from all kinds" (198). See Muller's critique of Foord on this point in Richard A. Muller, "Calvin on Christ's Satisfaction and Its Efficacy: The Issue of 'Limited Atonement,'" in *Calvin and the Reformed Tradition: On the Work of Christ and the Order of Redemption* (Grand Rapids, MI: Baker Academic, 2012), 85 n. 55.

The interpretation of "all" in 1 Timothy 2:4–6 presented here is that "all" refers to "all *sinners* without *distinction.*" Christ gave himself as a ransom for individual sinners from all kinds of backgrounds, regardless of ethnicity, class, economic income, or moral history.

QUALIFICATION ON THE MEANING OF "WORLD"

While Christ's death for "all without distinction" involves individuals, he is also said to have died for the "church" and the "world" as organic wholes.[128] That is to say, Christ does not die just for individuals who are clumped together into an aggregate group called "the elect." Paul certainly speaks of Christ's death for individuals (Gal. 2:20), but he also views his death organically: Christ died for his bride, the church (ἐκκλησίαν); as a Head (κεφαλή) for his body (σώματος) (Eph. 5:23–25); he bought the church of God (ἐκκλησίαν τοῦ θεοῦ) with his blood (Acts 20:28); God was in Christ, reconciling the world (κόσμον) to himself (2 Cor. 5:19). These are not collective terms for a group of individuals; they are organic terms, understood in relation to who Christ is as Bridegroom, Head, and cosmic Savior. This organic dimension must be allowed its full weight in relation to the "world" texts in Paul. As R. B. Kuiper writes,

> Christ does indeed save individuals, but by and through the salvation of individuals He saves the world. He who forgets this can never do justice to the universalistic passages of Scriptures. Christ is the Savior of the world.[129]

To see this more clearly, I return briefly to the analogy Paul uses between Adam and Christ in Romans 5:12–21. If the analogy holds, then Christ is presented as the Last Adam and therefore as the Head of a new humanity. As Herman Bavinck comments,

> the church is not an accidental and arbitrary aggregate of individuals that can just as easily be smaller or larger, but forms with him an organic whole that is included in him as the second Adam, just as the whole of humankind arises from the first Adam. The application of salvation must therefore extend just as far as its acquisition.[130]

---

[128] R. B. Kuiper, *For Whom Did Christ Die?* (Grand Rapids, MI: Eerdmans, 1959), 96: "The elect are not just so many individuals, but collectively they constitute the church. And men are not so many particles separated from one another as isolated units. On the contrary, they are members of that organism which is known as the human race."

[129] Ibid., 95.

[130] Bavinck, *Sin and Salvation in Christ*, 467.

All those connected to him are part of a new humanity, they belong to a new age, they have been saved for a new world: "that is, in Christ God was reconciling the *world* to himself" (2 Cor. 5:19). How true. In saving people, Christ came to save humankind—Jew and Gentile united to form one new man (Eph. 2:15). As B. B. Warfield writes,

> Thus the human race of man attains the goal for which it was created, and sin does not snatch it out of God's hands: the primal purpose of God with it is fulfilled; and through Christ the race of man, though fallen into sin, is recovered to God and fulfills its original destiny.

Abraham Kuyper provides a beautiful analogy that complements the theology of Romans 5:

> If we liken mankind, thus, as it has grown up out of Adam, to a tree, then the elect are not leaves which have been plucked off from the tree that there may be braided from them a wreath for God's glory, while the tree itself is to be felled, rooted up and cast into fire; but precisely the contrary, the lost are the branches, twigs and leaves which have fallen away from the stem of mankind, while the elect alone remain attached to it . . . what is lost is broken from the stem and loses its organic connection.[131]

As Augustine said of the elect, commenting on 1 Timothy 2:4: *omne genus hominum est in eis* ("The whole human race is in them").[132]

TRUE OPTIMISM: ESCHATOLOGICAL UNIVERSALISM

In the light of the aforementioned, the rendering of "all" and "world" in certain contexts as "all without distinction" does not equate to a miserly number of people. We should not spend so much time qualifying these texts that we end up minimizing them. There have been some treatments of definite atonement that convey the sense that Christ died for "only a portion of mankind" or that "most of the world" will be lost.[133] Pascal spoke unfortunately of "the *small number* of the Elect for whose salvation Jesus

---

[131] Abraham Kuyper, *E Voto dordraceno II*, 178, quoted (and translated, most probably) by B. B. Warfield, "Are They Few that Be Saved?," in *Biblical and Theological Studies*, ed. Samuel G. Craig (repr., Philadelphia: P&R, 1952), 336.

[132] Augustine, *On Rebuke and Grace*, in *NPNF*[1] 5:489.

[133] So R. A. Morey, *Studies in the Atonement* (Southbridge, MA: Crowne, 1989), 60, refers to God electing "*only a portion of mankind*" (emphasis original), and John MacArthur in *The MacArthur Study Bible* (Nashville: Word, 1997), 1955, commenting on 1 John 2:2, writes, "*Most of the world* will be eternally condemned to hell to pay for their own sins, so they could not have been paid for by Christ" (emphasis added). The wording in both cases is unfortunate at best and pessimistic at worst.

Christ died."[134] But such pessimism is absent in Paul (and in the rest of the NT)—the *paucitas salvandorum* is an unbiblical category. Particularism and parsimony are not equivalent conceptions.[135] "However few or many His people may be today or tomorrow, in the end His people will be the world."[136] While Paul does not believe in an "each and every" universalism, he nevertheless does not think that the elect can all fit into one sand bucket—his is an "eschatological universalism" that is genuinely *universal* in the right sense of the word. The God of the apostle is the same God of Abraham to whom was promised a "seed" as numerous as the sand on the seashore and the stars in the heavens (Rom. 4:17–18; cf. Gen. 22:17; 32:12; Ex. 32:13; Deut. 1:10–11; Jer. 33:22; Hos. 1:10; Gal. 3:8; Heb. 11:12; Rev. 5:9; 7:9). "Scripture is not afraid that *too* many people will be saved."[137] Abraham was promised to be "the heir of the *world*," and Paul believed it (Rom. 4:13).

It is in this regard that the terms "all" and "world," when rightly defined in each particular context, should be allowed their full *universal* weight. Reformed theologians have "as important a mission in preserving the true universalism of the gospel . . . as we do in preserving the true particularism of grace."[138] Our universalism is not a "spurious" universalism of the Semi-Pelagian, Arminian, Amyraldian, or Hypothetical Universalist mold—who, if the proponents are consistent, can offer at most only the hope of the *possible* salvation of the world, but one which will never actually eventuate—nor is our universalism the unwarranted hope held out to us by Barth or McCormack—whose trajectory of thought in this regard is contrary to a number of Pauline texts—rather, Reformed theology at its best champions a true, genuine, achievable, eschatological universalism.[139] "For the earth will be filled with the knowledge of the glory of the LORD as the waters cover the sea" (Hab. 2:14).

---

[134] Quoted by Lucien Goldmann, *Le Dieu caché: Etude sur la vision tragique dans les* Pensées *de Pascal et dans le théâtre de Racine* (Bibliothèque des idées; Paris: NRF Gallimard, 1955), 324, from *Deux pièces imparfaites sur la Grâce et le concile de Trente* (Paris: Vrin, 1947), 31, cited in (and translated by) Blocher, "Jesus Christ *the* Man," chapter 20 in this volume (emphasis added). Commenting on the "most common view of Paul's eschatological salvation," Boring, "Universal Salvation in Paul," 281, summarizes it as "most of humanity is left in the grave," or Christ's work affects "a minority of human beings" (285).

[135] B. B. Warfield, *The Plan of Salvation* (Grand Rapids, MI: Eerdmans, 1935), 97.

[136] Kuiper, *For Whom Did Christ Die?*, 95–96.

[137] Bavinck, *Sin and Salvation in Christ*, 465.

[138] Warfield, *Plan of Salvation*, 125.

[139] This is true of optimistic amillennialism as well as postmillennialism. Helpfully, Warfield, *Plan of Salvation*, 128–31, and Kuiper, *For Whom Did Christ Die?*, 96–97, both emphasize the need to see the salvation of the world as a process.

V. Avoiding a Non Sequitur: Definite Atonement and Evangelism

One of the accusations often leveled at the Reformed who hold to a definite atonement is that the doctrine necessarily dampens zeal for evangelism.[140] But this is a non sequitur. Particularistic and universalistic tendencies within Paul's soteriology sit cheek-by-jowl. He is the Apostle to the Gentiles who can speak of becoming all things to all people so that by all means he might save some (1 Cor. 9:22), while at the same time declaring that he endures all things for the sake of the elect (Acts 18:10; 2 Tim. 2:10; Titus 1:1). In Romans, Paul can say in all honesty that he wishes that he himself were accursed and cut off from Christ for the sake of his fellow countrymen and women (9:3), yet at the same time such a passionate desire does not blur his perspective on God's sovereign election: "For not all who are descended from Israel belong to Israel" (9:6). It is reasonable to suggest that the apostle holds the same perspective when it comes to the atoning work of Christ and evangelism. Within Paul's soteriology, Christ's atonement has a particular focus: the church, his bride (Acts 20:28; Eph. 5:25–27), the elect as a new humanity from all nations; yet such a perspective does not hinder or dampen the apostle's desire to preach the gospel to every creature under heaven (Col. 1:23). Thus, the suggestion that definite atonement leads necessarily to a hindrance in evangelism may reasonably receive the apostle's common retort: μὴ γένοιτο! On the contrary, definite atonement grounds and motivates the cause of evangelism, for what is offered to people is not the opportunity or possibility of salvation, but salvation itself.

Summary

In his epistles, Paul speaks of Christ's death in both particularistic and universalistic ways. It is the argument of this chapter that these texts present compatible elements in Paul's atonement theology. The universalistic texts do not counter the possibility of definite atonement in Paul; rather, they are complementary to it. Close attention to the universalistic texts themselves reveals that the meaning of "many," "all," and "world" cannot be simplistically interpreted in each instance as "all without exception" or "every single person."

My analysis reveals a number of important points when considering the

---

[140] For example, Knox, "Some Aspects of the Atonement," 266: definite atonement "cuts away the basis of a genuine offer of the gospel to all the world, and blunts the point of evangelism in preventing the pressing home of the claims of Christ on the consciences of the hearer (sic), by interdicting such phrases as 'Christ died for you,' 'God so loved you . . .'"

universalistic language in Paul. First, though Paul had the linguistic arsenal to state unambiguously that there was no one for whom Christ did not die, he chose not to use it. The terms "many," "all," and "world" remain undefined and ambiguous, dependent on context for their meaning.

Secondly, the meaning of the universalistic terms "many," "all," and "world" is influenced by various contextual factors: (1) an implicit union with Christ (Rom. 5:12–21; 2 Cor. 5:14–15); (2) an ecclesiological context in which the apostle is confronting false teaching that promoted an elitist and exclusivist culture in the church (1 Tim. 1:4–7; 4:1–8; Titus 1:10, 14–15; 3:9); (3) a literary context where the focus is on "all *kinds* of people" (1 Tim. 2:4–6; 4:10; Titus 2:11–14); (4) a redemptive-historical context whereby Paul is presented as Apostle to the Gentiles (Acts 22:15); (5) a theological context in which monotheism is the basis for the gospel being for all people (1 Tim. 2:5–6; cf. Rom. 3:27–31); and (6) inner-biblical connections with texts in the New and Old Testaments (1 Tim. 2:6; cf. Matt. 20:28//Mark 10:45; cp. Isaiah 53; Titus 2:14; cp. Ezek. 37:23). Attention to these factors constrains us from concluding that Paul has a distributive meaning to his universalistic terminology.

Thirdly, a text such as Colossians 1:20, in which the universal impact of Christ's atoning work is spotlighted, turns out to be inconsequential for discussions over the extent of Christ's substitutionary death: to argue retrospectively from the universal impact of Christ's death to a universal extent in his death is an illegitimate deduction. As Romans 8:19–23 demonstrates, the universal restoration of the whole creation is premised on a particular redemption—the adoption of the sons of God.

Fourthly, the "perishing" texts of Romans 14:15 and 1 Corinthians 8:11 (cf. Acts 20:28) were shown in the end to support definite atonement rather than universal atonement; and those who wish to employ them in defense of a universal atonement must answer to the repercussions for the perseverance of the saints: some for whom Christ died are saved and then finally lost.

With these points in mind, it is now reasonable to see how Paul's universalistic language is more than compatible with his particularism. Two important qualifications, however, are necessary. First, in arguing for a non-distributive meaning to the terms "many," "all," and "world," I do not wish to suggest that by these terms Paul means "many elect," "all the elect," or the "world of the elect." If there have been some Reformed interpreters who have argued like this, then their exegesis is unfortunate. Calvin has proved to be a better example to follow: he does not fall foul of interpreting the term "all" in 1 Timothy 2 as meaning "all the elect" on the one hand, or of arguing that the apostle intends the meaning "all without exception" on the other hand. Rather, there is a third option, "all sinners without distinction." As Calvin argued, discussion of predestination is irrelevant to the context, but neither does that drive him to conclude that "many" and "all" must therefore necessarily mean "everyone." Paul's language is deliberately undefined and ambiguous, and all sides in the debate should respect this.

The reason that at times Paul employs universalistic language in relation to the atonement is because he is confronting heresy in the church that promoted salvation for an elite and exclusive few. Paul is emphatic in such contexts: Christ died for *all*, for the *world*, for *Jew and Gentile*. The terms are redemptive-historical: Paul views the gospel as the end of the ages in which God's grace and love is to be proclaimed to all peoples of the earth. He is the "great universalizer of the gospel."[141] In this regard, the "all without distinction" meaning should be seen for what it actually is: all-inclusive, all-embracing—no one is left out: not Gentile, not women, not slave, not barbarian, not children, not elderly, not poor, not white, not black—not anyone!

Secondly, the organic dimension of those for whom Christ died must not be neglected in Paul's atonement theology. Paul presents Christ's death for individuals (Gal. 2:20), but also for organic wholes (Acts 20:28; Eph. 5:25; 2 Cor. 5:19). As Husband and Head, Christ died for his bride and body; as Cosmic Savior, he died for the world; and as the Last Adam, he died for a new humanity. In this regard, Christ truly is the Savior of the *world*—an innumerable number of people from every tribe and language and nation.

---

[141] Vos, "Biblical Doctrine of the Love of God," 448.

The Glorious, Indivisible, Trinitarian Work of God in Christ

DEFINITE ATONEMENT IN PAUL'S THEOLOGY OF SALVATION[1]

Jonathan Gibson

Introduction

In the previous chapter I argued, at the risk of oversimplification, that Paul's atonement theology is comprised of at least four groups of texts (with some overlap between them): (1) particularistic texts that concern Christ's death for a particular group ("me," "church," "his people," "us"); (2) universalistic texts that concern Christ's death for an undefined, ambiguous group ("many," "all," "world"); (3) "perishing" texts that concern Christ's death for people who may finally perish, either because they are exposed as false teachers or because they stumble into sin through a weak conscience; and (4) "doctrinal loci" texts that concern important doctrines which directly impinge upon the intent and nature of the atonement (such as eschatology, election, union with Christ, christology, Trinitarianism, doxology, covenant, ecclesiology, and sacramentology). These four groups of texts constitute

---

[1] I am grateful to Henri Blocher, Richard Gaffin, and Jonathan Moore for their helpful comments on an earlier draft of this chapter.

important components of a unified theological lens through which Christ's death may be viewed.

In discussions on the intent and nature of the atonement, particularistic, universalistic, and "perishing" texts are usually employed in a textual *quid pro quo* as each respective side tries to support their position. In my last chapter, I aimed to demonstrate that the universalistic and "perishing" texts in Paul's atonement theology complement rather than compromise the possibility of interpreting Christ's death as a definite atonement. Isolated exegesis of individual texts, however, does not prove or disprove the doctrine of definite atonement in Paul—a larger soteriological framework must be respected.

A NEW APPROACH

While a fully comprehensive treatment of the intent and nature of the atonement in Paul certainly requires a careful and thorough exegesis of the particularistic, universalistic, and "perishing" texts, here I present a different approach, one that aims to overcome the impasse that often arises when all sides engage in the debate. In this chapter I propose a biblico-systematic approach. Definite atonement, carefully and properly understood, is not a *biblical* doctrine per se, nor even a *systematic* doctrine per se; rather, definite atonement is a *biblico-systematic* doctrine. That is to say, the doctrine of definite atonement emerges from holding together various soteriological texts *while at the same time* synthesizing internally related doctrines, such as eschatology, election, union with Christ, christology, Trinitarianism, doxology, covenant, ecclesiology, and sacramentology.[2] Definite atonement is a theological conclusion reached on the other side of comprehensive synthesis.[3] When exegesis serves the domain of constructive theology—or put better, when there is a symbiotic relationship between exegesis and constructive theology—one may argue not only that Paul's theology allows for a definite atonement but that it can point in no other direction. My approach understands Paul's doctrine of the atonement through the lens of his soteriology, that is, through the wider framework of the saving work of God in Christ. As R. A. Morey has rightly commented, "The confusion surrounding this doc-

---

[2] As David Ford, *Theology: A Very Short Introduction* (Oxford: Oxford University Press, 1999), 103, comments, "salvation is a topic where most key theological issues can be seen to converge." As I mentioned in the previous chapter, the list is not intended to be exhaustive.

[3] For a recent attempt, see Jarvis J. Williams, *For Whom Did Christ Die? The Extent of the Atonement in Paul's Theology*, Paternoster Biblical Monographs (Milton Keynes, UK: Paternoster, 2013).

trine [of the extent of the atonement] often results from the failure to view it in the light of the whole plan of salvation."[4]

This is not to impose a "systematic" grid over the universalistic or "perishing" texts, one that "dominates" or "minimizes" the universalistic elements of Paul's atonement theology while privileging the particularistic texts. An accurate and comprehensive formulation of Paul's soteriology will *include* his universalistic and "perishing" texts as significant components in that lens. Nevertheless, these texts are but two of several constituents in Paul's soteriological framework, and should be neither privileged nor prejudiced as they sit alongside particularistic texts and "doctrinal loci" texts, the latter of which concern various doctrines which directly impinge upon his atonement theology, such as eschatology, election, union with Christ, christology, Trinitarianism, doxology, covenant, ecclesiology, and sacramentology. It is these latter loci that are often neglected, and the aim of this chapter is to let their voice be heard in the debate over the intent and nature of the atonement.[5] Indeed, I would argue that the doctrinal loci texts may serve a mediating role in the textual *quid pro quo*: on the one hand, they keep us from bland and reductionistic interpretations of the particularistic texts; on the other hand, they restrain us from naïve and simplistic interpretations of the universalistic and "perishing" texts.

PAUL'S SOTERIOLOGICAL PARADIGM

Commencing with an analysis of Ephesians 1:3–14, I discern five key components of Paul's soteriology, which help to form the main sections of this chapter. These components are then unpacked through careful exegesis of various Pauline texts. I will argue that in Paul the saving work of God is (1) indivisible; (2) circumscribed by God's electing grace; (3) encompassed by union with Christ; (4) Trinitarian; and (5) doxological. The first four exegetical sections each conclude with theological reflections as I bring Paul's soteriology into conversation with various positions on the intent and nature of the atonement, such as Semi-Pelagianism, Arminianism, Amyraldianism, Hypothetical Universalism, and the theology of Karl Barth.[6] It is my belief

---

[4] R. A. Morey, *Studies in the Atonement* (Southbridge, MA: Crowne, 1989), 57.

[5] Space precludes an analysis of the last three doctrines—covenant, ecclesiology, and sacramentology—but I would argue that these also lend supporting arguments to the particularistic trajectory in Paul's atonement theology.

[6] As the introduction in this book makes clear, and as will be seen below, it is important to appreciate the various positions on the intent and nature of the atonement and their nuanced differences—hence why I have distinguished five distinct schools of thinking, as well as the one presented in this chapter. At times some of these dovetail in the

that approaching the issue of the intent and nature of the atonement from the vantage point of doctrinal loci in Paul's soteriological paradigm provides helpful resources for progressing the debate.

The Saving Work of God in Christ

The chief task of Christian soteriology is to explain the saving work of God in Christ.[7] Soteriology, often referred to as the "economy of salvation," may appear to be a "systematic" category, but it does have biblical roots. The word "economy" is used in Ephesians 1:10: "as an economy [οἰκονομίαν] of the fullness of time, to unite all things in Christ, things in heaven and things on earth in him."[8] The verse is the high point of Paul's *berakah* paragraph in 1:3–14. The word οἰκονομία describes the manner in which God's plan is being worked out in human history.[9] As Fred Sanders writes, "When Paul talks about God's economy, his point is that God is a supremely wise administrator who has arranged the elements of his plan with great care."[10] It should be no surprise, then, to find in Paul's theology an ordered pattern to his presentation of the saving work of God in Christ. And this is exactly what we do find in Ephesians 1:3–14.

EPHESIANS 1:3–14

> Blessed be the God and Father of our Lord Jesus Christ, who has blessed us in Christ with every spiritual blessing in the heavenly places, even as he chose us in him before the foundation of the world, that we should be holy and blameless before him. In love he predestined us for adoption as sons through Jesus Christ, according to the purpose of his will, to the praise of his glorious grace, with which he has blessed us in the Beloved. In him we have redemption through his blood, the forgiveness of our trespasses, according to the riches of his grace, which he lavished upon us, in all wisdom and insight making known to us the mystery of his will, according to his purpose, which he set forth in Christ as a plan for the fullness of time, to unite all things in him, things in heaven and things on earth. In him we have obtained an inheritance, having been predestined according to the purpose of him who works all things according to the counsel of his will, so that we who were the first to hope in Christ might be to the praise of his glory. In him you also,

---

way that they deviate from the Bible's theology of the atonement; at other times, they deviate for different reasons and in different ways.

[7] John B. Webster, "'It Was the Will of the Lord to Bruise Him': Soteriology and the Doctrine of God," in *God of Salvation: Soteriology in Theological Perspective*, ed. Ivor J. Davidson and Murray A. Rae (Farnham, Surrey, UK: Ashgate, 2011), 15.

[8] My translation.

[9] Peter T. O'Brien, *The Letter to the Ephesians*, PNTC (Leicester, UK: Apollos, 1999), 113, 227–28.

[10] Fred Sanders, *The Deep Things of God: How the Trinity Changes Everything* (Wheaton, IL: Crossway, 2010), 130.

when you heard the word of truth, the gospel of your salvation, and believed
in him, were sealed with the promised Holy Spirit, who is the guarantee of
our inheritance until we acquire possession of it, to the praise of his glory.

This one-sentence-long paragraph (in the Greek) sketches five main components of Paul's soteriology.

(1) *The saving work of God is indivisible.* Paul paints his soteriology on
an eschatological canvas in which he describes God's salvation in four distinct but interrelated "moments," stretching from eternity past through history
and on into eternity future.[11] There is moment one: redemption predestined
(pre-temporal), when the Father elected us in Christ before the foundation
of the world and predestined us for adoption as sons (vv. 4–5); moment two:
redemption accomplished, conveyed by the pithy phrase "through his blood"
(v. 7), a reference to Christ's death on the cross; moment three: redemption
applied, the moment when redemption and forgiveness of sins became personally realized in our lives (v. 7), and we were sealed with the Holy Spirit
(v. 13); and moment four: redemption consummated (post-temporal), our
future inheritance that we will acquire one day (v. 14). This fourth moment
of redemption is the consummation of moments two and three.[12]

(2) *The saving work of God is circumscribed by God's electing grace.*
Election and predestination set in motion God's salvation plan. Put differently, the moment of redemption predestined serves as the beginning and
fountainhead of the other three moments of redemption. It is the moment that
initiates and shapes the others.

(3) *The saving work of God is encompassed by union with Christ.* God's
saving work was performed "in" and "through Christ." Eleven times in this
paragraph the phrase "in him," "in whom," or "through Christ" appears. To
mention a few: we were chosen "in him" (v. 4) and predestined "through
Jesus Christ" (v. 5); "in him" we have redemption (v. 7), and "in him" we

---

[11] Geerhardus Vos, *The Pauline Eschatology* (Grand Rapids, MI: Eerdmans, 1953), 42–61: "the shaping of soteriology by eschatology is not so much in the terminology; it proceeds from the actual realities themselves and the
language simply is adjusted to that" (46).

[12] Roger R. Nicole, "The Nature of Redemption," in *Standing Forth: Collected Writings of Roger Nicole* (Ross-
shire, UK: Mentor, 2002), 245–46, gives six ways in which the term redemption may be understood: (1) an all-
embracing term for the divine plan, including presuppositions and implications of this plan; (2) God's saving
purpose and activity; (3) objective basis for the sinner's restoration as found in the person and work of Christ;
(4) Christ's work as distinct from his person; (5) application of salvation, i.e., the subjective impartation of Christ's
saving benefits; (6) the ultimate consummation of the plan of grace and the believer's entrance into future glory.
When I speak in this chapter of the "moments of redemption," I am using the term "redemption" as referring to (2):
God's saving purpose and activity—redemption predestined, accomplished, applied, and consummated. In other
words, redemption is employed here as a general term for salvation.

obtained an inheritance (v. 11) and were sealed with the Holy Spirit (v. 13). Salvation, for Paul, occurs "through Christ" and "in union with" Christ.

(4) *The saving work of God in Christ is Trinitarian.* The blessings that have come to us are the work of the triune God: Father, Son, and Holy Spirit. The Father is active in the first moment of redemption, electing and predestining us (vv. 4–5); the Son secures the second moment, redemption and forgiveness of sins (v. 7); and then the Spirit, in the third and fourth moments, applies that redemption to us and serves as the guarantee of our future inheritance (vv. 13–14).

(5) *The saving work of God in Christ is doxological.* The purpose of God's saving work in Christ is for the "praise of his glory," a phrase repeated three times in this paragraph (vv. 6, 12, 14).[13]

Ephesians 1:3–14 is not the *summa* of Paul's soteriology, but it does provide a matrix, a paradigm, within which one can go exploring. What is in sketch form here can be filled out with greater clarity through an analysis of several Pauline texts. The five points above will serve heuristically as we explore the Pauline corpus.

I. The Saving Work of God Is Indivisible

TITUS 3:3–7

> For we ourselves were once foolish, disobedient, led astray, slaves to various passions and pleasures, passing our days in malice and envy, hated by others and hating one another. But when the goodness and loving kindness of God our Savior appeared, he saved us, not because of works done by us in righteousness, but according to his own mercy, by the washing of regeneration and renewal of the Holy Spirit, whom he poured out on us richly through Jesus Christ our Savior, so that being justified by his grace we might become heirs according to the hope of eternal life.

In Titus 3, Paul temporally locates God's salvation in the three moments of redemption accomplished, applied, and consummated. The moment of redemption accomplished is explicit and is denoted by the temporal adverb ὅτε ("when"; v. 4), which qualifies the main verb ἐπεφάνη ("appeared").[14] God's "goodness and loving kindness" (χρηστότης καὶ φιλανθρωπία[15]) refer here to

---

[13] Verse 6 is slightly different: "to the praise of the glory of his grace" (εἰς ἔπαινον δόξης τῆς χάριτος αὐτοῦ).

[14] Except in Acts 27:20, the verb ἐπιφαίνω occurs in soteriological contexts (Luke 1:79; Titus 2:11; here).

[15] Χρηστότης refers to God's "goodness, kindness, generosity" (BAGD) in relation to God's salvation (Rom. 2:4; 11:22 [3×]; Eph. 2:7); φιλανθρωπία refers to God's philanthropy toward mankind (BAGD). Together the words may be understood as God's "kindness-and-love-toward-mankind" that appeared in Christ's first appearing (George

Christ's first appearance, in which he "gave himself for us to redeem us from all lawlessness" (2:13–14). Syntactically, the verb ἔσωσεν in 3:5 is the center point of verses 3–7: "all that leads up to the verb and flows from it enters into the understanding of what is intended by it."[16] The preceding ὅτε clause is tied syntactically to this main verb in a protasis–apodosis relationship: when Christ appeared the first time to die and rise, God saved (ἔσωσεν) us (v. 5).[17]

Paul introduces the next (implied) moment of redemption applied in a prepositional phrase that is connected to the main verb ἔσωσεν: God saved us "by the washing of regeneration and renewal of the Holy Spirit" (διὰ λουτροῦ παλιγγενεσίας καὶ ἀνακαινώσεως πνεύματος ἁγίου).[18] The first pair of genitives focuses on the need for washing; the second pair of genitives, on the need for renewal. Together, the bathing of regeneration and renewal of the Holy Spirit envisage transformed human existence, a point in time that can have occurred only during our own lifetime experience.

In verse 7, Paul hints at the final moment of redemption consummated: ἔσωσεν is tied syntactically to a purpose clause in verse 7, which orients us toward the future. The purpose of God's salvific act in Christ and the Spirit's regeneration is "so that [ἵνα] being justified by his grace [δικαιωθέντες τῇ ἐκείνου χάριτι], we might become heirs [κληρονόμοι] according to the hope of eternal life [ἐλπίδα ζωῆς αἰωνίου]." "Heir" suggests an "anticipatory position," and "hope of eternal life" speaks of "a future unending life with God."[19]

So, in Titus 3, Paul locates God's salvation in three moments: the moment of redemption accomplished, when Christ appeared in history; the moment of redemption applied, when the Holy Spirit regenerates and renews us in our own lifetime experience; and the moment of redemption consummated, the hope of eternal life.

Continuing with the Titus text, we observe that these three moments of God's salvation are distinct but integrally connected. Paul maintains a *distinction* between the three moments and does not collapse one into the other. Our salvation is not a "done deal" at the "when" of the cross; rather, there

---

W. Knight III, *The Pastoral Epistles: A Commentary on the Greek Text*, NIGTC [Grand Rapids, MI: Eerdmans, 1992], 338).

[16] Ibid., 341.

[17] Interposed between the two clauses, two prepositional clauses (set in antithesis) provide the motivating basis for God's saving act: not because of works done in righteousness on our part (οὐκ ἐξ ἔργων τῶν ἐν δικαιοσύνῃ ἃ ἐποιήσαμεν ἡμεῖς), but according to his own mercy (ἀλλὰ κατὰ τὸ αὐτοῦ ἔλεος).

[18] Διά with the genitive is used with σῴζω nine times in the NT, but nowhere else does the NT speak as fully or explicitly of the means of salvation as it does here.

[19] Knight, *Pastoral Epistles*, 347.

is a specific "when" and "now" to our salvation. In fact, verse 3 restrains us from collapsing redemption applied into redemption accomplished, because (γάρ), Paul says, "we ourselves were once [ποτε] foolish, disobedient," etc. (cf. Eph. 2:1–3, 12–13). The believer's once-unregenerate state in time before conversion ensures the distinction between the moments of redemption accomplished and redemption applied, and counters any claims of an "eternal justification." Additionally, Titus 3:5 restrains us from seeing redemption already fully consummated by speaking of the "hope" (ἐλπίδα) of eternal life. The believer's "not yet" attainment of eternal life maintains a distinction between the moments of redemption applied and redemption consummated, thus withholding us from an "over-realized eschatology."

While the three moments of God's salvation are distinct, they are also *integrally connected.* Paul moves with such ease from the moment of redemption accomplished to the moment of redemption applied, despite the fact that there is a significant time lapse between the two, especially for believers living today. The connection is tighter still: the abundant outpouring of the Spirit in regeneration (v. 5) comes *through* (διά) the person of Christ in his atoning work as Savior (v. 6).[20] To state it in systematic terms: redemption applied flows from redemption accomplished. Thus, the two moments of salvation are distinct but integrally connected: not only does the moment of redemption accomplished lead to the moment of redemption applied, but the former is the *source* of the latter. There is more than mere chronological sequence going on here; there is cause and effect. Finally, these two moments of God's salvation are also connected to the future moment of redemption consummated: God saved us in order that (ἵνα) we might have the hope of eternal life (v. 7).

Two other Pauline texts unpack in more detail the relationship between the moments of redemption predestined, accomplished, applied, and consummated.

Romans 5:9–10

> Since, therefore, we have now been justified by his blood, much more shall we be saved by him from the wrath of God. For if while we were enemies we were reconciled to God by the death of his Son, much more, now that we are reconciled, shall we be saved by his life.

---

[20] While the text does not explicitly mention Christ's atoning work as such, he is described here as Savior (σωτῆρος), a title which can derive its definition only from what he actually did.

In Romans 5, Paul ties the moments of redemption accomplished and redemption applied together as he speaks about the present state of believers before God. The moment of redemption applied is seen in our justification (δικαιωθέντες; v. 9) and our reconciliation (κατηλλάγημεν; v. 10).[21] References to the moment of redemption accomplished occur in prepositional phrases that serve as explanation for the means by which God applied redemption to us: we have now (νῦν) been justified "by his blood" (ἐν τῷ αἵματι αὐτοῦ),[22] and we have been reconciled to God "by the death of his Son" (διὰ τοῦ θανάτου τοῦ υἱοῦ αὐτοῦ). The third moment of future salvation (redemption consummated) is conveyed by the future tense verb σωθησόμεθα ("shall we be saved"), a reference to the final day of judgment.

As with the other Pauline passages that I have analyzed, similarities surface: (1) each moment is held as distinct but integrally connected to the others; and (2) salvation is not viewed as fully completed at the moments of redemption accomplished or redemption applied, but remains an eschatological hope. In addition to these similarities, Romans 5:9–10 reveals a new link, an unbreakable bond. Paul's whole argument for the believer's assurance of salvation at the final judgment rests on the connection between redemption accomplished and applied on the one hand, and redemption consummated on the other. As in Titus 3:3–5, redemption applied occurs through redemption accomplished, but now the synergy of redemption accomplished and applied together *guarantees* redemption consummated: if God has already done the most difficult thing—reconcile and justify us by Christ's death—*how much more* (πολλῷ οὖν μᾶλλον) will he rescue us on that last day of his wrath. Paul stresses his point by twice using this greater-to-lesser argument.[23]

ROMANS 8:29–34

> For those whom he foreknew he also predestined to be conformed to the image of his Son, in order that he might be the firstborn among many brothers. And those whom he predestined he also called, and those whom he called he also justified, and those whom he justified he also glorified.

---

[21] Douglas J. Moo, *The Epistle to the Romans*, NICNT (Grand Rapids, MI: Eerdmans, 1996), 311–12, thinks that reconciliation here refers to Christ's accomplishment of reconciliation by Christ on the cross as well as the believer's acceptance of that reconciliation. In any case, redemption applied covers the end result here.

[22] The temporal marker νῦν locates the timing of our justification in our lifetime experience.

[23] Both arguments are exhibited by temporal participles (δικαιωθέντες and καταλλαγέντες, respectively), which set up the protasis, before σωθησόμεθα introduces the apodosis: "having been justified . . . how much more will we be saved; . . . having been reconciled . . . how much more will we be saved."

What then shall we say to these things? If God is for us, who can be against us? He who did not spare his own Son but gave him up for us all, how will he not also with him graciously give us all things? Who shall bring any charge against God's elect? It is God who justifies. Who is to condemn? Christ Jesus is the one who died—more than that, who was raised—who is at the right hand of God, who indeed is interceding for us.

In Romans 8:29–30, Paul presents a "golden chain" of God's salvation that stretches back to before the beginning of time, moves through time, and reaches forward to the end of time. Three moments of God's salvation in Christ are present in the chain: redemption predestined (προέγνω . . . προώρισεν), redemption applied (ἐκάλεσεν . . . ἐδικαίωσεν), and redemption consummated (ἐδόξασεν).[24] Redemption predestined serves as the "fountainhead" that initiates the process of God's salvation in eternity past and which consummates in glorification in eternity future. The demonstrative pronoun τούτους ("these"), the sustained use of καί ("also"), and the repetition of the key verbs (προώρισεν, ἐκάλεσεν, ἐδικαίωσεν) point to an exact correspondence between those who are foreknown, predestined, called, justified, and glorified. The extent of salvation at each stage is the same. It is interesting also to note the clipped way in which Paul refers to each of these links in the chain, especially the last three: God alone is presented as the agent at work, with no contribution from man supplied at any of the points in the chain.[25] For Paul, salvation, from beginning to end, is "of the Lord."

Although not present in the "salvation chain" of verses 29–30, the moment of redemption accomplished comes into focus in verse 32, as Paul responds to his own rhetorical question of verse 31: "If God is for us, who will be against us?" Paul speaks of Christ's death in antithetical terms: God did not spare his own Son (ὅς γε τοῦ ἰδίου υἱοῦ οὐκ ἐφείσατο) but (ἀλλά) gave him up for us all (ὑπὲρ ἡμῶν πάντων παρέδωκεν αὐτόν). The compressed sentence is full of rich truths for the doctrine of the atonement. The adjective ἰδίου ("own") adds drama to the sparing: this was God's *own beloved* Son whom he did not spare.[26] Not only did God not spare his own Son, but he

---

[24] I understand ἐδόξασεν to be a proleptic aorist, which is used to express the certainty of an event as if it has already occurred. John Murray, *The Epistle to the Romans*, 2 vols., NICNT (Grand Rapids, MI: Eerdmans, 1959), 1:320, refers to the first two actions as pre-temporal and the last three as temporal.

[25] Of course, both calling and justification for Paul do not occur irrespective of faith—the former is a precondition for faith; the latter is the result of faith—but, accurately speaking, these acts of God are not defined by human activity (Murray, *Romans*, 321).

[26] Moo, *Romans*, 540, among others (see n. 18), believes that there is an allusion here (and therefore a contrast) to the sparing of Isaac, Abraham's own son (same verb in LXX Genesis 22:16: φείδομαι).

"gave him up" (παρέδωκεν αὐτόν), a Pauline expression for Jesus's substitutionary death.[27] Octavius Winslow writes movingly, "Who delivered up Jesus to die? Not Judas, for money; not Pilate, for fear; not the Jews, for envy—but the Father, for love!"[28]

The focus on redemption accomplished in verse 32a serves as the protasis ("if") in Paul's "quasi" conditional sentence, and verse 32b becomes the apodosis ("then"). Together, both sentences combine to produce a similar *a maiori ad minus* argument to Romans 5:9–10. The interrogative particle πῶς, alongside the emphatic negative particle οὐχὶ and the emphatic conjunctive καί, heightens the logic: If God has, indeed (γε), given his Son for us, *how* will he *not also* (πῶς οὐχὶ καί), along with him, give us all things? The "all things" (τὰ πάντα) are all the blessings that we need on the path to final glorification,[29] which makes sense given the reference to glorification in Romans 8:30. Thus, Paul not only connects the moment of redemption accomplished in verse 32a to the moment of redemption consummated in verse 32b, but he presents the connection as an unbreakable bond. For Paul, it is inconceivable for God to accomplish redemption for people and not bring that accomplished redemption to its consummated end in glorification. For him, the former not only links to the latter; it *guarantees* the latter. In Paul's mind, how could it *not*? For, if God has already given *Christ* for us, how will he not also give us graces of lesser proportion?[30] As John Murray writes, "Since he is the supreme expression and embodiment of free gift and since his being given over by the Father is the supreme demonstration of the Father's love, every other grace must follow upon and with the possession of Christ."[31]

In Romans 5:9–10, redemption accomplished *and* applied guarantees redemption consummated. Romans 8:32 provides yet another new insight into Paul's soteriological framework: redemption accomplished *on its own* secures redemption consummated, without any reference to redemption applied. What Paul presents here is the *efficacy* of Christ's atoning work (without reference to its application): it cannot *but* produce its intended effect. Put

---

[27] Sometimes παραδίδωμι is passive referring to the Father's "giving him over" (Rom. 4:25), and other times it refers to the Son's own "giving himself" (Gal. 2:20; Eph. 5:2, 25). A similar root (δίδωμι) is used in other texts of Christ "giving himself" (Gal. 1:4; 1 Tim. 2:6; Titus 2:14).

[28] Octavius Winslow, *No Condemnation in Christ Jesus* (London, 1857), 358 (cited in Murray, *Romans*, 324).

[29] Moo, *Romans*, 541.

[30] This possibly helps to explain the difficult phrase σὺν αὐτῷ.

[31] Murray, *Romans*, 326.

another way, all those for whom Christ died cannot but be given all things in order to reach final glorification.

Another important insight for definite atonement exists in reference to those for whom the Son was given up. As we saw earlier, the demonstrative pronoun τούτους shows that the moments of redemption predestined, applied, and consummated all carry the same extent. In verse 32, Paul now shows that redemption accomplished also carries the same extent as the other moments of salvation. Paul presents redemption accomplished and redemption consummated as coextensive: if Christ was given up "for us all" (ὑπὲρ ἡμῶν πάντων), how will God not also freely, along with Christ (σὺν αὐτῷ), give "us" (ἡμῖν) all things in order to be glorified. This means that unless one wishes to affirm universal salvation, the word "all" must be limited in some way. The context provides the correct referent for "us all" (ἡμῶν πάντων): the "us" of verse 32 is the same as the "us" of verse 31 and those referred to in the preceding verses: those whom God foreknew, predestined, called, justified, and will one day glorify (vv. 29–30). The subsequent verses also support an intended and definite referent: the "all of us" are God's elect (ἐκλεκτῶν θεοῦ; v. 33) and those for whom Christ intercedes (ὃς καὶ ἐντυγχάνει ὑπὲρ ἡμῶν; v. 34). Murray brings the point to a helpful conclusion: "The sustained identification of the persons in these terms shows that this passage offers no support to the notion of universal atonement. It is 'for all of us' who belong to the category defined in the context that Christ was delivered up."[32]

SUMMARY

Let me summarize Paul's soteriological framework thus far. First, Paul presents four key moments of God's saving work in Christ: redemption predestined, accomplished, applied, and consummated. Set on a temporal canvas, salvation for Paul is thoroughly eschatological: from the moment of predestination, God's redemptive purposes move inexorably forward toward the

---

[32] Ibid., 325. Moo, *Romans*, 540, is correct to observe that the text does not say that Christ died "*only* for all you believers,"; and Norman F. Douty, *Did Christ Die Only for the Elect? A Treatise on the Extent of Christ's Atonement* (1978; repr., Eugene, OR: Wipf & Stock, 1998), 92, is correct when he writes, "To read [Paul] as meaning that God delivered Christ for all of us who believe *and for none else*, is injecting into the words what is not there." But the *mere proposition* that the text does not contain the word "only" cannot be used to counter the case for definite atonement in Romans 8, since the text has its own inherent logic, one which demonstrates clearly that (1) those for whom Christ died are the elect, and that (2) Christ's death is an *efficacious* substitutionary atonement that cannot but produce its intended effect. The *nature* of the atonement is in Paul's purview here, and its nature is one of ultimate efficacy: those for whom Christ died *will* make it to glory. Paul's argument is therefore tendential to definite atonement and can point in no other direction.

final moment when redemption will be fully consummated.[33] Second, each of these four moments are integrally connected yet always distinct, never collapsed into each other yet never separated either. For Paul, in moment one, our salvation has been predestined; in moment two, the whole of our salvation has been procured and secured, even though redemption is yet to be experientially applied (moment three) and eschatologically consummated in his presence (moment four). Paul ties these four moments together in such a way that moment one (redemption predestined) sets in motion God's salvation, while moment two (redemption accomplished) is the source from which moment three (redemption applied) derives, and the guarantee that moment four (redemption consummated) is inevitable. These four moments of salvation do not belong to separate theological "tracks" as if Christ's redemptive work were somehow disconnected from God's electing work; rather, Paul presents one theological "chain" whose "links" join together to present God's redemptive purposes in Christ as one whole, integrated salvation. The saving work of God is indivisible.

THEOLOGICAL REFLECTIONS:
GOD'S INDIVISIBLE SAVING WORK AND THE ATONEMENT

Affirming that the saving work of God is indivisible, where the moments of redemption are distinct but inseparable, keeps one from falling into two errors:

(1) *There is the error of collapsing the moment of redemption applied into the moment of redemption accomplished, as is the case in Karl Barth's theology.* For Barth, God's act of reconciliation is a grace that cannot be "split up into an objective grace which is not as such strong and effective for man but simply comes before him as a possibility, and a subjective grace which, occasioned and prepared by the former, is the corresponding reality as it actually comes to man."[34] Writing on justification and sanctification, Barth is at pains to avoid setting up "a dualism between an objective procuring of salvation there and then and a subjective appropriation of salvation here and now."[35] Such a

---

[33] Richard B. Gaffin, *Resurrection and Redemption: A Study in Paul's Soteriology*, 2nd ed. (Phillipsburg, NJ: P&R, 1987), 59: "eschatology is not only the goal of soteriology but also encompasses it, constituting its very substance from the outset."
[34] Karl Barth, *Church Dogmatics*, ed. G. W. Bromiley and T. F. Torrance, 14 vols. (Edinburgh: T. & T. Clark, 1956–1975), IV/1, 87–88 (hereafter *CD*).
[35] Barth, *CD* IV/2, 502–503: "The one is done wholly and immediately with the other" (502).

dualism, according to Barth, overlooks "the simultaneity of the one work of salvation, whose Subject is the one God by the one Christ through the one Spirit—'being more closely bound together than in a mathematical point.'"[36] On the basis of this unitary character of the one work of God in Christ, Barth rejected the concept of a temporal *ordo* in the divine *salus*, if by it is meant "a temporal sequence [of acts] in which the Holy Spirit brings forth His effects . . . here and now in men."[37] McCormack captures Barth's position succinctly:

> His insistence on the unitary character of the work of God in Christ and in the Holy Spirit means that the work of Christ *is* effective as such, that the work of the Spirit does not complete it or give to it an efficacy it does not otherwise have. The work of Christ and the work of the Spirit belong to a *single* movement of God toward the creature, a movement that entails both the accomplishment of the work of Christ and the awakening of individuals to this accomplishment.[38]

Though Barth was well intentioned, his view is seriously flawed for a number of reasons. In exchanging the *temporal* for the *simul*, Barth has collapsed redemption applied into redemption accomplished. What Paul holds as *temporally* distinct-but-inseparable moments on the eschatological canvas of his soteriology, Barth unites together as *simultaneously* distinct-but-inseparable moments. Barth's desire to avoid presenting what Christ has done as "proffered opportunity and possibility" is commendable, but the exchange of the *temporal* for the *simul* collapses redemption accomplished and applied into *one* temporal act. In doing so, Barth not only eliminates the Pauline distinction of the here-and-now work of the Spirit from the there-and-then work of Christ, but he also erases in man's existentialist experience the once-fallen state from the now-renewed state. This is at variance with several Pauline texts. Paul speaks of being "dead in trespasses and sins" and "children of wrath" at one time (ποτε) in the past (Eph. 2:1–3), previously foolish and disobedient and in need of washing and renewal (Titus 3:3–5). Resurrection, re-creation, regeneration, realm transfer—these were our needs, not our (unbeknown) possessions, *during our lifetime experience*. Barth's position

---

[36] Ibid., 503. It is not that Barth collapses the two acts into each other to such an extent that they lose their identity: ". . . we have here in this event two genuinely different moments. . . . The two belong indissolubly together. . . . But it is a connexion, not identity. The one cannot take the place of the other" (503).

[37] Ibid., 502.

[38] Bruce L. McCormack, "*Justitia Aliena*: Karl Barth in Conversation with the Evangelical Doctrine of Imputed Righteousness," in *Justification in Perspective: Historical Developments and Contemporary Challenges*, ed. Bruce L. McCormack (Grand Rapids, MI: Baker, 2006), 181 (emphasis original).

reduces the Spirit's work to a mere "awakening" of people to a reality that is *already* theirs,[39] which seriously underplays the Spirit's role in washing and renewing us (Titus 3:5).

(2) *In contrast to Barth, there is the opposite error of forcing a disjunction between the moments of redemption (as is the case in Semi-Pelagianism and Arminianism, Amyraldianism, and Hypothetical Universalism).* On these schemes, redemption accomplished is disjoined from redemption applied, such that the former does not of necessity influence the latter. So, for example, on the Arminian side, Roger Olson writes, "Arminians believe that Christ's death on the cross provided *possible* salvation for everyone, but it is *actualized* only when humans accept it through repentance and faith."[40] For Amyraut, "there is no necessary cause and effect relationship between salvation as procured by Christ and its application."[41] And, on the Hypothetical Universalist side, Gary Shultz writes, "All people are objectively reconciled to God, but not all people are subjectively reconciled to God, and therefore not all people are saved."[42] In such statements, Christ's atoning death for everyone does not of necessity lead to its being appropriated by everyone; these views fail to see the integral connections between the distinct-but-inseparable moments of redemption in Paul's soteriology. As we have seen in Paul, if Christ has secured the objective reconciliation, how will he not also ensure the subjective reconciliation?

These alternate approaches—of collapsing and disjoining the moments of redemption accomplished and redemption applied—present errors on either side of Paul's soteriology. Karl Barth eliminates the temporal distinctions, seeing only one unified act at one point in history, while Semi-Pelagians and Arminians, Amyraldians, and Hypothetical Universalists maintain the temporal distinctions but not the connections. In contrast to both, Paul presents distinctions between each of the moments of God's salvation, but he never allows for disjunctions between them. The saving work of God is indivisible.

---

[39] See Barth, *CD* IV/1, 751: Faith, then, "does not alter anything. As a human act it is simply the confirmation of a change which has already taken place, the change in the whole human situation which took place in the death of Jesus Christ and was revealed in His resurrection and attested by the Christian community." Christians are "those who waken up" to the reality that already belongs to the whole of mankind (*CD* IV/2, 554); they only see what there is for all in the death of Christ (*CD* IV/3.2, 486–97).

[40] Roger E. Olson, *Arminian Theology: Myths and Realities* [Downers Grove, IL: IVP Academic, 2006), 222.

[41] So Brian G. Armstrong's assessment of Amyraut's formulation (*Calvinism and the Amyraut Heresy: Protestant Scholasticism and Humanism in Seventeenth-Century France* [Madison: University of Wisconsin Press, 1969], 210).

[42] Gary L. Shultz, Jr, "The Reconciliation of All Things," *BSac* 167 (October–December 2010): 449.

II. The Saving Work of God Is Circumscribed by God's Electing Grace

Three Pauline texts illuminate the point.

EPHESIANS 1:4–5 AND 5:25–27

> . . . even as he chose us in him before the foundation of the world, that we should be holy and blameless before him. In love he predestined us for adoption as sons through Jesus Christ, according to the purpose of his will . . .

> Husbands, love your wives, as Christ loved the church and gave himself up for her, that he might sanctify her, having cleansed her by the washing of water with the word, so that he might present the church to himself in splendor, without spot or wrinkle or any such thing, that she might be holy and without blemish.

God's election and predestination shapes and guides his redemptive purposes in history. This can be seen by Paul's reuse of key terminology in his epistle. In chapter 1, Paul explains that God's purpose in electing us "in Christ" was so that we might "be holy and blameless before him" (εἶναι ἡμᾶς ἁγίους καὶ ἀμώμους κατενώπιον αὐτοῦ; v. 4). Then in chapter 5, Paul repeats the same terminology in describing the purpose of Christ's sacrificial self-giving for the church: so that she might be "holy and blameless" (ἵνα ἦ ἁγία καὶ ἄμωμος; v. 27, NIV). Thus the elective purpose of God the Father (1:4) and the redemptive purpose of God the incarnate Son (5:27) are one and the same: to present the elect as the Son's bride, holy and blameless, on the last day.[43] More specifically, Christ's death is the *means* to accomplish the electing purpose of the Father. In short, election circumscribes atonement.

GALATIANS 1:4

> . . . who gave himself for our sins to deliver us from the present evil age, according to the will of our God and Father . . .

This text supports the proposition above. Christ "gave himself" (τοῦ δόντος ἑαυτόν) for a particular group of people—for "our sins" (ὑπὲρ τῶν ἁμαρτιῶν ἡμῶν)—according to the will of God the Father (κατὰ τὸ θέλημα τοῦ θεοῦ

---

[43] There are of course other redemptive purposes in Christ's death (e.g., Titus 2:14).

καὶ πατρὸς ἡμῶν). In Ephesians, Christ gave himself for the church in order to present us holy and blameless; here in Galatians, the purpose of Christ's self-giving is to deliver his people from the present evil age (ὅπως ἐξέληται ἡμᾶς ἐκ τοῦ αἰῶνος τοῦ ἐνεστῶτος πονηροῦ). In both cases, God's purpose and will circumscribe the atonement for a particular group of people.

2 TIMOTHY 1:9–11

> ... who saved us and called us to a holy calling, not because of our works but because of his own purpose and grace, which he gave us in Christ Jesus before the ages began, and which now has been manifested through the appearing of our Savior Christ Jesus, who abolished death and brought life and immortality to light through the gospel, for which I was appointed a preacher and apostle and teacher ...

This passage contains connections similar to those already seen in Ephesians and Galatians. In verses 9–11, in a doxological "aside," Paul presents all four moments of salvation, stretching from eternity to eternity—some more explicit than others—with various links between them. In verse 9, two explanatory relative clauses describe God's actions toward us in our own lifetime experience: he saved us (τοῦ σώσαντος ἡμᾶς) and called us (καλέσαντος).[44] Theologians generally locate these actions in the soteriological category of redemption applied, a salvific act by God that occurs in our own lifetime experience.[45] The basis for this divine saving and calling is explained in antithetical terms: not according to our works (οὐ κατὰ τὰ ἔργα ἡμῶν) but according to God's own purpose and grace (κατὰ ἰδίαν πρόθεσιν καὶ χάριν). Paul then unpacks this χάριν in two explanatory relative clauses (τὴν δοθεῖσαν ... φανερωθεῖσαν), both of which are accompanied by temporal markers that spotlight two more moments of God's salvation plan. In the first clause, God's grace has been given to us "before times eternal" (ESV mg.) (πρὸ χρόνων αἰωνίων; cf. Titus 1:2)—the moment of redemption predestined (2 Tim. 1:9); in the second clause, God's grace was manifested (ἐπιφάνεια) "now" (νῦν), in the present age, a reference to the time of Christ's first appearing—the moment of redemption accomplished

---

[44] In Paul, this is an effective call (cf. Rom. 8:30; 9:11 [2×], 24; 1 Cor. 1:9; Gal. 1:6; 5:8; 1 Thess. 5:24).

[45] John Murray, *Redemption Accomplished and Applied* (Edinburgh: Banner of Truth, 1955), identifies nine components to this soteriological category of redemption applied: effectual calling, regeneration, faith and repentance, justification, adoption, sanctification, perseverance, union with Christ, and glorification. For the purposes of this chapter, I place glorification within a new soteriological category of redemption consummated, as it relates to a new distinct "moment" of God's salvation in history, albeit the end result of redemption applied.

(v. 10a).⁴⁶ The reference to "immortality" implies a final temporal element in the text: life and immortality (ζωὴν καὶ ἀφθαρσίαν) were inaugurated through Christ's first appearing, but their effects would carry on into the future—the moment of redemption consummated (v. 10b).

Taking a step back, the following theological connections may be discerned. Redemption applied (God's saving and calling us in our lifetime experience) is based on the grace of redemption predestined (God's purpose and grace given to us before time began), which is made manifest in redemption accomplished (Christ's work in his first appearing), which in turn secures redemption consummated (the immortal life that continues on into the future). As in Romans 8:29–34, the moment of redemption predestined acts as the "fountainhead" of the other moments of redemption: it is the "meritorious grounds" (κατά) for applying redemption (2 Tim. 1:9), and it circumscribes the revelation (φανερωθεῖσαν) of redemption accomplished (v. 10). This last point is significant for our discussion. For Paul, the gospel of Jesus Christ is the manifestation, not primarily of God's universal philanthropy, nor even of his salvific stance toward the world, but of his grace toward *the elect*. In other words, election circumscribes the saving work of God—not vice versa.

THEOLOGICAL REFLECTIONS: ELECTION AND THE ATONEMENT

These observations on 2 Timothy 1:9–11 reinforce the connections that I have already noted in Ephesians 1:4–5; 5:25–27, and Galatians 1:4, and serve to counter any attempt that would (1) *render election non-determinative for salvation* (i.e., as mere foreknowledge, as in Semi-Pelagianism and Arminianism),⁴⁷ or that would (2) *place the decree of election after the decree of redemption* (as in Amyraldianism),⁴⁸ or that would (3) *subordinate God's electing love for his elect to a universal compact* (as in Hypothetical

---

⁴⁶ Among the NT writers, ἐπιφάνεια is used only by Paul and refers exclusively to the appearing of Jesus in his first coming (here) or second coming (2 Thess. 2:8; 1 Tim. 6:14; 2 Tim. 1:10; 4:1, 8; Titus 2:13).

⁴⁷ For example, James Arminius, "A Declaration of the Sentiments of Arminius," in *The Works of James Arminius*, trans. James Nichols and William Nichols, 3 vols. (London, 1825; repr., Grand Rapids, MI: Baker, 1956), 1:653: "[God] knew from all eternity those individuals who *would*, through his preventing [prevenient grace], *believe*, and, through his subsequent grace *would persevere*" (emphasis original; cited in Olson, *Arminian Theology*, 184).

⁴⁸ For example, D. Broughton Knox, "Some Aspects of the Atonement," in *The Doctrine of God*, vol. 1 of *D. Broughton Knox, Selected Works* (3 vols.), ed. Tony Payne (Kingsford, NSW: Matthias Media, 2000), 265: "the decree of election is logically after the decree of atonement, where also, in fact, it belongs in the working out of the application of salvation." It would be inaccurate to call Knox an "Amyraldian" in every sense of the term—on the nature of the atonement he was more of a British Hypothetical Universalist. On this point, however, he was in line with Amyraut.

Universalism).[49] In each case, God's general universal love trumps his special love for the elect to the extent that the latter becomes a mere "afterthought."[50] On the contrary, front and center in Paul's soteriological framework is God's electing purpose and grace for his people. The gospel is the manifestation of this grace.

III. The Saving Work of God Is Encompassed by Union with Christ

A number of texts in Paul that concern the work of redemption speak, either implicitly or explicitly, of Christ's death and resurrection occurring in union with his people. When the concept is present, God's saving work is described in efficacious terms.

ROMANS 5:12–21

> Therefore, just as sin came into the world through one man, and death through sin, and so death spread to all men because all sinned—for sin indeed was in the world before the law was given, but sin is not counted where there is no law. Yet death reigned from Adam to Moses, even over those whose sinning was not like the transgression of Adam, who was a type of the one who was to come.
>
> But the free gift is not like the trespass. For if many died through one man's trespass, much more have the grace of God and the free gift by the grace of that one man Jesus Christ abounded for many. And the free gift is not like the result of that one man's sin. For the judgment following one trespass brought condemnation, but the free gift following many trespasses brought justification. For if, because of one man's trespass, death reigned through that one man, much more will those who receive the abundance of grace and the free gift of righteousness reign in life through the one man Jesus Christ.
>
> Therefore, as one trespass led to condemnation for all men, so one act of righteousness leads to justification and life for all men. For as by the one man's disobedience the many were made sinners, so by the one man's obe-

---

[49] For example, John Davenant, "A Dissertation on the Death of Christ, as to its Extent and special Benefits: containing a short History of Pelagianism, and shewing the Agreement of the Doctrines of the Church of England on general Redemption, Election, and Predestination, with the Primitive Fathers of the Christian Church, and above all, with the Holy Scriptures," in *An Exposition of the Epistle of St. Paul to the Colossians*, trans. Josiah Allport, 2 vols. (London: Hamilton, Adams, 1832 [English trans. of 1650 Latin ed.]), 2:555–56, said that God's special love to save the elect is "a kind of special design subordinate to the infallible fulfilment of this universal compact. . . . Lest, therefore, this universal compact should not bring the effect of salvation to any one, God, by a special and secret intention, hath taken care that the merit of the death of Christ should be applied to some for the infallible obtaining of faith and eternal life."

[50] Geerhardus Vos, "The Biblical Doctrine of the Love of God," in *Redemptive History and Biblical Interpretation: The Shorter Writings of Geerhardus Vos*, ed. Richard B. Gaffin (Phillipsburg, NJ: P&R, 1980), 456.

dience the many will be made righteous. Now the law came in to increase
the trespass, but where sin increased, grace abounded all the more, so that,
as sin reigned in death, grace also might reign through righteousness leading to eternal life through Jesus Christ our Lord.

The argument of Romans 5:12–21 is set against the backdrop of verses 1–11,
where Paul assures believers of God's future glory despite the trials and
tribulations that they face.[51] Believers can be assured of salvation on the
day of God's wrath (vv. 9–11), because (διὰ τοῦτο; v. 12) Christ's one act of
obedience is so much more powerful than Adam's one act of disobedience
(vv. 12–21). The comparison between Adam and Christ is exhibited in the
"just as [ὥσπερ] . . . so also [οὕτως καί]" positive comparisons (vv. 12, 18,
19, 21), as well as the "not as [οὐχ ὡς] . . . so is [οὕτως καί]" negative comparisons (vv. 15–17).[52] In verses 15–17, Paul presents three contrasts between
the work of Adam and the work of Christ.[53] Verse 15 presents a contrast of
degree: the work of Christ, described here as a gracious gift (χάρισμα), is so
much better in every way than the work of Adam: where Adam's trespass
(παραπτώματι) brought death to many (οἱ πολλοὶ ἀπέθανον), Christ's work
has brought the grace of God (ἡ χάρις τοῦ θεοῦ) and the free gift (ἡ δωρεά).
The potency of Christ's grace over Adam's sin is an "abounding plus"[54]
(πολλῷ μᾶλλον), which has "the power not only to cancel the effects of
Adam's work but to create, positively, life and peace."[55] Verses 16–17 consist of two contrasts: the first contrast is one of *consequence*, emphasizing
the *power* of each man's actions: Adam's sin (ἁμαρτήσαντος) brought condemnation (κατάκριμα) and death (θάνατος); Christ brought righteousness
(δικαίωμα) and life (ζωῇ). The other contrast is *numerical*, emphasizing the
grace of God: the judicial verdict of condemnation followed Adam's one sin
(ἐξ ἑνός), but the justification brought by Christ followed after many sins (ἐκ
πολλῶν παραπτωμάτων). Verse 17 acts as climax to the contrast of these two
key figures in world history: Adam introduced onto the world stage the reign
of death (ὁ θάνατος ἐβασίλευσεν), while Christ introduced the reign of life
(ἐν ζωῇ βασιλεύσουσιν).

---

[51] Paul most likely has one eye on Jewish suspicion about justification before God in the present, since the Jews relegated the verdict of justification to the last day (Moo, *Romans*, 293).
[52] In verse 16, οὕτως καί is missing through ellipsis, but the comparison between the one who sinned (ἑνὸς ἁμαρτήσαντος) and the gift (τὸ δώρημα) is still present.
[53] Moo, *Romans*, 334.
[54] Murray, *Romans*, 193.
[55] Moo, *Romans*, 337.

In verses 18–19, Paul brings his overall comparison to a conclusion: con-demnation (κατάκριμα) came to all people through the one trespass (δι' ἑνὸς παραπτώματος) of Adam; justification that leads to life (δικαίωσιν ζωῆς) came to all people through the one righteous act (δι' ἑνὸς δικαιώματος) of Christ (v. 18). Paul reiterates and elaborates the same point again in verse 19: the result of the epoch-initiating acts of Adam and Christ are stated in more personal terms: by Adam's one act of disobedience (διὰ τῆς παρακοῆς), many were constituted sinners (ἁμαρτωλοὶ κατεστάθησαν οἱ πολλοί); by Christ's one act of obedience (διὰ τῆς ὑπακοῆς),[56] many were constituted righteous (δίκαιοι κατασταθήσονται οἱ πολλοί).

All told, in order to provide the grounds for the believer's assurance of future salvation, Paul resorts to a grand comparison between the two history-making figures of Adam and Christ. As Henri Blocher writes,

> The grand parallel with Adam serves as the grounding of that assurance: if Adam's role was so dramatically efficacious in securing the condemnation of all people in him, and therefore the reign of death, how much more is Christ's work efficacious for those in him, leading to eternal life![57]

Implicit throughout Paul's argument is a union between Adam and all his descendants and a union between Christ and all his descendants: "there exists a life-giving union between Christ and his own that is similar to, but more powerful than, the death-producing union between Adam and his own."[58] The union is seen by the connection of Adam and Christ to "the many" (οἱ πολλοί; vv. 15b, 15c, 19a, 19b) and the "all" (πάντες; v. 18a, b) littered throughout this paragraph. The use of οἱ πολλοί and πάντες in verses 12–21 must be interpreted in the light of the ἑνός to whom they are connected. To argue for an exact denotation between the two groups related to Adam and Christ is to opt for the position of universalism, which, in the light of other Pauline texts (e.g., Rom. 2:12; 2 Thess. 1:8–9) is untenable. As Doug Moo states, "Paul's point is not so much that the groups affected by Christ and Adam, respectively, are coextensive, but that Christ affects those who are his just as certainly as Adam does those who are his."[59]

Respecting this careful distinction helps avoid the unwarranted position

---

[56] Most likely a reference to his ultimate act of obedience to death (ibid., 344).
[57] Henri A. G. Blocher, *Original Sin: Illuminating the Riddle*, NSBT (Leicester, UK: Apollos, 1997), 80.
[58] Moo, *Romans*, 318.
[59] Ibid., 343.

of universalism[60] or the confusing interpretation of "paradox."[61] Christ has *secured* the benefits of justification and life for all who are united to him—not for everyone. Paul's argument in Romans 5 also renders inadequate the view that Christ has made justification "available" and "possible" for everyone who will believe,[62] or that the benefit of Christ's obedience "extends to all men potentially" but "[i]t is only human self-will which places limits to its operation."[63] These options soften the language of 5:12–21. Christ's work cannot be reduced to mere potentiality: justification language in Paul is always used of the actual status conferred on the individual.[64] Moreover, any talk of the human will resisting the power of Christ's atonement surely flies in the face of the apostle's argument. Christ's one act of obedience is *so much more powerful* than Adam's one act of disobedience.

Of course, it may be argued that Romans 5:12–21 presents Christ's work as efficacious *only for those who believe*, and within the passage this is certainly true—it is for those who "receive" (λαμβάνοντες) the gift of righteousness (v. 17). On this basis, some conclude that the efficacy of Christ's work occurs only at the point of faith, and not before. While this may, at first glance, appear true, it ignores the fact that union with Christ (strongly assumed throughout Paul's paragraph here) *precedes* any reception of Christ's work by faith. As I will demonstrate below, it is this union with Christ that *leads* to the potent efficacy of Christ's work for those who belong to him and who receive the gift of righteousness.

Romans 6:1–11

What shall we say then? Are we to continue in sin that grace may abound? By no means! How can we who died to sin still live in it? Do you not know that all of us who have been baptized into Christ Jesus were baptized into

---

[60] So A. J. Hultgren, *Christ and His Benefits: Christology and Redemption in the New Testament* (Philadelphia: Fortress, 1987), 54–55. Bruce L. McCormack, "So That He Might Be Merciful to All: Karl Barth and the Problem of Universalism," in *Karl Barth and American Evangelicalism*, ed. Bruce L. McCormack and Clifford B. Anderson (Grand Rapids, MI: Eerdmans, 2011), 227–49, argues that Paul allows us to at least hope for universal salvation.

[61] So C. K. Barrett, *A Commentary on the Epistle to the Romans* (London: A. & C. Black, 1957), 108–11; C. E. B. Cranfield, *The Epistle to the Romans*, 2 vols., ICC, (Edinburgh: T. & T. Clark, 1975), 1:294–95, who acknowledges indebtedness to Karl Barth, *Christ and Adam. Man and Humanity in Romans 5* (New York: Collier, 1962), 108–109. M. Eugene Boring "The Language of Universal Salvation in Paul," *JBL* 105 (1986): 269–92, speaks of "language games."

[62] So R. C. H. Lenski, *The Interpretation of St. Paul's Epistle to the Romans* (1936; repr., Minneapolis: Augsburg, 1961), 383: "What Christ obtained for all men, all men do not receive"; P. E. Hughes, *True Image: The Origin and Destiny of Man in Christ* (Grand Rapids, MI: Eerdmans, 1989), 174–75.

[63] So J. B. Lightfoot, *On a Fresh Revision of the English New Testament*, 3rd ed. (London and New York: Macmillan, 1891 [1872]), 108, cited in his *Notes on the Epistles of St. Paul* (London, 1895), 291.

[64] Moo, *Romans*, 343.

his death? We were buried therefore with him by baptism into death, in order that, just as Christ was raised from the dead by the glory of the Father, we too might walk in newness of life.

For if we have been united with him in a death like his, we shall certainly be united with him in a resurrection like his. We know that our old self was crucified with him in order that the body of sin might be brought to nothing, so that we would no longer be enslaved to sin. For one who has died has been set free from sin. Now if we have died with Christ, we believe that we will also live with him. We know that Christ, being raised from the dead, will never die again; death no longer has dominion over him. For the death he died he died to sin, once for all, but the life he lives he lives to God. So you also must consider yourselves dead to sin and alive to God in Christ Jesus.

Let not sin therefore reign in your mortal body, to make you obey its passions. Do not present your members to sin as instruments for unrighteousness, but present yourselves to God as those who have been brought from death to life, and your members to God as instruments for righteousness. For sin will have no dominion over you, since you are not under law but under grace.

The union with Christ implied in Romans 5:12–21 becomes explicit in 6:1–11. As a basis for why believers should no longer live in sin but rather live for righteousness, Paul refers to the participation of believers in the redemptive events of Christ's death and resurrection. Using baptism as a symbol for our "conversion-initiation" into the Christian life,[65] Paul makes an exact correspondence between those who were baptized into Christ and those who were baptized into his death: ὅσοι ἐβαπτίσθημεν . . . ἐβαπτίσθημεν (v. 3; cf. Gal. 3:27). Paul speaks of believers being buried with Christ (συνετάφημεν . . . αὐτῷ) through baptism into death (διὰ τοῦ βαπτίσματος εἰς τὸν θάνατον), so that just as Christ was raised from the dead, we too might walk in newness of life (καινότητι ζωῆς; Rom. 6:4).[66] Why? Because our union with Christ straddles his death *and* resurrection, verse 5: "For if we have been united with him in a death like his [εἰ γὰρ σύμφυτοι γεγόναμεν τῷ ὁμοιώματι τοῦ θανάτου αὐτοῦ], we shall certainly be united with him in a resurrection like his [ἀλλὰ καὶ τῆς ἀναστάσεως ἐσόμεθα]." And, Paul notes that our union with Christ in his death (εἰ δὲ

---

[65] A term borrowed from James Dunn, *Baptism in the Holy Spirit*, SBT 15 (London: SCM, 1970), 145.

[66] The "time" of this dying and rising with Christ in some sense transcends time. The transition from death to life, old age to new age, occurred through the redemptive work of Christ on Good Friday and Easter Sunday, but the reality of this transition occurs only during the lifetime of individual believers (Moo, *Romans*, 365).

ἀπεθάνομεν σὺν Χριστῷ) leads to the hope of living with him in the future (καὶ συζήσομεν αὐτῷ; v. 8). In sum: for Paul, believers were united with Christ in his death and resurrection. Our union with him is what brings about our own spiritual death and resurrection. Paul reiterates this in another text relevant to our discussion.

2 CORINTHIANS 5:14–21

> For the love of Christ controls us, because we have concluded this: that one has died for all, therefore all have died; and he died for all, that those who live might no longer live for themselves but for him who for their sake died and was raised.
>
> From now on, therefore, we regard no one according to the flesh. Even though we once regarded Christ according to the flesh, we regard him thus no longer. Therefore, if anyone is in Christ, he is a new creation. The old has passed away; behold, the new has come. All this is from God, who through Christ reconciled us to himself and gave us the ministry of reconciliation; that is, in Christ God was reconciling the world to himself, not counting their trespasses against them, and entrusting to us the message of reconciliation. Therefore, we are ambassadors for Christ, God making his appeal through us. We implore you on behalf of Christ, be reconciled to God. For our sake he made him to be sin who knew no sin, so that in him we might become the righteousness of God.

Similar to Romans 6:1–11, Paul hints here of the union of believers with Christ at his death, and implies that this union effects the death of sinners to themselves: "one has died for all, therefore all have died" (εἷς ὑπὲρ πάντων ἀπέθανεν, ἄρα οἱ πάντες ἀπέθανον; 2 Cor. 5:14). Since most commentators and scholars agree that all three uses of πάντες in verses 14–15 are coextensive, the exact referent of πάντες not need detain us for now.[67] It is perhaps overfocus on the referent of πάντες in verses 14–15 that misses the simple meaning of the text, which turns on the conjunction ἄρα. Taking the conjunction in its consequential sense, we see that all those for whom Christ died[68] died to themselves *because of* Christ's death for them (v. 14). In the light of the ethical focus in verse 15, this seems the best reading of the aorist verb

---

[67] As I noted in my previous chapter, two observations suggest that the three successive uses of πάντες are all coextensive. The definite article (οἱ) before πάντες in verse 14b is anaphoric, pointing back to the πάντες of verse 14a; and, whether one takes καί as epexegetic or conjunctive in verse 15a, the following phrase ὑπὲρ πάντων ἀπέθανεν is identical in sense to verse 14a.

[68] The preposition ὑπέρ may have the general sense of representation ("for the benefit of, on behalf of") or substitution ("in the place of"). Drawing too sharp a distinction between these options seems unwarranted. See Murray J. Harris, *The Second Epistle to the Corinthians*, NIGTC (Grand Rapids, MI: Eerdmans, 2005), 421.

ἀπέθανον in verse 14b. "The death of one was the death of all,"[69] so that all who died might live for Another.

To make such a claim here, Paul *assumes* a union of believers with Christ in his death and in his resurrection.[70] The purpose of Christ's death is in order that (ἵνα) those for whom he died would no longer live for themselves (οἱ ζῶντες μηκέτι ἑαυτοῖς ζῶσιν) but (ἀλλά) for him who died and rose again for them (τῷ ὑπὲρ αὐτῶν ἀποθανόντι καὶ ἐγερθέντι). Admittedly, ἵνα "introduces an intended result, not an automatic outcome,"[71] but when verse 15 is read in correspondence with Romans 6:4–5, it is hard to reconcile how in Paul's soteriology there can be those who died with Christ but who are *not* raised with him to walk in newness of life and to live for him. Paul even goes so far as to say that if anyone is "in Christ" (ἐν Χριστῷ) he is a new creation (καινὴ κτίσις): the old has gone (τὰ ἀρχαῖα παρῆλθεν), the new has come (ἰδοὺ γέγονεν καινά; 2 Cor. 5:17). This is so precisely because those "in Christ" were united with him in his death *and* resurrection.[72] Christ's death-and-resurrection work was so potent in force that it effected a new creation in redemptive history, one that is appropriated to those united to him by faith during their lifetime experience.[73]

SUMMARY

We have seen that Christ's atonement is life-and-death decisive for those "in him" as their representative and as their substitute: "in this regard, 'for us,' 'for our sins,' and 'in him,' 'with him' are correlative and inseparable; the former functions only within the bond indicated by the latter."[74] That is to say, in Paul's soteriology, Christ's death *for* people cannot be viewed in separation from his union *with* those same people: "ὑπέρ is not without σύν and σύν is not without ὑπέρ."[75] Attending to this vital union between Christ and his people explains the potent efficacy of Christ's death, an efficacy

---

[69] Charles Hodge, *Commentary on the Second Epistle to the Corinthians* (Grand Rapids, MI: Eerdmans, 1953), 136.

[70] Interestingly, this verse has been neglected in Constantine R. Campbell's otherwise comprehensive treatment of union with Christ (*Paul and Union with Christ: An Exegetical and Theological Study* [Grand Rapids, MI: Zondervan, 2013]).

[71] Harris, *Second Corinthians*, 423.

[72] The phrase ἐν Χριστῷ should not be overlooked, and counters statements such as "all humanity is bound up with him, he died for all humanity and all humanity died in him" (T. F. Torrance, *The Atonement: The Person and Work of Christ* [Downers Grove, IL: IVP Academic, 2009], 183).

[73] Vos, *Pauline Eschatology*, 47: "There has been created a totally new environment, or, more accurately speaking, a totally new world, in which the person spoken of is an inhabitant and participator."

[74] Richard B. Gaffin, *By Faith, Not By Sight: Paul and the Order of Salvation* (Carlisle, UK: Paternoster: 2006), 36.

[75] W. T. Hahn, *Das Mitsterben und Mitauferstehen mit Christus bei Paulus: Ein Beitrag zum Problem der Gleichzeitigkeit des Christen mit Christus* (Gütersloh, Germany: C. Bertelsmann, 1937), 147, cited and translated in Gaffin, *Resurrection and Redemption*, 58.

in which redemption accomplished not only secures all the resources for redemption applied, but also guarantees the outcome of redemption consummated.[76]

Union with Christ as Key to Paul's Soteriology

Union with Christ is "the central truth of salvation for Paul, the key soteriological reality comprising all others."[77] In Paul, union with Christ does not just attend the moment of redemption accomplished; it traverses all four moments of God's saving work. In redemption predestined, we were chosen "in Christ" (Eph. 1:4; 2 Tim. 1:9); in redemption accomplished, we died "with Christ" (Rom. 6:5–6; Gal. 2:20) and were raised "with him" (Rom. 6:5–6; 2 Cor. 5:14–15); in redemption applied, we who were dead were made alive together "with Christ," raised "with him" and seated "with him" in heavenly places (Eph. 2:5–6); and, mysteriously, the Christ who was "outside us" now lives in us by faith (Col. 1:27); in redemption consummated, we will finally be "with Christ" (2 Cor. 5:8; Phil. 1:23; Col. 3:4).[78] These are distinct dimensions of the one single union with Christ. The dimensions are never to be separated from one another—arguably, it is this one union with Christ which unites the four moments of redemption together—but they are also to be held as distinct, with one not being collapsed into the other. For example, although Paul affirms that believers were elected "in Christ" (Eph. 1:4), we still needed to die "with Christ" and rise again "with him" (Rom. 6:3–5); until we believed, we were outside of Christ as "children of wrath" (Eph. 2:3), before being seated "with Christ" in heavenly places by faith (Eph. 2:6); and while we enjoy the status of "Christ in us" (Col. 1:27), we still hope for the day of being "with Christ" in person (Phil. 1:23).

In sum: Paul's soteriology is set on an eschatological canvas in which he presents four distinct-but-inseparable moments of God's saving work *in Christ*. Union with Christ distinguishes and connects these four moments together, and guarantees the efficacy of Christ's atoning work. As with the moments of redemption, so in union with Christ there is distinction in unity and unity in distinction.

---

[76] When I speak of the "efficacy" of the atonement, I do not mean to suggest that it is a potent "substance" or "force," but rather that it is *personally* powerful. That is, its power resides in the person who performed it.

[77] Gaffin, *By Faith, Not By Sight*, 36, who notes that the concept stems from the OT description of God being the "portion" of his people (Ps. 73:26; 119:57; Jer. 10:16) and, reciprocally, they being his "portion" (Deut. 32:9) (35).

[78] In respect to union with Christ, Gaffin refers to the first three moments as predestinarian, redemptive-historical, and existential (*By Faith, Not By Sight*, 37).

THEOLOGICAL REFLECTIONS:
UNION WITH CHRIST AND THE ATONEMENT

Affirming union with Christ as central to Paul's soteriology provides clarity on a number of key aspects of Christ's atonement:

(1) *Affirming the distinct-but-inseparable dimensions of the one union with Christ counters collapsing one aspect into another, as is the case in Karl Barth's theology.* Barth's presentation of faith as "awakening" to a reality that already belongs to the sinner[79] has the potential to eliminate the Pauline distinctions of being outside of Christ at one time and of being united with Christ through faith at a later point in time. In this regard, Barth has failed to maintain the distinct, *temporal* dimensions of the one union with Christ. For Paul, faith is that instrumental means by which the sinner experiences a realm transfer: he who was elected in Christ before time began (Eph. 1:4; 2 Tim. 1:9) was nevertheless outside of Christ at one point in his life (Eph. 2:1–3; cf. Rom. 16:7, by inference), before being united with Christ by faith at his conversion (Eph. 2:5–8; Col. 3:3).

(2) *Union with Christ counters attempts to force a disjunction between redemption accomplished and redemption applied, which in turn necessarily render the efficacy of Christ's death contingent upon faith.* Because Christ was united to his people in his death, talk of "potentiality" or "conditionality" in relation to the atonement is entirely inadequate, since it makes the effectiveness of the atonement dependent upon faith, either synergistic faith (as in Semi-Pelagianism and Arminianism)[80] or God-elected, monergistic faith (as in Amyraldianism and Hypothetical Universalism)—but either way, *human* faith. On the first construct, faith as it were "taps into" the atonement, or even serves as a "catalyst" for its activation;[81] on the second construct, election to faith works on a theological "track" disconnected

---

[79] Cf. Barth, *CD* IV/1, 751; *CD* IV/2, 554; *CD* IV/3.2, 486–97.

[80] This synergistic faith may take one of two forms: either a symmetrical synergism (equal cooperation between God and man's *free* will) as in Semi-Pelagianism, or an asymmetrical synergism (non-resisting, permissive cooperation of man's will which is already *freed* through God's prevenient grace) as in classic Arminianism. For this important distinction, see Olson, *Arminian Theology*, 158–78, esp. 164–66.

[81] So Olson, *Arminian Theology*, 222: "Arminians believe that Christ's death on the cross provided *possible* salvation for everyone, but it is *actualized* only when humans accept it through repentance and faith." I am not accusing Arminians of grounding salvation *in* faith; rather, the issue is whether faith is what *makes* the atonement effective. There is a distinction.

from the atonement.[82] Whichever option one chooses, one cannot escape the fact that each scheme ultimately renders the atonement impotent to save: Christ's acquisition of salvation is left *in suspenso* until a *human* condition is fulfilled.[83] Such a position not only smacks of anthropocentricism—"The center of gravity has been shifted from Christ and located in the Christian. Faith is the true reconciliation with God."[84]—but it is also contrary to the view that Christ's death is *effective* substitutionary atonement. As seen in Romans 5:12–21, Christ's redemptive work overcame the powerful effects of Adam's fall—sin and death; how much less, then, could a human will— whether free from birth or freed by prevenient grace—resist the dynamism of Christ's work fulfilling its intended purpose? Moreover, in contrast to Amyraldianism, as seen earlier in some Pauline texts (Eph. 1:4; 5:27; Gal. 1:4; 2 Tim. 1:9–11), election and the atonement do not operate on separate theological tracks: the former circumscribes the latter. And what God has joined together, let no one separate.

(3) *Affirming union with Christ at the moment of redemption accomplished counters any disjunction between the effect of Christ's substitutionary death and the effect of his resurrection*, as if Christ's death might lead to the spiritual death of some sinners, but not also to their resurrection to new life.[85] To suggest such a separation is to cause serious injury to Paul's doctrine of redemption accomplished. As Richard Gaffin helpfully states, "Strictly speaking, not Christ's death, but his resurrection (that is, his exaltation), marks the completion of the once-for-all accomplishment of redemption."[86] This is not

---

[82] So Lewis Sperry Chafer, *Systematic Theology, Volume III* (Dallas: Dallas Seminary Press, 1948), 187: "The highway of divine election is quite apart from the highway of redemption."

[83] So, for example, Amyraut wrote, "This will to render the grace of salvation universal and common to all human beings is so conditional that without the fulfilment of the condition it is entirely inefficacious" ("Ceste volonté de rendre la grace du salut vniuerselle & cómune à tous les humains estant tellement conditionnelle, que sans l'accomplissement de la condition, elle est entierement inefficacieuse") (Moïse Amyraut, *Brief Traitté de la Predestination et de ses principales dependances* [Saumur, France: Jean Lesnier & Isaac Debordes, 1634], 90). Although classic Arminianism posits prevenient grace *prior* to faith, it also cannot evade the charge that Christ's atonement is provisional and contingent and thus ultimately impotent, since even the *freed* will of man may still *resist* the efficacy of God's regenerative work that flows from the atonement (see James Arminius, "Declaration of Sentiments," *Works*, 1:659–60). Cf. also I. Howard Marshall, "Predestination in the New Testament," in *Grace Unlimited*, ed. Clark H. Pinnock (Minneapolis: Bethany Fellowship, 1975), 140: "The effect of the call of God is to place man in a position where he can say 'Yes' or 'No' (which he could not do before God called him; till then he was in a continuous attitude of 'No')."

[84] Herman Bavinck, *Sin and Salvation in Christ*, vol. 3 of *Reformed Dogmatics*, ed. John Bolt, trans. John Vriend, 4 vols. (Grand Rapids, MI: Baker, 2006), 469.

[85] Contra Harris, *Second Corinthians*, 421: "while all persons 'died' when Christ died, not all rose to new life when he rose from the dead." For Harris, "this death may be the death deservedly theirs because of sin, or an objective 'ethical' death that must be appropriated subjectively by individual faith, or a collective participation in the event of Christ's death by which sin's power was destroyed" (422).

[86] Gaffin, *Resurrection and Redemption*, 116.

to equate inseparability with indistinguishability. Christ's death and resurrection are *distinct* events in the life of Christ and the believer; but, to be faithful to Paul, there can be no *disjunction* between them: "if we have been united with him in a death like his, we shall certainly be united with him in a resurrection like his" (Rom. 6:5). There is more than mere analogy at play here.[87] As Sinclair Ferguson writes, "If we are united to Christ, then we are united to him at all points of his activity on our behalf."[88]

(4) *Being united with Christ means that Christ's substitutionary atonement is a* representative *atonement and not merely a bare "instead of" atonement.* To treat Christ's death as the latter is to view Christ as an arbitrary individual—albeit as the Son of God—who died for no one in particular because he had no intrinsic relationship with those for whom he died. In this case, he is no different from a substitute in a sport's game. Respecting union with Christ, however, means that Christ died as a *representative* substitute, one who was joined in his person to those for whom he died, with all his roles and offices at play. Christ died as a public man, not a private man. That is, Christ died as King for his people, as Husband for his bride, as Head for his body, as Shepherd for his sheep, as Master for his friends, as Firstborn for his brothers and sisters, as the Second and Last Adam for a new humanity.[89] As Murray put it, "Christ Jesus cannot be contemplated apart from his work nor his work apart from him."[90] This is what makes Christ's death efficacious substitutionary atonement, because, being united with his people, Christ died as *Someone*, as their representative.

This point carries with it a necessary corollary.

(5) *Union with Christ means that the particularity of the atonement must take place prior to the moment of redemption applied.* If union with Christ traverses all four moments of redemption, then one cannot introduce particularity into the atonement at the point of application.[91] Christ's atoning death is for a particular group of people precisely because it is an "in-union-with"

---

[87] Gaffin, again: "the solidaric tie between the realization of redemption in the life history of the believer and its past, definitive accomplishment is so strong and of such a nature that the former can only be understood and expressed in terms of the latter" (ibid., 59).
[88] Sinclair B. Ferguson, "The Reformed View," in *Christian Spirituality: Five Views of Sanctification*, ed. Donald L. Alexander (Downers Grove, IL: IVP Academic, 1989), 58.
[89] Henri A. G. Blocher, "The Scope of Redemption and Modern Theology," *SBET* 9.2 (1991): 102.
[90] Murray, *Romans*, 214.
[91] Contra Knox, "Some Aspects of the Atonement," 265.

death. The scope of redemption accomplished and redemption applied is therefore necessarily coextensive.[92]

IV. The Saving Work of God in Christ Is Trinitarian

John Webster writes that "Soteriology . . . has its place within the theology of the *mysterium trinitatis*, that is, God's inherent and communicated richness of life as Father, Son and Holy Spirit."[93] Webster's comment cannot be underestimated. A careful reading of the Pauline corpus reveals a tacit Trinitarianism that pervades virtually all of Paul's thought. In particular, he demonstrates a conjoining of Father, Son, and Spirit in the economy of salvation.

PAUL'S DOCTRINE OF THE TRINITY

Three texts stand out in particular for revealing Paul's doctrine of the Trinity, where the triadic pattern is expressed within the reality of the oneness of God. First, in 1 Corinthians 12:4–6, Paul explains that the Spirit's presence among God's people manifests itself in a rich diversity of gifts, a diversity reflected also in the very nature of God: Spirit, Lord, and God (the Father). This diversity should serve the unity of the body, since it is the same Spirit, Lord, and God. Second, this diversity in unity and unity in diversity is expressed in the creedal formulation of Ephesians 4:4–6, where Paul speaks of one Spirit, one Lord, and one Father. Third, the grace-benediction of 2 Corinthians 13:14 presents the activity of the three divine persons in concert. The grace of our Lord Jesus, seen in his death and resurrection for others, manifests the foundational love of God the Father, while the Spirit continually actualizes that love and grace in the life of the believer and the Christian community.[94]

That Trinitarianism is foundational to Paul's soteriology is corroborated by a number of texts in which Paul formulates his doctrine of salvation in Trinitarian terms, both implicitly and explicitly.[95] We may divide these into

---

[92] Contra Harris, *Second Corinthians*, 423: "There is universalism in the scope of redemption, since no person is excluded from God's offer of salvation; but there is a particularity in the application of redemption, since not everyone appropriates the benefits afforded by this universally offered salvation"; or Bruce A. Demarest, *The Cross and Salvation: The Doctrine of Salvation*, Foundations of Evangelical Theology (Wheaton, IL: Crossway, 1997), 193: "Christ . . . provided salvation for more people than those to whom he purposed to apply its saving benefits."
[93] Webster, "It Was the Will of the Lord," 20.
[94] Gordon D. Fee, *Pauline Christology: An Exegetical-Theological Study* (Peabody, MA: Hendrickson, 2007), 592.
[95] See soteriological passages such as Romans 8:3–4, 15–17; 1 Corinthians 6:11; 2 Corinthians 1:21–22; Galatians 4:4–7; 1 Thessalonians 1:4–6; 2 Thessalonians 2:13–14; Titus 3:4–7. Gordon D. Fee, *God's Empowering Presence: The Holy Spirit in the Letters of Paul* (Peabody, MA: Hendrickson, 1994), 48 n. 39, lists many other such texts, soteriological or otherwise: Romans 5:5–8; 8:9–11; 15:16–19, 30; 1 Corinthians 1:4–7; 2:4–5, 12; 6:19–20; 2 Corinthians 3:16–18; Galatians 3:1–5; Ephesians 1:3, 17–20; 2:17–22; 3:16–19; 5:18–19; Philippians 1:19–20; 3:3; Colossians 3:16. For an unpacking of some of these, see ibid., 841–42.

triadic texts (that is, Father, Son, and Spirit texts) and dyadic texts (that is, Father and Son texts and Son and Spirit texts). There is obvious overlap between some of them.

TRIADIC TEXTS: FATHER, SON, AND SPIRIT

Galatians 4:4–6

> But when the fullness of time had come, God sent forth his Son, born of woman, born under the law, to redeem those who were under the law, so that we might receive adoption as sons. And because you are sons, God has sent the Spirit of his Son into our hearts, crying, "Abba! Father!"

This passage provides an excellent example of the "Trinity-in-unity" at work in our salvation. The repetition of the phrase ἐξαπέστειλεν ὁ θεός ("God sent") with the respective objective clauses τὸν υἱὸν αὐτοῦ ("his Son") and τὸ πνεῦμα τοῦ υἱοῦ αὐτοῦ ("the Spirit of his Son"; vv. 4, 6) reveals the profound Trinitarianism in Paul's economy of salvation. God the Father sends his two Emissaries to accomplish and apply redemption: the Son to *redeem us* from under the law (ἵνα τοὺς ὑπὸ νόμον ἐξαγοράσῃ) in order "that we might receive adoption as sons" (ἵνα τὴν υἱοθεσίαν ἀπολάβωμεν); and the Spirit to *be in our hearts* (εἰς τὰς καρδίας ἡμῶν) so that as sons we might cry, "Abba! Father!" (κρᾶζον, αββα ὁ πατήρ).[96] The obedience of Son and Spirit to the Father ensures harmony of purpose: the "circle" of salvation that starts with the Father in sending the Son and the Spirit closes in communion with him as newly adopted sons cry, "Abba! Father!" It is notable also, that while the Son is designated simply as God's Son (τὸν υἱὸν αὐτοῦ), the Spirit sent from the Father is the Spirit of the Son (τὸ πνεῦμα τοῦ υἱοῦ αὐτοῦ), which implies that the Father's sending of the Spirit is in cooperation with the Son, whose Spirit he is.[97]

Romans 8:1–11

> There is therefore now no condemnation for those who are in Christ Jesus. For the law of the Spirit of life has set you free in Christ Jesus from the law of sin and death. For God has done what the law, weakened by the flesh, could not do. By sending his own Son in the likeness of sinful flesh and for

---

[96] While the participle κρᾶζον ("crying") is directly related to the Spirit (either as an attributive participle explaining what the Spirit does, or as an adverbial participle indicating the purpose or result of the main verb ἐξαπέστειλεν), few would dispute that the Spirit's cry here also becomes the believer's cry (cf. Rom. 8:15).

[97] Acts 2:33 reveals a similar triadic pattern in relation to the Spirit's outpouring: having been exalted to the right hand of God the Father (τῇ δεξιᾷ οὖν τοῦ θεοῦ ὑψωθείς), the Son receives from the Father (λαβὼν παρὰ τοῦ πατρός) the promise of the Holy Spirit (τήν τε ἐπαγγελίαν τοῦ πνεύματος τοῦ ἁγίου), whom he then pours out (ἐξέχεεν) at Pentecost.

sin, he condemned sin in the flesh, in order that the righteous requirement of the law might be fulfilled in us, who walk not according to the flesh but according to the Spirit. For those who live according to the flesh set their minds on the things of the flesh, but those who live according to the Spirit set their minds on the things of the Spirit. For to set the mind on the flesh is death, but to set the mind on the Spirit is life and peace. For the mind that is set on the flesh is hostile to God, for it does not submit to God's law; indeed, it cannot. Those who are in the flesh cannot please God.

You, however, are not in the flesh but in the Spirit, if in fact the Spirit of God dwells in you. Anyone who does not have the Spirit of Christ does not belong to him. But if Christ is in you, although the body is dead because of sin, the Spirit is life because of righteousness. If the Spirit of him who raised Jesus from the dead dwells in you, he who raised Christ Jesus from the dead will also give life to your mortal bodies through his Spirit who dwells in you.

This passage is similar to Galatians 4:4–6 in that it begins with the initiative of God the Father to save and ends with adopted sons of God crying, "Abba! Father!"—and all through the cooperative work of the Son and the Spirit. In Romans 8:1–11, the work of the Spirit and the Son are closely conjoined as together they perform God's salvation for sinners: the law of the Spirit of life (νόμος[98] τοῦ πνεύματος τῆς ζωῆς) sets us free (ἠλευθέρωσέν) in Christ Jesus (ἐν Χριστῷ ᾿Ιησοῦ)[99] from the law of sin and death (ἀπὸ τοῦ νόμου τῆς ἁμαρτίας καὶ τοῦ θανάτου; v. 2). The Son and the Spirit serve the Father in the economy of salvation: by sending the Son "in the likeness of sinful flesh and for sin" (ἐν ὁμοιώματι σαρκὸς ἁμαρτίας καὶ περὶ ἁμαρτίας), God the Father "condemned sin in the flesh" (κατέκρινεν τὴν ἁμαρτίαν ἐν τῇ σαρκί; v. 3)—redemption accomplished. He did this "in order that the righteous requirement of the law might be fulfilled in us, who walk not according to the flesh but according to the Spirit" (τοῖς μὴ κατὰ σάρκα περιπατοῦσιν ἀλλὰ κατὰ πνεῦμα; v. 4)—redemption applied. Thus we see the Son and the Spirit working in harmony at the Father's bidding in both moments of redemption. Of particular focus in this passage is the Spirit, who is essential to salvation: "Anyone who does not have the Spirit of Christ does not belong to him [Christ]" (v. 9). But if Christ is in us (εἰ δὲ Χριστὸς ἐν ὑμῖν), then "the Spirit is life" (πνεῦμα ζωή) in us (v. 10), and if the Spirit lives in us (εἰ δὲ τὸ πνεῦμα . . . οἰκεῖ ἐν ὑμῖν), then God, who raised Christ from the dead (ὁ ἐγείρας

---

[98] The best interpretation of νόμος here is probably "principle," "binding authority," or "power" (Moo, *Romans*, 474).
[99] The prepositional phrase is best read in relation to the verb ἠλευθέρωσέν rather than in relation to the genitive phrase τῆς ζωῆς, and carries an instrumental force.

Χριστὸν ἐκ νεκρῶν), will give life to our mortal bodies through his Spirit who dwells in us (διὰ τοῦ ἐνοικοῦντος αὐτοῦ πνεύματος ἐν ὑμῖν; v. 11). This is all so because the Spirit is the "Spirit of God" (πνεῦμα θεοῦ) and the "Spirit of Christ" (πνεῦμα Χριστοῦ; v. 9), and thus the Father and Son cannot act without the accompaniment of the Spirit.

Titus 3:4–6

> But when the goodness and loving kindness of God our Savior appeared, he saved us, not because of works done by us in righteousness, but according to his own mercy, by the washing of regeneration and renewal of the Holy Spirit, whom he poured out on us richly through Jesus Christ our Savior . . .

This text also reveals that all three persons of the Trinity are active in God's salvation, working in the moments of redemption accomplished and redemption applied. To paraphrase the text, when (ὅτε) God the Father's goodness and loving kindness to mankind appeared (ἐπεφάνη) (in the Son's death and resurrection; v. 4),[100] the Father saved us (ἔσωσεν) through (διά) the regenerating and renewing work of the Holy Spirit (λουτροῦ παλιγγενεσίας καὶ ἀνακαινώσεως πνεύματος ἁγίου; v. 5), whom the Father poured (ἐξέχεεν) out on us through (διά) the Son, Jesus Christ our Savior (Ἰησοῦ Χριστοῦ τοῦ σωτῆρος ἡμῶν; v. 6). The work of redemption here is a work of Father, Son, and Spirit, each working in harmony to achieve salvation. This can be seen most clearly in relation to the administration of the Spirit: as the subject of ἐξέχεεν, the Father is the primary agent in pouring out the Spirit, but he does so through (διά) the intermediate agency of the Son.[101] The christological implications are obvious,[102] but equally profound is the fact that Father, Son, and Spirit are all of one mind in applying redemption.

Dyadic Text: Father and Son

2 Timothy 1:9–10

> . . . who saved us and called us to a holy calling, not because of our works but because of his own purpose and grace, which he gave us in Christ Jesus before the ages began, and which now has been manifested through the

---

[100] As I mentioned earlier, "when" and "appeared" refer to Christ's first appearance (cf. Titus 2:13–14; Knight, *Pastoral Epistles*, 339).

[101] That the Son is involved in the administration of the Spirit is unsurprising when read in the context of other texts where Paul refers to the Spirit as the Spirit of Christ (Rom. 8:9; 2 Cor. 3:17; Gal. 4:6; Phil. 1:19).

[102] While elsewhere the Father is designated with the title of "Savior" (σωτῆρος; e.g., Titus 1:3; 3:4), here the Son is designated "Savior" (σωτῆρος).

appearing of our Savior Christ Jesus, who abolished death and brought life
and immortality to light through the gospel . . .

This is an example of a dyadic text in which the works of Father and Son are
conjoined. God the Father (θεοῦ) saved (σώσαντος) and called (καλέσαντος)
us according to his own (ἰδίαν) purpose and grace (πρόθεσιν καὶ χάριν),
a pre-temporal election that was given to us in his Son, Jesus Christ (τὴν
δοθεῖσαν ἡμῖν ἐν Χριστῷ Ἰησοῦ; v. 9). Then, in history, the Son incarnate,
Jesus Christ our Savior (τοῦ σωτῆρος ἡμῶν Χριστοῦ Ἰησοῦ), manifested
(φανερωθεῖσαν) the Father's gracious electing purpose (v. 10). So what the
Father purposes, the Son manifests—and therefore their work must carry the
same extent.

DISTINCT-BUT-INSEPARABLE ROLES IN THE TRINITY

While the analysis above demonstrates that Scripture testifies to the *harmony*
of purpose within the triune Godhead, it is important to also respect the
distinct roles of each person in the Godhead as they bring about the saving
purposes of God. Put simply: for Paul,

> human redemption is the combined activity of Father, Son, and Spirit, in
> that (1) it is predicated on the love of God, whose love sets it in motion;
> (2) it is effected historically through the death and resurrection of Christ
> the Son; and (3) it is actualized in the life of believers through the power
> of the Holy Spirit.[103]

This much is true, but John Owen provides a necessary qualification. When
one of the persons of the Trinity acts *"principally,* immediately, and by way
of eminency" in his distinct role it is never exclusive in relation to the other
persons of the Trinity; when one person of the Trinity acts, the others are not
somehow absent or passive or mere spectators.[104] The roles of each person in
the Trinity are not interchangeable, but neither are they independent.

In the moment of redemption predestined, while we were elected "in
Christ," God's Son, and predestined for adoption as sons "through Christ
Jesus," the Father was the primary agent in choosing us (Eph. 1:4–5). In the

---

[103] Fee, *Pauline Christology*, 589.
[104] John Owen, *Of Communion with God the Father, Son, and Holy Spirit, Each Person Distinctly, in Love, Grace, and Consolation* in *The Works of John Owen*, ed. W. H. Goold, 24 vols. (Edinburgh: Johnstone & Hunter, 1850-1853; repr., Edinburgh: Banner of Truth, 1967), 2:18: "When I assign any thing as *peculiar* wherein we distinctly hold communion with any person, I do not exclude the other persons from communion with the soul in the very same thing."

moment of redemption accomplished, while it was the Son who came in the likeness of sinful flesh, it was the Father who sent him (Rom. 8:3), and the Spirit who vindicated his appearance in the flesh (1 Tim. 3:16); and while the Son gave himself for our sins (Gal. 1:4; 2:20; Eph. 5:2, 25; 1 Tim. 2:6; Titus 2:14), it was the Father who set him forth as a propitiation (Rom. 3:25).[105] The Son secured our reconciliation (Rom. 5:9–11), but the initiative came from the Father (Rom. 5:8) in the power of the Spirit who raised Christ from the dead (Rom. 1:4; 8:11). *Ubi Filius, ibi Pater et Spiritus.*

In the moment of redemption applied, we were able to receive the promised Spirit through faith only because the Son incarnate became a curse for us (Gal. 3:13–14); the regenerative action of the Spirit occurred through the Son's work as Savior (Titus 3:5–6); and when the Spirit is active in us, it is the Father's love that he pours into our hearts when we trust in the Son (Rom. 5:1, 5). Elements of redemption applied—washing, sanctification, and justification—occur through the double agency of Jesus and the Spirit of God (1 Cor. 6:11). The Spirit's working in harmony with the Father and Son in both redemption accomplished and redemption applied makes sense given that he is the "Spirit of God" and the "Spirit of Christ" (Rom. 8:9): he is the agent through whom we belong to Christ (Rom. 8:9) and through whom God will give life to our mortal bodies (Rom. 8:11). *Ubi Spiritus, ibi Pater et Filius.*

God the Father's activity straddles the moments of redemption accomplished and applied: in the one, he sends his Son to redeem us from under the law (Gal. 4:4–5); in the other, he sends his Spirit to ensure our adoption as sons (Gal. 4:6). While the Son is prominent in redemption accomplished and the Spirit in redemption applied, neither is passive or absent from the other in either moment of salvation; and both perform their roles at the bidding of the Father. Sanders provides a neat summary that encapsulates the point:

> Christ the Son accomplishes redemption in his own (Spirit-created and Spirit-filled) work. The Holy Spirit applies that finished redemption to us in his own (Son-directed and Son-forming) work. The two works are held together by an inherent unity. The Son and the Spirit are both at work in both phases; nevertheless, the Son takes the lead in accomplishment, and the Spirit takes the lead in application.[106]

---

[105] Hebrews 9:14 speaks of the Son offering himself to the Father through the eternal Spirit. See Peter T. O'Brien, *The Letter to the Hebrews*, PNTC (Nottingham, UK: Apollos, 2010), 324, for a defense of πνεύματος αἰωνίου as a reference to the Holy Spirit, among other options.

[106] Sanders, *Deep Things of God*, 142.

And again,

> So the Son is active in applying redemption, but he acts by equipping the Spirit to do the application. They are always mutually implicated, though in each phase one of them sets the other one up to take the leading role. Just as Christ (enabled by the Spirit) accomplished redemption, so the Spirit (making Christ present in faith) applies it. Nowhere in the twofold economy is there a simple departure or complete absence of one of the agents. We are always in the Father's two hands at once.[107]

In short: "The Spirit serves the Son by applying what he accomplished, and the Son serves the Spirit by making his indwelling possible. Both Son and Spirit, together on their twofold mission from the Father, serve the Father and minister to us."[108] *Ubi Pater, ibi Filius et Spiritus.*

The Economic Trinity Reflects the Immanent Trinity

The "processions" seen here in the economic Trinity in Galatians 4:4–6 arise from the immanent (ontological) Trinity, from God *in se*. In other words, who God is in the history of redemption arises from who God is in himself. His act reflects his being. And if God's being lives in harmony—three persons in one God and one God in three persons mutually cohering and complementing each other—then when the same God acts in history in the economy of salvation, we should expect nothing less than the same harmony of purpose and love. As Augustine put it: *opera trinitatis ad extra indivisa sunt*: "the Father, and the Son, and the Holy Spirit, as they are indivisible, so they work indivisibly."[109] From redemption predestined to redemption consummated, our salvation is encompassed by the triune God.

Theological Reflections: The Trinity and the Atonement

The saving work of God in Christ is Trinitarian. "Christian salvation comes from the Trinity, happens through the Trinity, and brings us home to the Trinity."[110] More specifically, the works of the Trinity in the economy of salvation are indivisible. That is, the works of Father, Son, and Spirit are distinct but inseparable. Each person performs specific roles in the plan of salvation,

---

[107] Ibid., 148. Sanders's reference to the Father's "two hands" is taken from Irenaeus.
[108] Ibid., 149.
[109] Augustine, *On the Trinity*, in *NPNF*[1] 3:17–228 (20).
[110] Sanders, *Deep Things of God*, 10.

but never in isolation from the others. What follows from this is that each person works together for a common goal—to save sinners. Christ's intention in dying was to make atonement for all those whom the Father had chosen in him before the foundation of the world and to send his Spirit in time upon elect individuals to apply that redemption to them.

The Trinity and Christ's Intention in Dying

Affirming that the persons of the Trinity work together in harmony in the economy of salvation just as they relate to God *in se*—"The eternal Trinity is the gospel Trinity"[111]—provides significant theological force to Paul's purpose statements in relation to Christ's atonement. Frequently in Paul, mention of Christ's death is accompanied by a purpose clause (ἵνα/ὅπως) to express the goal for which Christ died. He died so that people would no longer live for themselves (2 Cor. 5:15); to make us spiritually rich (2 Cor. 8:9); "to deliver us from the present evil age" (Gal. 1:3); to redeem those under the law, "so that we might receive adoption as sons" (Gal. 4:5–6); to sanctify his church and present her to himself without spot or wrinkle, holy and blameless (Eph. 5:25–27); to redeem us from lawlessness and purify a people for himself (Titus 2:14). In the light of the tacit Trinitarianism observed, the purpose clauses in these soteriological texts take on a whole new significance: they are not expressing wishful thinking in the form of a purpose clause—an unrealized potential; rather, they demonstrate a primary, intended goal that *will* be realized. If the triune God—Father, Son, and Holy Spirit—are for these ends, who then can be against them?

Such a perspective illuminates the intentionality of the atonement and provides some resources for answering the dilemma as to whether the extent of redemption accomplished can be wider than redemption applied (as in Semi-Pelagianism, Arminianism, and Amyraldianism), or as to whether there can be twin intentions of the Trinity within the economy of salvation (as in some forms of Hypothetical Universalism). All sides affirm that the saving work of God in Christ is Trinitarian.[112] However, it is one thing to say that the Trinity is at work in the economy of salvation; it is another thing to affirm that the intent and scope of each person's work is the same in the economy of salvation. The issue

---

[111] Ibid., 156.

[112] For example, James Arminius spoke of the *pactum salutis*, and Amyraut and Hypothetical Universalists (such as John Davenant) affirmed a Trinitarian soteriology.

turns not on whether the Trinity is at work; the issue turns on whether the goals and purposes of each person in the Trinity are the same. Taking this into account, a Trinitarian approach moves us toward a doctrine of definite atonement, because, alongside union with Christ, it prohibits any discrepancy between the extent of redemption accomplished and that of redemption applied, and it raises questions over twin intentions in God's economy of salvation.

Trinitarian Problems within a Universal Atonement Scheme

Holding to a universal atonement presents various problems for Trinitarian theology.

DISSONANCE IN THE TRINITY

(SEMI-PELAGIANISM, ARMINIANISM, AND AMYRALDIANISM)

One of the main problems with Semi-Pelagianism, Arminianism, and Amyraldianism is that they introduce dissonance into the Trinity, such that the Son intends to die for all, but the Father elects only some and the Spirit draws only some. When this is done, not only is the atonement severed from election (pitting the Father against the Son), but a disjunction is forced between redemption accomplished and redemption applied (pitting the Son against the Spirit). To opt for this position is to "separate the Father and the Holy Spirit from the Son, when the very essence of God is that there is one purpose in which they are united."[113] This detracts from the indivisible, Trinitarian work of God in Christ: the Father and the Son united in their distinct works within the economy of salvation, as are the Son and the Spirit.[114] Despite protests to the contrary, these various positions on the atonement cannot evade the accusation of a dysfunctional Trinity, where dissonance rather than harmony is the sounding note.

UNDERPERFORMANCE BY THE SPIRIT;

CONFUSION IN THE SON (HYPOTHETICAL UNIVERSALISM)

Hypothetical Universalists evade the accusation above by arguing for a harmonious duality of the roles of Father, Son, and Spirit in the economy

---

[113] Roger R. Nicole, *Our Sovereign Savior: The Essence of the Reformed Faith* (Ross-shire, UK: Christian Focus, 2002), 65.

[114] This latter connection is often missed or neglected. As I have noted, the Spirit is given through the *Son's* authoritative administration at the Father's right hand, and therefore the Spirit's work cannot be more narrow or more expansive than the Son's work. As Paul says in 1 Corinthians 15:45, "the last Adam became a life-giving Spirit"— the most emphatic statement in Paul on the unity and inseparability of the work of the exalted Christ and the Spirit.

of salvation. So, for example, John Davenant argued that the Son had a universal intent that "conformed to the ordination of the Father,"[115] and yet, at the same time, Christ affirmed the particular will of God when he died, for how else could Christ have "exhibited himself as conformed to the eternal appointment of his Father, if, in his saving passion, he had not applied his merits in a peculiar manner infallibly to effect and complete the salvation of the elect?"[116] Curt Daniel presents a contemporary example of the same position:

> There are general and particular aspects about the work of each member of the Trinity. The Father loves all men as creatures, but gives special love only to the elect. The Spirit calls all men, but efficaciously calls only the elect. Similarly, the Son died for all men, but died in a special manner for the elect.[117]

In disagreeing with this position, it should be noted that Paul affirms other intentions in the particular atonement wrought by Christ on the cross (cf. Col. 1:19–20). Nevertheless, what he means by these is different from what Hypothetical Universalists mean. Closer analysis of their position reveals three main problems:

(1) *Despite what some Hypothetical Universalists may argue, the universal intent of the Spirit does not in reality correspond to the universal intent of the Father and the Son.* On the universal axis, the Father intends atonement for all, the Son dies for all and makes provision for all, but the Spirit does not bring the gospel to all. The unevangelized remain a problem for proponents of a universal atonement. In this regard, the Spirit underperforms and in so doing brings disharmony into the Trinity.

(2) *It seems difficult to avoid the fact that in Hypothetical Universalism the Son ends up with a "confused" or "split" personality.* In Hypothetical Universalist presentations, the person and offices of Christ are inadvertently

---

[115] Davenant, "Dissertation," 2:398.
[116] Ibid., 2:542.
[117] Curt Daniel, *The History and Theology of Calvinism* (n.p.: Good Books, 2003), 371. Similar arguments may be found in Gary L. Shultz, Jr., "Why a Genuine Universal Gospel Call Requires an Atonement That Paid for the Sins of All People," *EQ* 82.2 (2010): 118–20; idem, "God's Purposes in the Atonement for the Nonelect," *BSac* 165 (April–June 2008): 152; Robert P. Lightner, *The Death Christ Died: A Biblical Case for Unlimited Atonement*, 2nd ed. (Grand Rapids, MI: Kregel, 1998), 130; Knox, "Some Aspects of the Atonement," 262, 265; and Douty, *Did Christ Die Only for the Elect?*, 60: "A single transaction with a double intention."

divided. They force the conclusion that Christ died for everyone as their "general Savior" to offer an atonement that would never actually atone, yet, at the same time, they propose that Christ died for those united to him in all his offices and roles in order to accomplish an atonement that does actually atone. Not only does this bring into question the definition of "Savior,"[118] but it also presents a confused Christ. Turretin presses the point home:

> As if this was the design of Christ—I wish to obtain redemption for all to the end that it may be applied to them, provided they believe; and yet to multitudes I am resolved neither to reveal this redemption, nor to give those to whom it is revealed that condition without which it can never be applied to them (i.e., I desire that to come to pass which I not only know will not and cannot take place, but also what I am unwilling should take place because I refuse to communicate that without which it can never be brought to pass as it depends upon myself alone). Now if this would not be becoming in a wise man, how much less in Christ, supremely wise and good?[119]

Turretin has a point. In other words, "since Christ could not will to die absolutely for the elect without involving (by the law of contraries) a will not to die for the reprobate, it cannot be conceived how in one act he should will both to die for the reprobate and not to die for them."[120]

By dividing the person and offices of Christ, Hypothetical Universalists inadvertantly distort orthodox christology. In Paul, Christ is presented as Husband (2 Cor. 11:2; cf. Eph. 5:25), Head (Eph. 5:23), Firstborn (Rom. 8:29: Col. 1:15, 18), and Last Adam (Rom. 5:14; 1 Cor. 15:45). This is who the incarnate Son *is*, and therefore when he dies for sinners he dies as no mere private individual but rather as a public man, as Husband, Head, Firstborn, and Last Adam. The work of salvation is the act of his person.[121] In his life, death, resurrection, and ascension, Christ did not lay aside his person or offices or roles at any point. In dying for people on the cross, Christ could not fail to be for all of them who he was.

In short, just as there is no disjunction between the moments of God's

---

[118] If the term "Savior" is to have any meaning at all, Christ *really must* save those for whom he died, otherwise he does not really die for them as their "Savior"; the term itself becomes meaningless.

[119] Francis Turretin, *Institutes of Elenctic Theology*, ed. James T. Dennison, Jr., trans. George Musgrave Giger, 3 vols. (Phillipsburg, NJ: P&R, 1993), 2:467.

[120] Ibid., 460.

[121] T. F. Torrance, *Atonement*, xliv–xlv, agrees that soteriology cannot be divorced from christology, but for him, since Christ is God and man, his work must have reference to all humanity (similarly, Knox, "Some Aspects of the Atonement," 260). But this is a non sequitur. As Donald Macleod, *The Person of Christ* (Downers Grove, IL: InterVarsity Press, 1998), 202, notes: "His humanity is that of Everyman. But he is not Everyman. He is the man, Christ Jesus; and the only humanity united to him hypostatically is his own."

work in Christ, or between the persons of the Trinity within the economy of salvation, so there is no disjunction between christology and soteriology, between the person of Christ and the work of Christ. He is *one* person and never acts in his saving work separate from his person or with any of his offices or roles temporarily defunct.

(3) *The argument for twin levels of intent in the atonement also gives the impression that there exist two "economies" of salvation:* one for the non-elect, for whom God aims only to provide a "potential" atonement, if they were ever to believe; and one for the elect, for whom God provides an "actual" atonement, through Christ securing even the means required to appropriate that atonement. Not only is this problematic in the light of the fact that in Paul's soteriology election circumscribes atonement, but it lacks any textual support in Scripture. In Ephesians 1:10–11, Paul presents God as having one economy of salvation; at no point does he present us with a "hypothetical" economy of salvation that is never realized.

V. The Saving Work of God in Christ Is Doxological

Returning to the Ephesian *berakah* with which this chapter began, I note one final component of Paul's soteriology. Three times the apostle states the ultimate purpose for God's saving acts: "to the praise of his glory" (εἰς ἔπαινον τῆς δόξης αὐτοῦ). It is important to observe where in the paragraph the phrase appears. God the Father elects and predestines us in Christ "to the praise of his glorious grace" (εἰς ἔπαινον δόξης τῆς χάριτος αὐτοῦ; 1:6)— redemption predestined; we obtain an inheritance so that we who were the first to hope in Christ might be "to the praise of his glory" (εἰς ἔπαινον δόξης αὐτοῦ; 1:12)—redemption applied; and we are sealed with the Holy Spirit, who acts as a guarantee for our future inheritance "to the praise of his glory" (εἰς ἔπαινον τῆς δόξης αὐτοῦ; 1:14)—redemption consummated. God's glory accompanies his acts of predestining, applying, and consummating salvation. God saves people—really and truly—for the praise of his own glory. And herein lies the final obstacle, perhaps the biggest obstacle, for advocates of a universal atonement: a salvation intended but never realized can bring God no praise. There is a better option: a definite atonement that displays the indivisible, Trinitarian work of God in Christ whereby sinners are actually saved "to the praise of his glorious grace."

Conclusion

In this chapter I have sought to move beyond the impasse of the textual *quid pro quo* that often ensues between all sides in the debate over the intent and nature of the atonement. I have aimed for integration and synthesis of various texts that concern some of the doctrinal loci which directly impinge upon Paul's atonement theology, and which for too long have been neglected. Two implications follow from my findings.

First, no reasonable discussion of the intent and nature of the atonement can occur without doctrinal loci in Paul's soteriology being brought to the table. Analysis of various Pauline passages reveals that eschatology, election, union with Christ, christology, Trinitarianism, and doxology are significant interrelated components in the lens of the apostle's soteriology. For Paul, the saving work of God is (1) indivisible; (2) circumscribed by God's electing grace; (3) encompassed by union with Christ; (4) Trinitarian; and (5) doxological. When these five doctrinal loci are respected, *as well as the interconnections between them*, then definite atonement emerges as the most plausible position to hold on the intent and nature of the atonement in Paul.[122]

Second, these doctrinal loci in Paul's soteriology must be allowed their voice and influence in any discussion of the universalistic and "perishing" texts in the Pauline corpus. Attending to these doctrinal components in Paul's soteriology provides color and nuance to the interpretation of the particularistic texts, while at the same time providing some theological constraint to (a) the naïve and simplistic interpretation of the universalistic passages where "many," "all," and "world" are taken as "all without exception" in every case, and to (b) the superficial or hasty interpretation of the "perishing" texts where a brother "for whom Christ died" can be saved and then lost. The constraint is not externally imposed by a "Reformed scholastic"; rather, it is present in the fabric of the apostle's own theology. For example, to interpret the universalistic texts as meaning "everyone" not only requires strained exegesis in the respective contexts[123] but also introduces theological incoherence into Paul's thought-world. It privileges diversity at the expense of unity in Paul's soteriology. This is not to insist that the universalistic (and "perishing") texts

---

[122] I would suggest that the other doctrinal loci in Paul of covenant, ecclesiology, and sacramentology—which I have not the space to analyze here—also serve to strengthen further the case for definite atonement.

[123] See my previous chapter, "For Whom Did Christ Die?"

must be read *through* the lens of the framework presented here; as stated at the beginning, such texts are *themselves* important components *of* the lens. It is to insist, however, that the lines of influence between exegesis of individual texts (within a wider biblical theology) and a systematic construct of Paul's soteriology are bidirectional.[124]

---

[124] For further study, see D. A. Carson, "Unity and Diversity in the New Testament: The Possibility of Systematic Theology," in *Scripture and Truth*, ed. D. A. Carson and John D. Woodbridge (Grand Rapids, MI: Zondervan, 1983), 65–95, 368–75; Henri A. G. Blocher, "The 'Analogy of Faith' in the Study of Scripture: In Search of Justification and Guide-Lines," *SBET* 5 (1987): 17–38; and Moisés Silva, "Epilogue," in his *Explorations in Exegetical Method: Galatians as a Test Case* (Grand Rapids, MI: Baker, 1996), 197–215.

14

"Problematic Texts" for Definite Atonement in the Pastoral and General Epistles

Thomas R. Schreiner

Is definite atonement actually taught in the Scriptures, or do prejudiced interpreters read it into biblical texts? I. Howard Marshall asks the right question: "Is it possible to interpret the election statements in such a way as to be consistent with the universal statements without twisting the meaning of either?"[1] I will argue here that supporters of definite atonement can answer that question in the affirmative. A number of texts in the Pastoral Epistles, the Petrine Epistles, and Hebrews that speak to the issue of definite atonement will be considered. Many of the texts examined here are part of the arsenal of those who defend unlimited/general atonement. In this chapter, I will argue that (1) understanding some of these texts in a way that supports definite atonement is more persuasive exegetically and theologically; and (2) those texts which do concern God's salvific stance to all kinds of people (1 Tim. 2:4; 4:10) or to everyone (2 Pet. 3:9) do not in fact disprove the doctrine of definite atonement—God's desire for people to be saved and his intention to save only the elect are compatible elements in biblical soteriology.

---

[1] I. Howard Marshall, "Universal Grace and Atonement in the Pastoral Epistles," in *The Grace of God and the Will of Man*, ed. Clark H. Pinnock (Minneapolis: Bethany, 1995), 53.

Pastoral Epistles

CONTEXT OF 1 TIMOTHY

As most commentators agree, a mirror reading of 1 Timothy suggests that in this epistle the apostle Paul confronts some kind of exclusivism heresy. Perhaps Paul's opponents relied on genealogies to limit salvation to only a certain group of people, excluding from God's saving purposes those who were notoriously sinful or those from so-called inferior backgrounds (1:4; cf. Titus 3:9).[2] Paul writes to remind Timothy and the church that God's grace is surprising: his grace reaches down and rescues all kinds of sinners, even people like Paul who seem to be beyond his saving love (1:12–17).

GOD'S DESIRE TO SAVE ALL IN 1 TIMOTHY 2:1–7

Paul's reflections on his own salvation function as an important backdrop for the discussion of salvation in 1 Timothy 2:1–7, a key passage relating to definite atonement. Some contend that the emphasis on "all" precludes definite atonement.[3] Paul begins by exhorting his readers to pray "for all people" (ὑπὲρ πάντων ἀνθρώπων; v. 1). Does Paul refer here to every person without exception or to every person without distinction? The immediate reference to "kings and all who are in high positions" (v. 2) suggests that various classes of people are in view.[4] Is such a reading of 1 Timothy 2:1–2 borne out by the subsequent verses? Praying for all is "good" and "pleasing" (v. 3), for God "desires all people to be saved and to come to the knowledge of the truth" (ὃς πάντας ἀνθρώπους θέλει σωθῆναι καὶ εἰς ἐπίγνωσιν ἀληθείας ἐλθεῖν; v. 4). The same question arising in verse 1 surfaces here again: Does "all people" (πάντας ἀνθρώπους; v. 4) refer to every person without exception or to every person without distinction? The Reformed have traditionally defended the latter option.[5] Sometimes this exegesis is dismissed as special pleading and

---

[2] For a full analysis of the false teaching that Paul addresses in the Pastoral Epistles, see George W. Knight III, *The Pastoral Epistles: A Commentary on the Greek Text*, NIGTC (Grand Rapids, MI: Eerdmans, 1992), 10–12; I. Howard Marshall, *A Critical and Exegetical Commentary on the Pastoral Epistles*, ICC (Edinburgh: T. & T. Clark, 1999), 44–51; and Philip H. Towner, *The Letters to Timothy and Titus*, NICNT (Grand Rapids, MI: Eerdmans, 2006), 41–50. Gordon D. Fee, *1 and 2 Timothy, Titus*, NIBC (Peabody, MA: Hendrickson, 1984), 64, writes, "The concern [in 1 Timothy 2:3–4] is simply with the universal scope of the gospel over against some form of heretical exclusivism and narrowness."

[3] See, for example, Marshall, "Universal Grace and Atonement," 62–63; and Robert P. Lightner, *The Death Christ Died: A Biblical Case for Unlimited Atonement*, rev. ed. (Grand Rapids, MI: Kregel, 1998), 62–73.

[4] So Knight, *Pastoral Epistles*, 115.

[5] John Calvin, *Institutes of the Christian Religion*, ed. John T. McNeill, trans. Ford Lewis Battles (Philadelphia: Westminster, 1960), 3.24.16; John Owen, *The Death of Death in the Death of Christ* (Carlisle, PA: Banner of Truth, 1995), 233–35; and Knight, *Pastoral Epistles*, 119.

attributed to Reformed biases. Such a response is too simplistic, for there are good contextual reasons for such a reading. A focus on all people without distinction is supported by verse 7, where Paul emphasizes his apostleship and his ministry to the Gentiles: "For this I was appointed a preacher and an apostle (I am telling the truth, I am not lying), a teacher of the Gentiles in faith and truth." Hence, there are grounds in the context for concluding that "all people" zeros in on people groups, so that Paul is reflecting on his Gentile mission. In Acts 22:15 (NIV), when Paul speaks of being a witness "to all people" (πρὸς πάντας ἀνθρώπους), he clearly does not mean all people without exception; "all" refers to the inclusion of the Gentiles in his mission (Acts 22:21).[6]

The parallel with Romans 3:28–30 provides further evidence that Paul thinks particularly of all people without distinction in 1 Timothy 2:4.[7] Both Jews and Gentiles, according to Paul, are included within the circle of God's saving promises. Paul contends that both are justified by faith, for the oneness of God means that there can be only one way of salvation (cf. 1 Tim. 2:5). One of the advantages of the people group interpretation is that it centers on a major theme in Pauline theology, namely, the inclusion of the Gentiles.

Such an interpretation does not seem to be special pleading, for even interpreters unsympathetic to the Reformed position detect an emphasis on Gentile inclusion in response to some kind of Jewish exclusivism (1 Tim. 1:4). For example, Marshall says, "This universalistic thrust is most probably a corrective response to an exclusive elitist understanding of salvation connected with the false teaching. . . . The context shows that the inclusion of Gentiles alongside Jews in salvation is the primary issue here."[8] And Gordon Fee remarks on verse 7, "This latter phrase in particular would seem to suggest some form of Jewish exclusivism as lying at the heart of the problem."[9]

In sum, Paul reminds his readers of a fundamental truth of his gospel: God desires to save all kinds of people.[10] As William Mounce says, "the universality of salvation [is] the dominant theme" in the paragraph.[11] The

---

[6] If "world" in 1 Timothy 3:16 refers to human beings, the term refers to every person without distinction, not every person without exception, for it is obvious that many in the world did not believe.

[7] Cf. Romans 11:32, where "all" embraces Jew and Gentile, but not every person (cf. Gal. 3:28; Col. 3:11).

[8] Marshall, *Pastoral Epistles*, 420, 427. In his comment on 1 Timothy 2:4, Marshall says, "the emphasis on 'all' is presumably directed at the false teaching in some way" (425).

[9] Fee, *1 and 2 Timothy, Titus*, 67.

[10] The focus on all kinds of people ensures that whatever gender, class, economic status, social standing, or moral history, *no one* is excluded from God's salvation. The "all without distinction" position is an expansive, all-inclusive one, and should not be understood otherwise.

[11] William D. Mounce, *Pastoral Epistles*, WBC (Nashville: Thomas Nelson, 2000), 78.

idea of salvation is supported by the phrase "to come to the knowledge of the truth" (εἰς ἐπίγνωσιν ἀληθείας ἐλθεῖν; v. 4), which is simply another way of describing the gospel message of salvation (cf. 2 Tim. 2:25; 3:7; cf. Titus 1:1). The universal reach of salvation flows from a fundamental tenet of the OT and Judaism: there is only one God (cf. Deut. 6:4). Since there is only one God, there is only one way of salvation, for "there is one mediator between God and men, the man Christ Jesus" (εἷς καὶ μεσίτης θεοῦ καὶ ἀνθρώπων, ἄνθρωπος Χριστὸς Ἰησοῦς; 1 Tim. 2:5). God's saving intentions are universal, including both Jews and Gentiles.

Marshall objects to the Reformed interpretation of all kinds of people, arguing that dividing groups from individuals fails, "since in the last analysis divisions between individuals and classes of humankind merge into one another."[12] But the Reformed view does not exclude individuals from God's saving purposes, for people groups are made up of individuals. The exegetical question centers on whether Paul refers here to every person without exception or every person without distinction. We have already seen that there is strong evidence (even in Marshall) that the focus is on the salvation of individuals from different people groups. For example, in his paper, "Universal Grace and Atonement in the Pastoral Epistles," Marshall states,

> The pastor [Paul] is emphasizing that salvation is for everybody, both Jew and Gentile. . . . But it does not help the defender of limited atonement, any more than the view that "all" refers to "all kinds of people," for what the Pastor is telling his readers to do is to pray for "both Jews and Gentiles," not for the "the elect among Jews and Gentiles."[13]

Marshall fails to see that by arguing that prayers are to be made for "Jews and Gentiles" he inadvertently affirms what he earlier denies: the Reformed position of "all kinds of people." Moreover, Marshall actually misrepresents the Reformed view here, which is *not* that Paul teaches that our prayers should be limited to the elect. The Reformed position has consistently maintained that we are to pray for Jews and Gentiles, Armenians and Turks, Tutsis and Hutus, knowing that God desires to save individuals from every people group. Knowing this does not mean that we know who the elect are so that we limit our prayers to them.

---

[12] Marshall, *Pastoral Epistles*, 427.
[13] Marshall, "Universal Grace and Atonement in the Pastoral Epistles," 63.

The interpretation of "all without distinction" should be carried over into 1 Timothy 2:6. Here Christ is designated as the one "who gave himself as a ransom [ἀντίλυτρον] for all."[14] Clearly, we have the idea of Christ's substitutionary sacrifice, where he gives his life as a ransom for the sake of others.[15] It seems best to take the "all" (πάντων) in the same sense as we saw earlier (vv. 1, 4), meaning all kinds of people, since Paul particularly emphasizes his Gentile mission in the next verse (v. 7). Moreover, Paul most likely alludes here to Jesus's teaching that he gave "his life as a ransom [λύτρον] for many [πολλῶν]" (Matt. 20:28; Mark 10:45), which in turn echoes Isaiah 53:11–12. As Alec Motyer demonstrates elsewhere in this volume, the referent of "many" in Isaiah 53, though it encompasses an undefined but numerous group of people, is still necessarily limited—it refers to those for whom redemption is both accomplished *and* applied—and therefore cannot refer to every single person.[16] If these intertextual connections are correct, then Christ giving himself as a ransom for "all without exception" is ruled out.[17]

First Timothy 2:6 supports the notion that Christ purchased salvation for all kinds of individuals from various people groups. The verse and context say nothing about Christ being the *potential* ransom of everyone. The language in verse 6—"who gave himself" (ὁ δοὺς ἑαυτόν)—is a typically Pauline way of referring to the cross, and always refers to Christ's *actual* self-sacrifice for *believers* (Rom. 8:32; Gal. 1:4; 2:20; Eph. 5:2; Titus 2:14). It stresses that Christ gave himself as a ransom so that at the cost of his death he actually purchased those who would be his people. The reason Paul can speak of Christ's death in expansive, all-inclusive terms in 1 Timothy 2:6 is because he sees his ministry as worldwide (2:7; cf. Acts 22:15), his soteriology is universal in the right sense (2:5; cf. Rom. 3:28–30), and he is confronting an elitist heresy that was excluding certain kinds of people from God's salvation (1 Tim. 1:4). Paul wants to make it clear: Christ died for all kinds of people, not just some elite group.[18]

---

[14] Leon Morris, *The Apostolic Preaching of the Cross*, 3rd rev. ed. (Grand Rapids, MI: Eerdmans, 1965), 51, renders ἀντίλυτρον as "substitute-ransom."

[15] Cf. Marshall, *Pastoral Epistles*, 432; Mounce, *Pastoral Epistles*, 89–90.

[16] See J. Alec Motyer, "'Stricken for the Transgression of My People': The Atoning Work of Isaiah's Suffering Servant," chapter 10 in this volume.

[17] Hence, the major thesis of Gary L. Shultz, Jr., "A Biblical and Theological Defense of a Multi-Intentioned View of the Extent of the Atonement" (PhD diss., The Southern Baptist Theological Seminary, 2008), that Christ actually paid for the sins of all people without exception should be rejected.

[18] Some could say that Jesus is actually the ransom of all and opt for universalism, but as I point out below in the discussion on 1 Timothy 4:10, there are serious problems with a universalist reading.

1 Timothy 4:10

Interpreters have long debated the meaning of the Pauline affirmation that God "is the Savior of all people, especially of those who believe" (ὅς ἐστιν σωτὴρ πάντων ἀνθρώπων μάλιστα πιστῶν; 1 Tim. 4:10). One aspect of the debate centers on the meaning of the word μάλιστα. The ESV translates the word "especially," as do virtually all English translations. In 1979, however, T. C. Skeat argued that μάλιστα should be translated "namely," or "that is." Skeat defended his case by citing some examples from Greek papyrus letters, and then with a few NT examples. For instance, according to Skeat, when Paul asked Timothy to bring him "the books, and above all the parchments" (τὰ βιβλία μάλιστα τὰς μεμβράνας; 2 Tim. 4:13), the "parchments" define what books should be brought to him. Similarly, the "empty talkers and deceivers" (ματαιολόγοι καὶ φρεναπάται) are identified as "the circumcision party" (οἱ ἐκ τῆς περιτομῆς) using the word μάλιστα in Titus 1:10. Or, when Paul says that one should provide "for his relatives," he defines them as "members of his household" (εἰ δέ τις τῶν ἰδίων καὶ μάλιστα οἰκείων οὐ προνοεῖ; 1 Tim. 5:8). So here in 1 Timothy 4:10, according to Skeat, the text should be translated, "God, who gives salvation to all men—that is to say, to all who believe in Him."[19] Skeat's claim that μάλιστα means "that is" or "namely" certainly yields a coherent and plausible reading of some verses.

Nevertheless, the notion that μάλιστα means "that is" or "namely" should be rejected. Vern Poythress disputes every one of Skeat's examples, showing that his understanding of the term is flawed in both the Greek papyri and in the NT examples.[20] He shows that Skeat's readings are either ambiguous and therefore not proven, or they are mistaken. The ambiguous texts, which could possibly support Skeat's hypothesis, should not be introduced in favor of his interpretation. Poythress, correctly, objects that a new meaning for a word must not be accepted in ambiguous texts if an established meaning for the word makes sense in the text under consideration. He argues that the meaning "especially" or "particularly," an elative sense of μάλιστα, fits every example. In other words, the term μάλιστα should be rendered "especially" or "particularly"; it intensifies adverbially the word it modifies.

For the sake of space we will not rehearse here the extrabiblical evidence

---

[19] T. C. Skeat, "'Especially the Parchments': A Note on 2 Timothy iv. 13," *JTS* 30 (1979): 174. R. A. Campbell, "KAI MALISTA OIKEIWN—A New Look at 1 Timothy 5:8," *NTS* 41 (1995): 157–60, has added support to Skeat's position. So also Knight, *Pastoral Epistles*, 203–204.
[20] Vern S. Poythress, "The Meaning of μάλιστα in 2 Timothy 4:13 and Related Verses," *JTS* 53 (2002): 523–32.

provided by Skeat. Suffice it to say that Poythress demonstrates in every instance that Skeat's rendering is unpersuasive. The word μάλιστα is found six times in 2–4 Maccabees and never means "that is" or "namely" (2 Macc. 8:7; 3 Macc. 5:3; 4 Macc. 3:10; 4:22; 12:9; 15:4). The two examples in Acts also should be translated "especially." Acts 20:38 says that those who accompanied Paul to the ship were "especially sorrowful" (ὀδυνώμενοι μάλιστα) that they would not see him again. Acts 25:26 is particularly helpful. Festus, in introducing Paul to his guests, explains that he "brought him before you all, and especially before you, King Agrippa" (προήγαγον αὐτὸν ἐφ᾽ ὑμῶν καὶ μάλιστα ἐπὶ σοῦ, βασιλεῦ Ἀγρίππα; Acts 25:26). Any notion that μάλιστα means "that is" here is clearly wrong, for the plural "you" refers to the guests, and Agrippa is distinguished from them as the special guest of the occasion.

There are some instances where Skeat's interpretation is contextually possible. The saints who greet the Philippian believers could be identified as those who are part of Caesar's household (Phil. 4:22). But it is much more likely that the saints and those of Caesar's household are not coextensive. Hence, the saints with Paul greet the Philippians, and in particular or especially (μάλιστα) "those of Caesar's household" (δὲ οἱ ἐκ τῆς Καίσαρος οἰκίας). Similarly, it fits better with the lexical meaning of μάλιστα if, in Titus 1:10, "those of the circumcision party" are a subset of the "empty talkers and deceivers." All those of the circumcision party are empty talkers and deceivers, but there are also empty talkers and deceivers who do not belong to the circumcision group.[21] Similarly, 2 Timothy 4:13 fits with what μάλιστα means elsewhere, for it makes perfect sense to ask for books in general and then to specify that Timothy should particularly bring the parchments.

Other uses in Paul confirm that μάλιστα means "especially" or "particularly." For instance, Paul commands the Galatians to "do good to everyone, and especially [μάλιστα] to those who are of the household of faith" (Gal. 6:10). "Everyone" is a broader category than "the household of faith," for it includes those who are unbelievers. So, Paul admonishes the church to do good to all people but especially to fellow believers. Similarly, in Philemon 16, Paul admonishes Philemon to receive Onesimus as a brother in the Lord, adding "especially to me" (μάλιστα ἐμοί). Again, Skeat's translation would not fit at all here. In 1 Timothy 5:8, providing for one's own "and

---

[21] Hong Bom Kim, "The Interpretation of μάλιστα in 1 Timothy 5:17," *Novum Testamentum* 46 (2004): 360–68, shows that μάλιστα never means "that is" or "namely" in the Pastoral Epistles, and that the translation "especially" is correct. Surprisingly, Kim shows no awareness of Poythress's article on the subject.

especially [μάλιστα] for members of [one's] household" is naturally read as saying that the latter is a subset of the former. Those who are part of one's household have a special priority. So too, in 1 Timothy 5:17, "elders who rule well" (οἱ καλῶς προεστῶτες πρεσβύτεροι) should receive "double honor" (διπλῆς τιμῆς), and then Paul adds, "especially those who labor in preaching and teaching" (μάλιστα οἱ κοπιῶντες ἐν λόγῳ καὶ διδασκαλίᾳ). Given the meaning of μάλιστα elsewhere, it is likely that Paul commends a subcategory of elders—those who devote themselves to the preaching and teaching of the Word.

In conclusion, then, there is little doubt that μάλιστα means "especially" instead of "that is" or "namely" in 1 Timothy 4:10. Naturally the translation "that is" would appear to fit nicely with definite atonement, for then the verse would teach that God is the Savior of all people, that is, believers. The "all people" would be defined as believers, and thus there would be no sense that God universally saves all people. Lexically, however, this interpretation is quite implausible and hence it should be rejected. The ESV translates the verse well: God "is the Savior of all people, especially of those who believe."

Now at first glance 1 Timothy 4:10 could be interpreted to support universalism, since the verse says that God "is the Savior of all people." But a universalist meaning is ruled out by the addition of the words "especially believers," which are superfluous if all are saved, for it is difficult to see how believers are saved in a special way if all people without exception are saved. If universalism is true, all without exception are saved, and there is no unique salvation for believers. Furthermore, even in 1 Timothy, Paul teaches a final destruction of the impenitent, which does not fit with a universalist reading (e.g., 6:9).

But what does the verse mean if the ESV translation is accurate? The phrase "all people" (πάντων ἀνθρώπων) could be translated "all sorts of peoples," and then the focus would be on various people groups.[22] Naturally this fits well with what we have seen earlier in 1 Timothy 2:1–7 and Titus 2:11.[23] However, this still begs the question of how God may be the *Savior* of all kinds of people, and especially of believers.

---

[22] So, for example, Louis Berkhof, *Systematic Theology*, 4th ed. (Grand Rapids, MI: Eerdmans, 1941), 396–97; and Knight, *Pastoral Epistles*, 203.

[23] Steven M. Baugh, "'Savior of All People': 1 Tim 4:10 in Context," *WTJ* 54 (1992): 333. Though Reformed, Baugh rejects this interpretation here, but he embraces it in 1 Timothy 2:4.

Steven Baugh proposes an interpretation that appears to solve any dilemma for a Reformed position on definite atonement. He argues that the word "Savior" here does not refer to spiritual salvation, "but to God's gracious benefactions to all of humanity,"[24] or, "to God's care for all of humanity during our time upon earth."[25] Baugh notes many examples in Greco-Roman literature, and especially in Ephesian inscriptions, where Savior refers to the protection and preservation granted by kings, emperors, patrons, and other leaders. Paul counters the idea, according to Baugh, that those who were deceased were gods and saviors. Hence, identifying God as Savior denotes what is often called his common grace, which is granted to all people. Baugh understands the verse to say that God bestows his common grace on all people without exception. Perhaps we can think here of the provision of food, health, and the times of joy (cf. Acts 14:17). God's goodness has been especially manifested to those who are believers, for they have been given both material and spiritual blessings.

Baugh's interpretation solves the problem before us, for if the verse does not refer to spiritual salvation, there is no need to suggest that God secures the salvation of all people. Nevertheless, it is quite unlikely that Baugh's interpretation is correct, for there is a crucial problem with his interpretation. One of the major themes in the Pastoral Epistles is salvation. Paul refers to both God and Christ as "Savior" (σωτήρ) and uses the verb "save" (σῴζω) seven times (1 Tim. 1:15; 2:4, 15; 4:16; 2 Tim. 1:9; 4:18; Titus 3:5). God is identified as "Savior" six times in the Pastorals (1 Tim. 1:1; 2:3 4:10; Titus 1:3; 2:10; 3:4) and Christ four times (2 Tim. 1:10; Titus 1:4; 2:13; 3:6). The noun "salvation" (σωτήρια) is used twice (2 Tim. 2:10; 3:15), and the adjective "bringing salvation" (σωτήριον) once (Titus 2:11). What is striking is that there is not a single instance in the Pastorals where the salvation word group refers to anything besides spiritual salvation.[26] In other words, the term never means preservation, nor does it focus on material blessings. A survey of some examples will confirm this judgment.

In 1 Timothy 1:1, God as Savior is connected with the hope that belongs to believers in Christ, which makes it clear that spiritual salvation is in

---

[24] Ibid., 331. So also John Calvin, *Commentaries on the Epistles to Timothy, Titus, and Philemon*, trans. William Pringle (repr., Grand Rapids, MI: Baker, 2005), 112.

[25] Baugh, "Savior of All People: 1 Tim 4:10 in Context," 333.

[26] Fee, *1 and 2 Timothy, Titus*, 110, rightly says that such an interpretation of Savior is "found nowhere else in the NT." So also Knight, *Pastoral Epistles*, 203; and Shultz, "Multi-Intentioned View of the Extent of the Atonement," 138–39.

view. It is even clearer that spiritual salvation is intended in 1 Timothy 2:3–4, for God "our Savior" (τοῦ σωτῆρος ἡμῶν; v. 3) is the one "who desires all people to be saved" (ὃς πάντας ἀνθρώπους θέλει σωθῆναι; v. 4). Then Paul proceeds to speak of Christ as the "Mediator" (μεσίτης; v. 5), so there is no doubt that salvation from sin is the subject. A reference to spiritual salvation is evident in 1 Timothy 1:15: "Christ Jesus came into the world to save sinners" (Χριστὸς Ἰησοῦς ἦλθεν εἰς τὸν κόσμον ἁμαρτωλοὺς σῶσαι). Similarly, in 2 Timothy 1:10, Christ is identified as Savior (σωτῆρος), as the one "who abolished death and brought life and immortality to light through the gospel" (καταργήσαντος μὲν τὸν θάνατον φωτίσαντος δὲ ζωὴν καὶ ἀφθαρσίαν διὰ τοῦ εὐαγγελίου). The references to conquering death and the dawn of life through the gospel confirm a reference to spiritual salvation. In 2 Timothy 2:10, "salvation" (σωτηρίας) is linked with obtaining "eternal glory" (δόξης αἰωνίου). The Scriptures lead to "salvation through faith in Christ Jesus" (σωτηρίαν διὰ πίστεως τῆς ἐν Χριστῷ Ἰησοῦ; 2 Tim. 3:15). So too, the Lord will "save" (σώσει) Paul "into his heavenly kingdom" (εἰς τὴν βασιλείαν αὐτοῦ τὴν ἐπουράνιον; 2 Tim. 4:18).[27] God and Christ are both identified as Savior (σωτῆρος) in the introduction of Titus (1:3–4), and spiritual salvation is clearly in view, since in the context Paul refers to "God's elect" (ἐκλεκτῶν θεοῦ), "knowledge of the truth" (ἐπίγνωσιν ἀληθείας; v. 1), "eternal life" (ζωῆς αἰωνίου; v. 2), his "preaching" (κηρύγματι; v. 3), and "common faith" (κοινὴν πίστιν; v. 4). In Titus 2:10, God as "Savior" (σωτῆρος) is linked with his bringing "salvation for all people" (σωτήριος πᾶσιν ἀνθρώποις; v. 11) and "waiting for our blessed hope" (τὴν μακαρίαν ἐλπίδα; v. 13) of the coming of Christ as "God and Savior" (θεοῦ καὶ σωτῆρος). Both God and Christ are identified as Savior (σωτῆρος) in Titus 3:4–6, and this is linked with the truth that God "saved us" (ἔσωσεν ἡμᾶς; v. 5).

Lexically, then, there is little doubt that Paul refers to spiritual salvation in 1 Timothy 4:10. Surprisingly, Baugh does not consider how "salvation" and "Savior" are used elsewhere in the Pastorals, and he wrongly resorts to how the word is used in inscriptions in Ephesus instead of relying on the nearer and more important context—the Pauline usage in the Pastoral Epistles. A reference to spiritual salvation is confirmed by the context in which verse 10 appears. Paul explicitly contrasts spiritual and physical training

---

[27] Scholars dispute the meaning of "save" in 1 Timothy 2:15 and 4:16, but spiritual salvation is likely intended in these instances as well.

(vv. 7–8), prizing the former over the latter. Indeed, spiritual training is paramount, for it provides benefit both "for the present life and also for the life to come" (ζωῆς τῆς νῦν καὶ τῆς μελλούσης; v. 9). The reference to "the life to come" indicates that spiritual salvation is intended.

In conclusion, Baugh's interpretation is creative and solves the problem before us, but it fails lexically and does not account well for the meaning of "salvation" and "Savior" in the Pastoral Epistles, and therefore should be rejected.

What then is the best interpretation of 1 Timothy 4:10? We have seen thus far: (1) that the word μάλιστα means "especially"; (2) that universalism is excluded; (3) that "all people" probably focuses on people groups (both Jews and Gentiles); and (4) that "Savior" refers to spiritual salvation.

Further light may be shed on this difficult verse by seeing its parallelism with 1 Timothy 2:3–4:[28]

> . . . God our Savior, **who desires all people to be saved** and <u>to come to the knowledge of the truth</u> (2:3–4)
> . . . τοῦ σωτῆρος ἡμῶν θεοῦ, ὃς πάντας ἀνθρώπους θέλει σωθῆναι καὶ <u>εἰς ἐπίγνωσιν ἀληθείας ἐλθεῖν</u>

> . . . the living God, **who is the Savior of all people**, <u>especially of those who believe</u> (4:10)
> . . . θεῷ ζῶντι, ὅς ἐστιν σωτὴρ πάντων ἀνθρώπων <u>μάλιστα πιστῶν</u>

The phrase "God our Savior, who desires all people to be saved" (2:3b–4a) shares the same conceptual horizon with "the living God, who is the Savior of all people" (4:10b–c) and refers to God's salvific desire toward all kinds of people—in this sense God avails himself as Savior to all kinds of individuals from diverse people groups. The phrase "to come to the knowledge of the truth" (2:4b) mirrors "especially . . . those who believe" (4:10d), showing that salvation is a reality only for those who come to the knowledge of the truth through faith. It seems, then, that Paul is saying here that God is *potentially* the Savior of all kinds of people—in that, as the living God there is no other Savior available to people—but that he is *actually* the Savior of only believers. The additional comment, "especially of believers," intensifies the meaning of salvation. The possibility of God being a Savior for all kinds of

---

[28] We should also keep in mind the context of Jewish exclusivism (1 Tim. 1:4), which Paul was addressing.

people exists because there is only one living God (4:10b) and one Mediator available to people (2:5–6), but this possibility becomes a *reality* for those who believe. The phrase clarifies that believers are a subset of all people; they are a special category because they are actually saved.

But does such an interpretation disprove definite atonement? In the first place, this interpretation should not be confused with one that suggests two levels to the atonement: Christ dies for everyone to make them redeemable, and he dies for the elect to actually redeem them.[29] This introduces an unwarranted split-level into the atonement. The issue in 1 Timothy 4:10 is not two levels to the atonement, but rather the twin truths that God (the Father) is the *available* Savior for all kinds of people—God's salvific stance—while at the same time being the *actual* Savior for only those who believe (in Christ).

Secondly, 1 Timothy 4:10 illustrates that definite atonement may be affirmed alongside other biblical truths, such as God's salvific stance to the world and the possibility for people to be saved if they believe in Christ. Those who hold to a definite intention in the atonement to save only the elect also believe that God desires people to be saved (1 Tim. 2:3–4; cf. Ezek. 18:32), that he is available as Savior to all people (1 Tim. 4:10), that Christ's death is sufficient for the salvation of every person,[30] and that all are invited to be saved on the basis of Christ's death for sinners (1 Tim. 1:15). But it is a non sequitur to suggest that affirming any of these biblical truths somehow negates the truth that Christ intended to die only for his elect, actually paying for their sins alone. In biblical soteriology, these theological elements sit side by side.

Titus 2:11–14

Another text that pertains to definite atonement in the Pastorals is Titus 2:11–14. Verse 11 is particularly striking: "For the grace of God has appeared, bringing salvation for all people" (Ἐπεφάνη γὰρ ἡ χάρις τοῦ θεοῦ σωτήριος πᾶσιν ἀνθρώποις). We are again faced with the issue that has occupied us in 1 Timothy. Some maintain that "all people" (πᾶσιν ἀνθρώποις) refers to all people without exception, but it is more likely that Paul again refers to all people without distinction. A good case can be made for such a judgment, because Paul refers to people from various groups earlier in chapter 2: older

---

[29] See, for example, D. Broughton Knox, "Some Aspects of the Atonement," in *The Doctrine of God*, vol. 1 of *D. Broughton Knox, Selected Works* (3 vols.), ed. Tony Payne (Kingsford, NSW: Matthias Media, 2000), 260–66.

[30] The sufficiency of Christ's death is a statement of its intrinsic value unrelated to its design.

men (v. 2), older women (vv. 3–4), younger women (vv. 4–5), younger men (v. 6), and slaves (vv. 9–10). Indeed, verse 14 focuses particularly on Christ's redeeming work for believers: Christ "gave himself for us [ὑπὲρ ἡμῶν] to redeem us [λυτρώσηται ἡμᾶς]." The repeated use of the first person plural pronoun "us" (ἡμῶν, ἡμᾶς) in the text (2:12, 14) points to Christ securing salvation for his own. Furthermore, the ἵνα clause shows that Christ's intention was not merely to make salvation possible for everyone, but to actually redeem (λυτρώσηται) and purify (καθαρίσῃ) a special people for himself (ἑαυτῷ λαὸν περιούσιον).

Petrine Epistles

INTRODUCTION

Space precludes an exhaustive assessment of Peter's soteriology in his epistles,[31] but a quick survey reveals that they are rich in the theology of election and atonement (e.g., 1 Pet. 1:1–2, 8–9, 20; 2:24; 3:18).[32] For the purposes of this chapter, however, my focus concerns two Petrine texts that are often adduced to refute definite atonement: 2 Peter 2:1 and 3:9.

2 PETER 2:1

It seems to some as if 2 Peter 2:1 presents a case that is contrary to definite atonement, for in speaking of the false teachers, who initially embraced the gospel but have now denied it, Peter says that they are "denying the Master who bought them."[33] What is quite striking is that Peter says that Christ "bought them" (ἀγοράσαντα αὐτούς). What Peter means here has been interpreted in different ways. Some argue that the buying here is non-soteriological, and hence Peter does not teach that Christ redeemed the false teachers.[34] The problem of Christ actually purchasing believers who then lose the benefit of being purchased is thereby avoided. But this interpretation faces a severe lexical problem. We have no instance in the NT where

---

[31] I am assuming here that 1 and 2 Peter were written by the apostle Peter. Second Peter is particularly controversial. For a defense of Petrine authorship, see Thomas R. Schreiner, *1 and 2 Peter and Jude*, New American Commentary (Nashville: B&H Academic, 2003), 255–76.

[32] For a helpful treatment on 1 Peter, see Martin Williams, *The Doctrine of Salvation in the First Letter of Peter*, Society for New Testament Studies Monograph Series 149 (Cambridge: Cambridge University Press, 2010).

[33] For example, R. C. H. Lenski, *The Interpretation of the Epistles of St. Peter, St. John and St. Jude* (Minneapolis: Augsburg, 1966), 305, "Here we have an adequate answer to Calvin's limited atonement: the Sovereign, Christ, bought with his blood not only the elect but also those who go to perdition."

[34] Wayne Grudem, *Systematic Theology: An Introduction to Biblical Doctrine* (Grand Rapids, MI: Zondervan, 1994), 600; Owen, *Death of Death*, 250–52, emphasizes the non-soteriological solution, but he also recognizes that the language may be phenomenological.

the ἀγοράζω word group, when it is associated with the death of Christ, has a non-soteriological meaning (cf. 1 Cor. 6:20; 7:23; Gal. 3:13; 4:5). So, this interpretation looks like special pleading in which the word "bought" is redefined to salvage the theology of definite atonement. Gary D. Long defends another non-soteriological view. He argues that δεσπότης here refers to Christ as Creator and that ἀγοράζω is a creation term as well, referring to Christ's ownership of the false teachers.[35] But Long's view fails for the same reason as the view examined above, for we have already seen that the ἀγοράζω word group is soteriological in the NT.[36]

Another possibility is that the word "bought" bears its usual meaning, but those who were bought or redeemed fell away from the faith. The false teachers were truly redeemed by the blood of Christ but they apostatized and denied the faith that they had at first embraced. This is another way of saying, of course, that they lost or abandoned their salvation.[37] On this reading, some of those whom Christ has redeemed or purchased end up being damned. The apostasy view has the advantage of being a straightforward and clear reading of the text. Some of those whom Christ redeemed have fallen away and denied the faith. Space is lacking to interact in detail, either exegetically or theologically, with the notion that some of those who are redeemed may end up eternally damned.[38] I would argue that there are many texts which teach that those who truly belong to the Lord will never finally and ultimately fall away, since the Lord has promised to keep them (see e.g., John 10:28–29; Rom. 8:28–39; 1 Cor. 1:8–9; Phil. 1:6; 1 Thess. 5:23–24). Hence, the loss-of-salvation view should be rejected.

D. W. Kennard proposes another solution to the text before us.[39] The term "bought," says Kennard, is soteriological. The false teachers, therefore, were genuinely bought or redeemed by Christ. Kennard, however, departs from both standard Arminian and Reformed views in explaining the nature of redemption here, for he maintains that some of those who are redeemed will not be saved on the final day. At first glance one might conclude that

---

[35] Gary D. Long, *Definite Atonement* (Phillipsburg, NJ: P&R, 1977), 67–79. Like Owen, Long acknowledges the possibility of the phenomenological view. Cf. also Baugh, "'Savior of All People': 1 Tim 4:10 in Context," 331; and Calvin, *Epistles to Timothy, Titus, and Philemon*, 112.

[36] For criticisms of Long, see Andrew D. Chang, "Second Peter 2:1 and the Extent of the Atonement," *BSac* 142 (1985): 52–56.

[37] So, for example, I. Howard Marshall, *Kept by the Power of God: A Study of Perseverance and Falling Away* (Minneapolis: Bethany, 1969), 169–70.

[38] See Thomas R. Schreiner and Ardel B. Caneday, *The Race Set Before Us: A Biblical Theology of Perseverance and Assurance* (Downers Grove, IL: InterVarsity Press, 2001).

[39] D. W. Kennard, "Petrine Redemption: Its Meaning and Extent," *JETS* 39 (1987): 399–405.

this interpretation fits with Arminianism since some of those who are truly redeemed will lose their redemption, and hence will not be saved on the day of judgment. Kennard, nevertheless, introduces a wrinkle that distinguishes him from classical Arminianism, for on his scheme all the elect will certainly be saved and will never lose their elect status. According to Kennard, however, some of those who are redeemed are not elect.

How should Kennard's proposal be assessed? It would take us too far afield to consider his proposal in detail, for we would need to investigate the nature of redemption and election elsewhere in the NT. Suffice it to say that his reading, which separates election from redemption, is unpersuasive and lacks exegetical and theological support from the remainder of the NT. Traditional Arminian and Reformed scholars offer more plausible readings when they posit, respectively, that either those who are elect and redeemed may apostatize or that those who are elect and redeemed will surely be kept from apostasy by God himself.

Still another possible reading has been proposed. The term "bought" here refers to what Andrew Chang calls "spiritual redemption."[40] The atonement is unlimited in nature; the problem with the false teachers is their refusal to accept the salvation purchased for them. This view must be distinguished from the "loss-of-salvation" notion presented above, for Chang insists that no true believer can apostatize. The Arminian interpretation says that some were truly redeemed but repudiated their salvation. But Chang maintains that Peter describes the false teachers as "bought" in terms of potentiality. Theologically, this interpretation ends up saying that Christ purchased all potentially, but the purchasing does not take effect unless someone believes.

Chang's interpretation, though it may seem appealing at first glance, should be rejected. When we approach a text, it is vital to read it in context. We must attend to what the text we are investigating is trying to do, so that we read it on its own terms. Chang's interpretation fails to convince because he separates what Peter says about the false teachers being redeemed by Christ from what Peter says about their falling away, in 2 Peter 2:20–22. The false teachers are described as those who "have escaped the defilements of the world through the knowledge of our Lord and Savior Jesus Christ" (v. 20).[41] Verse 21 says that they "have known the way of righteousness."

---

[40] Chang, "Second Peter 2:1 and the Extent of the Atonement," 60.
[41] Actually, what Peter says here is true both of the false teachers and of their "converts" who have also fallen away. In defense of this view, see Schreiner, *1 and 2 Peter and Jude*, 360–61.

So, it is rather astonishing that Chang says, "The text gives no evidence that these false teachers professed to be believers."[42] Peter remarks that after having escaped, they have now been "entangled" and "overcome" (v. 20), so that "the last state has become worse for them than the first" (v. 20). They have "turn[ed] back from the holy commandment delivered to them" (v. 21). So, they are like unclean dogs and pigs, who have revisited their filth. Peter describes the false teachers as being purchased by Christ (v. 1), as knowing Jesus as Lord and Savior (v. 20), and as knowing the righteous way (v. 21). It is precisely here where it is evident that Chang's solution does not work, for Peter is not saying that the false teachers *potentially* knew Christ as Lord and Savior or that they *potentially* knew the righteous way. It is evident from Peter's language that the false teachers gave every indication initially that they were truly Christians. Chang's view lacks inner coherence and consistency, for he fails to integrate what Peter says about the false teachers being bought by Christ (v. 1) with their knowing Christ as Lord and Savior (v. 20) and knowing the way of righteousness (v. 21).

Is there a reading that treats this text plausibly, and consistently interprets what Peter says about the false teachers in both verse 1 and verses 20–22? I suggest there is: Peter's language is phenomenological. In other words, it *appeared as if* the Lord had purchased the false teachers with his blood (v. 1), though they actually did not truly belong to the Lord.[43] Similarly, the false teachers *gave every appearance* of knowing Jesus Christ as Lord and Savior (v. 20) and *appeared* to have known the righteous saving way (v. 21).[44] Such an interpretation is to be preferred to Chang's reading, for the same interpretation is proposed for verse 1 and verses 20–21. In both instances a phenomenological reading makes good sense of the text, whereas it does not work to speak of a potential redemption (v. 1) and a potential knowing of

---

[42] Chang, "Second Peter 2:1 and the Extent of the Atonement," 56.

[43] Ibid., 60, dismisses this view, which he identifies as the "Christian charity view," saying that "the text gives no support to this view." But he fails to see that verses 20–22 do support this view when these verses are integrated with verse 1. Indeed, the latter must not be segregated from the former, for both texts refer to the false teachers.

[44] Shultz, "Multi-Intentioned View of the Extent of the Atonement," 150 n. 180, contradicts himself in his exposition of 2 Peter 2. When referring to verse 1 and the notion that the false teachers were professing believers, he says, "There is no support for this view in the text, and there is good reason to believe that the false teachers were not professing believers." Shortly thereafter he says, "the false teachers are not apostate Christians or former Christians who have lost their salvation" (151). But he later says about verses 20–22, "These false teachers are unbelievers who once made false professions of faith without ever experiencing regeneration" (182). Contrary to Shultz, the false teachers were "apostate Christians," in the sense that they had fallen away from their earlier profession of faith. Shultz, like so many, fails to consider the role of verses 20–22 and what it says about the false teachers in his comments on verse 1. Hence, his dogmatic statement about there being no support for the phenomenological interpretation is false and contradicted by his own words, for if one believes that the false teachers had not lost their salvation (as Shultz does), they had at the very least renounced the profession of faith they had made previously.

Christ (vv. 20–21), for Peter says that they *knew* the Lord, and hence he does not refer to potentiality in verses 20–21. The issue is whether the language of being bought by Christ and knowing the Lord is plausibly interpreted as phenomenological.

Why would Peter use phenomenological language if the false teachers were not truly saved? Is this an artificial interpretation introduced to support a theological bias? I have already said that the Arminian reading of the text is straightforward and clear. One can understand why it has appealed to so many commentators throughout history. However, it is better to say that the false teachers gave every appearance of being saved. They *seemed* to be part of the redeemed community, but their apostasy demonstrated that they never truly belonged to God. The words of 1 John 2:19 fit them: "They went out from us, but they were not of us; for if they had been of us, they would have continued with us. But they went out, that it might become plain that they all are not of us." Similarly, Jesus said about those who prophesied in his name, exorcised demons, and performed miracles, but who lived lawless lives, "I never knew you" (Matt. 7:23). He does not say that he knew them once but that he does so no longer. On the contrary, they were never truly members of the people of God, yet for a time they gave the impression of being so. There are other texts which teach that some who truly appeared to be believers later turned out to have spurious faith (Mark 4:1–20; 1 Cor. 11:19; 2 Tim. 2:19).[45] Furthermore, Peter's use of phenomenological language makes sense, for the false teachers were vitally involved in the church. It was not as if outsiders who never claimed to be Christians arrived and began to propagate teachings contrary to the gospel. On the contrary, the false teachers were insiders who departed from what they were first taught. Hence, Peter underscores the gravity of what occurred. Those who were fomenting the false way were, so to speak, "Christians." They were to all appearances "bought" by Christ (2 Pet. 2:1) and seemed to "know" him as Lord and Savior (v. 20). Peter is not claiming that they were actually Christians, that they were truly redeemed (v. 1), or that they truly knew Jesus as Lord and Savior (v. 20), but that they gave every reason initially for observers to think that such was the case. Their subsequent departure showed that they were actually dogs and pigs (v. 22). In other words, they were never truly changed, and thus eventually they revealed their true nature.

---

[45] See here D. A. Carson, "Reflections on Assurance," in *Still Sovereign: Contemporary Perspectives on Election, Foreknowledge, and Grace,* ed. Thomas R. Schreiner and Bruce A. Ware (Grand Rapids, MI: Baker, 2000), 260–69, where he presents a very persuasive argument for a category of people in Scripture with spurious faith.

To sum up, 2 Peter 2:1 does not falsify definite atonement, for Peter does not intend to teach that Christ actually or potentially redeemed the false teachers. Instead, he uses phenomenological language, which is the same way we should interpret the language of their knowing Christ as Lord and Savior (v. 20). The false teachers initially *gave every impression* of being believers, and thus in turn *appeared* to have been "bought" (in a soteriological sense) by Christ. Hence, their subsequent defection was all the more surprising.

A right understanding of 2 Peter 2:1 actually supports definite atonement, since Christ did not *actually* buy these false teachers—for if he had, they would have persevered. Definite atonement refers not only to the *intended* target of the atonement—namely, the elect—but also to its *efficacy*: the atonement achieves its purpose, full and final salvation for the elect. What some fail to grasp in using 2 Peter 2:1 in support of a general atonement[46] is that to affirm general atonement here is to compromise the doctrine of the perseverance of the saints. For we have seen in 2 Peter 2 that what Peter teaches about the atonement (v. 1) cannot be separated from what he teaches about perseverance (vv. 20–22). No doctrine is an island, and to suggest general atonement in this verse is to distort the doctrine of Christian perseverance.[47] Therefore, to say that Christ died for the false teachers phenomenologically fits both exegetically *and* theologically.

2 PETER 3:9

Another verse that plays a significant role in the discussion of definite atonement is 2 Peter 3:9. God is "not wishing that any should perish, but that all should reach repentance" (μὴ βουλόμενός τινας ἀπολέσθαι ἀλλὰ πάντας εἰς μετάνοιαν χωρῆσαι). Here Peter explains that God's patience provides the reason why Jesus's coming is delayed. The reason for his patience is then explained: he does not want any to perish but all to repent. The idea that God is patient so that people will repent is common in the Scriptures (Joel 2:12–13; Rom. 2:4). God's slowness "to anger" is a refrain repeated often in the OT (Ex. 34:6; Num. 14:18; Neh. 9:17; Ps. 86:15; 145:8; Joel 2:13; Jonah 4:2; Nah. 1:3), but he will not delay his wrath forever.

We should note at the outset that perishing (ἀπολέσθαι) refers to eternal

---

[46] For example, Knox, "Some Aspects of the Atonement," 263; and Mark Driscoll and Gerry Breshears, *Death by Love: Letters from the Cross* (Wheaton, IL: Crossway, 2008), 172.

[47] Or, to avoid this, proponents must revert to the language of "potentiality," which, as we have seen, lacks coherence in the wider context.

judgment, as is typical with the term. Repentance (μετάνοιαν), correspondingly, involves the repentance that is necessary for eternal life. Peter does not merely discuss rewards that some will receive if they live faithfully. He directs his attention to whether people will be saved from God's wrath. We must also ask who is in view when he speaks of "any" (τινας) perishing and "all" (πάντας) coming to repentance. Notice that the verse says "patient *with you*" (μακροθυμεῖ εἰς ὑμᾶς). The "any" and "all" in the verse may be an expansion of "you" (ὑμᾶς) earlier in the verse. Peter does not reflect, according to one interpretation, on the fate of all people in the world without exception. He considers those in the church who have wavered under the influence of the false teachers. God desires that every one of them will repent.[48]

A restrictive meaning of "you" is certainly possible. But it seems more probable that the words "any" and "you" refer to God's desire for all without exception to be saved. John Murray rightly argues that there is no definite reference to the elect in the context, that the call to repentance suggests that some of those addressed might perish if they fail to repent, and hence Peter indiscriminately summons all to repent.[49]

It is evident, of course, that not all are saved. So, how do we explain a desire of God that is frustrated in part? Theologians have often and rightly appealed here to two different senses in God's will: there is a decretive will of God and a permissive will of God. God desires the salvation of all in one sense, but he does not ultimately ordain and decree that all will be saved. Is there a contradiction, though, in saying that God desires the salvation of all but decrees or determines the salvation of only some? Positing a contradiction is unconvincing, for the Scriptures teach us that there is "complexity" in the divine will.[50] For instance, in Romans 9, Paul explicitly affirms God's decretive will to elect some (Jacob and not Esau), and yet in 10:21 God stretches his hands out to all Israel in invitation because he longs for them to be saved. The two-sided dimension of God's will is also expressed in the apostle's ministry.

---

[48] So Owen, *Death of Death*, 236–37.

[49] John Murray, "The Free Offer of the Gospel," in *Collected Writings of John Murray. Volume 4: Studies in Theology* (Edinburgh: Banner of Truth, 1982), 129–30.

[50] John Calvin, *Commentaries on the Catholic Epistles*, ed. John Owen, trans. John Owen (repr., Grand Rapids, MI: Eerdmans, 1948), 22:419–20, defended the notion that God's will is "complex." Calvin says, "But it may be asked, If God wishes none to perish, why is it that so many do perish? To this my answer is, that no mention is here made of the hidden purpose of God, to which the reprobate are doomed to their own ruin, but only of his will as made known to us in the gospel. For God there stretches forth his hand without a difference to all, but lays hold only of those, to lead them to himself, whom he has chosen before the foundation of the world" (420). It is important to qualify that God's will is only "complex" in *how it appears to us*. Calvin, again, is helpful here: "God's will is one and simple in him" but it "appears manifold to us on account of our mental incapacity" (*Institutes*, 1.18.3). We need to refer the "complexity" to our perception and not to divine volition per se.

In 2 Timothy 2:10, Paul says he endures all things for the sake of the elect, yet in 1 Corinthians 9:22 he becomes all things to all people so that he might save some. The "complexity" in the divine will is therefore apparent.[51]

If the interpretation proposed here is correct, 2 Peter 3:9 should be understood to teach that God desires the salvation of everyone. Nonetheless, it is clear from many texts that he decrees the salvation of only some. The notion that Christ died to secure the salvation of some and actually paid for the sins of those whom he has chosen fits with divine election and with the application of the Spirit's work to the hearts of believers. The Father, Son, and Spirit work together in securing the redemption of God's people (cf. 1 Pet. 1:1–2). From eternity past God decreed that Christ's death would be effective for the elect. At the same time, sinners are indiscriminately offered full forgiveness because God desires all to be saved.

Hebrews

The main text in Hebrews that relates to definite atonement is Hebrews 2:9, where the author says that Jesus suffered "by the grace of God" (χάριτι θεοῦ) so that "he might taste death for everyone" (ὑπὲρ παντὸς γεύσηται θανάτου). Understandably this text has often been adduced to support unlimited atonement. I will argue, however, that such a reading of the text, though superficially attractive, does not fit well with the context of Hebrews 2.

Before addressing the meaning of Hebrews 2:9, a quick survey of Hebrews relative to the atonement is fitting. In Hebrews, Jesus is the Melchizedekian Priest who, in fulfillment of Psalm 110:1, "sat down at the right hand of the Majesty on high" after accomplishing "purification of sins" (1:3). Jesus, in contrast to the Levitical priesthood, brought "perfection," in that believers now "draw near to God" (7:19) through his sacrifice. His sacrifice is permanently effective, since he intercedes for believers on the basis of his death as the one who lives and reigns forever (7:24–25). The relationship between Jesus's death and his intercession is crucial. Clearly, Jesus's intercession as the Risen One is invariably effective since he intercedes on the basis of his death (cf. Rom. 8:31–34). But it would be illegitimate to posit a

---

[51] The "complexity" in God's will does not depend upon positing a distinction between θέλω and βούλομαι, as if the latter term refers to God's decreed will and the former to his preference. See especially the pointed comments of Marshall, "Universal Grace and Atonement in the Pastoral Epistles," 55–57. Cf. also Mounce, *Pastoral Epistles*, 86. But against Marshall, the distinction between God's decreed and desired will rests on a larger perspective than the individual reading of particular words, and hence is still a legitimate theological conclusion.

separation between his death and intercession. In other words, Jesus intercedes specially and exclusively for those for whom he died. Just as he does not intercede for all, so in the same way he died in a unique sense for those whom he came to save, pleading on the basis of his death for their salvation.

The author of Hebrews desired his readers to be full of assurance. Hence, he reminds them that Christ's blood cleanses their consciences (Heb. 9:14). Christ's sacrifice is the final and definitive sacrifice (9:25–28), and hence no further sacrifice is needed. Christ has effectively borne "the sins of many" (9:28). His one sacrifice renders the need for other sacrifices superfluous (10:1–4). Believers are "sanctified through the offering of the body of Jesus Christ once for all" (10:10; cf. 10:14). Since Christ's work on the cross is complete, he sits at God's right hand (10:12). Sin has been completely and decisively forgiven at the cross of Christ (10:14).

The texts on intercession and sanctification point to the truth that Christ specially died for those who are his own. Nevertheless, Hebrews 2:9 could easily be understood as pointing in the other direction, since it says that Jesus tasted death for all, and Psalm 8 presumably includes a reference to every human being (cf. Heb. 2:5–8).[52]

Yet when we actually examine the context of Hebrews 2, we find evidence suggesting that the death Jesus tasted "for everyone" (ὑπὲρ παντός) does not, in this context, refer to everyone without exception but to everyone without distinction.[53] First, in verses 5–8, though the author refers to human beings in general, he does not put any stress on all human beings without exception. Instead, the author focuses on Jesus Christ and teaches that only those who belong to him will enjoy the rule over all things described in Psalm 8. Second, verse 10 speaks of "bringing many sons to glory" (πολλοὺς υἱοὺς εἰς δόξαν ἀγαγόντα). Jesus's suffering was effective in its design and purpose, in that it actually brought "sons to glory." The focus clearly rests on what Jesus effectively accomplished through his death. Third, those redeemed are described as "brothers" (ἀδελφούς) of Jesus (vv. 11–12).[54] Those who are the beneficiaries of Jesus' death are identified as members of his family. Hence, the author does not call attention to the benefit of Jesus's death for all people

---

[52] So Lightner, *The Death Christ Died*, 71–72; and Shultz, "Multi-Intentioned View of the Extent of the Atonement," 144.

[53] Rightly, Owen, *Death of Death*, 238; and John Murray, *Redemption Accomplished and Applied* (Grand Rapids, MI: Eerdmans, 1955), 61.

[54] William L. Lane, *Hebrews 1–8*, WBC (Waco, TX: Word, 1991), 59, says that they are part of the "covenantal family."

in general but to the advantage that exists for those who are part of his family. Fourth, the particularity in Jesus's family is even clearer in verse 13, where the author, in citing Isaiah 8:18, depicts Jesus as saying, "Behold, I and the children God has given me" (ἰδοὺ ἐγὼ καὶ τὰ παιδία ἅ μοι ἔδωκεν ὁ θεός). Not any or all children are in view here, but specific children—the children God has given to Jesus. It seems, then, that Jesus's brothers are equivalent to the children God gave him. Jesus suffered to bring these to glory, suggesting that his death "for everyone" in context refers to those brothers whom God had ordained to be part of his family. Fifth, in verse 16 the author of Hebrews remarks that Jesus does not help angels, "but he helps the offspring of Abraham." The phrase "offspring of Abraham" (σπέρματος Ἀβραάμ) is most interesting. If the author had a general or unlimited atonement in view, we would expect a reference to the "offspring of Adam" or "the sons of Adam." Such a designation would emphasize the universality of Jesus's work for all human beings. But that is not the purpose of the author of Hebrews here. He focuses on the "offspring of Abraham," so that the emphasis is on God's chosen people—the children of Abraham. As we see elsewhere in the NT, the church of Jesus Christ is considered to be the seed of Abraham (cf. Gal. 3:6–9).[55] Many readers may interpret the text quickly and be guilty of thinking that the "offspring of Abraham" are equivalent to the "offspring of Adam." Clearly, the focus is not on the undifferentiated love of Christ but on his particular concern for the chosen seed of Abraham.

When we place this description of Abraham's offspring with the emphasis on the children God gave to Jesus and the use of the word "brothers," we have significant evidence that Jesus's death "for everyone" (v. 9) is particular rather than general. Hence, it supports definite atonement rather than general atonement. All of this fits with verse 17, which speaks of Jesus's High Priestly ministry "to make propitiation for the sins of the people" (εἰς τὸ ἱλάσκεσθαι τὰς ἁμαρτίας τοῦ λαοῦ). Given the focus on God's elect and Jesus's family in the context, it seems fair to conclude that here the emphasis is on the actual satisfaction accomplished in Jesus's death for those who would be part of his family.[56]

---

[55] Cf. here Harold W. Attridge, *The Epistle to the Hebrews*, Hermeneia (Philadelphia: Fortress, 1989), 94; and Philip E. Hughes, *A Commentary on the Epistle to the Hebrews* (Grand Rapids, MI: Eerdmans, 1977), 119.

[56] In support of interpreting ἱλαστήριον as "propitiation" here, see Lane, *Hebrews 1–8*, 66, and Hughes, *Hebrews*, 121–23; contra Attridge, *Hebrews*, 96 n. 192, who argues for "expiation." Shultz, "Multi-Intentioned View of the Extent of the Atonement," 144, says that all things cannot be subjected to Jesus if he did not pay for the sins of all, but such a theological deduction is not warranted by the argument of Hebrews 2.

To conclude, though Hebrews 2:9 may on first glance support general atonement, a closer look at the context suggests that definite atonement is in view.

Conclusion

This chapter has concentrated on texts that are often cited as disproving definite atonement. In the Pastorals, 1 Timothy 2:1–7, 4:10, and Titus 2:11 focus on salvation being accomplished for all without distinction, both Jews and Gentiles. God's saving purposes are not restricted to the Jews but extend to the entire world. Furthermore, the salvation Christ has accomplished is effective; he has truly ransomed some to be saved (1 Tim. 2:6; Titus 2:11, 14). He has not merely made salvation possible; he has actually saved those whom he has chosen.

Second Peter 2:1, which speaks of Jesus's redemption of the false teachers, is often cited in support of general atonement. I have attempted to show, however, that when we compare 2:1 with 2:20–22, the language of redemption is phenomenological. The false teachers appeared to be believers because of their initial embrace of the Christian faith. Their later defection showed that they were not true believers and therefore were not truly ransomed by Christ. Hence, 2 Peter 2:1 does not support general atonement, and to argue that it does is potentially to compromise Christian perseverance. Second Peter 3:9, which speaks of God's desire for all to repent, should be interpreted as expressing God's desired will, but God's will of desire does not negate the fact that he has decreed that only some will be saved. We have seen in this chapter that we must distinguish between God's desired will (his desire for all to be saved) and his decretive will (his determination that only some will be saved).

Finally, Hebrews 2:9 is regularly cited in defense of general atonement, since it speaks of Jesus's death "for everyone." When we consider Hebrews as a whole, the author emphasizes the effectiveness of Jesus's death, especially in tying together Jesus's intercession with his atoning sacrifice. Furthermore, there are significant indications in the context of Hebrews 2 that "everyone" refers to God's chosen people, for the author speaks of the sons who are brought to glory (v. 10), of Jesus's brothers (vv. 11–12), of the children that God gave to Jesus (v. 13), and of Abraham's offspring (v. 16). In context, the focus is on Abraham's family—the chosen people of God—which rules out a general atonement. Jesus's propitiation (v. 17), then, is specifically for his people.

III

DEFINITE ATONEMENT
IN THEOLOGICAL
PERSPECTIVE

15

Definite Atonement and
the Divine Decree

Donald Macleod

The focus of this chapter is the link between the divine intention of the atonement and its extent. Was it the eternal design of God that the cross should redeem every human being? Or was it his design to redeem the elect, a multitude so vast that no one can count them (Rev. 7:9), but still only a portion of the human race?

Wayne Grudem has expressed some unease over this approach, suggesting that it is a mistake to state the question in a way that focuses on the purpose of the Father and the Son rather than on what actually happened in the atonement: "If we confine the discussion to the purpose of the atonement, then this is just another form of the larger dispute between Calvinists and Arminians." He proposes, instead, that we should focus on the atonement itself: "Did Christ pay for the sins of all unbelievers who will be eternally condemned, and did he pay for their sins fully and completely on the cross? It seems that we have to answer no to that question."[1]

It is difficult to see how "what actually happened in the atonement" can of itself, and irrespective of the divine intention, offer any answer to the question whether it was for the ultimate benefit of all or for the benefit of only some. The crucifixion narrative as such provides no answer, nor does

---

[1] Wayne Grudem, *Systematic Theology: An Introduction to Biblical Doctrine* (Leicester, UK: Inter-Varsity Press, 1994), 601.

the essential nature of Christ's death as a sacrifice. Was the sacrifice for all or for some? Nor can we find an answer in the *effects* of Christ's sacrifice. It expiated sin, but for whom? It propitiated God, but for whom? It made peace with God, but for whom?

As a matter of historical theology the question of the extent of the atonement has always been formulated in terms of the divine decree. Grudem himself quotes Berkhof to this effect:

> The question does relate to the design of the atonement. Did the Father in sending Christ, and did Christ in coming into the world to make atonement for sin, do this with the design or for the purpose of saving only the elect or all men? That is the question, and that only is the question.[2]

In stating the question in these terms, Berkhof was merely following precedent. Nor was this way of stating the question confined to those advocating definite atonement. The Five Articles of the Remonstrants (1610) similarly anchored the discussion in an "eternal unchangeable purpose" (Article I), agreeably to which, "Jesus Christ, the Saviour of the world, died for all men and for every man" (Article II).[3] The response of the Synod of Dort was likewise formulated in terms of "the sovereign counsel and most gracious will and intention of God the Father" (Article II.8).[4]

As understood in Reformed orthodoxy, the divine decree is all-encompassing: God has freely and unchangeably ordained "whatsoever comes to pass" (WCF, 3.1). This includes the eternal destiny of human beings. Some are predestined to everlasting life and others foreordained to everlasting death (WCF, 3.3). The core idea here is discrimination, a fact accepted in one form or another by all Christian traditions except the Universalist. There are "some" and there are "others." The question is, At what point is this discrimination established?[5]

Arminianism

According to Arminianism as represented by the Remonstrant Articles, the eternal counsel of God made no distinction between man and man. The dis-

---

[2] Louis Berkhof, *Systematic Theology* (Edinburgh: Banner of Truth, 1958), 394 (emphasis original).
[3] See Philip Schaff, *The Creeds of Christendom. Volume III: The Evangelical Protestant Creeds*, 3rd ed., rev. and expanded (New York: Harper & Brothers, 1882), 545, 546.
[4] Ibid., 587.
[5] For a helpful overview of the various positions, see table 15.1, by B. B. Warfield, at the end of this chapter.

crimination takes place in time, when some human beings choose to accept the gospel and others choose to reject it. God elects the former and rejects the latter. There is no discrimination between some predestined to faith and others foreordained to be left in unbelief. Nor is there any decreed discrimination with regard to the outcome of the atonement. According to God's "eternal, unchangeable purpose," Christ "died for all men and for every man, so that he has obtained for them all, by his death on the cross, redemption and the forgiveness of sins."[6] John Wesley endorsed this position boldly, declaring that "Christ died, not only for those who are saved, but for those who perish."[7] More recently, Donald Bloesch has reiterated Wesley's contention that every human being is "a blood-bought soul."[8]

But how can blood-bought souls perish? Because, according to the nineteenth-century Scottish Arminian James Morison, while all objective legal obstacles to their salvation have been removed, other internal obstacles remain. These obstacles may be summed up in one word: *unbelief,* "which is now, therefore, the only barrier between human sinners and the enjoyment of pardon, justification, redemption, and reconciliation."[9] Morison seems to regard these remaining internal obstacles lightly. In reality they are formidable in the extreme, and, according to Arminianism, God has made no commitment to removing them. This goes back to the Remonstrants' doctrine of the divine decree: God has determined, by an eternal and unchangeable decree, to save out of the fallen human race those who, by the grace of the Holy Spirit, will believe in Christ. This sets forth clearly a doctrine of conditional election: an election of those who will come to faith, not an election *to* faith. Morison states it unambiguously: "Sinners are elected by God just on the same principle that they are justified by him. Tis as believers that they are justified; and tis as believers that they are elected, and I no more scruple to rejoice in conditional election than I scruple to glory in conditional justification."[10]

On this construction there is no commitment on God's part to overcome human unbelief. The Remonstrants do, indeed, speak of the grace of the Holy Spirit (*gratia praeveniens*), but this grace is not linked to any determination to renew the individual will; nor is it, as in Augustinianism, invincible. On

---

[6] Schaff, *Evangelical Protestant Creeds*, 546.

[7] John Wesley, *Sermons on Several Occasions*, 5 vols. (London: Wesleyan Conference Office, 1876), 3:428.

[8] Donald G. Bloesch, *Jesus Christ: Saviour and Lord* (Carlisle, UK: Paternoster, 1997), 168.

[9] James Morison, *The Extent of the Atonement* (London: Hamilton, Adams & Co., 1882), 2.

[10] Ibid., 104.

the contrary (Article IV of the Remonstrant Articles), many have resisted and overcome this grace, which amounts to no more than what the Reformed call "common" or "general grace." Morison denies that there is "over and above the universal influence, a peculiar kind of influence which God in sovereignty pleases to vouchsafe only to a few."[11] No such special grace is needed, since God has graciously endowed every man with ample ability to believe his gospel: "Nothing can be clearer than that all men are able to avail themselves of the propitiation, when it is presented to them."[12]

This is pure Pelagianism, though not every Arminian has spoken as unguardedly as Morison. Arminianism has had its own version of the "Calvin *versus* the Calvinists" debate ("Arminius against the Arminians") and some, like Philip Limborch and Charles Finney, have been accused of radical departure from the master's teaching. It is clear that Arminius himself (followed by Episcopius, Wesley, Watson, and Pope)[13] insisted strenuously on the necessity of grace: "I ascribe to grace," he wrote, "the commencement, the continuance and the consummation of all good,—and to such an extent do I carry its influence, that a man, though already regenerate, can neither conceive, will nor do any good at all, nor resist any evil temptation, without this preventing and exciting, this following and cooperating grace."[14]

This means that wherever there is faith, grace has gone before it (*prevenient* grace) as its indispensable condition; and this grace is *sufficient* to enable us to come to faith. But it is not in itself effectual, because every one of us is free to resist it. Arminius himself is plain on this: "I believe, according to the scriptures, that many persons resist the Holy Spirit and reject the grace that is offered."[15] More recently, Howard Marshall has put it thus: "The effect of the call of God is to place man in a position where he can say 'Yes' or 'No' (which he could not do before God called him; till then he was in a continuous attitude of 'No.')"[16]

This highlights once again the difficulties inherent in the Arminian doctrine of the divine decree and its associated rejection of the doctrine of defi-

---

[11] Ibid., 100.
[12] Ibid., 97.
[13] See Roger E. Olson, *Arminian Theology: Myths and Realities* (Downers Grove, IL: Inter-Varsity Press, 2006), 166–73.
[14] James Arminius, "A Declaration of the Sentiments of Arminius," in *The Works of James Arminius*, trans. James Nichols and William Nichols, 3 vols. (London, 1825; repr. Grand Rapids, MI: Baker, 1956), 1:664 (cited in Olson, *Arminian Theology*, 162).
[15] Ibid.
[16] I. Howard Marshall, "Predestination in the New Testament," in *Grace Unlimited*, ed. Clark H. Pinnock (Minneapolis: Bethany Fellowship, 1975), 140.

nite atonement. God predestines believers to salvation; he does not predestine individuals to become believers. And Christ secures universal redemption, but he does not secure such a ministry of grace as will ensure that the resistance of the human heart is overcome. Grace must be "improved upon" or "cooperated with." Otherwise it will not overcome our resistance. It is up to us, helped by grace, to say yes.

It is hard to reconcile this with the picture that the NT draws of the spiritual state of humanity. We are dead in sin (Eph. 2:1), utterly hostile to God (Rom. 8:7) and congenitally unable to see the gospel as anything but ridiculous (1 Cor. 2:14). If God does not regenerate us by a monergistic re-creative act in which we ourselves are "altogether passive" (WCF, 10.2), we will remain dead; and if he does not give us the gift of faith, not one single human being will ever be able to free himself from the shackles of unbelief. What advantage is it that a gracious offer is made to us if we cannot but resist and reject the offer? And what advantage is it that the outward legal obstacles have been removed if the internal obstacles still prevent us from taking advantage of the proffered salvation? As B. B. Warfield points out, it is precisely the sort of intimate special influence denied by Morison that lies at the heart of Reformed particularism.[17] It is God who touches us in the innermost core of our being and gives us faith. Every grace that might merit election is itself a result of this divine grace: a grace that we may indeed resist, but which in the case of the elect always proves invincible (the true meaning of the Latin *irresistibilis*). The love that provided a Savior also ensures that we come to him.

Arminian universalism suggests a complete lack of coordination within the divine decree. God decrees that his Son shall die to redeem the whole world, but he makes no provision to apply this redemption to a single soul. Beside this lies an even deeper tension. The work of the Son on the cross is universal and indiscriminate; the work of the Spirit in renewal is limited and particular. Yet the Spirit no less than the Son was author of the divine decree; and over and above that, the work of redemption is at every stage the work of the triune God. The Father, the Son, and the Holy Spirit are involved together at the cross, though each in his own way; and the Father, the Son, and the Spirit are similarly involved in the renewal of the individual soul. The decree covering the work of each person must be coextensive with the decree covering the work of each of the others.

---

[17] B. B. Warfield, *The Plan of Salvation* (Grand Rapids, MI: Eerdmans, 1935), 98.

The work of redemption, as revealed in the NT, is one organic whole, with one intended outcome: to conform God's elect to the image of his Son. It is with a view to this outcome that we are predestined, called, justified, and glorified (Rom. 8:28–30). This makes plain that within the plan of salvation there is an indissoluble link between the forensic and the ontological. All those embraced by electing love will be put right with God; and all those put right with God will be sanctified and glorified.

The peculiarity of Arminianism is that while it seems to provide for universal redemption from the guilt of sin, it makes no provision for redemption from its power. Yet, biblically, the one is as important as the other. Corrupt and depraved as well as guilty, we need to be transformed as well as forgiven. But according to the proponents of universal redemption, this is no part of God's "determination." The cross was focused exclusively on our guilt, ignoring our bondage.

This is all the more remarkable in view of the sentiments expressed in Charles Wesley's great hymn "And Can It Be?" In the final verse, Wesley asserts unmistakably the link between the cross and justification: "No condemnation now I dread." But prior to this he also says,

Long my imprisoned spirit lay
Fast bound in sin and nature's night;
Thine eye diffused a quick'ning ray,
I woke, the dungeon flamed with light;
My chains fell off, my heart was free;
I rose, went forth, and followed Thee.

This challenges every element in Arminian theology. The soul is in a dungeon, in chains. The heart is in darkness. But suddenly the dungeon is filled with light! Suddenly the chains fall off! Is this not invincible grace? And is it not discriminating grace? Who commands the quickening ray, and why does it illuminate only some dungeons and not others? Why are every person's chains not broken? There can be only one answer: "It pleased God, who separated me from my mother's womb, and called me by his grace" (Gal. 1:15, KJV).

Eternal Predestination

Over against Arminianism stands the doctrine of the Reformed Confessions, that the discrimination between the saved and the unsaved is ultimately a matter of the eternal counsel of God. Some men and angels are predestined to everlasting life, others are passed by (WCF, 3.3; 3.7).

Here we have to note, first of all, that election (soteriological predestination) is set in the context of cosmic predestination. God works out everything in accordance with his purpose (Eph. 1:11), including contingent events, the free actions of people, and even the sinful actions of people. Yet we have to be careful as to the relation between these two orders of predestination. It is in the salvation of his people that God has decreed to find personal satisfaction, and cosmic predestination is therefore the servant of soteriological predestination. This has a direct bearing on the question of the extent of the atonement. If the purpose of "all things" is to conform his people to the image of Christ (Rom. 8:28–29), the cross can hardly be an exception. It, too, must have been ordained as a means to this specific end. This is not to deny that by the decree of God some benefits also accrue to the non-elect as a result of the cross. But the great soteriological benefits (reconciliation and redemption) pass them by; and when we ask why, we cannot get beyond Jesus's own words: "Even so, Father: for so it seemed good in thy sight" (Matt. 11:26, KJV).

It is also noteworthy that election is "in Christ." Part of the meaning of this is immediately clear: for example, Christ is the *author* of election. As the eternal Son, *homoousios* with the Father, he is a full and equal partner to the decree. Predestination is Christ-shaped. But by the same token, the "passing by" (*preterition*) of others also accords with the mind of Christ. Limiting the saving benefits of the atonement to definite, special objects of God's love is not a violation of the mind of Christ but an expression of it. Conversely, when we come to the last judgment, where those "passed by" face final condemnation, this, too, is Christ-shaped. It is the Son of Man who pronounces the dread sentence, "Depart from me" (Matt. 25:41). Overwhelmingly solemn though this is, it carries the assurance that judgment will not be without mercy. In the last analysis it is the One who bore sin who will judge it.

It is also clear that Christ is the *executor* of election. He is the appointed Redeemer and bears full responsibility for ensuring that the plan of salvation does not fail. Fundamental to this is the responsibility to atone for his people's sins, but his responsibility does not end there. He is charged with effecting a complete salvation. He must bring us to God (1 Pet. 3:18). This is why the post-resurrection Christ continues to be redemption-active, using his glory to give eternal life to all those whom the Father has given him (John 17:2). The application, as well as the accomplishment of redemption, is his responsibility; the two are part of the one divine purpose, and they are of equal compass. It was all agreed in heaven, before he came; and what was agreed was that as the Good Shepherd he would lay the sheep on his shoulder and bring it home.[18]

But is Christ also the *ground* of election? Are we in Christ first, and then elect; elect because we are in Christ? This takes us to the extreme boundaries of revelation, but if we are elect because we are in Christ, then election ceases to be unconditional. It becomes conditional on our being in Christ. This means that love is not ultimate, whereas, biblically, love is the source of everything. God so loved the world that he gave us his Son; and God so loved us that he gave us to his Son. The impulse to redeem, born of love, comes first, and from it flows the plan of salvation, including, supremely, the provision of a Redeemer. We are elected (loved) to be in Christ; and he does his work as the Mediator of an elect. It is as *their* Redeemer he dies, in their place he suffers, and in their place he is forsaken by the Father. And it is they, precisely and specifically, whom he redeems from the curse of the law, having become accursed in their place (Gal. 3:13); and as an inherent element in that redemption, he has secured, again precisely for them, the promised Spirit (Gal. 3:14). As always, the forensic and the ontological are inseparably linked. God's love is set on securing both; and they are in fact secured, indissolubly, for every single object of his electing love.

Yet Reformed orthodoxy need feel no embarrassment when confronted with the Arminian doctrine of a universal love extended equally to every member of the human race. Arminians believe that God has provided a Savior suited to the needs of every human being and that he has commissioned his ambassadors to plead with every human being to accept the services of this Savior. This is all that Arminians believe; and the Reformed believe it all—every jot and tittle of it. But they also believe that there is a divine love that goes further than mere universal goodwill. There is a love that not only secures a warrant for the prisoner's release but that actually opens the prison doors and pulls the prisoner free. The Arminian does not, by contrast with the Reformed, believe that such a love is universal; rather, he believes that there is no such love: no, not for a single soul. God does not love anyone so much that he is determined to overcome their resistance and draw them

---

[18] John Owen, *Salus Electorum, Sanguis Jesu: Or The Death of Death in the Death of Christ*, in *The Works of John Owen*, ed. W. H. Goold, 24 vols. (Edinburgh: Johnstone & Hunter, 1850–1853; repr. Edinburgh: Banner of Truth, 1967), 10:209.

invincibly into his arms. But this is exactly what the Reformed believe. God has decreed that his redeeming love will do whatever it takes to draw into its own glory a multitude that no one can count; and it is precisely for their sake that he has ordained for himself the pain of sacrificing his own Son as an expiation for their sin.

Supra- and Infralapsarianism

There have been interesting differences of opinion, however, even among those who believe that the discrimination between the saved and the unsaved is ultimately a matter of the eternal counsel of God. These differences have arisen because theologians have ventured to enquire into the order of the divine decrees and have tried to ascertain at what point in that order the discrimination takes place. Did the decree to distinguish the elect from the non-elect come *before* the decree to permit the fall (the supralapsarian position)? Or did it come *after* the decree to permit the fall (the infralapsarian position)?

William Cunningham once referred to this debate as "that unnecessary and now obsolete controversy."[19] Karl Barth saw it differently and devoted eighteen pages of small print to the issue, before identifying himself with a seriously modified supralapsarianism.[20] The key question, as Barth points out, is the *objectum praedestionis*. As God elects, is his eye upon man as fallen or upon man as unfallen?[21]

According to the supralapsarian view, the object of election is man as not yet fallen, or even decreed to fall. This view clearly requires a doctrine of definite atonement. The decree to save some (passing others by) stands all-dominant at the top of the order of the divine decrees, leaving no place in the divine plan for any intention to redeem, in any sense, every member of the human race. As Barth points out, explaining the classic supralapsarian position, "To this proper divine will and decree of God everything else that God wills is subordinate, as an interrelated means to its accomplishment."[22] If even creation and the fall are decreed as means of furthering God's basic purpose of saving his elect, the cross must fall under the same rubric. Christ dies for those whom God has preordained to salvation.

---

[19] William Cunningham, *The Reformers and the Theology of the Reformation* (Edinburgh: T. & T. Clark, 1862), 363.
[20] Karl Barth, *Church Dogmatics*, ed. G. W. Bromiley and T. F. Torrance, 14 vols. (Edinburgh: T. & T. Clark, 1956–1975), II/2, 127–45 (hereafter *CD*).
[21] Ibid., II/2, 127.
[22] Ibid., II/2, 128.

Yet the supralapsarian position was never widely countenanced in Reformed theology. The Synod of Dort, for example, seems to allow that it may be held as a private opinion, but clearly endorses the infralapsarian view that the object of election is man as already created, fallen, and corrupt: the elect are chosen "from the whole human race, which had fallen through their own fault from their primitive state of rectitude into sin and destruction" (I:VII).[23]

In accordance with this, Turretin and the majority of seventeenth-century Reformed dogmaticians were heavily critical of supralapsarianism. One of the criticisms was that it was inherently illogical. It seemed clear to the infralapsarians, as Barth points out, that, "The revelation of the *misericordia Dei* [God's pity for the wretched] presupposes an already existent *miser* [wretched one], and the revelation of the *iustitia Dei* [the righteousness of God] presupposes an already existent *iniustitia* [unrighteousness]."[24] If the first in order of the divine decrees was that God would manifest his mercy in the salvation of the elect and his justice in the damnation of the reprobate (the usual vocabulary of this debate), then both election and reprobation clearly presuppose man's fallenness. This point was already made by Turretin: both the manifestation of mercy and the manifestation of justice "requires the condition of sin in the object, for neither mercy can be exercised without previous misery, nor justice without previous sin."[25]

There has sometimes been a disturbing symmetry in the way Reformed theology has stated the objective of the divine decree, as if God resolved to glorify himself equally in the revelation of his forgiving grace and in the revelation of his retributive justice. Such symmetry is not inherent in the doctrine of predestination. It may well be, on the contrary, that the whole truth can be expressed in the statement that God resolved to glorify his name by the revelation of his mercy in the salvation of the elect. This reflects an unconditional, determinative love committed to ensuring that all the elect come to share in the glory of the eternal Son (John 17:5). But there is no parallel, effectuating decree with regard to the non-elect. They are not singled out; they are passed by. They are not called to unbelief; they are left in it. There is indeed a sovereign element here, but it is a sovereign non-act, not a sovereign act. Their names are *not* put in the book of life; their eyes are *not*

---

[23] Schaff, *Evangelical Protestant Creeds*, 582.
[24] Barth, *CD* II/2, 130.
[25] Francis Turretin, *Institutes of Elenctic Theology*, ed. James T. Dennison, Jr., trans. George Musgrave Giger, 3 vols. (Phillipsburg, NJ: P&R, 1992), 1:346.

opened; their hearts are *not* renewed. The whole truth is present, therefore, in the statement that out of the mass of guilty sinners God has resolved to save his chosen.

This is why Reformed theology, when defining *reprobation*, drew a clear distinction between *preterition* and *condemnation*. The former (from the Latin, *praeterire,* to pass by) corresponds to election. In electing some, God *passes by* others, and this passing by is utterly sovereign and unconditional. But *condemnation*, the final assignation of the impenitent to eternal punishment, is not a sovereign but a judicial act: they are condemned to dishonor and wrath *for their sin* (WCF, 3.7). But this condemnation is a "strange" work (Isa. 28:21) which brings God no pleasure (Ezek. 18:23) and causes no joy in heaven. It is not done with relish, any more than was the case in God's judgment of Israel: "How can I give you up, O Ephraim? How can I hand you over, O Israel?" (Hos. 11:8). What will bring joy to God is the moment when he presents his elect faultless in the presence of his glory (Jude 24–25). This is the satisfaction he has decreed for himself, even at the cost of his own pain. Is the condemnation of some of his creatures part of that pain? We see through a glass, darkly. But if God is glorified in the damnation of sinners, part of that glory is that he shrinks from it; and another part of it is that though he shrinks from it, he does it, because the judge of all the earth must do right. It is an act of equity, not of malice.

A further criticism of supralapsarianism was that it exposed Reformed theology to the charge that it represented God as creating some men merely in order to damn them. This was how Wesley construed the Reformed doctrine of free grace, as if the cause of damnation lay simply in the will of God: "They are born for this—to be destroyed body and soul in hell . . . for what grace God gives, he gives only for this, to increase, not prevent, their damnation."[26] The supralapsarian construction of predestination is certainly open to Wesley's charge. It seems to make the decree to create men and permit them to fall a means of fulfilling the decree ordaining some men to eternal death.[27] This left Turretin profoundly uneasy. It was as if God reprobated men before they were "reprobable" through sin, and destined the innocent to punishment before any criminality was seen in them. It would mean not that

---

[26] Wesley, *Sermons on Several Occasions*, 3:421.
[27] Cf. William Perkins, *A Golden Chain*, chapter 7: "The means of accomplishing God's predestination are twofold: the creation and the fall." See *The Work of William Perkins*, ed. Ian Breward (Appleford, UK: Sutton Courtenay, 1970), 186.

he willed to damn them because they were sinners, but that he permitted them to become sinners in order to damn them; even that he decreed to create in order that he might destroy them.[28]

Over against this, Turretin protested that the creation and fall were not ordained as means to give effect to predestination, but presupposed as its antecedent condition: "Disease in the sick is the previous condition without which he is not cured, but it is not the means by which he is cured."[29] Nor does the physician make the patient sick simply in order that he might heal him.

In Turretin's mind this was linked to another difficulty. According to supralapsarianism, the objects of election are abstractions: not real humans in need of love and redemption, but mere potentialities, creatable but uncreated, liable to fall but not fallen. A nonentity, Turretin objected, cannot be the object of predestination.[30] And how, without sin in the object, could such an election be an election of mercy? Scripture consistently roots our salvation not in a cold, abstract divine sovereignty but in God's warm love and pity; and equally consistently it portrays that love as directed specifically at those already lost and in need of a Savior. In its very foundation this is a love that has to provide an expiatory sacrifice (*hilasmos*; 1 John 4:10); and if that was the condition of the world in general, a hopeless *massa corrupta*, it was no less the condition of every individual among the elect. According to Romans 5:6–11, for example, God's love is for those who were "powerless," "ungodly," "sinners," and "hostiles"; and in Romans 8:29 the objects of predestination are those who have lost the divine image and need to be re-conformed to the likeness of his Son. It was precisely to achieve this that Christ died.

But though prominent advocates of definite atonement have been supralapsarians (most notably Beza), the doctrine does not stand or fall with this particular view of the order of the divine decrees. As Muller points out, the results of the two positions are identical:

> the infralapsarian form does not argue that more human beings are brought into the kingdom, nor does it leave any opening for the human will in matters of salvation. It merely identifies the human objects of the eternal decree differently—as created and fallen rather than as creatable and liable.[31]

---

[28] Turretin, *Institutes*, 1:344.
[29] Ibid.
[30] Ibid., 1:343.
[31] See Richard A. Muller, "The Use and Abuse of a Document: Beza's Tabula Praedestinationis, the Bolsec Controversy, and the Origins of Reformed Orthodoxy," in *Protestant Scholasticism: Essays in Reassessment*, ed. Carl R. Trueman and R. Scott Clark (Carlisle, UK: Paternoster, 1999), 59.

In accordance with this, the Synod of Dort, for example, clearly espoused both infralapsarianism and definite atonement. Granted, on the infralapsarian view the decree to redeem the elect no longer stands at the top of the order of the divine decrees, as it does in supralapsarianism. But the elect are still a definite number, albeit chosen from within the human race conceived of as fallen, and God's plan of salvation is that they, and they only, will be saved. Furthermore, this divine determination to save his chosen is still the primary, all-controlling focus of the divine purpose. God works all things together to ensure that all those elected out of the *massa corrupta* will one day be conformed to the image of his Son. It is toward this outcome that all history moves, and whether the saving decree be supralapsarian or infralapsarian makes no difference to the size of the elect and redeemed community. Whenever (in the order of divine thought) the names were put in the book of life, every name in the Book will have his sins atoned for and his soul transformed.

Barth's "Purified Supralapsarianism"

In the twentieth century, Karl Barth lent the luster of his name to what he called a "purified supralapsarianism."[32] The purification has been such, however, as to produce a doctrine that none of the protagonists on either side of the seventeenth-century debate would recognize, because Barth took up his position only after stripping it of the presuppositions common to both parties. This meant that predestination no longer referred to an eternal election or non-election from among the individual descendants of Adam; nor did it imply that God set up a "fixed system" within which human beings would live out their temporal histories; nor again did it mean an exact equilibrium between God's final election of some and his final rejection of others. Above all, election was not a *decretum absolutum* in which God by a sovereign and utterly inscrutable act of his own good pleasure eternally fixed the number of the saved and of the lost.

This leaves little or nothing of the terms on which the debate between supra- and infralapsarians was originally conducted. The discrimination between the saved and the unsaved, the regenerate and the unregenerate, is no longer a matter of the divine will (if, indeed, there is any discrimination at all); and the doctrine of election has nothing to do with the election of some

---

[32] Barth, *CD* II/2, 142.

and the non-election of others. In effect, the whole Augustinian–Reformed doctrine of predestination is dismissed as misguided and in radical need of correction, a correction which at least one Barth scholar has suggested will stand forever as his greatest contribution to the development of church doctrine.[33]

Barth was fully aware that his doctrine was discontinuous with the previous theological tradition. But what was this "purified supralapsarianism"? It was supralapsarianism in the sense that Barth placed soteriology at the top of the order of the divine decrees, even to the extent of giving the order of redemption primacy over the order of creation. God's plan for the final destiny of the human race comes before his will to create, and before his will to permit the fall and the existence of evil. The determination of the elect comes before all else.

But then, having placed soteriology at the top of the order, Barth goes on to transfer election from soteriology to christology. The elect man is Christ, and as such he is the true object of predestination. However, this itself involves two distinct ideas. At the most fundamental level, God elects himself, which means that prior to the creation of the world he ordained that he would become the man Jesus Christ. Indeed his very reason for creating the world was that he would become this man, defining himself as the God who is *for us*, and who is for us in this way, burdened with our sins and afflicted by their curse and misery.

There is also, however, a subsequent election. Not only does God predestine his Son to come into existence as the Son of David, but he also makes him, incarnate as the Son of David, "a new object of the divine decree, distinct from God."[34] It is this elect man, Jesus Christ, who is foreordained to glory and honor. He is the object, the sole object, of God's good pleasure. Indeed, he *is* his good pleasure. He is his decree, the witness to God's affirmation of man and to God's foreordination of man to victory over death and sin. God is glorified not in the salvation or damnation of individuals, but in this man, Jesus Christ.

But Christ is not only the Elected One. He is also predestined to be the Rejected One, the object of God's No! as well as of God's Yes! This is Barth's

---

[33] See Bruce L. McCormack, "Grace and Being: The Role of God's Gracious Election in Karl Barth's Theological Ontology," in *The Cambridge Companion to Karl Barth*, ed. John B. Webster (Cambridge: Cambridge University Press, 2000), 92.
[34] Barth, *CD* II/2, 162.

version of the doctrine of double predestination. Christ, the elected one, is also foreordained to bear the divine penalty due to sin: "And he does so. But he does it in the person of the elected man Jesus. . . . The wrath of God, the judgment and the penalty, fall, then, upon him."[35]

Alongside the election of "this man, Jesus Christ" there is, however, another election: the election of the community. This community is the human race, created by God and fallen away from God: "It is to this man, to the plurality of these men, to each and all, that the eternal love of God is turned in Jesus Christ."[36] This is "the election of the many (from whom none is excluded) whom the electing God meets in this way."[37] Here Barth seems to embrace an explicit doctrine of universal redemption:

> whether you are a friend of God like Moses or an enemy like Pharaoh, whether your name is Isaac or Ishmael, Jacob or Esau, you are the man on account of whose sin and for whose sin Jesus Christ has died on the cross for the justification of God, and for whose salvation and bliss, and for whose justification, he has been raised from the dead.[38]

This is at the opposite pole from the idea of a discriminating eternal predestination of individuals, some elected to eternal life, some passed by. According to Barth, the whole human race is elect in Christ; and having also been rejected (reprobated?) in Christ we have, one and all, died with him, risen with him, and have been justified with him.

Barth saw his formulation as a "correction" to the "classical" doctrine of predestination.[39] It is hard to see, however, how an election focused so exclusively on the person of Christ can be reconciled with the NT concept of an election of grace. In Barth's supralapsarianism the object of election is the Son of God. But does his being the Son not preclude his being in any sense the object of an election grounded in mercy? How can the electing God make himself the object of an unconditional election of grace?

It is equally difficult to see how, remaining faithful to Scripture, we can dispense with the idea of an election of individuals and replace it with the idea of the election of "the community," whether that community be Israel, the church, or the entire human race. This is clearly what Barth advocates:

---

[35] Ibid., 124.
[36] Ibid., 195.
[37] Ibid.
[38] Ibid., 223.
[39] Ibid., 325.

"We have to remove completely from our minds the thought of an individual purpose in predestination."[40] Yet what Barth repudiates is, surely, what Scripture sets forth. Not only is there an election within elect Israel, but one individual, Jacob, is elect, while another individual, Esau, is not (Gen. 25:23). Yahweh "knew" Jeremiah before he was formed in the womb and set him apart before he was born (Jer. 1:5). The imagery of Revelation 20:15 belongs to the same order: it is "names," not communities, that are written in the book of life.

In accordance with this, it is in the *ordo salutis* that Scripture characteristically places the doctrine of predestination. This is particularly clear in Romans 8:29–30: "For those God foreknew he also predestined to be conformed to the image of his Son, that he might be the firstborn among many brothers and sisters. And those he predestined, he also called; those he called, he also justified; those he justified, he also glorified" (NIV). A similar soteriological setting for predestination can be seen in Ephesians 1:3–14, where God is said to have chosen "us," and to have chosen us to "every spiritual blessing in the heavenly places in Christ"—blessings which the apostle goes on to enumerate as holiness, adoption, redemption, forgiveness, and the sealing of his Spirit. In love, God chose *us*; he chose us to share in the core blessings of personal religion, and he undertook to intervene directly and intimately in our lives to ensure that these blessings actually reach us. This brings us back to the key issue raised by the Arminian controversy. Is there a direct, divine action on the human heart, rooted in God's own discretion and initiative, which accounts for the fact that some come to faith and others do not? Paul leaves us in no doubt. God made us alive together with Christ, God raised us up, and God seated us in the heavenly realms (Eph. 2:4–6).

A further difficulty with Barth's doctrine is that here, once again, we meet a fracturing of the unity between the immanent and the economical Trinity. The immanent Trinity, the electing God as he is in himself, makes no distinction between person and person. Election is universal: none are passed by. God "has mercy on the man Jesus and in him on all men by becoming man himself, by taking every man's burden in order to clothe man with his own glory."[41] Yet, in the execution of the decree by the Holy Trinity in the economy of redemption there is clear discrimination. Indeed, it

---

[40] Ibid., 143.
[41] Ibid., 219.

was this fact that Calvin took as his point of departure for his discussion of predestination: "In actual fact, the covenant of life is not preached equally among all men, and among those to whom it is preached it does not gain the same acceptance either constantly or in equal degree."[42] The factual basis of Calvin's approach is indisputable. But how can it be that in the eternal covenant the divine self-determination has as its object the salvation of all men,[43] while in the administration of the covenant there is no provision for the salvation of all men?

Barth's answer is that we cannot, with traditional supralapsarianism, view the plan of salvation as a system of "consistent theistic monotheism"[44] or as "a fixed system which anticipated the life-history and destiny of every individual as such."[45] The rhetorical force of this sentence depends on the word "fixed," suggesting that the traditional doctrine implies a deterministic scheme in which every event, including every human decision, is linked in an inexorable causal nexus. Yet such classic Reformed statements as the Westminster Confession of Faith (3:1) disown such determinism, laying down that divine foreordination offers no violence to the will of the creature; nor does it take away liberty or contingency, but rather establishes it.

This respect for liberty and contingency does not detract from the fact that foreordination is all-embracing (Eph. 1:11). Even less does it detract from the fact that God, without violating our wills, is involved in the application of redemption not merely in the remote sense in which he is involved in the fluttering of a butterfly's wings, but in the direct sense that he is the Author and Giver of faith. Barth denies this, repudiating the idea that the elect are, by the grace of God, delivered from the impotence and depravity to which they were subject by nature.[46] This is essentially the same denial of invincible grace as was urged by Arminianism. Yet it is precisely of such grace that Scripture speaks, and it is in its very nature particularist, implying a specific divine intervention in the lives of individual human beings.

But this still leaves us, on Barth's terms, with the tension between the decree of the immanent Trinity and the work of the economical Trinity. Why, if God elects all people to salvation, is the work of the economical Trinity not

---

[42] John Calvin, *Institutes of the Christian Religion*, ed. John T. McNeill, trans. Ford Lewis Battles, (Philadelphia: Westminster, 1960), 3.21.1.
[43] Barth, *CD* II/2, 116.
[44] Ibid., 129.
[45] Ibid., 134.
[46] Ibid., 328.

coextensive with the will of the immanent Trinity? This is the difficulty that haunts every theory of universal redemption.

The more one reflects on Barth's doctrine of election, the more the suspicion grows that it is not quite so original after all, and that to a large extent he is merely playing different word-games with the traditional terminology. This is particularly true of his view of Christ as the Rejected One. Prima facie, it looks as if Barth adopts the paradoxical position that Christ is both elect and reprobate, and the language startles because we assume that "reprobate" carries its usual connotation of "son of perdition," denied all grace, hardened, and condemned to eternal torment for his sins. If that were the case, Barth's doctrine would indeed be novel; and paradoxical. But this is not what Barth means. In effect, if not in intention, what he offers is an exposition of 1 Peter 1:19–20, with its portrayal of Christ as the one foreordained as the Lamb of God before the foundation of the world. It was implied in his assumption of the office of Mediator that Christ would not only *offer*, but would *be*, the *hilasmos* for our sins; or, in Barth's language, God "elects Jesus, then, at the head and in the place of all others. The wrath of God, the judgment and the penalty, fall, then, upon him."[47] In the supreme paradox, God makes himself the object of his own wrath.

Yet Christ is not appointed an eternal reprobate. Instead, there is a work given him to do, namely, to lay down his life as a ransom for many; there is a terminal point to that work, such that he himself can cry triumphantly, "It is finished!" (John 19:30); and at its terminus there lies not reprobation but resurrection glory and hyper-exaltation (Phil. 2:9). It is to such joy that the Messiah is predestined: to have the preeminence in all things. And in view of such an outcome he is emphatically the Elect One, not the Reprobate.

Where Barth does become original, however, is where he goes on to argue that the rejection of Christ is the rejection of every man. God has elected all to salvation, and God has elected all to rejection (in Christ); and in view of this rejection there is now no condemnation to any human being. On the basis of Christ's rejection, all are saved and there can be no place for any doctrine of definite (limited) atonement.

This is at least the logic of Barth's position. Behind the details, as Geoffrey Bromiley points out, looms an "incipient universalism."[48] Yet Barth re-

---

[47] Ibid., 124.
[48] Geoffrey W. Bromiley, *Introduction to the Theology of Karl Barth* (Edinburgh: T. & T. Clark, 1979), 97.

fuses to take the next step and adopt explicitly the doctrine of *apokatastasis*. That doctrine, in Barth's view, is an unwarranted inference from an optimistic estimate of man in conjunction with the infinite potentiality of grace.[49] The final extent of the circle of election is God's concern:

> If we are to respect the freedom of divine grace, we cannot venture the statement that it must and will be finally coincident with the world of men as such (as in the doctrine of the so-called *apokatastasis*). No such right or necessity can legitimately be deduced. Just as the gracious God does not need to elect or call any single man, so He does not need to elect or call all mankind.[50]

As Berkouwer points out, it is impossible to harmonize Barth's refusal to accept the *apokatastasis* with the fundamental structure of his doctrine of election.[51] If election is universal, why not salvation? This is not the place for a full evaluation of this tension, but it may be the place to note that Barth's rejection of the *apokatastasis* brings him right back to the very point he wished to avoid: the idea that the divine decree is ultimately a matter of God's "inscrutable good pleasure." Barth insists that because the decree is the decree of Jesus Christ it cannot be a *decretum absolutum*. On the contrary, everything is revealed in the face of Jesus Christ, and there is no mystery left: "Faith in predestination is faith in the non-rejection of man."[52]

It transpires, however, that the elect can be disobedient to their election, and for those who are thus disobedient "there does exist a definite sphere of damnation."[53] We are still left, then, with the dark mystery of reprobation: the condemnation of some to dishonor and wrath for their sins (in this case, the sin of rejecting their election). This means that we can no longer say, as Barth wishes to say, that the choice of the godless man is void.[54] Nor can we say that the wrath of God no longer has any relevance for him.[55] Behind the electing God, and behind the God who appoints himself to be rejected in the place of man, there is, after all, another God, who, at the Great Assize, will pronounce the dread sentence, "Depart from me, you cursed" (Matt. 25:41).

And yet, from the standpoint of Scripture, not *another* God, for it is Jesus Christ, the Son of Man, the electing God, who now gathers the nations

---

[49] Barth, *CD* II/2, 295.
[50] Ibid., 417.
[51] G. C. Berkouwer, *The Triumph of Grace in the Theology of Karl Barth* (London: Paternoster, 1956), 116.
[52] Barth, *CD* II/2, 167.
[53] Ibid., 27.
[54] Ibid., 306.
[55] Ibid., 125.

together and does what Barth insists the doctrine of election must never do: separate people into the blessed and the cursed, the sheep and the goats. Reprobation, too, is Christ-shaped.

Barth's doctrine of election offers no solution to the problem of evil. Evil remains an *anomia*: a lawlessness without reason; a darkness without light; a vile and virulent force which God incorporates into his tapestry, but which he never condones. The doctrine of universal election still leaves us with a universe from which evil will never be finally eradicated. Despite the fact that all men are elect in Christ, and all sin is expiated by his blood, there remains a residual humanity permitted to say a final No! to God's Yes! Before such a permission, we are speechless, and Barth has no more to say than had the proponents of the "classical" doctrines of predestination and definite atonement. He can merely quote, once again, the words of the Elect One: "yes, Father, for such was your gracious will" (Matt. 11:26).

The Electing God: *Incarnandus* or *Incarnatus*?

There remains the most distinctive aspect of Barth's doctrine: the capacity in which Christ acts as the electing God. Brunner attributed to Barth the view that the preexisting God-Man was the ground of election, and pointed out that if there were indeed an eternal preexistence of the God-Man, the incarnation would have been utterly unnecessary: "The idea of the preexistent *Divine Humanity* is an *ad hoc* artificial theory of the theological thinker, who can only carry through his argument that the Man Jesus is the Only Elect Human Being by means of this theory."[56] Bruce L. McCormack dismisses this as "a fairly drastic misunderstanding,"[57] but it is easy to see how the misunderstanding could arise. Barth supports his conception of Christ as the electing God with an exegesis of the prologue to John's Gospel, stressing the identity of the Logos *asarkos* (John 1:1) with the Logos *ensarkos* (John 1:14). In the light of this, the preexistent Logos who was "with God" (in, for example, the decree of predestination) is the same person as the Jesus of history; and Barth seems to move from this to the idea that it is this Jesus of history who is, in some sense, the electing God. This is clearly how McCormack understands Barth: Jesus Christ, the God-Human in his divine-human unity, is the subject (author) of election.[58]

---

[56] Emil Brunner, *The Christian Doctrine of God* (London: Lutterworth, 1949), 347.
[57] McCormack, "Grace and Being," 92.
[58] Ibid., 94.

McCormack falls back at this point on a distinction, clearly recognized by seventeenth-century Reformed theologians, between the Logos *incarnatus* (already incarnate) and the Logos *incarnandus* (to be incarnate). It was manifestly not the incarnate Logos who was the author of election. But was it the Logos *incarnandus*?

According to Reformed orthodoxy, Christ became *incarnandus* only as the object of election. He was ordained to be incarnate by the decree of God. This makes election prior to *incarnandus* and posits (in the order of thought) a prior state of the Logos in which not only was he not incarnate but he was not ordained to be incarnate; and this means a mode of being independent of his being as Redeemer. McCormack emphatically rejects this. It implies, he alleges, that God's decision to turn toward the human race was contingent and does not reflect what God is essentially. Ontologically, God is no longer defined as the God whose very being is actualized in the decision to become incarnate and to die on behalf of the human race.[59]

In such relatively uncharted waters one runs the risk of drastically misunderstanding both Barth and McCormack (who are not necessarily pursuing the same agenda). But the point at issue is a weighty one: whether the incarnation was discretionary or whether (from the standpoint of the highest conceivable supralapsarianism) the impulse to become incarnate is the very essence of God.

Suppose that, instead of arguing from John's prologue, Barth had argued from Philippians chapter 2: would he have reached the same conclusion? The key moment in the Philippians passage is the decision of the preexistent Christ to make himself nothing (v. 7, NIV). It clearly *was* a decision, one that involved his adding to the form of God the form of a servant, and obscuring his divine glory behind the veil of humanness. It was voluntary and discretionary even to the extent that the apostle can commend it as an example to the Philippian believers: "Your attitude should be the same as that of Christ Jesus" (v. 5, NIV). Indeed, not only are they to imitate his attitude (and his action), but they are to imitate his motives: he disregarded his own interests and focused on those of others.

It is true that this decision was taken by Christ from all eternity. Just as God never existed without being in love with his people, so the Son of God never existed without being of a mind to become man and to suffer and die

---

on their behalf. Yet, though eternal, that decision was contingent. It was not, like his eternal sonship, the necessary form of his being, but a chosen form, born of a decision freely taken, and in itself the first of a sequence of decisions which would take him eventually to Bethlehem, Gethsemane, and Calvary; just as, by another free decision, he chose not to take the nature of angels.

Christ, then, became incarnate not simply willingly (*volens*), but because he willed to (*voluit*). Does this make the incarnation arbitrary and prevent us from learning anything from it about what God really is? Surely not; otherwise all our free decisions would be arbitrary, whereas it is precisely our free decisions that declare what we really are. Christ's free decision to empty himself truly expressed his *morphe*; but his *morphe* did not necessitate it. It was a choice, a free choice, and had it not been such, it would not have been his glory.

At the same time, however, Christ's foreordination of himself to become incarnate rendered the incarnation certain. The same cannot be said of universal election as Barth construes it. If God predestined all men to salvation in Christ, that decree has clearly not been fulfilled, and that must surely call into question its very existence. Saving grace for each and all of Adam's descendants cannot be inferred from the being of God even as disclosed to us in the election of "this man, Jesus." Just as the incarnation was an act of the divine freedom, so the bestowal of grace on individuals is an act of the divine freedom. It is bestowed on all for whom the triune God purposed it and on all for whom, in accordance with that purpose, God the Son purchased it.

Hypothetical Universalism

Alongside the supra- and infralapsarian versions of predestinarianism there exists a third: Hypothetical Universalism, which attempts to proclaim the doctrine of universal redemption while at the same time retaining the doctrine of unconditional election. There are nuanced positions within Hypothetical Universalism that must be respected.[60] Some Hypothetical Universalists, such as John Davenant, for example, could argue for an infralapsarian position on the *ordo decretorum*, seeing election and reprobation as preceding

---

[60] See Richard A. Muller, "Davenant and Du Moulin: Variant Approaches to Hypothetical Universalism," in his *Calvin and the Reformed Tradition: On the Work of Christ and the Order of Salvation* (Grand Rapids, MI: Baker Academic, 2012), 126–60.

the decree to give Christ as Redeemer, while at the same time presenting the decree of redemption as referencing the elect and the reprobate in different ways in order to accomplish different ends. On this reading, God decreed that the cross should *purchase* salvation for all men on the condition that they believe, but also decreed that it should be *applied* to the elect only. This means that the discrimination between saved and unsaved is still rooted in the divine decree. Other Hypothetical Universalists argued that in the order of divine thought the discrimination follows redemption. The elect are chosen not only from among the fallen but from among the redeemed: hence the description, "post redemptionist."

This latter school of thought is usually associated with Moïse Amyraut (Amyraldus),[61] whose *Brief Traitté de la Predestination et de ses Principales Dépendances* (1634) led, in the oft-quoted words of Peter Bayle, to "a kind of civil war among the Protestant theologians of France."[62] Amyraut was cited to explain and defend his views at the French National Synod of Alençon in 1637.[63] It is clear from Quick's account that Amyraut believed unequivocally in absolute predestination, but within this predestination he distinguished two decrees.[64] First, there was a conditional decree "to save all men through Jesus Christ, if they shall believe in him." It was in this connection that Amyraut spoke of Christ dying "également pour tous" (equally for all): a form of words the Synod directed him not to use in the future because it was "an occasion of stumbling to many."[65] But besides this conditional decree to redeem the whole world there was a second, unconditional decree "to give Faith unto some particular Persons": in other words, to *apply* the redemption only to an elect chosen from among the redeemed.[66]

Amyraut had drawn inspiration from his beloved Scottish mentor, John Cameron, who had taught that, "Christ died for believers *absolutely*, for all men *conditionally*."[67] But even before Cameron and Amyraut there was already a significant group of English Hypothetical Universalists, foremost

---

[61] Warfield, *Plan of Salvation*, 94, for example, uses the term "Amyraldianism" as a generic description of Hypothetical Universalism.

[62] Brian G. Armstrong, *Calvinism and the Amyraut Heresy: Protestant Scholasticism and Humanism in Seventeenth-Century France* (1969; repr., Eugene, OR: Wipf & Stock, 2004), 80, hereafter cited as *CAH*.

[63] There is a useful summary of the proceedings in John Quick, *Synodicon in Gallia Reformata: or, the Acts, Decisions, Decrees and Canons of Those Famous National Councils of the Reformed Churches in France*, 2 vols. (London, 1692), 2:354–57.

[64] Ibid., 2:354.

[65] Ibid. Amyraut removed the words in his 1658 edition.

[66] Quick, *Synodicon in Gallia Reformata*, 2:354.

[67] John Cameron, *Praelectiones*, 3 vols. (Saumur, France: 1628), 3:196.

among whom was John Davenant, Bishop of Salisbury, the senior member of a delegation sent to the Synod of Dort with specific royal instructions to maintain the doctrine of universal redemption set forth in Article 31 of the Church of England's *Articles of Religion*: "The offering of Christ once made is that perfect redemption, propitiation, and satisfaction, for all the sins of the whole world, both original and actual." Davenant's efforts at the Synod were successful at least to the extent that he, Amyraut, and later Hypothetical Universalists, repeatedly professed themselves willing to subscribe to the Canons of Dort. In one of his communications from the Synod, Davenant indicated that, in compliance with his instructions, he had supported the doctrine of universal redemption ("our Blessed Saviour by God's Appointment did offer himself up for the redemption of mankind"), but he had also maintained *"God's and Christ's special intention to redeem effectually*, and to merit effectual Grace only to the Elect."[68] Davenant clearly commanded wide respect, and when asked by some continental Divines for his views on the "Gallican Controversy" he replied in a tract, "On the controversy among the French Divines of the Reformed Church, concerning the gracious and saving will of God towards sinful men."[69] While critical of some of Cameron's expressions, and even more so of his doctrine of "universal grace," Davenant did not disown his core thesis that "Christ died for all men individually, with some general intention."[70] Instead he declared that, "Christ is rightly said to have died for all men, inasmuch as on his death is founded a covenant of salvation, applicable to all men while they are in this world."[71]

Davenant's mature and extended deliverance on the subject appeared in his posthumous "A Dissertation on the Death of Christ, as to its Extent and special Benefits."[72] The core thesis of the "Dissertation" posits two divine wills: "There was in Christ himself a will according to which he willed that his death should regard all men individually; and there was also a will accord-

---

[68] See John Davenant, "Letters and Expresses from the Synod of Dort," appended to John Hales, *Golden Remains of the Ever Memorable Mr. John Hales of Eton College, &c* (London, 1688), 587, 590.

[69] See Morris Fuller, *The Life Letters and Writings of John Davenant* (London: Methuen, 1897), 193–200.

[70] Ibid, 195.

[71] Ibid.

[72] John Davenant, "A Dissertation on the Death of Christ, as to its Extent and special Benefits: containing a short History of Pelagianism, and shewing the Agreement of the Doctrines of the Church of England on general Redemption, Election, and Predestination, with the Primitive Fathers of the Christian Church, and above all, with the Holy Scriptures," in *An Exposition of the Epistle of St. Paul to the Colossians* (1627), trans. Josiah Allport, 2 vols. (London: Hamilton, Adams, 1832). This is the title of the English translation of the original Latin edition published in 1650 (Davenant had died in 1641). This translation (along with the "Tract") was appended by Josiah Allport to Davenant's commentary on Colossians. The "Dissertation" was reprinted separately (with different pagination) by Quinta Press (Oswestry, UK) in 2006. This reprint also includes the "Tract" on the Gallican controversy (201–209).

ing to which he willed that it should pertain to the elect alone."[73] However, unlike Cameron, who directed his polemics mainly at Beza and "the Divines" (his name for the Reformed orthodox), Davenant manifests a real concern over the threat posed by Arminianism, and particularly the position of the Dutch Remonstrant Grevinchovius, who argued that the passion of Christ was like a throw of the dice, leaving it entirely possible that the offer of the gospel would not be taken up by a single individual: "the redemption might be obtained for all, and yet applied to none."[74] Over against this, Davenant insisted that God had decreed from eternity infallibly to save the elect; and Christ would have been aware of this decree, which meant that in his will, as he offered himself, there was some effectual and singular intention of effectively saving these persons, the elect: "Therefore the intention of Christ in offering himself regarded the elect in a special manner."[75]

In what sense, then, is the death of Christ "the universal cause of the salvation of mankind?"[76] Davenant offers no single answer to this, and much of what he does say would command instant assent even among most advocates of definite atonement. He speaks, for example, of the death of Christ being "applicable to every man";[77] of the promises of the gospel "appertaining" to all to whom they are published; and of men having a "common right" to believe the gospel.[78] But sometimes he is on less certain ground, as when he accepts the idea that the passion of Christ renders God "placable" or "reconciliable."[79] In reality, surely, God was already placable or reconcilable prior to the cross, otherwise he could never have been reconciled to the world by the death of his Son. Divine placability is not a consequence of the cross, but its presupposition.

Davenant also speaks of the oblation of Christ as ratifying and confirming the evangelical covenant: "Whoever believes will be saved." There is no reason, however, why a believer in definite atonement should not present this covenant as lucidly and fervently as a believer in Hypothetical Universalism. When the former offers redemption to all, he knows that it was not ordained for all; but, equally, when the latter calls all men to faith, he knows that it was not ordained for all.

---

[73] Davenant, "Dissertation," 2:380.
[74] Ibid., 2:514.
[75] Ibid., 2:526.
[76] Ibid., 2:401.
[77] Ibid., 2:344.
[78] Davenant, "Dissertation," 2:411.
[79] Ibid., 2:443.

By far the most interesting part of Davenant's treatment is his doctrine of "ordained sufficiency." All Reformed theologians have agreed on the infinite *inherent* sufficiency of the sacrifice of Christ: sufficient in itself to redeem the whole world and many worlds besides. Davenant wants to go beyond this and to speak not only of an inherent sufficiency, but of an ordained sufficiency. By God's ordination and deliberate intention Christ was offered for the redemption of all mankind and *accepted* for the redemption of all mankind.[80] The sufficiency, he claims, is not confined to the intrinsic nature of the sacrifice but is extended to the divine intention: in the act of offering himself, it was Christ's intention to redeem all men. But the intention was conditional in the sense that Christ's redemptive act had to be completed by an additional act, external to the sacrifice itself, namely faith; and it was not part of the "ordained sufficiency" to secure this faith for all. The "ordained sufficiency," then, means only that Christ's death was the appointed means to save all men, but (as he conceded in his "Tract") this appointment was not accompanied by any "determinate will in God of producing that end by those means."[81] There was no divine resolve actually to save all men, but only "a general sufficiency" to effect the salvation of all.

It is hard to distinguish this "general sufficiency" from the "mere" sufficiency with which Davenant had professed himself dissatisfied. God ordained the means by which all people might be saved, but he did not ordain the grace by which all could avail themselves of these means. In sum, Davenant is always more confident discussing the absolute decree to save the elect than he is when discussing the hypothetical decree to save everyone.

The influence of Davenant was reflected in the presence at the Westminster Assembly of a small but articulate group of Hypothetical Universalists, including Edmund Calamy, John Arrowsmith, Lazarus Seaman, and Richard Vines.[82] The most vocal of these was Calamy, who expressly aligned himself with "our devines of the sinod of Dort" and declared,

> Christ did pay a price for all, absolute intention for the elect, conditionall intention for the reprobate, in case they doe believe; that all men should be *salvabiles, non obstante lapsu Adami*; that Jesus Christ did not only dy sufficiently for all, but God did intend in giving of Christ and Christ in

---

[80] Ibid., 2:403.
[81] Davenant, "Tract," part I.
[82] See Alexander F. Mitchell and John Struthers, eds., *Minutes of the Sessions of the Westminster Assembly of Divines* (Edinburgh: Blackwood, 1874), lv. Mitchell, the author of the introduction, describes them as disciples of Davenant.

giving himself did intend to put all men in a state of salvation in case they doe believe.[83]

The lay theologian Edward Polhill belonged to the same tradition,[84] but the most thorough exposition of English Hypothetical Universalism was Richard Baxter's *Universal Redemption of Mankind, by the Lord Jesus Christ*, published posthumously in 1694. Baxter is particularly explicit in his post-redemptionism, arguing that there was no discrimination between elect and non-elect prior to the satisfaction of Christ. When it came to the cross, "Neither the Law whose curse Christ bore, nor God as the Legislator to be satisfied, did distinguish between men as Elect and Reprobate . . . and so impose on Christ or require from him satisfaction for the sins of one sort more than of another; but for *Mankind* in general."[85] However, "Election and Redemption are not of the same extent, and not all [are] Elected that are Redeemed, but Redemption is Universal."[86] But, although universal, this redemption is entirely hypothetical: we are all *conditionally* pardoned whether we believe it or not.[87] As with Cameron and Amyraut, Baxter is prepared to affirm that, "Christ dyed equally for all Men," but he immediately adds, "Yet he never properly intended or purposed the actual justifying and saving of all."[88] Redemption may be universal, but the sovereign election of God operates within the community of the redeemed, conferring faith according to "the good pleasure of God and the Redeemer, which we call Predestination."[89]

Hypothetical Universalism clearly appeals to theologians who believe in eternal predestination but shrink from the idea that Christ died only for the elect. Yet it labors under serious difficulties of its own. The most serious difficulty relates to the division of the divine decree into two parts. Amyraut was clearly conscious of a problem here, and sought to distance himself from any suggestion that there are two decrees. In the mind of God, there is but one, "formed in God in one and the self-same Moment, without any

---

[83] Chad Van Dixhoorn, ed., *The Minutes and Papers of the Westminster Assembly 1643–1652*, 5 vols. (Oxford: Oxford University Press, 2012), 3:692. The Latin phrase, *salvabiles, non obstante lapsu Adami*, means, "salvable, notwithstanding the fall of Adam."
[84] See Edward Polhill, *The Divine Will Considered in Its Eternal Decrees and Holy Execution of Them*, in *The Works of Edward Polhill* (London, 1673; repr., Morgan, PA: Soli Deo Gloria, 1998), 111–211.
[85] Richard Baxter, *Universal Redemption of Mankind by the Lord Jesus Christ* (London, 1694), 36.
[86] Ibid., 279.
[87] Ibid., 40.
[88] Ibid., 63.
[89] Ibid., 42.

succession of Thought, or Order of Priority and Posteriority."[90] This observation is well founded. But can this one decree be simultaneously absolute and conditional? Surely, if the purpose of the one decree is the salvation of all those foreordained to eternal life, everything else in the plan must be subordinate to that? If so, those who advocate Hypothetical Universalism must take the paradoxical position that universal redemption is a means toward particular redemption.[91] Christ died for all, in order to save some. This is to concede that the divine intention from the beginning was to save those, and those only, who actually are saved.

Another difficulty lies in the use that Amyraut, in particular, makes of the distinction between the *secret* and the *revealed* will of God. Armstrong sees this distinction as the "very heart" of Amyraut's attempt to reformulate Reformed theology.[92] In reality, as Herman Bavinck points out, the distinction is as old as Tertullian, though later theologians expressed it variously.[93] On the one hand, there was the will of God's good-pleasure, or God's secret will, or God's decretive will; on the other, there was God's expressed will, or his signified will, or his revealed will, or his preceptive will. The most precise form of the distinction is that between the *decretive* will and the *preceptive* will, but whatever terminology we use it is entirely illegitimate to read the one will off from the other. The fact that God's *preceptive* will is that preachers should offer the redemption of Christ to everyone indiscriminately does not mean that it is therefore part of his *decretive* will that everyone is to be saved—any more than the fact that, since only the elect will believe, preachers should not summon the non-elect to faith. The logic is no different from that which applies to the sixth commandment. God's preceptive will is, "You shall not kill." It clearly is not his decretive will. Yet Amyraut (who preferred to speak of the *secret* and *revealed* will) spoke as if the revealed will were somehow an indicator of the secret will—almost, indeed, an alternative version of it.

The problem is that, rightly or wrongly, it is the *secret* will of God that is under discussion in the debate on the extent of the atonement. Did God in offering his Son intend to redeem even those he had not predestined to salva-

---

[90] Quoted in Quick, *Synodicon in Gallia Reformata*, 2:355.
[91] Cf. D. Broughton Knox, "Some Aspects of the Atonement," in *The Doctrine of God*, vol. 1 of *D. Broughton Knox, Selected Works* (3 vols.), ed. Tony Payne (Kingsford, NSW: Matthias Media, 2000), 261: "In intending to reconcile the elect only, the method God has chosen has been to make all men reconcilable."
[92] Armstrong, *CAH*, 192.
[93] Herman Bavinck, *God and Creation*, vol. 2 of *Reformed Dogmatics*, ed. John Bolt, trans. John Vriend (4 vols.) (Grand Rapids, MI: Baker, 2004), 242.

tion? The answer of Reformed orthodoxy has been a categorical no. But it has also said, no less categorically, that the secret counsel of God can never be our personal rule of conduct. We cannot postpone our response to the gospel until we know whether, according to his secret will, we are elect: we are bound by his revealed will, which commands instant faith and repentance. Nor can we defer complying with God's command to preach the gospel till we have some assurance that, according to his secret will, those before us have been foreordained to eternal life. Our rules of engagement are given in God's *revealed* will. Conversely, however, God's revealed will cannot govern our understanding of his secret decree, as if we could infer from the universal offer of the gospel the doctrine of universal redemption.

Yet, secret though God's decree is, we are not left entirely in the dark. The biblical revelation sheds light on its general principles, if not on its specific details. We know that God's ultimate concern is to conform men and women to the likeness of Christ and that his plan of salvation will ultimately include a multitude too numerous to count. Yet we also know from experience that this multitude will not include each and every member of the human race. It was to explain this fact that Calvin introduced his discussion of election in the *Institutes*: "In actual fact, the covenant of life is not preached equally among all men, and among those to whom it is preached, it does not gain the same acceptance either constantly or in equal degree."[94]

Hypothetical Universalists are likely to reply at this point that this is an abuse of logic, and it is here that scholars such as Armstrong raise the specter of "Reformed Scholasticism," extolling Amyraut as an example of an alternative theology, humane and warmly evangelical. In its Reformed variety, according to Armstrong, scholasticism meant building a system of theology by logical deduction from one central principle, in this case, predestination; and allied to this was an impatience with antinomies, and a determination to harmonize all the apparent contradictions within the system.

The danger is a real one, but Hypothetical Universalism does not by itself provide an infallible antidote. Granted, it cannot be accused of deriving its system from the doctrine of absolute predestination, but it does nevertheless have its own central dogma: the universal offer of the gospel. The idea of a divine decree limiting the extent of the atonement is rejected on the ground that unless Christ died in some sense for all, we cannot tell

---

[94] Calvin, *Institutes*, 3.21.1.

every man, "I have good news for you!" Amyraut himself was convinced that, "the orthodox methodology and doctrine had destroyed the effectiveness of Reformed preaching."[95] Richard Baxter declared categorically, "If Christ hath not satisfied for the Sins of all, then no Man hath a sufficient ground for his first justifying faith."[96] The same note is sounded by contemporary Amyraldians. For example, addressing the 2006 Conference of the Amyraldian Association, J. E. Hazlett "confessed" that in the days when he had seen the gospel through the filter of "Owenite scholasticism" he had always had a bad conscience about evangelistic preaching.[97] The reason for the bad conscience was simple: he could not reconcile the commission to offer Christ to everyone with the doctrine that he died only for the elect. But without letting go of the doctrine of election, he found peace in Hypothetical Universalism: "Our message is for *all without exception*. It is for *all indiscriminately* because of what Christ has done on the cross for *all indiscriminately*."[98]

Armstrong cites it as one of the virtues of Hypothetical Universalism that, over against the "Calvinist" passion for logical consistency, it adhered to the precept that, "it is not necessary for everything in theology to be perfectly reconciled and perfectly coherent, since man is at all times incapable of comprehending God and his actions."[99] But is the doctrine of two wills, one setting forth a universal purchase and the other a particular application, not precisely an attempt to reconcile the doctrine of unconditional election with the universal offer of the gospel? It was Reformed orthodoxy that refused to attempt any such reconciliation. The Canons of Dort, for example, laid down that the promise of the gospel together with the command to believe and repent ought to be proclaimed to all persons indiscriminately and without distinction (II:I), but they moved on almost immediately to declare that it was the will of God that Christ by the blood of the cross should effectually redeem all those and those only "who were from eternity chosen to salvation" (II:VIII). No attempt was made to reconcile those apparently "irreconcilable" truths. Nor were the great evangelists of Reformed orthodoxy embarrassed by the alleged inconsistency. They had received a commission to preach

---

[95] Armstrong, *CAH*, 167.

[96] Baxter, *Universal Redemption*, 168. Cf. Edmund Calamy in *Letters and Papers of the Westminster Assembly*, 3:694: "if the covenant of grace be to be preached to all, then Christ redeemed, in some sense, all—both elect and reprobate."

[97] J. E. Hazlett Lynch, "Evangelistic Preaching—Amyraldian Style," in *Christ for the World: Affirming Amyraldianism*, ed. Alan C. Clifford (Norwich, UK: Charenton Reformed, 2007), 153.

[98] Ibid. (emphasis original).

[99] Armstrong, *CAH*, 170.

the gospel to every creature, and they wasted no time prying into the secret counsels of the Almighty or arguing with him that there was no point in pleading with every sinner since only the elect were to be saved. No Hypothetical Universalist preacher could ever outdo the uninhibited evangelistic passion of, for example, C. H. Spurgeon's sermon, "Compel them to come in" (Luke 14:23).[100] Conversely, Reformed evangelists warned their hearers not to deflect the gospel by vain speculations as to whether their names were in the book of life. The hearer's duty, his imperious duty, was defined in the revealed, preceptive will of God, "Believe in the Lord Jesus Christ." How that could be reconciled with God's decretive will was none of the hearer's business; and even if it had been, Hypothetical Universalism provided no solution. How could they put their trust in a hypothetical redemption? How could they believe at all unless they were elected to faith?

But Hypothetical Universalism faced an even more challenging question. The content of the *absolute* divine will was clear: Christ through his death would effectively and infallibly redeem the elect. But what was the content of the *conditional* will? If by the eternal decree of God Christ died for all mankind equally, in what sense did he die for Judas? In what sense did he redeem the reprobate?

We have already seen the answers offered by such as Davenant and Calamy. Others merely repeated the Arminian phraseology that Christ removed the legal obstacles to the salvation of all men, or that his death opened a door of mercy for all men. But all this is hypothetical (as well as ambiguous). The one great obstacle to the salvation of all people is sin; and the cross did not, as such, remove that obstacle in the case of everyone. More fundamentally, Hypothetical Universalism cannot escape from the difficulty that it posits a serious dislocation within the divine decree. On the one hand, God decreed to redeem all men on condition that they receive the gospel; on the other, knowing that every human being is by nature indisposed to receive the gospel, he decreed to overcome this indisposition only in the elect. He will give *them* faith; the rest he will pass by—redeemed but reprobate. In effect there are two saving decrees: one to save everyone from the guilt of sin by the cross of Christ; and another, quite distinct, to redeem only some from its power. This, surely, exposes a lack of coherence in the divine mind? It also resurrects those other specters that haunt *Arminian* universalism:

---

[100] C. H. Spurgeon, *The New Park Street Pulpit*, 63 vols. (London: Passmore and Alabaster, 1884), 5:18–24.

the dislocation between the work of the earthly Christ and the work of the heavenly, and the dislocation between the atoning work of Christ and the sanctifying work of the Holy Spirit. Why, if all are redeemed, are multitudes left "salvable" but not saved?

The NT, by contrast, insists on a divinely ordained link between the sacrifice of Christ and the subjective transformation of the sinner. This is plain in such a passage as Ephesians 5:25–27, where Paul links the death of Christ to the sanctification of the church: "Christ loved the church and gave himself up for her to make her holy . . . and to present her to himself a radiant church, without stain or wrinkle or any other blemish, but holy and blameless" (NIV). Clearly, the intended outcome of the cross was not merely forgiveness, but holiness; or, as the WCF (8.5) expresses it, Christ "purchased not only reconciliation, but an everlasting inheritance in the kingdom of heaven, for all those whom the Father hath given unto him." He died to bring us to God (1 Pet. 3:18), not to leave us in limbo.

Richard Baxter offered his own variant on the significance of the *conditional* decree to redeem all men. By it, God intended to lay the foundation for an "Evangelical Covenant" offering each and every member of the human race a new and easier way of salvation. God no longer confronts us with the principle "Do and live." Instead, he now requires only evangelical, not legal, obedience. The term "evangelical covenant" already occurs in one of Davenant's letters from the Synod of Dort, where he speaks of the oblation of Christ confirming and ratifying "the *Evangelical Covenant*, which may and ought to be preached seriously to all Mankind without exception."[101] He uses the same terminology in his *Dissertation,* but he also speaks of "a new covenant" where the legal command, "Do and thou shalt live," is replaced by "Believe and thou shalt live." This new covenant is linked directly to the death of Christ: "Through the merit of the death of Christ, a new covenant was entered into between God and the human race."[102]

Baxter developed this idea. Christ having saved all mankind from the legal necessity of perishing, God renounced his right to punish, and delivered the whole human race up to Christ as their Lord and Ruler, "to be dealt with hereafter upon terms of Mercy and not upon the old terms of the Law of Works in meer rigour of justice."[103] These "terms of Mercy," according

---

[101] Hales, *Golden Remains*, 587.
[102] Davenant, "Dissertation," 404.
[103] Baxter, *Universal Redemption*, 26.

to Baxter, amount to a New Law "suited to his present State of Misery," and the tenor of this Law is that,

> whosoever will repent, Thankfully and heartily accept Jesus Christ to be his Saviour, Teacher, King and Head, believing him to be the Redeemer, and will Love him (and God in him) above all, and obey him sincerely, to the Death, shall upon his first acceptance be justified and Adopted, and upon his perseverance be justified at Judgment, saved from Hell, and Glorified.

Conversely, whoever rejects Christ "shall bear the Guilt and punishment of all his Sins against the Law, and for his refusal be sorelier punished."[104]

Other Hypothetical Universalists struck a similar note. Edward Polhill, for example, declared that the design of the atonement was to procure "salvation on gospel terms."[105] It quickly becomes clear, however, that these "terms of mercy" are themselves a new legalism and that the Baxterian construction fully deserves the label "Neonomianism."[106] At first glance, it may indeed look as if God has relaxed his demands. In reality, he wants more. The moral law in all its compass has been satisfied in Christ, and so far as law-keeping goes, that should suffice. But No! There is another law, and it, too, demands obedience, this time by the sinner himself. Nor is it an easy law. One must repent "thankfully and heartily"; one must love Jesus "above all"; one must obey him "sincerely," "even to death"; and one must "persevere" in such repentance, love, and obedience to the end.

Surely here, as much as with the Old Law, the principle applies that, "by the works of the law shall no flesh be justified" (Gal. 2:16, KJV)? Baxter's "easier terms" will serve only to perplex the sinner with doubts as to the quality of his faith, love, and obedience. In the cold light of day these graces will always look inadequate, and if we seek to be accepted by God not *per fidem* (through faith) but *propter fidem* (on account of faith) we shall have little peace. Our faith needs a solid rock. It cannot itself be that rock, and when we look at it, our only comfort is that Christ has expiated faith's own imperfections. Faith cannot look to faith or to repentance or love or obedience. Scarcely conscious of itself, it can look only to the Lord our Righteousness, and to his one great all-accomplishing and all-securing sacrifice.

---

[104] Ibid., 53.

[105] Polhill, *Divine Will Considered*, 165.

[106] For example, in *The Marrow of Modern Divinity* (London, 1645), Baxter's position is represented by Neomista, one of four dialogue partners, the others being Evangelista, Nomista, and Antinomista.

But this is not all. This New Law carries its own curse; and it is a curse even more terrible than the curse of the Old Law. Christ delivered us from the punishment due under the Old Law (the law of works), but he did not deliver us from the punishment due under the New Law, the law of evangelical obedience: "Christ dyed not for any Mans non-performance of the conditions of the Law of Grace."[107] Christ will not now judge anyone according to the law of works. Instead, people will be judged on the basis of their compliance or noncompliance with the terms of grace; and Baxter's conclusion is, "Christ by his Law hath made a far sorer punishment than before belonged to them, to be due to all those that believe not in him. . . . And for refusing their Lord-Redeemer shall they be condemned."[108] Failure to comply with the New Law ("believe in the Lord Jesus Christ") incurs a greater guilt than noncompliance with the law of works.

Is it not fatally incoherent that God should simultaneously decree that the cross of Christ should redeem all the non-elect *and* provide him with grounds for their greater condemnation?

Conclusion

Two main arguments underlie this essay.

First, God has one plan of salvation, in which the three divine persons agree together to save a vast multitude of named human beings and conform them to the likeness of the beloved Son. In accordance with this plan, God made this elect multitude central to his administration of the universe. He would be *their* God, and the Son would be *their* Mediator. By his obedience and sacrifice he would expiate their sins, reconcile them to God, deliver them from Satan's power, and secure for them the ministry of the Holy Spirit, who, by touching their hearts, would enable them to respond to the love of God and receive him into their lives through faith. It is one coherent plan, driven by one great fact: God's determination to bring his named ones to glory.

The second underlying argument is the organic unity of salvation itself. Christ came to save: not to make salvation possible, or to contribute to it, or to attend to some parts of it, but actually to save. This salvation has two aspects, the forensic and the ontological, and these two aspects are inseparable. The cross secures both reconciliation and transformation. Its final decreed

---

[107] Baxter, *Universal Redemption*, 33.
[108] Ibid., 44.

outcome is not mere salvability but *theosis*, Christ making absolutely certain that those he loved will "become partakers of the divine nature" (2 Pet. 1:4). He would not merely *procure* eternal life for them: he would *give* it to them (John 17:2), ensuring a complete, seamless salvation, culminating in that moment when he would present them faultless "in the presence of his glory with great joy" (Jude 24). That is his ultimate satisfaction, and it was the prospect of it that sustained him as he "poured out his soul to death" (Isa. 53:12).

One decree: there shall be a glorified church of God. One salvation: bearing the image of the heavenly.

Table 15.1: The Order of Decrees[109]

	SUPERNATURALISTIC									NATURALISTIC	
	EVANGELICAL						SACERDOTAL				
	PARTICULARISTIC			UNIVERSALISTIC							
	Consistently Particularistic		Inconsistently Particularistic								
	Supralapsarian	Infralapsarian	Amyraldian	Lutheran	Wesleyan	Pure Universalistic	Anglican	Roman	Orthodox Greek	Remonstrant	Pelagian
	Election of some to eternal life with God.	Permission of Fall = guilt, corruption and total inability.	Permission of Fall = corruption, guilt and moral inability.	Permission of Fall = guilt, corruption and total inability.	Permission of Fall = guilt, corruption and total inability.	Permission of Fall.	Permission of sin.	Permission of Fall = loss of supernatural righteousness.	Permission of Fall = loss of original righteousness, involving loss of knowledge of God and proneness to evil.	Permission of Fall = (physical) deterioration (followed by moral).	Gift of free will by virtue of which each may do all that is required of him.
	Permission of Fall = guilt, corruption and total inability.	Election of some to life in Christ.	Gift of Christ to render salvation possible to all.	Gift of Christ to render satisfaction for sins of the world.	Gift of Christ to render satisfaction for sins of the world.	Predestination of all to life.	Gift of Christ to make satisfaction for the sins of all men.	Gift of Christ to offer satisfaction for all human sins.	Gift of Christ to reconcile sinful mankind with God.	Gift of Christ to render gift of sufficient grace possible.	Gift of the law and gospel to illuminate the way and persuade to walk in it.
	Gift of Christ to redeem the elect and ground offer to all.	Gift of Christ to redeem his elect and ground offer to all.	Election of some for gift of moral ability.	Gift of means of grace to communicate saving grace.	Remission of original sin to all and gift to all of sufficient grace.	Gift of Christ to expiate the sin of all.	Establishment of Church as living agent for communicating God's sufficient grace.	Institution of the Church and the sacraments, to apply satisfaction of Christ.	Establishment of the Church "for the continual supply of the benefits of the cross."	Gift of sufficient (suasive) grace to all.	Gift of Christ to (expiate past sin and to) set good example.
	Gift of the Holy Spirit to save the redeemed.	Gift of the Holy Spirit to save the redeemed.	Gift of the Holy Spirit to work moral ability in the elect.	Predestination to life of those who do not resist the means of grace.	Predestination to life of those who improve sufficient grace.	Gift of the Spirit to apply the expiation of Christ to all.	Communication of this grace through the sacraments as indispensable channels.	Application of satisfaction of Christ through sacraments, under operation of second causes.	Instruction, justification and edification through the ordinances of the Church.	Salvation of all who freely cooperate with this grace.	Acceptance of all who walk in right way.
	Sanctification of all the redeemed and regenerated.	Sanctification of all the redeemed and regenerated.	Sanctification by the Spirit.	Sanctification through the means of grace.	Sanctification of all who cooperate with sufficient grace.	Salvation of all.	Salvation through the sacrament of baptism imparting life and of the Eucharist nourishing it.	Building up in holy life of all to whom the sacraments are continued.	Building up in grace through the seven sacraments.	Sanctification by cooperation with grace.	Continuance in right-doing by voluntary effort.

[109] Replicated from Warfield, *Plan of Salvation*, 33.

16

The Triune God, Incarnation, and Definite Atonement

Robert Letham

At root, the doctrine of definite atonement affirms that, in accordance with the loving eternal decree of the triune God, Christ the Son took human nature in the incarnation and offered himself through the Holy Spirit to the Father so as to make atonement for his elect people. Entailed in this is an unbreakable connection between the Holy Trinity, the incarnation of the Son, and the atonement. At the heart of this connection is the doctrine of the indivisibility of the being and acts of the triune God.

Three prominent models that oppose definite atonement strongly imply either discord in the Trinitarian relations, inversion of the divine attributes, or theological incoherence. By far the most significant of the three is the model of T. F. Torrance (1913–2007), which I will argue is ultimately incoherent. But before we consider his position in detail, we need to examine the claims of his younger brother, J. B. Torrance (1923–2003),[1] and the seventeenth-century French theologian Moïse Amyraut (Amyraldus) (1596–1664).

Discordance—Amyraut and Hypothetical Universalism

Moïse Amyraut, from the theological school of Saumur, in France, developed a position on the decrees of God that had direct bearing on the nature and intent of the atonement. His work built on that of his predecessor, John

---

[1] J. B. Torrance was my doctoral supervisor.

Cameron (1579–1625), and was largely in response to the opposition by the Synod of Dort (1618–1619) to Arminianism. Dort had affirmed definite atonement under the second head of doctrine but in a context in which its full sufficiency for the whole world was to the fore. Indeed, some at the Synod, including the English and Bremen delegations, were more than inclined to stress the universal scope and sufficiency of Christ's death.[2] Amyraut built on this Hypothetical Universalism. His position continues to be influential to this day.[3]

THE AMYRALDIAN THEORY

According to Amyraut, Christ died on the cross with the intention of saving all people. However, the Father, foreseeing that not all would believe, elected some to salvation. In turn, the Holy Spirit grants repentance and faith to the elect. As Robert Reymond points out, for Amyraldianism, "the actual execution of the divine discrimination comes not at the point of Christ's redemptive accomplishment but at the point of the Spirit's redemptive application."[4] This construction and others like it are sometimes known as Hypothetical Universalism.[5] Essentially, Amyraldianism seeks to maintain the particularity of election and the corresponding particularity of the application of redemption by the Holy Spirit, while also maintaining a universal atonement. For this reason, Warfield classes it as inconsistent Calvinism.[6]

HYPOTHETICAL UNIVERSALISM

Some English Hypothetical Universalists proposed a slightly different argument.[7] Edmund Calamy (1600–1666), a member of the Westminster Assembly, held that Christ died absolutely for the elect, and conditionally for the

---

[2] See W. Robert Godfrey, "Tensions within International Calvinism: The Debate on the Atonement at the Synod of Dort," (PhD diss., Stanford University, 1974); Anthony Milton, ed., *The British Delegation and the Synod of Dort (1618–1619): The Church of England Record Society: Volume 13* (Woodbridge, UK: Boydell, 2005); Robert Letham, *Assurance in Theological Context: Reformed Dogmatics 1523–1619* (Edinburgh: Rutherford Studies in Historical Theology, forthcoming), chapter 7, a revision of my University of Aberdeen doctoral thesis (1979).

[3] See Moïse Amyraut, *Brief Traitté de la Prédestination et Des Ses Principales Dépendances* (Saumur, 1634). Recent advocates of similar constructions have included R. T. Kendall, *Calvin and English Calvinism to 1649* (Oxford: Oxford University Press, 1979); and Alan C. Clifford, *Atonement and Justification: English Evangelical Theology 1640–1790: An Evaluation* (Oxford: Clarendon, 1990).

[4] Robert L. Reymond, *A New Systematic Theology of the Christian Faith* (New York: Thomas Nelson, 1998), 477.

[5] However, some Hypothetical Universalists differed from Amyraut in his ordering of the decrees, some such as John Davenant being infralapsarian, and argued that Christ died conditionally for all if they were to believe and unconditionally for the elect for salvation.

[6] B. B. Warfield, *The Plan of Salvation*, rev. ed. (1935; repr., Grand Rapids, MI: Eerdmans, 1973), 89–95.

[7] See Jonathan D. Moore, *English Hypothetical Universalism: John Preston and the Softening of Reformed Theology* (Grand Rapids, MI: Eerdmans, 2007).

reprobate, in case they believe. In this context, Calamy was able to preserve the congruence in the works of the Trinity and avoid a split between the atonement and the intercession of Christ. He insisted,

> I am farre from universall Redemption in the Arminian sence, but that that I hould is in the sence of our devines in the sinod of Dort; that Christ did pay a price for all, absolute for the elect, conditionall for the reprobate, in case they doe beleive; that all men should be *salvabiles, non obstante lapsu Adami*; that Jesus Christ did not only dy sufficiently for all, but God did intend in giving of Christ & Christ in giving himselfe did intend to put all men in a state of salvation in case they doe beleive.

Calamy distinguished his position from Arminianism: Arminians say that Christ paid a price placing all in an equal state of salvation. "They say Christ did not purchase any Impetration." Calamy insisted his view "doth neither intrude upon either [the] doctrine of speciall election or speciall grace." The point he made was that Arminianism asserted that Christ simply suffered; all people are placed in a potentially salvable situation, so that any who believe will be saved. In contrast, he himself believed that Christ's death saves his elect and grants a conditional possibility of salvation to the rest.[8] In distinction from Amyraut, Calamy held that for the elect the atonement was efficacious. While the debates on the scope of saving grace lasted several days at the Assembly, and there were a number of divines who sided with Calamy, none were driven out. A good reason for this was that Calamy's views were not seen as posing a major threat to the sovereign particularism of the decrees nor to the nature or intent of the atonement.

CRITIQUE OF AMYRALDIANISM AND HYPOTHETICAL UNIVERSALISM

First, Hypothetical Universalism of all kinds illustrates the point that the question about the intent of the atonement is inescapably one about its nature. The atonement *is* what God intends it to be. The atonement, for Amyraut and Hypothetical Universalists, cannot be intrinsically efficacious, since while Christ is said to die for all people without exception, the results do not accrue to all. Its effectiveness is therefore contingent on the human response of

---

[8] C. Van Dixhoorn, "Reforming the Reformation: Theological Debate at the Westminster Assembly 1643–1652. Volume Six. Appendix B: Minutes of the Westminster Assembly, Volume 3. Folios 1ʳ–192ʳ (18 November 1644 to 31 December 1646)" (doctoral thesis, University of Cambridge, 2004), 202–203; Robert Letham, *The Westminster Assembly: Reading Its Theology in Historical Context* (Phillipsburg, NJ: P&R, 2009), 177.

faith in a similar way to classical Arminianism. However, there is a crucial difference from Arminianism. In the latter, election is on the basis of fore-knowledge. God foresees that some will respond in faith to the offer of the gospel and chooses these to salvation. In effect, his election simply ratifies the choices men and women make, albeit assisted to some extent by preve-nient grace. With Amyraldianism, election is more than a rubber stamp to a human decision, since the decision is preceded by grace. However, both have in common that the atoning death of Christ does not of itself secure the salvation of anyone in particular, since it is contingent on the human response in the case of Arminianism or on the particular work of the Spirit in terms of Amyraldianism. Moreover, since the atonement is not intrinsically effica-cious, it cannot yield a doctrine of penal substitution.[9]

Second, the key problem with the Amyraldian position, and Hypothetical Universalism in general, is that it posits disruption in the Trinity. The electing purpose of the Father and the work of the Spirit are in conflict with the inten-tion in the death of the Son on the cross. This is contrary to the simplicity of God and the indivisibility of the Trinity.

A foundational axiom of classic Trinitarian theology is the doctrine of the simplicity of God, shared by both the Western and Eastern churches. This asserts that God is not divisible into parts less than the whole of who he is. It follows that each of the three Trinitarian persons is the whole God, and all that can be said to be God is present in each person. Hence, the three mutually indwell one another, occupying the same infinite divine space. God is three, but indivisibly one being.

From this, it follows that in all God does all three persons are directly involved. God's various actions, while particularly attributable—or *appropri-ated*—to one of the three are yet indivisibly those of all three working together in harmony. This is expressed in the formula *opera trinitatis ad extra indivisa sunt* (the external works of the Trinity are undivided). For instance, only the Son became incarnate, but he was sent by the Father and his human nature was conceived by the Holy Spirit. Only the Spirit was sent at Pentecost, yet he was sent by the Father and the Son. These points are clearly taught both

---

[9] See Charles Hodge, *Systematic Theology*, 3 vols. (1871–1873; repr., Grand Rapids, MI: Eerdmans, 1977), 2:726–28; Herman Bavinck, *God and Creation*, vol. 2 of *Reformed Dogmatics*, ed. John Bolt, trans. John Vriend (4 vols.) (Grand Rapids, MI: Baker Academic, 2004), 368–72; idem, *Sin and Salvation in Christ*, vol. 3 of *Reformed Dog-matics*, ed. John Bolt, trans. John Vriend, 4 vols. (Grand Rapids, MI: Baker Academic, 2006), 461–63 and Robert Letham, *The Work of Christ* (Leicester, UK: Inter-Varsity Press, 1993), 225–47.

by Augustine, the leading Trinitarian theologian of the Latin church, and by Gregory of Nyssa and Gregory of Nazianzus of the Greek church.

Crucial to Augustine is the fact, established by the fourth-century Trinitarian controversy, that the Son is of the same essence as the Father.[10] While to us the persons and works of the Trinity are revealed sequentially—for we cannot understand the true simultaneity of being and action[11]—since they are one in being the work of the Son and the Father is indivisible. This is a constant *leitmotiv* in Augustine's thought.[12] In the important *Tractate 20 on the Gospel of John* Augustine argues this at length. The inseparability of the works of the Trinity follows from the inseparability of the persons, "because the Father and the Son are not two Gods, but one God . . . and the Spirit of charity also one, so that Father, Son, and Holy Spirit is made the Trinity." Thus creation is by the Father through the Son in the Holy Spirit, and is not three separate actions.[13] Hence God has one will, one power, and one majesty.[14]

A question from Augustine's friend Nebridius is important here. Nebridius asks why, since the works of the Trinity are indivisible and so all three persons are engaged in all the works of God, only the Son became incarnate and not the Father and the Spirit also? In reply, Augustine connects the inseparable works of the Trinity with the appropriations. It is true that all three persons are involved in all the works and ways of God, Augustine agrees. The three do nothing in which all do not have a part. Nevertheless, each work is appropriately applied to one of the persons. In particular, the Son alone is the subject of the incarnation, but not without the direct engagement of the Father and the Holy Spirit. The works of the divine persons are inseparable but distinct. It was most suitable that the Son became incarnate, although Augustine cannot explain satisfactorily why this is so.[15] He says much the same in a sermon on Matthew 3:13, proving that the works of creation and grace are undertaken by all three persons while applied to one in particular. There is "a distinction of persons, and an inseparableness of

---

[10] Augustine, *On the Trinity,* 1.6.9, *PL* 42:825; Augustine, *On the Gospel of John,* Tractate 6, *NPNF*[1] 7:39, *PL* 35:1425–35.

[11] Augustine, *Trinity,* 4.21.30, *PL* 42:909–10.

[12] Ibid., 1.6.12, 1.8.15–17, 1.12.25–27, *PL* 42:827, 829–32, 838–40; Augustine, *Letter 169,* 2.5, *NPNF*[1] 1:540, *PL* 33:744; Basil Studer, *The Grace of Christ and the Grace of God in Augustine of Hippo: Christocentrism or Theocentrism?* (Collegeville, MN: Liturgical Press, 1997), 104.

[13] Augustine, *John,* Tractate 20, *NPNF*[1] 7:131–37, *PL* 35:1556–64.

[14] Ibid., Tractate 22, *NPNF*[1] 7:150, *PL* 35:1574–82. See Tractate 77, *NPNF*[1] 7:339, *PL* 35:1833–35.

[15] Augustine, *Letter 11, NPNF*[1] 1:228–30, *PL* 33:75–77.

operation."[16] Hence, when one person is named, sometimes all three persons are understood.[17]

A generation earlier, Gregory of Nyssa argued that God is one in essence, three in persons, divided without separation, united without confusion.[18] In a work entitled *On the Holy Trinity and of the Godhead of the Holy Spirit to Eustathius*, he argues that we know God not from his essence but from his works. The works of the three persons are one, and so we conclude that their nature is one. These works are inseparable, for it is impossible to separate the Holy Spirit from any work of the Father and the Son. The Trinity is one Godhead. It follows that the Son is inseparable from the Holy Spirit.[19]

Gregory of Nazianzus, who together with Gregory of Nyssa helped the resolution of the Trinitarian crisis, wrote,

> To us there is one God, and all that proceeds from him is referred to one, though we believe in three persons. For one is not more and another less God; nor is one before and another after; . . . but the Godhead is . . . undivided in separate persons. . . . When we look at the Godhead, or the first cause, or the monarchia, that which we conceive is one; but when we look at the persons in whom the Godhead dwells . . . there are three whom we worship.[20]

Consequently, the church down through the ages has confessed both the inseparability of the works of God and the appropriations. Since God is one, all three persons act together in all God's works. Yet each work is particularly attributable (appropriated) to one person. This does not deny that the other two persons were also involved in these acts. The Trinity works in harmony rather than in unison—but not in discord. The triune God is one being with one undivided will; to suggest a variety of conflicting purposes in the mind of God is to head in the direction of tritheism. This undermines the simplicity of God. Moreover, when the maxim *opera trinitatis ad extra indivisa sunt* is taken into consideration, Amyraldianism and Hypothetical Universalism present the whole Trinity as being in two minds, first determining that the incarnate Son should die on the cross for the salvation of the whole human race, but then in contrast determining that some, not all, be saved, and going on to put this latter determination into effect. Warfield asks,

---

[16] Augustine, *Sermon on Matthew 3:13, NPNF*[1] 6:259–66, esp. 262, *PL* 38:354–64.
[17] Augustine, *Trinity*, 1.9.18–19, *PL* 42:832–34.
[18] Gregory of Nyssa, *Against Eunomius*, 2.2–3, 7.4, *PG* 32:325–40.
[19] *NPNF*[2] 5:326–30, *PG* 46:235, *PG* 32:683–94, where it is listed erroneously as Letter 189 of Basil.
[20] Gregory Nazianzus, *Oration* 31.14, *PG* 36:148–49.

how is it possible to contend that God gave his Son to die for all men, alike and equally; and at the same time to declare that when he gave his Son to die, he already fully intended that his death should not avail for all men alike and equally, but only for some which he would select (which, that is, because he is God and there is no subsequence of time in his decrees, he had already selected) to be its beneficiaries?

Warfield continues, "it is impossible to contend that God intends the gift of his Son for all men alike and equally and at the same time intends that it shall not actually save all but only a select body which he himself provides for it." This necessarily implies a chronological sequence among the decrees, "the assumption of which abolishes God . . . and therefore the nature of the atonement is altered by them."[21]

This problem is highlighted in the writings of John Davenant (1576–1641), a member of the highly influential delegation from Great Britain to the Synod of Dort. From the premise of the need for universal gospel preaching to be grounded on a coterminous provision, he taught that the death of Christ was the basis for the salvation of all people everywhere.[22] The call to faith, given promiscuously, presupposes that the death or merit of Christ is applicable to all those who, under the condition of faith, are promised the benefit.[23] Each person is salvable.[24] Therefore the scope and intent of the atonement is universal. Christ paid the penalty not for the sins of particular individual persons but for the whole human race.[25] This is grounded on an evangelical covenant made by God in which he promises everlasting salvation to all on the condition that they believe in Christ and repent.[26] In this, the onus falls on the act of faith and repentance: if Peter had persisted in denying Christ, he would not have been saved, while the promise would have been effected if Judas had repented.[27] For Davenant this meant much more than the slogan accepted by many particularists—"sufficient for all, efficient for the elect"—who affirmed that the sufficiency of Christ's death was simply

---

[21] Warfield, *Plan*, 94.
[22] John Davenant, "Mors Christi in sacra Scriptura proponitur ut universal remedium omnibus & singulii hominibus ex ordinatione Dei & natura res ad salute applicabile," in *Dissertationes duae: prima de morte Christi, quatenus ad omnes extendatur, quatenus ad solos Electos restringatur: Altera de praedestinatione & reprobatione* (Cambridge: ex officinal Rogeri Danielis, 1650), 10. On Davenant, see also Moore, *English Hypothetical Universalism*, 206–209.
[23] Davenant, "Mors Christi," 17.
[24] Ibid., 11.
[25] Ibid., 16.
[26] Ibid., 17.
[27] Ibid., 11.

due to its infinite value. Instead, Davenant held that, by Christ's death, God actually provides salvation for all. The sufficiency is ordained by God in the evangelical covenant.[28]

This universal provision in the atonement, for Davenant, overshadowed and preceded a decree whereby God determined salvation for the elect. No actual reconciliation or salvation comes before a person believes.[29] In this, God makes available or withholds the means of application of salvation to nations or individuals, according to his will. Only the elect receive saving faith.[30] This decree, differentiating between elect and reprobate, conflicts with God's decision that Christ atone for each and every person by his death. God decides first one thing, then another.[31]

In short, the Hypothetical Universalist position, in whatever guise, is inherently incoherent. Moreover, it runs counter to classic Trinitarian theology. It must be regarded as axiomatic that the atonement is a loving provision of all three persons of the Trinity, working in indivisible harmony, in which the Father sends the Son, conceived and sustained by the Holy Spirit. In turn, on the cross the Son offers himself to the Father in the Holy Spirit (Heb. 9:14). The atonement is the loving provision of the indivisible Trinity for us and for our salvation. Its value is infinite, its achievement by the Son inseparable from the active participation of all the Trinitarian persons in their distinct ways.

Inversion—J. B. Torrance and the Attributes of God

J. B. Torrance, the younger brother of T. F. Torrance, shared his brother's views in a range of areas. In particular, he was also influenced by John McLeod Campbell (1800–1872). Campbell strongly opposed John Owen and Jonathan Edwards in their respective arguments for definite atonement. In particular, he rejected their making justice an essential attribute of God and mercy an arbitrary attribute; God must be just since that is his nature, whereas he exercises mercy in accordance with his sovereign will. Hence, Campbell claimed that they argued that God deals with people in general on the basis of

---

[28] Ibid., 37.
[29] Ibid., 55.
[30] Ibid., 69, 87.
[31] See Jonathan D. Moore, "The Extent of the Atonement: English Hypothetical Universalism versus Particular Redemption," in *Drawn into Controversie: Reformed Theological Diversity and Debates within Seventeenth-Century British Puritanism*, eds., Michael A. G. Haykin and Mark Jones (Göttingen, Germany: Vandenhoeck & Ruprecht, 2011), 124–61.

justice, while his love and mercy is granted to those he has selected to receive it on the basis of a decision of his will.[32]

J. B. Torrance set out these views in an article in 1983,[33] although he voiced them in a wide variety of settings. He insists that limited atonement as taught by Owen and Edwards is contrary to the teaching of the Bible, that God is essentially love. Consequently, the doctrine of atonement in Federal Calvinism cannot display the nature of God. He argues that Calvinism fell prey to a series of dualisms. Firstly, it divided nature and grace, exemplified by the contrast between the pre-fall covenant of works, in which Adam related to God by law, and the covenant of grace, which includes only the elect. From this, secondly, Torrance maintains, law is prior to grace both historically and theologically and so gives even the covenant of grace a legal cast. Related to this deep-seated dualism is the overpowering double decree, by which God is said to elect only some to salvation while rejecting the rest. The doctrine of limited atonement is a by-product of this radical dualism. It betrays a false view of God as a contract-God who deals with people primarily on the basis of law, rather than a covenant-God, who has committed himself unconditionally in love. Moreover, it fails to view the atonement and salvation as a whole christologically, for the incarnation is the supreme revelation of who God is.

CRITIQUE OF J. B. TORRANCE

Paul Helm answered Torrance's argument. Helm disputed Campbell's claim since, according to the Calvinist doctrine, "some experience love, some justice, neither both," for the elect do not themselves experience justice, as it is satisfied for them by the atonement of Christ.[34] On the philosophical and theological level, Helm stated that "a justice that could be unilaterally waived would not *be* justice, and mercy that could not be unilaterally waived would not be mercy."[35] In short, justice that is not applied equally to all is not justice; it would be arbitrary and capricious, dependent on the will of an unpredictable "god"—ironically, exactly the problem Torrance wanted to avoid. Justice, to be justice, is applied across the board. Moreover, mercy

---

[32] John McLeod Campbell, *The Nature of the Atonement and Its Relation to Remission of Sins and Eternal Life* (1856; repr., London: James Clarke, 1959), 51–75.
[33] J. B. Torrance, "The Incarnation and 'Limited Atonement,'" *EQ* 55 (1983): 82–94.
[34] Paul Helm, "The Logic of Limited Atonement," *SBET* 3.2 (1985): 47–54 (50).
[35] Ibid.

that is dispensed to each and every person and cannot but be so, is not mercy; there is something inherently surprising about mercy. Mercy is a sovereign decision and cannot be compelled or utilized out of necessity. Torrance's argument effectively inverts the justice and mercy of God. Moreover, as Helm argues, if we were to suppose that God exercises mercy on all, this would be as arbitrary as his choice to show mercy only to some.[36] Garry Williams agrees: "the universal equity that justice requires demands the kind of universal exercise that the very nature of mercy precludes." On the other hand, he cites Owen to establish that what is required for mercy to be an essential property of God is that he exercise it toward any person in particular.[37]

That Torrance's criticism of the Reformed teaching on the attributes of God is misplaced is evident from Herman Bavinck's classic treatment of the work of Christ more than seventy years earlier. Bavinck establishes that "there is no such thing as a conflict between God's justice and his love. In our sinful state it may appear to us that way, but in God all his attributes are one and fully consistent with one another." He continues, "So . . . we must reject the notion that Christ was solely a revelation of God's punitive justice" while "on the other hand, Christ must not be viewed as solely a demonstration of God's love."[38]

Torrance has virtually no biblical exegesis to support his claims. When he does venture tangentially in that direction, he makes serious semantic errors. One of his main arguments rests on a distinction between God's pure unconditional love (ἀγάπη) and love as desire (ἔρος), the latter of which Aristotle argued cannot be predicated of God. Hence, Calvinism, being enmeshed in Aristotelian philosophy, could not recognize love as inherent in God's nature.[39] Torrance misses the point established by Robert Joly that ἀγάπη was used interchangeably in the NT with other words for love, as it had been in Greek usage for more than a century, and that ἀγαπάω was a common word for love at the time.[40]

In contrast to Torrance, inter alia, Romans 3:21–26 points to the complementarity of God's love and justice in the atoning death of Christ. Paul

---

[36] Ibid., 51.
[37] Garry J. Williams, "Karl Barth and the Doctrine of the Atonement," in *Engaging with Barth: Contemporary Evangelical Critiques*, ed. David Gibson and Daniel Strange (New York: T. & T. Clark, 2009), 261.
[38] Bavinck, *Sin and Salvation in Christ*, 369.
[39] Torrance, "Incarnation and Limited Atonement," 84–85.
[40] Robert Joly, *Le vocabulaire chrétien de l'amour, est-il original? Φιλειν et 'Αγαπαν dans le grec antique* (Bruxelles: Presses Universitaires de Bruxelles, 1968). See also D. A. Carson, *Exegetical Fallacies* (Grand Rapids, MI: Baker, 1984), 51–54.

stresses later that the source of the atonement is the love of God (Rom. 5:8). Here he presents it as a demonstration of grace in the face of universal human guilt (Rom. 3:21–24, cf. 3:19–20). The justification resulting from Christ's death is given freely by grace (v. 24). Yet, at the same time, it demonstrates his justice and righteousness (vv. 25–26). There is no conflict: God's grace is given freely out of love, in conformity with his righteous law.

The underlying theology that gives support to Torrance's claim here is spelled out in great detail by his brother, T. F. Torrance, through the whole corpus of his voluminous writings.

Incoherence—T. F. Torrance's Definitive Universal Atonement without Universal Salvation

T. F. Torrance was a staunch critic of definite atonement. While his criticisms surface at various points in his vast oeuvre, he most clearly and extensively expounds his atonement theology in his recently published class lectures.[41]

T. F. Torrance's Doctrine of Atonement

(1) *There is an inherent congruence between the incarnation and the atonement.* Christ died for those with whom he was united in the incarnation. Christ took our nature, the nature of all people, so therefore he died on the cross for all men and women:

> Atonement and incarnation, however, cannot be separated from one another and therefore the range of representation is the same in both. In both, all people are involved. In the incarnation, Christ, the eternal Son, took upon himself the nature of man and all who belong to human nature are involved and are represented, all men and women without exception, so that for all and each, Jesus Christ stood in as substitute and advocate in his life and in his death. Because he is the eternal Word or *Logos* in whom all humanity cohere, for him to take human nature upon himself means that all humanity is assumed by his incarnation; all humanity is bound up with him, he died for all humanity and all humanity died in him.[42]

In short, taking as axiomatic that in the incarnation Christ assumed into union human nature as such, the nature of each and every human person, it follows for Torrance that he made atonement for each and every person.

---

[41] T. F. Torrance, *Atonement: The Person and Work of Christ*, ed. R. T. Walker (Milton Keynes, UK: Paternoster, 2009).
[42] Ibid., 182.

(2) *The promises and commands of the covenant are both fulfilled in Christ.* For Torrance, atonement in the fullest sense embraces Christ's whole incarnate life and work.[43] The life and death of Christ fulfills the one covenant of grace made by God with all creation.[44] Although this came to expression in history in Israel and the church, and in an utterly unique way in the one Servant, "it was as such fulfilled for all humanity."[45] This comes to focus in Christ's vicarious humanity. In the incarnation he took a fallen human nature, the kind we have, and within our nature sanctified it by penetrating its deepest recesses and healing it from within. This was so due to the *homoousion,* for the eternal Son, the living God, was present as man, living for us, believing for us, suffering for us, dying for us, and rising from the dead and ascending to the Father for us. He himself is the atoning sacrifice for sin, in his incarnate humanity lived out for us. In line with the first point above, Torrance considers the incarnation itself to be the governing factor in the atonement.

(3) *Christ's atoning death was effective.* It reconciles and justifies, as the NT consistently states. In doing so Christ bore the sins of all people everywhere. In this he reconciled them to God and achieved their justification, entailing a complete reversal of the moral situation, for it is the justification of the ungodly. In it, mankind, "in spite of sin, is put fully in the right with God, and it is such a total and final act that men and women are no longer required to achieve justification by themselves. . . . They enter into justification through Christ's death."[46] It is enacted in the obedient life of Christ in completed action.

Thus, "Christ died for all men and women, and the justification involved is total." It is complete in Christ and "is actualised in the individual through incorporation into the one body of Christ."[47] "All men and women are already involved in God's act of justification," while "anything else completely disintegrates substitutionary atonement and breaks up the wholeness of justification and destroys it."[48] This is the key to Torrance's doctrine of atonement. "Justification is extended in its actualisation among all humanity through incorporation into Christ by his Spirit."[49] In keeping with this note of defini-

---

[43] Ibid., 9.
[44] Ibid., 182.
[45] Ibid., 183.
[46] Ibid., 107.
[47] Ibid., 128–29.
[48] Ibid., 129.
[49] Ibid.

tive achievement, reconciliation has taken place in the person of Christ; it remains an enduring and perfected reality for all in him.[50] Furthermore, "there is no positive act of rejection or judgement extended toward any human being, but only the act of acceptance."[51] It follows that Christ has achieved in the atonement definitive justification and reconciliation with God for each and every human person.

(4) *The task of the church is to make this known*, to show that God loves each and every person in the world and has given proof of this by his Son taking their nature, healing it from within, and securing their salvation in his death, resurrection, and ascension.[52]

(5) *The gospel reveals sin, since it exposes man's need for grace*. The logic of Torrance's overall position would demand universal salvation. However, he does not accept that this is the case. Since the act of God in justifying, reconciling, and accepting the sinner is an affront to man's dignity and often arouses fierce antagonism, there remains the possibility of hell.[53] "If a sinner is reprobated, if a sinner goes to hell, it is not because God rejected them, for God has only chosen to love them, and has only accepted them in Christ. . . . If anyone goes to hell they go to hell, only because, inconceivably, they refuse the positive act of the divine acceptance of them, and refuse to acknowledge that God has taken their rejection of him upon himself."[54] It is unclear whether the "if" is conditional or concessive, or even hypothetical.

In reality, the gospel often proves offensive, for the fact of God's acceptance and his having dealt with their sin exposes men and women as sinners who need his grace. Many cannot accept this humiliating message. So in the end it is possible that some will suffer hell. God has accepted them, but they may conceivably not accept God. That for them would be hell: to know that God loves them, but to live in the conscious rejection of it.[55] Thus, for Torrance the knowledge of sin comes through knowledge of the gospel—the gospel unmasks sin by the announcement of forgiveness.

Torrance refers to hell and argues that annihilation is not possible because

---

[50] Ibid., 150.
[51] Ibid., 156.
[52] Ibid., 342–43, 390–91, 407–408.
[53] Ibid., 157–58.
[54] Ibid., 156–57.
[55] Ibid., 110.

in the incarnation God has gathered all people into a relation of being with him. The sinner cannot escape God's love, for "his love refuses to allow the sinner to escape being loved." His being in hell is not the result of God choosing to damn him but is the result of his own decision to choose himself against the love of God.[56] He is forever imprisoned in his own refusal of being loved, and "that is the very hell of it."[57]

So Torrance does not accept universal salvation, despite the tenor and direction of his thought. Christ united himself with all people in the incarnation, and died for them all. But it is possible for people to reject his love. Damnation in hell involves confrontation by the love of God—this is hell.[58]

Torrance's Criticisms of "Limited Atonement"

It is hardly surprising that for Torrance limited atonement, as he calls it, is contrary to the thrust of the whole of Scripture.

(1) *Limited atonement denies that God loves the human race by its doctrine of election* in which he selects a few and rejects the many.[59] In doing so it denies that essentially God is love, and it elevates his justice and will, making God arbitrary.

(2) *It departs from classical christology by driving a wedge between the incarnation and the atonement.*[60] With limited atonement, Christ's incarnation is not sufficient of itself but is simply a preliminary to the real business of the cross, where the elect alone are the beneficiaries and consequently sustain a legal and contractual relationship to God, rather than a filial one.

(3) *It misses the underlying point that the atonement is a mystery.* As the high priest on the Day of Atonement disappeared within the veil—the real business of the day taking place out of sight—so the atonement took place in God's immediate presence and thus cannot be spelled out or spied out. It cannot be enclosed in doctrinal formulations.[61] In asserting the mystery of the atonement and opposing what he regards as the rationalistic construction of

---

[56] T. F. Torrance, *The School of Faith: The Catechisms of the Reformed Church* (London: James Clarke, 1959), cxv.
[57] Ibid., cxvi.
[58] Ibid., cxv–cxvii.
[59] Torrance, *Atonement*, 181–83.
[60] Ibid., 182–85.
[61] Ibid., 2–3.

limited atonement, Torrance claims that there is no logical relation between the death of Jesus and the forgiveness of sins today.[62]

(4) *Limited atonement is a forensic doctrine that obscures the centrally personal nature of atonement.* Here Torrance is especially indebted, like his brother, to John McLeod Campbell. Campbell wrote of Christ repenting vicariously on behalf of the human race. He did this by acquiescing in God's judgment on human sin, by submitting to it in his mind and life, and confessing man's sin.[63] So Torrance states that "in vicarious penitence and sorrow for the sin of mankind, Christ met and responded to the judgement and vexation of the Father, absorbing it into his own being."[64] In this the relation between the Father and the Son is paramount, a filial relationship rather than a forensic, contractual obligation. This was the crux of Campbell's opposition to the Calvinism of Owen and Edwards.[65] With limited atonement, Torrance argues, a detached forensic doctrine ignores this filial intimacy.[66] To the contrary, the *person* of Christ atones; it is not an act of atonement *in abstracto*: *Christ* is the atonement.[67]

(5) *The crux of Torrance's opposition to limited atonement is found in the relationship between incarnation and atonement.* "Because he is the eternal Word or *Logos* in whom all humanity cohere, for him to take human nature upon himself means that all humanity is assumed by his incarnation; all humanity is bound up with him, he died for all humanity and all humanity died in him."[68] Therefore it follows, says Torrance, that "we repudiate the idea that the humanity of Christ was merely instrumental in the hands of God and the idea that the atonement on the cross was merely a forensic transaction, the fulfilment of a legal contract."[69] Rather, the life and death of Christ fulfills the one covenant of grace made by God with all creation.[70] Although this came to expression in history in Israel and the church, and in an utterly unique way in the one Servant, "it was as such fulfilled for all humanity."[71] We shall

---

[62] Ibid., 4.
[63] Campbell, *Nature of the Atonement*, 114–296.
[64] Torrance, *Atonement*, 70.
[65] Campbell, *Nature of the Atonement*, 51–75.
[66] Torrance, *Atonement*, 72.
[67] Ibid., 73–75.
[68] Ibid., 182.
[69] Ibid.
[70] Ibid.
[71] Ibid., 183.

argue shortly that this argument rests on a decree of election in Christ that is universal in scope.

Bound up with this universal election is the claim that the entire divine judgment was exacted in Christ at the cross for all people. Since it is impossible to separate Christ from God on the grounds of the *homoousion*, God's judgment has been fully enacted, Christ exhaustively bearing the wrath of God on behalf of the whole human race. There is no separation, as there is with definite atonement, between divine judgment exacted on Christ on behalf of some, and a final judgment in which a further judgment will be poured out. Rather, God's judgment was completely exhausted at the cross. There is no God of wrath lurking behind Christ who will judge humanity apart from the cross.[72]

However, it would be misleading to consider Torrance's position here in purely logical categories, for he considers that it is a major error to do so. It lies at the root of what he terms "the Latin heresy," which has bedeviled Western theology. This is what reduces the atonement to an external forensic transaction. Instead, Torrance considers that the atonement should be understood from a center in God, in the light of the incarnation and the vicarious humanity of Christ. This has its own logic, and it is necessary to submit to this.[73]

Critique of T. F. Torrance's Argument

(1) Arbitrary Choice of NT Texts

Torrance takes two sayings of Jesus as the basis for his doctrine of atonement, Mark 10:45 and Matthew 20:28, where Jesus states that he came to serve and to give his life a ransom for many, and Matthew 26:26–28 and parallels, which record his words at the Last Supper. These are "all important sayings" and, as such, "taken together with all that he had previously spoken, and understood in the context of what he was actually doing at the last supper and clearly set himself to suffer, must form the basis of our doctrine of atonement and redemption."[74] These are certainly important sayings. They feature dominantly in Jesus's treatment of his death. But why should these

---

[72] Ibid., 185.
[73] See C. D. Kettler, *The Vicarious Humanity of Christ and the Reality of Salvation* (Lanham, MD: University Press of America, 1991), 121–42; E. M. Colyer, *How to Read T. F. Torrance: Understanding His Trinitarian and Scientific Theology* (Downers Grove, IL: InterVarsity Press, 2001), 81–123; and P. D. Molnar, *Thomas F. Torrance: Theologian of the Trinity* (Farnham: Ashgate, 2009), 101–86.
[74] Torrance, *Atonement*, 6–7.

two sayings be singled out from the rest of the NT witness—from the whole Pauline corpus, and the statements of Peter and John—and made the basis of "our doctrine of atonement"? This seems arbitrary. Moreover, Torrance misses the intertextual connections to Isaiah 53 in these passages, where "the many" are those to whom the Servant *applies* the atonement.

(2) Linguistic Errors

Torrance's lectures abound with biblical exegesis. Much of it is both profound and intensely illuminating. However, his sources are outdated, the latest being from the middle of the last century. He relies heavily on G. Gerhard Kittel and C. H. Dodd.[75] He makes no reference in the entire set of lectures to Leon Morris, whether on propitiation or on the blood of Christ, where he also ignores the work of Alan Stibbs and Wilfrid Stott.[76] He relies too much on etymologizing and falls foul of the criticisms of James Barr,[77] and possibly D. A. Carson.[78]

(3) Colored by a Vehement Aversion to "Federal Calvinism"

Throughout Torrance's voluminous writings a recurring theme is the argument that Calvin's theology was, to a great extent, perverted by covenant theology in the ways we have already explored. While Torrance himself owed much to his reading of Athanasius and Cyril and cannot simplistically be labeled as part of a school of thought other than his own, this antagonism[79] at times finds him misreading important historical evidence. Donald Macleod, in an illuminating dialogue with Torrance, points to his misreading of Calvin on the extent of the atonement in the latter's *Concerning the Eternal Predestination of God*. Torrance claims that Calvin there rejected the slogan "sufficient for all, efficient for the elect"; Macleod demonstrates that this is not so.[80]

---

[75] Ibid., 99 n. 8, 139.

[76] Ibid., 178–79; Leon Morris, *The Apostolic Preaching of the Cross* (London: Tyndale Press, 1955), 112–28, 179–213; Alan M. Stibbs, *The Meaning of the Word "Blood" in Scripture* (London: Tyndale Press, 1948), 3–32; and W. Stott, "The Conception of 'Offering' in the Epistle to the Hebrews," *NTS* 9 (1962): 65–67.

[77] James Barr, *The Semantics of Biblical Language* (repr., London: SCM, 1983), 107–60, who singles out Torrance not only in this chapter on etymologies but throughout the book, exposing the many occasions in which Torrance confuses language and thought (see 171–77, 184–87, 191, 193–94, 199, 201–205, 235, 254, 259, 264, 277, 279). On the other hand, Torrance is correct, in my estimation, to counter Barr by pointing out his nominalism, by which words and language are effectively self-referential, rather than referring beyond themselves to realities. See the discussion in Molnar, *Torrance*, 333–34.

[78] Carson, *Exegetical Fallacies*, 25–66.

[79] It is seen particularly in his *Scottish Theology: From John Knox to John McLeod Campbell* (Edinburgh: T. & T. Clark, 1996).

[80] See the presentation by Macleod, listed as "198 Donald Macleod 'Review of Scottish Theology by Tom Torrance,'" www.tapesfromscotland.org/Rutherfordhouseaudio.htm. On the same site see "199 Tom Torrance 'Reply to

(4) Irrationalism or Anti-Rational?

Torrance argues that the atonement takes place in the mystery of God, behind the veil, as the high priest in the OT entered the inner sanctuary, out of sight. This leads Torrance to assert it to be ultimately a mystery and to oppose clear doctrinal pronouncements that he dislikes, on the grounds that they are rationalistic attempts to explain this mystery.[81] While Torrance is right to stress that these matters transcend our understanding, nevertheless, up to a point, they have been revealed. Moreover, Torrance's claim of mystery flies in the face of his own persistent attempts to understand it. It appears to belittle the place of logic which, while not of final authority, is indispensable in thinking clearly about God's revelation. At times, in his rejection of logical attempts to explain this mystery, Torrance fallaciously dismisses his opponents on the grounds that their intellects have not been crucified with Christ.[82] There can be no arguing with that! Advocates of definite atonement need to repent! In this instance, Torrance's recourse to mystery seems close to irrationalism and obfuscation.

(5) Covenant as Universal

Torrance is correct in wanting to view the atonement in a covenantal context.[83] It is indeed true that the promises and commands of the covenant are both fulfilled in Christ. Torrance sees "atonement in the fullest sense [as] embracing the whole incarnate life and work." However, he views this through a grid in which the incarnational union is the focus of the whole of soteriology, from election onward. As we shall see, due to these premises, he understands the covenant of grace in a universalizing way.

(6) Absolutization of the Incarnation

For Torrance, the person of Christ atones, but not through an act of atonement *in abstracto*: *Christ* is the atonement.[84] This places the atonement within

---

Donald Macleod'" and "200 Tom Torrance and Donald Macleod dialogue" (accessed 18 April 2013). For Torrance's claims for Calvin, see *Scottish Theology*, 107. See Calvin's comments on 1 John 2:2 in *Concerning the Eternal Predestination of God*, trans. J. K. S. Reid (Cambridge: James Clarke, 1961), 148–49; *Calvin's Commentaries: The Gospel According to St. John 11–21 and the First Epistle of John*, ed. David W. Torrance and Thomas F. Torrance, trans. T. H. L. Parker (Grand Rapids, MI: Eerdmans, 1959), 244; and John Calvin, *Ioannis Calvini Opera Exegetica: Volumen XX: Commentarii in Epistolas Canonicas*, ed. Kenneth Hagen (Genève: Librairie Droz, 2009), 154–56.
[81] Torrance, *Atonement*, 2, 4, 88.
[82] Ibid., 188 n. 70.
[83] Ibid., 8–9.
[84] Ibid., 73–75.

Christ, as he heals fallen humanity from within. All is conflated into the incarnation.[85] But why, then, was the cross necessary? Certainly, this was the work of the *incarnate* Son of God but, as Paul insists, his death and resurrection are "of first importance" (1 Cor. 15:3). It is Christ's person *as he offered himself up to the Father on the cross* and *was raised from the dead by the Father* that is the ground of atonement—although certainly not in abstraction from his life, his work, or his obedience, or from who he is. It is hard to think of any passage in the NT where Torrance's assertion that "we are not saved by the atoning death of Christ" is even remotely implied.[86] On the contrary, there is an abundance of NT evidence that this is the ground of atonement and, indeed, of salvation as a whole.[87]

Torrance is correct about the coherence of incarnation and atonement. The question surrounds the scope of the atonement and therefore the incarnation. It is clear that the elect do not have a distinctive nature from that of the rest of humanity. Torrance's doctrine of atonement is, however, governed by the incarnation: since Christ took a human nature into union, a nature common to all, he therefore died for all. In effect, the atonement takes place from within the incarnate humanity of Christ, who heals our nature from within by his assumption of it. This is a theory described by R. P. C. Hanson, in connection with Athanasius, whose position via Cyril lies at the root of Torrance's own, as "a kind of sacred blood-transfusion, or an act of mass-transference almost independent of our act of faith."[88] The dogma of *enhypostasia* undermines Torrance's argument—ironically, since it is of great importance to his own theology—for, as Donald Macleod points out, "the only humanity united to him [Christ] hypostatically is his own."[89]

(7) Universalist Tendency

On this point, Torrance's argument can be summarized as follows:

 A. Atonement and incarnation cannot be separated from one another.
 B. Therefore the range of representation is the same in both.

---

[85] Ibid., 97.
[86] Ibid., 73.
[87] For example, Romans 3:21–26; 1 Corinthians 15:3–4; Galatians 3:13–14; Hebrews 1:3; and 1 Peter 1:18–19 and 2:21–25, to list a mere handful of such places.
[88] R. P. C. Hanson, *The Search for the Christian Doctrine of God: The Arian Controversy 318–381* (Edinburgh: T. & T. Clark, 1988), 451.
[89] Donald Macleod, *The Person of Christ* (Downers Grove, IL: InterVarsity Press, 1998), 202–203.

That incarnation and atonement are inseparable is obvious. However, does it necessarily follow that the range of representation is identical in both? If Christ represents his elect, he must still be incarnate. God being just, atonement was required for human sin by one who took Adam's place. This can hardly be said to separate the atonement from the incarnation. Rather, it pushes the issue back to who exactly Christ represents. Again, Torrance argues in the following way:

A. Christ is the eternal Word in whom all humanity coheres.
B. Consequently he assumed all humanity in the incarnation, and
C. He represented all men and all women without exception in the atonement.

This argument hinges on a decree of universal election, related to Barth's doctrine that election is exhaustively in Christ, who is both electing God and elect man, both reprobate and elect.[90] Torrance affirms that "election is identical with the life and existence and work of Jesus Christ, *and what he does is election going into action*."[91] As such, each and every person is elect in Christ. However, if the decree is discriminatory, God chooses some (whether few or many) rather than each and every person without exception, and represents these, while assuming human nature as such in the incarnation. Ultimately, Torrance's doctrine of atonement rests on assumptions of a universal decree of election, entailing universal representation by Christ.

Torrance is correct about the effectiveness of Christ's atoning death, and his discussion is outstanding. However, since he argues that Christ bore the sins of all people at all times, and did so efficaciously, *it seems inescapable, Torrance's protests to the contrary, that the result is universal salvation*. It is hardly credible that Torrance could hold to the congruence of election, covenant, incarnation, and atonement; to the decisive efficacy of the atonement as God's act of justification and reconciliation for each and every member of the human race; and yet retain the possibility—even hypothetical—of eternal damnation. To my mind, his thought leads in one of two directions. First, it could in theory point to a conditional atonement as in Arminianism. However, Torrance emphatically and correctly rejects this possibility on the grounds that it places the fulcrum of salvation on

---

[90] Karl Barth, *Church Dogmatics*, ed. G. W. Bromiley and T. F. Torrance, 14 vols. (Edinburgh: T. & T. Clark, 1956–1975), II/2, 1–506.
[91] Torrance, *Atonement*, 183.

the side of man, in the human response of repentance and faith.[92] It is also contrary to his persistent emphasis on the definitive accomplishment of the atonement. The other alternative, given the universal dimension of election, covenant, incarnation, and atonement, together with their decisive efficacy, is universal salvation. That Torrance steps back from this is greatly to his credit, for it flies in the face of the consistent witness of Scripture that not all will be saved. But it is also evidence of the internal incoherence of Torrance's doctrine.

(8) Marginalization of Faith

Torrance has an uncompromisingly objective doctrine of justification. However, its decisive finality in the person of Christ for each and every person would appear to render faith superfluous. It would also eradicate any transition from wrath to grace in the life experience of all men and women, since that has been refracted in the experience of Christ. Again, Torrance's dialectic of the cross means that, following Barth, God does not let any positive decision to reject man fall on man himself, for that he takes entirely on himself. So "there is no positive act of rejection or judgement extended toward any human being, but only the act of acceptance."[93] Therefore if a sinner is reprobated and goes to hell, it is not because God rejected him, for God has only chosen to love him.[94] It is because, inconceivably, the sinner refuses the positive act of divine acceptance.

(9) Incoherence

Many, if not most, of the penetrating criticisms leveled at Barth by Oliver Crisp are pertinent here. Crisp's conclusion for Barth is, "if all humanity have been (derivatively) elected and efficaciously atoned for by Christ . . . then their soteriological status simply cannot be uncertain."[95] It is simply incoherent for Torrance to say what he says about the definitive justification and reconciliation for all people and yet to deny universal salvation. Moreover, if it is possible for people to reject Christ and what he has done, it cannot be definitive and effective for them and cannot have been complete in Christ's

---

[92] Ibid., 187.
[93] Ibid., 156.
[94] Ibid., 157.
[95] Oliver D. Crisp, "On Barth's Denial of Universalism," *Themelios* 29.1 (2003): 18–29. See also idem, "On the Letter and the Spirit of Karl Barth's Doctrine of Election," *EQ* 79.1 (2007): 53–67; and "Karl Barth and Jonathan Edwards on Reprobation (and Hell)," in *Engaging with Barth*, 300–322.

person. It simply will not do to dismiss criticism on this point by the assertion that Torrance's claims stem from a center in God and that the critics have an uncrucified epistemology; this is to break down rational discourse on the basis of a privileged and precious gnosis.

(10) A One-Dimensional View of the Love of God

Torrance has a lack of nuance to his view of the love of God. He refers to God's "one equal love for each and every human being."[96] This fails on two counts. First, it misses the clear and repeated declarations of Scripture that God's covenantal love is discriminating. Second, it fails to distinguish between the differing ways in which God's love is exercised. Gerald Bray points to this when he denies that it is appropriate to equate the love God has for the world in general with what he displays to his chosen people, with whom he has entered into covenant. Bray writes,

> Consider the following: I love my parents, I love my wife, I love my chil-dren, I love my brothers and sisters, I love my friends. Are we talking about the same thing when we use the word "love" in this way? Of course not. I have sexual intercourse with my wife, which is perfectly appropriate in the context of loving her. But if I were to have sex with my mother, my daugh-ter or my sister it would be an abomination—worse even, than having sex with a friend. . . . It is the nature of the relationship which determines what "love" will mean in any particular context.[97]

(11) Blunting the Urgency of Gospel Proclamation

If the apostolic task was to let everyone know what had already been done for them by Christ, why the urgency of gospel proclamation as recorded in Acts and the rest of the NT? The corollary of Torrance's position seems to be that it would be better never to preach the gospel. Since Christ has made effective atonement for all, all will be saved unless they reject the news that this is so. Gospel preaching will not change anything for the better as far as they are concerned. However, it could make things infinitely worse if, having heard that Christ had died for them, they spurn this glad news and therefore suffer hell. In contrast, the missionary imperative in the NT sprang, inter alia, from the point that knowledge of sin comes through the law, before which the

---

[96] Torrance, *Atonement*, 191.
[97] Gerald Bray, *The Personal God* (Carlisle, UK: Paternoster, 1998), 45.

whole world stands guilty (Rom. 3:19–20), and, following that, the decisive need for repentance and faith.[98]

Positive Statement

While we have been critical of Torrance's construction of the atonement and his objections to definite ("limited") atonement, there is much to learn from his brilliant and profound understanding of the *homoousion,* the vicarious humanity of Christ and the crucial matter of union with Christ.[99] Torrance is correct that we need to understand the atonement in a Trinitarian context, and in integral connection with the incarnation. The atonement bears an organic relationship with the whole movement of God's grace in salvation.

As such, the atoning death of Christ is the outflow of a loving decision by the Trinity—the Father, the Son, and the Holy Spirit. All three persons work together in harmony. In the eternal counsels of the Trinity, the loving and gracious decision was made to head up the created order in Christ, the incarnate Son, who would take into permanent and eternal union human nature. In this way, as Christopher Wordsworth put it in his ascension hymn, "man with God is on the throne." Christ has taken our humanity to the right hand of the Father. In union with Christ we are now seated in heavenly places, made by grace a partaker of the divine nature. In this sense, all that was to be accomplished for the redemption of the human race from sin, including the atonement, was and is of cosmic and universal significance and extent.

In this eternal decision and indivisible purpose of the three Trinitarian persons—some have called this a "covenant of redemption"[100]—is embraced the whole panorama of humanity's creation, fall into sin, and deliverance by the incarnate Son. His incarnation is crucial in this, for it was in his incarnate and mediatorial life that he offered himself up on the cross to the Father in and by the same Spirit (Heb. 9:14). Throughout that time, as God manifest in

---

[98] Thomas Smail, *The Giving Gift: The Holy Spirit in Person* (London: Hodder and Stoughton, 1988), 109–12, criticized Torrance on the basis that he was undermining the integrity of the human response of faith and so conflating the work of the Holy Spirit with the work of Christ. Kettler, *Vicarious Humanity*, 139–41, argues, correctly, that this fails to appreciate Torrance's point that the genuine human response of faith occurs *in Christ*, so that Christ's vicarious human faith does not obliterate ours but is the place in which it can occur.

[99] See my book *Union with Christ* (Phillipsburg, NJ: P&R, 2011).

[100] Typically, as constructed by theologians in the Reformed tradition, this has been open to the charge that it includes the subordination of the Son, and tends toward tritheism by treating the Trinity as engaged in a divine committee meeting. Moreover, it can reasonably be asked whether the term "covenant" adequately safeguards the unity of the Trinity. See Letham, *Work of Christ*, 52–53; and Letham, *Westminster Assembly*, 235–36. However, if it is understood in terms of classic Trinitarianism, the three working with one indivisible will, the formulation can be acceptable. Certainly, the intention behind it—that redemption stems from an eternal commitment of the triune God—is eminently biblical and correct.

the flesh, he took Adam's place, living an obedient and sinless life, such that his offering was without blemish and spot, remedying the defect caused by the first Adam. As the Second and Last Adam, he brought into being a new humanity by his resurrection, under the direction of the Holy Spirit (1 Cor. 15:20–28, 35–49). The result is that all united to him are made partakers of the divine nature and live and reign with him forever, over the new creation that is the great and consummate goal of God.

The key to this is that all Christ is and did is in union with his people, or more specifically his church. From conception to the cross, from the grave into eternity, all he did and does is not only in our place as a substitute, or on our behalf as our representative, but in union with us, such that our sins became his, and his righteousness is ours. He took our place, bearing our guilt on the cross. This was no mere legal fiction; because of the union he sustained from eternity with us, he bore our sin in his body on the tree, having been made sin for us (2 Cor. 5:21). At the same time, due to that union, all that he is is ours—his righteousness (1 Cor. 1:30), his resurrection (1 Cor. 15:12–58), his ascension (Eph. 2:4–7), his sonship (Rom. 8:15–16; Gal. 4:4–6). Bearing in mind our sinful rebellion and the depths of depravity that this incurred, this great purpose is nothing short of a determination of the pure love that forever flows from God's heart, in the unity of his triune being (Rom. 5:8; John 3:16; Phil. 2:6–8). The Bible in general, and the NT in particular, always attributes this as being given to those who believe, to the sheep of Christ who follow him, and warns strenuously of the eternal perils of unbelief due to the sin by which the race has ruined itself. This atonement is glorious, even more glorious in the knowledge that it achieves what the triune God's great plan purposed.

17

The Definite Intent of Penal Substitutionary Atonement

Garry J. Williams

Introduction

In this chapter and the next I examine the connection between the penal character of the atonement and its definiteness. This first chapter outlines how critics of definite atonement undermine its penal substitutionary nature, and how the Old and New Testaments describe atonement made for the specific sins of specific people. The next chapter is a consideration of the double payment argument for definite atonement. The common criticism that the argument over-stretches the metaphor of atonement as the payment of a debt to God occasions a consideration of the role of God in the atonement and the nature of punishment itself. I attempt the beginnings of a biblical penology that yields a more nuanced understanding of the payment metaphor, and that vindicates both a double punishment argument and its metaphorical representation.

Penal Substitutionary Atonement Is Definite

Penal substitutionary atonement rightly understood entails definite atonement. Conversely, insistence on an atonement made for all without exception undermines belief in penal substitutionary atonement. This chapter will illustrate these connections by means of a close engagement with two advocates of the view that the atonement itself was intended for all and was narrowed only in the limitation of its application to believers. The first is James Ussher (1581–1656), Archbishop of Armagh from 1625. Ussher is an important figure in the history of the debate over the intention of the atonement because of his influence on other key figures, especially Bishop John Davenant (1572–1641), an influential member of the English delegation at the Synod of Dort. The second is D. Broughton Knox (1916–1994), who was Principal of Moore Theological College in Sydney and George Whitefield College in Cape Town. Knox had and still has a significant direct and indirect influence among Anglican evangelicals in Australia, South Africa, and England. Each of these two authors will illustrate a different aspect of the connection between penal substitutionary and definite atonement. Ussher will illustrate the effect of universalizing the atonement itself on our understanding of the *object* for whom or for which Christ bore punishment, and Knox will illustrate the effect on our understanding of the *nature* of the punishment that Christ bore.

As the examples of Ussher and Knox will show, the Reformed have disagreed among themselves over the intent of the atonement. My argument for definite atonement should not be taken as an attempt to disenfranchise others who share central Reformed convictions, and for whom I am grateful to God for many reasons. Enough Reformed blood has been spilled by friendly fire. This chapter is simply intended to show brothers that at this point they are wrong, and that their positions, logically applied, will have consequences that they themselves would surely find alarming.

Ussher: Exposition

There has been debate about Ussher's position on the atonement, but the evidence in the primary texts is clear: he is rightly designated a "Hypothetical Universalist" given his insistence that Christ's death was intended to make satisfaction for every person, should he or she believe. His view on this issue is found in two short works. The first is a letter that he wrote on March 3, 1617, that was circulated without his permission. In its published form it bears the title *Of the True Intent and Extent of Christs Death, and Satisfaction upon the Crosse*. The second is a short work written in defense of the letter,

An Answer of the Said Arch-Bishop of Armagh, to Some Exceptions Taken Against His Aforesaid Letter.[1]

Ussher feels the difficulty of this "tricky topic" ("*Lubricus locus*").[2] He quickly identifies two unacceptable "extremities": the undue extension or contraction of the benefit of satisfaction.[3] Those who extend the atonement too far imply that God really ought to forgive everyone even prior to faith, since the universal atonement has been completed.[4] Those who contract the intent of the atonement to the elect err because they make gospel preaching untrue in its demand that *all* trust that Christ died for them. Ussher identifies his own position in the letter as a "*middle* course" between these extremes.[5]

Three features of Ussher's doctrine are pertinent here. First, it is evident that his underlying concern was with the preaching of the cross. He uses an analogy to explain why a satisfaction that is infinite in value but not universal in intent cannot be a basis for the offer of hope in gospel preaching: "To bring newes to a *bankrupt* that the *King of Spain* hath treasure enough to pay a thousand times more than he owes, may be true, but yields but cold comfort to him the miserable *Debtor*: sufficiency indeed is *requisite*, but it is the word of *promise* that gives comfort."[6] In other words, the satisfaction of Christ must have been intended for all if it is to be sincerely and powerfully preached to all. Bare sufficiency cannot comfort the sinner.

Second, Ussher's own view is that Christ did not by his death actually secure pardon for anyone, but only made sin forgivable: "The *satisfaction* of Christ, onely makes the sinnes of mankind *fit for pardon*."[7] He employs the Roman Catholic distinction between venial and mortal sin to explain this point. Apart from the cross, all sins are mortal in the sight of God, since even the smallest sin demands infinite punishment, but the satisfaction of Christ renders all sins venial in that they may be forgiven.[8] God is thus placable, but not actually appeased until a sinner believes. General satisfaction is thus the "*first* act" of the priestly office of Christ which makes the sins of all people

---

[1] The letters are printed in *The Judgement of the Late Arch-Bishop of Armagh, and Primate of Ireland* (London: John Crook, 1658), 1–16 and 17–36.
[2] Ussher, *Judgement*, 1; the phrase "*Lubricus locus*" was classically used, for example by Cicero (*De Officiis*, i.19) and Pliny (*Letters*, i.8), to refer to a difficult or treacherous situation. Ussher cleverly plays on the use of "locus" for a topic of Christian theology.
[3] Ibid., 3.
[4] Ibid., 2.
[5] Ibid., 3.
[6] Ibid., 28.
[7] Ibid., 4.
[8] Ibid.

pardonable, putting "the sonnes of men onely in a *possibility* of being justi-fied." The actual deliverance from God's wrath depends on intercession, the *"second* Act" of Christ's priesthood. This second act brings the change from potential to actual discharge. Interestingly, Ussher turns at this key moment to Aristotelian vocabulary: the application of satisfaction "produceth this *potentia in Actum* [from potency to action]."[9] It is noteworthy that we find an opponent of definite atonement casting his argument in such terms; Aristotle was evidently not the exclusive property of John Owen.

Third, Ussher teaches that Christ did not make satisfaction for any in-dividual specifically, but for human nature *qua* nature. He makes this point in the context of defending the separation of satisfaction from intercession. One of the standard arguments for definite atonement is the required unity of Christ's satisfaction and intercession: as Ussher reports it, "He *prayed* not for the world, Therefore, He *payed* not for the world."[10] Ussher rejects the unity of satisfaction and intercession, insisting that they are "divers parts" of Christ's priesthood.[11] He explains their diversity by introducing a dis-tinction between satisfaction for human *nature* and intercession for human *persons*: "the one may well appertain to the *common nature*, which the son assumed, when the other is a *speciall* Priviledge vouchsafed to such *par-ticular* persons only, as *the father hath given him*."[12] Ussher then expands on this distinction: "the *Lamb of God, offering himselfe a sacrifice for the sinnes of the whole world*, Intended by giveing sufficient satisfaction to Gods Justice, to make the *nature of* man, which he assumed, a fit subject for mercy."[13] However, "he intended not by *applying* this all-sufficient remedy unto every person in particular to make it *effectual* unto the salvation of all, or to procure thereby *actual* Pardon for the sins of the *whole world*."[14] Ussher compares the universality of satisfaction with the universality of sin: Christ is "a *kind of universal cause* of the restoring of our Nature, as *Adam* was of the depraving of it."[15] Ussher repeats the point in the later work: *"by Christs satisfaction* to his Father he made the Nature of Man a fit subject for mercy."[16]

---

[9] Ibid., 32. For previous use of the distinction, cf. Thomas Aquinas, *Summa Contra Gentiles*, 1.16.7.
[10] Ibid., 13.
[11] Ibid.
[12] Ibid., 14.
[13] Ibid.
[14] Ibid., 14–15.
[15] Ibid., 15.
[16] Ibid., 30.

Ussher: Systematic Critique

On Ussher's view, Christ is a person and made satisfaction as a person, but he did not make satisfaction *for* persons as such. Crawford Gribben explains: "The implication of Ussher's thought, though he does not put it quite so succinctly, is that Christ was not an actual substitute for any in his death, but that he becomes a substitute for any given individual at the moment of their conversion."[17] The central problem here is Ussher's idea of human nature *qua* nature as the object of the atonement. For substitution to have a nature as its object, that nature would have to sin and would have to bear guilt and, potentially at least, punishment. Natures, however, cannot sin or bear guilt or punishment *qua* natures. Sins are committed *in* a nature, but they are not committed *by* a nature. Natures can do nothing of their own accord. It is persons who act in a nature, persons who sin in a nature, and persons who bear the resulting guilt and punishment in that nature. A substitution for sin therefore requires a shared nature as a minimum, but it also requires intentional identification with the persons who have sinned. Moreover, Christ cannot have made satisfaction for human nature *in abstracto* since it does not exist *in abstracto*. Unless we subscribe to a strong Platonist realism, human nature does not exist apart from the persons in whom it is instantiated. Even if natures do exist in the abstract, it is not obvious that guilt can pertain to abstract natures *qua* natures. While I agree with Article 11 of the 1675 Helvetic Consensus that all Adamic persons are guilty even for the mere possession of a fallen nature prior to their own sinning in that nature, this is not because the nature has sinned and is guilty as a nature: it is because another *person* has acted in it as their federal representative, and because they, as persons, are conceived in it. Even a strong traducianist idea of the unindividuated "soulic mass" of humanity existing in Adam and passed on from him would still find it existing only in the *person* Adam and individuated through persons begotten from him. It is right to speak of fallen and guilty human nature, but the guilt pertains only to persons in that nature. Substitution and satisfaction must, therefore, be made for persons in human nature, not for human nature alone.

If sin, guilt, and punishment cannot actually be borne for a human nature *qua* nature, then the suffering borne by Christ in Ussher's account cannot rightly be identified as a punishment at all. Here we find the logical, albeit

---

[17] Crawford Gribben, "Rhetoric, Fiction, and Theology: James Ussher and the Death of Jesus Christ," *The Seventeenth Century*, 20.1 (2005): 70.

466 DEFINITE ATONEMENT IN THEOLOGICAL PERSPECTIVE

unintended, consequence of Ussher's Hypothetical Universalism: if Christ suffered for human nature, then his suffering can have been only a non-penal affliction. In the classical vocabulary, insistence on Ussher's position results logically in Christ bearing *afflictio* (affliction) instead of *poena* (punishment), despite the language that he himself uses. Ussher's position overtly modifies only the object of Christ's substitutionary suffering, but that modification in turn implies a change in its very nature. The consistent application of Ussher's Hypothetical Universalism thus logically denies penal substitutionary atonement because such atonement cannot be made for a nature. Any insistence that Christ both atoned for human nature and bore punishment would leave the justice of God in question because the connection between sin and punishment would be severed: Christ bore punishment for a nature that cannot, by definition, have been guilty *qua* nature. Given that punishment can be borne only for persons, then on what basis in divine justice did Christ suffer, if he suffered for human nature?

Ironically, the consistent application of Ussher's view results in an account of the sufferings of Christ that is close to a particular strand of Arminianism. While I would argue that Hugo Grotius did not develop a new doctrine of the atonement, other Arminians clearly did.[18] For example, Philip van Limborch denies the strictly penal character of the atonement.[19] In relating the cross to the sacrifices commanded in Leviticus 4 and 5, he follows the epistle to the Hebrews when he implies the unreality of the transferal of sin under the old covenant: "hands were placed on the head of the victims, as if [*quasi*] the sins of men were transferred onto them by this ritual, Leviticus 1:4; 16:21." This is unremarkable, but then Limborch emphasizes the identity of the antitype with the type in just this respect: "For the type to correspond correctly to its antitype, it is necessary that the death endured by Christ should have the character of a most serious evil [*gravis mali*] inflicted upon Christ, as if [*quasi*] by it the punishment our sins deserved was transferred onto him." Again: "when the cruel death was imposed upon Christ on account of our sins it was as if [*quasi*] the punishment for our

---

[18] For this interpretation of Grotius, see Alan Gomes, "Hugo Grotius' *Defensio fidei catholicae de satisfactione Christi adversus Faustum Socinum*: An Interpretive Reappraisal," paper presented to the Evangelical Theological Society Far West Regional Meeting (1988), online at http://www.tren.com [accessed 24 July 2002]; and Garry J. Williams, "A Critical Exposition of Hugo Grotius's Doctrine of the Atonement in *De satisfactione Christi*" (unpublished doctoral thesis, University of Oxford, 1999), chapter 3.
[19] The evidence from Limborch is used by Gomes; see "Reappraisal," 27, and his "Faustus Socinus: *De Jesu Christo Servatore*, Part III: Historical Introduction, Translation, and Critical Notes" (PhD diss., Fuller Theological Seminary, 1990), 319–20 n. 34.

sins was transferred onto him."[20] Here Limborch repeats the qualificatory *quasi* with reference to Christ himself, showing that he thinks that Christ bore a serious evil to free sinners, rather than the punishment they deserved. Ussher's position consistently applied would leave him close to Limborch because the consequence of detaching punishment from persons is that it is no punishment at all. The Ussherian Hypothetical Universalist thus faces a choice. He can protect a universal account of the atonement by maintaining that Christ suffered for human nature, but only at the expense of embracing the Arminian denial that he bore actual punishment. Or else he can maintain that Christ bore punishment but surrender the idea of a universal atonement for human nature. If this idea is surrendered, then the consequence follows that Christ suffered for particular persons, and the choice must be made between universal salvation and particularism: Did he suffer for every person, or only for the elect?

Another way of illustrating the problem with the implications of Ussher's view is in terms of the exact meaning of the description "penal substitutionary atonement." The classical idea is not that something was substituted for punishment but that one person was substituted for others, to bear their punishment. Christ himself was the penal substitute; it was not his supposedly non-penal suffering that was substituted for punishment.[21] The abbreviation "penal substitution" should not be taken to imply that the atonement was the substitution of the penalty itself. There is such a thing as penal substitution in that sense, but the classical theological idea is that it was our very punishment that fell on Christ. Christ's suffering was in some ways different from that faced by his people, for example in its temporal duration and in his lack of despair, but such differences arose because he was the eternal Son of God, not because he bore something other than their punishment. This point is made clearly in the title of Robert L. Dabney's book, *Christ Our Penal Substitute*. Dabney's phrasing shows nicely that the substitute was the person Christ and that his substitution was in the realm of penalty, rather than that the punishment was replaced by something else.[22] This observation is not an arbitrary

---

[20] Philip van Limborch, *Theologia Christiana* (Amsterdam: Henricus Westenius, 1695), 3.20.5, 252a–b (my translation).

[21] For an intricate exploration of this distinction, see John Owen, *Of the Death of Christ, the Price He Paid, and the Purchase He Made*, in *The Works of John Owen*, ed. W. H. Goold, 24 vols. (Edinburgh: Johnstone & Hunter, 1850–1855; repr., Edinburgh: Banner of Truth, 1967), 10:430–79.

[22] There is much that is excellent in Dabney's account, though I will address a problem with it in the next chapter that is not entirely dissimilar to the problem with Ussher.

assertion on my part; it finds its basis in the language of Scripture itself. In Mark 10:45, for example, we find that the life of the Son of Man was substituted for others, not that the penalty was changed. The Son of Man came "to give his life as a ransom in the place of many" (δοῦναι τὴν ψυχὴν αὐτοῦ λύτρον ἀντὶ πολλῶν). The ransom was a life for lives (ψυχὴ ἀντὶ ψυχῶν), not a punishment for punishments (τιμωρία ἀντὶ τιμωριῶν).

A final problem with Ussher's position is its (no doubt unintended) christological consequence. If Christ suffered for human nature, then human nature must be a moral entity capable of bearing sin, guilt, and punishment. If human nature is a moral entity capable of bearing these things, then it must be a moral agent. The classical christological category of a person acting in a nature is disrupted by this conclusion because a human nature has taken on the property of a person as an acting subject. Chalcedonian christology rejects the idea of natures as agents, since it implies Nestorianism: two ontological Sons, divine and human, acting through a Christ united merely in appearance. It is no small thing to reckon that a nature can be capable of bearing sin, guilt, and punishment.

Knox: Exposition

As with Ussher, Knox's driving concern was the preaching of the gospel:

> The preacher is not concerned with the intended application of the atonement, which at the time of the preaching still lies hidden in the counsel of God. Thus, from the point of view of the preacher presenting the gospel (which is the same as our point of view), all have an equal interest in the death of Christ. Were it not so, and not true that Christ had died for all men, it would not be possible to extend a universal offer; for the offer, if it is to be a true offer, must rest on true and adequate grounds, which cannot be less than the death of Christ for those to whom the offer is being made.

Knox goes so far as to assert that the preacher "is at liberty, and indeed obliged, to press home the offer, and to say to each sinner individually, 'Christ has died for you.'"[23]

Knox unequivocally affirms penal substitutionary atonement.[24] Yet he is equally emphatic that the extent of this saving work was universal: "the work

---

[23] D. Broughton Knox, "Some Aspects of the Atonement," in *The Doctrine of God*, vol. 1 of *D. Broughton Knox, Selected Works* (3 vols.), ed. Tony Payne (Kingsford, NSW: Matthias Media, 2000), 261.
[24] See, for example, ibid., 109, 247, 249, 252.

of Christ extends uniformly to the whole of humanity." He argues this from Christ sharing humanity with all, from his perfect righteousness fulfilling the moral demand on all, his victory won for all, and his bearing the curse that rested upon all.[25] For Knox, the particularity of the atonement is located in its application rather than its nature: "the particularism which is characteristic of Calvinism ought not to be applied at the point of the making of the atonement, but at its application."[26] A passage in *Everlasting God* shows that, for Knox, limitation can in fact be located only within the application rather than in the accomplishment of redemption:

> Our Lord bore every man's penalty, the punishment that every man deserves. It is impossible to conceive of the limitation of our Lord's work on the cross, as though he would have borne more suffering, more punishment had his merits been applied in the mind and purpose of God to more sinners. The atonement is not quantitative, as though God added up the sins of the elect and placed the penalty for these and these only on Jesus; but the atonement is qualitative. Our Lord experienced fully the penalty for sin.[27]

Here we see the link between the nature and the intent of the atonement in Knox: the inapplicability of quantitative measures to penalty-bearing precludes any idea of the cross being intended for more or fewer sinners. Rather, in the words of William Cunningham, quoted by Knox, "The atonement, viewed by itself, is just vicarious suffering, of infinite worth and value, and, of course, intrinsically sufficient to expiate the sins of all men."[28] Quantitative ways of thinking are inappropriately pecuniary.[29] For Knox, the rejection of a pecuniary penology undermines the idea of definite atonement.

Knox: Systematic Critique

Knox is correct to claim that the punishment borne by Christ was not made up of discrete portions that were added up to make it what it was. Considered internally, Christ's death was infinitely valuable penal suffering because it was the infinitely glorious Son of God who suffered in his human nature. It was not made up of separable parcels of punishment. This is no revolutionary

---

[25] Ibid., 260.
[26] Ibid., 265.
[27] D. Broughton Knox, *Everlasting God*, in *The Doctrine of God*, vol. 1 of *D. Broughton Knox, Selected Works* (3 vols.), ed. Tony Payne (Kingsford, NSW: Matthias Media, 2000), 109.
[28] Knox, "Some Aspects of the Atonement," 261.
[29] Ibid., 265.

concession: Herman Bavinck, who defends definite atonement, affirms that "in the doctrine of satisfaction, we are dealing with factors other than those that can be measured and weighed."[30]

It does not follow, however, that all particularity is reserved only for the application of redemption, since there is another way of asserting the particularity of the punishment itself without appealing to the internal divisibility of punishment. All that is needed for the punishment to be particular is for the Father to have purposed the penalty borne by Christ as the penalty for the specific sins of particular people. It was the Father's intention that constituted the sufferings of Christ what they were. The sufferings of Christ, as the infinitely precious sufferings of his soul and body, had the internal characteristics necessary to atone for any and every sin. But they did not exist only in the realm of their own interiority—nothing does. They were constituted, like all created things, in the realm of the divine will. A properly covenantal ontology recognizes the primacy of God's will in constituting reality, together with its result in the internal properties of things. This is not to broach the question of the relationship between God's own essence and will that has recurred in the history of theology, nor is it to embrace the voluntarist answer to that question. We are not concerned here with the relationship between God's essence and will within himself, but with the basis of all created essences in the divine will and purpose. Whatever view we take of the intellectualist-voluntarist question in our doctrine of God, it is clear that created essences cannot find their reality outside of the divine will. The sufferings of Christ were what they were because of God's eternal intention for them in the covenant of redemption. An ontology that appreciates the importance of divine constitution thus creates the space for the particularity of the atonement that Knox thinks that the internal properties of punishment exclude. It is worth noting that it does so without any appeal to pecuniary metaphors, despite the insistence of David Allen that "the argument that the rejection of limited atonement entails the need to deny penal substitution ultimately rests on a confusion between *commercial* debt and *penal* debt."[31] As we have seen, a proper ontology of the atonement can establish that entailment without any reliance on financial language or concepts. I will explore in the next chapter whether there is more

---

[30] Herman Bavinck, *Sin and Salvation in Christ*, vol. 3 of *Reformed Dogmatics*, ed. John Bolt, trans. John Vriend, 4 vols. (Grand Rapids, MI: Baker Academic, 2006), 402.
[31] David L. Allen, "The Atonement: Limited or Universal?," in *Whosoever Will: A Biblical-Theological Critique of Five-Point Calvinism*, ed. David L. Allen and Steve W. Lemke (Nashville: B&H Academic, 2010), 102.

to be said for the use of commercial metaphors than many would allow, but there is no need of them to sustain the argument here.

Interestingly, Knox explicitly tries to separate the nature of the atonement from God's purpose and will for it, making the former unlimited and the latter limited: "The extent of Christ's work is not limited in itself, but only in the intentions and purposes of God, and consequently in the application of its benefits."[32] Knox attempts here a distinction between three elements: (1) the work of Christ itself, (2) God's intent for the work of Christ, and (3) the application of the work of Christ. The work of the cross itself is unlimited, but then there is a limited purpose for it in the mind of God, which has as its consequence a limited application. I agree that the cross is in one sense simply an infinite penalty for sin, but it is not possible to shutter off the Father's intent for the work of the cross (2) from its nature (1). The distinction between the cross (1) and its application (3) is a viable one, but the distinction between the cross (1) and the divine intent regarding the cross itself (2) is untenable. Nothing has its life apart from God's determination of its nature. At root, Knox's distinction relies on a defective ontology that separates things as they are in themselves from God's determinations regarding those things. Wayne Grudem maintains a similar separation when he argues that we should focus on "what actually happened in the atonement" rather than "the purpose of the atonement."[33] The separation is unsustainable: with an ontology that gives proper place to the constitutive role of God's will, the prior, determinative divine intention for the sufferings of Christ *makes* them what they are and thus makes them definite in nature. If the intention of God does not determine what a thing is, what does?

The Specificity of the Atonement in Scripture

I have identified some systematic problems with the accounts of Ussher and Knox, but they share a more fundamental difficulty: their indefiniteness cannot comport with the way that the Bible speaks of atonement. On both their views the suffering of Christ in itself is not identifiable as punishment for the sin and sins of particular persons: any narrowing occurs only in its application. By contrast, biblical portrayals of atonement locate the particularity in

---

[32] Knox, "Some Aspects of the Atonement," 261.
[33] Wayne Grudem, *Systematic Theology: An Introduction to Biblical Doctrine* (Leicester, UK: Inter-Varsity Press, 1994), 601.

the sacrifice itself, not simply in its application. When a sacrifice was made, it was made for the particular sin and sins of specific individuals. The effect of this section will thus be to show that the biblical descriptions preclude any accounts of the atonement that describe sin or punishment indefinitely, including, but not limited to, those of Ussher and Knox.

As an aside, I should explain my use of the statement that biblical atonement was made "for the particular *sin* and sins of specific individuals." Definite atonement, despite insisting that Christ bore the specific "sins" of individuals, also coheres with generic and singular ideas of "sin," and should not be taken to exclude them. Theologically, it is right to speak of the singular "sin" that pervades human nature as well as persons, because sin pertains to persons who exist in that nature. The fact that it is a person who sins does not imply that sin has nothing to do with human nature. Further, it is right to speak of the singular habit of sin as well as its plural acts. Both of these aspects of sin can and must be included in hamartiology and, therefore, in the doctrine of the atonement. For these reasons I refer to both the "sin and sins" of individuals, rather than just to their "sins."

SELECT NT TEXTS

Turning to the biblical data, we find that the NT speaks of sin in the singular. This might be taken by an advocate of universal atonement as an argument for viewing the sin borne by Christ as generic and universal *rather than* specific and individual. John the Baptist proclaims Jesus with the words, "Behold, the Lamb of God, who takes away the sin of the world!" (John 1:29).[34] Here sin is spoken of in the context of the atonement, and it is identified with the singular phrase τὴν ἁμαρτίαν τοῦ κόσμου. Paul, in describing the work of Christ, uses the singular of ἁμαρτία: "By sending his own Son in the likeness of sinful flesh and for sin [περὶ ἁμαρτίας], he condemned sin [τὴν ἁμαρτίαν] in the flesh" (Rom. 8:3); "For our sake he made him to be sin who knew no sin [τὸν μὴ γνόντα ἁμαρτίαν ὑπὲρ ἡμῶν ἁμαρτίαν ἐποίησεν], so that in him we might become the righteousness of God" (2 Cor. 5:21).[35] The writer to the Hebrews does the same, for example: "he has appeared once for all at the

---

[34] This verse is of course used to argue for a universal atonement. The correct interpretation of the Johannine "world"—that it marks the staggering wonder of Jesus being the Savior of Samaritans and Greeks as well as Jews (as in 4:42)—is beyond my scope here.

[35] It should be noted that if the second occurrences of ἁμαρτία in the Greek of 2 Corinthians 5:21 and Romans 8:3 are translated "sin offering" rather than "sin," then those occurrences are not germane here.

end of the ages to put away sin [εἰς ἀθέτησιν (τῆς) ἁμαρτίας] by the sacrifice of himself" (9:26); "the bodies of those animals whose blood is brought into the holy places by the high priest as a sacrifice for sin [περὶ ἁμαρτίας] are burned outside the camp. So Jesus also suffered outside the gate in order to sanctify the people through his own blood" (13:11).

It is not possible, however, to appeal to such texts to argue that Christ died only for sin considered generically and universally, because the purpose of the singular references is not to exclude the plural sense of specific sins committed by particular people. For example, more than half of the occurrences of ἁμαρτία in Paul's letters are in Romans 5–7, where he uses it to personify sin, rather than to distinguish the universal from the individual.[36] In his descriptions, sin, an active agent, seizes the opportunity presented by the law, brings death as its wages, but is finally defeated by Christ. The personification also serves to highlight the role of the Devil as the active personal agent behind sin. These are Paul's purposes in using the singular, rather than the exclusion of the idea of the plural sins of individuals. Indeed, Paul uses the plural to describe the work of Christ in one of his most emphatic statements: "For I delivered to you as of first importance what I also received: that Christ died for our sins [ὑπὲρ τῶν ἁμαρτιῶν ἡμῶν] in accordance with the Scriptures" (1 Cor. 15:3). He also uses another plural term for sin in an atonement context: Jesus "was delivered up for our trespasses" (διὰ τὰ παραπτώματα ἡμῶν; Rom. 4:25).

In John's Gospel we find Jesus switching easily from the singular to the plural for sin. In 8:21, he warns, "you will die in your sin" (ἐν τῇ ἁμαρτίᾳ ὑμῶν). The reference here may be generic, though most commentators think that the singular denotes the specific sin of unbelief.[37] Even if the generic interpretation is correct, it is not very marked because when Jesus refers back to this warning in verse 24 he does so using the plural: "I told you that you would die in your sins" (ἐν ταῖς ἁμαρτίαις ὑμῶν). This shows that we should not think that singular terms for sin exclude any reference to its plural manifestations.

Similarly, the singulars in Hebrews do not exclude the plural. Just after speaking of Christ putting away "sin" in 9:26, for example, the writer describes him as "having been offered once to bear the sins of many" (εἰς τὸ πολλῶν ἀνενεγκεῖν ἁμαρτίας"; 9:28), following the plural of the Septuagint

---

[36] So C. E. B. Cranfield, *The Epistle to the Romans*, 2 vols. (Edinburgh: T. & T. Clark, 1975; repr., 1990), 1:191.
[37] See further, Andreas Köstenberger, *John* (Grand Rapids, MI: Baker Academic, 2004), 258 n. 32.

of Isaiah 53:12. The Hebrew has the singular (חֵטְא־רַבִּים), though even the prophet used a parallel phrase in the plural in verse 11: "he shall bear their iniquities" (וַעֲוֹנֹתָם הוּא יִסְבֹּל). We can tell from the use of the plural elsewhere in the letter that the writer to the Hebrews did not use it only when he was following the Septuagint: "After making purification for sins [τῶν ἁμαρτιῶν], he sat down at the right hand of the Majesty on high" (1:3); "he had to be made like his brothers in every respect, so that he might become a merciful and faithful high priest in the service of God, to make propitiation for the sins [τὰς ἁμαρτίας] of the people" (2:17); "when Christ had offered for all time a single sacrifice for sins [ὑπὲρ ἁμαρτιῶν], he sat down at the right hand of God" (10:12). The writer also describes the typical work of the OT Aaronic priesthood in terms of plural sins (5:1, 3; 7:27), and uses παράβασις in the plural in 9:15: "a death has occurred that redeems them from the transgressions committed under the first covenant." Although none of these NT writers was self-consciously addressing our question, they evidently held that Jesus died bearing specific sins committed by particular people.

LEVITICAL OFFERINGS

The sacrificial language in these and so many other NT passages points us back to the wealth of OT material pertaining to the Mosaic sacrificial system, much of which is explored elsewhere in this volume. I intend, therefore, to take just three offerings from Leviticus 1–6 as case studies in the specificity of the Mosaic offerings. The ensuing argument is not intended to imply that the specificity of these offerings is disputed by others; it serves simply to highlight the strength of this under-attended material.

The opening chapters of Leviticus describe the regular offerings from the perspective of the worshiper, beginning with the burnt offering (more literally, "the offering that ascends"). The burnt offering, like other sacrifices, is described as a "pleasing aroma to the LORD" (1:9). Paul uses the Septuagint translation of this phrase (ὀσμὴν εὐωδίας) to describe Christ's sacrifice in Ephesians 5:2. Thus he identifies the burnt offering as a type of Christ's death. In addition, the NT idea of the Father sending the Son to die (Matt. 21:37–39; John 3:16; Rom. 8:32) echoes the narrative of Genesis 22 in which Isaac is referred to as a burnt offering (v. 2).[38]

---

[38] Gordon Wenham makes the point from John and Romans in *The Book of Leviticus* (Grand Rapids, MI: Eerdmans, 1979), 64.

There are two features of the burnt offering ritual that indicate the particularity of the sacrifice. First, the animal to be offered was brought by the one for whom it was offered. Unless he was bringing a small bird, the worshiper himself killed the animal, gutted it, cut it up, and washed its entrails and legs, while the priest sprinkled the blood and placed the carcass on the fire. Thus from the outset of the offering the sacrifice was connected to the specific worshiper. The second feature, the laying of a hand on the animal, underscores this. The meaning of the act in the early chapters of Leviticus is disputed. The main alternatives see it as indicating the transfer of sin (as 16:21), or identifying the offering with the specific worshiper. For my present purposes it is not necessary to choose between these interpretations, since either underscores the fact that the sacrifice was particular to the worshiper.[39]

The wording of Leviticus 1 further indicates that the sacrifice procures the acceptance of the specific worshiper: "He shall bring it to the entrance of the tent of meeting, that he may be accepted [לִרְצֹנוֹ] before the LORD" (1:3). John Hartley thinks that the third masculine singular suffix here refers to the acceptance of the offering itself ("that it may be acceptable").[40] This would be possible grammatically, but the reference to the offerer is supported by the use of the second masculine plural suffixes in 19:5, 22:19, 29, and 23:11 (לִרְצֹנְכֶם), which cannot refer to the thing offered.[41] Similarly, in 1:4 the related verbal form is used with a preposition indicating that the offerer is the indirect object: "it shall be accepted for him" (וְנִרְצָה לוֹ). As Jacob Milgrom notes, "the two dative suffixes attached to this and the following verb, *kipper*, both mean 'for, on behalf of,' thereby emphasizing the indispensability of the hand-leaning by the offerer himself."[42] This type of Christ's death was evidently an offering for a specific person.

The second offering to be considered is the purification offering, also a type of Christ's atonement.[43] It too is described in the words used by Paul as a "pleasing aroma" (Lev. 4:31), and Christ's blood is said to have a purifying effect (for example in Hebrews 9–10; 1 Pet. 1:2; Rev. 7:14). The offering was performed for inadvert offenses of impurity such as childbirth (Lev. 12:6)

---

[39] This ritual action also marks the particularity of the peace offering (3:2, 8, 13).
[40] John Hartley, *Leviticus*, WBC 4 (Nashville: Thomas Nelson, 1992), 12, 13.
[41] So Nobuyoshi Kiuchi, *Leviticus*, Apollos Old Testament Commentary 3 (Nottingham, UK: Apollos: IVP, 2007), 56.
[42] Jacob Milgrom, *Leviticus 1–16: A New Translation with Introduction and Commentary*, Anchor Bible 3 (New York: Doubleday, 1991), 153.
[43] The traditional term is "sin offering." For the designation "purification offering," see Wenham, *Leviticus*, 88–89; and Milgrom, *Leviticus 1–16*, 253–54.

or a more serious male bodily discharge (15:15). Chapter 4 describes the different offerings required of different parties: the priest was to offer a bull (vv. 3–12), as was the congregation (vv. 13–21), while a leader would offer a male goat (vv. 22–26) and one of the people a female goat or female lamb (vv. 27–35). Leviticus 5:1–13 describes offerings to deal with failure to testify despite adjuration, touching uncleanness, and rash oaths, graduated according to the means of the worshiper.

As with the burnt offering, the ritual action of the purification offering indicates the specificity of the sacrifice. In each of the offerings described in chapter 4, hand-laying emphasizes the tie between the worshiper and the sacrifice (vv. 4, 15, 24, 29, 33). In chapter 5 the graduated offerings required confession (v. 5), tying the sacrifice to the offense.

Again as in chapter 1, the wording of 4:1–5:13 also suggests the specificity of the offerings. Each of the descriptions of the four categories of worshiper in chapter 4 begins with a reference to a single offense that uses the word "one" (the feminine of אֶחָד; vv. 2, 13, 22, 27), and the word is then used again with the graduated offering (5:4, 5). All of the descriptions end with a statement concerning the intended effect of the offering on the worshiper, and most add a reference to the effect on the offense. As Roy Gane argues, these statements about the offerer show that Milgrom is wrong to limit the effect of the purification offerings to the cleansing of the sanctuary: the offerings purify the worshipers.[44]

In addition to the wording, I discern several carefully wrought patterns in 4:1–5:13, consisting of four elements, each of which serves to underscore the specificity of the offerings. The four elements are: the use of the word "one" for the offense; the presence or absence of reference to the intended effect of the offering on the specific sin; the variation in the preposition used with the noun for the sin (חַטָּאת), and the presence or absence of the specifying relative clause "which he has committed" modifying the noun.[45] The careful crafting of these four elements produces four patterns, which are mapped in fig. 17.1 and then explained.

---

[44] See Milgrom, *Leviticus 1–16*, 254–58; and Roy Gane, *Cult and Character: Purification Offerings, Day of Atonement, and Theodicy* (Winona Lake: Eisenbrauns, 2005), esp. chapters 6 and 12. Gane denies any function for these sacrifices in purifying the sanctuary, a role he reserves for the Day of Atonement.

[45] Gane provides useful tabulations of the components of language governed by כִּפֶּר in Pentateuchal references to the purification offering; see esp. *Cult*, 110–11.

§ 1: Leviticus 4:1–35

4:2 "one"

מִן + אֶחָד

"The priest shall make atonement for him/them . . ."*

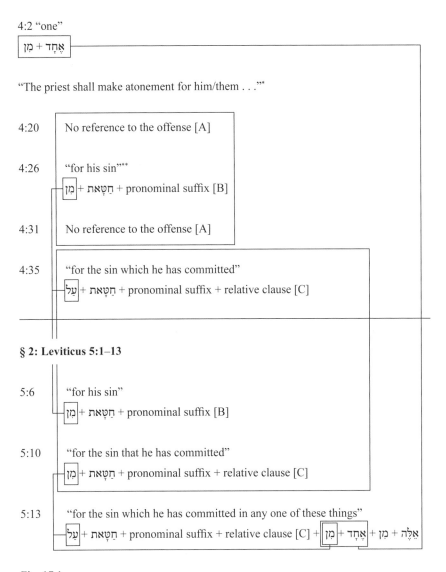

4:20	No reference to the offense [A]
4:26	"for his sin"*** מִן +‎ חַטָּאת + pronominal suffix [B]
4:31	No reference to the offense [A]
4:35	"for the sin which he has committed" עַל +‎ חַטָּאת + pronominal suffix + relative clause [C]

§ 2: Leviticus 5:1–13

5:6	"for his sin" מִן +‎ חַטָּאת + pronominal suffix [B]
5:10	"for the sin that he has committed" מִן +‎ חַטָּאת + pronominal suffix + relative clause [C]
5:13	"for the sin which he has committed in any one of these things" עַל +‎ חַטָּאת + pronominal suffix + relative clause [C] +‎ אֵלֶּה + מִן + אֶחָד +‎ מִן

Fig. 17.1

* I am persuaded by Jay Sklar that כִּפֶּר denotes ransom payment and purgation; see his *Sin, Impurity, Sacrifice, Atonement: The Priestly Conceptions*, Hebrew Bible Monographs 2 (Sheffield, UK: Sheffield Phoenix, 2005), chapter 4. I hereby follow his later advice about translating "to atone" but adding a footnote to explain the meaning (157 n. 76). Perhaps "make a purifying payment" might be a happy alternative.
** I use the ESV translations here, but see below on the privative sense of מִן, "from his sin." Considering this and the point in the previous footnote, we might translate 4:26, "the priest shall make a purifying payment for him from his sin."

In the first pattern, the ways in which the offense is referred to (or not) form two chiasms that bridge the sections 4:1–35 and 5:1–13, with the pattern A-B-A in 4:20, 26, and 31, and C-B-C in 4:35, 5:6, and 10 (shown inside the two boxes). In the second pattern, the prepositions מִן and עַל are arranged chiastically, also bridging the two sections. Milgrom thinks that they are equivalent in their causal meaning and are varied only for their sound, to prevent a "cacophonic clash" with מֵאַחַת in 5:13.[46] Gane rightly counters that מִן has a privative sense that עַל lacks, shown by the syntactically parallel uses denoting cleansing (טהר) from a flow of blood (12:7) and from sin (16:30).[47] But there is a further literary reason for the alternation here, since it creates this repetition of the מִן-עַל-מִן chiasm. In the third pattern, references to the offense grow in length within each section with the addition of the relative clauses. In the fourth pattern, 5:13 stands apart as a closing summary. It repeats the C pattern with עַל, but also twice uses the preposition מִן. The first time, it is prefixed to the word "one" (אֶחָד) as it was in 4:2, which has the effect of closing the section as it began, with a reference to singular sin.

These literary observations show that the references to specific offenses committed by particular people at the beginning and end of each of the descriptions of the purification offerings are far from accidental. They deliberately employ elegantly varied forms of expression to make the same point again and again: the sacrifices were offered for and were effective for the specific offenses of particular people. Gane notes the marked connection between the worshiper and the offering in these chapters:

> The beneficiary (obj. of עַל) is the same as the one to whom the evil belongs, as indicated by the possessive suffix on the term for evil (Lev. 4:26, etc.), and/or the subject of the verb חָטָא in a relative clause following מן (5:10; Num. 6:11). So evil is removed from its personal source.[48]

Similarly, Jay Sklar comments that the phrase כִּפֶּר + עַל + personal object confirms that "the rescuing or ransoming of the guilty party is not simply an indirect aspect of כֹּפֶר. Rather, it is a כֹּפֶר *for their life*, it is כִּפֶּר *for them*."[49]

The third offering to be examined is the reparation offering (אָשָׁם), which Isaiah 53:10 identifies with the death of the Suffering Servant. As Wenham

---

[46] Milgrom, *Leviticus 1–16*, 251, 307.
[47] See further, Gane, *Cult*, 125–26.
[48] Ibid., 135.
[49] Sklar, *Sin*, 75.

explains, the distinctive feature of this sacrifice is satisfaction or compensation.[50] I discern in 5:14–26[6:7] a similar verbal arrangement to the purification offering. This is evident in the introductory mention of the "one" offense committed (5:17, 22), and in the goal statements (see fig. 17.2).

§ 3: Leviticus 5:14–26[6:7]

"The priest shall make atonement for him . . ."

5:16   No reference to the sin [A]

5:18   "for the mistake that he made unintentionally"

        עַל + שְׁגָגָה + pronominal suffix + relative clause [C]

5:26   "before the Lord, and he shall be forgiven for any of the
        things that one may do and thereby become guilty"

        סלח + לְ + pronominal suffix + עַל + אֶחָד + מִן + כֹּל + relative clause

Fig. 17.2

Here we find again increasingly detailed summary descriptions marking the connection to the worshiper, with the first two closely parallel to patterns A and C. The final statement in 5:26 is different, because the specification of the sin is moved from the atonement clause to the result clause describing forgiveness, perhaps to emphasize the new statement that the atonement is made "before the Lord." The preposition עַל is used with "one" (אֶחָד), echoing 5:17 and especially 5:22 where the same combination is found, and closing the section as 5:13 did. As with the purification offerings, then, the bond between the worshiper, his sin, and his offering is deliberately articulated using a finely drawn literary pattern. Levitical atonement was definite atonement.

Applying the Biblical Data to Ussher and Knox

The evidence of the biblical types and antitype thus shows that atonement in Scripture pertains *in its very making* to the specific sin and sins of particular

---

[50] Wenham, *Leviticus*, 111.

people. The fundamental difficulty with Ussher and Knox is that their positions conflict with these biblical accounts of atonement. Scripture does not teach an atonement made simply for human nature (Ussher), nor does it teach a general atonement that is indistinguishable because it is unquantifiable (Knox). Rather, it teaches that, as he made atonement, Christ bore the punishment for the specific sin and sins of particular persons. Ussher and Knox admit the specificity and particularity only in the application of the atonement, but the descriptions in Scripture locate the specificity and particularity in the sacrifice of Christ itself.

Conclusion

We have seen the systematic problems with indefinite atonement in Ussher and Knox. Ussher relies on an untenable understanding of human nature as the object for which Christ atoned, while Knox builds from a flawed account of Christ's penal suffering as indistinguishable because it is not quantifiable. By contrast, penal substitutionary atonement in Scripture is definite atonement, made for the specific sin and sins of particular people. When measured by Scripture, only definite atonement counts as penal substitutionary atonement.

The problems with Ussher's and Knox's views are neither unique to them nor of purely historical interest. *Any* attempt to insist that Christ died for all without exception raises the specter of God punishing the same sin twice when he punishes the lost. One way of avoiding this consequence is to embrace universalism: Christ died bearing the specific sin and sins of all individuals and all will be saved. Ironically, such universalism would preserve the nature of the atonement, but it is not an option given the biblical teaching on hell. For those advocates of an indefinite atonement who see this, the only other option if they are to avoid implying that God violates the principles of justice is to redefine the object or nature of the atonement. Perhaps it was awareness of this argument that drove Ussher to limit substitution to a substitution for human nature, and Knox to deny the possibility of specifically identified punishment. It is the same awareness that ought logically to impel any other non-universalist arguing for an indefinite atonement to modify the object or the nature of the atonement. The theo-logic remains the same: any attempt to maintain an indefinite atonement will, if it refuses universalism, ultimately have to result in redefinitions of sin and punishment. I am, therefore, not surprised to have met in debate otherwise orthodox preachers and theologians proposing exclusively generic definitions of singular "sin" and denying that Christ bore the punishment for specific sins as they seek to avoid the logic of the case for definite atonement. But no such redefinitions can stand at the bar of Scripture: the biblical evidence shows that the Father sent his Son, the Son came to offer himself, and the Spirit mediated his offering for the specific sin and sins of particular people. Given this, the case against an indefinite atonement can be avoided only by universalism or by sacrificing the biblical doctrine of penal substitution.

Note again that we do not need to have recourse to a pecuniary metaphor to posit the specificity of punishment and the resulting problem of double punishment. In the next chapter I will examine whether the metaphor has a role to play, but for now it is sufficient to note that without any financial language the identification of the cross as punishment in the constitutive will of God sustains the double punishment argument. So long as God has identified this punishment as the punishment for these sins, then he cannot punish them again. An indefinite atonement must either embrace universalism or it must contradict the biblical doctrine of penal substitution.

I noted at the outset how Ussher and Knox are rightly driven by a desire to preach the cross faithfully. We do well to end on that most important topic. The consequences of an indefinite atonement for the preaching of the cross are grave. Ussher did preach to sinners that Christ died for them: "Your sins crucified him."[51] So, I presume, did Knox. But both their views imply that, as he laid down his life, Christ did not identify his suffering with my sins, or your sins, or anyone else's. At best Ussher might preach, "Christ suffered for your nature"; or Knox, "Christ suffered an indistinguishable penalty that may be applied to you." Of course I am not saying that this is what they did preach, but it is all that they ought to have preached, given their views. To put it frankly, any preacher who consistently holds to an indefinite atonement without universalism ought logically to resort to some similarly modified preaching of the nature of the atonement. That they do not is a reminder of how the Lord graciously protects us from the logical consequences of those errors that we all undoubtedly hold somewhere in our own theological systems.

It is the doctrine of definite atonement that provides a firm foundation

---

[51] See, for example, James Ussher, *Eighteen Sermons Preached in Oxford, 1640* (London: Joseph Crabb, William Ball, Thomas Lye, 1660), 386.

for preaching the cross as Scripture describes it. Ussher is right that the "bare sufficiency" of the atonement cannot actually comfort the sinner, but it is not the sinner outside of Christ who should find comfort. The sufficiency of the cross shows the sinner outside of Christ the one place where refuge from God's wrath can be found. It assures him that there is no sin too evil to be forgiven, no sin too bad for the blood of Christ. It is then, as the sinner is united to Christ and believes, that he actually finds the comfort of forgiveness. The believing sinner can be assured that Christ died effectively for him because he bore the punishment for the specific sins of his particular people, among whom he is now numbered. Definite atonement does not undermine the powerful preaching of the cross of the Scriptures. On the contrary, it alone can sustain the liberating assurance of penal substitutionary atonement: "Christ bore the punishment *for your sins*."

18

Punishment God Cannot Twice Inflict

THE DOUBLE PAYMENT
ARGUMENT *REDIVIVUS*

Garry J. Williams

The Double *Payment* Argument

It is possible to find statements of the double payment argument for definite atonement that create the impression that it rests on a conception of God, sin, and the work of Christ that is entirely commercial. When, for example, John Owen turns to argue from the nature of the satisfaction of Christ to a definite conception of the atonement, he lays out his understanding of satisfaction in thoroughly financial terms: "*Satisfaction* is a term borrowed from the law, applied properly to things, thence translated and accommodated unto persons; and it is *a full compensation of the creditor from the debtor*." He then develops this definition with reference to the death of Christ:

> First, the *debtor* is *man*; he oweth the ten thousand talents, Matt. xviii. 24. Secondly, The *debt* is *sin*: "Forgive us our debts," Matt. vi. 12. Thirdly, That which is required in lieu thereof to make satisfaction for it, is *death*: "In the day that thou eatest thereof, thou shalt surely die," Gen. ii. 17; "The wages of sin is death," Rom. vi. 23. Fourthly, The *obligation* whereby the debtor is tied and bound is the *law*, "Cursed is every one," etc., Gal. iii. 10; Deut. xxvii. 26; the justice of God, Rom. i. 32; and the truth of God, Gen. iii.

484 DEFINITE ATONEMENT IN THEOLOGICAL PERSPECTIVE

3. Fifthly, The *creditor* that requireth this of us is *God*, considered as the party offended, severe Judge, and supreme Lord of all things. Sixthly, That which interveneth to the destruction of the obligation is the *ransom* paid by Christ: Rom. iii. 25, "God set him forth to be a propitiation through faith in his blood."[1]

At the end of the chapter, Owen uses this financial framework to state the double payment argument against universal redemption: "Is it probable that God calls any to a second payment, and requires satisfaction of them for whom, by his own acknowledgement, Christ hath made that which is full and sufficient?"[2] Francis Turretin paints a similarly pecuniary picture when he writes of the debt of sin being "so taken away from the first debtors that payment cannot anymore be demanded from them."[3] Given such formulations of the double payment argument, it is not surprising that it is often rejected on the ground that it depends for its power on commercial concepts that are, properly speaking, inapplicable to the atonement.

This rejection is found in the work of both critics and defenders of the doctrine of definite atonement. Among the critics, Alan Clifford comments that Owen "explains and reinforces his teleology of the atonement" by "making the sufferings of Christ commensurate with the sins of the elect in a quantitative, commercialistic sense." He finds in Owen a "strict commercialist position."[4] Similarly, David Allen maintains that the doctrine of limited atonement "confuses a pecuniary (commercial) debt and penal satisfaction for sin."[5] For Allen, Owen "falsely understood redemption to involve literal payment to God so that the atonement itself secures its own application," and made this the controlling model in his book *The Death of Death in the Death of Christ*.[6]

In Owen's century, James Ussher defended his own Hypothetical Universalism against the double payment argument by objecting that it mistakes the metaphorical for the literal: "But if this *Justice* (you will say) be

---

[1] John Owen, *Salus Electorum, Sanguis Jesu: Or The Death of Death in the Death of Christ*, in *The Works of John Owen*, ed. W. H. Goold, 24 vols. (Edinburgh: Johnstone & Hunter, 1850–1855; repr., Edinburgh: Banner of Truth, 1967), 10:265–66 (emphasis original).
[2] Owen, *Death of Death*, in *Works*, 10:273.
[3] Francis Turretin, *Institutes of Elenctic Theology*, ed. James T. Dennison, trans. George Musgrave Giger, 3 vols. (Phillipsburg, NJ: P&R, 1993), 2:466.
[4] Alan C. Clifford, *Atonement and Justification: English Evangelical Theology 1640–1790: An Evaluation* (Oxford: Clarendon, 1990), 112–13.
[5] David L. Allen, "The Atonement: Limited or Universal?," in *Whosoever Will: A Biblical-Theological Critique of Five-Point Calvinism*, ed. David L. Allen and Steve W. Lemke (Nashville: B&H Academic, 2010), 83.
[6] Ibid., 89.

satisfied, how comes it to passe that God *exacts payment again* from any? *I Answer*, We must take heed we stretch not our *similitudes* beyond their just extent." Ussher feared that if we do stretch the similitude then we will "be forced to say (as some have done) That wee cannot see how *satisfaction and forgivenesse can stand together*" because a full payment leaves no room for forgiveness.[7] If God has been paid the full price for sin, then he does not forgo it, and therefore does not forgive. We see in this anxiety about the commercial conception of the atonement the extraordinary impact made on the history of Reformed thought by Faustus Socinus. When Ussher warns that some have stretched their similitudes too far and have been forced to deny the compatibility of satisfaction with remission, he is most likely referring to the Socinians. Socinus argued that "to forgive and to receive satisfaction are no more able to coexist than day and night, light and darkness."[8] For Socinus, satisfaction would involve giving God what he is owed, leaving no room for forgiveness. Ussher holds that any argument for a definite atonement based on a payment made by Christ invites this Socinian riposte.

In nineteenth-century Virginia as much as in seventeenth-century Ireland, the purportedly biblical theology of Socinus had a mesmeric effect. Unlike Ussher, Robert L. Dabney defended the belief that "Christ's redeeming work was limited in intention to the elect."[9] But he too feared surrendering ground to the Socinians. He refused to "attach any force" to the double payment argument and treated it as inextricably bound to a pecuniary understanding of satisfaction:

> Christ's satisfaction is not a pecuniary equivalent; but only such a one as enables the Father, consistently with His attributes, to pardon, if in His mercy He sees fit. The whole avails of the satisfaction to a given man is suspended on his belief. There would be no injustice to the man, if he remaining an unbeliever, his guilt were punished twice over, first in his Savior, and then in him.[10]

We see here what might at first blush appear to be two conflicting priorities for the Reformed defender of penal substitutionary and definite

---

[7] James Ussher, *The Judgement of the Late Arch-Bishop of Armagh, and Primate of Ireland* (London: John Crook, 1658), 31.
[8] Faustus Socinus, *De Jesu Christo Servatore*, in *Fausti Socini Opera Omnia*, Bibliotheca Fratrum Polonorum 1–2 (Irenopoli [Amsterdam]: [n. pub.], post 1656), iii.2, 1:193 (my translation).
[9] Robert L. Dabney, *Systematic Theology* (1871; repr., Edinburgh: Banner of Truth, 1985), 527.
[10] Ibid., 521. I have corrected the mistaken capitalization of "his" and "him."

atonement. On the one hand, the need to answer the Socinian attempt to render satisfaction and remission incompatible might lead to a denial of commercial concepts in the doctrine of the atonement. On the other, the refutation of a universal (and thus ineffectual) atonement might be thought to require just such commercial conceptions. Is then the double payment argument a powerful weapon too dangerous to use? In fact the potential pitfalls are even greater, because a full payment for sin by Christ might not only be incompatible with remission; it might also be thought to procure an immediate release from sin and therefore to render all the elect innocent, even before their conversion, a thought inimical to the apostle Paul, for whom the elect Ephesians were once "by nature children of wrath, like the rest of mankind" (Eph. 2:3).

Aim of This Chapter

My purpose in this chapter is to reexamine and restate the double payment argument. Much of the attention will focus on whether the argument is so inextricable from commercial concepts and their dangerous implications that it must be abandoned. I will demonstrate that while the argument can be reworked without the commercial concepts, it is possible to reach a more nuanced understanding of them that renders the double *payment* version safe to handle. After a general discussion of how metaphors function, I will explore the specific metaphor of punishment as payment to God as creditor. In the course of this exploration I will attempt to develop a biblical penology that will show what we should and should not infer from the metaphor. We will see that God should be regarded as creditor, but not only as creditor, and that we should avoid certain putative implications of the payment metaphor: the ideas of punishment as restoration and restitution, the claim that punishment is quantifiable, and the notion that it is an identical return for sin. The biblical data will show that punishment should be defined as *suffering inflicted as a fitting answer to sin*. This definition will establish against its critics a double punishment argument that could proceed without any commercial language, showing that the argument does not rely on an overextended metaphor. But it will also show that the language of payment remains useful because it expresses the idea of punishment as a fitting answer. Ironically, we will see that it is the Hypothetical Universalist critics of definite atonement who misapply the payment metaphor. Lastly, an objection to the double payment argument made by Lutheran theologians will be addressed.

Housekeeping the Metaphors

When we speak of God as creditor, of sin as debt, of man as debtor, and of the atonement as ransom, we are speaking metaphorically. Contrary to what we might expect having read some of his critics, John Owen knew this. Sin, he explains, is considered two ways in Scripture: as a debt and as a crime. When it is considered as a debt, God is the creditor, as in the Lord's Prayer (Matt. 6:12) and the parable of the unforgiving servant (Matt. 18:23–35). Citing the warning about paying the last penny in Matthew 5:25–26, Owen argues that debt makes us "liable to prison for non-payment; and so doth sin (without satisfaction made) to the prison of hell." Owen traces our debt back to the first man, Adam, in whom we all contracted our great debt as in a trustee. Then, before he turns to the understanding of sin as crime, he comments, "But this use of the words 'debt' and 'prison,' applied to sin and punishment, is metaphorical."[11]

Owen's point should be obvious, but we have been trained to view metaphors with suspicion. I recall being rather shocked when as a young student of theology I first read J. I. Packer's argument that the doctrine of penal substitutionary atonement is a "theological model."[12] Such a statement from a writer like Packer surprised me because it smacked of a denial of the reality of the atonement. I had been infected by the anti-metaphorical sentiment of philosophers such as John Locke, who argued that "all the artificial and figurative application of Words Eloquence hath invented, are for nothing else but to insinuate wrong *Ideas*, move the Passions, and thereby mislead the Judgment." In discourses intended to inform or to instruct, Locke avers, they are "wholly to be avoided."[13] I had of course failed to grasp that to call a description metaphorical is simply to describe *how* it refers to reality, not to question the reality to which it refers. We are mistaken when we speak of "mere metaphors" or dismiss something as "only a metaphor." Mary, for example, would rightly have drawn no comfort from noting that Simeon

---

[11] John Owen, *Vindiciae Evangelicae*, in *Works*, 12:515.
[12] J. I. Packer, "What Did the Cross Achieve? The Logic of Penal Substitution," in *Celebrating the Saving Work of God: Collected Shorter Writings of J. I. Packer, Volume 1* (Carlisle, UK: Paternoster, 2000), 97.
[13] John Locke, *An Essay Concerning Human Understanding*, ed. Peter H. Nidditch (1975; repr., Oxford: Clarendon, 1979), III.x.34, 508.

was "only" using a metaphor when he said that a sword would pierce her soul (Luke 2:35). As Janet Martin Soskice puts it in her classic work on the subject, to say "that an utterance is a metaphor is to make a comment on its form and is not to say that it has a particular and questionable 'metaphorical meaning.'"[14]

How do metaphors work? They are figures of speech in which a word denoting one thing is directly—not by the comparison of simile—applied to another. In an influential work, I. A. Richards labeled the thing to which the metaphor is applied the "tenor" and the term used to describe it the "vehicle."[15] In Simeon's metaphor, the suffering of Mary was the tenor, the piercing sword the vehicle. Basic to the function of metaphors is the idea that certain aspects of the vehicle apply to the tenor while others do not. These applicable aspects are termed the "grounds" of the metaphor, and the differences are the "gaps."[16]

To read any metaphor rightly we must distinguish the grounds and gaps carefully. The importance of doing so with biblical metaphors arises from the importance of the subject matter: misconstrue the metaphors, and we misconstrue God. For example, when Moses states that God is a consuming fire, we must not think that God is a chemical process produced by the chain reaction that results from the combination of an oxidizer, heat, and fuel. Rather, he is the God who punishes those who break his covenant because he defends his own name (Deut. 4:23–24). This is not to suggest a reductionist view of metaphors, as if we might simply translate them out of our language with no loss by providing a nonfigurative list of the grounds. Soskice explains the way in which metaphors are indispensable because of their generative power: "A good metaphor may not simply be an oblique reference to a predetermined subject but a new vision, the birth of a new understanding, a new referential access. A strong metaphor compels new possibilities of vision."[17] Simeon's sword is an example. With the phrase "a sword will pierce"—just one noun and one verb—he evokes a sense of Mary's vulnerability and of the pain penetrating into the very core of her being.[18] To explain all of the thoughts

---

[14] Janet Martin Soskice, *Metaphor and Religious Language* (Oxford: Clarendon, 1985), 69–70.
[15] See I. A. Richards, *The Philosophy of Rhetoric* (Oxford: Oxford University Press, 1965), chapters 5–6.
[16] For this distinction, see Craig Williamson, ed. and trans., *A Feast of Creatures: Anglo-Saxon Riddle-Songs* (Philadelphia: University of Pennsylvania Press, 2011), 27.
[17] Soskice, *Metaphor*, 57–58.
[18] The metaphor is clear, but the event(s) it refers to elicits some debate; for a comprehensive listing, see Darrell Bock, *Luke*, 2 vols. (Grand Rapids, MI: Baker, 1994; repr. 2002), 1:248–50.

and feelings that these two words evoke in nonfigurative language would be cumbersome indeed, and may not even be possible. There are distinguishable grounds here, but this does not mean that the metaphor can simply be eliminated.

Parsing the Trope

With these clarifications in place we turn to consider the specific metaphor of punishment as debt repayment. Immediately a new possibility opens before us: that we have neither to reject the metaphorical description of payment as punishment nor to embrace all that it might possibly imply. Instead, our task is one of theological exploration: to map the grounds and gaps of the commercial metaphor. Given how common an appeal to the limits of the similitude is as an answer to the double payment argument, it is surprising that there has not been closer examination of its inner workings. This may be part of a wider and yet more curious lacuna: the absence of any sustained treatment of penology among advocates of penal substitutionary atonement. There are evangelical defenses of retributive punishment as an essential presupposition of the doctrine, but these tend to proceed by demolishing the two alternatives (utility and reform) rather than by meditating on the nature of true punishment itself. As Oliver O'Donovan comments, that "encourages a style of argument that looks like a race of hobbled horses: none of the beasts are capable of finishing the course, so the victory goes to the jockey who knocks his rivals down before his own nag falls at the first jump."[19]

It is O'Donovan himself who has paid the closest attention to the nature of punishment in the context of his work on political theology. He is sharply critical of using the metaphor of debt and payment to understand punishment: "we ought to make our minds up once and for all to have done with the metaphor."[20] Given that the language of the metaphor is biblical, I take it that his point is not that the vocabulary itself should be expunged, but that we should not give it a formative role in understanding punishment. But even that seems to me to be a step too far: the metaphor must be there to do something. It is not merely decorative. The need is not to deny it *any* conceptual role, but to give it the right one. We cannot think that the financial

---

[19] Oliver O'Donovan, "Payback: Thinking about Retribution," in *Books and Culture: A Christian Review* <http://www.booksandculture.com/articles/2000/julaug/7.16.html > [accessed 17 December 2012].
[20] Oliver O'Donovan, *The Ways of Judgment* (Grand Rapids, MI: Eerdmans, 2005), 112.

metaphors are used to make points unrelated to the nature of sin, punishment, and the atonement, because it is in those contexts that the key Greek terms (such as λύτρον, λυτρόω, λύτρωσις, ἀπολύτρωσις, ἀντίλυτρον, ἀγοράζω, ἐξαγοράζω, περιποιέομαι, ὀφείλημα, ὀφειλέτης, and ὀψώνιον) are used.[21] Rather than being persuaded to abandon the metaphor, my aim here is to listen to criticisms of it, especially from Hugo Grotius and O'Donovan, in order to distinguish its grounds and gaps.

GOD AS CREDITOR AND RULER

The metaphor of punishment as payment identifies God as a creditor in the atonement, the one owed the debt of punishment. Socinus uses this description of God to argue against the orthodox view. If God is a creditor (*creditor*) and offended party (*pars offensa*), he can therefore freely will to forgive sin without satisfaction: "there is no creditor who, according to the strict letter of the law, is not able to forgive his debtor either part of the debt or the whole debt, having received no satisfaction."[22] Grotius responded by arguing that in the doctrine of the atonement God should not be considered as a creditor or an offended party, but as ruler (*rector*).[23] For a ruler, satisfaction is necessary not because he is owed it, but because he must act in all instances "for the sake of a community [*causa communitatis alicuius*]."[24] Because God is ruler, his penal laws may be relaxed, but only with compelling reasons and in a particular way such that they maintain their authority, that is, by satisfaction.

By denying the idea of God as creditor and offended party, Grotius is thought by many to replace the idea of punishment for retrospective retributive reasons with the idea of punishment only for the prospective good of the community. There is a long line of writers who describe Grotius as the founder of such a "governmental" theory of the atonement, with a diminishing level of attention paid to the text of his works as the years pass. The reading was disseminated by Ferdinand Christian Baur in an influential article in *Bibliotheca Sacra*, where he states that for Grotius "the real object of consideration is not past sin, but future."[25] In one of the few books on the theology

---

[21] For a classic treatment of the redemption terminology, see Leon Morris, *The Apostolic Preaching of the Cross*, 3rd ed. (Grand Rapids, MI: Eerdmans, 1965; repr. 1992), chapter 1.

[22] Socinus, *De Jesu Christo*, iii. 1, 1:186 (my translation).

[23] Hugo Grotius, *Defensio fidei catholicae de satisfactione Christi adversus Faustum Socinum Senensem*, in *Hugo Grotius Opera Theologica*, ed. Edwin Rabbie, trans. Hotze Mulder (Assen/Maastricht: Van Gorcum, 1990), chapter 2.

[24] Ibid., ii.16, 142/143.

[25] Ferdinand Christian Baur, trans. Leonard Swain, "The Grotian Theory of the Atonement," *BSac* 9 (1852): 262.

of Grotius, Joachim Schlüter asserts that "for Grotius the end of *satisfactio* is above all this, that men might be warned away from future sins."[26] This interpretation is quite wrong, but instructive for our purposes. It reminds us of the need to tread with care in handling metaphors: the misinterpretation of Grotius arises from inferring a substantive denial of retribution from his refusal to give the metaphors a constructive theological function. Even though he excludes the creditor metaphor, Grotius lists the innateness of divine justice as one of the points on which he disagrees with Socinus.[27] He expresses the importance of it as a cause of punishment in a letter to Antonius Walaeus:

> The causes demanding punishment must not only be located outside God [*extra Deum*], but also in God himself [*in ipso Deo*], in so far as there evidently resides in him [*in ipso residet*] that natural justice and the hatred of sin, which I defend against Socinus in more than one place.[28]

It is true that in his great treatise on just war, *De iure belli ac pacis*, Grotius denies the justice of any war that is caused solely by a desire for retribution and does not serve other ends.[29] But he explicitly contrasts this with God, because "the actions of God can be based upon the right of the Supreme Power, particularly where a man's special desert is concerned, even if they have in view no end outside themselves." Grotius underscores the uniqueness of God in punishing for retribution alone:

> God is said to have made all things for His own sake [*propter se*], that is by right of the highest freedom, not seeking or regarding any perfection outside Himself [*extra se*]; just as God is said to be "self-existent" [αὐτοφυής] because He is not born of anyone. Assuredly, Holy Writ bears witness that the punishments of those that are irretrievably lost are not exacted by God for any other purpose, when it says that He derives pleasure [*voluptatem*] from their woe, and that the impious are derided and mocked by God.[30]

---

[26] Joachim Schlüter, *Die Theologie des Hugo Grotius* (Göttingen, Germany: Vandenhoeck & Ruprecht, 1919), 43 (my translation).

[27] See Grotius, *De satisfactione*, v.13, 180/181. For a sustained interpretation of Grotius on the atonement, see my "A Critical Exposition of Hugo Grotius's Doctrine of the Atonement in *De satisfactione Christi*" (unpublished doctoral thesis, University of Oxford, 1999).

[28] C. Molhuysen and B. L. Meulenbroek, eds., *Briefwisseling van Hugo Grotius*, Rijks Geschiedkundige Publicatiën 64, 17 vols. (Gravenhage: Nijhoff/Instituut voor Nederlandse Geschiedenis, 1928–2001), 1:400, no. 412; reproduced in Grotius, *De satisfactione*, 465, no. 10 (June 29, 1615) (my translation).

[29] Hugo Grotius, *De jure belli ac pacis libri tres*, ed. J. B. Scott, trans. F. W. Kelsey et al., The Classics of International Law 3 (Washington, D.C.: Carnegie Institution of Washington, 1913 [vol. 1]; Oxford: Clarendon, 1925 [vol. 2]), I.20.iv.1–2, 1:316–17, 2:466–67.

[30] Ibid., II.20.iv.2, 1:317, 2:467.

God alone creates for himself and exists from himself, and he alone may act for himself. Hence, in his discussion of Romans 3:25–26 in *De satisfactione*, Grotius argues that the cross demonstrates both grace and "that justice which is the guardian of right order and also of retribution [ἀνταποδόσεως]."[31] There *are* writers who take up the emphasis on governmental grounds for the atonement and deny the role of God's inherent justice and retribution, especially among later Arminians and New England theologians, but Grotius is not one of them.

In a further challenge to the textbook caricatures parroted in the historiography, we find a governmental emphasis among Reformed writers. Like Grotius, Owen sets out the idea that God will punish sin because he, as the moral Governor of the universe, is bound to do so to maintain the authority of his law. Against the Socinian Crellius, for example, he argues that had God decided not to punish sin, he would have injured not only himself but the creation as well, since the infliction of punishment belongs to God "as he is the ruler of all and the judge of sinners, to whom it belongs to preserve the *good of the whole*, and the dependence of his creatures on himself."[32]

This material from Grotius and Owen illustrates well the danger of pigeonholing theological positions on the basis of their attitude toward the payment metaphor. We have been led to believe that God-as-creditor or offended party means retribution, whereas God-as-governor means consequentialism: the metaphors are bound to conflicting penal theories. Yet Grotius, who does not regard God as creditor or offended party, maintains retribution, while Owen, who does regard God as creditor, maintains punishment for governmental ends. There are important arguments to be had about which theologian has the most appropriate weighting of the two concepts, but if we take the lowest common denominator of Grotius and Owen as sustainers of a retributivist *and* governmental approach, then they both point us in the right direction. That they could both do so while making such different use of the metaphor of God as creditor reminds us again to attend to what an author says about the tenor of the metaphor rather than just the vehicle.

It is easy to see why a denial of the constructive function of the metaphor has been mistaken for a denial of retributive punishment. The language of repayment and offense is so closely connected to the idea of retribution that

---

[31] Grotius, *De satisfactione*, i.43, 118/119.
[32] John Owen, *A Dissertation on Divine Justice*, in *Works*, 10:567.

a refusal of the vehicle can be taken as a refusal of the tenor. The theory of metaphors would suggest that, rather than denying the constructive role of the metaphor *in toto*, Grotius should have distinguished its grounds from its gaps. That way he could still have rejected the oppositive Socinian reading of satisfaction and remission, but more plainly retained the idea of satisfaction to God's innate justice. The commercial metaphor should be retained because it helps to make clear that sin is not first and foremost against an order external to God, but against his own holy being, his *iustitia inhaerens* (inherent justice), and so needs to be dealt with in relation to him. As a debt exists in relation to a creditor personally, so punishment is deserved from God's personal being. *He* is the creditor, the one to whom we are "in debt." God does not relate to the law as a human judge relates to it, as if a personal interest in any case would be a bad thing. God, unlike the civil ruler, is supremely interested in sin against the law, because it is his law, expressive of his own holy being. The metaphor of governor alone risks picturing justice as purely for the common good and not for God; the metaphor of creditor alone risks undermining the reality of remission. It seems preferable that a mutually informing combination of the metaphors of God as ruler and creditor should be employed in expressing the biblical doctrine of the atonement, such as we find in Owen.

PUNISHMENT AS RESTORATION

Having considered God as creditor, we now come to the idea of punishment as payment, or repayment, and first to several ideas that ought not to be inferred from it. The metaphor of payment might be taken to imply that punishment simply restores the world to its prior state. The effect of punishing is to put everything right, leaving the creation as it was before the sin was committed. Just as repaying a debt can return a bank balance exactly to its previous amount, so punishing effectively rewinds the clock on creation. As G. W. F. Hegel describes it, *"coercion is annulled by coercion,"* suggesting a world as if nothing had happened.[33] This idea of punishment as the restoration of a prior state does not fit with the biblical picture, because, as O'Donovan argues, "redemption itself does not carry us back to the state of innocence

---

[33] G. W. F. Hegel, *Outlines of the Philosophy of Right*, ed. Stephen Houlgate, trans. T. M. Knox (Oxford: Oxford University Press, 2008), § 93, 97. Alan White translates the verb *aufgehoben* as "suspended" in his edition (Newburyport, MA: Focus, 2002), 77. "Annulled" is more appropriate, given Hegel's argument that coercion is "self-destructive."

before the first sin."[34] The re-creation will far surpass the pre-fall creation, partly because it will embody the remembered triumph over sin. The risen Jesus still bears the wounds of the cross (John 20:27). The New Jerusalem has the Lamb as its light, victorious but once slain (Rev. 13:8; 21:23), and at its center stands a tree that memorializes his healing work (22:2). There will be no crying, but it will not be as if sin never happened. The commercial metaphor should not be taken to imply that punishment simply erases sin.

PUNISHMENT AS RESTITUTION

The metaphor of payment also lends itself to the idea that punishment is a form of restitution, a return to the victim of what has been taken from him. O'Donovan warns against such identification: "If you take what the thief stole and return it to its rightful owner, that is not punishment, merely restitution."[35] The observation is an ancient one: even though Thomas Aquinas classes human punishment as an act of commutative or exchange justice, he too differentiates it from restitution.[36] Restitution "restores the balance when the taking of something has upset it. This is done by repaying the exact amount in question."[37] Thomas cites the example of a thief: when someone steals, he creates a double injustice, the injustice of inequality in the thing taken (*inaequalitas ex parte rei*), and the injustice of sin (*culpa iniustitiae*). These two injustices must not be confused, and they are to be dealt with differently. The injustice of inequality in the thing is remedied by strict restitution. For the injustice of sin, "the remedy is applied by punishment [*per poenam*], the imposition of which is for a judge. And so, before he is judicially condemned, a man is not bound to restore more than he took."[38] Restitution and punishment thus differ: restitution restores the inequality of the thing, but punishment serves to restore the "balance of justice [*aequalitas iustitiae*]."[39] Punishment imposed as a result of public condemnation by a judge is *poena*, contrasted with *restitutio*.

When the Socinian claims that penal satisfaction conflicts with the reality of remission and the need for application, he relies on the identification

---

[34] O'Donovan, *Ways*, 112.

[35] Ibid., 111.

[36] For the classification, see Thomas Aquinas, *Summa Theologiae: Latin Text and English Translation, Introductions, Notes, Appendices, and Glossaries*i, ed. Thomas Gilbey, 61 vols. (London: Blackfriars in conjunction with Eyre and Spottiswoode; New York: McGraw-Hill, 1964–1981), II-2.80.1, 39:7; 108.2, 41:121.

[37] Ibid., II-2.62.3, 37:109.

[38] Ibid., II-2.62.3, 37:110/111.

[39] Ibid., II-2.108.4, 41:126/127.

of punishment with financial restitution. When a sum owed has been repaid, there is no need for forgiveness and the debtor must be released immediately: he can no longer be treated as a debtor. We do not need to react to the Socinian claim by denying any idea of satisfaction as payment, but by carefully identifying the grounds and gaps of the metaphor. Specifically, the distinction between punishment and restitution creates the necessary space to resist Socinus. When we use the metaphor of punishment as debt payment, we do not identify it point-for-point with financial restitution. Punishment is suffering borne for sin; it is not financial compensation. The absence of forgiveness and the need for immediate discharge are implications of the financial vehicle that should not be applied to the tenor. Note that we do not simply cry "Metaphor!" and pack our bags, leaving behind *all* the possible inferences. Instead we locate the metaphor within its wider biblical and systematic theological context. We read it alongside the substantive conceptual distinction between financial restitution and punishment, and biblical statements about the reality of remission (e.g., Col. 1:13–14) and the unconverted remaining under the wrath of God (e.g., Eph. 2:1–3). The demarcation of gaps and grounds is thus determined by the patient reading of the metaphor in the context of the rest of Scripture, according to the historic Protestant principle *Scripturam ex Scriptura explicandam esse* (Scripture is to be explained from Scripture).

PUNISHMENT AS QUANTIFIABLE

We saw earlier how critics of the double payment argument find that it entails a quantitative view of punishment. Is punishment quantifiable in some sense? An amount of money can be quantified in different ways. It may be quantified as a whole, in that its total value can be delimited and measured. Or it may be quantified in that it can be subdivided into different quantit*ies* that are also distinguishable and mensurable. It is obviously the case that human punishments are in a sense quantifiable; for example, prison sentences can be measured in years. Yet O'Donovan shows that the idea of mensurability ought not to lead us to think that there is an ideal scale or index of punishments that every society ought to share. Because acts have different meanings in different societies, the correspondence between crime and punishment is "a symbolic construct of some kind."[40] The point is important but not obscure. For example, in 1546, Pierre Ameaux was

---

[40] O'Donovan, *Ways*, 121.

punished for accusing John Calvin of preaching false doctrines by having to walk around Geneva in just his shirt. In twenty-first-century London or New York, walking around in just a shirt would be no shame at all, and thus no suffering. Nor, presumably, would it have been for some of the impoverished refugees pouring into Geneva: the punishment gained its meaning from the fact that Ameaux was a member of the city's elite Little Council. Again, imagine the difference between a punishment of such public exhibition being imposed on a Muslim woman who always wears a *burqa* in public and on an Olympic beach volleyball player. Even if we have the most sophisticated understanding of our own culture and its symbolic language, it is very hard to know how much suffering any given punishment would produce in an individual, since there is no fixed correlation between the external imposition of punishment and the internal suffering of the one punished. Reactions to suffering vary, and a contrite criminal will bear a punishment quite differently from a recidivist. A society can measure years in prison, but it can never accurately gauge the degree of suffering borne by any prisoner. None of this means that there is no notion of appropriate weights of punishment, and therefore no possibility of a punishment being unjustly excessive; the argument is simply that while human punishments may be quantifiable, they are not always easily so.

Contrast God: he knows exactly what suffering an individual bears because he knows us better than we know ourselves, which means that divine punishments can have a perfection about them that is absent from human punishments. Scripture reveals that the eternal punishment of the lost will be quantifiable in its degree of severity at any one moment, because various texts indicate that there will be differing punishments for the lost, according to their guilt (Matt. 11:21–24; Luke 12:35–48). The suffering of the lost will also be notionally divisible into different time periods, and thus into quantities, because both heaven and hell will be temporal realities, God alone being the atemporal Creator of time. But because its duration will be eternal, the punishment of the lost will be unquantifiable as a whole, a thought at which we can but shudder. As Jonathan Edwards argues, this is because the sin being punished is infinitely heinous:

> 'Tis requisite that God should punish all sin with infinite punishment; because all sin, as it is against God, is infinitely heinous, and has infinite

demerit, is justly infinitely hateful to him, and so stirs up infinite abhorrence and indignation in him.[41]

We are not, however, focusing on the punishment of the lost, but on the substitutionary punishment of Christ in their place, which broaches a further kind of unquantifiability. The substitutionary sufferings of Christ were not identical in every respect with those deserved by his people, in that they were not temporally eternal. Owen states the qualification: Christ's suffering was "essentially the same in weight and pressure, though not in all accidents of duration and the like; for it was impossible that he should be detained by death."[42] The sufferings of Christ were therefore quantifiable in temporal duration, since he suffered in his state of humiliation until he cried, "It is finished" (John 19:30). The NT also indicates that Christ experienced the punishment that he bore differently from the way the lost will, because he did not despair. While he experienced the terrible and clouding effects of being forsaken by his Father, he endured the cross "for the joy that was set before him" (Heb. 12:2). As Turretin asks, "if faith was fixed in his heart, how could despair fall upon him?"[43] Edwards also explains how Christ's experience must have been different because, though forsaken, he was still loved by the Father: "Christ suffered the wrath of God for men's sins in such a way as he was capable of, being an infinitely holy person who knew that God was not angry with him personally, knew that God did not hate him, but infinitely loved him."[44] Christ bore punishment, but he knew that he was bearing it without being personally guilty: it was an imputative punishment from his Father who loved him, indeed who delighted especially in this his obedient act of offering his life in the place of his people. Nonetheless, the sufferings of Christ were, as Turretin describes them, "infernal on account of their dreadfulness and intensity."[45] While he suffered for a limited period of time, and while he never despaired, the suffering he bore was, as Owen states, "*solutio ejusdem*, payment of the same thing that was in the obligation."[46] Indeed, the penal humiliation of Christ met and surpassed the punishments

---

[41] Jonathan Edwards, *The "Miscellanies": 501–832*, in *The Works of Jonathan Edwards*, ed. Ava Chamberlain, 26 vols. (New Haven and London: Yale University Press, 2000), Misc. 779, 18:435.

[42] Owen, *Death of Death*, in *Works*, 10:269–70.

[43] Turretin, *Institutes*, 2:356.

[44] Jonathan Edwards, *The "Miscellanies": 833–1152*, in *The Works of Jonathan Edwards*, ed. Amy Plantinga Pauw, 26 vols. (New Haven and London: Yale University Press, 2002), Misc. 1005, 20:329.

[45] Turretin, *Institutes*, 2:355.

[46] Owen, *Death of Death*, in *Works*, 10:267.

of the lost because he is the Son of God. He came down to human form from the infinite heights of glory. As Edwards expresses it, "none ever stooped so low as Christ, if we consider either the infinite height that he stooped from, or the great depth to which he stooped."[47] His experience of penal humiliation was immeasurable.

Here we are reminded of the importance of understanding the person of Christ for grasping the magnitude of his work. The temporally limited punishment borne by Christ was of infinite, unquantifiable value because of the dignity of his human nature subsisting in union with his divine person. Christ was one; as the Chalcedonian definition states, "our Lord Jesus Christ is to us One and the same Son, the Self-same Perfect in Godhead, the Self-same Perfect in Manhood."[48] There is distinction but no division in Christ, so that when he died, the eternal Son died according to his human nature. We cannot say that "his humanity" died, as if to ascribe to it a life apart from the eternal Son. His human nature is anhypostatic: it has no personal existence from itself. And it is enhypostatic: it finds its personhood as the human nature of God the Son. This is why Cyril of Alexandria, whose role as cynosure for Chalcedon is widely underestimated, wrote so emphatically and frequently of the humanity of the Son as *his* humanity: the Word "became flesh, that is became man, appropriating a human body to himself in such an indissoluble union that it has to be considered as his very own body and no one else's."[49] As John McGuckin explains, "the divine Word was the direct and sole personal subject of all the incarnate acts."[50] Cyril's view of the single subjectivity of Christ, which became Chalcedon's, means that everything that Christ did was an act of God the Son: "even the suffering might be said to be his because it was his own body which suffered and no one else's."[51] Thus we may—indeed must—say that "God died" on the cross. We must ascribe the properties of one nature to the other because they are both united in the one person, or else we imply a Nestorian (or at least Diodoran) two-Sons Christology. This does not mean that the natures are mixed or that God literally

---

[47] Jonathan Edwards, *A History of the Work of Redemption*, in *The Works of Jonathan Edwards*, ed. John F. Wilson, 26 vols. (New Haven, CT: Yale University Press, 1989), 9:322.
[48] Quoted in T. Herbert Bindley and F. W. Green, eds., *The Oecumenical Documents of the Faith* (London: Methuen, 1950), 234.
[49] Cyril of Alexandria, *On the Unity of Christ*, ed. and trans. John Anthony McGuckin (Crestwood, NY: St. Vladimir's Seminary Press, 1995), 63.
[50] John McGuckin, *St. Cyril of Alexandria and the Christological Controversy: Its History, Theology, and Texts* (Crestwood, NY: St. Vladimir's Seminary Press, 2004), 154.
[51] Cyril of Alexandria, *Unity*, 118.

died. As Turretin explains, the properties are shared as the properties of the one person; they are not mixed together: "The communication is not only verbal, but is rightly called 'real'; not indeed with respect to the natures (as if the properties of the one nature were really communicated to the other), but with respect to the person."[52]

It is this real communication that explains the infinite value of the death of Christ. When Christ died, the eternal Son of God died in *his* human nature: it was therefore *his* death. The suffering of Christ was of infinite value because it was the suffering of his humanity hypostatized in union with his divine person. Christ's suffering was therefore as valuable as his divine nature: infinitely valuable. Being infinitely valuable, it was unquantifiably valuable. Any moment of the suffering of Christ was infinitely and unquantifiably valuable because it was the suffering of the Son of God. It was not only unquantifiably precious as a temporal whole, but unquantifiably precious when considered in any slice of time. Herein lies the wonder of the gospel that the church is tasked to preach to the ends of the earth: it is the good news of a sacrificial offering so powerful that no sin can be deemed too great for its atoning efficacy. The metaphor of payment cannot be taken to imply that the penal substitutionary suffering of Christ was measurable into discrete parcels of defined and limited value, assignable as portions to the different persons for whom he died.

The critics of Owen conclude that, if the punishment borne by Christ was not quantifiable, then it must have been general and indefinite. They insist that we face a choice: quantifiable and definite, or unquantifiable and indefinite. It is true that the double punishment argument is viable only if the idea of definiteness is retained; if unquantifiability means indefiniteness, then the argument fails. But the choice is a false one, since it is both possible and necessary to hold together the idea of an unquantifiable punishment and an inherently definite atonement: unquantifiability does not mean indefiniteness. A sustained consideration of the idea of return in the payment metaphor will enable us to see why.

Punishment as Identical Return

The language of punishment as a form of "paying back" the sinner might suggest that sin is repaid in the sense that it comes back upon the sinner himself as a return identical to his sin. The problem with this idea of punishment as the

---
[52] Turretin, *Institutes*, 2:322.

repetition of the sin upon the sinner is that the sin, being a sin, must not be re-peated. As O'Donovan points out, there is something very troubling about the idea that what a criminal deserves is for his sin to be committed back against him, as if what justice *really* requires is that we torture a torturer or rape a rapist, and only decency prevents us.[53] It would be blasphemous to ascribe such a "justice" to God, who is "of purer eyes than to see evil" (Hab. 1:13).

The inadequacy of identifying punishment as sin returned upon the sin-ner has long been recognized. In the *Nicomachean Ethics*, Aristotle believes in justice as some kind of exchange, but he rejects the Pythagorean ideal of simple "reciprocity" (τὸ ἀντιπεπονθός) as an adequate summary.[54] Thomas also discusses the idea of punishment as a return of sin, under the label "re-taliation" (*contrapassum*, which he uses for Aristotle's τὸ ἀντιπεπονθός). He describes retaliation as an "exact concordance of a reaction with the anteced-ent action [*aequalem recompensationem passionis ad actionem praeceden-tem*]," taking a life for a life or an eye for an eye as examples of such strict return.[55] The concept of *contrapassum* is memorably illustrated by Dante in the *Inferno*. The poet sees Bertrand de Born being punished for dividing Henry II of England from his son by having his head divided from his body: "Because I divided persons so joined, I carry my brain divided, alas, from its origin which is in this trunk. Thus you observe in me the counter-suffering [*contrapasso*]."[56] Thomas argues that justice does not always involve retali-ation. The requirement of commutative justice is that "the equivalent recom-pense be made, namely that the reaction as repayment [*passio recompensata*] matches the action [*aequalis actioni*]."[57] In other words, the criminal must suffer what he has inflicted. But this may require that the suffering inflicted in punishment be a quite different species from the sinful act. For example, it will not be sufficient just to take back from a thief what he has stolen. By taking back only what has been removed, the original loss would be greater than the suffering inflicted, because "he who inflicted loss on another would suffer no loss of property in return."[58] Only if the thief offers several times

[53] O'Donovan, *Ways*, 110–11.
[54] Aristotle, *Nichomachean Ethics*, book 5, section 5, in *The Complete Works of Aristotle: The Revised Oxford Translation*, ed. Jonathan Barnes, Bollingen Series 71.2, 2 vols. (1984; repr., Princeton, NJ: Princeton University Press, 1995), 2:1787.
[55] Aquinas, *Summa Theologiae*, II-2.61.4, 37:98/99, citing Exodus 21:23–24.
[56] Dante, *The Divine Comedy of Dante Alighieri, Volume 1: Inferno*, ed. Robert M. Durling and Ronald L. Martinez, trans. Robert M. Durling (New York: Oxford University Press, 1996), Canto 28, ll.139–42, 439.
[57] Aquinas, *Summa Theologiae*, II-2.61.4, 37:100/101.
[58] Ibid., II-2.61.4, 37:101.

what restitution would have required will he add to restitution the requisite suffering, the *passio* that responds justly to his *actio*.

Whatever the metaphor of repayment may mean, these arguments show that justice is not satisfied by the simple reenactment of the sin against the sinner. Punishment is not a return in that sense. Nor is it a perfect "echo" or "mirror" of sin. A perfect echo neither adds to nor removes from the original sound; in a perfect reflection nothing is lost or altered by the absorption or scattering of light. The perfect echo or mirror of a sin would be a sin.

PUNISHMENT AS AN ANSWER RETURNED TO SIN

Is there, then, no sense in which punishment is a return paid back for sin? In this section I will explore two lines of exegetical evidence to show that while punishment is not an identical return, it does correspond to sin in some strong sense. The first concerns the *lex talionis*, which O'Donovan notes "has seemed to promise an objective rule for the correspondence of punishment to crime."[59] Resisting this conclusion, he argues that it actually has a narrow function in Scripture: in Pentateuchal law it is used in only a limited number of contexts (Ex. 21:23–22:15; Lev. 24:20, and Deut. 19:21), and its single practical application is in the death penalty.[60]

O'Donovan stops here, but the evidence beyond the Pentateuch in fact suggests that the *lex talionis* principle had a more considerable influence. Narratives from Genesis to Kings suggest that the *lex talionis* had a more extensive role in divine action in history than it had in the law and practice of Israel herself. Indeed, the principle of the *talio* is not limited to Israel or the Sinai administration of the covenant, since it is established when God speaks to Noah at the beginning of the new creation in Genesis 9. God says to this new Adam, now progenitor of the surviving race, "Whoever sheds the blood of man, by man shall his blood be shed" (v. 6). The return here is blood for blood, an idea underscored by the chiastic patterning in the Hebrew, evident still in the translation: shed-blood-man / man-blood-shed.

Perhaps the most remarkable instance of the *talio* comes soon afterwards in the Babel narrative of Genesis 11. J. P. Fokkelman highlights the two symmetrical patterns in the text. The first is a parallel pattern with the same sequence of elements repeated in the account of human sin and God's response:

---

[59] O'Donovan, *Ways*, 120.
[60] Ibid., n. 31.

v. 1 "the whole earth had one language" [A]
    vv. 3, 4 "'Come, let us'" [B]
        v. 4 "'let us build'" [C]
            v. 4 "'let us make a name'" [D]
                v. 4 "'lest we be dispersed over the face of the
                    whole earth'" [E]
    v. 6 "they have all one language" [A']
        v. 7 "'Come, let us'" [B']
            v. 8 "they left off building" [C']
                v. 9 "Therefore its name was called Babel" [D']
                    v. 9 "the LORD dispersed them over the face of all
                    the earth" [E'][61]

The second is a concentric pattern or chiasm, where the description of God's punishment mirrors the description of the people's sin:

v. 1 "the whole earth had one language" [A]
    v. 2 "settled there" [B]
        v. 3 "they said to one another" [C]
            v. 3 "'Come, let us make bricks'" [D]
                v. 4 "'Come, let us build ourselves'" [E]
                    v. 4 "'a city and a tower'" [F]
                        v. 5 "And the LORD came down to see" [X]
                    v. 5 "the city and the tower" [F']
                v. 5 "which the children of man had built" [E']
            v. 7 "'Come, let us . . . confuse'" [D']
        v. 7 "'one another's speech'" [C']
    v. 8 "from there" [B']
v. 9 "the language of all the earth" [A'][62]

Within this second structure there is an even more detailed chiastic patterning in the consonants of the exhortative verbs for the human "let us make [נִלְבְּנָה]" (v. 3) and the divine "let us . . . confuse [נָבְלָה]" (v. 7): l-b-n is reflected by n-b-l. All of this patterning emphasizes the way in which the punishment imposed by God does indeed correspond in some way to the people's sin. As Fokkelman states it, "God's reaction and its effects are minutely attuned to man's action and its causes."[63] He himself makes the connection to the *lex talionis*: "The polarity of the story, with its poles men-God, action-reaction,

[61] Based on Fokkelman's analysis of the Hebrew in *Narrative Art in Genesis*, The Biblical Seminar 12, 2nd ed. (Sheffield, UK: JSOT Press, 1991), 20.
[62] Based on the Hebrew in ibid., 22.
[63] Ibid., 31.

hubris-nemesis, articulated so delicately and completely by the doubly-symmetrical structure, is the literary realization of a kind of *talio*."[64]

Not just in their literary structure but also in their content, the punishment inflicted on the builders by God functions as a point-for-point answer to their sin. The desire of the people to remain in one place involved rejecting the Adamic task of filling the earth given to Noah in 9:1. This sin was answered by the scattering of the people. The building of the tower revealed an idolatrous desire to become gods, as shown by a later oracle against the king of Babylon in Isaiah 14, where the king is depicted saying, "I will ascend above the heights of the clouds; I will make myself like the Most High" (v. 14). The cessation of the building through the confusion of tongues answered this attempt to reach the heavens. The desire for a famous name was sinful because it was to be created by men themselves; they did not wait for the name that God would *give* to Abraham (Gen. 12:2). The name "Babel" answered this desire by giving them a name that we still remember today, but not the name they would have chosen, since it sounds like the Hebrew for "confused" (בָּלַל). When God comes down, he meets sin with an exact, deserved, and comprehensive answer.

The second line of exegetical evidence for the idea of punishment as return is the language used in Scripture for eschatological punishment. In Romans 12, the apostle Paul quotes Deuteronomy 32:35 and applies it to the future wrath of God. He uses the verb ἀνταποδίδωμι (translating the Hebrew שִׁלֵּם) to refer to final punishment, a compound verb redolent with the idea of return, in this case hostile return:

> Repay no one evil for evil, but give thought to do what is honorable in the sight of all. If possible, so far as it depends on you, live peaceably with all. Beloved, never avenge yourselves, but leave it to the wrath of God, for it is written, "Vengeance is mine, I will repay [ἐγὼ ἀνταποδώσω], says the Lord." (vv. 17–19)

Paul uses the same verb in 2 Thessalonians 1, again referring to the last judgment:

> God considers it just to repay with affliction those who afflict you [ἀνταποδοῦναι τοῖς θλίβουσιν ὑμᾶς θλῖψιν], and to grant relief to you who

---

[64] Ibid., 32; for other examples of such patterning, see the rest of that chapter.

are afflicted as well as to us, when the Lord Jesus is revealed from heaven with his mighty angels in flaming fire, inflicting vengeance on those who do not know God and on those who do not obey the gospel of our Lord Jesus (vv. 6–8).

The idea of return is further underscored here by Paul's statement that God will repay affliction to the afflicters (pairing the verb θλίβω with the noun θλῖψις). While O'Donovan is right that punishment cannot be conceived as the identical return of the sin itself upon the sinner, this exegetical evidence requires some notion of punishment as a corresponding return for sin. The emphasis of these texts is that punishment is a proportionate and fitting response to sin. As Fokkelman comments on Genesis 9:6, the patterning "convinces the reader of the fitness of *this* punishment for *this* crime."[65] This is the central ground of the payment metaphor: punishment as a fitting answer returned to sin.

Jonathan Edwards draws out how punishment is not just an answer to sin, but contradicts it:

Sin casts contempt on the greatness and majesty of God. The language of it is that he is a despicable being, not worthy to be honored or feared, not so great that his displeasure is worthy to be dreaded; and that his threatenings of wrath are despicable things. Now the proper vindication or defense of God's majesty in such a case, is for God to contradict this language of sin in his providence towards sin that speaks this language, or to contradict the language of sin in the event and fruit of sin.

He continues,

The proper vindication of God's majesty from this, is for God to show by the event that he is worthy that the sinner should have regarded him and feared him, by his appearing in the fearful, dreadful event to the person guilty, that he is an infinitely fearful and terrible being. The language of sin [is] that God's displeasure is not worthy that the sinner should regard it. The proper vindication of God from this language is to show, by the experience of the event, the infinite dreadfulness of that slighted displeasure. In such a case the majesty of God requires this vindication.[66]

O'Donovan, though he eschews the idea of punishment as exchange or payment, has done the most significant recent work on the idea of punishment as a communicative act:

---

[65] Ibid., 35.
[66] Edwards, *"Miscellanies": 501–832*, Misc. 779, 18:439.

Since an act of judgment is true by correspondence to the act on which it reflects, punishment is an "expressive" act, telling the truth about an offense. Yet the truth told is ontologically distinct from the reality told of. The relation between them cannot be an exchange, which only occurs between commensurables. If I stand in front of a house and utter the statement "This is a house," my statement corresponds to the thing I see; yet the statement is in no sense *exchanged* for the house, since it is an entity of a different order. It *represents* it. In the same way the expressive act which fines or imprisons or even executes a convicted offender corresponds as a statement corresponds; it is of a different order from the act of robbery, kidnapping, or murder that was committed. Materially, there is a reciprocation of coercion to coercion; morally, the two acts are quite different.[67]

This understanding of punishment as an answer to sin effectively maintains both the correspondence and the moral distinction between them: punishment answers *this* sin, and it *answers* this sin.

A punishment, therefore, corresponds to a sin if it is a proper answer to it. This is why punishment is often materially the same as sin, because material identity may be the best way to answer the sin clearly. Biblical texts about men digging holes and falling into them or being trapped by their own snares do not mean that the punishment is morally identical to the sin, because what it says is opposite to the sin. Sin is always a lie, but the suffering inflicted in punishment is always a truthful reply. Goods stolen may be best answered by goods deprived, but the deprivation of goods is not theft. Punishment takes the form of suffering inflicted on the sinner because the person of the sinner, body and soul, is the appropriate sphere in which to answer the sin. The sin attaches to the sinner as his act, arising from his will, and so he is the proper place in which to punish it. As O'Donovan explains, "Punishment is thus justified in general because the person, property, or liberty of the condemned party is the only possible, or the most apt, *locus* for the enactment of a judgment."[68]

The idea of truthful answer shows why certain punishments would be unjust even if they did involve material correspondence. Take a hypothetical example of a disproportionate punishment inflicted by a human government. Imagine that a youth who has spray-painted an obscenity on someone's wall has that same obscenity tattooed across his forehead as a punishment.

---

[67] O'Donovan, *Ways*, 110.
[68] Ibid., 109.

If we thought of return simply in terms of material identity, we might think that there is something appropriate about permanently marking the face of a young man who has marked someone else's property, especially with the same word. But understood as a communicative act, the tattooing would be out of proportion to the crime because it would permanently deface a man created in the image of God, suggesting that a human person is no more important than a wall. The punishment, despite its material correspondence, would speak wrongly about the crime.

Unquantifiable and Definite Atonement

I have argued that the metaphorical description of punishment as repayment of a debt cannot be rejected *tout court*, but must be understood very carefully if we are not to reach mistaken and misleading conclusions about the nature of punishment, and therefore of the atonement. The metaphor must not be taken to identify punishment as simple restoration, as restitution, or as an identical return for sin. Nor does it imply a quantifiable atonement: while the punishment of the lost is quantifiable in terms of its degree and across any bounded period of time, it is not quantifiable as a whole, and the penal substitutionary suffering of Christ is unquantifiable as a result of his divinity. These are the gaps of the metaphor. Nonetheless, the metaphor may rightly be taken to imply, among other things, that punishment corresponds to sin as a fitting answer returned to it. This may or may not involve material identity, and it never involves moral identity, but just as a complete payment entirely discharges a debt, so a proper punishment conclusively refutes a sin.

With these distinctions in place it is now possible to address the claim of some critics of the double payment argument that a definite atonement must entail a quantifiable atonement and, vice versa, that an unquantifiable atonement must itself be indefinite. While this view is held by Hypothetical Universalists like Ussher, advocates of particular redemption, such as Andrew Fuller, also state it:

> If the speciality of redemption be placed in the atonement *itself*, and not in the sovereign *will of God*, or in the design of the Father and the Son, with respect to the persons to whom it shall be applied, it must, as far as I am able to perceive, have proceeded on the principle of *pecuniary* satisfactions. In them the payment is proportioned to the amount of the debt; and

being so, it is not of sufficient *value* for more than those who are actually liberated by it.[69]

For Fuller, a non-pecuniary atonement must *in itself* be indefinite, its definiteness arising only in its intended application. For Fuller, we should not ask, "Whose sins were imputed to Christ?"[70] The specificity of Christ's death arises only from its results, not its nature. He is clear that "*in itself*" the death of Christ was sufficient for all, and that any limitation occurs only in "the *appointment* or *design* of the Father and the Son," which means in its "sovereign application."[71] For Fuller, therefore, particular redemption is "a branch of the great doctrine of election."[72] Here is the crux: Fuller distances the nature of the atonement from its design and application.

Dabney maintains a similar identification of the double payment argument with the idea of quantifiable satisfaction. He rejects the argument by insisting that "Christ's satisfaction is not a pecuniary equivalent."[73] He denies that satisfaction is "a web of the garment of righteousness, to be cut into definite pieces, and distributed out, so much to each person of the elect." He counters, "This is all incorrect. Satisfaction was Christ's indivisible act, and inseparable vicarious merit, infinite in moral value, the whole in its unity and completeness, imputed to every believing elect man, without numerical division, subtraction or exhaustion." At this point, Dabney contrasts "expiation" with applied "reconciliation," asserting that expiation "is single, unique, complete; and, in itself considered, has no more relation to one man's sins than another," whereas reconciliation limits its scope to believers: "as it is applied in effectual calling, it becomes personal, and receives a limitation."[74]

My argument in the previous chapter stands against this insistence on an internally unspecified penal satisfaction narrowed only by its application: the sacrifice for sin in Scripture is itself specific. I now add a further argument from the understanding of punishment outlined in this chapter: the nature of punishment as suffering imposed by God to answer sin requires a definite

---

[69] Andrew Fuller, "Six Letters to Dr. Ryland," Letter 3, in *The Complete Works of Rev. Andrew Fuller*, ed. Joseph Belcher, 3 vols. (Harrisonburg, VA: Sprinkle, 1988), 2:708.
[70] Ibid., Letter 3, in *Works*, 2:708.
[71] Ibid., Letter 4, in *Works*, 2:710; Letter 3, in *Works*, 2:708.
[72] Andrew Fuller, *Three Conversations: Imputation, Substitution, and Particular Redemption*, in *Works*, 2:694.
[73] Dabney, *Systematic Theology*, 521.
[74] Ibid., 528. Dabney uses the term "atonement" for the narrower reconciliation, and "expiation" or "satisfaction" for the undifferentiated offering.

atonement. The notion of a punishment that is not an actual, defined answer to any sin committed by any individual is a contradiction in terms. If the penal substitution of Christ has no relation to one man's sin, then it is not in itself actually an answer to any sin, and is therefore not penal at all. In such an atonement God shouts out an unassigned "No" to nothing in particular, which in the parallel decree of election and in its later application is turned into an answer to something specific. But an unspecified "No" is not an answer to anything; it is without meaning. For substitutionary suffering to be punishment, it must in itself answer actual sins committed by actual people. A "punishment" with no particular sin preceding it in view would be akin to the nightmare consequence of the Benthamite dream: a supposed punishment, serving some end, but detached from any crime; like an innocent man hung from the gallows as an object lesson. Such punishment, in itself an actual return for nothing, is not really punishment. It is instead just the meaningless noise of suffering. It is *afflictio* not *poena*. This conclusion follows not from the quantifiability of debt payments but from the nature of punishment as an answer to sin. Fuller and Dabney certainly do not view Christ's work as mere affliction. They consistently and often powerfully affirm its penal character. My own early studies of the atonement were greatly helped by reading Dabney's *Christ Our Penal Substitute*. Nevertheless, I cannot see how anyone who excludes the identification of Christ's satisfaction itself with the specific sins of specific individuals can avoid the logical outcome of denying its truly penal character.

The only alternative to this endgame for the opponent of the double payment argument is to insist that the cross was after all in some stronger sense actually an answer to specific sins. There are strands of this in Fuller. For example, in his account of Jewish sacrifices he explains that "every sacrifice had its special appointment, and was supposed to atone for the sins of those, and those only, on whose behalf it was offered."[75] Note here how the atonement and offering itself was specific. Fuller then quotes the prayer of Christ in John 17:9 and 19, as if this explanation should be applied to his sacrifice too. He also writes of the "*designation*" of sacrifices by Hezekiah.[76] In some passages Dabney affirms the specificity of Christ's satisfaction. For example, on the same page that he argues that Christ's expiation had no more reference

---

[75] Andrew Fuller, *Reply to the Observations of Philanthropos*, § 4, in *Works*, 2:491.
[76] Fuller, *Three Conversations*, in *Works*, 2:690 (emphasis original).

to one man's sins than another, he writes that his sufferings "made a true satisfaction for all those who actually embrace them by faith."[77]

These passages show that while Fuller and Dabney insist on a satisfaction that is internally indefinite, they struggle to do so consistently. Their position is in trouble either way, given the nature of punishment. If they deny the specificity, then the truly penal character of the atonement is undermined. If they affirm it with full force, describing a sacrifice that has in its offering a special, designated appointment and true satisfaction for the elect, then the double punishment argument *redivivus* does its work: sin has been answered, and cannot justly be answered again.

A similar difficulty applies to the Hypothetical Universalist position. In his widely cited analogy of a king pardoning a debtor or criminal on the basis of his son bearing punishment, John Davenant rejects the double payment argument by appealing to the conditional application of Christ's work: "the enduring of the punishment was ordained to procure remission for everyone under the condition of obedience, and not otherwise."[78] We might conclude from this that Davenant envisages some kind of restriction in the punishment bearing itself, but actually he posits no such reservation: the conditionality is all in the application. He is unequivocal: Christ "sustained the punishment due not only to the sins of certain individual persons, but of the whole human race."[79] He explicitly denies that the offering of the Son was conditional:

> God gave his Son to the world, and the Son gave himself to the Father a ransom to take away the sins of the world, gratuitously and absolutely. A condition indeed is annexed in the preaching of the Gospel, not to the giving, but to the eternal life which is to follow from the beneficial application of the thing given.[80]

The punishment-bearing, ransoming, self-giving work of the Son was thus absolute. Davenant is resolved not to water down the penal character of the atonement. He does, however, limit the death of Christ itself as an act of procurement to the elect only. Christ's death did not purchase the conditions of application for the lost, but only for those predestined to life:

---

[77] Ibid.
[78] John Davenant, *A Dissertation on the Death of Christ*, trans. Josiah Allport (Oswestry, UK: Quinta, 2006), 52.
[79] Ibid., 40.
[80] Ibid., 58.

He willed that it should so pertain to the elect alone, that by the merit of it all things which relate to the obtaining of salvation, should be infallibly given to them. And in this sense we confess that the oblation of Christ is of the same extent as the predestination of God.[81]

But this argument narrows only the atonement as procurement, not the atonement as penal substitution. If the penal substitution, ransom, and self-giving is indeed absolute, then the double punishment argument applies despite any conditionality: God has answered the specific sins of every individual. The creation, seen and unseen, has witnessed the suffering that answers the sin. No man can answer again for that which has already been answered.

Who Really Stretches the Similitude?

Having been drilled to think that definite atonement relies on a commercial conception of sin, we may be surprised to discover one writer who defends it precisely by maintaining that the atonement is *not* to be regarded as a payment. According to his argument, it is the opponents of definite atonement who really stretch the similitude of satisfaction as payment. He defends definite atonement by taking a stand against a commercial conception of satisfaction. What is his name? *Mirabile dictu*—it is John Owen.

Owen considers the claim that satisfaction was made "on such a condition as should *absolutely suspend* the event." He explains that this kind of condition would "render it uncertain whether it should ever be for us or no." Hypothetical Universalists posit this kind of conditionality when they claim that unbelief can prevent the atonement benefiting one for whom it was made. Here is Owen's response to this notion, and with it the *coup de grâce* in which he points out that it is the Hypothetical Universalist himself who, by making the atonement refusable, identifies it with a financial payment:

Such a constitution may be righteous in pecuniary solutions. A man may lay down a great sum of money for the discharge of another, on such a condition as may never be fulfilled; for, on the absolute failure of the condition, his money may and ought to be restored to him, whereon he hath received no injury or damage. But in penal suffering for crimes and sins, there can be no righteous constitution that shall make the event and efficacy of it to

---

[81] Ibid., 54. Strangely, this strand of teaching in Davenant about a limited intent for the cross as procurement may mean that he has a more definite account of the atonement than advocates of a definite atonement, such as Dabney and Fuller, who locate the specificity exclusively in the application of Christ's work.

depend on a condition absolutely uncertain, and which may not come to pass or be fulfilled; for if the condition fail, no recompense can be made unto him that hath suffered. Wherefore, the way of the application of the satisfaction of Christ onto them for whom it was made, is *sure* and *steadfast* in the purpose of God.[82]

Owen draws a sharp contrast between pecuniary payment (*solutio*) and penal suffering: money can simply be refused and returned, but penal suffering can never be undone. The irony is palpable: *it is not the defender of definite atonement who relies too much on the similitude of payment, but its opponent.* The opponent claims that the death of Christ can fail to effect salvation, which means that its intention can be refused, and refusability without injustice is a feature of pecuniary payments. By contrast, a penalty borne by a person cannot be returned. The personal, physical, and spiritual suffering of Christ cannot be undone. Because the suffering has been borne and cannot be returned, it must take effect. Christ *has* died. Owen's argument, which should leave his critics aghast, is that definite atonement is *not* best served by reliance on the pecuniary metaphor, since a payment made in money can be refused and returned. Rather, it is the language of completed penal suffering that most clearly expresses why God will not punish sin twice and thus establishes the definiteness of the atonement.

If Owen rejects absolutely suspending the atonement on conditions, how does he avoid the Socinian charge, noted at the outset of this chapter and put to Owen by Richard Baxter, that satisfaction would have to be applied immediately upon being made? Where is the need for repentance and faith?[83] For Owen the gift of faith is itself a certain result of the work of Christ, produced by it *ipso facto*, yet "not in an immediation of time but causality."[84] Owen articulates the compatibility of identical satisfaction and delayed application on the basis of the covenant of redemption. It is the intention of God in the covenant that constitutes the sufferings of Christ as satisfaction, and therefore that covenant can also stipulate how the satisfaction will be applied. While Owen insists that Christ suffers the very penalty due to sinners without

---

[82] John Owen, *The Doctrine of Justification by Faith*, in *Works*, 5:217.

[83] Carl R. Trueman addresses this dilemma in "Atonement and the Covenant of Redemption: John Owen on the Nature of Christ's Satisfaction," chapter 8 in this volume.

[84] John Owen, *Of the Death of Christ, the Price He Paid, and the Purchase He Made*, in *Works*, 10:450 (emphasis original). Note that the term *ipso facto* can be confusing because it has different senses in different authors. Charles Hodge, for example, rejects it in relation to satisfaction, but it is clear that he equates it with *temporal* immediacy. See his *Systematic Theology*, 3 vols. (1871–1873; repr., Grand Rapids, MI: Eerdmans, 1954, 1986), 2:472, 557.

relaxation (the *solutio ejusdem* without *relaxatio*), he grants that the person bearing the penalty is changed in a relaxation of the law.[85] This change creates the space for a delayed application that would be missing if the sinner himself made satisfaction. In short, both the nature of the suffering of Christ as satisfaction and the timing of its application are covenantally constituted.[86]

It is worth noting that Owen also uses the covenantal constitution and change of person to answer the Socinian and Baxterian charge that identical satisfaction and gracious remission are incompatible. God did not receive satisfaction from the sinner but graciously provided it himself in Christ, and graciously relaxed the law that demanded it from the sinner.[87] In that sense, forgiveness is real because God himself graciously willed to bear the cost of sin.

The Lutheran Objection

I turn lastly to consider a reply to the double payment argument—to my mind less substantial—that originates from the Lutherans of the later sixteenth century. Unlike the case against relying on the financial metaphor mounted by Ussher and Allen, inter alia, this objection could be used as much against a double punishment as a double payment argument.

In 1586, Theodore Beza and Jacobus Andreae presented respectively the Reformed and Lutheran positions before Duke Frederick of Württemberg, who was engaged in a controversial attempt to impose the Lutheran Formula of Concord on his territory of Montbéliard. Beza and Andreae argued about 1 John 2:2: "He is the propitiation for our sins, and not for ours only but also for the sins of the whole world." In the record of the dispute, Beza proposes that the verse emphasizes the openness of the new covenant to the Gentiles, rather than the universal intention of the atonement: "John does not join together the elect with the damned, but distinguishes between Jews and Gentiles, so that he understands by the name 'world' the Gentiles with the Jews, but only the elect in both people."[88] He continues by arguing that "one drop of the blood of Christ would be enough for the sins of the whole world, even of the damned. But Christ did not die for the sins of the damned, otherwise

---

[85] Owen denies the relaxation of the penalty in *Death of Death*, in *Works*, 10:269, and affirms it of the person in ibid., 273.
[86] See John Owen, *Of the Death of Christ*, in *Works*, 10:458.
[87] Ibid., 444–46.
[88] Jacobus Andreae, *Acta Colloquij Montisbelligartensis* (Wittenberg: Myliander, 1613), 446 (translations are mine).

the damned also would be saved."[89] See how Beza's argument uses the logic of double payment: if Christ had died for all, none could be damned. After expressing his revulsion at this limitation of the atonement, Andreae produces what would become a standard Lutheran reply:

> Those assigned to eternal destruction are not damned because they sinned; otherwise also all the elect would be damned, since all have sinned and are wanting the glory of God: but they are damned for this reason, because they refuse to embrace Jesus Christ with true faith, who suffered, was crucified and died no less for their sins, than for the sins of Peter, Paul and all the saints. This is the eternal and unchangeable truth, against which the gates of hell will not prevail. As Christ clearly testifies, when he says: "This is the judgement, that light came into the world, and the world loved darkness more than light." Likewise, "The Holy Spirit will convict the world concerning sin, because they do not believe in me."[90]

The notion that the lost will be punished for the sin of unbelief and not for sin in general allows Andreae to hold that Jesus died for every general sin of every individual, and yet not all must be saved, because unbelievers may still justly be condemned for their unbelief since Christ did not die for it. This reply concedes the point about justice but responds to it by limiting the sins for which Christ died.

This is a radical innovation in eschatology, as Beza pointed out to Andreae:

> To me what you say is in fact plainly new, and previously unheard—that men are not damned because they have sinned—since sin is the sole cause of eternal damnation, the reason why the rebellious are abandoned to their own wickedness, and damned.[91]

Several arguments serve to disprove Andreae's position. First, while there are texts that speak of punishment for unbelief (for example, 2 Thess. 1:8), there are others that indicate that the lost will be punished for all of their deeds, not just their unbelief. Paul writes that "we must all appear before the judgment seat of Christ, so that each one may receive what is due for what he has done in the body, whether good or evil" (2 Cor. 5:10). And in Revelation the dead are judged "according to what they had done" (20:13). Indeed, it is hard to imagine how the sin of unbelief could be isolated as the one sin for

---

[89] Ibid., 447.
[90] Ibid., 447–48. Andreae is quoting from John 3:19 and 16:8–9.
[91] Ibid., 448.

which Christ did not die; it is rather the root of other sins that are all done in the realm of unbelief: without faith it is impossible to please God (Heb. 11:6). When in Matthew 25 Christ explains why the goats are sent away, he identifies their individual sins: "I was hungry and you gave me no food, I was thirsty and you gave me no drink" (v. 42). These sins were sins of rejecting Christ, but they were committed as sins of omission against his people ("the least of these"; v. 45). They were general sins, but they were also sins of unbelief. On Andreae's view, would Christ have atoned for them?

Second, Andreae's position generates a grave moral problem, because it implies that those who have never heard the gospel are condemned for not believing it. Andreae allows that all of their other sins have been borne by Christ. Why then are they not saved? It can only be because of their unbelief in rejecting the gospel. But they have not heard the gospel and so have had no opportunity to accept or reject it. Andreae faces a dilemma: either those who have not heard are condemned for their general sins, and there is the injustice of double payment, or they are condemned for their unbelief, and there is the injustice of punishing beyond the bounds of responsibility.

Third, Andreae's position, though partly driven by a desire to account for universal biblical texts, actually creates a different problem with the universal language of Scripture. The difficulty does not concern texts describing the people for whom Christ died, but those referring to the sin(s) for which he died. Every biblical affirmation that sins have been borne by Christ must now be understood to contain a tacit restriction: *except the sin of unbelief*. This is a restriction hard to sustain.

Lastly, this Lutheran position cannot be maintained if we believe that God punishes all sin. Imagine a non-Christian who has been committing the sin of unbelief. By God's grace, he is converted at age forty, and now believes. Andreae's position states that Christ did not die for the sin of unbelief, which means that he did not die for this man's sin of unbelief committed over forty years. Nor will the man himself, now a Christian, be punished for it. If, however, God punishes all sin, and if the man is forgiven for his prior unbelief, then Christ must have died for it. This is certainly the case if the punishment of sin is necessary from God's holy nature, but even if God does not have to punish sin he has still revealed that he will do so. Hence Owen, even before he came to believe in the stronger kind of necessity for punishment, rejected the claim that Christ could have died only for some sins. He quotes

Psalm 130:3 to show that if Christ died for only some of the sins of all men, then none can be saved, "for if God enter into judgment with us, though it were with all mankind for one sin, no flesh should be justified in his sight."[92] If God punishes all sin, then Christ must have died for the sin of unbelief, and if he did that for all without exception, then all without exception must be saved. Beza's alternatives remain: either universalism or definite atonement.

Conclusion

The description of punishment as the repayment of a debt to God as creditor is a biblical metaphor. Like all biblical language, it must be understood carefully within the breadth and depth of Scripture. It should not be understood to identify punishment as simple restoration, as restitution, or as an identical return for sin. Nor should it be taken to imply that the penal substitutionary suffering of Christ is quantifiable. Part of the glory of his death that we are to proclaim to all men, women, and children is its unlimited power. We are to preach to the lost that Christ's blood is immeasurably powerful to cleanse all who will come to him, no matter what they have done.

Positively, the metaphor expresses the personal relation of punishment to God's holy being, and the correspondence of sin to punishment as a fitting answer returned to it. These truths could be expressed without any commercial language, demonstrating that the double *punishment* argument does not depend for its force on the payment metaphor. Indeed, Owen shows that it is the opponent of definite atonement who depends on over-stretching the metaphor by implying the refusability of satisfaction. Nonetheless, we ought not to proceed by purging biblical metaphors, but by understanding them rightly. The nature of punishment, reflected in the idea of repayment, requires that for suffering to *be* punishment it must be an answer returned to specific sins committed by specific people. The atonement must in itself be definite. The nature of punishment as answer also establishes the double punishment argument: when God has given an answer to a sin, it has been given. Payment God cannot twice demand; punishment God cannot twice inflict. Christ's blood has spoken an answer to the sins of his people, including their sins of unbelief. Nothing more remains to be said.

---

[92] Owen, *Death of Death*, in *Works*, 10:173. For his later view that punishment is necessary given the holy being of God, see his *Dissertation on Divine Justice*, in *Works* 10:481–624. Turretin provides a shorter and simpler form of essentially the same position in his *Institutes*.

19

The New Covenant Work of Christ

PRIESTHOOD, ATONEMENT, AND INTERCESSION

Stephen J. Wellum

Introduction

One crucial biblical-theological issue at the center of the doctrine of definite atonement is the priestly work of Christ. Most would affirm with John Murray that our Lord's work is presented in Scripture as a priestly work: "The atonement must more broadly be subsumed under the Mediatorial work of Christ, and more specifically under the priestly office. But there is one Mediator, and Christ alone was called a High Priest after the order of Melchizedek."[1] Or, as Hugh Martin ably stated more than a century ago, "It is not enough to maintain that Christ's Priesthood is a real and veritable office; it must be regarded and set forth as pre-eminently *the* office—the foundation office—which Christ as a Redeemer executes."[2] Yet, many who affirm

---

[1] John Murray, "The Atonement," in *Collected Writings of John Murray. Volume 2: Lectures in Systematic Theology* (Carlisle, PA: Banner of Truth, 1977), 148.
[2] Hugh Martin, *The Atonement: In Its Relations to the Covenant, the Priesthood, the Intercession of Our Lord* (Edinburgh: James Gemmell, 1882), 53. This is not to downplay the fact that Christ also fulfills the role of Prophet and King—hence the famous *munus triplex*—nevertheless, as Martin argues, "His Priesthood is a more fundamental office than these—its necessity, its duties, and the discharge of these duties lying closer to the heart of his interposition for our salvation than aught that pertains to either of the other offices which He fulfills" (54). For a similar view in Calvin, see Stephen Edmondson, *Calvin's Christology* (Cambridge: Cambridge University Press, 2004), 89–114.

that Christ's work is a priestly work, including general atonement advocates, deny the repeated argument by defenders of definite atonement that Christ's High Priesthood necessarily entails a particular redemption. Robert Letham captures the priestly argument well:

> Christ's role as High Priest is a whole. It is one unified movement of grace towards humanity whereby he takes our place in obeying the Father, in atoning for our sins and bringing us to God. He makes very clear that he prays for us besides dying for us. This is a dominant theme in his high-priestly prayer to the Father in John chapter 17. In that prayer he says to the Father that he does not pray for the world but for those whom the Father had given him. . . . His intercession is limited. He prays for his own and not for the world. It follows that his atoning death is intended for those the Father had given him and not for all in an indiscriminate fashion. If we see the intercession as particular and the cross as universal, we are positing a disruption in the heart of Christ's high-priestly work.[3]

Let me flesh out the argument a bit more. Our Lord, as the Great High Priest of the new covenant, willingly and gladly offered himself as our substitute in deliberate obedience to his Father's will. In so doing, his intent was not only to achieve the redemption of a particular people but also to secure everything necessary to bring those same people to the end for which his death was designed, namely, the full forgiveness of sin and all the blessings of the new covenant, including the gift of the Spirit who effectively applies his work to those whom the Son represents. Furthermore, due to his powerful resurrection and ascension, our Lord's work as the Great Priest-King continues as he rules at the Father's right hand and intercedes for the elect, thus guaranteeing their eternal salvation. However, as the argument goes, all general atonement views must divide Christ's unified priestly work, redefine Christ's relation as Priest to his people, and ultimately make ineffective his work as the Head of the new covenant—all points which Scripture will not allow.

The priestly argument for definite atonement is nothing new. Almost every defense of particular redemption includes it.[4] Yet it is rarely dealt with by its critics, or if it is discussed at all, only aspects of it are men-

---

[3] Robert Letham, *The Work of Christ* (Downers Grove, IL: InterVarsity Press, 1993), 236–37.

[4] See John Owen, *The Death of Death in the Death of Christ* (1648; repr., Carlisle, UK: Banner of Truth, 1983). In many ways, Owen's entire treatise unpacks this argument. See also Francis Turretin, *Institutes of Elenctic Theology*, ed. James T. Dennison, Jr., trans. George Musgrave Giger, 3 vols. (Phillipsburg, NJ: P&R, 1993), 2:403–86; Herman Bavinck, *Sin and Salvation in Christ*, vol. 3 of *Reformed Dogmatics*, ed. John Bolt, trans. John Vriend, 4 vols. (Grand Rapids, MI: Baker, 2006), 455–75; Louis Berkhof, *Systematic Theology* (Grand Rapids, MI: Eerdmans, 1941), 361–405; Tom Barnes, *Atonement Matters: A Call to Declare the Biblical View of*

tioned, aspects which are usually divorced from its full biblical-theological presentation.[5] The purpose of this chapter is once again to lay out this argument as a crucial biblical-theological piece in the overall defense of definite atonement. I shall proceed in three steps. I shall (1) discuss two crucial methodological/hermeneutical matters that are central to the argument; (2) demonstrate that the OT priest does a particular and unified work, viz., those he represents, he also intercedes for and instructs; and (3) establish that our Lord as the Head and Mediator of the new covenant, in a far greater way than OT priests, achieves a particular and completely effective work for his covenant people.

I. Being Biblical: Two Crucial Methodological/ Hermeneutical Issues

Everyone desires to be biblical in discussions regarding the extent of the atonement, but this simply raises the larger question of how. Obviously this is a huge area, and I cannot discuss it in depth. Yet, minimally, one cannot be biblical unless one exegetes texts and draws theological conclusions by following the Bible's own story line according to its own intra-systematic categories.[6] For our purposes, if we are going to make headway in this debate, the entire discussion must be placed within the two intra-systematic categories of Scripture: (1) the typological pattern of "priesthood" and (2) the priesthood placed within the biblical "covenants," specifically the old and new covenants. Let me briefly discuss each of these in turn.

(1) Priesthood and Typology

To say that Christ is our "Great High Priest" not only drives us to set his work in the context of the OT, it also introduces the discussion of typology since he is presented as the antitypical fulfillment of the OT priest(s). But what exactly is biblical typology, especially given diverse understandings of it? I cannot give a full exposition here, but others have pointed in the right

the Atonement (Darlington, UK: Evangelical Press, 2008); and Michael S. Horton, *The Christian Faith* (Grand Rapids, MI: Zondervan, 2011), 486–520.
[5] See, for example, Donald M. Lake, "He Died for All," in *Grace Unlimited*, ed. Clark H. Pinnock (Minneapolis: Bethany, 1975), 31–50; Terry L. Miethe, "The Universal Power of the Atonement," in *The Grace of God and the Will of Man*, ed. Clark H. Pinnock (Minneapolis: Bethany, 1995), 71–96; and Bruce A. Demarest, *The Cross and Salvation*, Foundations of Evangelical Theology (Wheaton, IL: Crossway, 1997), 189–93.
[6] See Michael S. Horton, *Covenant and Eschatology* (Louisville: Westminster John Knox, 2002); cf. Richard Lints, *The Fabric of Theology* (Grand Rapids, MI: Eerdmans, 1993).

direction.[7] For our purposes, I want to list three features of typology that are important for our discussion.

First, typology is symbolism rooted in *historical-textual* realities. As such, it involves an *organic* relation between "persons, events, and institutions" (i.e., the type) in one epoch of redemptive history and their counterparts in later epochs (i.e., the antitype). Second, typology is predictive and thus divinely given and intended. God intended for the "type" to point beyond itself to its fulfillment or "antitype." Typologies are not mere "analogies" but are tied to recurrent patterns pointing forward to a culminating repetition of a pattern that ultimately finds its fulfillment in Christ. By these patterns God is providing the interpretative-conceptual categories to instruct us about the work of Christ, and trying to understand Christ's work apart from them will inevitably lead to *unbiblical* conclusions. Third, as one moves from type to antitype, the fulfillment in Christ always involves an *a fortiori* escalation. For example, as one moves from Adam, David, or the OT priests to Christ, it always leads to a *greater* reality. That is why our Lord is presented in the NT not merely as another Adam, David, or priest, but the *Last* Adam, David's *greater* Son, and our *Great* High Priest, who transcends and fulfills the early type in almost every way imaginable.

How do these observations relate to our discussion? In a number of ways. Typological structures are one of the crucial ways Scripture unpacks christology across the Bible's story line and grounds the uniqueness of the fulfillment era associated with the inauguration of the new covenant. By typology, Scripture unpacks both the unity and *discontinuity* of God's plan, especially vis-à-vis each covenant's priests. When the antitype finally arrives, the types are brought to their *telos* as the greater realities of fulfillment are inaugurated and the types give way to Christ's superior work. Thus, for example, in the case of the OT priest, we learn why and how he serves as the people's representative before God (Heb. 5:1). We discover the particularity of that office in relation to the covenant people and how the priest identifies with, atones for, intercedes on behalf of, and instructs a *particular* people. In all these ways,

---

[7] For a definition of typology, see Graham A. Cole, *He Who Gives Life: The Doctrine of the Holy Spirit*, Foundations of Evangelical Theology (Wheaton, IL: Crossway, 2007), 289: "The idea that persons (e.g., Moses), events (e.g., exodus), and institutions (e.g., the temple) can—in the plan of God—prefigure a later stage in that plan and provide the conceptuality necessary for understanding the divine intent (e.g., the coming of Christ to be the new Moses, to effect the new exodus, and to be the new temple)." For a helpful discussion of typology, see Paul M. Hoskins, *Jesus as the Fulfillment of the Temple in the Gospel of John* (Eugene, OR: Wipf & Stock, 2006), 18–37; and Richard M. Davidson, *Typology in Scripture* (Berrien Springs, MI: Andrews University Press, 1981).

our Lord Jesus fulfills this office/role, yet he is greater. In Christ, we do not have a priest limited to a particular time and place, one who must first deal with his own sins before he can deal with ours. Rather, he is perfect in every way, God the Son incarnate, who identifies with us in his incarnation, who is the Head and Mediator of the new covenant, and as such he is our Great High Priest who represents a *particular* people and *effectively* accomplishes for them all that is entailed by the new covenant. Unlike OT priests, our Lord accomplishes a priestly work which, in the words of Hebrews, is able to save his people completely (7:25, NIV). But note: Scripture knows nothing of a priestly work which is not also a unified work of provision *and* intercession for a specific people. To view Christ as our *greater* Priest entails that his work, especially under the new covenant, is an effective work which provides and secures everything necessary for the salvation of those in that covenant.

(2) Priesthood and Covenants

One must also think of Christ's priestly work, including its design, in relation to the biblical covenants since the concepts of "priest" and "covenant" are inseparable. This is precisely the argument of Hebrews 7:11, where the crucial parenthesis helps us understand the relationship between the priesthood and the covenant: "for on the basis of it [the Levitical priesthood] the law [old covenant] was given to the people" (AT). Here the author contends that the old covenant is grounded in the Levitical priesthood. That is why, given this relationship, the author argues in verse 12 that the OT, in announcing the coming of a *new* Priest (Psalm 110; cf. Hebrews 7), also anticipates the arrival of a *new* covenant (Jer. 31:31–34; cf. Hebrews 7–8), since a change in priesthood *necessarily* requires a change of covenant.[8]

Why? The answer is straightforward: at the heart of the covenant relationship is the reality that God dwells with his people. But given the biblical portrayal of God as personal, holy, and just, how can he dwell with his people without ultimately bringing judgment upon them? How can the Lord live among his people without destroying them by the flame of his holiness? These questions are faced and answered in Exodus 32–34. In the golden calf incident and the reinstitution of the covenant, the answer is this: God can be our covenant God only by the provision of the priesthood, tabernacle, and entire sacrificial system (see Lev. 17:11). God can establish his covenant,

---

[8] See Peter T. O'Brien, *The Letter to the Hebrews*, PNTC (Grand Rapids, MI: Eerdmans, 2010), 258.

given our sin, only by the blood of the covenant, the provision of his grace (Ex. 24:6–8).

What is the significance of this for our discussion? Everything. In order to understand the nature of Christ's priestly work, including its intent/design, it must be viewed in the light of covenantal structures, particularly the new covenant. As Sam Waldron and Richard Barcellos rightly note,

> The New Covenant is clearly the context or framework of the work of Jesus Christ. The work of Jesus Christ has no saving power divorced from the New Covenant. . . . Jesus' whole work was a covenant work; His blood covenant blood, His priesthood covenant priesthood, His office as Mediator a covenant office. The question about the scope, extent, or design of the death of Christ ought not to be answered, therefore, without reference to this covenant.[9]

The question to ask, then, is this: "What is the scope, extent, and design of the new covenant? Is it a general covenant made with everyone, making salvation possible for everyone, if they will take it? Or, is it a limited covenant made only with certain persons and assuring their eternal salvation?"[10] Or, to ask it another way: Who does our Lord, as the High Priest of the new covenant, represent in his death and apply the fruits of that covenant to? Does he represent all people without exception, or does he represent a particular people who are effectively brought to salvation and receive all the benefits of that covenant? As I will argue below, to reach any other conclusion than the latter is to remove the work of Christ from its new covenant context, which is precisely the problem with all general atonement views. Christ's atoning work cannot be extended to all people without also extending the new covenant benefits and privileges to all, which minimally includes regeneration, forgiveness of sins, and the gift of the Spirit. All general atonement views must either redefine the nature of the new covenant or argue that Christ dies as the covenantal Head of another covenant, whatever that is. However, if Christ's priestly death is understood *biblically*, such a view is unsustainable.

What is important to note though is how often general atonement advocates divorce their position from these biblical intra-systematic categories. They discuss at length "world" and "all" texts, the universal call of the

---

[9] Samuel E. Waldron with Richard C. Barcellos, *A Reformed Baptist Manifesto* (Palmdale, CA: Reformed Baptist Academic Press, 2004), 59–60.
[10] Ibid., 60.

gospel, and so on, but there is little discussion of the cross's design in the Bible's own categories of "priest" or "covenant." For example, Paige Patterson charges defenders of definite atonement as following "a logical system"[11] rather than Scripture, but his view discusses nothing of Christ's priestly death in its new covenant context. Or, David Nelson begins well by saying that he wants "to set the doctrine of the atonement in the grand redemptive narrative of Scripture. This includes the trajectory set with the Abrahamic, Davidic, and new covenants, and the continual calls to trust Yahweh that form the basis for justification before a righteous God (Gen. 15:6; Hab. 2:4)."[12] However, he does none of this when he discusses the intent of the atonement.[13] In Bruce Demarest's discussion he covers familiar territory, nevertheless he concludes by saying, "in terms of the Atonement's *provision* Christ died not merely for the elect but for all sinners in all times and places,"[14] without ever wrestling with the new covenant context of that death. Yet, before I develop this argument further, let me first turn to a discussion of the OT priest, who serves as the pattern for Christ's priestly work, and demonstrate how his work is particular and unified in terms of provision and intercession.

II. The Unified Work of the Old Covenant Priest[15]

Hebrews 5:1 is a helpful summary of the work of the OT high priest—"For every high priest chosen from among men is appointed to act on behalf of men in relation to God, to offer gifts and sacrifices for sins." Three points are stressed. First, every OT high priest was *selected* from among the people

---

[11] Paige Patterson, "The Work of Christ," in *A Theology for the Church*, ed. Daniel L. Akin (Nashville: B&H Academic, 2007), 585–86. Cf. I. Howard Marshall, "Universal Grace and Atonement in the Pastoral Epistles," in *Grace of God and the Will of Man*, 52, who says something similar yet fails to wrestle with these biblical categories.

[12] David P. Nelson, "The Design, Nature, and Extent of the Atonement," in *Calvinism: A Southern Baptist Dialogue*, ed. E. Ray Clendenen and Brad J. Waggoner (Nashville: B&H Academic, 2008), 127.

[13] See also Millard J. Erickson, *Christian Theology*, 2nd ed. (Grand Rapids, MI: Baker, 1998), 829; David L. Allen, "The Atonement: Limited or Universal?," in *Whosoever Will: A Biblical-Theological Critique of Five-Point Calvinism*, ed. David L. Allen and Steve W. Lemke (Nashville: B&H Academic, 2010), 68–109; Gary L. Shultz, Jr., "A Biblical and Theological Defense of a Multi-Intentional View of the Extent of the Atonement" (PhD diss., The Southern Baptist Theological Seminary, 2008); cf. idem, "Why a Genuine Universal Gospel Call Requires an Atonement That Paid for the Sins of All People," *EQ* 82.2 (2010): 111–23; idem, "The Reconciliation of All Things in Christ," *BSac* 167 (October–December, 2010): 442–59; and idem, "God's Purpose in the Atonement for the Nonelect," *BSac* 165 (April–June 2008): 145–63. Robert L. Lightner, *The Death Christ Died: A Case for Unlimited Atonement*, 2nd ed. (Grand Rapids, MI: Kregel, 1998), 118–23, discusses covenants but more in a dismissive way. Norman F. Douty, *Did Christ Die Only for the Elect? A Treatise on the Extent of Christ's Atonement* (1978; repr., Eugene, OR: Wipf & Stock, 1998), 19–21, briefly discusses covenants yet never wrestles with the relationship between the old and new covenants, their nature, and the subjects of each covenant.

[14] Demarest, *Cross and Salvation*, 191.

[15] I will limit my discussion of the priest to the old and new covenants. However, a full biblical theology of priests would take us back to Adam as "an archetypal Levite." See Ken A. Mathews, *Genesis 1–11:26* (Nashville: B&H Academic, 1996), 52; and G. K. Beale, *The Temple and the Church's Mission*, NSBT (Downers Grove, IL: InterVarsity Press, 2004), 29–121.

and thus was in solidarity with those he represented. In fact, in Israel, not any Israelite could serve in the office of priest, not even every Levite. The office of priest was reserved for Aaron and his direct descendants, and even members of the tribe of Levi were excluded from the priestly office (Ex. 29:9, 44; Num. 3:10; 18:1–7), even on the basis of certain physical defects (Lev. 21:16–23). In other words, the priest was a carefully chosen individual who came from among the covenant people of Israel.

Second, the high priest's appointment was for the purpose of *representing* a particular people before God, viz., all those under the old covenant. This representative work is beautifully portrayed in the clothing of the high priest— clothing which was not simply for aesthetics but also was instructive in regard to the work of the priest.[16] From head to toe, the priest's garments were designed to teach Israel and later generations something of the priest's work as the representative of the people. For example, the priest's breastplate contained twelve gems with the names of the twelve tribes of Israel set on them (Ex. 28:17–21). Each time he went into the presence of God "he would carry these gems with him (Ex. 28:29), indicating that he was there on behalf of the people with whom Yahweh had entered into covenant."[17] Never did the priest ever represent and mediate for a people other than the covenant people of God. Hugh Martin forcefully argues this point: "Priesthood rests on personal relation,"[18] and in the case of the OT priests, "They acted for individuals; and besides such action, they had no priestly action whatsoever, no official duty to discharge. . . . Indefiniteness, generality, vagueness, unlimitedness, universality, are ideas with which no theory of their office can possibly cohere."[19]

Third, the sphere in which the high priest represents the people is in matters related to God, specifically "to offer gifts and sacrifices for sins." In this way, the priest serves as the representative mediator of the people before God due to their sin, which stresses that the priest's work, at its heart, is propitiation and expiation.[20] Involved in this mediatorial work are six truths.

---

[16] See Carol Meyers, *Exodus* (New York: Cambridge University Press, 2005), 240, who rightly notes that the "priestly office and priestly garb are inextricably related."

[17] Letham, *Work of Christ*, 106.

[18] Martin, *Atonement*, 58.

[19] Ibid., 65. The *particular* representative role of the priests is further reinforced in Numbers, where the Levites serve as representatives for the firstborn Israelites (3:11–13). In fact, the Lord instructs Moses to count the Levites (3:14–39) and all the firstborn males in Israel (3:40–43) for the purpose of substituting the Levites for the firstborn males. This highlights not only the substitutionary nature of the priests' work but also its scope: the OT understands representation and substitution in particular terms.

[20] Some have argued that "gifts" merely refers to peace and cereal offerings, while "sacrifices" refers to animal sacrifices. However, O'Brien, *Hebrews*, 190, notes that "the terms are probably being used synonymously, even as a fixed phrase for sacrifices generally. . . . Thus, the prepositional phrase, *for sins*, qualifies the whole, not simply

(1) The OT priests performed their work in a particular place (tabernacle, temple) and for a particular people (Num. 3:7–8). Nowhere in the OT does the priest make atonement for all the nations or function as a universal mediator. The covenantal blessings of atonement are provided only for those within the covenant community.[21]

(2) As the priests offered sacrifices for sins before God, there was no separation between the provision of atonement and its application to the people. As the atonement is first applied to the altar in order to propitiate God, the sacrifice did not merely remove a barrier; it also effected something in the very dwelling place of God.[22] By this action the priest made the people acceptable to God by applying the sacrificial blood to the altar. This is also seen on the Day of Atonement, where the high priest atoned for the people and applied the same blood to the altar in order to cleanse the people and the sanctuary from any defilement before God (Lev. 16:15–19). In this way, there was no division between the provision of atonement and its application to the people.[23] No priest, under the old covenant, offered a sacrifice without simultaneously applying its blood to the altar. As this is brought to fulfillment in Christ, and as Hebrews so ably proclaims, the ineffectual nature of the old covenant was not due to the bifurcation between provision and application but the inferior nature of the sacrifices (Heb. 10:4, 11). However, in Christ, we have the perfect Priest and sacrifice. His death achieves a complete atonement *and* application to his new covenant people.

(3) In the priestly offering of sacrifices there was always a separation of the covenant people from the nations. This is first seen in the Passover where, as Paul Hoskins notes, the Passover sacrifice brought about a "separation between God's people and Pharaoh's people"[24] so that God's intended

---

the latter term." The heart of the priest's work dealt with the people's sins before God. This is not to say that the priest did not serve in other capacities, since the priest also had a prophetic function as evidenced by the Urim and the Thummim (Ex. 28:30; Lev. 8:8). The priests were also teachers of the covenant (Lev. 10:10–11; Deut. 33:10; cf. 2 Chron. 35:3; Ezek. 22:26; Hag. 2:11–13; Mal. 2:5–9), since they instructed God's people regarding holiness (cf. Leviticus 11–15). See Gordon J. Wenham, *The Book of Leviticus*, NICOT (Grand Rapids, MI: Eerdmans, 1979), 159. Note: in their teaching capacity a particular work is also done. An OT priest did not instruct people in a general way. Cf. R. K. Duke, "Priests, Priesthood," in *Dictionary of the Old Testament: Pentateuch*, ed. T. Desmond Alexander and David W. Baker (Downers Grove, IL: InterVarsity Press, 2003), 651.

[21] David T. Williams, *The Office of Christ and Its Expression in the Church* (Lewiston: Mellen, 1997), 14, notes, "Indeed, the sacrificial system, although it encompassed those who had identified with Israel by sojourning in their midst, obviously did not apply to those outside the covenant. The covenant was therefore essential to the relationship with God; there are however hints that it would in due course be extended to the nations (e.g., Isa. 19:21)."

[22] See Richard D. Nelson, *Raising Up a Faithful Priest* (Louisville: Westminster John Knox, 1993), 76–78.

[23] See Geerhardus Vos, *Biblical Theology* (Carlisle, UK: Banner of Truth, 1975), 164, who notes the intertwined nature of the provision and application of the atonement.

[24] Paul M. Hoskins, *That Scripture Might Be Fulfilled* (Longwood, FL: Xulon, 2009), 93.

purpose was to redeem Israel and not Egypt (Ex. 12:43–49). This truth is also seen in the entire sacrificial system, which functioned as a God-given barrier between Israel and the nations.

(4) Under the old covenant, the sacrifices offered were "relatively" efficacious for the people in the sense that God never intended the sacrificial system to effect *ultimate* salvation; they functioned as types/shadows of a greater Priest and sacrifice to come (Heb. 10:1–18). Yet with that said, the Passover and later sacrifices were efficacious in that they preserved the life of the firstborn in Exodus, and later, they purified the people, the priest, and the dwelling of God. Under the provisions of the old covenant, when combined with faith in the promises of God, and acknowledging their typological status, Hugh Martin rightly notes, "For whomsoever a Levitical priest sacerdotally officiated, he was completely successful—completely successful in averting evil, or procuring the privilege, which his official office contemplated."[25] As one moves from the old to the new covenant, it becomes even more pronounced how Christ's priestly work provides for and is effectively applied to all those he represents as the new covenant Head. But nowhere does the OT priest offer sacrifices for those outside the covenant people, nor does he offer sacrifices that do not effectively achieve their intended purpose (under the old covenant's limitations) for those who trust God's promises and act in obedience to him.

(5) The OT priest's role is always in terms of the application of his office to the one he represents, specifically in terms of offering and intercession. First, in terms of offering, it is significant that the OT priest does not kill the animal himself.[26] Instead, it is the worshiper who slays the animal (Lev. 1:1–5; cf. 1:11; 3:2, 8; 4:15, 24, 29, 33) and it is the priest who applies the blood accordingly. In this way, the priest applies the sacrificial blood for everyone who brings his offering to him, and there is not a single sacrifice where the blood is not applied to the worshiper (see Lev. 1:5, 11; 3:2, 8; 13; 4:16, 25, 30, 34; 5:9; 7:14). It is reasonable to assume the same pattern continues with Christ, the antitypical Priest. He not only offers himself for us thus securing our perfect redemption; he also applies it to us effectively, which is precisely why he is a greater Priest. Second, in terms of intercession, the OT priest also intercedes for all those he represents. In Numbers 6:22–27,

---

[25] Martin, *Atonement*, 65.
[26] The only exception is a sin offering made for a guilty priest (Lev. 4:4) or in the case of turtledoves or pigeons (Lev. 1:14–16).

the Lord instructs Moses to speak to Aaron about how he and the priests are to pronounce benedictions on Israel declaring the covenant blessing of the Lord. This too is instructive regarding the priest's work, since the blessing spoken by the priest is "more than just a pious wish, but an effective and power-laded formula."[27] Prior to the establishment of the Levitical priesthood, Moses acts in this fashion as the covenant mediator and intercessor (Exodus 32–34). Later in the prophetic anticipation of our Lord, Isaiah presents the Suffering Servant as both offering and Intercessor (Isa. 53:12). This is why Owen stated so emphatically,

> To offer and to intercede, to sacrifice and to pray, are both acts of the same sacerdotal office, and both required in him who is a *priest*; so that if he omit either of these, he cannot be a faithful *priest* for them: if either he doth not offer for them, or not intercede for the success of his oblation on their behalf, he is wanting in the discharge of his office by him undertaken. Both of these we find conjoined (as before) in Jesus Christ.[28]

Yet, general atonement advocates, especially Amyraldians and Hypothetical Universalists, posit a disruption in Christ's priestly work at this point: Christ dies for all without exception but only intercedes for the elect—a point that is plausible only if Christ's work is stripped of its *priestly, covenantal* specificity.

(6) The OT priest also served as the guardian of the Holy Place (tabernacle, temple), which maintains the purity and holiness of Israel.[29] The priestly duty, then, included a defensive posture toward anyone who attempted to enter God's house in a non-prescribed way (Num. 3:5–10; cf. 18:1–7; 25:1–9; Ex. 32:26–29). This too was part of the design of the priesthood: to mediate God's presence to the people, to protect the people from God's wrath, and to avenge the enemies of God, beginning with the house of Israel. In this defensive posture, it is difficult to think that the priest represents those he stands against in judgment. In fact, this theme is strongly emphasized in Christ's work: our Lord is zealous for God's house (John 2:17), he lays down his life for his sheep (John 10:11) and friends (John 15:13), and simultaneously crushes the head of Satan and all those who belong to him (John 12:31; Col.

---

[27] Nelson, *Raising Up a Faithful Priest*, 45.
[28] Owen, *Death of Death*, 71.
[29] See Richard C. Gamble, *The Whole Counsel of God. Volume 1: God's Mighty Acts in the Old Testament* (Phillipsburg, NJ: P&R, 2009), 444–45; Nelson, *Raising Up a Faithful Priest*, 25–31; and Beale, *Temple*, 66–121.

2:13–15; Heb. 2:14–18). As our Great High Priest, Jesus brings redemption to his people and judgment upon his enemies, but if so, then the atonement is an act of salvation and judgment, not merely a general atonement for all.[30]

III. The Unified Work of Christ, Our New Covenant Priest

The NT is clear that our Lord is the fulfillment of the OT priest in his entire unified work. Uniquely, the book of Hebrews unpacks this glorious truth in a twofold manner, related to typological structures.[31] Let us look at both of these ways and see how our Lord, as the High Priest of the new covenant, offers an atonement for a particular people and effectively secures everything necessary to bring those people to eternal salvation.

Christ Fulfills the Office and Work of the OT Priest

The first way that Christ's greater priesthood is argued in Hebrews is by comparing and contrasting the qualifications of the Levitical priest with Christ, thus establishing the fact that Jesus meets every qualification for that office yet is supremely greater (5:1–10; 8:1–10:18). Five points of similarity and difference are stressed.

(1) Just as the OT priest had to meet certain qualifications and had to be *selected* for this role, so Christ had to be *divinely called* by the Father and *appointed* to this office and work (5:4–6; cf. Psalm 2; 110)—an appointment ultimately rooted in God's eternal plan.

(2) Just as the OT priest *represented* a particular people before God, so Christ as the Head and Mediator of the new covenant represents all those under that covenant, and does so effectively. I will return to this point below.

(3) Just as the OT priest offered sacrifices for sins (5:1; 8:3), including his own (something that could never ultimately take away sins; 10:4, 11), so Christ offered himself. Yet his work achieved a definitive, once-for-all-time atonement (7:27; 9:12; 10:15–18) so that, unlike the OT priest, "he is able to save completely those who come to God through him" (7:25, NIV).

(4) Patterned after the OT priest, yet greater, Christ provides *and* applies his work to the people. Hebrews illustrates this point in two ways. First, as

---

[30] David Schrock has suggested to me that this is the proper place for *Christus Victor* and a multi-intentioned atonement. Yet, our Lord, in this view, does *not* provide a substitutionary sacrifice for the non-elect.

[31] Hebrews, like no other NT book, presents Christ as our Great High Priest. Some scholars have argued that Hebrews imposes this concept of priest on Jesus since in the Gospels Jesus never claimed this office for himself. For a response to this charge, see Letham, *Work of Christ*, 110–12.

Jesus enters the heavenly sanctuary (8:4–5; 9:24), he applies his blood to the altar and inaugurates a new covenant that is complete and effectual. Given these OT patterns, it is unlikely that he is doing this for the non-elect. Instead, our Lord enters God's throne room as the representative of his new covenant people. Second, the link between our Lord's accomplishment and its effects upon his people is underscored in Hebrews 9:11–15. As William Lane notes, the introductory clause in verse 15, "For this reason" (Καὶ διὰ τοῦτο), establishes a strong causal relationship between the achievement of Christ's priestly work (vv. 11–14) and the effects of that work in his new covenant people (v. 15).[32] In other words, Jesus's priestly work achieves *and* applies new covenant realities to *all* those in that covenant, which requires a particular redemption. The other alternatives are either universalism or the conclusion that Christ failed in his priestly office, both of which are unbiblical options.[33]

(5) While the OT priests' work was a unified work yet imperfect, Christ's work is both unified and perfect in provision, intercession, instruction, and guardianship.[34] In regard to intercession, our Lord, as priest, effectively prays for his people *before* the cross (Luke 22:31–32; John 17:6–26) and *after* his ascension (Rom. 8:32–34; Heb. 7:24–25; 1 John 2:1–2), guaranteeing that all the new covenant blessings are applied to them. There is no evidence that he intercedes salvifically for the non-elect, as is seen clearly in several NT passages.

In John 17:6–19, our Lord effectively prays for his disciples, those whom the Father has given him, but *not* for the world (vv. 9–10). In verses 20–26, Jesus then prays for all future believers, once again given to him by the Father (v. 24; cf. 6:37–44). This intercession is consistent with Jesus's teaching previously: he is the Good Shepherd who dies for the sheep (10:11, 15); he has other sheep that he will bring in the future (10:16); all of his sheep are given to him by his Father (10:29); his sheep receive eternal life due to his death; and *not* all people are his sheep (10:26–27). All of this is consistent with his office as Priest, in which he offers himself for a particular people and intercedes for them.

---

[32] William L. Lane, *Hebrews 9–13*, WBC 47b (Waco, TX: Word, 1991), 241.

[33] See Owen, *Death of Death*, 110–24, who makes this same argument.

[34] Space prohibits the development of how Christ is Instructor and Guardian of his people, yet John develops these points. Those whom the Father has given the Son he dies for and effectively saves (6:37–40; 10:11, 14); those same people hear his voice and receive his instruction (10:16, 26–30; 17:17), but those who are not his people do not hear his voice and reject his word (5:46–47; 8:42–47; 10:26–27). As Priest and Guardian, Jesus lays down his life for the sheep yet stands in judgment upon those who are not his sheep (10:11–30).

The same truth is taught in Romans 8:28–39. Here the unified work of Christ as Priest is developed with the intent of grounding our confidence in the God of sovereign grace. Those whom God has chosen, effectively called, justified, and who will be glorified (vv. 28–30) are confident because in the Son's death for us "all," the Father gives us *all* things, which, in this context, includes the entire application of salvation to us from calling to glorification. No one, then, can bring a charge against God's elect because it is Jesus who has died *and* intercedes *for us*. In his priestly office, Jesus offers himself and intercedes for us with a certain result: an effective redemption.

Hebrews 7:23–28 makes the same point. The reason why Jesus is so much better than the OT priest is because of who he is. In his offering of himself and in his glorious resurrection he achieves a permanent priesthood which secures a better covenant (see Hebrews 8–10). As a result, Jesus completely saves those who come to him *because* he always lives to intercede for them. As Lane comments, "The perfection and eternity of the salvation he mediates is guaranteed by the unassailable character of his priesthood. . . . The direct result of his intercessory activity is the sustaining of the people and the securing of all that is necessary to the eschatological salvation . . ."[35]

A Problem with General Atonement Views

A crucial problem with all general atonement views is that they fragment Christ's priestly work of offering and intercession. Either they must view Christ's work apart from these typological patterns and not discuss the atonement within the constraints of these biblical categories, or they must separate Christ's intercession from his death, thus dividing his priestly work. For example, Robert Lightner rightly acknowledges that Christ's intercession is savingly for the elect only, but then he contends that this does not take place until the elect believe, thus limiting Christ's intercession to his *heavenly* intercession.[36] This argument fails on at least three counts. First, it fails to view

---

[35] Lane, *Hebrews 9–13*, 189–90. For a discussion as to the nature of this intercession, see O'Brien, *Hebrews*, 275–78. O'Brien argues that, given Christ's definitive sacrifice, his intercession is more in terms of the application of the benefits of his sacrifice than in providing the basis for the forgiveness of sins (which has already been achieved). He concludes, "Whatever precise form the ascended Lord's intercessions for his people take, we may assume that they cover anything and everything that would prevent us from receiving the final salvation he has won for us at the cross" (278). Here is another way of underscoring the fact that Christ's priestly work involves both provision and application to those he represents. This requires either a definite atonement or the false conclusion that Christ failed in his intercessory role if a general atonement occurred.

[36] See Lightner, *Death Christ Died*, 102–104. Douty, *Did Christ Die Only for the Elect?*, 32–38, makes a similar argument. He agrees that Christ's atonement–intercession is inseparable due to his priestly office and that Christ intercedes only for believers (elect), but then he sharply distinguishes Christ's provisional/hypothetical work for

Christ's priestly work as unified—those he represents in his atoning death he also intercedes for effectively. Second, it fails to acknowledge that Christ intercedes for his own, including those who would later believe, during his *earthly* ministry—an intercession that does not fail, since Christ loses none of his people (John 6:39; 10:14–18, 26–30; 17:20–24). Third, it divorces Christ's unified priestly work from its new covenant context and thus has Christ dying for people who cannot be described as new covenant members, a point I will return to below.

On the other hand, Gary L. Shultz, Jr., argues that Christ's intercession may be viewed as salvific for the non-elect. His strongest appeal is to Luke 23:34, where Jesus prays for the forgiveness of his crucifiers. Shultz, on the basis of this text, contends that "intercession unto salvation is something that is available to all but only effectual for those who are in Christ."[37] However, he can sustain this argument only by removing Christ's intercession from *biblical* categories. All we know of priests is that they intercede for those they represent covenantally. What about Luke 23:34? Is it proof that Christ intercedes salvifically for the non-elect? No, and for five reasons.

First, such an interpretation goes against the entire Scriptural presentation of the intercession of the priest. Second, as Owen rightly observed, one cannot conclude from a specific prayer for a handful of people that this is a prayer "for all and every man that ever were, are, or shall be."[38] Third, as the obedient Son, Jesus not only fulfills the law by praying for his persecutors, he effectively requests the delay of judgment or the decrease in punishment based on *the people's relative ignorance*. The act of crucifixion demanded God's judgment (Acts 2:23–24), but Christ's prayer is answered by the Father showing his patience and forgiveness by not bringing full judgment at this point, thus allowing history to continue and God's ultimate purpose to save his elect to be realized.[39] Fourth, there is good evidence that as a general prayer for those who put him on the cross, it was answered in that the

---

all without exception from its application to the elect. He states, "Christ's actual intercession is not to be correlated with His provisional atonement, but only with His atonement as applied through faith. He prays, not for all for whom He provided atonement, but only for those who have received it" (35). On this point, my criticism of Lightner also applies to Douty.

[37] Shultz, "Defense of a Multi-Intentional View," 155 n. 195.

[38] Owen, *Death of Death*, 83. D. A. Carson, *Love in Hard Places* (Wheaton, IL: Crossway, 2002), 78, rightly contends that one must not apply this prayer to everyone who was involved in Jesus's betrayal and execution, for example, Judas Iscariot (see Mark 14:21).

[39] Carson, *Love in Hard Places*, 78, admits that the manner in which the Father answers Jesus's prayer is not transparent. A possible way is that "the Father showed his forbearance and forgiveness by not wiping them out on the spot." See also Klaas Schilder, *Christ Crucified* (Grand Rapids, MI: Eerdmans, 1940), 129–47.

centurion, the thief on the cross, and many of the Jews who crucified Christ were converted (Luke 23:40–43, 47; Acts 2:37–41), thus underscoring that Christ, as the Great High Priest, did effectively intercede for those who would become his own.[40] Fifth, for sake of argument, if Shultz is right, it not only fails to take seriously that the centurion, the thief on the cross, and those in Acts 2 actually are converted, but it also entails that Christ failed in his priestly work, i.e., those for whom he died and interceded for salvifically have not been redeemed. But this conclusion goes against everything Scripture says about the priestly work of Christ as perfect and effective.

General Atonement Responses and Counter-Critique

How do general atonement advocates respond to the above argument? At least in two ways. First, in terms of representation, they admit, it is true that the OT priest represented a particular people, but now in Christ this representation is expanded to the entire human race tied to Christ's incarnation.[41] Second, some appeal to the fact that the OT priest offered sacrifices for Israel as a "mixed" group (i.e., believers and nonbelievers), hence warrant for a general atonement.[42] I offer three counterpoints.

(1) If we think of priests in biblical categories, we have to affirm that the OT priest represented only the covenant people. Nowhere in the OT does the priest make atonement for the nations or function as a universal mediator. Covenantal blessings of atonement and forgiveness are given to God's people, and the entire law–covenant separated and distinguished Israel from the nations.

(2) What about appeal to the incarnation? Hebrews 2:5–18 is crucial here. In this text the Son is presented as greater than the angels because he does a work that no angel can do, namely, take on our humanity, undo the work of Adam, and restore us to the purpose of our creation by his atoning work. On the surface it seems like this text leads to a general atonement— "so that . . . he might taste death for everyone" (2:9), but as the argument unfolds, it becomes clear that his cross-work cannot be divorced from his role as the Priest and Mediator of the new covenant (2:17–18; cf. Hebrews 5–10).

---

[40] See Carson, *Love in Hard Places*, 78, who also suggests this possibility.
[41] See A. H. Strong, *Outlines of Systematic Theology* (Valley Forge, PA: Judson, 1907), 771–76; Douty, *Did Christ Die Only for the Elect?*, 21–29.
[42] See Mark Driscoll and Gerry Breshears, *Death by Love: Letters from the Cross* (Wheaton, IL: Crossway, 2008), 179; cf. Nelson, "Design, Nature, and Extent of the Atonement," 129–30.

Furthermore, as the covenant Head, his death does *not* fail in "bringing many sons to glory" (2:10), which is then identified with the people of God (v. 17), who are spoken of as *Abraham's descendants* (v. 16). The result of Christ's cross, then, has an effective, particular focus with expansion to those who are not merely Abraham's ethnic seed but Abraham's spiritual children (Jew *and* Gentile), but not all without exception.[43] Otherwise the entire priestly work and Christ's representative Headship would not achieve what it was intended to achieve, namely, the reversal of sin and death and the ushering in of a new creation, the defeat of the Evil One, and the guaranteed bringing of many sons to glory.

One cannot conclude from Christ's incarnation and death that he comes as the Last Adam to provide salvation for all without exception. Instead, Scripture teaches that our Lord takes on our humanity to win for us a new creation and to redeem the offspring of Abraham, sons and daughters of faith from every tribe, nation, and tongue. That is why Donald Macleod is right to remind us that even though Christ's humanity is that "*of* Everyman," "he is not Everyman."[44] Christ's humanity is that of his own; "although the incarnation unites Christ to human nature it does not unite him to *me*."[45] Furthermore, individuals are only united to Christ, and he only serves as their covenantal Mediator by "covenant-election-calling-faith-repentance-sealing,"[46] which is all grounded in Christ's atoning work. We have no Scriptural grounds, especially when speaking of Christ as our new covenant Head, to say that he acts for all without exception unless we want to render asunder his priestly work and make the cross ineffective in bringing his new covenant people to salvation.

(3) What about the OT priest offering sacrifices for a "mixed" people? Does this warrant a general atonement? No, and for three reasons. First, under the old covenant, the priest atoned for the sins of the covenant people alone, which moves in a particular direction, not a universal one. Second, the work of the priest was typological and thus *ultimately* ineffectual by design (see Heb. 10:4). No doubt, under the old covenant, priest and sacrifice served a

---

[43] See Barnes, *Atonement Matters*, 214–17. Christ as covenantal Head is intimately associated with union with Christ. However, our union with Christ is not *de facto* due to his incarnation. Even though Christ shares a common nature with us, he does *not* share new covenant blessings of forgiveness of sins to everyone through his flesh. This comes only by rebirth by the Spirit and through faith. In contrast to Adam, those whom Christ represents are believers, born of the Spirit.

[44] Donald Macleod, *The Person of Christ* (Downers Grove, IL: InterVarsity Press, 1998), 202.

[45] Ibid., 203.

[46] Ibid.

number of purposes, rooted in God's purposes for Israel as a physical nation set apart to bring forth the Messiah and to serve as a tutor for later generations (1 Cor. 10:6, 11), but one must carefully move from type to antitype, especially vis-à-vis the question of the atonement's extent. As Tom Barnes rightly notes,

> The breadth of this typological work with the entire nation was never meant to define the extent of the atonement through Jesus Christ. As Paul clarifies in Romans 4 and 9 the purpose of God when it comes to his sovereign gracious salvation of individuals was always more particular than the typological purpose accomplished throughout all Israel.[47]

Third, this argument fails to see the *discontinuity* between the old and new covenants and thus how much *better* (i.e., effective) the new covenant is, completely due to the greater work of our Lord Jesus Christ. In other words, for the sake of argument, let us grant that the general atonement argument is correct, that just as the OT priests atoned for "mixed" Israel, so now Christ atones for *all* humanity without exception. The problem with this argument is threefold. First, at the most basic level, what warrant is given for the move from the *particular* focus of the mixed covenant community to *all* of humanity (a non-covenantal universal framework), given the covenantal context of Christ's work? Furthermore, if consistent, general atonement advocates should affirm Christ's intercession for a mixed group in the NT—elect and non-elect—but the NT teaches that Christ's intercession is only for the elect. Second, and more significantly, it makes the new covenant no more effective than the old was to Israel. If the promise of forgiveness, which is at the heart of the new covenant (Jer. 31:34), is given to all humanity but not all are saved, then how is the new covenant more effectual than the old? Parallel to the old, there are covenant members within the new covenant who fail to receive what the covenant was intended to achieve, namely, eternal salvation. Yet this is contrary to the entire argument of Hebrews regarding the effectual work of our Lord and thus the new covenant; for all those for whom Christ died, he successfully leads to God's eternal rest, unlike the covenant mediators before him.[48] Third, it fails to acknowledge that the new covenant is not

---

[47] Barnes, *Atonement Matters*, 82.
[48] Regarding the nature and structure of the new covenant, my interpretation is slightly different from Reformed covenant theology, which makes an important distinction between those who are *in* the covenant and those who are *of* the covenant. The two categories necessarily overlap, but they are not necessarily identical. The former may be adults who enter the covenant by profession of faith, or children of believers who enter the covenant by

the same as the old in terms of the subjects of the covenant, once again due to our Lord's greater work. It is this last point which I want to develop now as we turn to the second way in which Hebrews unpacks the supremacy of our Lord's priestly work.

CHRIST TRANSCENDS THE OT PRIEST AND INAUGURATES A NEW COVENANT

The second way in which Christ's priesthood is shown to be *greater* in Hebrews is by demonstrating how it *transcends* the entire Levitical order: Christ comes in a *new* order, i.e., in the order of Melchizedek. As noted above, this fact demands a change in covenants, since a change in priesthood *necessarily* requires such a change (Heb. 7:11–12). Many implications of this incredible truth could be unpacked, but for our purposes one crucial question must be asked: Who are the subjects of the new covenant? Under the old covenant, its subjects were primarily the nation of Israel as a "mixed" entity, but what about the new? Does Christ, as the new covenant Head, represent all people without exception (a "mixed" group) and thus make salvation possible for them, or does he represent a particular people who are effectively brought to salvation and receive all the benefits of that covenant including the Spirit's work of application?[49] Scripture affirms the latter and not the former. Three points will develop this argument.

(1) The NT is clear that Christ's priestly work is a new covenant work (Luke 22:20; 1 Cor. 11:25; Hebrews 5–10). He is the Mediator of this covenant alone and no other.

(2) What is "new" about the new covenant? First and foremost, what is new is that Christ is the fulfillment of the previous covenants and covenant mediators; he is better and greater! But with that said, for our purposes we can also think of the new covenant's *newness* in terms of changes in *structure* and *nature* from the old. Structurally, under the old covenant, God dealt with

---

birth, but in both cases there is recognition that neither outward profession nor birth are in themselves sufficient to guarantee experience of the covenant as a communion of life. The latter are those who are eternally elect and who exercise saving faith in Christ (see Berkhof, *Systematic Theology*, 284–89). By this important distinction, Reformed theology is able to argue that Christ's death is specifically for his church and completely effective in saving the elect (those *of* the covenant), while simultaneously providing other blessings short of salvation for those *in* the covenant.

[49] Reformed theologians would not ask the question precisely in this way since they view the new covenant church as a "mixed" group of those *in* the covenant but not *of* the covenant, hence the distinction between the visible and invisible church. I am asking the question, not with this distinction in mind but in terms of those who advocate a general view of the atonement. Does the Scripture teach that the new covenant includes in it "all without exception," or does it teach instead that the new covenant includes a specific people known as the church?

his people in a mediated or "tribal-representative" fashion.[50] Despite remnant themes and an emphasis on individual believers, the OT pictures God working with his people in a "tribal-representative" structure whose knowledge of God and whose relations with God were uniquely dependent on specially endowed leaders. Hence, the emphasis on the Spirit of God being poured out, not on each believer, but distinctively on prophets, priests, and kings. Given this hierarchical structure of the covenant community, when these leaders did what was right, the entire nation benefited, but also, sadly, vice versa. But Jeremiah anticipates a day when this tribal structure will change (Jer. 31:29–30). As D. A. Carson observes,

> In short, Jeremiah understood that the new covenant would bring some dramatic changes. The tribal nature of the people of God would end, and the new covenant would bring with it a new emphasis on the distribution of the knowledge of God down to the level of each member of the covenant community. Knowledge of God would no longer be mediated through specially endowed leaders, for *all* of God's covenant people would know him, from the least to the greatest.[51]

Related to this anticipation is the OT promise of the gift of the Spirit and his unique work in the new covenant (Ezek. 11:19–20; 36:25–27; Joel 2:28–32; cf. Num. 11:27–29). What the prophets anticipate is that in the new covenant there will be a universal distribution of the Spirit on *all* flesh, namely, *all* those within the covenant community.[52] Thus, all those under the new covenant enjoy the promised gift of the eschatological Spirit (Eph. 1:13–14). In the NT, the Spirit is presented as the agent who gives us life and enables us to follow God's decrees, and all those in the new covenant have the Spirit. The NT is clear: the work of the Spirit is grounded in the cross-work of Christ (John 7:39; 16:7; Acts 2:33). As a result of Christ's new covenant work, the Spirit is sent to all those in the covenant; the Spirit is one of the blessed gifts of the new covenant purchased for us by the atoning death of Christ (cf. Titus 3:5). He is the precious seal, down payment, and guarantee

---

[50] See D. A. Carson, *Showing the Spirit* (Grand Rapids, MI: Baker, 1987), 150–58; cf. D. A. Carson, "1–3 John," in *Commentary on the New Testament Use of the Old Testament*, ed. G. K. Beale and D. A. Carson (Grand Rapids, MI: Baker, 2007), 1065.

[51] Carson, *Showing the Spirit*, 152.

[52] Once again, Reformed covenant theologians would differ slightly with my interpretation and argue that *all* should be understood not as *all* those within the covenant community but "all without distinction" within the covenant community, thus preserving the distinction between people *in* and *of* the covenant. However, they still maintain that the *all* of the new covenant does not include "all without exception" as the general atonement view claims.

of the promised inheritance. To be "in Christ" is to have the Spirit, for, as Paul reminds us, "if anyone does not have the Spirit of Christ, they do not belong to Christ" (Rom. 8:9, NIV).

In addition to the structural changes there is also change in the *nature* of the covenant people. The new covenant is *not* like the old precisely because all those in it know the Lord, not in a mediate but in an immediate way, and all have the law written on their hearts (i.e., regeneration) and experience the full forgiveness of sin (Jer. 31:34). This is not to say that no one in the OT never experienced regeneration; rather it demonstrates that *every* new covenant member is a regenerate person, unlike the "mixed" nature of the old. Under the old covenant there was a distinction between the physical and spiritual seed of Abraham; however, under the new covenant this is not the case. In other words, there is no "remnant" in the new covenant: all within it know God and experience regeneration and justification. That is why the new covenant is so much better than the old: it is effective and it will not fail, which is directly tied to Christ's greater priesthood. Thus, due to Christ's priestly work we have a full, effective, and complete salvation, unlike the types and shadows of the old.[53]

Why is this important? Given that Jesus is the Mediator of the new covenant, and it is a completely effective covenant in terms of provision *and* application, it is difficult to deny, unless we want to affirm universalism, that Christ's priestly work is particular and effective. In other words, *all* those in the new covenant—of whom Jesus acted as the covenant Mediator—are, in time, regenerated, justified, and brought to glory. Not one of them will be lost since our Lord, as the *greater* Priest, does not fail. For those for whom he died as covenant Head, his work is effectively applied by the Spirit, the same Spirit whose new covenant work is effectively secured by Christ's atoning death.

(3) If this analysis is correct, there are at least two problems for general atonement advocates. First, what covenant does Christ mediate? Biblically, Jesus is the Head of the new covenant, but if so, then, contrary to Scripture, general atonement advocates must view the new covenant as no more effective than the old since many people in that covenant never have new covenant blessings applied to them—e.g., regeneration, justification, the giving of the Spirit, and so on. But Scripture not only does not seem to suggest this

---

[53] See William L. Lane, *Hebrews 1–8*, WBC 47a (Waco, TX: Word, 1991), 200–211.

"mixed" understanding of the subjects of the new covenant; it also seems to suggest that our Lord, as the *greater* priest, does not fail to apply his work to *all* those in that covenant. In the end, general atonement advocates either have to redefine the people of the new covenant and place faith and repentance (tied to the work of the Spirit) outside of the priestly work of Christ, or argue that Christ is the Head of another covenant—but what precisely is that covenant?[54]

Second, general atonement advocates respond by sharply dividing the provision of salvation from its application.[55] No doubt everyone distinguishes between the objective work of Christ and its subjective application; it is simply not true that definite atonement advocates collapse the distinction. The real issue is that general atonement defenders fail to acknowledge that provision *and* application are central to the new covenant work of Christ. As the Great High Priest, our Lord not only dies for those who belong to the new covenant; he also secures all the benefits of the new covenant, which includes the Spirit's work of application.[56] Our Lord both provides and applies, which is why his work is *greater*. Yes, the Spirit's work takes place throughout history as the elect are brought to saving faith, but the certainty of that work is rooted in the plan of the triune God of sovereign grace: the Father's election of a people; the Son's achieving and securing everything necessary for the elect's salvation; and the work of the Spirit, sent by the Father and Son, to apply the benefits of the Son's work to *every* subject of the new covenant.[57]

---

[54] One general atonement advocate who discusses the covenantal context is Douty, *Did Christ Die Only for the Elect?*, 19–38. His discussion, however, fails to wrestle with Christ's work in new covenant terms, viz., as the Head of a particular people for whom he effectively achieves salvation and secures every new covenant blessing including the work of the Spirit. Douty does what all general atonement advocates do: he extends the new covenant blessing of forgiveness to all humanity but then robs the new covenant of its particularity, perfection, permanency, and security.

[55] See Strong, *Outline*, 773; Demarest, *Cross and Salvation*, 189–93; Douty, *Did Christ Die Only for the Elect?*, 58–60; and Lightner, *Death Christ Died*, 124–35.

[56] Lightner, *Death Christ Died*, 130–35, argues that the Spirit is given to all people universally, yet, biblically, the Spirit's work is organically linked to the new covenant. General atonement advocates must affirm two kinds of new covenant people: (1) those whose sins are paid for and who receive the Spirit; (2) those whose sins are paid for and who do not have the Spirit. But this not only reduces the new covenant to a "mixed" company like the old; it also does not explain why some subjects of the new covenant receive the Spirit and others do not, especially since Scripture presents the Spirit as the *effective gift* of the new covenant.

[57] As noted in a number of places throughout the chapter, the alert reader may ask whether there is an unintended consequence of my argument for definite atonement from the nature and subjects of the new covenant, namely, have I not undercut a Reformed covenantal defense of particular redemption given the view of the new covenant church consisting of a "mixed" people? My response is twofold: (1) It is my conviction that my understanding of the new covenant provides a firmer biblical-theological grounding for definite atonement. For a more detailed defense of it, see Peter J. Gentry and Stephen J. Wellum, *Kingdom through Covenant: A Biblical-Theological Understanding of the Covenants* (Wheaton, IL: Crossway, 2012). (2) I also think that Reformed covenantal theologians who differ with me on this point can legitimately hold to definite atonement since they affirm that Christ is the Head and Mediator of the new covenant and that Christ has died only for those under that covenant (i.e., the church, visible and invisible), *not* the non-elect, who are not the church, contra the general atonement view. Furthermore, they also affirm that Christ died effectively only for the elect (i.e., invisible church) even though there are many non-salvific

Concluding Reflection

I have sought to unpack a crucial biblical-theological argument for definite atonement from the unified work of Christ as our Great High Priest. It is not a new argument, but it is an important one. It seeks to argue that general atonement advocates fail to locate the priestly work of our Lord in its *covenantal* context. If they did, they would defend a particular view of the cross. They would not break the crucial link between Christ and his people. They would rightly see that Christ, as the *Great* Priest, acts as Representative, Substitute, Instructor, Guardian, and Intercessor of his people, not only paying for their sins but securing everything necessary, including the work of the Spirit, to apply his work to them and to bring them to their eternal rest. Ultimately what is at stake in the debate over the extent of the atonement is a Savior who saves, a cross that effectively accomplishes and secures all the gracious promises of the new covenant, and a redemption that does not fail.

---

blessings that the cross achieved for the non-elect in the visible church by virtue of the genealogical principle given in the Abrahamic covenant and continuing in the new covenant. It must be acknowledged that one very important argument in the defense of a "covenantal mixed community" over against my view is the appeal to the warning passages of Scripture (e.g., Heb. 6:4–6; 10:26–29). For how I would handle these texts in response, see Thomas R. Schreiner and Ardel B. Caneday, *The Race Set Before Us: A Biblical Theology of Perseverance and Assurance* (Downers Grove, IL: InterVarsity Press, 2001).

20

Jesus Christ *the* Man

TOWARD A SYSTEMATIC THEOLOGY
OF DEFINITE ATONEMENT

Henri A. G. Blocher

*In necessariis, unitas; in non necessariis (*or *dubiis), libertas; in omnibus, caritas* (in articles of faith that are necessary, unity; in non-necessary [*or* doubtful] ones, freedom; in all, charity)—the well-known maxim Martin Luther coined is always relevant.[1] One should add still another clause: *in secundariis seu subtilibus, benigna sed exacta diligentia* (in matters secondary [*not* indifferent] or subtle, a gracious attention combined with exactness). "For whom did Christ die and make atonement?" belongs to the fourth category, as signaled by dissent among divines otherwise in communion.

Away with all partisan spirit, then, whatever its guises! We should try hard to hear the other conviction, with its strong points and its underlying concerns. Andrew Fuller set a fine example of "Christian forbearance"[2] in this regard and warned against both "idolizing a sentiment" and lazy neglect or "scepticism."[3]

To start on that path, we should spell out the guiding principles of our enquiry. The essay consists of five sections. First, a *prolegomena* section

---

[1] Often ascribed to Rupertus Meldenius, whose *Parænesis votiva* of 1626 ends with similar words, but it comes from Luther's sermon preached on March 10, 1522 (Luther's *Werke*, Weimar Ausgabe, vol. X [third tome], 14).

[2] Andrew Fuller, *Reply to the Observations of Philanthropos*, in *The Complete Works of the Rev. Andrew Fuller* (London: Henry G. Bohn, 1848), 225, columns a and b. "Philanthropos" was the pseudonym of Daniel Taylor, a General Baptist theologian who had criticized Fuller's explanation of Christ's atonement as definite.

[3] Ibid., 233b. As in all quotations in this chapter, emphases are original to the authors unless otherwise noted.

will state, however briefly, which conception of systematic theology is put to work.[4] Second, a glance at past exchanges will highlight motives and arguments. A central section, third, will revisit issues that appear to be cardinal in debate, and sections four and five will offer suggestions that may contribute to a progress in mutual understanding.

I. Prolegomena: Introducing Systematic Theology

Short definitions of systematic theology could be "an ordered discourse on God and his works" or the Anselmian *"fides quærens intellectum"* (faith seeking understanding). A fuller statement would be D. A. Carson's:

> ... the branch of theology that seeks to elaborate the whole and the parts of Scripture, demonstrating their logical (rather than merely historical) connections and taking full cognizance of the history of doctrine and the contemporary intellectual climate and categories and queries while finding its sole ultimate authority in the Scriptures themselves, rightly interpreted. Systematic theology deals with the Bible as a finished product.[5]

We speak of God because he first spoke to us. Systematic theology is located midway between the foundational gift of God's Word and its application by its ministers to human needs; it gathers and "digests" the contents to facilitate communication. Both positive and speculative tasks are involved in the study of the atonement.

The "threefold cord" of Scripture, Reason, and Tradition, as Anglicans say, could be called the umbilical cord of systematic theology, for these three provide food and form. I rest content with the triad, though Richard Bauckham's essay offers an attractive "New Model: Scripture, Tradition and Context."[6]

TRADITION

The conditioning of systematic theology by tradition is inescapable: we should give thanks for it. We sit on the shoulders of giants. To dream of solving at one stroke an issue that has divided them for centuries is foolish. Yet, tradition may serve ministerially as *norma normata* (a rule that is

---

[4] A somewhat fuller development, which had to be cut out from this chapter, should appear later in article form.
[5] D. A. Carson, "Unity and Diversity in the New Testament," in *Scripture and Truth*, ed. D. A. Carson and John D. Woodbridge (Grand Rapids, MI: Zondervan, 1983), 69–70.
[6] Richard Bauckham, "Tradition in Relation to Scripture and Reason," in *Scripture, Tradition, and Reason: A Study in the Criteria of Christian Doctrine*, ed. Richard Bauckham and Benjamin Drewery (Edinburgh: T. & T. Clark, 1988), 140–45 (quoted: heading, 140; diagrams, 141). This is the most intelligent essay I have read on the topic.

ruled), not as the *norma normans* (the rule that rules). Carson admonishes, "Genuine Christianity, however biased, culture-bound, faulty, or weak it may be in any specific expression, must embrace some kind of commitment that desires to be 're-formed' by Scripture whenever such reductionism is pointed out."[7] "Reformation" is no empty word. On such a topic as the extent of the atonement, if one invokes the authority of the "best" tradition, this conviction welcomes corrections; it wishes for sharpened notions and procedures. I will not hide my traditional roots: I share J. I. Packer's adherence to what he names "reformed Augustinianism" and follows as being "Christianity at its purest"[8]—but still fallible and reformable.

With Bauckham, we should see that "the persistence of features of the tradition which originated to meet the needs of superseded contexts can sometimes prove unexpectedly useful in new contexts."[9] This entails the ability of every individual, *coram Deo*, to transcend conditionings and assess traditions for Truth[10]—and so the traditions of John Owen, John Davenant, Moïse Amyraut, Andrew Fuller, et al. on the nature of the atonement!

REASON

Reason is God-given sensitivity to necessary connections: if A, then B. Though essentially receptive, it functions actively: the mind reconstructs within itself the links it is seeking for in its objects, and "discovers"—hence the two meanings of invention (finding in nature and producing as a new thing); hence also the idealist illusion that the mind creates the order it displays. The perception of links implies both taking items together (comprehension) and discerning between them (intelligence).[11] The necessity that binds A and B is the key of rational coherence, consistency, systematic character: such words signify that the various elements "hold together."

That theology should be systematic,[12] and so use reason, agrees with

---

[7] D. A. Carson, "The Role of Exegesis in Systematic Theology," in *Doing Theology in Today's World. Essays in Honor of Kenneth S. Kantzer*, ed. John D. Woodbridge and Thomas E. McComiskey (Grand Rapids, MI: Zondervan, 1991), 61.

[8] J. I. Packer, "Is Systematic Theology a Mirage?," in *Doing Theology in Today's World*, 28.

[9] Bauckham, "Tradition in Relation," 143. Cf. 135, 144, 145.

[10] Ibid., 133–34; Bauckham helpfully maintains that "we can transcend our tradition" (though "only in dependence on our rootedness in it"). J. I. Packer, "Infallible Scripture and the Role of Hermeneutics," in *Scripture and Truth*, 331, says, of the thesis that we cannot really enter the meaning of what people of other cultures expressed, it "seems to be, to speak plainly, nonsense."

[11] The etymology of *intelligere* is, we are told, *inter-legere*, to choose between; in the Hebrew Bible, *bînâ*, intelligence, is cognate of *bén*, between. In the NT, *sunesis*, with its prefix, corresponds to the synthetic aspect.

[12] Carson, "Unity and Diversity," 69, recalls, "Warfield pointed out a long time ago that at one level 'systematic theology' is 'an impertinent tautology.'"

Scripture. John M. Frame summarizes evidence showing that biblical writ-ers relied on rational inferences and drew logical consequences.[13] Whence consistency, then? From Trinitarian monotheism, with the God of absolute unity expressing himself in his *Logos*.

Yet, the use of reason in systematic theology suffers from severe limi-tations.[14] We know in part, "we see through a mirror, in enigmatic modes" (1 Cor. 13:12, AT). Though the apophatic stress finds little encouragement in Scripture (cf. 1 John 5:20, *dianoia*!), I bow before the mystery of the divine being and the divine ways. It is incomprehensible. Antagonism may be healthy, and no "real" contradiction.[15] Furthermore, reason is no neutral, autonomous judge. Theologians do not see contradiction in the same place—even Reformed theologians on the extent of Christ's atonement!

On *mystery*, I suggest a distinction between the mysteries of light and the one opaque mystery. Trinity, incarnation, creation (as the power of the infinite God, who possesses all being, to raise before him a dependent being who still remains distinct, upon whom God puts a high price)—these truths remain incomprehensible, we approach them in fear and trembling, but they bring delight to the regenerate mind, harmony to our intelligence. The sovereign permission of evil, sin and its consequences, however, remains opaque. Rea-son has to humble itself and acknowledge its failure even to apprehend the mystery, what marks out evil as evil, the alien reality. Now, this has relevance for our debate: the evil of persons rejecting the offer of salvation in Christ is included in the sovereign permission, that opaque mystery.

Cumulative evidence casts away reasonable doubt; Scripture's perspicu-ity engraves certainty, sealed in our hearts by the Spirit. But on less central matters, we cannot do without *tendential logic*. Not tight: it brings out affini-ties, preferences, better harmony with the data; the tendency of the theory leads in that direction. *It may also mislead.*[16] Yet this logic warrants choices, provided one remains ready to reform them. The logic one applies to the ex-tent of the atonement is of the "tendential" kind. Jonathan D. Moore provides an illustration of the difference with strict logic: he shows how the wording of the Westminster Confession (after the Canons of Dordt) allowed the English

[13] John M. Frame, "Logic," in *Dictionary for Theological Interpretation of the Bible*, 462b.
[14] Of which ibid., 462a–463a, is remarkably conscious.
[15] Yves Congar, *Vraie et fausse réforme dans l'Eglise* (Unam Sanctam 20; Paris: Cerf, 1950), 238–44, applies J. A. Möhler's distinction of *Gegensatz* and *Widerspruch* along such lines.
[16] Cf. Raymond Boudon, *L'Art de se persuader des idées douteuses, fragiles ou fausses*, Points/Essais 242 (Paris: Fayard, 1990), esp. 72–102, 187–97.

Hypothetical Universalists to consider that their view, *in all strictness*, had not been ruled out, and to subscribe. Yet "the whole exegetical approach and systematic structures of the finally codified Westminster theology are inimical to it." "Structurally speaking" this required "a contorted reading of the Confession,"[17] but it was not impossible. The tendency of Westminster Calvinism leads to particular redemption, but not with mathematics-like rigor.

Though common grace ensures that reason still functions, especially in earthly enterprises (Luke 16:8b), reason's dependence on "faith" presuppositions and on contextual conditioning warns against uncritically espousing what counts as "rational" in the "world." Without making any concession to irrationalism, I adopt the following guidelines, in Frame's wording. While consistency remains a value: (1) "The primary goal of exegesis [I add: and of systematic theology] is not logical consistency but faithfulness to the text"; (2) "We must not simply push our logic relentlessly to the point where we ignore or deny a genuine biblical teaching"; (3) "If no explicit logical consistency can be obtained without conflict with other biblical teaching, then we must remain satisfied with paradox."[18]

SCRIPTURE

The Word of God, without which any attempt at systematic theology would be futile, reaches us in the form of canonical Scripture. No modern objection or reinterpretation should prevail over the high bibliology of orthodox Christianity. Prophets and apostles have uttered the words written down in the sacred books of both old and new covenants under such a divine superintendence that the result is both human and divine discourse, fully the one and fully the other. Satisfactory accounts of the nature and role of Scripture are found in the line of John Calvin, François Turretin,[19] Benjamin B. Warfield, and the two volumes edited by Carson and Woodbridge.[20] Drawing on

---

[17] Jonathan D. Moore, "The Extent of the Atonement: English Hypothetical Universalism versus Particular Redemption," in *Drawn into Controversie: Reformed Theological Diversity and Debates within Seventeenth-Century British Puritanism*, ed. Michael A. G. Haykin and Mark Jones (Göttingen, Germany: Vandenhoeck & Ruprecht, 2011), 149 and 151. I admire this magnificent piece of scholarship—a model.

[18] John M. Frame, "The Problem of Theological Paradox," in *Foundations of Christian Scholarship: Essays in the Van Til Perspective*, A Chalcedon Study, ed. Gary North (Vallecito, CA: Ross, 1976), 325; the sentences quoted are italicized in Frame's text.

[19] Though Turretin made marginal concessions on inerrancy (the exception among seventeenth-century orthodox divines), probably born of his desire to maintain a united front among the Reformed.

[20] Carson and Woodbridge, *Scripture and Truth*, and then D. A. Carson and John D. Woodbridge, eds., *Hermeneutics, Authority, and Canon* (Grand Rapids, MI: Zondervan, 1986). See also, *"But My Words Will Never Pass Away": The Enduring Authority of the Christian Scriptures*, ed. D. A. Carson, 2 vols. (Grand Rapids, MI: Eerdmans, forthcoming).

the resources of speech-act theory and highlighting the diversity of Scripture (genres, modes, and levels), as is associated with Kevin J. Vanhoozer's name,[21] has enriched and deepened our understanding—mine, indeed.

The *norma normans* rules, and we truly hear the Word of God in Scripture when we interpret aright. The axiom of sound hermeneutics—"Scripture is its own interpreter"—entails that Scripture itself must determine our interpretation. It implies that the character of Scripture should govern our way of reading it. It involves searching for the "natural sense" (Calvin), "whereby," Packer writes, "the exegete seeks to put himself in the writer's linguistic, cultural, historical, and religious shoes."[22]

As the word is used, "exegesis" concentrates on the meaning of particular passages, what the writers *meant*, whereas systematic theology is to expound what God *means* by the whole of Scripture today. The faithful transition from *meant* to *means* is possible because of the unity of history, unfolding under God's control. The question arises of the way one goes from exegesis to systematic theology. Packer recommends what he calls "retroduction"[23]: a complex interplay of parts and whole, analysis and synthesis, framing hypotheses and testing them, examining old and new offers, with a mutual control of exegesis and systematic theology in spiral progress.

The discipline of biblical theology deals with partial wholes (if this oxymoron be accepted!) and effects first-rank syntheses. "Ideally, therefore, biblical theology stands as a kind of bridge discipline."[24] Systematic theology should remain as close as possible, symbiotically, to biblical theology—to be schooled in biblical ways of thinking. The difference lies not only in scale and degree: systematic theology cares for the legacy of tradition and meets contemporary thought.

Biblical theology, as a discipline, follows the flow of salvation-history. Should we accept Carson's contrast: "The categories of systematic theology are logical and hierarchical, not temporal"?[25] I am struck, on the contrary,

---

[21] Starting with his groundbreaking essay, Kevin J. Vanhoozer, "The Semantics of Biblical Literature: Truth and Scripture's Diverse Literary Forms," in *Hermeneutics, Authority, and Canon*, 53–104.

[22] Packer, "Infallible Scripture and the Role of Hermeneutics," 345.

[23] Packer, "Is Systematic Theology a Mirage?," 32.

[24] D. A. Carson, "Systematic Theology and Biblical Theology," in *New Dictionary of Biblical Theology*, ed. T. Desmond Alexander and Brian S. Rosner (Leicester, UK: Inter-Varsity Press, 2000), 94b.

[25] Carson, "Systematic Theology and Biblical Theology," 102b, and, "its organizing principles do not encourage the exploration of the Bible's plot-line, except incidentally." Similarly, in Carson, "Role of Exegesis," 45: "it is organized on atemporal principles of logic, order, and need."

by the persistence of a basically chronological sequence as the backbone of traditional dogmatics. Our final comments below, on the atonement debate, will capitalize on the value of historical succession.

Though systematic theology does not forsake the biblical plot line, the tendency toward logical order is not denied. It harbors the danger of an excessive flattening of concrete diversity. Its temptation is to disregard whatever healthy antagonisms Scripture contains. Thinking them through requires humbling gymnastics and the acceptance of unsolved problems. One such antagonism, relevant to our debate, is that of the two themes, both of them massively attested in Scripture: of *peace* and of the *sword* (alluding to Matt. 10:34). The good news of peace, reconciliation, fullness, all in unity, is central; but no less that of election, separation, judgment, necessary decision (a "cutting"). Theology, guided by the twofold maxim *sola Scriptura, tota Scriptura*, strives to think through both.

II. Historical Theology: A Quick Glance at Past Exchanges

For clarity's sake, the decisive difference on the atonement should be identified first. Between advocates of definite atonement and Hypothetical Universalism in the Reformed tradition,[26] this difference has not been the acceptance or rejection of Peter Lombard's *dictum*, "sufficient for all, efficient for the elect," though mild criticisms were heard.[27] Definite atonement defenders, as a rule, ratified that use of words. The difference has not been discordant appreciations of the intrinsic value of Christ's redemptive offering; definite atonement theologians affirmed an *infinite* value, because of Christ's deity, which would not have required any addition had the price been paid for all human individuals. Leaving aside the so-called hyper-Calvinists, who remained marginal,[28] the difference has not been over the universal offer of salvation, such that everyone who responds in faith will receive the fruit of

---

[26] I am using "Hypothetical Universalism" as an "umbrella" term, for both the English form and Amyraut's (they differ on the order within the decree). *Universalism*: the vicarious satisfaction was made for every human individual who ever lived; *hypothetical*: the hypothesis that this individual will believe must be validated for salvation to issue. Lee Gatiss offers a luminous account of their tenets and differences in his recent monograph, *For Us and for Our Salvation: "Limited Atonement" in the Bible, Doctrine, History, and Ministry* (London: Latimer Trust, 2012), 90–99.

[27] From Théodore de Bèze, first (but concerned with Latin precision); see Pieter L. Rouwendal, "Calvin's Forgotten Classical Position on the Extent of the Atonement: About Sufficiency, Efficiency, and Anachronism," *WTJ* 70 (2008): 319–20. Rouwendal writes, "Beza remarked that this, if rightly understood, was true, but it was said 'very roughly and ambiguously, as well as barbarously'" (319).

[28] Roger R. Nicole, "Covenant, Universal Call, and Definite Atonement," *JETS* 38.3 (September 1995): 407, lists the main champions of this unfortunate choice, that, "no call can rightly be offered except to the elect": J. Hussey, J. Gill, J. Brine, Kl. Schilder, H. Hoeksema.

the atonement.[29] It has not been the acceptance or rejection of such propositions as "Christ died for all humans" and "He bore the sins of the world" *if*
all possible senses are considered; many definite atonement champions were
ready to undersign those statements in some sense.[30] It has not been about the
existence of benefits flowing from Christ's work of redemption, inclusive of
religious advantages (also the free offer of salvation), accruing to all human
persons, whether elect or not; definite atonement defenders have affirmed
them and attributed them to universal purposes of God in the death of Christ,
expressive of his love for all. John Murray, for instance, could write,

> The unbelieving and reprobate in this world enjoy numerous benefits that
> flow from the fact that Christ died and rose again . . . , the benefits innumer-
> able which are enjoyed by all men indiscriminately are related to the death
> of Christ and may be said to accrue from it in one way or another.[31]

Herman Bavinck stresses the universal significance of particular redemption
and summarizes: "Common grace is indeed subservient to special grace." He
recalls Pascal's thought that, without Christ, the world would be destroyed
or be a hell.[32] One can question the *consistency* of those agreements between
definite atonement and Hypothetical Universalism theologians, but one cannot deny that they have existed for many generations.

Where, then, does the decisive difference lie? In the relationship with
election. Is the purpose of the atonement identical for all, elect and reprobate? Hypothetical Universalism answers yes; definite atonement answers
no.[33] Or, in the transaction that took place on the cross, which is described
by such phrases as "bearing sins," "satisfying divine justice," "paying the

---

[29] For example, Donald Macleod, "*Amyraldus redivivus*: A Review Article," *EQ* 81.3 (2009): 220, "Belief in the full, free and indiscriminate offer of the gospel has been a core dogma of Reformed orthodoxy from the beginning. It has not merely been conceded. It has been insisted on, as a dogma of such importance that any doctrine inconsistent with it would have to be instantly jettisoned."

[30] Rouwendal, "Calvin's Forgotten," 323, on Voetius's authority, distinguishes the "particular" view and what he calls the "classical" one, and the difference is this: "Did Christ die in any sense for all men or not? Classic: yes; Particular: no." Is the distinction so helpful? Apart from Voetius, Rouwendal himself writes that "Beza [Particular] did not take a very great step" when he moved beyond Calvin [Classical, for Rouwendal] (325). William Cun-ningham, *Historical Theology: A Review of the Principal Doctrinal Discussions in the Christian Church since the Apostolic Age, Volume 2* (1862; repr., London: Banner of Truth, 1960), 333, 335, refers to such loose language by particular Calvinists.

[31] John Murray, *Redemption Accomplished and Applied* (Grand Rapids, MI: Eerdmans, 1955), 61–62. This teach-ing is ordinary, as in Turretin: Franciscus Turretinus, *Institutio theologiae elencticae*, pars secunda (New York and Pittsburgh: Robert Carter, 1847), locus XIV, qu. 14,11 (p. 403).

[32] Herman Bavinck, *Sin and Salvation in Christ*, vol. 3 of *Reformed Dogmatics*, ed. John Bolt, trans. John Vriend, 4 vols. (Grand Rapids, MI: Baker Academic, 2006), 470–71 (§ 407). Bavinck does not give a reference for Pascal's thought; it is § 556 in Brunschvicg's order of the *Pensées*.

[33] I adopt Rouwendal's way of pinpointing the difference, in his presentation, between Hypothetical Universalism and the "classical" position ("Calvin's Forgotten," 323).

ransom-price," are the reprobate included as well as the elect? Hypothetical Universalism: yes; definite atonement: no. Or, did atonement secure eternal life in such a way that those for whom it was accomplished according to its main purpose and operation shall infallibly receive it at the end? Definite atonement: yes; Hypothetical Universalism: no.

AUGUSTINE

Before Augustine, one hardly meets a clear statement taking sides. Despite the emphasis on free will among the Fathers, one encounters exegesis of favorite Hypothetical Universalism texts that seems to open the way for definite atonement interpretation. Turretin on 1 Timothy 4:10 claims Chrysostom, Œcumenius, Ambrose, on his side: they explained that Christ is the Savior of all for this present life, but of believers only for eternal life;[34] he quotes Jerome himself on Matthew 20:28: the Lord "did not say that he was giving his life for all, but for many, i.e., for those who would will to believe (*credere voluerint*)."[35] Augustine's case is complex, and no unified doctrine of atonement stands out clearly in his writings. His emphasis on the divine desire that all should be saved is repetitious, but other lines would lead to definite atonement. On 1 John 2:2 he differs from Hypothetical Universalism: he explains "the whole world" in terms of the *church* scattered in all nations (*in omnibus gentibus*).[36] Raymond A. Blacketer points to several other passages, with the same import.[37] Augustine's critics from Marseilles attacked him for holding a doctrine similar to definite atonement; so Prosper of Aquitaine writes him,[38] and Augustine did not respond by affirming Hypothetical Universalism. Those who later passionately claimed Augustine as their patron championed a definite atonement position.[39] So did the Jansenists, who were condemned on that article.[40] The tendential logic of

---

[34] Turretin, *Institutio theologiae elencticae*, locus XIV, qu. 14,14 (p. 405). He quotes to the same effect Thomas Aquinas.
[35] Ibid., qu. 14,17 (p. 406), with the further comment from the *Glossa ordinaria*, "not all, but those predestined."
[36] Augustine, *In Epistolam Ioannis Tractatus*, 1.8.
[37] Raymond A. Blacketer, "Definite Atonement in Historical Perspective," in *The Glory of the Atonement: Biblical, Historical, and Practical Perspectives*, ed. Charles E. Hill and Frank A. James III (Downers Grove, IL: InterVarsity Press, 2004), 308–10. Bavinck, *Sin and Salvation in Christ*, 457 (§ 404) offers references, but I confess my disappointment when I tried to check them.
[38] Prosper of Aquitaine, *Epistula Prosperi ad Augustinum*, 6, in *Œuvres de saint Augustin 24: Aux moines d'Adrumète et de Provence*, Latin text and trans. J. Chéné, Bibliothèque augustinienne (n.p.: Desclée de Brouwer, 1962), 404.
[39] Blacketer, "Definite Atonement in Historical Perspective," 310–11; Bavinck, *Sin and Salvation in Christ*, 457 (§ 404), who basically relies on Petavius (Denis Pétau).
[40] Jansenius may be credited with a form of definite atonement doctrine. But what about Pascal? Roger R. Nicole, in his magisterial article, "John Calvin's View of the Extent of the Atonement," *WTJ* 47 (1985): 209, protests against

Augustine's views on predestination and grace was leading in the definite atonement direction.

JOHN CALVIN

What Calvin really thought and taught on the matter is a hotly disputed issue. After the exact survey by Roger Nicole,[41] we must be content with a few lines that may supplement treatments in the present volume. Statements abound that Christ died for "us," for us poor sinners (a few times: "for all poor sinners"), for the world, for the human race (Latin, *genus*; French, *genre*); Calvin regularly adds that faith is the necessary condition for participation in the fruit of the atonement: unbelievers deprive themselves of the saving benefits that are offered to all. The following passage summarizes Calvin's ordinary teaching:

> . . . whether all participate in the good which our Lord Jesus Christ secured for us? No: for unbelievers have neither part in it nor portion. It is, therefore, a special privilege for those whom God draws to himself. And also St. Paul shows that faith is required, or else Christ will bring us no benefit. Though, therefore, Christ be in general the Redeemer of the world, his death and passion bring no fruit but to those who receive what St. Paul here demonstrates.[42]

Hypothetical Universalism? History shows firm supporters of definite atonement using similar terms, and rigorous scholars have concluded that Calvin's are loose enough to allow for a definite atonement–compatible meaning![43] Weighty arguments cast doubt on the Hypothetical Universalism reading.

Calvin, when commenting on passages appealed to by Hypothetical Universalism supporters (1 John 2:2), does not interpret them in their way; he binds together atonement and intercession and recalls that Christ did not pray for the world (John 17:9); there were defenders of definite atonement around Calvin, and closest of all, his assistant and heir Théodore de Bèze—and we do not hear the faintest echo of any disagreement. In his book against Tilemann Heshusius, Calvin does say of Christ's blood that it "was not shed to expiate the sins" of unbelievers, but the interpretation is not straightforward.

J. B. Torrance's placing Pascal among adversaries of definite atonement: "he infelicitously conjoins the name of the Jansenist Pascal." Pascal's position is controversial. In his *Pensées*, § 781 (Brunschvicg) he apparently separates in thought between the Lamb's redemption (for all) and the Lord's application (to the elect).

[41] Nicole, "John Calvin's View of the Extent of the Atonement," 209.

[42] Fourth sermon on the Epistle to the Ephesians, on 1:7–10 (John Calvin, *Ioannis Calvini Opera quae supersunt omnia*, ed. J. W. Baum, A. E. Cunitz, and E. Reuss, 59 vols. [Braunschweig, Germany: Schwetschke, 1863–1900], cited as *CO*, 51:287–88).

[43] See especially Nicole, "John Calvin's View of the Extent of the Atonement," 215–20.

William Cunningham, who first pointed to the passage, remained cautious: the statement is isolated; "we do not found much upon it."[44]

A hundred times, while rambling through Calvin's writings, I have felt the same frustration: now a magnificent opportunity for him to clarify his position—and he bypasses it. *As if* with intent! We cannot imagine that the issue had not emerged for him; he must have known about the controversies.[45] *If* he deliberately avoided taking sides, we may imagine motives. His concern for Protestant unity was paramount; he may have feared that the issue would be divisive. He may have concluded that the biblical evidence was not clear-cut (he shunned speculation). He may have felt that the precise point in debate did not *preach* well. We may even mention the "existential" slant in Calvin's theology.[46] Such motives may have prevented the tendential logic of his doctrine, which indicated at times arguments for definite atonement, from coming out in the open.

Recent works wishing to rehabilitate Hypothetical Universalism among the Reformed (Paedobaptists and Baptists), stress the historical argument. One example could be the copious plea by David Allen.[47] He enlists many worthies among critics of "limited atonement/particular redemption." Many quotations fail to convince because the flexibility of the language used by definite atonement supporters is not recognized, but his remarks are thought provoking. Two prestigious names will be considered here, one Baptist, one Presbyterian: Andrew Fuller and, briefly, Charles Hodge.

ANDREW FULLER

Andrew Fuller, William Carey's theologian, is a towering figure for Baptist Calvinism. Allen claims him for the position he champions and so describes Fuller's stance:

> . . . when Andrew Fuller modified his views as a result of his interaction with General Baptist Dan Taylor, he explicitly says that he agreed with

---

[44] William Cunningham, *Historical Theology: A Review of the Principal Doctrinal Discussions in the Christian Church since the Apostolic Age, Volume 2* (1862; repr., Edinburgh: Banner of Truth, 1960), 396.
[45] In his nuanced treatment, "The Quest for the Historical Calvin," *EQ* 55 (1983): 101, Tony [A. N. S.] Lane considers that Calvin had "not a fully-developed position on this matter." Maybe Calvin *refrained* from developing one.
[46] Calvin is most interested in subjective effects, for example, comfort for anguished consciences. The third sermon on the prophecies of Isaiah, on Isaiah 53:4–6, *CO* 35:625, explains the necessity of Christ's judicial death in terms of our attitude toward our sins.
[47] David L. Allen, "The Atonement: Limited or Universal?," in *Whosoever Will: A Biblical-Theological Critique of Five-Point Calvinism*, ed. David L. Allen and Steve W. Lemke (Nashville: B&H Academic, 2010), 61–107. "Historical Considerations" runs from pages 67–78, and history is already much involved in pages 62–66.

him on "the universal extent of Christ's death" (*The Complete Works* . . . , 550). Moreover, in Fuller's treatment of substitution in his *Six Letters to Dr. Ryland*, he seeks to answer the questions of "The persons for whom Christ was a substitute; whether the *elect only*, or mankind in general." He argues that Christ substituted for mankind in general, but he maintained this in conjunction with his belief that Christ did such with an effectual purpose to save only the elect (*Works*, 2:706–709).[48]

In contrast to "intrinsic sufficiency," this implies "extrinsic sufficiency," which "speaks to the atonement's actual infinite ability to save all and every human, and this because God, indeed, wills it to be so, such that Christ, *in fact*, made a satisfaction for all humankind."[49] A close rereading of the relevant passages,[50] however, suggests that some complements are needed to achieve a proper balance.

Fuller, in the last letter to Dr. Ryland, emphasizes his disagreements with Richard Baxter and writes, "I consider redemption as inseparably connected with eternal life, and therefore as applicable to none but the elect, who are redeemed from *among* men."[51] The particularity of redemption, distinct from the sufficiency of atonement, Fuller drew from Galatians 3:13, Romans 3:24, and Revelation 5:9 and 14:3–4.[52] He explains, "If it be a proper definition of the substitution of Christ that he died *for* or *in the place of others, that they should not die*, this, as comprehending the designed end to be answered by his death, is strictly applicable to none but the elect."[53] And again,

> . . . as Christ did not lay down his life but by *covenant*—as the elect were given to him, to be as the *travail of his soul, the purchase of his blood*—he had respect in all that he did and suffered to this recompence of reward. It was for the covering of *their* transgressions that he became obedient unto death.[54]

---

[48] Ibid., 62–63 n. 2. In my 1848 edition of Fuller's *Works* (n. 2 above), Allen's references are 248a and 320b–322a.
[49] Ibid., 64: "*Intrinsic sufficiency* speaks to the atonement's internal or infinite abstract ability to save all men (if God so intended), in such a way that it has no direct reference to the actual extent of the atonement." The labels are not adequate: "intrinsic sufficiency" is correctly defined, but *extrinsic* normally means that the attribute *does not belong to the thing itself*, and "extrinsic sufficiency" would deprive the atonement of its own value as the death of the Son–Substitute; this would fit Scotist *acceptatio* theory, not Reformed orthodoxy!
[50] They are: (1) section IV of Fuller's "Reply to Philanthropos [alias Daniel Taylor]," 223b–233b; (2) letters IX–XIII by Agnostos [alias Andrew Fuller] on the same controversy, 247a–255b; (3) letters III–VI of the "Six Letters to Dr. Ryland," 320b–325b; (4) conversations II and III of the "Three Conversations on Imputation, Substitution, and Particular Redemption," 312a–317b, between Peter, James (speaking for Fuller), and John.
[51] Fuller, *Works*, 324b.
[52] Ibid., 250a and b.
[53] Ibid., 321a.
[54] Ibid., 321b.

He follows those "worthy men" who have "admitted that Christ might be said, in some sense, to have died for the whole world";[55] the language of Scripture is "indefinite."[56] He wishes to rule out "such notion of election or of the limited extent of Christ's death, as that it shall be in vain for any of the sons of men *truly* to *seek* after God. If they are *willing* to be saved *in God's way*, nothing shall hinder their salvation."[57] There is no lack of provision for forgiveness.[58] I fail to discern, in Fuller's developments, Allen's emphasis on an actual transaction making satisfaction precisely for the sins of the non-elect.[59] He pens a balanced summary:

> . . . concerning the death of Christ. If I speak of it *irrespective of the purpose of the Father and the Son, as to the objects who should be saved by it,* merely referring to what it is in itself sufficient for, and declared in the gospel to be adapted to, I should think that I answered the question in a scriptural way by saying, It was for *sinners as sinners;* but if I have respect to the *purpose* of the Father in giving his Son to die, and to the *design* of Christ in laying down his life, I should answer, *It was for the elect only.*[60]

This scheme looks nearer to Allen's "intrinsic sufficiency"—and, indeed, Fuller quotes from John Owen thrice on the perfect sufficiency of Christ's atonement[61]—than to his "extrinsic sufficiency."

"John" concludes the discussion between "Peter," the more conservative Calvinist of his time, and "James," the spokesman for Fuller's contribution, by minimizing their disagreement.[62] The conversation, however, has brought to light a fine issue: can one separate, in thought, the *nature* of the atonement and its *intention*, in God's and Christ's intention? "Peter" argues, "Intention enters into the nature of atonement,"[63] and "James" counters the claim. Systematic theology should scrutinize the point. And a related problem stands out from Fuller's disquisitions: the way sufficiency should

---

[55] Ibid., 249a (letter X).
[56] Ibid., 251a (letter XI).
[57] Ibid., 249a (letter X).
[58] Ibid., 248a (letter X).
[59] "Moderate-Calvinists," so Fuller for Allen, "understand the term *sufficient* to mean not only that Christ's death *could have* satisfied the sins of all unbelievers had that been God's intention but that His death in fact *did* satisfy the sins of all humanity"; against "high-Calvinists" who say, "Jesus only satisfied the sins of the elect" ("The Atonement: Limited or Universal?," 90–91). Incidentally, I regret this use of the verb "satisfy." Atonement satisfies *the demands of justice*, which requires the *punishment* of sins.
[60] Fuller, *Works*, 321a.
[61] Ibid., 223 footnote (with Witsius), 315a (Conversation III), and 321 footnote (cf. 314a).
[62] Ibid., 317a and b.
[63] Ibid., 315a.

be conceived.[64] Allen rightly observes, "The debate over the nature of this sufficiency is *the key debate* in the extent question."[65]

CHARLES HODGE

Charles Hodge belongs to the same category in Allen's presentation.[66] And, indeed, we find him quite close to Fuller. He puts forward the same disjunction: "The secret purpose of God in providing such a substitute for man, has nothing to do with the nature of his work, or with its appropriateness."[67] Hodge argues against a "double payment" objection to the "Augustinian" combination of particular redemption and universal call: it would only avail with a *pecuniary* satisfaction, and Hodge denies that "the satisfaction of Christ was in all respects analogous to the payment of a debt, a satisfaction to commutative or commercial justice."[68] He does rule out double *judicial* payment: "If the claims of justice are satisfied they cannot be again enforced. . . . What reason can there be for the infliction of the penalty for which satisfaction has been rendered?"[69] though his explanation lacks clarity and one can doubt the cogency of his metaphors.[70]

Hodge maintains a "special reference to the elect";[71] "There is a sense in which He died for all, and there is a sense in which he died for the elect alone";[72] "He did not come merely to render their salvation possible, but actually to deliver them from the curse of the law, and from the power of sin";[73] "it secured the actual salvation of those for whom He wrought."[74] This, the main concern of definite atonement defenders, contrasts with Allen's key word "save*able*."[75] Hodge's "universalistic" statements aim at justifying the universal offer, which he grounds on Christ's "relation to man, to the whole human family,"[76] on God's provision of "such a substitute for man."[77]

---

[64] Thomas J. Nettles, *By His Grace and for His Glory: A Historical, Theological, and Practical Study of the Doctrines of Grace in Baptist Life* (Grand Rapids, MI: Baker, 1986), 302–304, accurately represents the views of Fuller and other Baptists.
[65] Allen, "Atonement: Limited or Universal?," 66.
[66] Ibid., 63 n. 4, and 85.
[67] Charles Hodge, *Systematic Theology*, 3 vols. (1871–1873; repr., Grand Rapids, MI: Eerdmans, 1986), 2:555.
[68] Ibid., 554 (cf. 557). Fuller, *Works*, 312b, 316b, had opened the way.
[69] Hodge, *Systematic Theology*, 2:472.
[70] Ibid., 555–56.
[71] Ibid., 544.
[72] Ibid., 546.
[73] Ibid., 548.
[74] Ibid., 552.
[75] Allen, "Atonement: Limited or Universal?," 64 (authors write "saveable," as here, or "savable"). The atonement creates the *possibility* of salvation. Of course, this is the meaning of "Hypothetical" Universalism.
[76] Hodge, *Systematic Theology*, 2:545.
[77] Ibid., 554.

Note the singular form, *not* for each and every individual: he may have in view the *corporate* dimension, to which we shall come back. His exegesis inclines toward definite atonement readings,[78] and he reaches the balanced statement, "Christ, therefore, did not die equally for all men. He laid down his life for his sheep; He gave Himself for his Church. But in perfect consistency with all this, He did all that was necessary, so far as a satisfaction to justice is concerned, all that is required for the salvation of all men."[79] Allen too quickly enlists Hodge on his side.

KARL BARTH AND BRUCE L. McCORMACK

The twentieth century witnessed the emergence of an original form of Reformed theology whose voice deserves to be heard in our debate. Karl Barth and his followers share with Reformed stalwarts a common heritage, and yet with a radically different way of doing theology.[80] A Barthian renaissance has taken place in English-speaking countries, involving scholars with an evangelical background—a further reason for us to devote some space to a possible Barthian contribution in definite atonement/Hypothetical Universalism discussions. Barth himself did not invest much in this regard. It will best suit our purpose, rather than studying Barth himself,[81] to focus on a leading contemporary interpreter of Barth, and one deeply interested in the relationship with evangelical theology: Princeton professor, Bruce L. McCormack.

McCormack has aroused controversy on a central issue of Barthian interpretation, and it has some bearing on our topic. His "creative" thesis, whose seed was sown by Eberhard Jüngel,[82] ascribes to Barth a radically new, christologically determined, ontology. God did not only choose, from all eternity, to become a man in Jesus Christ, but he thereby freely constituted his own being: "The eternal event in which God chose to be 'God for us' is, at the

---

[78] Ibid., 558–61.

[79] Ibid., 556–57.

[80] On the somewhat paradoxical relationship, two recent symposia may be mentioned: Sung Wook Chung, ed., *Karl Barth and Evangelical Theology: Convergences and Divergences* (Grand Rapids, MI/Milton Keynes, UK: Baker Academic/Paternoster, 2006); and David Gibson and Daniel Strange, eds., *Engaging with Barth: Contemporary Evangelical Critiques* (Nottingham, UK: Apollos, 2008).

[81] Garry J. Williams, "Karl Barth and the Doctrine of the Atonement," in *Engaging with Barth*, 249–70, deals critically with the extent of reconciliation (*Versöhnung*) in Barth's theology.

[82] McCormack pays tribute to the Tübingen theologian in his essay, "Karl Barth's Historicized Christology: Just How 'Chalcedonian' Is It?" as republished in his *Orthodox and Modern: Studies in the Theology of Karl Barth* (Grand Rapids, MI: Baker Academic, 2008), 221 n. 49: "This is perhaps the appropriate place to note—with gratitude—the impact that Jüngel's little book [*Gottes Sein ist im Werden*] has had on my thinking (both as a reader of Barth and with regard to the systematic issues involved)."

same time, the eternal event in which God gave (and continues to give) to himself his own being—and vice versa."[83] No *Logos asarkos* except as *incarnandus*, "rejection of free-floating talk of the 'eternal Son' as a mythological abstraction . . ."[84] McCormack speaks of God's giving himself his own being;[85] this doctrine "makes God so much the Lord that he is even the Lord over his own 'essence.'"[86] The same is also the human ontological ground: "It is an eternal decision in which both the being of God *and the being of the human* are constituted by way of anticipation."[87]

This interpretation of Barth, which also embodies McCormack's conviction, has been challenged. McCormack has replied with a chronological scheme—before 1939–1942, though new insights were breaking through, Barth was the prisoner of older metaphysics—and even after, he was not always consistent.[88] I tend to agree with him that such a reading has extracted what is most Barthian in Barthianism.[89]

Everything flows from the christological principle: there is no knowledge that does not proceed exclusively from this center, which is also all-inclusive, Jesus Christ, God and man. We may not conceive of God (and of humanity), in the slightest measure, as other than this Event—it would require another source of knowledge! There can be no other ontology than that determined by Incarnation. Since Barth and McCormack still work with a duality of time and eternity, they speak of God's eternal decision or election, but it is identical with the Event. In an earlier version of his thesis, McCormack could write, "the actions and relations of the eternal Son in time (in the incarnation) are 'built-into' the being of God in eternity through election."[90] Now it

---

[83] Bruce L. McCormack, "The Actuality of God: Karl Barth in Conversation with Open Theism," in *Engaging the Doctrine of God: Contemporary Protestant Perspectives*, ed. Bruce L. McCormack (Grand Rapids, MI/Edinburgh: Baker Academic/Rutherford, 2008), 210.

[84] Bruce L. McCormack, "Grace and Being: The Role of God's Gracious Election in Karl Barth's Theological Ontology," as republished, "in a slightly different form," in *Orthodox and Modern*, 193–94. This essay (2000) was the major manifesto of McCormack's reading.

[85] For example, McCormack, "Actuality of God," 210 (twice).

[86] McCormack, "Historicized Christology," 216.

[87] Bruce L. McCormack, "*Justitia aliena*: Karl Barth in Conversation with the Evangelical Doctrine of Imputed Righteousness," in *Justification in Perspective: Historical Developments and Contemporary Challenges*, ed. Bruce L. McCormack (Grand Rapids, MI/Edinburgh: Baker Academic/Rutherford, 2006), 191.

[88] Just to take one comparatively recent article, "The Actuality of God": "I am not suggesting that Barth was ever absolutely consistent" (211 n. 57); "Barth does seem at times to contradict this" (215); Barth did use "omnicausality" several times, "dangerous" talk (235 n. 123); "residue of classical metaphysics" in *CD* II/1 (236), "ambiguities"; "instability" in *CD* II/1, and Barth in a "predicament" (237, 238); "the confusions which lie at the heart of Barth's doctrine of God in *Church Dogmatics*, II/1" (239).

[89] For a brief assessment, see Henri A. G. Blocher, "Karl Barth's Christocentric Method," in *Engaging with Barth*, 46–47 n. 172.

[90] Bruce L. McCormack, *For Us and Our Salvation: Incarnation and Atonement in the Reformed Tradition*, Studies in Reformed Theology and History (Princeton, NJ: Princeton Theological Seminary, 1993), 34.

is even clearer: there is no prior being of God.[91] Barth and McCormack thus fall back on the Aristotelian doctrine of God as *actus purus, purissimus, et singularis*.[92] Unity must then prevail: creation and reconciliation cannot be *really* different works. If, in *Church Dogmatics* II/1, Barth was "able to speak of the work of reconciliation and redemption as a 'fundamentally new work' in comparison with the work of creation," this has become "an impossible thing" in his mature thought.[93] Dualities are condensed: ontology and history, creation and reconciliation, the person and work of Christ—"Jesus Christ *is* his history"[94]—"reconciliation" and "redemption" (appropriated to the Spirit in Barth). McCormack lucidly states, "What Barth has done is transfer the concept of irresistible grace out of the realm of the Holy Spirit's work in calling, justifying, and regenerating the individual into the realm of Christ's work."[95] Participation in Christ is not of the Spirit but of the God-man's work.[96]

What are the consequences for the extent of the atonement? The nature of atonement is reinterpreted: no longer as the satisfaction of the demands of divine justice or wrath,[97] but as the destruction of the old sinner followed by resurrection.[98] Since creation is ultimately one Act with reconciliation, "in Jesus Christ the God-man" and grounded on the covenant of grace, and since participation in him is not a new work, every human individual is "in Christ." Election does not separate "two distinct groups of people": "In truth . . . the division that is described by the 'man of sin' on the left hand and the elect of God on the right hand is a division that cuts through the existence of every human individual at its very root."[99] In Christ, *each and every human being is judged (destroyed) and reconciled to God*. The nonsymmetrical duality of

---

[91] In "The Actuality of God," 239 n. 133, McCormack quotes from Barth's (unsatisfactory) effort at correlation of being and will: Barth does not grant priority to either, and writes, "Rather, it is as He wills that He is God, and as He is God that He wills." McCormack adds, "I would say, on the contrary, 'It is as He wills that He is God,' and leave it at that."

[92] Ibid., 214–15.

[93] McCormack, *"Justitia aliena,"* 234.

[94] McCormack, "Actuality of God," 222; a symptom of the ontological understanding of reconciliation, despite the use of forensic language.

[95] Ibid., 230 (all italics in McCormack's text).

[96] McCormack, *"Justitia aliena,"* 191.

[97] Already in *For Us and Our Salvation*, 30, McCormack had perceived the change. In *Kirchliche Dogmatik* (hereafter *KD*) II/1, he saw "a potentially disastrous weakness. At a crucial point, he [Barth] repeated the error of the sixteenth- and seventeenth-century Reformed theologians and made the death of Christ a satisfaction offered to the divine righteousness." But in *KD* IV/1, Barth could "rectify" this error, and penal substitution "was placed in a more clearly subordinate position" (the important quotation is found on the next page, from *KD* IV/1, 279 [English 253]); Barth says of satisfaction offered to the wrath of God, "The latter idea is quite foreign to the New Testament." Cf. Williams, "Karl Barth and the Doctrine of the Atonement," 257.

[98] McCormack, *"Justitia aliena,"* 187.

[99] Ibid., 188.

God's *Yes* and *No* within the Event, replaces the duality of final destinies. The outcome would seem to be actual universalism, *apokatastasis*, but Barth refrained from an unambiguous statement of the same; he typically confided to Jüngel, "I don't teach it, but I don't say, either, that I don't teach it."[100]

Barthianism, in McCormack's version, shares concerns of both definite atonement and Hypothetical Universalism supporters. With Hypothetical Universalism, he charges Calvin and Reformed orthodoxy with an overemphasis on God's righteousness and its separation from mercy: they "make God's mercy the prisoner, so to speak, of His righteousness, until such time as righteousness has been fully satisfied."[101] "I have tried to show," he writes, "that a christologically grounded doctrine of God will accomplish all that is important and legitimate in the open theistic program, namely, the substitution of the living God of the Bible for a timeless, impassible deity."[102] For him, "God does not specifically decree an earthquake here, a tsunami there, as particular events."[103] On the other hand, the desire of magnifying Christ's work of reconciliation, *ephapax* ("once for all"), to which nothing can be added, is shared by Reformed definite atonement orthodoxy and Barthianism. The latter stresses that "what Jesus Christ accomplishes is not merely the possibility of reconciliation but the reality of it"[104]—the truth definite atonement advocates see jeopardized in Hypothetical Universalism. McCormack goes on: "It is not only the case that the work of the Holy Spirit does not complete a work of Jesus Christ which was incomplete without it; the work of the Holy Spirit does not even make effective a work of Jesus Christ which is ineffective without it!"[105] Depending on the interpretation of "effective," the proposition is either compatible or incompatible with definite atonement.[106]

McCormack's contribution draws attention to two important factors. First, on the role of Scripture: alongside proclamations of biblical authority, Barth and Barthians depart from the "obvious meaning" of passages on election and the final state. I cannot imagine Barth ascribing to Paul, historically, as the meaning Paul intended, as the content of Paul's thought, the theologi-

---

[100] Eberhard Jüngel, "La Vie et l'oeuvre de Karl Barth," in Pierre Gisel, ed., *Karl Barth. Genèse et réception de sa théologie* (Geneva: Labor et Fides, 1987), 56.
[101] McCormack, *For Us and Our Salvation*, 27.
[102] McCormack, "Actuality of God," 240.
[103] Ibid., 225.
[104] McCormack, "*Justitia aliena*," 179 (all italics in McCormack's text).
[105] McCormack, "Actuality of God," 229.
[106] If the proposition entails the rejection of "application" as a distinct work, as McCormack expressly rejects it in "*Justitia aliena*," 192 ("application" translates *Zueignung*), Reformed orthodoxy cannot subscribe. If "effective" means that the saving effect is certain, having been secured by the cross, this is the teaching of definite atonement.

cal thesis Barth expounds.[107] He would appeal to the *Object* of the biblical witness, beyond the human words. "For Barth," Garry Williams writes, "the key move is not exegetical but hermeneutical."[108] This is correct if we include the dogmatic position on Scripture and the Word of God. McCormack calmly denies the classical doctrine of inspiration: he discards "an understanding of biblical inspiration which would require that all biblical statements ultimately find their source in a single Author,"[109] while sketching a caricature of the classic evangelical view.[110] The second factor is the view of time and eternity. Though McCormack pleads that the proposition "we are 'in Christ' long before the appearance of Jesus in time . . . does not mean . . . that history has been rendered insignificant,"[111] the question must be raised. Ontologized history and historicized ontology might amount to the loss of both ontology and history! For Barth, time is *eternalized* in Jesus Christ, and its diversity is condensed into one: since his time "is the only moved and moving time . . . it does indeed mean suspension, the total relativizing of all other time and of its apparently moved and moving content."[112] Is the tendency foreign to orthodoxy? It might affect the extent of the atonement.

WEIGHING UP BARTH AND MCCORMACK

The Barthian proposal is too original to be embraced in the same move as the others. It is also too powerful for any adequate treatment here and would require a discussion of the whole system or anti-system. I only offer a few thoughts to explain why I cannot recommend it, globally, as an option for evangelical theology.

The christological concentration is a grandiose simplification, a refashioning of the whole edifice that achieves an imposing symmetry. The drawing power of Barth's offer proceeds from the prestige of that achievement, from

---

[107] One remembers, of course, Barth's sharp disjunction between *Paulus dixit* and *Deus dixit*, and his assertion that the Bible is vulnerable (fallible, erring) also in its theological structures.

[108] Williams, "Karl Barth and the Doctrine of the Atonement," 269.

[109] McCormack, "Actuality of God," 195.

[110] Ibid. He goes on, against the idea of harmonization: "But evangelical [as defined by McCormack] theology surrendered the notion of a mechanical dictation a long time ago, and it is hard to imagine any other explanation of the process of inspiration which would allow for and require a single-Author theory. Most today are quite content to acknowledge that inspiration is wrongly construed where divine authorship excludes or even only suppresses human activity in the production of biblical writings." Evangelical (in our sense) theology, as represented by writers such as J. I. Packer or Edmund Clowney, *both* maintains the single "primary" Author *and* denies that it entails not only "mechanical dictation" (that old hat!) but any suppression of human activity.

[111] Ibid., 192, since, he argues, God's being "is constituted eternally, in and for itself, by that which God will undergo as human in time."

[112] Barth, *CD* I/1, 116 [*KD* I/1, 119]; "suspension" translates *Stillstand.*

the rigor of the development from a unique starting point, and from its ability to honor Scripture. But on all three counts, objections may be raised.

The beauty of concentration may cloak a forced identification of things that should be kept distinct. So "punishment" and "reprobation." Nowhere in Scripture (and tradition) is Christ called "reprobate." Nowhere is he said to have *repented* in our stead.[113] The fusion under the label *das Nichtige* of ontological "nothingness" and moral/relational/dramatic evil slides back down the slope of myth—it is against biblical uniqueness. Remaining diversity falls prey to dialectics: unbelief is ontologically impossible, and yet real; we are participants in Christ, the Christ-Event is all-inclusive, and yet: "However true it may be that 'in Christ' I am no longer the 'man of sin,' yet in myself I find that I am."[114] "Clearly, Barth has stretched the relationship of our true being in Jesus Christ and our lived existence to the breaking point."[115] The problem with such paradoxes is not only the consistency of the "in myself" dimension, but the cash-value of the statements. The ambiguities on *apokatastasis* may belong here.[116]

Is the method rigorous? When facing the one all-inclusive Event, how can Barth discern what he can say of Christ's deity and of his humanity? *De facto*, he draws from other sources: "all theologians, including Barth, maintain some kind of implicit or explicit criteria for distinguishing the characteristics that should be predicated of Christ's deity on the basis of his humanity from those that should not."[117] Barth's appeal to the theme *actus purus* is a legacy of philosophical theology and lacks roots in original Christianity.[118] Actually, he relies on the witness of Scripture and on tradition, theological and philosophical, but, since they are all fallible in his sight, this recourse lacks rigor. The incarnate Christ is the center or culmination, not the starting point, of revelation. God prepared his coming, to enable godly people to interpret the Event aright. God *first* spoke through the prophets, before he spoke finally "in (the) Son." God's discourse through the prophets and the Son (entrusted to his apostles) is the infallible Word by which the Christ Event is to

[113] McCormack echoes this language of Barth in *For Us and Our Salvation*, 21.
[114] McCormack, "*Justitia aliena*," 193.
[115] Ibid., 194.
[116] One possible reason why Barth refrained from affirming *apokatastasis* (seldom mentioned) is that statements which he penned rule out any survival or post-existence after death, and interpret eternal life as the eternalization of *this life* (though other statements communicate another impression); the difference between believers and unbelievers *is final*.
[117] Williams, "Karl Barth and the Doctrine of the Atonement," 255.
[118] I leave aside the question of whether talk of God's decision constituting his being represents unfathomable profundity or sheer nonsense. I suspect no mortal can tell.

be interpreted. (By God's grace, Barth also received from Scripture precious glimpses of divine truth.)

The third criterion, precisely, is conformity to the teaching of Scripture. It looks impossible to reconcile Barth's doctrine of election, and whatever flows from it, with the "natural" sense of the biblical authors. Our *prolegomena* ruled this out. The "precious glimpses," however, may include the definitive fullness of Christ's work. Barthians quote universalistic-looking texts without due regard for context (e.g., Rom. 11:32; 1 Cor. 15:22). But they have something biblical to teach us when they magnify the cosmic scope of reconciliation, with the christological "hymn" of Colossians 1:15–20, when they highlight the theme of "all" and "peace."

III. Definite Atonement and Hypothetical Universalism

(1) On the Use of Scripture

If we now narrow down our focus on discussions between friends of Beza and Owen on one side, Amyraut and Baxter on the other, the biblical (exegetical) arguments would seem to be the first for us to examine. The verdict of Scripture is decisive. Although this essay is not devoted to exegesis, some reflections are apropos.

Supporters of definite atonement and Hypothetical Universalism have shared the same presuppositions and procedures regarding Scripture. Contrary to stereotypes, the degree of "scholasticism" was about the same on both sides, and, for instance, "Owen was supremely a biblical theologian, deeply engaged with the biblical data and willing to change or develop his position as exegetical considerations were brought to bear."[119] The suspicion has been common that particularists were imposing a logic born of dogmatic tenets (election) upon texts; reciprocally, defenders of Hypothetical Universalism have been thought by their critics to read into the biblical text "modern" ideas of love and responsibility. Only a painstaking examination of the passages involved and of the commentaries offered could settle the issue. The confrontation has never been simply that of dogmatic system versus Bible, logic versus exegesis. Some independent scholars have concluded, for instance, in favor of a "particular" reading. A telling example would be that of the arch-liberal Albert Schweitzer. His reconstitution of Jesus's intentions led him to

---

[119] Moore, "Extent of the Atonement," 132.

conclude that Jesus was thinking of dying only for a specific community, not for all.[120] Schweitzer wrote before the Qumran finds, and one element in the Dead Sea documents brings some support to the thesis. The "many" (πολλοί) of Mark 10:45 (and parallels) echoes the *rabbîm* (רבים) of Isaiah 53, almost a technical term there for the beneficiaries of the Servant's sacrifice. Now, the Qumran dissenters, through their *pèšèr*, appropriated the word from the prophecy and chose it for self-identification: the members are the *rabbîm* (*Rule of the Community*, 1 QS). The Qumran community, which styled itself as the community of the new covenant (appropriating Jeremiah 31), whose "sons of light" were about to wage war against the sons of darkness, was little inclined toward universalism! If the word "many" (in relationship with Isaiah 53) had *particular* connotations in first-century Judaism, it could in Jesus's *logion*.

Passages of fullness and wider embrace abound, and particularists could avow that they feel embarrassed with some of them: the tendential logic of such texts favors a universalist reading. But defenders of Hypothetical Universalism overstep the mark if they suggest that it is the only possible reading, and that the matter is thereby settled. Not seldom, advocates of Hypothetical Universalism overlook quite natural understandings.

Allen, for example, charges particularists with ignoring Hebrews 2:9: Jesus tasted death for every man.[121] But "man" is no part of the original. Hints in the context suggest a specific meaning: the beneficiaries are the sons whom God will lead to glory, those "sanctified," whom Christ calls his brothers in the *ekklèsia* (ἐκκλησία); in verse 16 the writer expressly distinguishes categories for whom Christ did and did not intervene: not for angels, but *for Abraham's seed*—the equivalence for "the elect." Allen also mentions 2 Corinthians 5:14, and Gary L. Shultz, Jr., develops the argument: "That the word 'all' refers to all people, and not just believers, is clear from how Paul distinguishes the 'all' from 'they who live' in 2 Cor. 5:15."[122] Leaving aside other remarks, it is surprising that Shultz does not see a simple solution, which Fuller had provided long ago: "My answer is, that, upon *my* hypothesis [definite atonement], Christ died for more than actually live at any period of time; part of them being, at every period, in a

---

[120] Albert Schweitzer, *La Mystique de l'apôtre Paul*, trans. M. Gueritot (Paris: Albin Michel, 1962), 57.

[121] Allen, "Atonement: Limited or Universal?," 97 n. 110.

[122] Gary L. Shultz, Jr., "Why a Genuine Universal Gospel Call Requires an Atonement That Paid for the Sins of All People," *EQ* 82.2 (2010): 116 n. 21.

state of unregeneracy."[123] They who lived when Paul was writing were not *all* the believers for whom Christ died. The import of the verses that seem to prove that Christ died for reprobates, 2 Peter 2:1 and Hebrews 10:29, is relativized by the fact that such precise language is used only for *apostates*. This opens the possibility: "as they claim," or, "as implied by the official status they enjoyed as baptized members of the church." Finally, an observation weakens the advantage Hypothetical Universalism draws from the "fullness" texts: the "all" note is struck with about the same force and frequency in statements about the cross and in statements about application, life conferred, and ultimate destiny. Romans 5:18, for example, speaks of justification actually accruing to all, not a mere offer or availability. Hypothetical Universalism leads one to expect another scheme: all at the cross, some only in application.

Regarding passages that mention a specific category of beneficiaries—Christ gave himself for his church, etc.—Allen warns against "the negative inference fallacy."[124] Fair enough. Nevertheless, the tendential logic that springs from such rather favors definite atonement. "For us" is vague, and hardly decides the point. But some contexts provide interesting hints. The Good Shepherd allegory (John 10) does not only mention that he gives his life for his sheep (vv. 11, 15). Almost polemically, it delimits the category of these sheep: they are his own (ἴδια, repeated), whom he calls individually by name (v. 3), and who distinguish themselves from others by responding to *his* voice (v. 5), who are also found in the other "fold," the nations (v. 16), and of whom he severely tells the Jewish leaders, "you are not . . . my sheep" (v. 26)—with such an emphasis in the whole discourse, the declaration "I lay down my life for the sheep" takes on a particular resonance.

Piecemeal exegesis does not yield a clear-cut answer to the choice between definite atonement and Hypothetical Universalism. The evidence must be "digested" by *theological* reflection. Scripture remains *norma normans*, but must be intelligently taken as a structured whole.

(2) The Love of the Triune God and the Invitation He Extends

Among the motives of Hypothetical Universalism, the desire to magnify the love of God for all his creatures is prominent. It is reflected in the universal

[123] Fuller, *Works*, 252b (letter XII).
[124] Allen, "Atonement: Limited or Universal?," 93.

call, "Come to me and you shall be saved." The love for all was expressed though the gift of Christ for all, and thus, payment having been made for all, the offer can be brought to all. Definite atonement looks like a denial of this maximum generosity. If the gift was not for all, God does not love all, and since the payment was not made for all, how can the offer be sincere?

Some of the Reformed, it seems, have denied the universal love of God. Though they could quote verses such as Psalm 5:5 and "Esau I have hated" (Mal. 1:3), their denial is so opposed to the drift of Scripture and the "analogy of faith" that I rule it out of court. The vast majority of definite atonement theologians have firmly held to the doctrine of the love of God extending to the non-elect, as a beautiful article by Andrew Swanson expounds (based on R. L. Dabney, W. T. Shedd, and John Howe).[125] The real issue is whether God loves all individuals with identical love, in which case one could expect the atonement to be intended indiscriminately for each and every one. Paul Helm summarizes the logic of John McLeod Campbell and J. B. Torrance on the topic (whom he criticizes): "Any attribute necessary to God is necessarily exercised by God equally on all of whom it is logically possible to exercise it."[126] This deprives God of his freedom. Equalitarian love smacks of humanism. Bavinck already denounced "a petit-bourgeois love, against which Nietzsche rightly fulminated."[127] God's free election implies a difference between the love for the ones and the love for the others. Donald Macleod notes that "Reformed theology has never excluded such language as that Christ died for all men or that God loves all men. But it has insisted that there is a special love which has not only 'redeemed all men, on condition that they believe,' but has also resolved to bestow that very faith itself."[128] Packer coins memorable aphorisms: "God loves all in some ways" and "God loves some in all ways."[129] This could not be denied even on Arminian grounds.

We must, however, sharpen the issue. Should we speak of a universal salvific will? And if we should, does it require a universal extent, *pro omnibus et singulis*, of the atonement? The love of God for all also refers to their ultimate salvation. Such statements as Ezekiel 18:32 and 2 Peter 3:9

---

[125] Andrew Swanson, "The Love of God for the Non-Elect," *Reformation Today* 51 (May–June 1976): 2–13.
[126] Paul Helm, "The Logic of Limited Atonement," *SBET* 3.2 (Autumn 1985): 53.
[127] Bavinck, *Sin and Salvation in Christ*, 469 n. 144.
[128] Macleod, "*Amyraldus redivivus*," 218.
[129] J. I. Packer, "The Love of God: Universal and Particular," in *The Grace of God and the Bondage of the Will. Volume 2: Historical and Theological Perspectives on Calvinism*, ed. Thomas R. Schreiner and Bruce A. Ware (Grand Rapids, MI: Baker Books, 1995), 419.

(an implicit restriction to the elect is little likely) declare such a will. Yet other texts seem to say the opposite (1 Sam. 2:25 in an old book and 1 Pet. 2:8 in a foundational epistle). Since God, the *auctor primarius*, does not contradict himself, we must distinguish two senses of "will." I choose to speak of God's will of *desire* (which also generates his precepts), and God's will of *decree*. The inescapable teaching of Scripture is this: God "desires" that all enter Life, but he "decrees" that some will not. This decree is *permissive*: God (in whose hand is even the king's heart; Prov. 21:1) moves no creature to anti-God dispositions; the creature misuses created freedom against the fountain of all goodness, and bears the guilt; yet, God remains sovereign (Eph. 1:11), and therefore the creature's refusal to repent is (permissively) part of the divine design.

"This is a hard teaching. Who can accept it?" The permissive character of the sovereign decision over the "vessels of wrath" makes it possible for it to coexist with the salvific "desire" and universal love. Yet, it is no rational solution. I cannot understand why the Lord of lords so decides about men and women he loves. I have argued elsewhere that this mystery must remain opaque, a thorn in the flesh of our reason, *the* occasion for humble trust. The riddle is the riddle of evil, and adherents of both definite atonement and Hypothetical Universalism must face it, in humble trust.

If the divine will is twofold, what is the consequence for the atonement? Does a similar duality affect it? Actually Shultz stresses the plurality of intentions. He argues, "Paul's gospel ministry can certainly be motivated both by God's general intentions in the atonement for all people, as well as his particular, salvific intentions for the elect."[130] For him, the universal intention, and actual transaction, required the "payment of the penalty for all the sins of every person who has ever lived."[131] But this is not obvious. First Timothy 4:10, *the* verse which expressly points to a twofold salvific function of God's saving work, does *not* distinguish between the "hypothetical" provision for all and "actual" communication to believers only, but between two kinds, or levels, of benefits. The immediate context, from verse 7b, introduces the duality: bodily exercise does bring some profit—we could speak of a temporal "salvation"—but the exercise of godliness is

---

[130] Shultz, "Why a Genuine Universal Gospel Call," 118 n. 28 (his PhD dissertation was written in defense of a "Multi-Intentioned View of the Extent of the Atonement").
[131] Gary L. Shultz, Jr., "God's Purposes in the Atonement for the Nonelect," *BSac* 165.658 (April–June 2008): 147; cf. "Why a Genuine Universal Gospel Call," 122.

fruitful at both levels, earthly and (Paul could have said) μάλιστα heavenly. Paul does not restrict the benefits of godliness to the higher level, since some affect also life in the body. The duality obtains with God the Father's saving work: it secures the goods of present life *for all* (common grace rooted in the cross), and life of the coming age *for believers only*.[132] The adverb μάλιστα cannot signify the difference between potential and actual.[133] The verse neither rules out the Hypothetical Universalism proposition nor supports it.

(3) Three "Knots" in the Debate on Definite Atonement

I see three "knots" in this debate. The first one relates to Trinitarian harmony within the economy of salvation, from the Father's design to the Spirit's work among humankind. The second one focuses on the conditions required for a genuinely universal offer of salvation. The third, less often discussed, deals with the possibility of this personal assurance: "Christ died for *me*" (see Gal. 2:20).

Trinitarian Harmony

The argument of Trinitarian harmony has been put forward in favor of definite atonement. The Father decided to save only the elect; the Spirit regenerates only the elect; consistency leads one to expect that Christ died redemptively only for the elect. Recently, however, Hypothetical Universalism advocates have used the argument, in boomerang fashion, against definite atonement, emphasizing the universal salvific will of the Father. Shultz claims that the Spirit reaching out to unbelievers, convicting the *world* (John 16:7–11), shows that the reference is to all.[134] He quotes from Robert P. Lightner: "The Holy Spirit's work could not reach out beyond the elect if the death of Christ did not have this universal scope since the Spirit's ministry was procured in and through the cross."[135] This dependence is clearer, however, for the

---

[132] Turretinus, *Institutio theologiae elencticae*, II[a], locus XIV, qu. 14,14 (p. 405), refers to Acts 17:28 and Psalm 36:6 for the wider and lower meaning of "salvation" for all, and cites Chrysostom, Œcumenius, Primasius, Ambrosius, and Thomas Aquinas in favor of this understanding. Thomas R. Schreiner, in the present volume, follows another path. His argument, that "Savior" (etc.) always refers to final salvation in the Pastoral Epistles does carry weight but is not decisive: the NT obviously focuses on life eternal (the predominance of the higher meaning is *thematic* rather than *lexical*). It does not rule out the weaker meaning, which belonged to contemporary usage, if clues are found in the context that favor it. This, I argue, is the case.

[133] See Vern S. Poythress, "The Meaning of μάλιστα in 2 Timothy 4:13 and Related Verses," *JTS* 53 (2002): 523–32.

[134] Shultz, "Why a Genuine Universal Gospel Call," 118–19.

[135] Ibid., 120 (the reference given is to Robert P. Lightner, *The Death Christ Died: A Biblical Case for Unlimited Atonement*, 2nd ed. [Grand Rapids, MI: Kregel, 1998], 130).

regenerating work of the Spirit than in the case of impenitent unbelievers. The "conviction" (ἐλέγχειν, to convict) of John 16:8–11 is the judicial demonstration of the world's guilt (NEB: "confute"), not the persuasion that leads to faith.

All could agree that a duality harmoniously affects the roles of Father, Son, and Spirit. The Father, in his benevolence, desires the salvation of all, but he decrees the salvation of some only. (Why so? The opaque mystery of his permission of evil, in this case of the evil of final impenitence.) The Spirit does move among all human beings and exerts pressure on their consciences (e.g., through miracles, Matt. 12:28–32); he only regenerates the elect of the Father. The incarnate Son dies "in some sense" for all, and ensures that the offer of salvation be extended to all; the connection made in Scripture between his death and his church, or his sheep, warrants saying that he dies in a particular sense for his own; they only enjoy the life he gained for them, as the Father has decreed and the Spirit applies. The decisive issue is whether the sense ("some sense") in which Christ died for all requires the "payment of the penalty for all the sins of every person who has ever lived."[136] This tenet of Hypothetical Universalism thins down the difference between the sense "for all" and the "particular" sense in the Son's case, while it cannot do so for the Father's will and the Spirit's work.

Universal Offer

The last named weakness shall not prove too embarrassing if the core proposition receives adequate vindication: universal offer requires a payment *pro omnibus et singulis*. The universal offer is not, for us, in dispute.[137] Proclaiming that it would be void without such a payment may be intimidating, but it certainly falls short of proof.[138] Roger Nicole has shown that in human affairs, for example, when a firm advertises an offer, the "provision" need not be equal to the amount which would be distributed if *all* asked for the thing. Coextensive provision is no obligation, neither assistance to render people able to accept—with disability "self-induced."[139] There is one "essential prerequisite": that the thing offered be actually granted if the terms

---

[136] Shultz's wording, "God's Purposes," 147.
[137] Note with Cunningham, *Historical Theology, Volume II*, 344, that "hyper-Calvinists" did not refuse universal call because of "limited atonement."
[138] Norman F. Douty, *The Death of Christ: A Treatise Which Answers the Question: "Did Christ Die Only for the Elect?"* (Swengel, PA: Reiner, 1972), 35–37, expresses it with trenchant force (quoting from Ussher and Davenant).
[139] Nicole, "Covenant, Universal Call," 408–409.

be observed.[140] So with definite atonement: whosoever will may come and shall be saved—without any exception.

The difficulty Hypothetical Universalism defenders denounce looks more psychological than analytical. One *feels* that God cannot "sincerely" offer Judas or Jezebel a cancellation of their debts as a benefit from the cross, if the price was not paid for them on the cross. But the same difficulty arises when one thinks that God offers Judas or Jezebel (code names for any non-elect individuals) something they are unable to get, since they are unable to repent. God has decided not to operate repentance in their hearts—this truth, Reformed theologians who hold to Hypothetical Universalism acknowledge. (And God has foreknown with absolute certainty that Judas and Jezebel will not repent.[141])

At the same time, defenders of definite atonement, when they stress, as Fuller did, that the cross makes all the required provision for the universal offer have hardly elucidated the *how*.[142] Is it enough to appeal to our ignorance of who is elect to justify an indiscriminate call? For God who knows invites all.

What about Christ's death and *this* individual? Telling someone "Jesus Christ died for your sins," Nicole candidly specifies, is "not strictly legitimate unless there is some assurance that the people involved are in fact among the elect."[143] Shultz grows indignant: "part of the gospel is telling an unbeliever that 'Christ died for you.'"[144] He argues that Paul includes "Christ died for our sins" in the summary of what he preached to the Corinthians as unbelievers.[145] This carries little weight, since Paul does not reproduce the wording, *verbatim*, he had used in evangelism; and if he said "for us" then, it may have meant his team and anyone who would join them. Critics can go even further: how can *I* seek refuge in Christ if I am not sure he died for me? The direct connection was precious for the apostle (Gal. 2:20), or for Pascal, who could hear Jesus telling him, "I was thinking of you in my agony; I shed such drops of my blood for you."[146] Does one need Hypothetical Universalism thus to bind a given individual to the Savior?[147]

---

[140] Ibid., 409–10.
[141] Fuller, *Works*, 229b, 248a, 249b, highlighted the import of divine foreknowledge.
[142] See Nettles's acute critique, *By His Grace and for His Glory*, 305–307.
[143] Nicole, "Covenant, Universal Call," 410.
[144] Shultz, "Why a Genuine Universal Gospel Call," 115 n. 18.
[145] Ibid., 114–15.
[146] In "le Mystère de Jésus," *Pensées* (Brunschvicg § 553).
[147] In Pascal's case, of course, the statement could be interpreted of a Jansenist *particular* reference of Christ's atoning death.

Two considerations should quieten emotions regarding the way to tell the gospel. In the looser sense, many definite atonement defenders have accepted "Christ died for all," and, so, *for you*. On the other hand, nowhere do we see the apostles use this form of words when addressing unbelievers. On rigorous definite atonement grounds, it is adequate to tell anyone, "Christ invites you: 'Come to me'; if you do so, you will find that he paid for your sins on the cross, and thus lifted your condemnation for ever." Not an awful distance! Could one legitimatize "Christ died for you" through the idea of presumptive election? Actually, Pascal framed such a thesis:

> All men in the world are under obligation . . . to believe that they belong to the small number of the Elect for whose salvation Jesus Christ died and to think the same of each of the men who are living on earth, however wicked and godless they be, so long as there remains in them a fragment of life—leaving to God's inscrutable secret the discernment between Elect and reprobate.[148]

Personal Assurance

How to reach personal assurance is a delicate issue. It is not bound to the extent of the atonement. As the Reformers warned, as soon as one starts speculating on one's election, one stands on the brink of a deadly abyss. There is no fixed point apart from faith in Christ. Only by looking to him can we overcome the "temptation of predestination." Assurance is consubstantial with the very movement of faith, casting ourselves upon his mercy. This is valid for Amyraut as it is for Owen (and for Arminius). Concerning the link with the atonement, Turretin's analysis is noteworthy for clarity and precision. Faith unfolds in two stages, and "Christ is not revealed and promised in the Gospel as having died for me in particular but only generally [*tantum in genere*] for those who believe and repent."[149] The first moment, faith in Christ as a response to his invitation (*refugio ad Christum*), does not yet include the assurance that he died *for me*; this comes at the next stage, as a reflex act of faith (*actu fidei reflexo et secundario*).[150] Such an account proceeds from the truth that "Christ died for all who believe and repent [*pro omnibus credentibus et poenentibus mortuus est*]," and applies it.[151]

---

[148] In Lucien Goldmann, *Le Dieu caché: Etude sur la vision tragique dans les* Pensées *de Pascal et dans le théâtre de Racine* (Paris: NRF Gallimard, 1955), 324, from *Deux pièces imparfaites sur la Grâce et le concile de Trente* (Paris: Vrin, 1947), 31.
[149] Turretinus, *Institutio theologiae elencticae*, II^a, locus XIV, qu. 14,46 (p. 419).
[150] Ibid., qu. 14,50 et 49 (pp. 421 and 420).
[151] Ibid., qu. 14,51 (p. 421).

Asking about the "for me" of the cross draws attention to the fine point: is the *intention* of the act or sacrifice an essential part of the act or sacrifice? In the "Conversation" Fuller stages on particular redemption (Conversation III), "Peter" includes the intention (*for whom*, precisely, did Christ die?) within the *nature* of the atonement, whereas "James" locates the intention of making the atonement effectual for some in *application*, in God's design as to application.[152] We should, as a rule, mark off intention *about* an action from the intention *of* the said action. When something is accomplished and no precise object specified, the use that may be made (or not) of its fruit does not belong to its nature. But the intention *to do* what one does constitutes the very soul of the act, without which it would no longer be an act. Between those two poles, what of Christ's atonement? Christ's self-sacrifice is meant for the benefit of others; bearing sins as a substitute seems to imply the reference to beneficiaries as essential to the act. Fuller prefers a less direct relationship and, though he maintains "particular redemption," sees the intention of the atonement as such a satisfaction of justice that will make possible the universal offer of salvation and application to the elect.[153] Does it account for the language of Scripture? The question engages our next two topics: arguments about "double payment" and "sufficiency."

(4) Does Hypothetical Universalism Involve Unacceptable "Double Payment"?

Supporters of definite atonement have objected to Hypothetical Universalism, whether Amyraldian or "English," that it implies *double payment* in the case of reprobates, something unworthy of divine justice. If Christ paid the legal debt of Judas/Jezebel, and God, at the last judgment, demands it from them, and sends them to punishment that they should pay for their sins—this is not right. Augustus M. Toplady's "Faith Reviving," expresses the argument in poetic terms:

Complete atonement Thou hast made
And to the utmost farthing paid
Whate'er Thy people owed.
Nor can God's wrath on me take place

---

[152] Fuller, *Works*, 314b, 315a, 316b.
[153] Similarly Hodge, *Systematic Theology*, 2:555: "The secret purpose of God in providing such a substitute for man, has nothing to do with the nature of his work."

When sheltered 'neath Thy righteousness
And covered by Thy blood.

If Thou my pardon hast secured
And freely in my room endured
The whole of wrath divine,
Payment God cannot twice demand
First from my bleeding Surety's hand
And then *again* from mine.[154]

The argument has been the target of vehement criticism. Allen brings against it a threefold charge: "it confuses a pecuniary (commercial) debt and penal satisfaction for sin"; it ignores that "the elect are still under the wrath of God until they believe (Eph. 2:4)"; and "it negates the principle of grace in the application of the atonement—nobody is *owed* the application."[155] In his view, "John Owen falsely understood redemption to involve literal payment to God so that atonement itself secures its own application. . . . He has distorted and thus contradicted Scripture . . ."[156]

Allen's second and third objections attack a caricature of the "double payment" argument: Christ's payment itself being of grace, grace reigns! Within an Owenic framework, however, other dimensions of reconciliation may be associated to "payment" and suspend the enjoyment of its benefits; this raises no logical problem if, in the end, all dimensions (legal, personal) concord. But there is a serious problem if they do not, if Judas's debt was paid and yet he refuses reconciliation (Hypothetical Universalism). Since the fruit of Christ's atonement is found *in him*, the Mediator and Head of his people, there is nothing incongruous if union with him is the condition of enjoyment, and "the elect are still under the wrath of God until they believe." He who paid is "owed" the application: *he* has the right to raise from their spiritual death those who were given to him by the Father (John 6:37, 39; 17:6, 9, 12); the application is *his* reward, the fruit of the "labor of his soul," and he can claim the "satisfaction" of freely justifying them (Isa. 53:11)—this perspective is fairer to definite atonement logic.

Is the pecuniary, debtor-creditor, scheme inadequate? This complaint is shared by Fuller, and by Hodge in biting words: "an entire mistake or mis-

---

[154] Quoted by J. I. Packer, "Sacrifice and Satisfaction," in *Our Savior God: Studies on Man, Christ, and the Atonement*, ed. James M. Boice (Grand Rapids, MI: Baker, 1980), 137 (emphasis added).
[155] Allen, "Atonement: Limited or Universal?," 83.
[156] Ibid., 89.

representation of the attribute of justice, to which, according to Augustinians, the satisfaction of Christ is rendered."[157]

Note the locus of dissent. Theologians in Owen's line (Owen himself, thrice cited by Fuller, as we saw) have repudiated a literal understanding of the payment made; the intrinsic value of Christ's offering explodes any book-keeping attempt. The real issue is the import of the payment metaphor and whether it creates a problem for Hypothetical Universalism in the "Judas/ Jezebel" case. I find it worrying that a main language of Scripture for guilt and atonement be summarily dismissed. Metaphors are not to be pressed unduly, but neither are they to be despised; they cognitively guide interpretation. This language "translates" easily in sacrificial and judicial languages.[158] Can we drive a wedge between "commercial" and judicial languages in Scripture? Debtors incur condemnation; if unable to satisfy the demands of their creditors, they become slaves and suffer imprisonment—the condition of sinners under the law (Gal. 3:23; cf. Matt. 18:30). Reciprocally, fines are inflicted as penalties. "Ransom" evokes both pecuniary and judicial images. The double payment argument can be stated in judicial terms, and so it is by Cunningham.[159] A righteous judge will not inflict twice the penalty which a given crime has deserved.

How do Hypothetical Universalism advocates deal with the argument, set on the judicial plane? They follow John Davenant, who affirmed that it was in God's power "to annex conditions" and illustrated his thought with the parable of the king whose son would discharge the debt of traitors; he would stipulate "that none should be absolved or liberated except those only who should acknowledge the King's Son for their Lord and serve him"; nobody would object to rebels being punished, "because the payment . . . was or-dained to procure remission for every one under the condition of obedience, and not otherwise."[160] Turretin replied that it was a lame argument, because a human "Prince, even if it be his most ardent wish, cannot give to the prisoner the will to apply the ransom to himself—and this Christ can."[161] Davenant's "conditions annexed" sound attractive because they correspond to the way

---

[157] Hodge, *Systematic Theology*, 2:554. Cf. 557: the mistake "arises from confounding a pecuniary and a judicial satisfaction."
[158] I worked on atonement metaphors in my "Biblical Metaphors and the Doctrine of the Atonement," *JETS* 47.4 (December 2004): 629–45.
[159] Cunningham, *Historical Theology, Volume II*, 352–57.
[160] Quoted by Allen, "Atonement: Limited or Universal?," 84–85.
[161] Turretinus, *Institutio theologiae elencticae*, II[a], locus XIV, qu. 14,33 (p. 413).

things go among humankind: among men the decision of beneficiaries happens outside the grace afforded, but not so with *God's* grace!

Is it conceivable that God/Christ should pay for the sins of Judas and Jezebel, and yet leave them to their (self-induced) inability to meet the condition of faith, while he could create faith in them? Maybe, though it is harder than simply offering forgiveness to them. But then, three issues must be explored. The first one, on the conditions for substitution, we consider later. The second one is whether scriptural data on atonement, and the role of faith, warrant the "annexed conditions" concept. The third one is whether one can still say that Christ judicially paid for all the sins of the finally lost.

Christ is the Author, through his death, of a perfect salvation. His finished work takes away the sin of the world, a world "reconciled." Objective redemption lacks nothing. Do not "annexed conditions" take away from fullness? Something else must be done, in addition to what Christ did, that the person be saved. This remains even if the condition is met by a divine gift, as long as this gift is not secured by the atonement itself. Calling it "application" is slightly misleading: it is the subject's contribution, added to Christ's, which causes the application of saving benefits. Does anyone, Hypothetical Universalism advocates will reply, deny the condition of faith?[162] Definite atonement supporters affirm the condition of faith, but since it is secured, and thus made certain (not immediate), by Christ's death, it is not added as another condition and does not detract from completeness. Faith is no additional efficient cause (required by annexed conditions), but strictly instrumental. Application is only application.

Can Hypothetical Universalism maintain that Christ paid for *all* the sins of all humans? Judas's or Jezebel's final hardening is not included, being the ground of their condemnation. In Davenant's illustration, the rebels are punished mainly because of their later disobedience, for which the king's son had *not* paid the price. Allen strongly rejects the charge, and quotes from Neil Chambers: Owen is guilty of "polemical reductionism," "for unbelief is not just an offense like any other, it is also a state, which must be dealt with not only by forgiveness but by regeneration," and the latter bears only indirect relation to the cross.[163] Is this to the point? Inasmuch as unbelief is also a sin, whatever else it may be, its condemnation implies either the legal problem

---

[162] Barthians, of course, tend to do so (with some ambiguities), since they wish to maintain the fullness of reconciliation.
[163] Allen, "Atonement: Limited or Universal?," 88.

of double payment (penalty), or that no payment had been made for it on the cross. Amyraldians give the impression that they conceive of the payment for the sins of this or that individual as somehow "suspended" in mid-air until the gift of faith makes it effectively "for" this individual; yet they say, in agreement with Scripture, that payment was actually made for sinners on the cross. The tension is serious, near the heart of Hypothetical Universalism.

Shultz correctly understands "reconcile" in Colossians 1 (NIV): "Those in hell will be reconciled in that they will no longer be able to rebel against God and because they will acknowledge Jesus for who He is."[164] He then claims, "In order for Christ to reconcile all things to the Father, He had to pay for all sin, including the sins of the nonelect. Otherwise some sin would be outside His atoning work and thus outside His cosmic triumph."[165] Presumably, Shultz would not advance that Jesus Christ bore the sins of the fallen angels (principalities, etc.), and, therefore his cosmic triumph does not require his payment for the sins of all his enemies. Reconciliation in Colossians 1 (restoration of order, pacification) involves satisfaction of justice, payment for sin, but Shultz misses that the everlasting punishment of impenitent sinners *is* the satisfaction of justice; in Matthew 5:25–26, Jesus warns about it in terms of payment: to "the last penny."

(5) Is "Sufficiency" Sufficient?

"Sufficiency," since Peter Lombard, has been used by all parties; but has it helped to make them more lucid? Allen, as already quoted, is right: "The debate over the nature of this sufficiency is *the key debate* in the extent question."[166] It has been combined with slippery concepts such as "possibility" and "ability." Sloppy logic has sometimes muddied waters. For example, Lewis Sperry Chafer writes of the atonement, "It is *actual* as to its *availability*, but *potential* as to its *application*."[167] This reader finds himself in wonderland, for application means that a benefit becomes *actual* in experience, and availability, as the suffix *-ability* indicates, regards what is virtual or *potential*! Analysis should dispel deceptive haziness.

Is Christ's atonement sufficient for all? "To suffice" for something means

---

[164] Shultz, "God's Purposes," 157.
[165] Ibid.
[166] Allen, "Atonement: Limited or Universal?," 66.
[167] Lewis Sperry Chafer, "For Whom Did Christ Die?," *BSac* 137.548 (October–December 1980 [reprint of 1948 article]): 316.

to provide in a situation all the factors that will bring about the "something." If A is sufficient for B, when A, then B. If, A being present, B does not happen, we say that A was not sufficient for B. Is Christ's atonement sufficient for the salvation of all? Allen complains that for Carson "sufficiency" means only "that Christ's death *could have* satisfied the sins [*sic*] of all unbelievers had that been God's intention."[168] Yes, we should more sharply distinguish between *intrinsic value* and *sufficiency* proper. But is sufficiency better established with Hypothetical Universalism? Hardly. A is there, and B does not follow: atonement was made, we are told, for Judas and Jezebel (A), and yet, they are not saved (B does not follow). Even for John and Priscilla, who are saved, the "annexed condition" of faith had to be added: A was not entirely sufficient.[169] We come near that "insufficient sufficiency" which Pascal mocked in his second Provincial letter, the mongrel concept Thomists had forged to distance themselves from Jansenists and please Jesuits.[170]

Advocates of definite atonement have been most concerned by the lack of a sufficient provision in the Hypothetical Universalism scheme—"provision" being a mixture of actuality and possibility. Nicole recalls Loraine Boettner's simile: the definite atonement bridge is narrower, but it does bring you across the river; the Hypothetical Universalism bridge is very broad, but it is not long enough (sufficient) to reach the other side. Nicole, with delightful humor, compared the wider bridge to a famous bridge in France: "the only thing it is good for is dancing."[171] He was alluding to the Saint-Bénézet bridge in Avignon, which goes only halfway over the river Rhône, and to the old folk song: "Sur le pont d'Avignon, on y danse, on y danse." What do reprobates lose with definite atonement compared with Hypothetical Universalism? As to the elect, the advantage of definite atonement is manifest. The atonement is sufficient for their salvation, since it made certain the gift of faith.

The same obtains with parallel categories. Hypothetical Universalism discourse asserts that Christ's death made salvation *possible* or *available*: "All living people are in a saveable state because there is blood sufficiently shed for them (Heb. 9:22)."[172] Definite atonement supporters find this lan-

---

168 Allen, "The Atonement: Limited or Universal?," 90.

169 Nettles, *By His Grace and for His Glory*, 311, writes, "The third misinterpretation of 'sufficient' consists of an apparent necessity of separating objectivity from effectuality in order to maintain the concept of sufficiency for the whole world."

170 Pascal, *Lettres écrites à un Provincial* (Paris: Librairie de Paris, 1933), esp. 13 (whole letter 12–23).

171 Roger R. Nicole, "Particular Redemption," in *Our Savior God*, 168–69. Cf. Bavinck, *Sin and Salvation in Christ*, 467 (§ 405): "In logic there is the rule: 'The greater its extent, the weaker the grasp.'"

172 Allen, "Atonement: Limited or Universal?," 64; "possible" (65), "savable" (66).

guage far below the biblical mark. Christ is not the Author of the possibility of salvation, but of salvation indeed! Hodge shared their concern: "So the righteousness of Christ did not make the salvation of men merely possible, it secured the actual salvation of those for whom He wrought."[173] "Owen's burden," Macleod discerns, "is not that the cross avails only for a few, but that the cross actually saves, in the full sense of the word."[174] Contrary to current labels, definite atonement is intended as a defense of *unlimited* atonement— unlimited in its import and efficacy!

Talk of "possibility" is not innocent. Possibility is no self-evident notion, and nurtures sophistry. Taken absolutely, according to Aristotelian genealogy, it is pagan; incompatible with biblical monotheism. There is a scriptural way to construe and handle the category, but how delicate! In what sense is any event "possible" if God did not decree it? In what sense is the salvation of the non-elect "possible" if it has been absolutely certain from the foundation of the world that they shall not be saved? Questions to ponder.

After reviewing debates on "double payment" and "sufficiency," I acknowledge it as wisdom to keep the nature and intent of the atonement tightly connected: the atonement's value and efficacy must not be conceived in abstraction from the "for whom" dimension in God's design.

IV. Christ the Redeemer Lamb as *the* Man

The objections leveled at Hypothetical Universalism may leave unaffected the feeling that a particular atonement is a dubious foundation for a universal offer. The articulation between the two must be brought to light if definite atonement is to carry full conviction.

Jesus Christ died as the Substitute. But *how* could he substitute *validly*, in compliance with the principles of justice that express God's own righteousness? It is not self-evident. In Davenant's illustration, the king's son pays for the traitors. We should not accept this element too easily, as if it raised no problem. *The voluntary character of the vicarious payment does not warrant brushing the problem aside—precisely because the matter is not pecuniary, but judicial.* The problem is with the Judge: will not the Judge of all the earth do right and refuse to treat the righteous one as if he were a criminal (Gen. 18:25)? Scripture nowhere teaches that any individual might substitute for

---

[173] Hodge, *Systematic Theology*, 2:552.
[174] Macleod, *"Amyraldus redivivus,"* 219.

any individual under condemnation. Scripture rules out such a violation of justice (Deut. 24:16; Jer. 31:29–30; Ezekiel 18). The Socinian objection to penal substitution is not deprived of force.

Jesus *did not* die as any individual instead of other individuals. Scripture affirms individual responsibility but also a *community* dimension of human life, with consequences for justice. Scripture reveals a specific structure among humankind that was inadequately described as "corporate personality" and which I call community *headship*.[175] Individuals are members of one another; their being joined together produces entities that enjoy a significant degree of organic unity: one individual, no *mere* individual, expresses that unity and acts for the body. The *Head* recapitulates the reality of the group. This grounds a legitimate judicial transfer. The Head takes responsibility for the body. The structure is found at various levels, with the organic bond stronger or weaker, and therefore the prerogatives of headship more or less conspicuous. The law takes into account substitution. In the marriage community, Numbers 30:15[16] spells out that the husband, the head of the community, may have to *bear his wife's sin*, the phrase for undergoing the penalty; similarly, parents for children, kings for people. Christ validly substituted for sinners because such a structure made it valid.

The witness fills the Bible. Christ offered himself as the Shepherd for *his* sheep, the King for *his* people, the Master for *his* friends, the Head for *his* body, the Bridegroom for *his* bride, the New and the Last Adam for *his* new creation and new humanity. Turretin stressed that Christ acted both as our Pledge (*Vas*) and our Head (*Caput*), and these should not be separated; and neither should his death and his resurrection: he had to die as our Pledge and rose again as our Head.[176] Thomas Aquinas, already, and though his idea of satisfaction is different, answered the difficulty "he who sinned must satisfy" (no transfer) by the proposition, "the Head and the members are assimilated to [*sunt quasi*] one mystical person. Therefore, the satisfaction of Christ belongs to all believers as his members."[177]

This insight is difficult to square with Hypothetical Universalism, and one spots a tension with Fuller's insistence that Christ's death, considered irrespective of "the appointment of God, with regard to its application," was

---

[175] Cf. my sketch in Henri A. G. Blocher, *Original Sin: Illuminating the Riddle*, NSBT (Leicester, UK: Apollos, 1997), 96–99.
[176] Turretinus, *Institutio theologiae elencticae*, II^a, locus XIV, qu. 14,20 (p. 407).
[177] Thomas Aquinas, *Summa Theologiae*, III^a, qu. 48, art. 2, first difficulty and solution *ad primum* (my translation).

578 DEFINITE ATONEMENT IN THEOLOGICAL PERSPECTIVE

"for men, not as elect or non-elect, but as *sinners*,"[178] and, whereas Christ "did undergo the whole curse of the law, and wrath of God due to sin," it was only "made a *price* for them" in God's further design.[179] If Christ's headship is constitutive for his role, how can the sufficiency of his work be abstracted from it? What is this "sin," in Fuller's sentence, against which the wrath of God was discharged? Scripture says that he bore *our* sins, and *our* iniquities were laid upon him. The "price paid" metaphor refers to the transaction itself, not to later application. In the wake of Witsius, Cunningham perspicaciously observed that substitution under capital punishment, *pro aliquo mori* (dying for somebody else), is "enervated" if no precise class be in view.[180] Though Fuller did *not* teach Grotius's "rectoral" theory of the atonement, did he make one step in that fatal direction? The rectoral doctrine offers misleading talk of sin being punished, since it denies the transfer of our sins on Christ—there was no sin on the Crucified to punish. God mounted on the cross a pedagogical show, *against* justice. Evangelical theology should steer clear of "rectoral" associations and focus on Christ the legitimate Substitute, since he is the Shepherd, the King, the Master, the Head, the Bridegroom, the New Adam.

At this juncture, a new dawn of understanding is breaking on our horizon and reveals aspects that meet truly biblical concerns among Fuller's and Hypothetical Universalism's supporters. Christ died as the Head of the new humanity—"humanity" suggests a rather universal scope. Considering the largest community in which the structure of headship is established, and with most radical import—the human *genus*—we may affirm both definite atonement and a universal reference. Augustine wrote of the elect, "The whole human race [*genus*] is in them."[181] Christ's headship as the New Adam grounds such propositions as these: "Man" in the generic sense (*anthrôpos*, *homo*) was redeemed on the cross; the *world* was reconciled (2 Cor. 5:19); every human being qua human being is concerned. For Christ assumed humanity. As its new Head, he was in his death, as Pilate unwittingly prophesied, *the Man* (John 19:5).

How is humanity involved? We avoid the snare of Platonic hyper-realism and we should not view humanity as an "essence" existing beyond,

[178] Fuller, *Works*, 313a (Conversation II).
[179] Ibid., 315a (Conversation III).
[180] Cunningham, *Historical Theology, Volume II*, 351–52.
[181] Augustine, *De Correptione et Gratiâ*, *NPNF*[1] 5:489. He is explaining 1 Timothy 2:4.

apart from, concrete individuals. Such a solidarity, nevertheless, such a bond of organic unity obtains between men and women, under their Head, that the singular "humanity," "humankind," or "Man" (generic sense) answers to a dimension of reality. *This* is appropriated by Jesus Christ as the new Head and Redeemer. He creates in himself Jews and Gentiles "into one new ἄνθρωπος" (Eph. 2:15; cf. 4:13). Considering the dimension of unity of humankind, he deserves to be called "the Savior of the world" (John 4:42).

The conditions of Christ's headship should be scrutinized. They are complex: the new humanity is not another humankind created *ex nihilo*; God re-creates in Christ the old. Hence we discern two main moves or stages. Incarnation: the Son entered the solidarity of flesh and blood (Heb. 2:14), he joined the Adamic race and was born of a woman, to rescue the "children" God had given him (Heb. 2:13; cf. John 6:37, 39). But he was not born "in Adam," under Adam's headship. The Spirit's miracle in his conception marked him as a New Beginning, a new Head, a new Adam—though the new creation was incipient at this stage. Scripture hints nowhere at any ontological change affecting the body of humankind as an effect of incarnation; human beings are not yet "in Christ" at this stage (cf. Rom. 16:7), and all die "in Adam." The new humanity emerges on Easter Day—second stage. The firstborn of Mary becomes the Firstborn from the dead, the Firstfruits of the new creation. All believers in him are joined to him their new Head, by the agency of his Spirit: "in Christ" they share in the new creation (2 Cor. 5:17). The new, re-created humanity inherits the titles, calling, and organic unity which belonged to the Adamic *genus*.[182]

What about those who do *not* believe? They are not "in Christ," do not bind themselves to the new Head. They die in Adam. Yet, the bond of human solidarity entails that Christ's work, since he is the Head of the *genus*, concerns them: they are called to him, to join him in the transition from old Adamic death to new creation life. Unless they espouse the movement of humanity's re-creation as recapitulated in Christ, they cut themselves off from humanity as a *genus*: they confirm for themselves the Adamic condemnation.

---

[182] This insight I see missing in Nettles's rigorous argument in *By His Grace and for His Glory*. His emphasis on a "quantitative . . . element in the atonement" (320), meaning that Christ satisfied for the exact quantity of the sins of the elect (ruling out the sins of the reprobate), since Scripture attests a *gradation* in punishments (318), does not warrant a one-to-one correspondence, through simple addition, between sins and punishment. God's justice *is* exact, but how God determines what punishment is fit for "the sin of the world" as borne by the Substitute, I do not claim to fathom. (Nettles acknowledges a difference: Christ's punishment included no remorse [319].)

Because of the complexity, two complementary perspectives are justified. From one vantage point, believers appear to be individuals escaping, through personal faith, the solidarity of the old race (Acts 2:40: "Save yourselves from this crooked generation"). From the other, unbelievers appear to be individuals refusing the new solidarity of salvation in the Head, Christ. Abraham Kuyper captured the latter in a pictorial allegory:

> If we liken mankind, thus, as it has grown up out of Adam, to a tree, then the elect are not leaves which have been plucked off from the tree that there may be braided from them a wreath for God's glory, while the tree itself is to be felled, rooted up and cast into fire; but precisely the contrary, the lost are the branches, twigs and leaves which have fallen away from the stem of mankind, while the elect alone remain attached to it. . . . what is lost is broken from the stem and loses its organic connection.[183]

This botanical image is biblical: Israel represents the whole human race, both in grace and in judgment—its figure is precisely the olive tree from which unbelievers are severed individually (Rom. 11:17–21). Israel, the vine, is assumed in Christ—"I am the vine"—and fruitless branches also are being cut off (John 15:2, 6).

Highlighting the organic dimension, the corporate character, of humanity illuminates the foundation in atonement of universal invitation, and why faith is required for enjoyment. The vision enables us to render greater justice to the "peace" theme of Scripture, the theme of the reconciliation of all things—without forgetting the "sword." Beyond quantitative, statistical, considerations,[184] "peace" is a qualitative restoration, an expression of the Good News. God's victory over evil is complete, through the blood of the cross—*Agnus Victor*!

V. Preserving the Truth of Time

Turretin's proposition is worth quoting again: "Christ is not revealed and promised in the Gospel as having died for me in particular, but only *in genere* for those who believe and repent."[185] The statement respects historical

---

[183] Abraham Kuyper, *E Voto dordraceno II*, 178, as quoted (and translated, most probably) by B. B. Warfield, "Are They Few That Be Saved?," in *Biblical and Theological Studies*, ed. Samuel G. Craig (repr. Phillipsburg, NJ: P&R, 1952), 336.

[184] We are not *obligated* to believe that the finally saved shall be few, or even a minority. Such a restriction as is found in Matthew 7:14 may apply only to the generation of contemporary Israelites (cf. Romans 11). Cf. Warfield, ibid.

[185] Turretinus, *Institutio theologiae elencticae*, II[a], locus XIV, qu. 14,46 (p. 419).

sequence. I suspect that a premature intermingling of eternal and temporal perspectives has obfuscated the meaning of definite atonement; distinguishing between them removes stumbling blocks in the way of its reception.

Orthodox theology has run the risk of undermining the significance, the "consistency," of the successive events which realize salvation in time. A tendential logic of that kind flourished when an emphasis on God's sovereignty was combined with a Platonic notion of eternity ("pure present," "for God" there is no succession, neither past nor future).[186] While Scripture reveals the antecedence of God's purpose to enhance the significance of temporal events, to protect them from nihilistic dissolution, the impression then prevailed that nothing counted but the heavenly decision. History was mere manifestation, secondary. A symptom was the doctrine of eternal justification, which a minority espoused. This tendential logic was checked by biblical adherence, and deleterious effects were minimal,[187] yet the presentation of some doctrines was weakened. Without surrendering to "process" the superiority of divine duration, we maintain the truth of time under God: differences between past and future, promise and fulfillment, not-yet-accomplished and accomplished indeed, count for God.

If we uphold the validity of historical sequence, we tell the story of atonement and avoid the appearance of restriction. The Son incarnate, *the Man*, gives himself a ransom as the Head, the Head of "the many" who will acknowledge him and join him through faith. At this stage, the reference of his substitution is not indefinite, for the qualification is well defined, but it is historically open, just as is the gospel call. Whosoever will may come and become a member of the new humanity for whom Christ fully paid the price. *Sub specie æternitatis*, the list is known to God, the names of the "firstborn" were written on heavenly tablets from the foundation of the world (Heb. 12:23; Rev. 13:8; 17:8), but this does not weaken the truth of human history[188]—all Augustinians acknowledge this for the gospel call; why not of atoning substitution?

---

[186] Cf. Henri A. G. Blocher, "Yesterday, Today, Forever: Time, Times, Eternity in Biblical Perspective," *Tyndale Bulletin* 52.2 (2001): 183–202.

[187] Barth affirms in *KD* III/2, § 47, the presence of past and future in God's eternity, but all simultaneous, without succession! Cf. Klaas Runia, *De Theologische Tijd bij Karl Barth, met name in zijn anthropologie* (Franeker, Netherlands: T. Wever, 1955), esp. 29–30 and 44–70. Runia shows that Abraham Kuyper contradicted himself on succession in eternity (237–38 n. 124); Runia himself finally renounces including succession but confesses doing so "hesitatingly" (254).

[188] God's exercise of his sovereignty should not be conceived after the model of creaturely causation. God includes in his plan, in advance, the role of created freedom. This is how it is both true that the Father has set the times and dates (Acts 1:7) and that we are to speed the coming of the Day (2 Pet. 3:12).

Conclusion

Too subtle? On rather subtle issues, subtlety is relevant—hopefully it might bring into closer fellowship minds desirous to honor the Lord and Savior of the world. May the God of peace, who through the blood of the eternal covenant brought back from the dead the Great Shepherd of the sheep, use frail considerations to lead his servants together in ways well pleasing to him.

IV

DEFINITE ATONEMENT
IN PASTORAL PRACTICE

21

Slain for the World?

THE "UNCOMFORTABILITY" OF
THE "UNEVANGELIZED" FOR A
UNIVERSAL ATONEMENT

Daniel Strange

"Worthy are you to take the scroll and to open its seals,
for you were slain, and by your blood you ransomed people for God
from every tribe and language and people and nation,
and you have made them a kingdom and priests to our God,
and they shall reign on the earth."

Revelation 5:9–11

Introduction

No doctrine is an island. With the question of the intent and extent of the atonement, we are not dealing with an atomistic or isolated doctrinal point that has no bearing on other doctrinal loci. Rather, it is a question that is one part of theologically interconnected, organic, and systemic "wholes," hierarchically ordered on various hermeneutical and theological presuppositions. These are "basic" beliefs that are cherished deeply. Given that these hermeneutical presuppositions interpret evidence before us, even the biblical evidence that we believe to be so blindingly "obvious," the danger of incommensurability between differing positions is always near, and the possibility of persuasion frustratingly distant. In such a scenario perhaps a new strategy is needed to break this stalemate and offer the possibility of breaking through the seemingly impregnable defenses of the rival position.

Those familiar with the apologetic method known as "presuppostionalism" will know that in this scenario of competing, hermetically sealed positions, which can be likened to "worldviews," the "truth" of a position can be demonstrated not by "direct" arguments which point to one's own worldview, but rather by "indirect" arguments which demonstrate the truth of one's position by pointing to fundamental flaws in the competing worldview. This is sometimes called an argument with a "transcendental" thrust, or alternatively, an argument for the "impossibility of the contrary." In this chapter, I wish to take the somewhat novel approach of applying this method, not to an *inter*-Christian/non-Christian encounter, but to the *intra*-evangelical debate on the intent and extent of the atonement. I will seek to defend a definite atonement, by demonstrating not the "impossibility" of a universal atonement but, perhaps less dramatically, the "uncomfortability" of a universal atonement. To put it more colloquially, I want to put a "stone in the shoe"[1] of those who hold to universal atonement with the aim of making them more epistemologically aware of the systemic implications of this doctrine and so to reexamine their commitment to it.

The particular "stone" I wish to use comes in the form of a question hurled at orthodox Christians throughout history, most famously by Porphyry in the third century and by John Hick in the twentieth.[2] But it is also a question asked countless times to countless "ordinary" Christians in countless apologetic contexts in between. It concerns the fate of those who never hear about Christ through no apparent fault of their own—the so-called "unevangelized." Such a question could well be called the problem of evil in its soteriological form. The "heaviness" of this stone, particularly at an emotional and pastoral level, has been too much for some to bear, especially as it has seemingly gained in weight in the last century with the increasing proximity and knowledge of other cultures and religions. Indeed it is this stone that Hick tells us was the tipping point for his paradigmatic shift in the "theology of religions," that moved him from particularist to pluralist, a "Copernican revolution" he calls all Christians to make.[3]

In no way wanting to diminish the pastoral and emotional difficulties wrapped up in the question of the unevangelized, I wish to use this question to help us answer another one: the question of the intent and extent of

---

[1] I take this phrase from Greg Koukl's book *Tactics* (Grand Rapids, MI: Zondervan, 2009), 38.
[2] Porphyry, quoted by Augustine in a letter to Deogratias, *NPNF*[1] 1:416; John Hick, *God and the Universe of Faiths* (Oxford: Oneworld, 1993), 122–23.
[3] Hick, *God and the Universe of Faiths*, 120–33.

the atonement. While the category of the unevangelized presents no "easy" answers for those who hold to definite atonement, for those who hold to universal atonement, the unevangelized present peculiar and, to my mind, insurmountable theological difficulties.

My contention is that unless proponents of universal atonement deny the *fides ex auditu* (faith comes by hearing) and embrace some form of soteriological inclusivism (with its deeply problematic ramifications for evangelical exegesis, doctrine, and mission), universal atonement is in actuality a "limited" atonement, not simply in its "quality" (in offering only the "possibility" of salvation), but also in its "quantity" or "scope." To put it a little more provocatively, for those who never hear the gospel, not only is universal or "unlimited" atonement susceptible to the claim of *not* presenting a sincere or "well-meant" offer of the gospel, but actually for this category of humanity, it makes no offer at all, thus making it "limited." As a result, further questions might be raised as to this atonement's "objective" qualitative nature[4] (especially if a "penal" rather than "governmental" theory of atonement is espoused), and ultimately of God's character and sovereignty. Christ has provided a *de jure* salvation for all, but *de facto* it is not accessible to all and is limited in its scope.

To reappropriate Hick's infamous analogy, for proponents of universal atonement, I wish to argue that the category of the unevangelized is an epicycle too far in their Ptolemaic system, and that what is called for is a "Copernican Revolution," a paradigmatic shift that embraces a definite atonement.

This chapter will be divided into two parts, reflecting my chosen apologetic methodology. First, I will present an "offensive" argument by describing and analyzing the question of the unevangelized within the sphere of universal atonement, and then, second, I will present a "defensive" argument by examining the same question within the sphere of definite atonement.

(1) The Question of the Unevangelized in Relation to a Universal Atonement

That the category of the unevangelized is an apologetic "stone in the shoe" for those who hold to universal atonement, is by no means an original argument. It is John Owen's second argument of sixteen against "the general

---

[4] That is, does Christ's cross-work *actually* procure salvation, rather than just *potentially* procure salvation?

ransom" idea in *The Death of Death in the Death of Christ*: "From the fact that the gospel, which reveals faith in Christ to be the only way of salvation, is not published to all men."[5] It is worth quoting his objection at length here:

> If the Lord intended that he should, and [he] by his death did, procure pardon of sin and reconciliation with God for all and every one, to be actually enjoyed upon condition that they do believe, then ought this good-will and intention of God, with this purchase on their behalf by Jesus Christ, to be made known to them by the word, that they might believe; "for faith cometh by hearing, and hearing by the word of God," Rom. X. 17: for if these things be not made known and revealed to all and every one that is concerned in them, namely, to whom the Lord intends, and for whom he hath procured so great a good, then one of these things will follow;—either, first, That they may be saved without faith in, and the knowledge of, Christ (which they cannot have unless he be revealed to them), which is false, and proved so; or else, secondly, That this good-will of God, and this purchase made by Jesus Christ, is plainly in vain, and frustrate in respect of them, yea, a plain mocking of them, that will neither do them any good to help them out of misery, nor serve the justice of God to leave them inexcusable, for what blame can redound to them for not embracing and well using a benefit which they never heard in their lives? Doth it become the wisdom of God to send Christ to die for men that they might be saved, and never cause these men to hear of any such thing; and yet to purpose and declare that unless they do hear of it and believe it, they shall never be saved? What wise man would pay a ransom for the delivery of those captives which he is sure shall never come to the knowledge of such payment made, and so never be better for it? Is it answerable to the goodness of God, to deal thus with his poor creatures? To hold out towards them all in pretence the most intense love imaginable, beyond all compare and illustration,—as his love in sending his Son is set forth to be,—and yet never let them know of any such thing, but in the end to damn them for not believing it? Is it answerable to the love and kindness of Christ to us, to assign to him at his death such a resolution as this:—"I will now, by the oblation of myself, obtain for all and everyone peace and reconciliation with God, redemption and everlasting salvation, eternal glory in the high heavens, even for all those poor miserable, wretched worms, condemned caitiffs, that every hour ought to expect the sentence of condemnation; and all these shall truly and really be communicated to them if they will believe. But yet, withal, I will so order things that innumerable souls shall never hear one word of all this that I have done for them, never be persuaded to believe, nor have the object of faith that is to be believed proposed to them, whereby they might indeed

---

[5] John Owen, *The Death of Death in the Death of Christ* (1684; repr., Edinburgh: Banner of Truth, 1959), 28.

possibly partake of these things?" Was this the mind and will, this the design and purpose, of our merciful high priest? God forbid.[6]

In Owen's argument a series of potential possibilities revolve around the relationship between universal provision of atonement and the question of access to that provision. If one believes that Christ died for all, but one also recognizes that some do not have access to this knowledge, then there is a tension created which can only be resolved theologically in two ways, both of which, for Owen at least, are unthinkable. On the one hand, either people can actually be saved without hearing about Christ (which he does not even entertain as a possibility), or, on the other hand, the atonement must be construed in such a way that both the character of God and the unity of the economy of the Godhead is questioned—"that this good-will of God, and this purchase made by Jesus Christ, is plainly in vain." We will explore both of these consequences starting with the second one first.

A) The Importance of Demonstrating Universal Accessibility in the Defense of a Universal Atonement

The second consequence which Owen describes pertains to "the design and purpose, of our merciful high priest."[7] Illustrating his argument, Owen imagines a prince who has "a full treasure" and intends to redeem all his captives, but does not take the time to tell all the captives they have been redeemed, thus leaving them in their state of bondage. He asks, "would not this be conceived a vain and ostentatious flourish, without any good intent towards the poor captives?"[8] Herman Bavinck notes that in such a situation God's justice is potentially denigrated "by saying that he causes forgiveness and life to be acquired for all and then fails to distribute them [to all]."[9] Robert Reymond's conclusion is similar in not wanting to posit what he believes would be a divergence within the economy of God between his sovereign "providence" and his sovereign "provision":

> Clearly the matter of who hears the gospel is under the providential governance of the sovereign God, and he has so arranged gospel history that

---

[6] Ibid., 126–27.
[7] Ibid., 127.
[8] Ibid.
[9] Herman Bavinck, *Sin and Salvation in Christ*, vol. 3 of *Reformed Dogmatics*, ed. John Bolt, trans. John Vriend, 4 vols. (Grand Rapids, MI: Baker, 2006), 469–70.

many people will never hear about Christ. It is unthinkable to suppose then that God sent his Son to save people who, by the ordering of his own providence, never hear the gospel in order that they may believe and be saved.[10]

But is this dilemma avoidable? From within a broader Arminian context, the answer here is yes, for an immediate response to this possibility might be the claim that theologians like Owen and Reymond are still operating within a deterministic Reformed framework which, in terms of the doctrines of sovereignty and providence, decretally foreordains that some will not have access to the gospel. Thus within such a framework there inevitably arises the problem of a Janus-like conflict within the divine economy, which pits an ordained universal provision against an ordained limited accessibility. That Reformed writers like Owen and Reymond would reject such a position and "resolve" the dilemma by propounding a limited provision is obvious.[11]

However, within an Arminian soteriological framework, it might be claimed that, just as God's universal salvific will can be frustrated by human libertarian freedom, so the same can be said regarding a soteriological "universal accessibility": God may desire everyone to hear the gospel, but this desire for everyone to hear may be frustrated. Getting the gospel to those people is *our* task, and this missionary task can succeed or fail. Could it not be argued that one of the primary motivations for two thousand years of Christian mission and their urgency has been the belief that Christian men and women are the means by which the unevangelized hear the gospel, and the fact that many have not heard is *our* responsibility? Therefore, while both for God and Christians, universal accessibility to salvation may be desired, it is not a logical entailment of universal atonement. Thus it could well be suggested that the dilemma that Owen and Reymond create in their argument is shown to be something of a false dichotomy and one that can be bypassed.

Does this possible Arminian resolution stand? On closer inspection, I believe that it does not, and that Owen's original dilemma remains especially for those who wish to hold to an objective "penal" substitution. While there is obviously a close connection between God's universal salvific will and universal atonement (as the saving will of God is revealed in Christ's work on the cross), there would appear to be some crucial differences between the two concepts. In the doctrine of universal atonement, we are not dealing

---

[10] Robert L. Reymond, *A New Systematic Theology of the Christian Faith* (Nashville: Thomas Nelson, 1998), 676–77.
[11] Although it appears less obvious to Amyraldians or Hypothetical Universalists.

with an abstract "wish" that can be frustrated but with the actual making of this wish come true, an objective reality that has occurred in history: Christ died for all. To reiterate the question: is there a necessary link between Christ dying for everyone, and everyone hearing about Christ dying for everyone? The question is not whether a universal redemptive provision is universal in its efficacy, for Arminians admit that man's freedom to resist salvific grace limits its efficacy. Rather, the question is whether a universal redemptive provision can be limited in its scope in some way or another (for example, the failure of Christian mission to take the gospel to certain parts of the world). I would briefly like to offer what I think must be the response here, by sketching the contours of universal atonement particularly in its Arminian form, but applicable also, I would argue, in the Amyraldian and Hypothetical Universalist forms.[12]

At the heart of the doctrine of universal atonement and within an Arminian synergistic soteriological framework[13] are two sets of linked ideas: objective accomplishment and subjective application, and universal possibility and particular actuality. Whatever Jesus's death accomplished, only Jesus could accomplish it, but each individual must still accept that free gift: "It is clear . . . that Christ's death is universal in its sufficiency and intention, but it is limited in its application. This limitation is imposed not by God but by man. The individual human being, created in the image of God with free will, must accept the benefits of the atonement."[14] Therefore, in Arminian soteriology, one sees a symbiosis between objective and subjective sides: a positive subjective response is needed to make effective the objective accomplishment, but there could not be the possibility of a subjective response without the objective provision. Because there is a degree of conditionality in this schema, an objective universalism is avoided, for universal atonement leads to universalism only if "God's sovereignty means that every act of God must be 'efficacious' and 'cannot be frustrated by man,' thereby negating

---

[12] For example, Lewis Sperry Chafer, *Systematic Theology, Volume III* (Dallas: Dallas Seminary Press, 1948), 196, argued that Christ's finished work is *"actual* in its availability, but *potential* in its application." And John Davenant, "A Dissertation on the Death of Christ, as to its Extent and special Benefits: containing a short History of Pelagianism, and shewing the Agreement of the Doctrines of the Church of England on general Redemption, Election, and Predestination, with the Primitive Fathers of the Christian Church, and above all, with the Holy Scriptures," in *An Exposition of the Epistle of St. Paul to the Colossians*, trans. Josiah Allport, 2 vols. (London: Hamilton, Adams, 1832 [English trans. of 1650 Latin ed.]), 2:384, held to both an unconditional and absolute universal satisfaction, but one which could only profit people "conditionally . . . if they should believe."

[13] As contrasted with the Reformed monergistic framework.

[14] Terry L. Miethe, "The Universal Power of the Atonement," in *The Grace of God and the Will of Man*, ed. Clark H. Pinnock (Grand Rapids, MI: Zondervan, 1989), 75.

any possible human freedom as being consistent with divine sovereignty."[15] There is enough biblical evidence to suggest that not everyone has accepted God's free gift in Christ. Conversely, while there is the possibility that no one would accept Christ's free offer of grace, this is only a logical possibility, since the Bible suggests that many do indeed accept this offer.

It is the close link between the objective and subjective sides of the Arminian soteriology which seems to tie universal atonement to universal accessibility. For although Christ's death has achieved something objectively independent of the believer (i.e., the possibility of salvation which did not exist before Christ's death), in terms of its salvific potential the subjective offer of this objective achievement would seem to be necessary to make the provision truly "universal." It would appear that to make a "genuine" universal offer one needs every recipient to be in a position to either accept or reject that offer. But can a universal offer be genuine yet frustrated? It can in terms of its efficacy, for it can be accepted or rejected. But can it be also only potential in scope? To affirm this would appear to disrupt the delicate balance between objective and subjective, with the subjective totally defining and therefore subsuming the objective. In my understanding of universal atonement, though, particularly in its penal substitutionary version, I do not think this is what Arminian theologians mean when they claim that Christ's death is objectively universal and "unlimited." To put it another way, without the universal possibility to accept or reject Christ, Christ's death is now "limited" to those who hear about it and those who do not. But can an "unlimited" or "universal" atonement, which declares that "Christ died for all," properly be called such when there are effectively terms and conditions in the "small print" that read, ". . . *subject to one's hearing about it*"? Proponents of universal atonement often criticize the definite atonement position for not being able to hold to both definite atonement and a universal "well-meant" gospel call.[16] However, concerning the unevangelized it would seem that they themselves are in the same "limiting" position, for the unevangelized have no offer at all.

This is not all, for there arises another objection in Christ dying for people who never have access to the possibility of accepting or rejecting this provision. This objection is a variation of another classic "theme"

[15] Ibid.
[16] Roger R. Nicole both rehearses and responds to this objection in "Covenant, Universal Call, and Definite Atonement," in *Standing Forth: Collected Writings of Roger Nicole* (Ross-shire, UK: Mentor, 2002), 335–36.

against universal atonement, that it "eviscerates Christ's cross work of its intrinsic infinite saving worth"[17] and remains opaque on the precise nature of Christ's objective procurement. Concerning this objection, Reymond notes that an atonement of universal extension "must make clear precisely what Christ did do at the cross if he did not actually propitiate, reconcile and redeem,"[18] and that what we actually have in this particular doctrinal construction is a work that procured "nothing that guarantees the salvation of anyone, but only made everyone in some inexplicable way salvable."[19] In this criticism, Arminians advocating a "penal substitution" are accused of being inconsistent, while those advocating some form of "governmental" or "rectoral" theory of atonement, while being more consistent, are accused of misunderstanding the fundamental nature of Christ's "penal" substitutionary work.[20]

In terms of the unevangelized, this critique is seen in an acute form, for if the usual accusation is one of opacity concerning the objectivity of atonement in a universal provision, then the unevangelized intensify the "inexplicability" further. In what way is this category of people even salvable if they do not have the opportunity to respond to what was done for them? Surely for God to immediately "save" them would be a violation and overriding of the libertarian freedom all men and women have, to accept or reject God's offer of salvation in Christ. Again the precise nature of Christ's objective provision in universal atonement is called into question.

At this point in the story, and in what must rank as one of the most unlikely cases of doctrinal cobelligerence, the implications of Owen's argument regarding the necessity of accessibility receive support from a number of advocates of universal atonement who argue precisely for the *necessary* connection between universal atonement and universal accessibility. The late Clark Pinnock is one such example. Although one may ultimately question whether he actually does safeguard a constitutive model of atonement,[21] his language bespeaks objectivity:

---

[17] Reymond, *Systematic Theology*, 682.
[18] Ibid., 681–82.
[19] Ibid., 682.
[20] See ibid., 473–78, 681–83; Robert Letham, *The Work of Christ* (Leicester, UK: Inter-Varsity Press, 1993), 167–69, 229–33. Roger E. Olson, *Arminian Theology: Myths and Realities* (Downers Grove, IL: InterVarsity Press, 2006), 221–41, notes that historically Arminianism has had no "one" theory of the atonement, and that advocates of both "penal substitution" and "governmental" theories (which Olson still thinks is "substitutionary") can be found.
[21] See my previous work, *The Possibility of Salvation among the Unevangelized: An Analysis of Inclusivism in Recent Evangelical Theology* (Carlisle, UK: Paternoster, 2001), esp. chapters 3 and 7, on Pinnock's Christology.

In his death and resurrection, humanity *de jure* passed from death to life, because God had included it in the event. Its destiny had been objectively realized in Christ—what remains to be done is a human response and salvation *de facto*. . . . we only have to accept what has been done and allow the Spirit to conform our lives to Christ.[22]

It is Pinnock himself who makes the move from universal atonement to universal accessibility. "If Christ died for all the opportunity must be given for all to register a decision about what was done for them. They cannot lack the opportunity merely because someone failed to bring the gospel of Christ to them."[23] Here he quotes favorably the apologist Stuart Hackett, who articulates the issue nicely:

If every human being in all times and ages has been objectively provided for through the unique redemption in Jesus, and if this intended provision is in fact intended by God as for every such human being, then it must be possible for each human individual to become personally eligible to receive that provision—regardless of his historical, cultural, or personal circumstances and situation, and quite apart from any particular historical information or even historically formulated theological conceptualization—*since a universally intended redemptive provision is not genuinely universal in the requisite sense unless it is also and for that reason universally accessible.*[24]

Given what I have already said, I believe Pinnock and Hackett are internally consistent in making this necessary connection between universal atonement and universal accessibility.[25] But can universal accessibility be defended theologically and biblically?

B) The Problems of Demonstrating Universal
Accessibility in a Defense of Universal Atonement

If Owen's second scenario is a dead end—"That this good-will of God, and this purchase made by Jesus Christ, is plainly in vain, and frustrate in respect

---

[22] Clark H. Pinnock, *Flame of Love: A Theology of the Holy Spirit* (Downers Grove, IL: IVP Academic, 1996), 95–96.
[23] Clark H. Pinnock, *A Wideness in God's Mercy: The Finality of Jesus Christ in a World of Religions* (Grand Rapids, MI: Zondervan, 1992), 157.
[24] Stuart Hackett, *The Reconstruction of the Christian Revelation Claim* (Grand Rapids, MI: Baker, 1984), 244.
[25] I disagree, therefore, with another advocate of universal atonement, Gary L. Shultz, Jr., "Why a Genuine Universal Gospel Call Requires an Atonement That Paid for the Sins of All People," *EQ* 82.2 April (2010): 113 n. 8, who dismisses Pinnock et al. for making this connection: "The atonement's payment for all sin did not procure an opportunity for anyone to be saved apart from hearing the gospel, which is part of the reason the gospel needs to be proclaimed to all people." Without further explanation by Shultz, which he does not give in this particular article, I do not see how he avoids the implications we have teased out based on Owen's second scenario concerning the justice of God, the potential division within the divine economy, and the precise nature of Christ's objective provision.

of them"—then defenders of universal atonement have to retrace their steps and come back to Owen's first scenario: "That they may be saved without faith in, and the knowledge of, Christ." As I have already mentioned, Owen declares this to be another dead end, with no investigation necessary. However, given the options available, defenders of universal atonement may want to explore this avenue a little further. Indeed, I wish to argue that they must, for given the necessary link established between universal atonement and universal accessibility, and given the reality that there are people in human history who have not heard the proclamation of the gospel through a human messenger in this life, this option becomes the *only* one available to them. In their respective defenses of definite atonement, William Cunningham and Herman Bavinck note this:

> The idea very naturally occurs to men, that, if Christ died for all the human race, then some provision must have been made for bringing within all men's reach, and making accessible to them, the privileges or opportunities which have been procured for them. And as a large portion of the human race are, undoubtedly, left in ignorance of Christ, and of all that He has done for them, some universalists have been led, not very unnaturally, to maintain the position,—that men may be, and that many have been, saved through Christ, or on the ground of his atonement, who never heard of him, to whom the gospel was never made known.[26]

> [Universal atonement] leads to the doctrine, as the Quakers rightly observed, that if Christ died for all, then all must be given the opportunity, in either this world or the next, to accept or reject him, for it would be grossly unjust to condemn and to punish those whose sins had all been atoned for solely because they lacked the opportunity to accept Christ by faith.[27]

Those who are familiar with his work will know that a theologian like Pinnock, having laid the foundations for universal accessibility, has few qualms in crashing through Owen's no-entry sign and boldly going down Owen's first route, although he immediately recognizes some heavy theological construction work is necessary:

---

[26] William Cunningham, *Historical Theology: A Review of the Principal Doctrinal Discussions in the Christian Church since the Apostolic Age, Volume 2* (1862; repr., Edinburgh: Banner of Truth, 1960), 367.
[27] Bavinck, *Sin and Salvation in Christ*, 470. Bavinck cites here the Dutch translation of Robert Barclay's defense of Quakerism, *An Apology for the True Christian Divinity* (1678). Barclay's fifth and sixth propositions, "Concerning the Universal Redemption by Christ, and also the Saving and Spiritual Light wherewith every man is enlightened" are a strong defense of the benefits of Christ's atonement being the "light" and "seed" of the gospel which is preached *in* every creature, even those who do not hear the gospel outwardly.

This raises a difficult question. How is salvation within reach of the un-evangelized? How can anyone be saved without knowing Christ? The idea of universal accessibility, though not a novel theory, needs to be proven. It is far from self-evident, at least biblically speaking. How can it best be defended?[28]

Before discussing the merits and demerits of various defenses of universal accessibility, I wish to pause at this point in order to reiterate my contention that, for those who hold to universal atonement, a theory concerning universal accessibility is not a speculative theological luxury or "extra" but rather a theological necessity which is inextricably linked to any defense of a universal atonement. This needs to be recognized by defenders of the doctrine. It is to be remembered that what we are speaking of here is not an optimistic or pessimistic "agnosticism" that *some* or even *many* who never hear the gospel will be saved, but rather a crucial theological mechanism whereby *all* people who have ever lived are able to freely respond to what Christ has done for them. Given the significance of such a mechanism, agnosticism would seem theologically unsatisfactory.

The problem regarding universal accessibility, however, is that it is, in Pinnock's own words, "far from self-evident, at least biblically speaking." Various theories have been put forward in order to demonstrate universal accessibility, but in each case they are speculative and appear to raise more problems than they solve. Donald Lake is a good example here in his defense of universal atonement. In his final section on world missions he writes,

> A valid offer of grace has been made to mankind, but its application is limited by man's response rather than God's arbitrary selection. God knows who would, under ideal circumstances, believe the gospel, and on the basis of his foreknowledge, applies that gospel even if the person never hears the gospel during his lifetime.[29]

Lake's explanatory brevity here, as well as the substance of his argument, simply raises further questions as to the nature of these "ideal circumstances." Similarly, a number of evangelical Wesleyan theologians believe they have laid a solid theological foundation in linking the universal benefits of the atonement to a "universal enabling" or "prevenient" grace, based on a num-

---

[28] Pinnock, *Wideness*, 157.
[29] Donald M. Lake, "He Died For All: The Universal Dimensions of the Atonement," in *Grace Unlimited*, ed. Clark H. Pinnock (Minneapolis: Bethany, 1975), 43.

ber of texts (the *locus classicus* being John 1:9: "The true light, which gives light to everyone, was coming into the world"). However, as with Lake, the precise nature of how this "prevenient" grace can be responded to, is not detailed. Much more biblical and theological rigor is needed here.[30]

It is scholars like Clark Pinnock and John Sanders who have seen the necessary link between universal atonement and universal accessibility, and who also have given the most detailed arguments in demonstrating universal accessibility. Their "inclusivist" positions argue that people can be ontologically saved by Christ while being epistemologically unaware of him. Combining his own commitment to "open theism," a strong version of Wesleyan "prevenient" grace, and a protestantization of the Roman Catholic Karl Rahner's "supernatural existential," Pinnock's "pneumatological inclusivism"[31] grounds universal accessibility in what he calls a "cosmic covenant," a formulation that he believes combines foundational biblical axioms of both universality and particularity. From the divine side, the omnipresent work of the Spirit presents opportunities for all men and women to respond to God. From the human side, this response is elicited through what Pinnock calls the "faith principle." Drawing on biblical examples of the nature of faith in the OT and also the category of "holy pagans," Pinnock draws an analogy between the faith of those who were chronologically pre-messianic and the faith of those who are informationally pre-messianic. His contention is that through "general revelation" people have enough information about God to respond freely to the Spirit's overtures. In later writing, he takes this "faith principle" further by speaking of an "ethical" principle whereby good works may signal a positive response to the promptings of the Spirit at a noncognitive level even though cognitive beliefs may actually be "false." "Authentic faith and holy action may flow from persons inhabiting an unpromising religious and doctrinal culture. Someone might be an atheist because he or she does not understand who God is, and still have faith."[32]

In my monograph, I have described and critiqued Pinnock's inclusivism in great detail, arguing that he significantly redefines the orthodox interpretation of the four *solas* of the Reformation (*solus Christus, sola fide, sola*

---

[30] For a discussion of prevenient grace, see Strange, *Possibility of Salvation*, 93–96.
[31] My own name for his position and the subject of my monograph, *Possibility of Salvation*.
[32] Clark H. Pinnock, "An Inclusivist View," in *More Than One Way? Fours Views of Salvation in a Pluralistic World*, ed. Dennis L. Okholm and Timothy R. Phillips (Grand Rapids, MI: Zondervan, 1995), 118.

gratia, and *sola Scriptura*), as well as illegitimately reconfiguring the relationship between the second and third persons of the Trinity.[33] As a result, my conclusion there was that Pinnock's version of inclusivism cannot be considered as a viable evangelical argument for both Reformed and Arminian evangelicals.

While I am not insisting that all defenders of universal atonement subscribe to a theological construction as "radical" as that of Pinnock's, there remain a number of more general difficulties in demonstrating the principle of universal accessibility.

First, the Bible consistently stresses not only the necessity of the new birth by the Spirit, but the necessity of receiving this through the hearing and acceptance of the gospel proclaimed. However one wishes to interpret the "times of ignorance" (Acts 17:30–31) and the "mystery of Christ" (Eph. 3:4–10), the overwhelming emphasis in the NT, both exegetically (in terms of specific texts) and redemptive-historically (in terms of broader themes and trajectories), is the need in this epoch of redemptive history to put one's faith in Jesus Christ as heard through the medium of the human messenger. There is scant explicit NT evidence for any other version of saving faith apart from conscious faith in Christ, nor is there explicit evidence that this knowledge of Christ can be known via some other medium than the "word of Christ."[34] Universal accessibility, therefore, remains in the arena of theological speculation, but a speculation that is "forced upon" defenders of universal atonement as they seek to show how everyone who has ever lived *must* have the chance to respond to Christ's saving work.[35]

Second, the theological basis that necessitates some mechanism for a universal accessibility can be questioned. As I have already noted, many Wesleyan theologians use texts such as John 1:9 as exegetical evidence for some form of internal Christ-given "universal enabling." However, I do not believe these texts can bear the weight put upon them. For example, one of the most detailed historical and lexical studies of John 1:9 is that

---

[33] Strange, *Possibility of Salvation*, esp. chapters 6–9.

[34] For more evidence supporting this claim, see John Piper, *Let the Nations Be Glad: The Supremacy of God in Missions* (Leicester, UK: Inter-Varsity Press, 1993), 115–67. In terms of the salvation of OT believers and their disanalogous relationship to the unevangelized, see Strange, *The Possibility of Salvation*, chapter 6; and Adam Sparks, *One of a Kind: The Relationship between Old and New Covenant as the Hermeneutical Key for Christian Theology of Religions* (Eugene, OR: Pickwick, 2010).

[35] Interestingly, Wesleyan scholar Randy Maddox, *Responsible Grace: John Wesley's Practical Theology* (Nashville: Kingswood, 1994), 33–34, notes that Wesley himself in his later thought indicated that the unevangelized could be saved on the basis of their response (made possible through "prevenient" grace) to the revelation they had received.

of E. L. Miller.[36] After surveying the possible options, Miller argues exegetically that "it is in all likelihood the light that was coming into the world (not every person) and that the verse thus bears a clear incarnational teaching."[37] Moreover, intra-textually, "the idea of a universal revelation by which people in general are illuminated with respect to some basic knowledge of God or spiritual truths is otherwise utterly inimical to the Johannine literature."[38] Miller's conclusion is that of a restrictive and "external" interpretation, which is fully consistent with the Johannine literature: "the 'light' of 1:9 is to be conceived as a *special* revelation, radiating specifically from the incarnate Logos and holding consequences and benefits only for those whose lives are touched by it."[39] Such gracious "universal enabling" appears Scripturally thin.[40]

The third general difficulty is the motivation to mission and evangelism if everyone has access to respond to Christ outside of the human messenger. Universal accessibilists have been insistent that the nerve to missionary agency is not cut, and, given the plethora of motivations for missionary activity, I would not want to overstate my case here.[41] However, with John Piper, while *the* nerve to missionary motivation might not be cut, *an* important nerve certainly is:

> Nevertheless there is a felt difference in the urgency when one believes that preaching the gospel is absolutely the only hope that anyone has of escaping the penalty of sin and living for ever in happiness to the glory of God's grace. It does not ring true to me when William Crockett and James Sigountos argue that the existence of 'implicit Christians' (saved through general revelation without hearing of Christ) actually "should increase motivation" for missions. They say that these unevangelized converts are "waiting eagerly to hear more about God." If we would reach them "a strong church would spring to life, giving glory to God and evangelizing their pagan neighbours." I cannot escape the impression that this is a futile

---

[36] E. L. Miller, "The True Light Which Illumines Every Person," in *Good News in History*, ed. E. L. Miller (Atlanta: Scholars Press, 1993), 63–82.

[37] Ibid., 79.

[38] Ibid.

[39] Ibid., 80.

[40] For more on this, see Thomas R. Schreiner, "Does Scripture Teach Prevenient Grace in the Wesleyan Sense?," in *The Grace of God, the Bondage of the Will. Volume 2: Historical and Theological Perspectives on Calvinism*, ed. Thomas R. Schreiner and Bruce A. Ware (Grand Rapids, MI: Baker, 1995), 365–82; and Strange, *Possibility of Salvation*, 93–105.

[41] For example, see John D. Ellenberger, "Is Hell a Proper Motivation for Missions?," in *Through No Fault of Their Own*, ed. William V. Crockett and James G. Sigountos (Grand Rapids, MI: Baker, 1991), 217–28. For a version of Reformed accessibilism on this point, see Terrance L. Tiessen, *Who Can Be Saved? Reassessing Salvation in Christ and World Religions* (Leicester, UK: Inter-Varsity Press, 2004), 259–94.

attempt to make a weakness look like a strength. On the contrary, common sense presses another truth on us: the more likely it is that people can be saved without mission the less urgency there is for missions.[42]

In a similar scenario to the issue of the "well-meant" offer as discussed above, while a disincentive to mission is often an argument leveled at proponents of definite atonement,[43] it is actually universal accessibility that provides a disincentive to mission.

SUMMARY

In summary then, in the category of the unevangelized, proponents of universal atonement are caught between a Scylla and Charybdis with no apparent path through which to navigate. On the one hand, if they accept *fides ex auditu*, that people can be saved only through *hearing* of Christ from a gospel messenger, then their definition of "universal" atonement is called into question, especially if they wish to hold to its objective character. On the other hand, if they accept that all people must have the opportunity to respond to what Christ has done because of his objective universal atonement, then they must deny that it is only through the medium of the proclamation of the gospel by human messengers that salvation comes, and approve some other theory of universal accessibility, theories which seem to counter the biblical testimony and which lead to some problematic theological and pastoral conclusions for evangelicals. Faced with these uncomfortable alternatives, I would encourage them to look once again at the doctrine of definite atonement, which I do not believe entails these dilemmas.

(2) The Question of the Unevangelized in Relation to a Definite Atonement

A bare summary of how the doctrine of definite atonement relates to the question of the unevangelized shows a much greater intra-systematic consistency and, even more importantly, a unified intra-Trinitarian will and purpose. God has ordained and providentially arranged that those sinners for whom Christ died and procured salvation will always hear the gospel of Christ and ir-

---

[42] Piper, *Let the Nations Be Glad*, 118, citing Crockett and Sigountos, *Through No Fault of Their Own*, 260.
[43] So D. Broughton Knox, "Some Aspects of the Atonement," in *The Doctrine of God*, vol. 1 of *D. Broughton Knox, Selected Works* (3 vols.), ed. Tony Payne (Kingsford, NSW: Matthias Media, 2000), 261, 266.

resistibly come in repentance and faith, through the regenerating work of the Spirit. Ordinarily, as this gospel is heard through a human messenger, those who remain outside this redemptive channel fall outside of the saving intent of the atonement. Furthermore, even *if* one wanted to tentatively speculate (and I note again here, seemingly *contrary* to the NT evidence) that God has employed and even now employs, occasionally or more frequently, "extraordinary" means to communicate and apply the benefits of Christ's cross-work (dreams, visions, angels, theophanies) to his elect who *never* come into contact with a human messenger, God is neither constrained nor obligated to provide access to salvation *universally*, as he is for those who defend universal atonement.[44]

The above summary is meant to be a description rather than an apologetic defense. I recognize that while defenders of universal atonement may agree with the logical consistency of the position, they will still question the exegetical and theological presuppositions on which this statement rests. To fill in a little more of the picture here, I finish with two points relating definite atonement to aspects of "universality," and which I hope further enhance and persuade for its truth.

A) The Universality of Sin and the Particularity of Grace in a Defense of Definite Atonement

First, I wish to note that definite atonement resonates with both the universality of sin and the particularity of saving grace. Some construals of universal atonement and universal accessibility can sound in a different key from that of Scripture. As Carson notes,

> The tone of the Bible . . . is that if we human beings are lost, it is because of our sin. Our guilt before God justly earns his wrath. If we are not consumed, it is of the Lord's mercy. . . . The love of God is presented as surprising, undeserved, unmerited, lavish . . . the condemnation of guilty rebels that seems so transparently obvious in the Bible's story line is not transmuted into a different kind of story, a "pity the perpetrator" story: they may be guilty, but if they do not have free access to a way of escape surely it would be unjust to condemn them?[45]

[44] Examples of those who postulate more than one modality for special revelation include Tiessen, *Who Can Be Saved?* and Christopher R. Little, *The Revelation of God among the Unevangelized: An Evangelical Appraisal and Missiological Contribution to the Debate* (Pasadena, CA: William Carey Library, 2000).
[45] D. A. Carson, *The Gagging of God: Christianity Confronts Pluralism* (Leicester, UK: Apollos, 1996), 289–90.

Biblical anthropology presents the effects of the fall as being so severe that the only universal thing we merit is judgment:

> The justice of God is questioned by some critics who protest that election-love is discriminatory and therefore a violation of justice. But all love is preferential or it would not be love. . . . The modern misjudgment of God flows easily from contemporary theology's occupation with love as the core of God's being, while righteousness is subordinated and denied equal ultimacy with love in the nature of deity.[46]

J. I. Packer is not "unfair" when he comments that these accessibilist arguments seem more influenced by American principles of fairness than by anything else.[47]

The universality of sin and the particularity of grace are seen clearly in the history of revelation and the revelation of history. Despite protestations as to the narrowness of those who fall within special revelation, and of those who do not as being "through no fault of their own," the genesis of history reveals a time when special revelation was indeed universally known and as accessible as general revelation. Indeed, as I have argued elsewhere, general revelation and special revelation were and still are properly designed to be inseparable: God's works needing to be interpreted by God's words.[48] The entrance of sin had consequences for the accessibility of saving revelation. While all people are guilty for suppressing the revelation they have, and will be judged accordingly,[49] in the sovereign providence of God, he has graciously preserved and sustained redemptive knowledge of himself within some streams of humanity and not within others. Owen and Reymond both give exegetical examples of such historical discrimination, with each referring to Acts 16:6–8 where the Holy Spirit forbade Paul and his companions to speak the word in Asia.[50] If this discrimination is acknowledged, is it not legitimate to hold to a discrimination in the atonement too? Indeed, to do so means that the particularity of revelation and redemption are coextensive and remove the problem of the unevangelized.

---

[46] Carl Henry, "Is It Fair?," in *Through No Fault*, 253–54.

[47] Words spoken by Packer at "Evangelical Affirmations" conference, Trinity Evangelical Divinity School, 1989, and quoted by John Sanders in his *No Other Name: Can Only Christians Be Saved* (London: SPCK, 1994), 136 n. 6.

[48] See Daniel Strange, "General Revelation: Sufficient or Insufficient?," in *Faith Comes by Hearing: A Response to Inclusivism*, ed. Christopher W. Morgan and Robert A. Peterson (Nottingham, UK: Apollos, 2008), 40–77.

[49] See, for example, the "more bearable" judgment for Tyre and Sidon than Chorazin and Bethsaida in Luke 10:13–14, and the "few blows and many blows" of Luke 12:48.

[50] Owen, *Death of Death*, 128; Reymond, *Systematic Theology*, 676.

However, does a belief in particularity of revelation, grace, and atonement not produce a disincentive for mission?

B) THE UNIVERSALITY OF, AND MOTIVATION FOR, CHRISTIAN MISSION IN A DEFENSE OF DEFINITE ATONEMENT

The connection between definite atonement and Christian mission is, I believe, a strong one. A number of issues need to be distinguished here.

First, we can speak of definite atonement and the universal proclamation of the gospel. Even the staunchest defenders of definite atonement have expressed their commitment to the universal and indiscriminate dissemination of the gospel:

> God has commanded the gospel to be preached to every creature; He has required us to proclaim to our fellow-men, of whatever character, and in all varieties of circumstances, the glad tidings of great joy,—to hold out to them, in His name, pardon and acceptance through the blood of atonement,—to invite them to come to Christ, and to receive Him,—and to accompany all this with the assurance that "whosoever cometh to Him, He will in no wise cast out."[51]

> 1. The general publishing of the gospel unto "all nations" with the right that it hath to be preached to "every creature," Matt. 28:19; Mk. 16:15; because the way of salvation it declares is wide enough for all to walk in. There is enough in the remedy it brings to light to heal all their diseases, to deliver them from all their evils. If there were a thousand worlds, the gospel of Christ might, upon this ground, be preached to them all, there being enough in Christ for the salvation of them all, if so be they will derive virtue from him by touching him in faith; the only way to draw refreshment from this foundation of salvation.[52]

Second, definite atonement is compatible with matters of responsibility, urgency, and privilege, what might be called the harmonious overtones that accompany the divine call to proclaim the gospel to all peoples. Caricatures of definite atonement often state that if Christ died only for some and God is going to save only his elect, then there is no point in preaching the gospel to all. However, as Helm has noted, "Scripture does not invite us to break up the causal nexus of events as revealed and to speculate about each link in

---

[51] Cunningham, *Historical Theology, Volume II*, 345.
[52] Owen, *Death of Death*, 185.

the chain."[53] Lake is misinformed concerning a biblically faithful Reformed theology when he says that "the doctrine of election has served to solve the problem of those who died without ever hearing the gospel: if they were part of the elect, they were saved without hearing; if not numbered among the elect, their hearing was of no consequence."[54] As the servants of the king in Jesus's parable of the wedding banquet, we are to "Go to the street corners and invite to the banquet anyone you find" (Matt. 22:9, NIV). This is our responsibility. Moreover, the need for Christians to take the gospel to peoples and nations who have never heard the gospel remains urgent. Furthermore, that God has chosen to call his people through the instrumentality of the human messenger is not only an awesome responsibility but also an "unspeakable privilege."[55]

Finally, in a definite atonement we have the grounds for both missionary motivation and confidence. Historically, for missionary pioneers like William Carey, such a doctrine served as a spur and not a brake in his motivation and vision.[56] The book of Revelation presents a wonderfully certain picture of a people objectively ransomed by the blood of Christ, "from every tribe and language and people and nation" (5:9), "a great multitude that no one could number, from every nation, from all tribes and peoples and languages" (7:9), and who all give glory to God in their rich diversity.

Far from dampening the motivation to mission, definite atonement provides great confidence for Christian mission. The message we proclaim is not that of a gospel offer which construes the atonement as providing merely the possibility of salvation or the opportunity of salvation, for "it is not the opportunity of salvation that is offered; it is salvation. And it is salvation because Christ is offered and Christ does not invite us to mere opportunity but to himself."[57] Moreover, in the spirit of the Lord's words to Paul—"I have many in this city who are my people" (Acts 18:10)—we are confident in the unity of the triune God's sovereign economy of salvation, for we know that wherever we proclaim the gospel, God's Spirit has gone before, relating to all personally through the ever-present revelation of

---

[53] Paul Helm, "Are They Few that Be Saved?," in *Universalism and the Doctrine of Hell*, ed. Nigel M. De S. Cameron (Carlisle, UK: Paternoster, 1993), 280.

[54] Lake, "He Died for All," 43.

[55] Piper, *Let the Nations Be Glad*, 159.

[56] It is said that Revelation 5:7–9, quoted at the beginning of this chapter, was the passage that sent Carey to India, for he knew that there were people ordained to eternal life there.

[57] John Murray, "The Atonement and the Free Offer of the Gospel," in *Collected Writings of John Murray. Volume 1: The Claims of Truth* (Edinburgh: Banner of Truth, 1976), 83.

himself both externally in creation and history and internally in the *imago Dei*. While this revelation is both sinfully suppressed and substituted, it is never totally erased, so that all know God and are "without excuse." But more, in God's amazing graciousness and mercy, and in a myriad of ways, we are confident that he has been preparing his own people, those for whom Christ died, to receive the gospel message we proclaim, in saving repentance and faith.

22

"Blessèd Assurance, Jesus Is Mine"?

DEFINITE ATONEMENT
AND THE CURE OF SOULS

Sinclair B. Ferguson

Jesus taught definite atonement. He speaks of himself as the "good shepherd [who] lays down his life for the sheep" (John 10:11, 15). He knows and is known by his "own" sheep, just as the Father knows him and he knows the Father (John 10:14–15). Jesus's sheep listen to his voice and follow him (John 10:27). He gives them eternal life, and they will never perish; no one can snatch them out of his hand (John 10:28). The Father has given them to him; no one can snatch them out of his Father's hand (John 10:29).

Here *definite* atonement is *efficacious* atonement: the sheep are first the Father's; they are given to the Son; he lays down his life *for his own sheep*; they are kept in the hands of the Son and the Father; no sheep for whom Christ lays down his life ever perishes (John 10:28). But in addition, Jesus makes the implicit explicit: those who do not come to faith were never his "own sheep": "You do not believe because you are not part of my flock" (John 10:26, AT). Our Lord's logic here is striking. It is not, "You do not believe *and therefore* you are not part of my flock." Rather, it is, "You do not believe *because* you are not part of the flock for which I lay down my life."

Thus alongside *efficacious* atonement, Jesus speaks of a *divine discrimination* between the sheep (those given, died for, called, drawn, and kept), and those who are not part of his flock.

Gospel ministers serve as under-shepherds and assistant bishops to Christ the "Shepherd and Overseer" (1 Pet. 2:25). Theirs is a deeply theological calling. Like Calvin, they seek to become better theologians in order to be better pastors. Two comments are in order here.

First, and in the nature of the case, the minister is a general practitioner in theology, not an academic specialist. The pastor is a church builder, not an architect. But to serve well on the building site of the church, he needs a full, working knowledge of the architecture of the gospel. In particular, since his calling is to preach Scripture in the light of its usefulness (2 Tim. 3:16–4:5), he must be familiar with everything that is "profitable" and must not "shrink from declaring . . . the whole counsel of God" (Acts 20:20, 27). He must also be equipped not only to teach truth but to discern and refute error (Titus 1:9), so that he can protect the flock of God from fierce wolves (Acts 20:29–31).

Secondly, in any ministry that claims to stand in the apostolic succession, the exposition and application of the biblical teaching on the atonement demands a central place. Paul gives us the vision in summary statements: "I decided to know nothing among you except Jesus Christ and him crucified" (1 Cor. 2:2); "Far be it from me to boast except in the cross of our Lord Jesus Christ" (Gal. 6:14). As under-shepherd, the pastor must expound what the Chief Shepherd did in laying down his life for his sheep.

But surely *definite* atonement is a sophisticated and controversial point of theology, and therefore one unlikely to impact pastoral ministry?

The NT emphasizes that the atonement knows no ethnic limitations (Gal. 3:26–28), and yet it is also "definite." In his death Christ actually atones for the sins of his people; reconciliation is a finished work. This is woven into the warp and woof of the NT's teaching in much the same way that the work of the Trinity flavors and colors its message. In a similar if perhaps less obvious way, how one thinks about the nature, effects, and extent of the atonement has an inevitable impact, directly or indirectly, on preaching, teaching, and pastoral counseling. If part of the minister's task is to help his congregation to sing in joyful wonder in response to the gospel,

Amazing love! how can it be,
That Thou, my God, should'st die for me?[1]

then the meaning of his dying "for me" cannot be ignored.

The position adopted throughout this volume is that Christ died for the elect, and that the atonement he made, *whatever its broader ramifications*, was "definite," i.e., intended for specific individuals and essentially efficacious. Its purpose was not to make salvation possible for all (and logically, therefore, potentially efficacious for none), but to make a particular, effective atonement: the Shepherd laid down his life for his sheep; all of his sheep will be called, justified, and glorified (Rom. 8:30).

Christ and the Atonement

The inner dynamics of expounding "Christ and him crucified" involve Jesus's identity as the Son of God, the reality of his incarnation and humiliation, his life of obedience, and especially the multivalent character of his death and resurrection. This is underscored in Paul's epitomizing statement in Romans 3:21–25. Here the big gospel words—redemption, propitiation, justification—should not be thought of as theories or metaphors of the atonement; they describe what the atonement actually is, and identify Christ in terms of his work. He *is* the propitiation for our sins, and the redemption is *in him*. The gospel Benefactor and the gospel blessings can never be separated from one another. Thus to possess them one must possess or be "in" him; to receive them one must "receive" him. John Murray expresses it finely:

> The apostle conceives of this redemption as something that has its permanent and abiding tenancy in Christ; it is "the redemption that is in Christ Jesus." The redemption is not simply that which we have in Christ (Eph. 1:17) but it is the redemption of which Christ is the embodiment. Redemption has not only been wrought by Christ but in the Redeemer this redemption resides in its unabbreviated virtue and efficacy. And it is redemption thus conceived that provides the mediacy through which justification by God's free grace is applied.[2]

This "redemption" in Christ is by implication fourfold: *from the guilt of sin* (securing justification); *from the wrath of God* (securing reconciliation); *from*

[1] From the hymn by Charles Wesley, "And Can It Be That I Should Gain?"
[2] John Murray, *The Epistle to the Romans*, 2 vols., NICNT (Grand Rapids, MI: Eerdmans, 1960), 1:116.

the dominion of sin (securing freedom from sin's reign but not yet its presence); and *from the oppression of the powers of darkness*.[3]

The "propitiation" in view has a Godward focus (Rom. 3:25). It is the counterpoint to Paul's extended exposition of the wrath of God being revealed against all unrighteousness and ungodliness (Rom. 1:18–3:20). By nature, all have sinned, stand condemned, and face God's wrath. In Christ as propitiation, we who (with Saul/Paul) were "children of wrath, like the rest of mankind" (Eph. 2:3), discover that he "delivers us from the wrath to come" (1 Thess. 1:10).[4]

This propitiation is essential to all other aspects of Christ's atoning work. Neither kingly nor prophetic ministries can be effective without the priestly sacrifice.[5] Since salvation is embodied in Christ, it becomes ours through Spirit-given faith-union with him.[6] In the unique conceptualization of the NT, we believe not only "in" or "on" Christ but actually "into" (πιστεύειν εἰς) Christ (cf. John 14:1).[7]

Within this context the focus of the minister's gospel proclamation is Christ himself, clothed in the gospel.[8] As Calvin never tired of saying, salvation is ours not only "through" Christ but actually "in" Christ.[9] Everything we need for salvation is in him. United to him, all that is in him for us becomes ours.

If, in terms of Jesus's own teaching, he effectively accomplished this for definite individuals, what are the implications for day-to-day pastoral ministry? There are several, but our focus here is on the topic of Christian assurance, not least because it has been vigorously argued that definite atonement militates against it, both theologically and existentially.

What follows is a discussion of definite atonement and Christian assurance in conversation with John McLeod Campbell, the nineteenth-century

---

[3] Cf. Romans 8:31, where Paul's use of the interrogative personal pronoun "who" surely embraces celestial as well as terrestrial opponents (cf. Rom. 16:20; Col. 2:15; Heb. 2:14–15).

[4] The oft-repeated comment that in the NT the verb καταλλάσσω ("to reconcile") never has God as its object too frequently carries the sleight-of-hand implication that therefore the *atonement* does not terminate on God. But propitiation, in its very nature, must terminate on God, not man.

[5] See Sinclair B. Ferguson, "Christus Victor et Propitiator: The Death of Christ, Substitute and Conqueror," in *For the Fame of God's Name: Essays in Honor of John Piper*, ed. Sam Storms and Justin Taylor (Wheaton, IL: Crossway, 2010), 171–89.

[6] Cf. Calvin's striking statement that, "As long as Christ remains outside of us, and we are separated from him, all that he has suffered and done for the salvation of the human race remains useless and of no value to us" (*Institutes of the Christian Religion*, ed. John T. McNeil, trans. Ford Lewis Battles [London: SCM, 1960], 3.1.1).

[7] According to Rudolph Bultmann, "πιστεύω κλτ.," *TDNT*, 6:203, this usage is "neither Greek nor LXX [i.e., found in the Septuagint]."

[8] Calvin, *Institutes*, 3.2.6.

[9] See, for example, Calvin's comments in his commentaries on Romans 6:11; 1 Corinthians 1:5.

Scottish Presbyterian pastor-theologian. McLeod Campbell (as he is usually known) argued that limitation of the atonement "takes away the warrant which the universality of the atonement gives to every man that hears the gospel to contemplate Christ with the personal appropriation of the words of the apostle, 'who loved me, and gave himself for me.'"[10]

John McLeod Campbell

Campbell was born near Oban in 1800, the son of a Church of Scotland minister. He became minister of the Parish of Row (Rhu) in 1825. Five years later he was charged with two counts of teaching contrary to the subordinate doctrinal standards of his church, the Westminster Confession of Faith (WCF): first, that Christ died for all humanity; and second, that assurance was of the essence of faith and necessary for salvation.[11] In 1831, the General Assembly deposed him (by a vote of 119 to 6). Much of the remainder of his life was spent serving an independent congregation in Glasgow.

In 1855, Campbell published *The Nature of the Atonement.* A second edition followed in 1867, with reprints since.[12] His reputation as a thinker was sufficiently rehabilitated for the University of Glasgow (his alma mater) to award him an honorary Doctor of Divinity in 1868, four years before his death in 1872. His views seem to have had little contemporary influence in Scotland,[13] but were more widely appreciated in England.[14]

Campbell's views were resurrected in mid-twentieth-century Scotland and beyond largely through the influence of the brothers T. F. Torrance and

---

[10] John McLeod Campbell, *The Nature of the Atonement* (Edinburgh: Handsel, 1856; repr., Grand Rapids, MI: Eerdmans, 1996), 71.

[11] Contra WCF, 8.7; 10.1; 18.3. For a short autobiographical view on these two issues, see John McLeod Campbell, *Reminiscences and Reflections: Referring to His Early Ministry in the Parish of Row, 1825–31*, ed. D. Campbell (London: Macmillan, 1873), 152–57. For details of his trial, see John McLeod Campbell, *The Whole Proceedings before the Presbytery of Dumbarton and Synod of Glasgow and Ayr. In the case of the Rev. John McLeod Campbell, Minister of Row, including the libel, answers to the libel, evidence, and speeches* (Greenock: R. B. Lusk, 1831).

[12] The most recent edition being the one noted in n. 10 above.

[13] Major writers on the atonement in Scotland, such as William Cunningham, George Smeaton, and Hugh Martin, seem largely to have ignored him. Cunningham was a witness for the prosecution in his presbytery trial (Robert Rainy and James Mackenzie, *The Life of William Cunningham* [Nelson: London, 1871], 152–57; also Campbell, *Whole Proceedings*, 17–19). George Smeaton described Campbell's view as "extravagant and strangely constituted . . . it has no warrant or foundation in Scripture, the phraseology of which alone can direct us in our theological thinking" (*Christ's Doctrine of the Atonement* [Edinburgh: T. & T. Clark, 1871], 494). Hugh Martin gave much attention to this doctrine but was in fact critiqued for ignoring Campbell. In the next generation, T. J. Crawford, while regarding Campbell's work as "able and interesting" concluded that it "is encompassed with difficulties which seem to be insuperable" (*The Doctrine of Holy Scripture Respecting the Atonement* [Edinburgh: Blackwood & Sons, 1871], 323; see 316–31 for his extended discussion). A. B. Bruce regarded Campbell as introducing "something very like absurdity" (*The Humiliation of Christ* [Edinburgh: T. & T. Clark, 1881], 318). James Denney, while not wholly uncritical, resonated in later life with Campbell's denial of the atonement as a *penal* substitution (*The Christian Doctrine of Reconciliation* [London: Hodder & Stoughton, 1917], 262).

[14] Notably in R. C. Moberly's influential *Atonement and Personality* (London: John Murray, 1901), 396–410.

J. B. Torrance, many of whose published writings constitute a sustained support for Campbell's theology and share his deep antipathy to "Federal Calvinism." Indeed, T. F. Torrance's late work, *Scottish Theology*,[15] bore the subtitle "From John Knox to John McLeod Campbell," and devoted almost one tenth of a work covering four centuries—and the climactic section of the entire book—to Campbell.[16]

The Nature of the Atonement is a sustained critique of the doctrine of penal substitution, motivated by Campbell's astute observation that penal substitution and definite atonement are two sides of the same coin. Though Campbell may be little known today beyond those who have an interest in Scottish theology, J. I. Packer is right to comment that "potentially the most damaging criticism of penal substitution came not from Socinus, but from McLeod Campbell."[17] By implication, then, his work is also "potentially the most damaging criticism" of definite atonement. Indeed it was intended to be so.

Context for *The Nature of the Atonement*

Campbell's concerns over the nature of the atonement arose not so much from the ivory tower of academia as from real-life ministry and from the burden of his own flock's lack of assurance.[18] Early in his ministry he discovered that his preaching of the gospel was being heard as if it were a demand for greater (self) righteousness.[19] Over a period of time he became convinced that this turning of grace into a demand, and the lack of assurance of Christ experienced by his parishioners, were fruits of (what he saw as) Federal theology's twofold emphasis on particular (and in that sense "limited") atonement and that assurance was the fruit of recognizing evidences of grace as marks that one was among the elect. Thus, as Campbell himself noted, from around 1828, universal atonement became more prominent in his preaching, accompanied by an emphasis on the assurance of Christ's love for all.[20]

---

[15] T. F. Torrance, *Scottish Theology* (Edinburgh: T. & T. Clark, 1996).

[16] It is striking in this context that T. F. Torrance's own revered teacher H. R. Mackintosh seems to have viewed Ronald A. Knox's critique of the concept of "vicarious repentance" as unanswerable (*Some Loose Stones: Being a Consideration of Certain Tendencies in Modern Theology, Illustrated by Reference to the Book Called "Foundations"* [London: Longmans, Green, London 1914], 160–73). Knox has R. C. Moberly's exposition of this teaching particularly in view. For the reference to Mackintosh, see J. K. Mozley, *The Doctrine of the Atonement* (Duckworth: London 1915), 196 n. 1.

[17] J. I. Packer, "What Did the Cross Achieve? The Logic of Penal Substitution," *Tyndale Bulletin* 25 (1974): 42.

[18] Only later did his specific hostility to so-called Federal Calvinism as a theological system develop.

[19] See his *Memorials of John McLeod Campbell, D.D.*, ed. Donald Campbell, 3 vols. (London: Macmillan, 1877), 1:145.

[20] Ibid., 1:50.

Campbell's son Donald records two marked stages in the development of his opinions:

> His anxious meditation on the religious state of his people, and his experience of the small effect of his earlier teaching, led him to this conclusion—that, in order that they might be free to serve God, with a pure disinterested love to Him, "their first step in religion would require to be, resting assured of His love in Christ to them as individuals, and of their individually having eternal life given to them in Christ." This was the essence of the doctrine of "Assurance of Faith," which aroused opposition in Glasgow at the end of 1827. And the controversy in which he was thus involved led him to a further step. This "assurance," which he saw to be the necessary beginning of true religious life, must rest upon something outside of the moods and feelings of the individual; it must have its foundation in the record of God which the Gospel contained. Hence, he was led to the closer consideration of the extent of the Atonement; and he came to the conclusion, that, unless Christ had *died for all*, unless he was indeed the gift of God to every human being, there was no sufficient warrant for calling upon men to be assured of God's love to them.[21]

The narrative of Campbell's trial and deposition makes for unhappy reading. Earlier in the conflict he argued that his teaching was not inconsistent with his church's subordinate standards, the Westminster Confession of Faith.[22] But some who had a deep affection for him, and a real sympathy with his pastoral concern for the free offer of the gospel and for the Lord's people to enjoy full assurance, nevertheless regarded his language as "rash."[23] Moreover, in a remarkable interchange that took place immediately after his deposition, his friend Alexander Scott asked him, "Could you sign the Confession now?" "No," he replied, "the Assembly was right. Our doctrine and the Confession were incompatible."[24]

---

[21] Ibid.

[22] See Campbell, *Whole Proceedings*, 50–66.

[23] The comment is that of Thomas Chalmers, whom (in addition to Edward Irving) Campbell had first consulted in 1828, "in the hope that the grounds of my convictions would commend themselves to them" (see *Memorials* 1:52). Chalmers, who was not unsympathetic to Campbell's concerns, and was himself profoundly committed to the universal offer of the gospel, appears to have had a deep personal concern for him. Interestingly his perspective on Campbell was not so different from that of Robert H. Story: "He [i.e., Campbell] ought to have done as day after day I entreated him, at once disavow the expressions and express his resolution never to use them, but as Scripture warranted . . ." (*Memoir of the Life of Rev. Robert Story* [London: Macmillan, 1862], 190). Within a month of Campbell's deposition, Chalmers wrote to the Countess of Elgin, "I grieve for poor Campbell. He was probably right in *idea*, but if he obstinately persist in couching that right idea in a wrong phraseology, he may not be the less dangerous as an expounder of truth. The man whose sound views may save himself, might still, by abandoning the form of sound words, mislead others. Yet I cannot help being in great heaviness on his account" (William Hannah, ed., *Letters of Thomas Chalmers* [1853; repr., Edinburgh: Banner of Truth, 2007], 349).

[24] See James L. Goodloe IV, *John McLeod Campbell: The Extent and Nature of the Atonement*, Studies in Reformed Theology and History 3 (Princeton, NJ: Princeton Theological Seminary, 1997), 35.

Critique of Campbell

There are features in Campbell that resonate powerfully and attractively. For one thing, he recognized a real pastoral issue—a deep lack of assurance of salvation in many people within his church. That is a long-standing and widespread pastoral burden. He did not shirk the issue. For another, he sought to respond theologically. He never severed theology from praxis. This is surely a great *desideratum* in a minister of the gospel. That said, however, closer examination of Campbell's work exposes a number of major flaws.

Campbell's critique of definite atonement is self-confessedly not exegetical (although he held that it was exegetically sustainable). It seeks to be logical and theological. But the argumentation rarely proceeds on the basis of careful or substantial exegesis, and theological *a priori* appears to trump handling texts in context.[25]

Campbell's primary objection is to *limited* atonement. His driving motivation is that a doctrine of equal and universal love is a necessary *a priori* of the gospel of the atonement: *"That cannot be the true conception of the nature of the atonement which implies that Christ died for an election from among men."*[26] Significantly, he acknowledges that if the atonement is interpreted in terms of penal substitution, then definite ("limited") atonement follows.[27] *Penal* substitution must be excluded from any right doctrine of the atonement.[28] Campbell's criticisms of penal substitution (and therefore by implication "definite" atonement) include the following:

(1) *Penal, substitutionary, definite atonement makes justice a necessary attribute of God but love an arbitrary one.* In Federal theology, Campbell main-

---

[25] Thus, for example, without any careful exegetical or contextual reflection, such words as Hebrews 10:19–21, clearly addressed to *believers*, are read as if addressed equally to *unbelievers* (see Campbell, *Memorials*, 1:65).

[26] Campbell, *Nature of the Atonement*, 71 (emphasis original).

[27] Ibid. Cf. also 68.

[28] T. F. Torrance appears to seek to redeem Campbell at this point: "*The penal element as infliction under the wrath of God, which Christ as Mediator fully experienced, was by no means rejected but discerned in a deeper dimension*" (*Scottish Theology*, 301–302; emphasis original). But this is hardly what Campbell himself means. Torrance's claim made earlier that "Campbell unquestionably held to 'the Catholic and Reformed' doctrine of the atonement" (295) is, surely, breathtaking. *Pace* Torrance, Campbell cannot so easily be turned into a devotee of Athanasius, Calvin, and prospectively Barth. Equally untenable is the claim that the high "Federal Calvinist," Samuel Rutherford, speaks "in anticipation of Campbell" and viewed Christ as "repenting for us in his passive obedience" (305; cf. ibid., 100). Jason Goroncy, "'Tha mi a' toirt fainear dur gearan': J. Mcleod Campbell and P. T. Forsyth on the Extent of the Atonement," in *Evangelical Calvinism: Essays Resourcing the Continuing Reformation of the Church*, ed. Myk Habets and Bobby Grow (Eugene, OR: Wipf & Stock, 2012), 255 n. 6, accepts this reading of Rutherford on the basis of Torrance's work. What makes Torrance's claim particularly eyebrow-raising is that the words he cites as Rutherford's (from *Christ Dying and Drawing Sinners to Himself*) *are not Rutherford's words at all* but those of John Towne, whom Rutherford is in the process of contradicting! Rutherford is thus made to affirm the very thing he denies.

tains, God "must" be just to all. Justice is therefore "necessary," while love is "arbitrary." God, however, does not love arbitrarily. God *is* love. In a word, behind the orthodox ("Federal") "Calvinistic" view of the atonement lies a distorted view of God. For, in Campbell's words, "Nothing can be clearer to me than that *an arbitrary act cannot reveal character.*"[29] This point is further pressed home by appeal to Jesus's command to love our enemies (Matt. 5:44).[30] But if we are to love all of our enemies, does this not imply the universal (and equal) love of God? The atonement he provides must therefore be universal.

While this argument has beguiling features, its flaws are substantial. For one thing, the use of the term "arbitrary" lends emotional not logical power to the argument. "Arbitrary" implies "by a decision of the will." In the context of the Campbell "school," "arbitrary" always seems to carry the emotive, secondary, and sinister sense of "capricious."

Here Campbell is guilty of confusing *character* and *relationship*. The former exists independently of the latter, but is manifested variously in the context of the latter. A just and loving person never expresses those attributes without reference to each other, or irrespective of context. Thus, according to Scripture, it is just for the *loving* God to hate sin, and even to reveal that he hates sinners. No intelligible interpretation of Malachi 1:2–3 ("I have loved Jacob but Esau have I hated") can make these words mean that God loves Jacob and Esau in the same sense and in the same way (irrespective of whether these proper nouns represent individuals or nations). Moreover, this point remains valid irrespective of the specific use Paul makes of this text in Romans 9:13.

Furthermore, the Jesus who in Matthew 5:44 commands love of enemy also in 7:23 himself says to some, "I never knew you; depart from me, you workers of lawlessness." The loving God revealed in Scripture dismisses individuals from his presence into "outer darkness" (Matt. 8:12) and exposure to his wrath, yet ever remains the God of (holy) love.[31]

In this general context, Campbell and his "school" are guilty of confusing "justice" with "punitive justice." The two are not the same. The former is an essential attribute (God is eternally just within the eternal fellowship

---

[29] Campbell, *Nature of the Atonement*, 73 (emphasis original). The oddity of such a thought, which Campbell (with others) regards as profoundly significant, is its implication: that a woman's choice to marry a particular man (an "arbitrary" not a "necessary" act) tells us nothing about her character. Further, the logic would also imply that if her character is love, she will love all men equally! See n. 31 below.
[30] Ibid., 45.
[31] Note the even stronger language in Matthew 25:41.

of the Trinity); the latter is a relational response (God righteously exercises punitive justice only within the context of sin).[32] Moreover, in giving "love" absolute priority on the basis of 1 John 4:8, disrespect is shown to the fabric of Scripture. For 1 John 1:5 has earlier stressed that "God is light." The Scriptures never abstract love from holiness. Here, at least in Campbell's more recent advocates, a hidden (Barthian?) motif ("God is the One who *loves in freedom*"[33]) masks a neglect of the Johannine and biblical motif ("God is the One who *loves in holiness*").

At root here in Campbell, and a recurring feature in his "school," is an illegitimate extrapolation from a particular biblical statement to a general theological position, without reference to broader exegetical and biblical-theological considerations. In this instance, the Christ who calls us to love our enemies is the Lamb from whose wrath kings, great ones, and generals flee (Rev. 6:12–17). Distinguishing love, far from being an idiosyncratic feature of Federal theologians in the seventeenth century, is rooted in Scripture and the historic orthodoxy of the church. It is finely expressed in Aquinas's summary of Augustine's Tractate CX on John 17:21–23: "God loves all things that He has made, and amongst them rational creatures more, and of these especially those who are members of his only-begotten Son; and much more than all, His only begotten Son himself."[34]

What Campbell set himself against is not merely, as he erroneously assumes, "Federal Calvinists," but an entire Christian tradition.

(2) *Closely connected to Campbell's complaint that the "older Calvinism" gave priority to justice over love, is his criticism that it also made the divine-human relationship essentially legal rather than filial.* Commenting on Galatians 4:5–6, he wrote:

> Therefore, when we contemplate the Son of God, in our nature, dealing on our behalf with the condemnation of sin, and the demand for righteousness, which are in the law, we are to understand that He is not thus honouring in humanity the Law of God for the purpose of giving us a perfect legal standing as under the law, but for the purpose of taking us from under the

---

[32] God is eternally, trinitarianly, just; but there is no *punitive* justice inherent in God's being. Justice is an essential attribute, capable of exercise among the members of the Trinity; punitive justice is that attribute in action with respect to sin and evil.

[33] Karl Barth, *Church Dogmatics*, ed. G. W. Bromiley and T. F. Torrance, 14 vols. (Edinburgh: T. & T. Clark, 1956–1975), II/1, 257 (title § 28).

[34] Thomas Aquinas, *Summa Theologiae*, trans. Fathers of the English Dominican Province, 5 vols. (Notre Dame, IN: Ave Maria, 1948), 1.20.3.

law, and placing us under grace—redeeming us that we may receive the adoption of sons. So that not a legal standing, however high or perfect, but a filial standing, is that which is given to us in Christ.[35]

In his view, classical atonement theology is permeated with a kind of legality from which his own doctrine brought deliverance. In the "older Calvinism," justification becomes a forensic rather than a real standing; but the true standing for which we have been created is not legal but filial, namely, sonship.[36]

Here it seems to have eluded Campbell that in Scripture the filial relationship is itself a *legal* standing ("adoption," a category uniquely Pauline, is almost certainly borrowed from the Roman legal system).[37] But more than that, this critique fails to account for the extent to which the filial relationship, so dominant in Calvin (as his frequent use of *adoptio* makes clear), is also prevalent in the literature of "the older [Federal] Calvinism" of the seventeenth century.[38] In fact the Westminster Confession of Faith holds a place of distinction in being the first such systematic exposition of the Christian faith to contain an entire chapter on adoption.[39]

Furthermore, the notion that the "older Calvinism" consistently viewed the Edenic relation as fundamentally legal, but not gracious, is equally questionable. John Owen, whose view of the atonement is specifically in Campbell's crosshairs, held the contrary view, as did others.[40] Indeed the Westminster Divines made clear that the original divine-human relationship was constituted out of the "condescension" of God, so that even the so-called covenant of works was a gracious arrangement. It was, after all, implicitly

---

[35] Campbell, *Nature of the Atonement*, 76.
[36] Ibid.
[37] See, inter alia, Francis Lyall, *Slaves, Citizens, and Sons: Legal Metaphors in the Epistles* (Grand Rapids, MI: Zondervan, 1984), 67–99, esp. 81–88.
[38] See, for examples, William Ames, *The Marrow of Sacred Divinity* (Leyden, 1623), chapter 37; John Owen, *The Doctrine of Justification by Faith*, in *The Works of John Owen*, ed. W. H. Goold, 24 vols. (Edinburgh: Johnstone & Hunter, 1850–1853; repr., Edinburgh: Banner of Truth, 1965), 5:205–23. Cf. Joel Beeke, *Heirs with Christ: The Puritans on Adoption* (Grand Rapids, MI: Heritage Reformed Publishing, 2010).
[39] WCF, 14. Later, perhaps under the influence of the use of Francis Turretin's *Institutes of Elenctic Theology*, ed. James T. Dennison, trans. George Musgrave Giger, 3 vols. (Phillipsburg, NJ: P&R, 1992–1997), as a theological summa (especially his treatment in his Sixteenth Topic, Justification), adoption tended to be treated by systematic theologians as simply an aspect of justification. Even so, Turretin expounds it at some length in *Institutes*, 2:666–69. Moreover, it was among Federal theologians in the nineteenth century that considerable interest was shown in the Christian's sonship.
[40] Owen, *Justification*, in *Works*, 5:277: "Grace is the original fountain and cause of all our acceptation before God in the new covenant. *Ans.* It was so also in the old. The creation of man in original righteousness was an effect of divine grace, dignity, and goodness; and the reward of eternal life in the enjoyment of God was of mere sovereign grace: yet what was then of works was not of grace;—no more is it at present." See also Samuel Rutherford, *The Covenant of Life Opened* (Edinburgh, 1655), 35, 194.

618 DEFINITE ATONEMENT IN PASTORAL PRACTICE

a promissory covenant. Campbell had simply not read widely enough in the sources.[41]

(3) *Campbell further argues that, contrary to the "older Calvinism," forgiveness is prior to repentance. Indeed it is actually prior to the atonement itself.*[42] This criticism is intended as a massive statement about the priority of grace. If repentance is antecedent to forgiveness, and is a condition for receiving it, then grace cannot be "free." Indeed, it is argued, it was for this reason that Calvin taught that repentance *follows*, rather than *precedes*, forgiveness.[43]

While this may sound grace-full, it is in fact a sleight of hand. Either that, or Jesus and the apostles require correction. For both launch the gospel with the proclamation of "repentance and forgiveness of sins" (Luke 24:47); "Repent and be baptized every one of you . . . *for the forgiveness of your sins*" (Acts 2:38); "*If* we confess our sins, he is faithful and just to forgive us our sins" (1 John 1:9).[44] Here is the apostolic conditional clause to which Campbell and his "school" appear to be so allergic.

Furthermore, if forgiveness precedes repentance, I am surely already forgiven. What necessity, then, for an atonement—or, for that matter, faith? By contrast, in the apostolic teaching, while there is grace in the heart of God toward sinners, it is only *in Christ* that there is forgiveness and pardon (Eph. 1:7).[45] And only when we are united to Christ is it ours. For outside of Christ we remain "by nature children of wrath, like the rest of mankind" (Eph. 2:3). This union takes place within the context of faith and repentance (a two-sided coin of grace-bestowed response to the word of the gospel). The gospel never places either justification or forgiveness *prior* to union with Christ. To do so would be to confuse God's gracious disposition with his righteous pardon.

Calvin himself is appealed to in this context to corroborate Campbell:

> John Calvin, in the *Institutes* (Book III, chapter 3) . . . drew a distinction between legal repentance and evangelical repentance. Legal repentance said, "Repent, and if you repent, you will be forgiven. This made the imperative

---

[41] WCF, 7.1. For extended discussion, see Andrew A. Woolsey, *Unity and Continuity in Covenantal Thought: A Study in the Reformed Tradition to the Westminster Assembly* (unpublished doctoral thesis, University of Glasgow, 1988), 1:54, 83–86; 2:263–64, 299. For an accessible introduction, see Philip G. Ryken, *Thomas Boston as Preacher of the Fourfold State* (Carlisle, UK: Paternoster, 1999), 104–108.
[42] Campbell, *Nature of the Atonement*, 44–46.
[43] Cf. the argument of J. B. Torrance in his "Introduction" to *Nature of the Atonement*, 13–15.
[44] Emphasis added.
[45] Cf. the wise pastoral comments of John Owen, *Communion with God the Father, the Son, and the Holy Ghost*, in *Works*, 2:32.

prior to the indicative, and made forgiveness conditional upon an adequate repentance . . ."[46]

In other words, Campbell argued that making repentance prior to forgiveness inverted the evangelical order of grace, whereas in the NT *forgiveness is logically prior to* repentance.[47]

But this is again a misstep. For one thing, it is a flawed exposition of Calvin. For him, repentance means the "regeneration" of the whole of our lives—a *lifelong* process rooted in (and therefore subsequent to) the forgiveness with which the Christian life begins.[48] No "Federal Calvinist" would quibble at this. But, when Calvin is thinking about the way the Christian life *begins* and forgiveness is received, he notes, "Repentance proceeds from a sincere fear of God. *Before the mind of the sinner can be inclined to repentance, he must be aroused by the thought of divine judgment.*"[49] This is a very different perspective from the contention that forgiveness *precedes* repentance.

For another, this fails to take account of the gospel order of Pentecost: "Repent and be baptized every one of you in the name of Jesus Christ *for the forgiveness of your sins*" (Acts 2:38); and of the apostle John: "*If* we confess our sins, he is faithful and just to forgive us our sins" (1 John 1:9).

Moreover, if forgiveness is not conditional upon atonement, the forgiveness of sins is, by implication, possible for God without an atonement.[50] But again this will not do, especially since "without the shedding of blood there is no forgiveness of sins" (Heb. 9:22). Here Campbell (and his followers) confuse a divine *disposition* of grace with a divine *act* of forgiveness. But in Scripture forgiveness is not an attribute but an act inherent in justification.[51]

---

[46] Torrance, "Introduction" to *Nature of the Atonement*, 11–12.

[47] Ibid. See his sermon "Confession," in *Responsibility for the Gift of Eternal Life*, Compiled by Permission of the late Rev. John Campbell, D. D., From Sermons Preached Chiefly at Row, in the Years 1829–31 (London, 1873), 61, where he speaks of "a real substantial forgiveness, independent of all returning."

[48] Calvin's actual definition of repentance gives no credence to the Campbell–Torrance perspective at this point. It is found in *Institutes*, 3.3.5: "A real conversion of our life unto God, proceeding from sincere and serious fear of God; and consisting in the mortification of our flesh and the old man, and the quickening of the Spirit." In fact, while Calvin does not deny the value of the legal/evangelical distinction to which J. B. Torrance refers, he immediately states, "yet the term repentance (insofar as I can ascertain from Scripture) must be differently taken"!

[49] Calvin, *Institutes*, 3.3.7 (emphasis added). Cf. the emphasis in 3.3.5.

[50] Cf. Campbell, *Nature of the Atonement*, 20–21, where he discusses this.

[51] In addition it should be noted that in "Federal" theology it is understood that (i) God's love is not conditioned by Christ's death; (ii) the conditions for forgiveness (repentance and faith) are given by God in grace; and (iii) what "guards" the sheerness of grace is *not* that there is no "if" in gospel proclamation, but rather that faith and repentance are noncontributory to salvation. This is underscored by Paul's striking turn of phrase in Romans 4:16: "That is why it depends on faith, in order that the promise may rest on grace." The logic in this particular context is that rather than distort grace, the necessity of faith (and repentance by implication) preserves grace; it does not obscure or distort it.

This brings us to Campbell's peculiar reworking of the very nature of the atonement.

(4) *For Campbell, the atonement is not a work of penal substitution that justly grounds forgiveness but rather a perfect confession of our sins.* "Atonement" is effected by Christ as the God–Man who has perfect oneness with both God and man. As such he fully enters into and absorbs the pain of God's attitude toward our sin and what it deserves. Because of his oneness of mind with the Father, he fully tastes its horror and thus effects "a perfect confession of our sins. This confession, as to its own nature, must have been *a perfect Amen in humanity to the judgment of God on the sin of man . . .*" In essence, then, Jesus experiences

> the full apprehension and realization of that wrath, as well as of the sin against which it comes forth into His soul and spirit, into the bosom of the divine humanity, and, so receiving it, He responds to it with a perfect response—a response from the depths of that divine humanity—and *in that perfect response He absorbs it.* For that response has all the elements of a perfect repentance in humanity for all the sin of man—a perfect sorrow—a perfect contrition—all the elements of such a repentance, and that in absolute perfection, all—excepting the personal consciousness of sin—and by that perfect response in Amen to the mind of God in relation to sin is the wrath of God rightly met, and that is accorded to divine justice which is its due, and could alone satisfy it.[52]

This is a perfect repentance, although lacking any consciousness of personal sin.[53] Christ is indeed a deeply suffering Savior. What he did was vicarious; Campbell claims it was an expiatory atonement. What it was *not* was penal substitution.[54]

Campbell himself hints that his "vicarious repentance" perspective may have been first stimulated by a speculative comment made by Jonathan Ed-

---

[52] Campbell, *Nature of the Atonement*, 118 (emphasis original). Torrance, *Scottish Theology*, 305–307, argues that Campbell's "repentance" may be captured by the Latin word *poenitentia*, an internal penal infliction that he endured in his soul." But the issue is "who imposes the penal character of the infliction?" For further, see Campbell's chapter "Repentance," in *Responsibility*, 46–65.

[53] Campbell, *Nature of the Atonement*, 118; a point on which Campbell's view was virtually universally criticized in the nineteenth century. Campbell sees an illustration of such "atonement" in the zeal of Phinehas in Numbers 25:10–13. But the atonement made in that context was not Phinehas's zeal but the penal death of the perpetrators of ungodliness (108–110, 115).

[54] Elegantly stated by John R. W. Stott, *The Cross of Christ* (Downers Grove, IL: InterVarsity Press, 1986), 142: "In this way 'sin-bearing' has dissolved into sympathy, 'satisfaction' into sorrow for sin, and 'substitution' into vicarious penitence, instead of vicarious punishment."

wards, to the effect that only "either an equivalent punishment or an equivalent sorrow and repentance" could atone for sin.[55] Edwards gave no further thought to the latter possibility. But Campbell developed it. Indeed, he believed it was vindicated by the fact that the first thing an awakened sinner seeks to do in order to have peace with God is to seek to repent and to do so perfectly. Perfect repentance, he states, would be "the true and proper satisfaction to offended justice."[56] This, he holds, Christ provided. There is, therefore, no imputation of our guilt and punishment as such to Christ; only his sympathy with the Father's disposition toward our sin. As one of us, Christ therefore perfectly repents for us. In this he offers a perfect and pure intercession.

The problem with this is, of course, that the NT knows no such category as the perfect vicarious repentance of Christ. To speak of Christ's "repentance" may or may not be a helpful theological construct,[57] but to see a concept of which the Bible itself never speaks as the central key to the atonement is, surely, cavalier. It is to fail to do theology out of a center in the actual text of Scripture, and to ignore the central thrusts of the biblical teaching. "The LORD has laid on him the iniquity of us all" (Isa. 53:6) is surely not to be interpreted to mean that Christ entered sympathetically into the Father's hostility to our sin;[58] nor does it consist with the perspective of Galatians 3:13 that Christ became "a curse" for us; nor account for the strongly judicial language used both in the Passion narrative and by Paul in Romans 8:32, that the Father "handed over" or "gave up" the Son to a *judicial* process. He "tasted death" (see Heb. 2:9) specifically as the "wages of sin" (Rom. 6:23).[59] In particular, Campbell's theology does scant justice to the cry of *God-forsakenness*—the litmus test, as R. C. Moberly noted, of

---

[55] Campbell cites and discusses Edwards in *Nature of the Atonement*, 119. For the full text of Edwards in context, see Jonathan Edwards, *"The Miscellanies" 501–832*, in *The Works of Jonathan Edwards*, ed. Ava Chamberlain, 26 vols. (New Haven, CT: Yale University Press, 2000), Misc. 779, 18:439. A. B. Bruce, *The Humiliation of Christ*, 4th ed. (Edinburgh: T. & T. Clark, 1900), 318, 438–39, speculated that the ultimate source of Edwards's speculation might be Rupert of Duytz (1075–1129).

[56] Campbell, *Nature of the Atonement*, 124.

[57] The consensus is that a repentance without a consciousness of personal sin is an incoherent notion. But see Geerhardus Vos, *Biblical Theology: Old and New Testaments* (Grand Rapids, MI: Eerdmans, 1948), 344.

[58] The words "Stricken, smitten by God, and afflicted . . . the LORD has laid on him the iniquity of us all . . . it was the will of the LORD to crush him" (Isa. 53:4, 6, 10), "I will strike the shepherd, and the sheep of the flock will be scattered" (Matt. 26:31; citing Zech. 13:7) can hardly be reduced to Christ absorbing the disposition of the Father toward sin but not becoming the object of his wrath against sin. Scripture does not relieve us of the double perspective toward which Campbell felt so much antipathy.

[59] The NT focus is not on Christ's repentance, nor on his realization of divine wrath, but on the death he died (John 10:7–18; Rom. 5:9–10; 1 Cor. 15:3; 2 Cor. 5:21; Heb. 2:9, 14, 17; 9:11–14; 10:19; 1 Pet. 1:18–19, 2:24; 3:18). It is the shedding of blood—Christ laying down his life in death as propitiation, as a penal substitute (Rev. 1:5; 5:9)—that stands front and center for the apostles (1 Cor. 15:3).

622 DEFINITE ATONEMENT IN PASTORAL PRACTICE

any view of the atonement.[60] For Campbell, the words have become a cry of horror in sharing the divine response to sin, and no longer a cry of God-forsakenness.

The critique—one that has reemerged in our own time—is that penal substitution is unworthy of God. But this is to ignore the concord in the Trinity. For the Lord Jesus himself answers the perceived problem of Trinitarian disharmony, or antagonism. There is none. He "lays down" his life[61] "for the sheep." And this is the "reason the Father loves me" (John 10:17). In him, simultaneously, "heaven's love and heaven's justice meet."[62]

Within Campbell's system there seems to be no rationale for the cross *as such*. Perhaps Gethsemane is necessary, but why the death of the cross? Contrary to Calvin, Campbell refuses to see the cross as an expression of the holy judgment of God upon his Son, when Christ appears before the Father in the character of a sinner, yet also as simultaneously the very moment when the Father loves the Son. There is both agony and ecstasy at the cross. We cannot—as Campbell wants to do—avoid the profound two-dimensionality of it all. Here the Father "turns his face away"[63] as his Son appeared before him having been "made . . . to be sin" by him (2 Cor. 5:21). But here the Father also might be heard singing quietly, "If ever I loved thee, my Jesus, 'tis now."[64]

The all too familiar axiom of Gregory Nazianzus, "that which he has not assumed he has not healed" (originally set within the context of debate over the *natures* of Christ),[65] is also apropos by extension within the context of the *work* of Christ: the unassumed remains the unhealed and unredeemed. If Christ did not experience what we deserve to experience for our sin—namely, God's wrath (Rom. 1:18) and the divine curse (Gal. 3:13)[66]—there is no atonement for it. Our deepest problem is not that we do not share the Father's horror of sin, or his understanding of what it deserves. Rather we deserve what sin actually deserves. Unless Christ bears this for me, he cannot redeem me. It is not enough that in some sense he absorbs the wrath of God, but does not bear it. To be our Savior he must bear the wrath to which we are

---

[60] Moberly, *Atonement and Personality,* 407. For Campbell's exposition, see *Nature of the Atonement*, 200–207.
[61] Again, clearly the reference is to death, not to a sympathetic view of the horror of sin.
[62] From the hymn by Elizabeth C. Clephane, "Beneath the Cross of Jesus."
[63] From the hymn by Stuart Townend, "How Deep the Father's Love for Us."
[64] From the hymn by William R. Featherstone, "My Jesus, I Love Thee."
[65] Gregory Nazianzus, *Select Letters of Saint Gregory Nazianzus, NPNF²* 7:51. The letter, written to his fellow priest Cledonius, is a critique of the christology of Apollinarius.
[66] The latter text is set within a covenantal context: note the dual motifs of (i) the fulfillment of the Abrahamic covenant and (ii) the use of blessing/cursing language, which is virtually definitive of covenant (i.e., federal) operations.

liable and "deliver us from the wrath to come" (1 Thess. 1:10). Furthermore, one is bound to ask, Why would vicarious repentance have any effect on the Evil One such as to set his prisoners free?

In sum, for Campbell the cross is not *penal* substitution. It is Christ's vicarious "Amen" to God's judgment on sin. The cross is not the suffering the Holy Father brings on his Son, but rather the suffering of a participation in what God feels toward sin. In a sense it is God feeling his own feelings in man. Our Lord's interpretation of his passion as his Father saying "I will smite the shepherd . . ." (Mark 14:27, KJV; cf. Zech. 13:7) becomes of no consequence, *for in Campbell's system there is no smiting by the Father at all.*

In all this Campbell confesses he finds a double relief. Intellectually, it is a relief not to see a double consciousness in both Father and Son.[67] Morally and spiritually, it is a relief not to be required to see a legal fiction having taken place at Calvary.[68] But unfortunately Campbell's empathetic Christ does not deliver me from the wrath to come, because while he has felt its terror, he has never borne it in my place.

But if Christ has not borne my condemnation, and only entered into a wholly empathetic view of what sin deserves, how can I be confident that "there is . . . no *condemnation* for those who are in Christ Jesus" (Rom. 8:1)? Agreement with condemnation, sensing how righteous yet awful it is, is not the same as bearing it. There is an ongoing sleight of hand in Campbell's theology here. It claims to deliver what it does not have the theological capital to purchase and provide.

This leads to a fifth point.

(5) *Campbell's contention, stated (if possible) more vigorously by his later followers, is that only his view of the atonement sets us free to enjoy assurance of salvation. Definite atonement militates against the assurance that characterized early Reformed theology*: "This it does because it takes away the warrant which the universality of the atonement gives to every man that hears the gospel to contemplate Christ with the personal appropriation of the words of the apostle, 'who loved me, and gave himself for me.'"[69] In view here is the issue that Campbell and his followers regard as the death knell of

[67] Here Campbell is set in opposition to Calvin (*Institutes*, 2.16.2).
[68] Campbell, *Nature of the Atonement*, 222.
[69] Ibid., 71.

the Federal scheme: "How can I have assurance of salvation if I do not know that Christ died for me?"

At the pastoral level, one occasionally encounters this issue in individuals who display a spiritual pathology that does not easily yield to the medicine of the gospel. In general, however, this is largely a question raised in the academy rather than in the life of the church, and it tends to be something of a straw man. But it is also indicative of some theological and pastoral confusion. For (a) the warrant for faith and the assurance it brings in its exercise is not the knowledge that Christ died for us but the promise that he will save to the uttermost those who come to God through him (Heb. 7:25); and (b) assurance of salvation is not rooted in the knowledge of either election or the identity of those for whom Christ died; it comes exclusively through faith in Christ as he offers himself to us in the gospel as able to save all who come to him. As framed, the problem is largely a pseudo problem. The assurance of faith is not attainable prior to the actual exercise of faith. And this assurance comes not by knowing Christ died for me but by trusting him to save me.[70]

Here Federal theology with its doctrine of limited atonement has been unjustly seen as the "whipping boy" for lack of assurance. But this is certainly a myth.[71] The truth is that assurance of salvation was actively discouraged in the church since at least the time of Gregory the Great (540–604), who, at the doorway to the Middle Ages, regarded it as basically impossible for the ordinary believer and even undesirable. Medieval theology would develop an *ordo salutis* terminating in the idea of the justification of the man who had been *made justus* (hence justi-fication) by the working of grace. But how could one know one was fully *justus* and therefore justifiable? The Counter Reformation Council of Trent (1545–1563) agreed, when it specifically decreed, "No one is able to know with certainty of faith, without possibility of error on his part, that he himself has obtained the grace of God."[72] The formidable Roman Catholic theologian Cardinal Robert Bellarmine

---

[70] Hence the relevance of Samuel Rutherford's conviction that the reprobate have the same warrant to believe in Christ as do the elect. In this connection it is often overlooked that on no occasion recorded in the NT did the apostles preach the gospel in terms of "Christ died for you, therefore believe." Paul's statement, "The Son of God who loved me and gave himself for me" (Gal. 2:20) is an expression of faith, not one that arises apart from faith.

[71] Not least since Martin Bucer's commitment to limited atonement—unlike Calvin's—never seems to be placed in question nor seen as the *bête noire* of assurance. See Jonathan H. Rainbow, *The Will of God and the Cross: An Historical and Theological Study of John Calvin's Doctrine of Limited Redemption* (Allison Park, PA: Pickwick, 1990), 49–63.

[72] *Nullus scire valeat certitudine fidei, cui non potest subsesse falsum, se gratiam Dei esse consecutum* (*Canons and Decrees of the Council of Trent*, session 6, chapter 9).

(1542–1621)[73] could then write with all the authority of the Church of Rome that "The principal heresy of Protestants is that saints may obtain to a certain assurance of their gracious and pardoned state before God."[74]

Over against this, and far from being guilty as charged by Campbell and his "school," the Federal theologians actually placed great emphasis on the fact that Christians may experience "infallible assurance" through the use of the ordinary means of grace. This was their confessional position.[75]

Many a young (and old!) minister can empathize with the pastoral challenges Campbell encountered: a lack of joyful assurance of salvation among his people; men and women who feel they are not "good enough" for God. But far from being the specific result of Federal theology, this is a widespread phenomenon. It is in fact the natural bent of fallen men and women who are at heart legalists,[76] and who therefore see the way to salvation in terms of their efforts to fulfill the demands of the law and attain worthiness of heaven in their lives. Who can ever feel "good enough" on that basis? That was the root problem with the whole medieval system of grace. If this were the fruit of specifically Federal theology, penal substitution, and definite atonement, it would hardly have been all-pervasive in medieval Europe, nor would it have continued to prevail in contexts where Federal theology is unknown (and may even be repudiated).

Campbell and his followers characteristically argue that while Calvin held that assurance is of the essence of faith, the "older Calvinism" taught that assurance is not of faith's essence. The following two statements are seen as epitomizing the contrast:

> *Calvin*: Now we shall possess a right definition of faith if we call it a firm and certain knowledge of God's benevolence toward us, founded upon the truth of the freely given promise in Christ, both revealed to our minds and sealed upon our hearts through the Holy Spirit.[77]

> *The Westminster Confession of Faith*: This infallible assurance doth not so belong to the essence of faith, but that a true believer may wait long, and conflict with many difficulties, before he be partaker of it.[78]

---

[73] Bellarmine was proclaimed a *Doctor Ecclesiae* in 1931.
[74] Cardinal Robert Bellarmine, *De Justificatione*, 3.2.3.
[75] WCF, 18; *The Larger Catechism*, qu. 80.
[76] As, strikingly, the major antinomians in the Protestant tradition confessed themselves to have been.
[77] Calvin, *Institutes*, 3.2.7.
[78] WCF, 18.3.

The conclusion drawn is that what Calvin so clearly affirms, "Federal Calvinism" denied. But this reading pays scant attention to either the nature or the context of these two statements. Here we should carefully notice an important distinction: Calvin is providing a *definition* of *faith*; the Westminster Divines are describing the *experience* of *assurance*.[79] The contrast drawn therefore is methodologically flawed, and compares apples to oranges. In fact the Westminster Divines defined faith in Calvinian terms as "accepting, receiving and resting on Christ alone for justification, sanctification and eternal life, by virtue of the covenant of grace."[80] Patently, their discussion of assurance then describes how faith works out in experience. *That*, as Calvin himself clarifies in *Institutes*, 3.2, presents a very different picture. For faith is not an abstraction that perfectly matches its definition. Calvin, if anything, has even stronger words than those of the Federal theologians of the Westminster Assembly:

> Surely, while we teach that faith ought to be certain and assured, we cannot imagine any certainty that is not tinged with doubt, or any assurance that is not assailed by some anxiety. On the other hand, we say that believers are in perpetual conflict with their own unbelief. Far, indeed, are we from putting their consciences in any peaceful repose, undisturbed by any tumult at all.[81]

Further, "unbelief is, in all men [i.e., who are believers] always mixed with faith."[82] Thus only "He who, struggling with his own weakness, presses toward faith in his moments of anxiety, is already in large part victorious."[83] Again, "I have not forgotten what I have previously said, the memory of which is repeatedly renewed by experience [N.B.!]: faith is tossed about by various doubts, so that the minds of the godly are rarely at peace—at least they do not always enjoy a peaceful state."[84]

Calvin's explanation for this is altogether in keeping with the Federal theologians who followed. Significantly, it occurs shortly *before* his definition of faith: "Experience obviously teaches that until we put off the flesh, we attain less than we should like."[85] The fact that the Christian is situated within

---

[79] Contrary to the way in which their words have too frequently been read, the Westminster Divines treated assurance as *normal* and lack of assurance as the *exception*, and therefore an *abnormal* condition, albeit a real and sometimes stubborn pastoral issue.
[80] WCF, 14.2.
[81] Calvin, *Institutes*, 3.2.17 (emphasis added).
[82] Ibid., 3.2.4.
[83] Ibid., 3.2.17.
[84] Ibid., 3.2.37.
[85] Ibid., 3.2.4.

a conflict between flesh and spirit (and Spirit) provides for Calvin the resolution of the paradox: "In order to understand this, it is necessary to return to that division of flesh and spirit which we have mentioned elsewhere."[86] The Christian experiences faith within the context of the "not-yet-ness" of full and final salvation.[87] In Christ we are no longer dominated by the flesh but by the Spirit. But we are not yet delivered from the flesh. So long as this eschatological tension exists for the believer, there will be, in Calvin's view, a possible gap between the definition of faith and the actual experience of the believer:

> The greatest doubt and trepidation must be mixed up with such wrappings of ignorance, since our heart especially inclines by its own natural instinct toward unbelief. Besides this, there are innumerable and varied temptations that constantly assail us with great violence. But it is especially our conscience itself that, weighed down by a mass of sins, now complains and groans, now accuses itself, now murmurs secretly, now breaks out in open tumult. And so, whether adversities reveal God's wrath, or the conscience finds in itself the proof and ground thereof, thence unbelief obtains weapons and devices to overthrow faith.[88]

Yet, Calvin insists, faith triumphs, for one simple reason: faith is not an abstraction; it is personal trust in Jesus Christ—it is *fiducia*. Here Calvin and the much-maligned Federal theologians speak with one voice: the least and weakest faith receives the same strong Christ. He saves completely those who come to God by him. Thus,

> The root of faith can never be torn apart from the godly breast, but clings so fast to the inmost parts that, however faith seems to be shaken or to bend this way or that, its light is never so extinguished or snuffed out that it does not at least lurk as it were beneath the ashes. . . . though it be assailed a thousand times, it will prevail over the entire world.[89]

Compare these words: "Faith . . . may be often and many ways assailed and weakened, but gets the victory; growing up in many to the attainment of a full assurance through Christ, who is both the author and finisher of our faith."[90]

---

[86] Ibid., 3.2.18.

[87] Cf. ibid., 3.2.18–21.

[88] Ibid., 3.2.20.

[89] Ibid., 3.2.21.

[90] WCF, 14.3. Again, contrary to what is often hinted at, Calvin also gives some place to the so-called practical syllogism (Calvin, *Institutes*, 3.14.18). Cf. Richard A. Muller, "Calvin, Beza and the Later Reformed on Assurance of Salvation and the 'Practical Syllogism,'" in his *Calvin and the Reformed Tradition: On the Work of Christ and the Order of Salvation* (Grand Rapids, MI: Baker Academic, 2012), 244–76.

The former statement comes from Calvin, the latter from the Federal theology of the Westminster Confession of Faith. Far from contradicting each other they are in harmony, indistinguishable from each other in the way they balance the definition of faith with the actual experience of the believer.[91] For both, assurance is the singular fruit of the gospel and the birthright of every Christian.

Definite Atonement and Christian Assurance

Space forbids further elucidation, negatively or positively, of the various aspects of the implications of definite atonement for pastoral ministry. But in brief one can conclude that the doctrine of definite atonement, Christocentrically understood, is well able to sustain a believer's assurance.

First, it is the contention of this chapter, and this book as a whole, that not only is definite atonement able to sustain the doctrine of Christian assurance, it in fact *grounds* it. Christ's propitiation of God's wrath at Calvary (Rom. 3:25) ensures that we will not—cannot!—receive God's wrath on the last day (Rom. 5:9–11). As Calvin observed, commenting on Romans 8:32,

> since Christ, by expiating their sins, has *anticipated* the judgment of God, and by His intercession not only abolishes death, but also covers our sins in oblivion, so that no account is taken of them . . . *so there remains no condemnation*, when the laws have been satisfied and the penalty *already paid.*[92]

The point is well captured by Toplady in his hymn, "From Whence This Fear and Unbelief?"

> If thou hast my discharge procured,
> And freely in my room endured
> The whole of wrath divine;
> Payment God cannot twice demand,
> First at my bleeding Surety's hand,
> And then again at mine.

The *good news* of the gospel is based on the premise of the illegitimacy of a "double payment." We are as justified before God as Christ is—because it

---

[91] In the light of this evidence, the scholarship that has so vigorously contrasted the two would appear to be open to the charge of a prejudicial "proof-texting" in its reading of *both* Calvin *and* the later "Calvinism."

[92] John Calvin, *Romans and Thessalonians*, Calvin's New Testament Commentaries (1539; repr., Grand Rapids, MI: Eerdmans, 1960), 184–85 (emphasis added).

is with his justification alone that we ourselves are justified. It is precisely from this that our assurance comes. Moreover, it is what provides us with a personal touch of his grace as we participate in the Lord's Supper— "my body, my blood, given for *you*" (Matt. 26:26–29; Mark 14:22–26; Luke 22:17–20).

A second implication follows when we understand that "the redemption that is in Christ Jesus" is in the one "whom God put forward as a propitiation by his blood, to be received by faith" (Rom. 3:24–25). Here, the God who puts forward is God the Father, the blood is that of God the incarnate Son, the faith is the fruit of God the Spirit's ministry. The unity and harmony of the three persons of the Trinity in both accomplishing and applying redemption are evident. In this complex of activity no wedge can be driven between the purpose of the Father, the atoning work of the Son, and the effective purposes of the Spirit without compromising the coherence of the Trinity. By contrast, *any* form of indefinite (universal) atonement short of absolute universalism in effect limits the efficacy of the Son's work and debilitates the power of the Spirit's ministry.

This may seem a point of negation only. But it implies a deep Trinitarian dysfunction with deleterious implications for our doctrine of God. For with an indefinite, universal atonement the ineffectiveness of the Father's intention, and/or of the Son's propitiation, and/or of the Spirit's ministry is the inevitable result—and the inevitable implication is a lack of harmony in the purposes or activities of the members of the Trinity. In stark contrast, many passages in the NT underscore the harmonious and concerted ministry of all three persons of the Trinity.[93] The Patristic doctrine of the appropriations remains true (each person playing a distinctive role in the accomplishment of salvation). But so too does the maxim *opera ad extra trinitatis indivisa sunt*—all three persons of the Trinity communally engage in the work of each person in the Trinity.[94]

---

[93] For example, Romans 8:3–4, 9–17; 14:17–18; 1 Corinthians 6:17–20; Galatians 4:4–6; Ephesians 1:3–14; 5:18–20; Philippians 3:3; 2 Thessalonians 2:13–14; Titus 3:4–7; 1 Peter 1:2.

[94] It might appear that Hypothetical Universalism is able to sustain Trinitarian unity. In this scheme the Trinitarian decree of *impetration* involves the Son dying for all "if they should believe," but the decree of *application* of redemption is limited to the elect. Thus in both decrees the members of the Trinity are at one. But while the conditional clause ("if they should believe") appears to guarantee the absolute harmony of the Trinity (since the condition is in man, not in God), its actual effect leaves a disruption in the unity of the Father and the Son. For within this schema the Father sets forth his Son as a real propitiation for the sins of some for whom that propitiation never actually propitiates. This remains a non-propitiating propitiation, which creates a double jeopardy. The unity claimed at the level of decree turns out to be illusory at the level of the actions of the Father and the Son. The atonement made by Christ apparently will never atone before the Father. The atonement takes place within the relations in the Trinity (it is the work of the person of the divine Son—albeit in his humanity—in relation to the divine Father). Thus in the

At stake here, of course, is the Christian's confidence in the deep harmony of the three persons of the Trinity. Any disharmony of intention, function, or accomplishment undermines assurance of salvation. And it destroys a joyful confidence that the disposition of each person of the Trinity shares absolutely in the determination of the other two persons to redeem us. Positively stated, the knowledge of the absolute harmony of purpose, sacrifice, and application in the *opera ad extra trinitatis* leads to the confident communion of the believer with each person of the Trinity in terms of that person's appropriation as well as in terms of fellowship with the whole Trinity.[95]

Conclusion

By way of concluding observation, it is surely one of the peculiarities of the contention that "Federal Calvinism" is the root cause of (i) hearing the gospel as demand rather than as gift, and (ii) lack of assurance, that the proponents of this view never seem to consider that these phenomena were and are by no means isolated to Scotland! Thus, for example, evangelical Anglican ministers, serving in a context formed by the (non-federal!) *Thirty-nine Articles*, have regularly encountered the same issues in pastoral ministry, as do ministers of the gospel throughout the world from South Korea to Latin America. If there is a historical culprit here, it is far more likely to be the lingering influence of *medieval* theology with its maxim *"facere quod in se est"* ("do what lies within you")—or, in its popular form, "heaven helps those who help themselves."[96] Nor should it be forgotten how deeply embedded in post-seventeenth-century thought is the influence of English Deism (and its "father," Lord Herbert of Cherbury [1583–1648], older brother of the great metaphysical poet George Herbert), in which repentance merits forgiveness. Behind all, of course, lies the fundamental bent of the fallen human heart. After all, even the theologian Nicodemus heard Jesus's words about the *gift* of the birth from above as a *demand* for man's contributory action in redemp-

---

Hypothetical Universalism scheme there is an action of the Son (atonement accomplished for all) which does not receive the corresponding responsive action of the Father (being atoned). Thus unity at the level of decree masks an inherent disunity at the level of the action of the incarnate Son with respect to the Father. If it is responded that the Son atoned only conditionally ("if they should believe"), then the incoherence of this non-atoning atonement still leaves the same impression of an incoherent activity of the Trinity that is present in other non-particularist views.
[95] A theme to which John Owen (surely the greatest theologian among the English-speaking "Federal Calvinists") gives classical expression in his *Of Communion with God the Father, Son, and Holy Ghost, Each Person Distinctly, in Love, Grace, and Consolation, or, The Saints' Fellowship with the Father, Son, and Holy Ghost Unfolded* (London, 1657).
[96] See Heiko A. Oberman, *The Harvest of Medieval Theology* (Cambridge, MA: Harvard University Press, 1983), 129–45.

tion: "How can a man *do* this? Can he enter into his mother's womb . . . ?" Such blindness to grace is not "federal" but natural.

Contrary to Campbell's contention, and that of his "school," definite atonement does not divest the Christian of his or her assurance. Definite atonement spotlights the illegitimacy of a double payment for our sin and highlights the Trinitarian harmony displayed in the gospel. Both together serve to ground a believer's assurance: all those for whom Christ died will come to faith, and will never be plucked from his or his Father's hand, being kept by the power (or Spirit) of God for salvation on the last day. Blessèd assurance indeed—and a true cure for souls.

23

"My Glory I Will Not Give to Another"

PREACHING THE FULLNESS OF DEFINITE ATONEMENT TO THE GLORY OF GOD

John Piper

The Glory of the Cross

If the ultimate end for which God created the world is the display of his glory, and if the apex of his glory is the splendor of his grace, and if the achievement of Christ on the cross is the climactic display of this splendid grace, and if John Murray is right that "the glory of the cross is bound up with the effectiveness of its accomplishment,"[1] then the title of this chapter points to the ultimate nature of the topic before us. When we do not preach the full atoning effect of the cross—when this fullness does not underpin our free offer of the gospel to all sinners and our application of God's blood-bought promises to all his children—we diminish the glory of the cross and fall short of God's ultimate purpose in creation.

I do not mean that this diminishment necessarily cancels a person's Christian faith, or even removes God's blessing from someone's ministry. God is merciful to use us in spite of many failings. I am sure that in many

---

[1] John Murray, *Redemption Accomplished and Applied* (Grand Rapids, MI: Eerdmans, 1955), 75.

ways I fall short of God's purpose to glorify himself in the cross. The point is not to nullify or undermine anyone's faith or ministry. The point is to summon all of us to move toward magnifying more fully the majesty of the glory of the grace of God in the cross of Christ—and to do that by believing and proclaiming the full glory of Christ's death in effectively purchasing his elect, expiating their guilt, and propitiating God's wrath against them. Murray *is* right: "the glory of the cross is bound up with the effectiveness of its accomplishment."

The End for Which God Created the World

Reading the *Dissertation Concerning the End for Which God Created the World* by Jonathan Edwards was a worldview-transforming experience for me when I was in my twenties. I found the book—with its unparalleled saturation with Scripture—totally compelling, and I have spent most of my life trying to herald its main message.[2] That message is clear: "All that is ever spoken of in the Scripture as an ultimate end of God's works is included in that one phrase, 'the glory of God'; which is the name by which the last end of God's works is most commonly called in Scripture."[3] God does nothing without this as his chief end. The words of God in Isaiah 48:11 fly like a banner over every divine deed: "For my own sake, for my own sake, I do it, for how should my name be profaned? My glory I will not give to another."

The glory of God is at the heart of the gospel. Faith sees and savors "the light of the gospel of the glory of Christ, who is the image of God" (2 Cor. 4:4). That is a remarkable phrase: "the gospel of the glory of Christ"—or as Paul says again two verses later, "the light of the knowledge of the glory of God in the face of Jesus Christ." Whether he speaks of "the glory of Christ, who is the image of God" or "the glory of God in the face of Christ," the reality is the same. God's glory revealed in Christ and his work is essential to what the gospel is. When we are dealing with the glory of God, we are

---

[2] See, for example, the case for this message in John Piper, *God's Passion for His Glory: Living the Vision of Jonathan Edwards* (Wheaton, IL: Crossway, 1998); "The Goal of God in Redemptive History," appendix 2 in *Desiring God: Meditations of a Christian Hedonist*, 25th anniversary ed. (Colorado Springs: Multnomah, 2011), 313–26; and *Let the Nations Be Glad: The Supremacy of God in Missions*, 3rd ed. (Grand Rapids, MI: Baker, 2010), 11–40.

[3] Jonathan Edwards, *Dissertation Concerning the End for Which God Created the World*, in *The Works of Jonathan Edwards*, general ed. Harry S. Stout, 26 vols. (New Haven, CT: Yale University Press, 1989), 8:526. The most thorough exegetical work in recent times defending Edwards's viewpoint is James M. Hamilton, *God's Glory in Salvation through Judgment: A Biblical Theology* (Wheaton, IL: Crossway, 2010). Similarly, Thomas R. Schreiner has developed his NT theology around the unifying theme of "Magnifying God in Christ": *A New Testament Theology: Magnifying God in Christ* (Grand Rapids, MI: Baker Academic, 2008).

dealing with a reality that is not only ultimate in the aim of history, but central to the gospel.

The Central Task of Ministry and the Aim of Preaching

All of this means that the central task of Christian ministry is the magnifying of the glory of God. The aim is that the fullness of the revelation of the glory of God be displayed for God's people, and that they be helped to respond joyfully with the fullest admiration possible.

This means that preaching, which is essential to the life of the church, aims in every sermon to magnify the glory of God in Jesus, and to satisfy the deepest need of people to know and admire God. The fullness of what we need to know about God is found with clarity and surety in only one place, the Bible. Therefore, every sermon will be expository in the sense that it will try to bring the revelation of God's glory to light through the meaning of biblical texts. And at the heart of all those texts is the supreme revelation of the glory of God through the manifestation of his grace in the work of Jesus Christ on the cross. Which brings us to the great reality of the atonement in relation to the glory of God in preaching.

The Death of Christ as the Climax of the Glory of God's Grace

Now I can be more specific than I have been so far. I have said that God does all that he does to uphold and magnify and display his glory. Now I can go further and say that all his works exist to display the glory of his *grace*, and the cross of Christ is the climactic revelation of the glory of his grace, which is the apex of the glory of God.

What we are about to see from Scripture is that the revelation of the glory of God's grace was planned before creation and came to its climax in *the death of Christ for sinners*. In conceiving a universe in which to display the glory of his grace, God did not choose "Plan B." The death of Christ was not an afterthought or adjustment. For this the universe was planned. Everything leading to it, and everything flowing from it, is explained by it. To support this claim, consider several key texts.

Let us begin with Revelation 13:8. John writes, "All who dwell on earth will worship [the beast], everyone whose name has not been written before the foundation of the world in the book of life of the Lamb who was slain." Before the world was created there was a book called "the book of life of the

Lamb who was slain." The Lamb is Jesus Christ, the crucified. So the book is the book of Jesus Christ crucified. Therefore, before God made the world, he had in view Jesus Christ slain, and he had in view a people purchased by his blood, whose names were written in the book.

Next, consider 2 Timothy 1:9. Paul looks back into eternity before the ages began and says that God "saved us and called us to a holy calling, not because of our works but because of his own purpose and grace, which he gave us [that is, he gave us this *grace*] in Christ Jesus before the ages began." God gave us *grace*—undeserved favor toward sinners—in Christ Jesus before the ages began. We had not yet been created. We had not yet existed so that we could sin. But God had already decreed that grace—an "in Christ" kind of grace, blood-bought grace, sin-overcoming grace—would come to us in Christ Jesus. He planned all that before the creation of the world.

So there is a "book of life of the Lamb who was slain," and there is "grace" flowing to undeserving sinners who are not yet created. That is the plan. Why that is the plan is answered by Paul in Ephesians 1:4–6 and by John in Revelation 5:9–12. Before I look at these texts, the answer can be summed up as follows: This is the plan because *the aim of creation is the fullest display of the greatness of the glory of the grace of God. And that display would be the slaying of the best being in the universe—Jesus Christ—for countless millions of undeserving sinners.*

In Ephesians 1:4–6, Paul says,

> [God] chose us *in him* [that is, in Christ] before the foundation of the world, that we should be holy and blameless before him. In love he predestined us for adoption as sons *through Jesus Christ*, according to the purpose of his will, *to the praise of his glorious grace.*

From eternity to eternity, the goal of God in the history of redemption is to bring about the praise of the glory of his grace. But what is most relevant at this point is to notice that this plan happened "in Christ" (v. 4) or "through Jesus Christ" (v. 5) before the foundation of the world.

What does it mean that "in Christ" we were chosen and that our adoption was to happen "through Jesus Christ"? We know that in Paul's mind Christ suffered and died as a Redeemer so that we might be adopted as children of God (Gal. 4:5). Our adoption could not happen apart from the death of Christ.

Therefore, what Paul means is that to choose us "in Christ" and to plan to adopt us "through Jesus Christ" was to plan (before the foundation of the world) the suffering and death of his Son for sinners. And this was for the purpose of the praise of the glory of the grace of God (see Eph. 1:6, 12, 14). Which means that the death of Jesus for sinners is the climax of the revelation of the glory of God's grace.

Now consider the confirmation of this in Revelation 5:9–12. Here the hosts of heaven are worshiping the Lamb precisely because he was slain:

> And they sang a new song, saying, "Worthy are you to take the scroll and to open its seals, *for you were slain*, and by your blood you ransomed people for God from every tribe and language and people and nation." . . . Then I looked, and I heard around the throne . . . myriads of myriads and thousands of thousands, saying with a loud voice, "Worthy is the Lamb *who was slain*, to receive power and wealth and wisdom and might and honor and glory and blessing!"

The hosts of heaven focus their worship not simply on the Lamb but on "the Lamb *who was slain*." And they are still singing this song in Revelation 15:3: "And they sing . . . the song of the Lamb." Therefore, we can conclude that the centerpiece of worship in heaven for all eternity will be the display of the glory of the grace of God in the slaughtered and resurrected Lamb.

Definite Atonement as a Significant Part of the Glory of Christ's Achievement

The question before us in this chapter is whether definite atonement is a significant part of the glory of God's grace which he intends to display in the atoning work of his Son. And if so, how does it affect our preaching for evangelizing the world and building up the body of Christ for the glory of God?

My answer is yes, the definite atoning work of Christ is a significant part of the glory of God's grace. And to know this, by the working of God's Spirit, inflames the cause of world missions and enables us to preach in such a way that our people experience deeper gratitude, greater assurance, sweeter fellowship with God, stronger affections in worship, more love for people, and greater courage and sacrifice in witness and service. Preaching, which aims at these things to the glory of God, will speak of the cross in its fullness, not denying any of its universal implications, but also not denying its precious, definite, effective, invincible power to save God's elect.

Two key texts that we have already seen (Eph. 1:4–6 and Rev. 5:9)[4] point in this direction—that a significant part of the glory of Christ's achievement is that it secures not the potential but the actual, total, and eternal salvation of God's elect. We saw from Ephesians 1:4–6 that God's ultimate goal to glorify himself in creation reached its high point in the display of his grace "through Jesus Christ" (v. 5), that is, "in the Beloved" (v. 6). Now let us follow Paul's thought a little further into the definiteness of Christ's saving work that displays the glory of God's grace.

From verse 5 we see that God predestined *sinners* to adoption as sons: "He predestined us for adoption as sons through Jesus Christ." I showed above that the words "through Jesus Christ" mean through the redeeming work of Jesus Christ (cf. v. 7) This is how we know that God had *sinners* in view when he predestined his chosen ones for adoption. They needed redeeming. What this means, then, is that the redeeming work of Christ on the cross is what secures the passage of a person from lost sinner to adopted son, from being a child of wrath (2:3) to being a child of God. Thus the glory of God's grace, displayed in the achievement of the cross, is also displayed in the blood-bought passage of a lost person from death to life.

What is involved in that passage is explained by Paul in Ephesians 2:4–5. We see there that it is God's grace that makes the dead live. "God, being rich in mercy, because of the great love with which he loved us, even when we were dead in our trespasses, made us alive together with Christ—by grace you have been saved." Paul breaks into the flow of his sentence (signified in English with a parenthetical dash) to make sure that we realize that the act of making the spiritually dead to live is the work of God's grace. This is what is involved in the transition from being a child of wrath to being a child of God. One must be made alive spiritually. And Paul says that this is the work of God's grace. This is why it is often called sovereign grace: it raises the dead. The dead do not raise themselves. God does by his grace. And it is this "glorious grace" that will be praised for all eternity.

---

[4] Space forbids a detailed treatment of Revelation 5:9, but observe in passing that the wording points to definite atonement, and the context shows that this definite atoning work gives rise to Christ's glorification: "Worthy is the Lamb who was slain, to receive . . . glory!" (5:12). What did his being "slain" accomplish? The heavenly beings sing to Christ, "You were slain, and by your blood you ransomed people for God *from* every tribe." The phrase "from every tribe" (ἐκ πάσης φυλῆς) points to the selective work of the ransoming. It does not say that he ransomed every tribe, but "ransomed people for God *from* every tribe." The ransom distinguished them.

What makes this so relevant for definite atonement is that God does not raise everyone from spiritual death. He raises those whom he "predestined for adoption as sons" (1:5). And since the grace by which he does this is "through Jesus Christ" (that is, through his atoning work), the quickening they experience is secured for them by the death of Christ on their behalf. This means that in the atonement God designed and secured spiritual life, and its resulting faith, for those whom he predestined to sonship.[5] The atonement does not make possible the spiritual quickening of all people; it makes certain and effective the spiritual quickening of the elect. That is the conclusion of Paul's teaching on grace in Ephesians 1:4–6 and 2:4–5.

So in answer to the question, Is definite atonement a significant part of the glory of God's grace which he intends to display in the atoning work of his Son? we may say, yes. And our first reason for this answer is that the way God planned to magnify the glory of his grace is by predestining sinners to sonship through that blood-bought grace (1:5–6). And the way he planned to bring sinners to sonship was by the power of this grace in raising them spiritually from the dead and making them alive in Christ (2:5).

Thus the "glory of his grace," which has been God's aim from all eternity, includes the glorious design and power of the atonement to secure the faith and salvation of his elect. The blood-bought grace of God makes alive the dead, brings them into union with Christ, awakens faith, and saves his own to the uttermost. In other words, it is not just redemption accomplished at the cross that brings glory to God, but redemption accomplished *and applied* to the believer that is "to the praise of his glorious grace" (Eph. 1:6).

The Love of God and Definite Atonement

Before turning to a discussion of the new covenant and its relation to definite atonement and the glory of Christ, this is a suitable place to raise the question of how definite atonement relates to the love of God. It is suitable here because the text I just dealt with (Eph. 2:4–5) says that God's making us alive is owing to his "great love": "God . . . *because of the great love with which he loved* us . . . made us alive together with Christ." Discussing the love of God at this point is not an interlude in the argument but an extension of it.

---

[5] For a more extended argument for the assumption that the spiritual quickening, or "new birth," referred to in Ephesians 2:5 is the way that God brings about saving faith, see John Piper, *Finally Alive: What Happens When We Are Born Again* (Ross-shire, UK: Christian Focus, 2009), 99–108.

Paul's understanding of the unique love of God for his elect, expressed in the effective work of the atonement for them in particular, shows how essential definite atonement is in the glory of the cross, which is the greatest act of divine love (Rom. 5:8).

In a sense, I have been talking about the love of God from the very beginning of this chapter, because the *grace* of God is an expression of his *love*. It is the form love takes when it meets guilty people. But here in Ephesians 2:4, Paul makes explicit that the working of grace to make spiritually dead people alive is an expression of God's "great love." This is a unique expression in the Bible. God's *great love* "with which he loved us" prompted him to make us alive when we were dead.

This means that there is a unique love of God for his elect that accounts for the unique effect of definite atonement in saving them. We have already seen that the sovereign grace that makes the dead live is a blood-bought grace flowing to the elect from the divine purpose of the cross. We are made alive because the atonement secures it. Now we add this insight: this divine purpose of the cross is an expression of God's "great love" for his elect. Others are not made alive. Therefore, this love is a distinguishing love. It is not given to all. It is given to sinners who are predestined for sonship.

We see this again in Ephesians 5:25: "Husbands, love your wives, as Christ loved the church and gave himself up for her." A husband loves his wife in a way that is different from the way he loves other women. And Christ loves his bride, the church, in a way that is different from the way he loves other people. He "gave himself up for her." In my preaching, this has been one of the most effective ways to help my people feel the preciousness of definite atonement as an expression of God's distinguishing love for them. What would it be like for a wife, I ask them, to think that her husband only loves her the way he loves all other women? It would be disheartening. He chose her. He wooed her. He took the initiative because he set his favor on her from all the others. He has a distinguishing love for her—a great love—that is unique. She is his own loved treasure like no other woman. And so God's elect are his own loved and blood-bought people as none others are.

I tell my people, you will never know how much God loves you if you continue to think of his love for you as only one instance of his love for all the world. To be sure, God loves the world (John 3:16), but there is a "great love" for his children which he does not have for the world. Nor should anyone say (changing the metaphor from bride to children) that he has this special love for his children because they believe in him. That is backwards. Rather, spiritually dead children of wrath were made alive and brought to faith *because* he had this special love for them (Eph. 2:4). This is the wonder of it. God set his electing, atoning love on us *before* we were able to do anything to commend ourselves to him.

When we preach, we long for our people to feel loved with the fullness of God's love for them. The Arminian and Amyraldian ways of thinking make this experience difficult, if not impossible. They obscure the truth that it was precisely the distinguishing "great love" of God (Eph. 2:4), expressed in the death of Christ, by which God brings his elect to life and gives them faith.

Both views make it harder for the children of God to read Galatians 2:20 with the personal sweetness God intended: "I have been crucified with Christ. It is no longer I who live, but Christ who lives in me. And the life I now live in the flesh I live by faith in the Son of God, *who loved me and gave himself for me.*" He loved *me.* He gave himself for *me.* The preciousness of this personal love is muted where it is seen as an instance of the same love that Christ has for those who finally perish. It is not the same.

When John said of Jesus, "Having loved *his own* who were in the world, he loved them to the end" (John 13:1), he did not mean that this personal love for "his own" was the same as the love he had for everyone. He had a "great love" for his own. There was none greater. "Greater love has no one than this, that someone lay down his life *for his friends*" (John 15:13). Whatever blessings flow to the world from the cross of Christ, and they are many, there was in its design a "great love" specifically intended to rescue "his own."

The Father had chosen his own out of the world and given them to the Son. "Yours they were, and you gave them to me" (John 17:6). He loved them to the end and kept them, so that none was lost. "This is the will of him who sent me, that I should lose nothing of all that he has given me" (John 6:39). To that end, he consecrated himself the night before his death: "For their sake I consecrate myself, that they also may be sanctified in truth" (John 17:19). And then he prayed for them—only for them, not for the world—since this was part of the "great love" he had for "his own": "I am praying for them. I am not praying for the world but for those whom you have given me, for they are yours" (John 17:9). And then he died for *them.* "I know my own and my own know me . . . and I lay down my life for the sheep" (John 10:14–15).

He "[laid] down his life for his friends" (John 15:13). This is what it means that "having loved his own . . . he loved them to the end" (John 13:1).

And in the mind of Christ, this achievement for "his own" was no small part of the glory he was bringing to the Father in his saving work. "I *glorified* you on earth, having accomplished the work that you gave me to do" (John 17:4). It was the perfect and complete salvation of "his own" that caused him to say to the Father, "All mine are yours, and yours are mine, and I am *glorified* in them" (John 17:10). This glory was not the glory of a salvation made *available*, but a salvation made *real* and *effective* in the lives of "his own." The love of God for his elect is greater than the love he has for the world. As Geerhardus Vos comments, "The divine love for the elect is different not only in degree but specifically from all other forms of love, because it involves a purpose to save, of which all the other forms fall short."[6] Therefore, the greatness of this special love—expressed in the definite effectiveness of the atonement—is a significant part of God's glory in saving his people through the death of Christ.

The New Covenant and Definite Atonement

Having dealt with the love of God for his people in relation to definite atonement,[7] I turn now to the theme that has been most compelling for me as it relates to definite atonement and its personal and pastoral implications. This is a continuation of the argument that definite atonement is indeed a significant part of the glory of Christ's achievement on the cross.

In my pilgrimage toward understanding the Scriptures in regard to definite atonement, the most compelling truth has been the NT teaching concerning the new covenant. Specifically, I have been helped by the truth that the blood of Christ obtained the promises of the new covenant, which include God's regenerating work leading to faith and salvation. In other words, what Christ secured when he died was not only the possibility that all who believe will be saved, but also—and this is what makes the atonement definite—that all who are "called" *will* believe (Rom. 8:30; 1 Cor. 1:24). The blood of Christ did not merely purchase possibilities; it purchased actualities.

---

[6] Geerhardus Vos, "The Biblical Doctrine of the Love of God," in *Redemptive History and Biblical Interpretation: The Shorter Writings of Geerhardus Vos*, ed. Richard B. Gaffin (Phillipsburg, NJ: P&R, 1980), 456. One of the most helpful discussions of the love of God is D. A. Carson, *The Difficult Doctrine of the Love of God* (Wheaton, IL: Crossway, 2000).

[7] When I discuss the free offer of the gospel, I will return to the theme of the love of God for the unbelieving world.

The faith of God's chosen and called was purchased by "the blood of the covenant" (Matt. 26:28).

The promise of the new covenant, that a heart of unbelief would be replaced by a heart of faith (Ezek. 11:19; 36:26), was invincibly obtained by the death of Jesus. The term *definite atonement* refers to this truth—when God sent his Son to die, he had in view the definite acquisition of a group of undeserving sinners, whose faith and repentance he obtained by the blood of his Son. This is a divine purpose in the cross—to purchase and create the saving faith of a definite, freely chosen, unworthy, rebellious group of sinners.

This is a more glorious way to save sinners than if Christ had died only to offer sinners the possibility of actualizing salvation by means of a faith that rises decisively from human self-determination. To be sure, the Arminian view portrays sinners as needing divine assistance in order to believe—prevenient grace. But in that view the sinner provides the decisive impulse, not God. God only assists; the sinner decides. Thus, the blood of the covenant does not decisively secure the faith. The decisive cause of faith is human self-determination. The atoning work of Christ, they say, sets up this possibility. But it does not secure the outcome. But if saving faith is decisively a gift of God (Eph. 2:8[8]; Phil. 1:29), then the atoning work of Christ is seen in a different light.

The gift of faith is free to us, but it cost Christ his life. And what he bought was not only the possibility of faith but the production of faith by the work of the Holy Spirit as promised in the new covenant (Titus 3:5). The glory of this achievement is lost when we replace the decisive causation of Christ's death with our decision (whether it be human-initiated faith as in Arminianism, or God-elected faith as in Amyraldianism).[9] "What do you have that you did not receive? If then you received it, why do you boast as if you did not receive it?" (1 Cor. 4:7). Our saving faith was "received." It is a gift of God. It was purchased for us by Christ, more specifically, by the blood of the covenant. Therefore, let the one who boasts, boast in the Lord (1 Cor. 1:31). Thus our boast in his glory rests in significant measure on his atoning purchase of our faith.

One reason this understanding of definite atonement has helped me so

---

[8] Admittedly, the pronoun τοῦτο ("this") in verse 8b is neuter while πίστις ("faith") in verse 8a is feminine. The neuter pronoun refers back to the whole of "salvation by grace through faith," which means faith is included in the "gift of God" (Peter T. O'Brien, *The Letter to the Ephesians* [Leicester, UK: Apollos, 1999], 175).

[9] While Amyraldians would not wish to say that ultimate human self-determination is the decisive factor in a person's salvation, nevertheless their presentation of the atonement is similar to that of Arminianism: something "outside" of the atonement is the decisive factor that secures a person's salvation, even if it is a faith that God himself brought about. On either scheme, Christ's atoning death only provides the possibility of salvation; faith is the decisive factor that "activates" the atonement.

much is that the new covenant is so all-embracing. Every grace and every gift and every promise that the church enjoys now and forever comes to her through her participation in the new covenant. *If the blood of Christ bought the faith by which the church enters into that covenant, then every blessing she enjoys from that covenant is owing to that particular purpose of God in the cross.* In other words, the definite, invincible, atoning effect of the cross to secure the faith of God's elect is the ground of our eternal enjoyment of every blessing of the new covenant.

This is the astonishing truth that Paul expressed in 2 Corinthians 1:20: "All the promises of God find their Yes in him. That is why it is through him that we utter our Amen to God for his glory." Because of our union with Christ—because we, Gentiles and Jews, are "in him," the seed of Abraham (Gal. 3:16)—all the promises made to God's people are ours. We will see that this is possible because Christ is the Minister of a new covenant. And he is such because his blood is the "blood of the covenant" (Matt. 26:28; Mark 14:24; Luke 22:20). In other words, the atoning work of Christ on the cross secures for the people of God all the blessings of the new covenant, including a new heart of faith.

The last half of 2 Corinthians 1:20 connects this achievement of the cross with the glory of God: "That is why it is through him that *we utter our Amen to God for his glory.*" The glory of God consists largely in the display of Christ's achievement in obtaining all the promises of God for his people. Let us look more closely now at the new covenant.

A Closer Look at the New Covenant

God spoke through Jeremiah that

> the days are coming, declares the LORD, when I will make a *new covenant* with the house of Israel and the house of Judah, not like the covenant that I made with their fathers. . . . my covenant that they broke, though I was their husband, declares the LORD. For this is the covenant that I will make with the house of Israel after those days, declares the LORD: I will put my law within them, and I will write it on their hearts. And . . . I will forgive their iniquity, and I will remember their sin no more. (Jer. 31:31–34)

One fundamental difference between the promised new covenant and the old one "made with their fathers" is that they broke the old one, but in the new covenant, God will "put [his] law within them" and will "write it on their hearts" so that the conditions of the covenant are secured by God's sovereign initiative. The new covenant will not be broken. That is part of its design. It lays claim on its participants, secures them, and keeps them.

God makes this point even more clearly in the next chapter of Jeremiah:

> I will give them one heart and one way, that they may fear me forever, for their own good and the good of their children after them. I will make with them an everlasting covenant, that I will not turn away from doing good to them. And I will put the fear of me in their hearts, that they may not turn from me. I will rejoice in doing them good. (Jer. 32:39–41)

God makes at least six promises in this text: (1) I will make with them an everlasting covenant; (2) I will give them the kind of heart that secures their fearing me forever; (3) I will never turn away from doing good to them; (4) I will put the fear of me in their hearts; (5) I will not let them turn away from me; and (6) I will rejoice in doing good to them.

Here in Jeremiah 32 it becomes even clearer than in the chapter before that God is taking the sovereign initiative to make sure that the covenant succeeds. God will not leave it finally in the power of the fallen human will to attain or sustain membership in the new covenant. He will give a new heart— a heart that fears the Lord. It will be decisively God's doing, not man's. And he will act in this covenant so that "they may not turn from me" (v. 40). Thus John Owen comments, "This then is one main difference of these two covenants—that the Lord did in the old only require the condition; now, in the new, he will also effect it in all the federates, to whom this covenant is extended."[10] Similarly, Ezekiel prophesies in the same way: God will take the initiative and give a new heart and a new spirit:

> I will give them one heart, and a new spirit I will put within them. I will remove the heart of stone from their flesh and give them a heart of flesh. (Ezek. 11:19)

> I will give you a new heart, and a new spirit I will put within you. And I will remove the heart of stone from your flesh and give you a heart of flesh. And I will put my Spirit within you, and cause you to walk in my statutes and be careful to obey my rules. (Ezek. 36:26–27)

---

[10] John Owen, *Salus Electorum, Sanguis Jesu: Or The Death of Death in the Death of Christ*, in *The Works of John Owen*, ed. W. H. Goold, 24 vols. (Edinburgh: Johnstone & Hunter, 1850–1853; repr. Edinburgh: Banner of Truth, 1967), 10:237.

An unregenerate heart of stone is the deep reason why Israel did not trust God's promises, or love him with all their heart and soul and mind and strength. If the new covenant is to be more successful than the old covenant, God will have to take out the heart of stone and give his people a heart that loves him. In other words, he will have to take a miraculous initiative to secure the faith and love of his people. This is exactly what Moses says God will do:

> The LORD your God will circumcise your heart and the heart of your off-spring, so that you will love the LORD your God with all your heart and with all your soul, that you may live. (Deut. 30:6)

In other words, in the new covenant God promises that he will take the initiative and will create a new heart, so that people are made members of the new covenant by his initiative, not their own. If someone enjoys participation in the new covenant with all its blessings, it is because God forgave his iniquity, removed his heart of stone, gave him a tender heart of flesh that fears and loves God, and caused him to walk in his statutes. In other words, the new covenant promises regeneration. It promises to create faith and love and obedience where before there was only hardness.

The Blood of Jesus Obtains the Promises of the New Covenant

What we find when we come to the NT is that Jesus is the Mediator of this new covenant and that he secured it by his own blood. This is the connection between the atonement and the new covenant: Jesus's blood is the blood of the covenant. The design of his death was to establish this covenant with all the terms we have just seen.

According to Luke 22:20, at the Last Supper Jesus took the cup after they had eaten and said, "This cup that is poured out for you is the new covenant in my blood." Paul recounts this in 1 Corinthians 11:25: "He took the cup, after supper, saying, 'This cup is the new covenant in my blood.'" I take this to mean that the promises of the new covenant are purchased by the blood of Christ. Or to use the language of Hebrews, "This makes Jesus the guarantor of a better covenant" (Heb. 7:22). "He is the mediator of a new covenant, so that those who are called may receive the promised eternal inheritance" (Heb. 9:15).

The language of sovereign, enabling grace that we saw, for example, in Jeremiah 32:40–41, as part of the new covenant, is echoed in Hebrews 13:20–21:

> Now may the God of peace who brought again from the dead our Lord Jesus, the great shepherd of the sheep, by the blood of the eternal covenant, equip you with everything good that you may do his will, working in us that which is pleasing in his sight, through Jesus Christ, to whom be glory forever and ever. Amen.

In his keeping of the new covenant, and in his commitment to honor Christ's blood of the covenant, God equips us with everything good and works in us what is pleasing in his sight. He does it through Jesus "to whom be glory forever and ever." In other words, "everything good" that the church receives from God, and every good that we are enabled to do because of God, is owing to the blood-bought new covenant promises. Therefore, Jesus gets glory forever as the one who purchased those promises for us.

Again, lest that last sentence pass by too quickly, notice (as with 2 Cor. 1:20) how Hebrews 13:20–21 points to the focus of this chapter ("My Glory I Will Not Give to Another"). Take note of why the writer says, "through Jesus Christ, to whom be glory forever and ever." The word "through" shows that God's "working in us that which is pleasing in his sight" is secured by Jesus Christ in his capacity as the one who shed "the blood of the eternal covenant" (v. 20). Therefore, the immediate ground for glorifying Christ is the blood-bought, God-wrought changes in the human soul that please God. In other words, a significant part of the glory of Christ is the glory of the effectiveness of his atoning work in providing what we could not provide on our own to please God—for example, faith (see Heb. 11:6).

The point I am making is that not all the promises of the new covenant depend on the condition of faith. Rather, one of the promises made in the new covenant is that the condition of faith *itself* will be given by God. This means that the new covenant people are created and preserved by God. "I will put the fear of me in their hearts, that they may not turn from me" (Jer. 32:40). God puts the fear of God in us in the first place. And God keeps us from turning away. He creates his new people and keeps his new people. And he does this by the blood of the covenant, which Jesus said was his own blood (Luke 22:20).

The upshot of this understanding of the new covenant is that there is a definite atonement for the new covenant people. In the death of Christ, God secures a definite group of unworthy sinners as his own people by purchasing the conditions they must meet to be part of his people. The blood of the covenant—Christ's blood—purchases and guarantees the new heart of faith and repentance. God did not do this for everyone. He did it for a "definite" or a "particular" group, owing to nothing in themselves. And since he did it through Jesus Christ, the Great Shepherd, who laid down his life for the sheep, we say, "to him be glory forever and ever." This achievement is a significant part of the glory of the cross of Christ.

A Modern Appearance of an Old Error

Before turning more specifically to the preaching that flows from the glory of God expressed in definite atonement, I should deal with a current presentation of what is sometimes called "four-point Calvinism," popularized by a well-known preacher, Mark Driscoll,[11] and by a teacher of preachers, Bruce Ware,[12] and one of his former doctoral students, Gary L. Shultz, Jr.[13]

Ware and Shultz call their position the "multiple intentions view" and Driscoll calls his view "unlimited limited atonement." Driscoll expresses clearly his dependence on Ware as he spells out his view, and the language used by both of them is similar, so in these three men I am dealing, it seems, essentially with one view. In my assessment, the effort of Ware and Driscoll to hold on to a kind of "definite (indefinite) atonement" obscures the biblical teaching on this doctrine.

The problem with their view is not the concept of multiple intentions, but rather what they actually claim about those intentions. For example, Ware claims that "those in hell, who never put their faith in Christ and so were never saved, are under the just judgment of God for their sin, even though *Christ has paid the penalty for their sin.*"[14] And Driscoll claims that "all those in hell will stand reconciled to God, but not in a saving way as the universalists falsely teach."[15] These are extraordinary claims—to say that the penalty of the damned was (in some sense) paid for by the death of Christ, and the damned in hell are (in some sense) reconciled to God.

[11] Mark Driscoll, pastor at Mars Hill Church in Seattle, and Gerry Breshears, professor of Systematic Theology at Western Seminary in Portland, Oregon, articulate their view in *Death by Love: Letters from the Cross* (Wheaton, IL: Crossway, 2008), 163–81.
[12] Bruce Ware, who teaches theology at The Southern Baptist Theological Seminary in Louisville, Kentucky, has given me permission to quote him from unpublished documents he has written, including, "Extent of the Atonement: Outline of the Issue, Positions, Key Texts, and Key Theological Arguments."
[13] Under Ware's guidance, Shultz wrote his doctoral dissertation, Gary L. Shultz, Jr., "A Biblical and Theological Defense of a Multi-Intentional View of the Extent of the Atonement" (PhD diss., The Southern Baptist Theological Seminary, 2008), in *Dissertations and Theses: Full Text* [database on-line]; publication number AAT 3356774. He has written an article on this theme: "Why a Genuine Universal Gospel Call Requires an Atonement That Paid for the Sins of All People," *EQ* 82.2 (2010), 111–23. I have not read Shultz's dissertation but only the article.
[14] Bruce Ware, personal correspondence, March 5, 2011, quoted with permission.
[15] Driscoll and Breshears, *Death by Love*, 174.

Did Christ Pay the Penalty for the Sin of Those in Hell?

To maintain that the sins of all people were paid for, one must believe that people in hell have also had their sins paid for. Ware explains in what sense he believes that Jesus paid the penalty for the sins of those who are in hell for rejecting Jesus:

> Those in hell, who never put their faith in Christ and so were never saved, are under the just judgment of God for their sin, even though *Christ has paid the penalty for their sin* (e.g., 2 Pet. 2:1; 1 John 2:2), just as the elect, before they put their faith in Christ and so are "children of wrath" (Eph. 2:3), are under the just judgment or "curse" of God for their sin (Gal. 3:10), even though Christ has paid the penalty for their sin (e.g., John 10:11, 15; Gal. 3:13; Eph. 5:25).[16]

Even though Ware says that Christ "has paid the penalty for" the sin of those in hell, nevertheless, he also believes that they will be paying the penalty for their own sin forever:

> Since the non-elect never believe in Christ and so never are saved, they retain their guilt before a holy God along with the obligation they have, by divine justice, to pay the penalty for their own sin—which they do eternally, since their sin's guilt can never be paid fully by them.[17]

How can this be? How can there be a "double payment" for sin? Ware's answer is in the analogy between the elect before they are converted and the non-elect in hell. Ware argues that Christ has clearly and particularly paid the penalty for the elect, yet they are still "children of wrath" before they put their faith in Christ. So if the elect can be under God's wrath, when that wrath has already been propitiated at the cross, then the non-elect can be under God's wrath in hell, even though Christ has also already propitiated God's wrath for their sin. But when you scrutinize this analogy, it breaks down at the very point where it needs to work for Ware's argument.

Sentence versus Execution

In the first place, for the elect to be born "children of wrath" (Eph. 2:3) and to be condemned already (John 3:18) prior to conversion does not mean that

---

[16] Bruce Ware, personal correspondence, March 5, 2011, quoted with permission.
[17] Ibid.

the elect were *enduring* the *actual* wrath of God that is equivalent to what the non-elect experience in hell. It means that the *sentence* of God's wrath still hung over them. Until the point of faith, they were heading to hell, where God's wrath would then be *executed* on them. Thus there are not "two payments" for the elect's sins: God's wrath for their sins that Christ propitiated at the cross, and the abiding wrath of God in their pre-conversion state. The latter refers to the *sentence* of judgment that was fixed over them prior to their conversion, a sentence that was executed on Christ when God's wrath was poured out at the cross. The wrath that hung over us in our pre-conversion state and which would have broken upon us for real in hell after the eschatological day of judgment, if we had not believed in Christ, broke on Christ two thousand years ago. Thus, there are not two judgments for our sin here, only one. Ware has failed to distinguish between a penal sentence and the actual execution of that sentence.

But why does the sentence of God's wrath still hang over the elect in their pre-converted state, if Christ has already propitiated God's wrath? This leads to a second point.

The Judicial Nature of the Death of Christ

If we keep in mind the judicial (rather than pecuniary) nature of Christ's death in dealing with God's wrath, we can conceptualize a time gap between the judicial act that deals with his wrath (at the cross) and the actual application of that accomplishment to the elect (at conversion). In this understanding there is no "double payment" that lasts from the point of a person's conception until conversion. There is only one payment (punishment) for that person's sins: God's wrath. This wrath, which is due to them and which remains on them prior to conversion, was propitiated when Christ died, *but the application of that propitiation is delayed.* That is, the *one* penalty for the elect person's sins was judicially paid for by Christ when he propitiated God's wrath at the cross; but the *application* of that wrath-removing event is not applied immediately but only at the point of saving faith. Until then, the judgment that the person is under—God's wrath—remains in place until they appropriate Christ's wrath-averting death through faith.

In what sense, then, are the elect under the wrath of God between conception and conversion? It is not unlike a prisoner on death row, who, awaiting his death sentence remains under the judgment of the state. Unbeknown to him someone offered to die in his place last week and was executed soon after, but the paperwork to release him has taken a week to process. Even though the penalty was meted out a week ago, the prisoner was not immediately released but only at a later stage when the substitutionary death could be processed and applied. This scenario does not constitute a "double payment"; it merely demonstrates a delay between the one payment and its application.[18]

Same Payment for the Unconverted Elect and the Non-Elect in Hell?

Thirdly, there is a profound difference between the way the atonement relates to God's wrath for the non-elect in hell and the way the atonement relates to God's wrath for the elect before conversion. When we say that Christ paid the penalty for the elect, we mean that he secured every providence and every grace needed to bring the elect to himself. The future, damning outcome of his wrath is eliminated. This does not mean that we need to deny that the sentence of God's wrath "remains" (μένει; John 3:36) on the elect before they are united to Christ by faith, as we have noted above.

But alongside this wrath that "remains" on the elect before their conversion, there are other massive realities limiting the future execution of that wrath. There is calling love and regenerating love, which were obtained by the blood of Christ when the penalty for the sin of the elect was paid. None of this can be said of the non-elect in hell. They will experience the wrath of God in hell forever. Therefore, the analogy in Ware's argument between the meaning of "paid the penalty for" the non-elect in hell and "paid the penalty for" the elect before conversion does not work. For the elect, Christ's payment, motivated by electing love, unleashes calling love and regenerating love, which irrevocably pursue the elect unbeliever and overcome his unbelief. But if that is not what "paid for" means for the non-elect, what then does it mean?

A "Fully Satisfactory Payment" for the Non-Elect?

In sum, the fact of the elect being "children of wrath" between conception and conversion, even though Christ had propitiated God's wrath at the cross,

---

[18] See John Owen, *Of the Death of Christ*, in *Works*, 10:458: "Hence it is that the discharge of the debtor doth not immediately follow the payment of the debt by Christ; not because that payment is refusable, but because in that very covenant and compact from whence it is that the death of Christ is a payment, God reserveth to himself this right and liberty to discharge the debtor when and how he pleaseth."

does not provide an analogy for there being "two payments" for the sin of the non-elect—one made by Christ on the cross and the other made by them in hell—as Ware wishes to claim. Ware's analogy of the elect in their pre-converted state being under the wrath of God does not solve the dilemma of a "double payment." Glaring questions remain unanswered: What does Ware *mean* when he says that Christ has *paid the penalty* for the sins of the non-elect? And how *can* God exact a double punishment for the same sin? I do not think that Ware takes seriously enough the problem of saying that Christ paid the penalty of the non-elect *and yet* they themselves pay the penalty. One or the other of these two payments loses its ordinary meaning. Given Ware's insistence on the reality of Christ's paying the penalty for the sins of the damned, the inevitable result for the reader is a minimizing of the meaning of Christ's substitutionary sin-bearing work.

Are People in Hell Now Reconciled to God through Christ?

Another claim that Ware and Driscoll make is that people in hell are now reconciled to God through Christ. They both draw attention to the effect of Christ's blood in "reconciling" those in hell to God. They are referring to Colossians 1:18–20:

> And he is the head of the body, the church. He is the beginning, the first-born from the dead, that in everything he might be preeminent. For in him all the fullness of God was pleased to dwell, and through him to reconcile to himself all things, whether on earth or in heaven, making peace by the blood of his cross.

Ware and Driscoll say that this text teaches the "reconciliation" of absolutely all things, including demons and humans in hell, and that this peacemaking work of Christ happens "by the blood of his cross." Therefore, it is one of God's "multiple intentions" of the atonement, which is valid not just for the elect but for all.

Neither Ware nor Driscoll is a universalist. The reconciliation of all things, as they see it, does not mean the final salvation of all people. But such "reconciliation," they say, is true even of people who are in hell. They are "reconciled" to God. What does this mean? The answers to this question, it seems to me, involve Driscoll and Ware in a worse tangle of linguistic im-probability than the ones they are trying to avoid. Driscoll writes,

God will overcome all rebellion through Jesus' blood and the triumph of the Lamb who is the Lion. In this sense all those in hell will stand reconciled to God, but not in a saving way as the universalists falsely teach. In hell unrepentant and unforgiven sinners are no longer rebels, and their sinful disregard for God has been crushed and ended.[19]

This last sentence stretches language to the breaking point. On the one hand, we are told that hell has "unrepentant sinners" in it. But then we are told that they are no longer rebels. But what meaning does "unrepentant" have except that people rebel against the command to repent? In addition, Driscoll says concerning these "unrepentant" people that their "sinful disregard for God has been . . . ended." Are we to imagine another kind of disregard for God than a sinful kind? A disregard that has no sinfulness in it? Or are we to understand that *all* disregard for God has been ended? The disregard of the "unrepentant" surely means to regard poorly, that is, to feel no humble reverence or proper esteem for God. But that kind of sinning has not been ended if there are *unrepentant* people in hell.

Ware expresses his understanding of universal reconciliation based on Colossians 1:18–20 as follows:

This reconciliation must be one which includes a sense in which those outside of Christ, consigned to eternal punishment in hell, are at peace with God. Since they are not saved and do not have right standing before God, the peace that they have is simply this: they now have seen God for who He is and Christ as the only Savior and Lord; they have bowed their knees before God and have confessed with their mouths that Jesus Christ (alone!) is Lord (Phil. 2:10–11); and through this work done at the judgment of God in the end, the deception is removed, their rebellion is over, and they now know and accept the truth of what they rejected the whole of their lives: God is God, Christ is Lord, and they are rightly accountable before Him for the sin of their lives. As a result, there is peace—no more rebellion, no more deception, no more lies. The truth is known and accepted by these hell-bound sinners, and they go to hell knowing now that God is holy and was right, they are sinful and were wrong, and their judgment is fully just.[20]

There are two kinds of problems with this remarkable interpretation of the meaning of "reconciliation." One is that the word *reconciliation* does not

---

[19] Driscoll and Breshears, *Death by Love*, 174.

[20] Personal correspondence from Bruce Ware, dated March 5, 2011, quoted with permission.

carry these meanings. And the other is that not all of these descriptions of those in hell are true.

First, to say that those in hell are "at peace with God" in this context ("making peace by the blood of his cross") is breathtakingly inappropriate. The parallel language in Ephesians shows how precious this blood-bought peace is:

> [Jesus] himself is our peace, who has made us both one and has broken down in his flesh the dividing wall of hostility by abolishing the law of commandments expressed in ordinances, that he might create in himself one new man in place of the two, so making peace. (Eph. 2:14–15)

To say that blood-bought peace describes the relationship between God and those in hell surely must eventually make a heaven of hell or rob heaven of peace.

Second, the peace that those in hell have, according to Ware, is this: "They now have seen God for who He is and Christ as the only Savior and Lord." The demons during Jesus's lifetime saw Jesus for who he was. This was before the cross, and it had no enmity-removing effect on them: "Ha! What have you to do with us, Jesus of Nazareth? Have you come to destroy us? I know who you are—the Holy One of God" (Luke 4:34). There is no reason to think that in hell the recognition of Jesus as Savior and Lord will diminish enmity. And there is no linguistic warrant for calling such an enmity-increasing recognition of Jesus *peace*.

Third, the peace of the damned, says Ware, is that "they have bowed their knees before God and have confessed with their mouths that Jesus Christ (alone!) is Lord (Phil. 2:10–11)." The devils already confessed Jesus as Lord (see above). This is not the unique work of the blood of Christ. And there is no reason to believe that when the entire unrepentant world joins the demons in this begrudging confession, there will be less than intensified enmity and hatred. That is not what *reconciliation* means, especially in this cross-centered context.

Fourth, Ware's claims about what will happen on the day of judgment are, at best, misleading. "The deception is removed"? Only in the most superficial way is this true. In the way that really counts (seeing Christ as glorious because of his atoning work; 2 Cor. 4:4), it is not true. People who have really disbelieved that Jesus is God and Lord will realize that they were wrong. True. But there is a deeper deception that will not be removed. And it is the essence of what is removed from sinners when there is blood-bought reconciliation.

"The rebellion is over"? There is no sense in which this is true that corresponds to the meaning of the word *reconciliation*. If anything, rebellion increases when people see Christ more clearly, if not with the spiritual recognition of his beauty. The sense in which rebellion ceases is that people and demons in hell no longer have access to the saints. Their rebellion is contained. They are removed from God's new creation. This is not reconciliation. It is ultimate banishment and alienation. This is not the peace Jesus purchased with his blood. This is the removal of those who would not make peace with God.

Another View on the Reconciliation of All Things

In those last sentences I have signaled what my view of Colossians 1:20 is. Paul said, God's aim was "to reconcile to himself all things, whether on earth or in heaven, making peace by the blood of his cross." I agree with Ware and Driscoll that this does not imply universal salvation.[21] What I disagree with is that Paul means "all things" will be reconciled to God in *this* heaven and earth in which we live *now*, with all its demons and human rebels.

Rather, I think he means that the blood of Christ has secured the victory of God over the universe in such a way that the day is coming when "all things" that are in the *new* heavens and the *new* earth will be entirely reconciled to God with no rebel remnants. Before that day comes, all those who refuse to be reconciled by his blood will be cast into "outer darkness" (Matt. 8:12), so that they are not reckoned to be a part of the new heavens and the new earth. The rebels in hell will simply not be part of the "all things" which fill the new heavens and the new earth. They are "outside" of the new reality, in the "darkness."

Heinrich Meyer argued similarly on Colossians 1:20:

> . . . through the Parousia the reconciliation of the whole which has been effected in Christ will reach its consummation, when the unbelieving portion of mankind will be separated and consigned to Gehenna, the whole creation

---

[21] Such salvation would not cohere with teachings of Scripture. Jesus says that there are some who "will go away into eternal punishment, but the righteous into eternal life" (Matt. 25:46). Paul said there are some who "will suffer the punishment of eternal destruction, away from the presence of the Lord" (2 Thess. 1:9). John says of these that "the smoke of their torment goes up forever and ever" (Rev. 14:11).

in virtue of the Palingenesia [new creation] (Matt. xix.28) will be transformed into its original perfection, and the new heaven and the new earth will be constituted as the dwelling of δικαιοσύνη [righteousness] (2 Pet. iii.13) and the δόξα [glory] of the children of God (Rom. viii.21); while the demoniac portion of the angelic world will be removed from the sphere of the new world, and cast into hell. Accordingly, in the whole creation there will no longer be anything alienated from God and object of his hostility, but τὰ πάντα [all things] will be in harmony and reconciled with him.[22]

Perhaps there is a very good reason why Paul omits the term καταχθονίων ("under the earth") when he says that Christ will "reconcile to himself all things, whether on earth or in heaven." He does not say, "whether on earth or in heaven or *under the earth*," as he does in Philippians 2:10. Indeed there is a good reason for not saying this. The reason would seem to be that there will be an "outer darkness"—an "under the earth"—that does indeed have *unreconciled* beings in it. But this does not take away from "all things" being reconciled in heaven and on the earth in the age to come. In God's new universe (the new heaven and the new earth) there will be no whiff of rebellion. All of that is in another dimension. "Outside" in "darkness." Real. But not part of the *new* reality. In the new reality all things are reconciled to Christ by his blood.

Summing Up the Problem with Ware and Driscoll's View

In sum, the position that Ware and Driscoll put forward involves a significant departure from the ordinary use of biblical language, and a tangle of linguistic improbabilities. To be sure, the texts that Ware and Driscoll believe drive them away from the traditional Reformed view of definite atonement (Col. 1:20; 2 Pet. 2:1; 1 John 2:2; etc.) must be explained in biblically faithful ways. That, in part, is what this book is for. It is not the purpose of this chapter to give all those explanations (though I have been tempted to do so, and have many thoughts about those texts).

Is a Revision of the Historic Reformed View of Definite Atonement Necessary?

What begs to be answered in this chapter is the persuasion that God's multiple intentions in the atonement, as Ware, Driscoll, and Shultz develop them, de-

---

[22] H. A. W. Meyer, *Critical and Exegetical Hand-Book to the Epistles to the Philippians and Colossians, and to Philemon* (1883; repr., Winona Lake, IN: Alpha, 1980), 241–42.

mand a revision of the Reformed view of the atonement, and that their view makes the free, sincere offer of the gospel to all men more consistent and compelling. I think both aspects of this persuasion are mistaken.

John Murray, late professor of systematic theology at Westminster Theological Seminary, Philadelphia, represents the traditional Reformed view of definite atonement. Nevertheless, he carefully observes that God has multiple intentions in it, yet not in a way that undermines definite atonement. His careful analysis shows that one need not abandon definite atonement in order to embrace the intentional benefits that come to the non-elect because of it. Murray writes,

> The design of Christ's death is more inclusive than the blessings that belong specifically to the atonement. This is to say that even the non-elect are embraced in the design of the atonement in respect of blessings falling short of salvation which they enjoy in this life.[23]

When Murray says that "the non-elect are embraced in the design of the atonement," he does not mean that the non-elect are atoned for, but that the definite atonement for the elect produces benefits for others. For our purposes in this chapter, it is especially important to note that one of the benefits that come to everyone, including those who are not elect, is the free offer of the gospel, or what Murray calls "the unrestricted overture of grace."

> Many benefits accrue to the non-elect from the redemptive work of Christ. . . . It is by virtue of what Christ has done that there is a gospel of salvation proclaimed to all without distinction. Are we to say that the unrestricted overture of grace is not grace to those to whom it comes?[24]

The Gauntlet Thrown Down

This is the kind of claim that Shultz takes issue with in his article, "Why a Genuine Universal Gospel Call Requires an Atonement That Paid for the Sins of All People," and helps to spotlight one of the most crucial issues in relation to preaching and definite atonement. Shultz, like many before him, says we simply cannot preach the gospel freely and sincerely where we do not assume that Christ died to pay for the sins of all people. In other words,

---

[23] John Murray, "The Atonement and the Free Offer of the Gospel," in *Collected Writings of John Murray. Volume 1: The Claims of Truth* (Carlisle, PA: Banner of Truth, 1976), 64.
[24] Ibid., 63–64.

he would say, the Reformed view of definite atonement defended in this book is inimical to faithful gospel preaching. Shultz writes,

> [T]he Bible makes clear that Jesus' payment for the sins of all people, elect and nonelect, was necessary for the universal gospel call to take place. One of the primary intentions God had in sending the Son to die for the sins of all people was to render the gospel genuinely and rightly offered to all people. Even though not all people will be saved, Christ died to provide the basis by which all people could be saved if they would trust in Christ. Particular redemption [i.e., definite atonement], by limiting the atonement only to the elect, is unable to account for the universal gospel call. Therefore the truth of the universal gospel call offers strong support for understanding the atonement as unlimited in its extent.[25]

Thus the gauntlet is thrown down: "Particular redemption," Shultz says, "by limiting atonement only to the elect, is unable to account for the universal gospel call." This is not true. In fact, I will argue that *only* particular redemption can account for a fully biblical, universal gospel offer. The fullness of Christ's achievement on the cross can be offered only if it has been fully achieved. And only definite atonement expresses the fullness of that achievement. Shultz continues, "If Christ did not pay for the sins of the non-elect, then it is impossible to genuinely offer salvation to the non-elect, since there is no salvation available to offer them."[26]

Shultz really issues two challenges. One is, can definite atonement provide the basis for a *valid* offer of the gospel to *all*? The other is, can definite atonement provide the basis for a *sincere* offer of the gospel to *all*? The biblical answer to both is yes. But our method in demonstrating our answer to these challenges must be different. Let us deal first with the question of validity. Can definite atonement provide the basis for a *valid* offer of the gospel to *all*—even to those whose sins are not paid for and for whom God has not been propitiated?

Definite Atonement and a Valid Offer of the Gospel to All

What is essential for a valid offer of salvation? Here is the answer of Roger Nicole: "Simply this: that *if the terms of the offer be observed, that which is*

---

[25] Shultz, "Why a Genuine Universal Gospel Call," 114. This is not the only argument Shultz makes in his article, but the others are of the kind that are answered in previous chapters of this book. Our concern is with the legitimacy of preaching the gospel freely to all people from the standpoint of definite atonement.
[26] Ibid., 122.

offered be actually granted. In connection with the gospel offer, the terms are that a person should repent and believe. Whenever that occurs, salvation is actually conferred."[27] An offer is valid if the one who offers always and without fail gives what is offered to everyone who meets the terms of the offer. This God does without fail. No one ever believed on Jesus and then perished (John 3:16).

But Shultz objects that "it is impossible to genuinely offer salvation to the non-elect, since there is no salvation available to offer them." Is that true? I would argue not. There is a massive, full, effective, glorious salvation, accomplished once for all. And it is there to be offered freely and to be embraced by all who will have it as their treasure. If we follow John Murray's insightful line of thinking, we will see not only what is actually there to offer, but also what is the only ground of a fully biblical offer.

Murray asks, "What is offered in the gospel?" and answers,

> It is Christ who is offered. More strictly *he* offers himself. The whole gamut of redemptive grace is included. Salvation in all of its aspects and in the furthest reaches of glory consummated is the overture. For Christ is the embodiment of all. Those who are his are complete in him and he is made unto them wisdom from God, and righteousness, and sanctification, and redemption. When Christ invites us to himself it is to the possession of himself and therefore of all that defines his identity as Lord and Saviour.[28]

This is crucial. Christ is the one offered in the gospel. All other blessings are in him. If we receive him, we have them. He is offered freely to all. He gives himself to all who come. The offer is valid because he is really there as the embodiment of all that is promised. He is offered freely, and he never denies himself to any who meet the terms of the offer—"to all who did receive him, who believed in his name, he gave the right to become children of God" (John 1:12).

Now comes the really amazing part. What is offered to the world, to everyone who hears the gospel, is not a love or a saving achievement designed for all and therefore especially for no one; but rather, what is offered is the absolute fullness of all that Christ achieved for his elect. This fullest of all possible achievements is offered to all—because *Christ* is offered to all. And

---

[27] Roger R. Nicole, "Covenant, Universal Call, and Definite Atonement," *JETS* 38.3 (September 1995), 409–10 (emphasis added).
[28] Murray, "Atonement and the Free Offer of the Gospel," 82 (emphasis original).

thus definite atonement turns out to be the only ground of a fully biblical offer of the gospel. Murray, again:

> [I]f Christ—and therefore salvation in its fullness and perfection—is offered, the only doctrine of the atonement that will ground and warrant this overture is that of salvation wrought and redemption accomplished. And the only atonement that measures up to such conditions is a definite atonement. In other words, an atonement construed as providing the possibility of salvation or the opportunity of salvation does not supply the basis required for what constitutes the gospel offer. It is not the *opportunity* of salvation that is offered; it is salvation. And it is salvation because Christ is offered and Christ does not invite us to mere opportunity but to himself.[29]

In the gospel, we do not offer people a *possibility* of salvation, we offer Christ, and in him the infinite achievement that he accomplished for his people by his death and resurrection.

The basis of the *validity* of this offer, therefore, is (1) that Christ is the one we offer, (2) that he really did accomplish and secure all the benefits we offer including himself as the supreme treasure, and (3) that the promise is true that whoever receives him will have him and all his blood-bought benefits.

Definite atonement fulfills these conditions for a *valid* offer of the gospel. It says (1) that Christ really is the all-powerful, all-wise, all-satisfying, divine Son of God offered in the gospel; (2) that by his death and resurrection he has acted out God's discriminating, definite, electing, regenerating, faith-creating, every-promise-guaranteeing, new-covenant love, and thus has purchased and secured irreversibly for the elect everything needed to bring them from deadness in sin to everlasting, glorified life and joy in the presence of God; and (3) that everyone, without *any* exception, who receives Christ as supreme treasure—who believes in his name—will be united to Christ in the embrace of this electing love, and enjoy him and all his gifts forever.

Therefore, on the basis of this definite atonement we preach Christ to the world. We offer Christ freely to all. We say, "Believe in the Lord Jesus, and you will be saved" (Acts 16:31). We say, "If anyone thirsts, let him come to Christ and drink. Whoever believes in him 'Out of his heart will flow rivers of living water'" (see John 7:37–38). And we say, "God so loved the world, that he gave his only Son, that whoever believes in him should not perish but have eternal life" (John 3:16).

---

[29] Ibid., 82–83 (emphasis original).

In other words, we offer Christ in all his personal glory and with all his saving benefits to everyone who will believe. We make no distinctions. We do not try to discern who the elect are. We do not look for evidences of God's calling. That is the historic difference between biblical Reformed theology and Hyper-Calvinism.[30] We indiscriminately preach to everyone: "Receive Christ, and your sins will be covered. Receive Christ, and your condemnation will be removed."

Definite Atonement and a Sincere Offer of the Gospel to All

But Shultz (among others) now raises his second challenge. Not just can this universal offer be valid, but can it be *sincere*? Can definite atonement provide the basis for a *sincere* offer of the gospel to all? The answer is yes. The offer of the gospel based on definite atonement is totally sincere and without any deceit at all. It has full integrity. We tell the world with complete openness, "Christ has purchased a people for himself. He invites you to be a part of it. He holds out his hands to you. If you will come, you will be satisfied in him forever. If you will receive Christ, you will have Christ! All that he has done will count for you. He desires that you come. So come!"

Someone will say, "It cannot be a sincere offer because Christ knows which people, hearing this sermon, will and will not come." This objection applies to everyone who believes in the foreknowledge of God, whatever they believe about the atonement. If God's foreknowledge cancels the sincerity of his invitations, then there are no sincere invitations at all. In other words, even the Amyraldian and Hypothetical Universalist must deal with the issue that God commands everyone everywhere to repent and believe the gospel (Acts 17:30–31), while also granting repentance and faith to only some (Phil. 1:29; 2 Tim. 2:25).

But the bottom-line objection to the sincerity of the gospel offer, for those who believe in definite atonement, is not what God *knows*, but what God *desires*. Does he desire that all come? The answer is yes. But in order to see this biblically, we must notice that God is able to desire something sincerely and, for wise and holy reasons, nevertheless decide that what he desires will not come to pass.

---

[30] Iain Murray writes in *The Forgotten Spurgeon* (Edinburgh: Banner of Truth, 1973), 47: "Hyper-Calvinism in its attempt to square all truth with God's purpose to save the elect, denies that there is a universal command to repent and believe, and asserts that we have only warrant to invite to Christ those who are *conscious* of a sense of sin and need."

For example, Jesus says, "O Jerusalem, Jerusalem, the city that kills the prophets and stones those who are sent to it! How often would I have gathered your children together as a hen gathers her brood under her wings, and you were not willing!" (Luke 13:34). Yet Jesus also says concerning his ministry that the awakening of sinners to the knowledge of the Father and the Son is decisively in his hands: "All things have been handed over to me by my Father, and no one knows the Son except the Father, and no one knows the Father except the Son and *anyone to whom the Son chooses to reveal him*" (Matt. 11:27). So Jesus desires the salvation of the lost, but does not always use the power at his disposal to open their eyes. Similarly, God says in Ezekiel 33:11, "As I live, declares the Lord GOD, I have no pleasure in the death of the wicked, but that the wicked turn from his way and live." And yet we learn from Paul that the power to grant repentance is in the hand of God. "God may perhaps *grant* them repentance leading to a knowledge of the truth" (2 Tim. 2:25). God does not delight in the death of the wicked, as Ezekiel says, and yet, for wise and holy reasons, he withholds the working of his power to "grant them repentance."

What this means is that the sincere offer of the gospel and definite atonement are not contradictory. God desires the salvation of the lost, but he does not save all of them. Another way to say it is that there are what appear to be "levels" in God's willing. At one level, he sincerely *desires* that everyone be saved.[31] And at another deeper level, his wisdom counsels otherwise, to save only some.

We see this clearly in Lamentations 3:31–33: "The Lord will not cast off forever, but, though he cause grief, he will have compassion according to the abundance of his steadfast love; for he does not afflict *from his heart* or grieve the children of men." In other words, at one level, God does, in fact, choose to "afflict . . . or grieve the children of men," but at another level ("from his heart"), he does not desire it. I have tried to show more fully elsewhere the complexity of the will of God, and the love of God as it appears to us.[32] God desires and wills and loves in different ways at different times and in different relations.[33]

---

[31] Murray, "Atonement and the Free Offer of the Gospel," 70 n. 1, says it this way: "This universal love should be always so conceived as to leave room for the fact that God, for sovereign reasons, has not chosen to bestow upon its objects that *higher* love which not merely *desires*, but *purposes* and works out the salvation of some" (emphasis added).

[32] John Piper, *Are There Two Wills in God? Divine Election and God's Desire for All to Be Saved* (Wheaton, IL: Crossway, 2013).

[33] For a thorough treatment of the various ways God loves, see Geerhardus Vos, "The Biblical Doctrine of the Love of God," in *Redemptive History and Biblical Interpretation: The Shorter Writings of Geerhardus Vos*, ed. Richard B. Gaffin (Phillipsburg, NJ: P&R, 1980), 425–57.

John Calvin saw these things clearly—"that in a wonderful and ineffable manner nothing is done without God's will, not even that which is against this will"[34]—and cautioned his critics that their objections were "hurled not against me but against the Holy Spirit." He gave several biblical examples, such as Eli's sons not obeying their father because "it was the will of the LORD to put them to death" (1 Sam. 2:25), and Amos 3:6, which asks, "Does disaster come to a city, unless the LORD has done it?" But Calvin also warned that

> God's will is not therefore at war with itself, nor does it change, nor does it pretend not to will what it wills. Even though his will is one and simple in him, it appears manifold to us because, on account of our mental incapacity, we do not grasp how in diverse ways it wills and does not will something to take place.[35]

The point is: Jesus can really and sincerely invite all people to come to him, while knowing that in the infinite wisdom of God it has been determined that some will not come. God will pass over them, and not give them the gift of repentance. This seems clearly implied in Jesus's words to the towns of Chorazin and Bethsaida: "Woe to you, Chorazin! Woe to you, Bethsaida! For if the mighty works done in you had been done in Tyre and Sidon, they would have repented long ago in sackcloth and ashes" (Matt. 11:21). In other words, Jesus knew what miraculous deeds would lead them to repentance, and he did not do those deeds. He sincerely desires all to be saved, yet he does not always act to bring all to salvation. There are wise and holy reasons for why his desire does not rise to the level of effective volition.

The ultimate wise and holy reason why Jesus and the Father do what they do is always the same—they act for the sake of displaying the fullness of God's glory. If the gospel is hidden from some and revealed to others, God knows how this will magnify the glory of his justice and the glory of his grace. God desires "to show his wrath and to make known his power . . . in order to make known the riches of his glory for vessels of mercy" (Rom. 9:22–23). His wrath ultimately serves the glory of his mercy—which, as we saw at the beginning of this chapter, is the ultimate aim of God in creation (Eph. 1:6).

I conclude, then, that Shultz is mistaken: a universal gospel offer based on definite atonement is not only valid, but also sincere. And I also conclude that

---

[34] John Calvin, *Institutes of the Christian Religion,* ed. John T. McNeil, trans. Ford Lewis Battles (Philadelphia: Westminster, 1960), 1.18.3.
[35] Ibid.

definite atonement provides the *only* basis for the kind of gospel offer that is fully biblical. In fact, Murray shows that unless we offer the fullest achievement of the greatest love of God, our overtures to sinners are impoverished:

> It is not the general love of God to all mankind, the love manifested in the gifts of general providence, that is offered to men in the gospel. . . . When Christ invites us to himself he invites us to the embrace of his love on the highest level of its exercise and therefore to the love wherewith he loved the church and gave himself for it. . . . We thus see how impoverished would be our conception of the free overture of Christ in the gospel if the appeal were simply to the undifferentiating and general love of God.[36]

The spread of the gospel to all people, even to the non-elect, is an expression of the general love of God for the whole world. But this general love is not what is offered to the world in the gospel. The offer of the gospel is the fullest and most glorious achievement of God's love for his elect. This is offered in the gospel because Christ is offered in the gospel. J. I. Packer puts it like this: "The basis on which the New Testament invites sinners to put faith in Christ is simply that they need Him, and that He offers Himself to them, and that those who receive Him are promised all the benefits that His death secured for His people."[37]

Yes. All of them. All the benefits that his death secured for his people. The sure and all-satisfying experience of the electing, regenerating, faith-creating, justifying, sanctifying, preserving, glorifying love of God. Every blessing in the heavenly places (Eph. 1:3). All the promises of God (2 Cor. 1:20). All things working together for their good (Rom. 8:28). No good thing withheld (Ps. 84:11). And in the end, sinless and all-satisfying fellowship with God (1 Pet. 3:18). This is the gospel offer. And it cannot be offered like this where its definite and irreversible achievement for God's people is not believed. The glory of our human offer in preaching is the glory of Christ's full achievement in dying.

Definite Atonement and Missions

It should be obvious, but I will make it explicit: this vision of the atonement and the free offer of the gospel propels us into the global work of

---

[36] Murray, "Atonement and the Free Offer of the Gospel," 83.
[37] J. I. Packer, *Evangelism and the Sovereignty of God* (Downers Grove, IL: InterVarsity Press, 1961), 68.

missions with compassion and confidence: compassion, because we have
been so loved ourselves and because God has put within us a longing for
others to join us in this great salvation; confidence, because contained in the
atonement itself is the power of the gospel to raise the spiritually dead and
bring people to faith.[38] We are carried in our passion for the nations by the
spectacular person of Christ and the stupendous achievement of his cross. We
do not hesitate to say to every person in every people group that God loves
you, and he offers you in Christ the fullest possible redemption in everlasting,
all-satisfying fellowship with himself. This message is valid, and this offer
is sincere, to every person on the planet. And it is breathtakingly glorious.
How could we not want to bring this news to every person and every people
group in the world!

Preaching Definite Atonement for the Body of Christ

That Christ died and rose again to accomplish this definite, full, and irreversible atonement for his people is the glory of his *cross*, which is the climax
of the glory of *grace*, which is the apex of the glory of *God*. This is how I
began this chapter. And I said there that not only does this vision of the atoning work of Christ inflame world missions, but it also enables us to preach
in such a way that our people experience deeper gratitude, greater assurance,
sweeter fellowship with God, stronger affections in worship, more love for
people, and greater courage and sacrifice in witness and service. Let me flesh
this out briefly.

With the vision of Christ's achievement displayed and defended in this
book, we will aim in all our preaching to magnify the glory of Christ by
helping our people realize the unspeakably great benefits that come to them
because of this achievement. Our aim will be to help our people know and
experience the reality of a definite, full, and irreversible atonement. If God
gives us success, here is some of what it will mean for us and our people.

*Knowing and experiencing the reality of definite atonement affects us
with deeper gratitude.* We feel more thankfulness for a gift given to us in
particular, rather than feeling like it was given to no specific people and we
happened to pick it up. The world should be thankful that God so loved the
world that he gave his only Son so that whoever believes in him may not

---

[38] Recall from earlier in the chapter the connection between the quickening power of grace in Ephesians 2:4–5 and its relation to the atoning work of Christ in 1:4–7.

perish but have eternal life. But those who belong to Christ should be far more thankful because the very faith that unites us to Christ for all his promises was purchased and secured by the blood of the new covenant.

Knowing and experiencing the reality of definite atonement affects us with greater assurance. We feel more secure in God's hands when we know that, before we believed or even existed, God had us in view when he planned to pay with his blood, not only for a free offer of salvation but also for our actual regeneration and calling and faith and justification and sanctification and glorification—that it was all secured forever for us in particular. The rock solid assurance of Romans 8:32–39 ("Who shall bring any charge against [us]! . . . What shall separate us! . . .") is rooted in the unbreakable link between the definite atonement that Christ made ("He who did not spare his own Son but gave him up for us all") and the promises purchased for those for whom he died ("Will he not also with him graciously give us all things?").

Knowing and experiencing the reality of definite atonement affects us with sweeter fellowship with God. A pastor may love all the women in his church. But his wife feels a sweeter affection for him because he chose her particularly out of all the other women, and made great sacrifices to make sure he would have her—not because he offered himself to all women and she accepted, but because he sought her in particular and sacrificed for her. If we do not know that God chose us as his Son's "wife" and made great sacrifices for us in particular and wooed us and wanted us in a special way, our experience of the personal sweetness of his love will not be the same.

Knowing and experiencing the reality of definite atonement affects us with stronger affections in worship. To be loved with everlasting love, before creation and into the future ages, is to have our affections awakened for God, which will intensify worship and make it more personal than if we thought we were loved only with the same love as God has for those who will never come. To look at the cross and know that this love was not only for the sake of an offer of salvation to all (which it is), but more, was the length to which God would go so that *I*, in particular, would be drawn into the new covenant—that is the bedrock of joy in worship.

When the psalmist says in Psalm 115:1, "Not to us, O LORD, not to us, but to your name give glory, for the sake of your steadfast love and your faithfulness!" he makes it clear that the worship of God—the glorification of God—springs from a vital sense of his "steadfast love and faithfulness."

When a church is faithfully and regularly taught that they are the definite and particular objects of God's "great love" (Eph. 2:4), owing to nothing in them, the intensity of their worship will grow ever deeper.

Knowing and experiencing the reality of definite atonement affects us with more love for people and greater courage and sacrifice in witness and service. When a profound sense of undeserved, particular, atoning love from God combines with the unshakable security of being purchased—from eternity, for eternity—then we are more deeply freed from the selfish greed and fear that hinder love. Love is laying down one's conveniences, and even one's life, for the good of others, especially their eternal good. The more undeservingly secure we are, the more we will be humbled to count others more significant than ourselves, and the more fearless we will be to risk our lives for their greatest good. Definite atonement is a massively strengthening truth for the humble security and bold fearlessness of the believer. In that way, it releases and empowers love.

Preach the Fullness of Definite Atonement

The list of benefits could go on, but the implication for preaching is clear. Preaching, which aims at world evangelization and serves to strengthen the people of God in the ways we have seen, should speak of the achievement of the cross in its fullness. The aim of this preaching is to join God in his ultimate purpose in all things—to display the fullness of his glory. We have seen that the apex of God's glory is the splendor of his grace as it reaches its climax in the glory of the cross. And the glory of the cross is the fullness of its definite achievement. Therefore, we diminish the glory of the cross and the glory of grace and the glory of God when we diminish definite atonement. But when it is preached and embraced in its biblical fullness, the glory of the work of Christ, the glory of the freedom and power of grace, and the glory of the being of God himself are wonderfully magnified.

Select Bibliography

Allen, David L. "The Atonement: Limited or Universal?" In *Whosoever Will: A Biblical-Theological Critique of Five-Point Calvinism*. Edited by David L. Allen and Steve W. Lemke, 61–107. Nashville: B&H Academic, 2010.

Amyraut, Moïse. *Brief Traitté de la Predestination et de ses principales dependances*. Saumur, France: Jean Lesnier & Isaac Debordes, 1634; 2nd ed., 1658.

Anderson, James W. *"The Grace of God and the Non–Elect in Calvin's Commentaries and Sermons."* PhD diss., New Orleans Baptist Theological Seminary, 1976.

Armstrong, Brian G. *Calvinism and the Amyraut Heresy: Protestant Scholasticism and Humanism in Seventeenth-Century France*. Madison: University of Wisconsin Press, 1969.

Barnes, Tom. *Atonement Matters: A Call to Declare the Biblical View of the Atonement*. Darlington, UK: Evangelical Press, 2008.

Baugh, Steven M. "'Savior of All People': 1 Tim 4:10 in Context." *WTJ* 54 (1992): 331–40.

Bell, Charles M. "Calvin and the Extent of the Atonement." *EQ* 55.2 (1983): 115–23.

Bell, Richard H. "Rom 5:18–19 and Universal Salvation." *NTS* 48 (2002): 417–32.

Blacketer, Raymond A. "Definite Atonement in Historical Perspective." In *The Glory of the Atonement: Biblical, Historical and Practical Perspectives. Essays in Honor of Roger Nicole*. Edited by Charles E. Hill and Frank A. James III, 304–23. Downers Grove, IL: InterVarsity Press, 2004.

Blocher, Henri A. G. "Biblical Metaphors and the Doctrine of the Atonement." *JETS* 47.4 (December 2004): 629–45.

———. "The Scope of Redemption and Modern Theology." *SBET* 9.2 (1991): 80–103.

Boersma, Hans. "Calvin and the Extent of the Atonement." *EQ* 64.4 (1992): 333–55.

Boring, M. Eugene. "The Language of Universal Salvation in Paul." *JBL* 105.2 (1986): 269–92.

Campbell, John McLeod. *The Nature of the Atonement*, with a new introduction by J. B. Torrance. Edinburgh: Handsel, 1856. Reprint, Grand Rapids, MI: Eerdmans, 1996.

Carson, D. A. *The Difficult Doctrine of the Love of God*. Leicester, UK: Inter-Varsity Press, 2000.

Chafer, Lewis Sperry. "For Whom Did Christ Die?" *BSac* 137.548 (October–December 1980 [reprint of 1948 article]): 310–26.

Chang, Andrew D. "Second Peter 2:1 and the Extent of the Atonement." *BSac* 142 (1985): 52–63.

Clendenen, E. Ray, and Brad J. Waggoner, eds. *Calvinism: A Southern Baptist Dialogue*. Nashville: B&H Academic, 2008.

Clifford, Alan C. *Amyraut Affirmed: Or, "Owenism, a Caricature of Calvinism."* Norwich, UK: Charenton Reformed, 2004.

———. *Atonement and Justification: English Evangelical Theology 1640–1790: An Evaluation*. Oxford: Clarendon, 1990.

———. *Calvinus: Authentic Calvinism, a Clarification*. Norwich, UK: Charenton Reformed, 1996.

Daniel, Curt, *The History and Theology of Calvinism*. N.p.: Good Books, 2003.

Davenant, John. "A Dissertation on the Death of Christ, as to its Extent and special Benefits: containing a short History of Pelagianism, and shewing the Agreement of the Doctrines of the Church of England on general Redemption, Election, and Predestination, with the Primitive Fathers of the Christian Church, and above all, with the Holy Scriptures." In *An Exposition of the Epistle of St. Paul to the Colossians*. Translated by Josiah Allport. London: Hamilton, Adams, 1832.

Douty, Norman F. *The Death of Christ: A Treatise Which Answers the Question: "Did Christ Die Only for the Elect?"* Swengel, PA: Reiner, 1972.

———. *Did Christ Die Only for the Elect? A Treatise on the Extent of Christ's Atonement*. 1978. Reprint, Eugene, OR: Wipf & Stock, 1998.

Driscoll, Mark, and Gerry Breshears. *Death by Love: Letters from the Cross*. Wheaton, IL: Crossway, 2008.

Ferguson, Sinclair B. "Christus Victor et Propitiator: The Death of Christ, Substitute and Conqueror." In *For the Fame of God's Name: Essays in Honor of John Piper*. Edited by Sam Storms and Justin Taylor, 171–89. Wheaton, IL: Crossway, 2010.

Foord, Martin. "God Wills All People to Be Saved—Or Does He? Calvin's Reading of 1 Timothy 2:4." In *Engaging with Calvin: Aspects of the Reformer's Legacy for Today*. Edited by Mark D. Thompson, 179–203. Nottingham, UK: Apollos, 2009.

Gatiss, Lee. "A Deceptive Clarity? Particular Redemption in the Westminster Standards." *RTR* 69.3 (2010): 180–96.

———. *For Us and for Our Salvation: "Limited Atonement" in the Bible, Doctrine, History, and Ministry*. London: Latimer Trust, 2012.

———. "'Shades of Opinion within a Generic Calvinism': The Particular Redemption Debate at the Westminster Assembly." *RTR* 69.2 (2010): 101–18.

Godfrey, W. Robert. "Reformed Thought on the Extent of the Atonement to 1618." *WTJ* 37 (1975–1976): 133–71.

———. "Tensions within International Calvinism: The Debate on the Atonement at the Synod of Dort, 1618–1619." PhD diss., Stanford University, 1974.

Gomes, Alan W. "*De Jesu Christo Servatore*: Faustus Socinus on the Satisfaction of Christ." *WTJ* 55 (1993): 209–31.

Goodloe, James L., IV. *John McLeod Campbell: The Extent and Nature of the Atonement*. Studies in Reformed Theology and History 3. Princeton, NJ: Princeton Theological Seminary, 1997.

Guy, Fritz. "The Universality of God's Love." In *The Grace of God and the Will of Man*. Edited by Clark H. Pinnock, 31–49. Minneapolis: Bethany, 1995.

Habets, Myk, and Bobby Grow, eds. *Evangelical Calvinism: Essays Resourcing the Continuing Reformation of the Church*. Eugene, OR: Wipf & Stock, 2012.

Hall, Basil. "Calvin against the Calvinists." In *John Calvin*. Edited by G. E. Duffield, 19–37. Grand Rapids, MI: Eerdmans, 1966.

Hartog, Paul. *A Word for the World: Calvin on the Extent of the Atonement*. Schaumburg, IL: Regular Baptist Press, 2009.

Helm, Paul. *Calvin and the Calvinists*. Edinburgh: Banner of Truth, 1982.

———. "The Logic of Limited Atonement." *SBET* 3.2 (1985): 47–54.

Hodge, A. A. *The Atonement*. 1867. Reprint, London: Evangelical Press, 1974.

Kendall, R. T. *Calvin and English Calvinism to 1649*. Studies in Christian History and Thought. New York: Oxford University Press, 1979.

Kennard, D. W. "Petrine Redemption: Its Meaning and Extent." *JETS* 39 (1987): 399–405.

Kennedy, Kevin D. "Hermeneutical Discontinuity between Calvin and Later Calvinism." *SJT* 64.3 (2011): 299–312.

———. *Union with Christ and the Extent of the Atonement in Calvin*. New York: Peter Lang, 2002.

Knox, D. Broughton. "Some Aspects of the Atonement." In *The Doctrine of God*. Vol. 1 of *D. Broughton Knox: Selected Works*. Edited by Tony Payne. 3 vols., 260–66. Kingsford, NSW: Matthias Media, 2000.

Kuiper, R. B. *For Whom Did Christ Die?* Grand Rapids, MI: Eerdmans, 1959.

Lake, Donald M. "He Died for All: The Universal Dimensions of the Atonement." In *Grace Unlimited*. Edited by Clark H. Pinnock, 31–50. Minneapolis: Bethany Fellowship, 1975.

Leahy, Fredrick S. "Calvin and the Extent of the Atonement." *Reformed Theological Journal* 8 (1992): 54–64.

Letham, Robert. *The Work of Christ*. Leicester, UK: Inter-Varsity Press, 1993.

Lightner, Robert P. *The Death Christ Died: A Biblical Case for Unlimited Atonement.* 2nd ed. Grand Rapids, MI: Kregel, 1998 (1967).

Long, Gary D. *Definite Atonement.* Phillipsburg, NJ: P&R, 1977.

Macleod, Donald. "*Amyraldus redivivus*: A Review Article." *EQ* 81.3 (2009): 210–29.

Marshall, I. Howard. "Predestination in the New Testament." In *Grace Unlimited.* Edited by Clark H. Pinnock, 127–43. Minneapolis: Bethany Fellowship, 1975.

———. "Universal Grace and Atonement in the Pastoral Epistles." In *The Grace of God and the Will of Man.* Edited by Clark H. Pinnock, 51–69. (Minneapolis: Bethany, 1995).

Martin, Hugh. *The Atonement: In Its Relations to the Covenant, the Priesthood, the Intercession of Our Lord.* Edinburgh: James Gemmell, 1882.

McCormack, Bruce L. *For Us and Our Salvation: Incarnation and Atonement in the Reformed Tradition.* Studies in Reformed Theology and History. Princeton, NJ: Princeton Theological Seminary, 1993.

———. "So That He Might Be Merciful to All: Karl Barth and the Problem of Universalism." In *Karl Barth and American Evangelicalism.* Edited by Bruce L. McCormack and Clifford B. Anderson, 227–49. Grand Rapids, MI: Eerdmans, 2011.

Miethe, Terry L. "The Universal Power of the Atonement." In *The Grace of God and the Will of Man.* Edited by Clark H. Pinnock, 71–96. (Minneapolis: Bethany, 1995).

Moore, Jonathan D. *English Hypothetical Universalism: John Preston and the Softening of Reformed Theology.* Grand Rapids, MI: Eerdmans 2007.

———. "The Extent of the Atonement: English Hypothetical Universalism versus Particular Redemption." In *Drawn into Controversie: Reformed Theological Diversity and Debates within Seventeenth-Century British Puritanism.* Edited by Michael A. G. Haykin and Mark Jones, 124–61. Göttingen, Germany: Vandenhoeck & Ruprecht, 2011.

Morey, R. A. *Studies in the Atonement.* Southbridge, MA: Crowne, 1989.

Muller, Richard A. "Arminius and the Reformed Tradition." *WTJ* 70.1 (2008): 19–48.

———. "Calvin and the 'Calvinists': Assessing Continuities and Discontinuities between the Reformation and Orthodoxy." Parts I and II. In *CTJ* 30.2 (1995): 345–75 and 31.1 (1996): 125–60.

———. "Calvin on Christ's Satisfaction and Its Efficacy: The Issue of 'Limited Atonement.'" In his *Calvin and the Reformed Tradition: On the Work of Christ and the Order of Salvation,* 70–106. Grand Rapids, MI: Baker Academic, 2012.

———. "How Many Points?" *CTJ* 28 (1993): 425–33.

———. "A Tale of Two Wills? Calvin and Amyraut on Ezekiel 18:23." *CTJ* 44.2 (2009): 211–25.

———. "Toward the *Pactum Salutis*: Locating the Origins of a Concept." *Mid-American Journal of Theology* 18 (2007): 11–65.

———. "Was Calvin a Calvinist?" In his *Calvin and the Reformed Tradition: On the Work of Christ and the Order of Salvation*, 51–69. Grand Rapids, MI: Baker Academic, 2012.

Murray, John. *The Atonement*. Philadelphia: P&R, 1962.

———. "The Atonement." In *Collected Writings of John Murray. Volume 2: Lectures in Systematic Theology*, 142–50. Carlisle, PA/Edinburgh: Banner of Truth, 1977.

———. "The Atonement and the Free Offer of the Gospel." In *Collected Writings of John Murray. Volume 1: The Claims of Truth*, 59–85. Carlisle, PA/Edinburgh: Banner of Truth, 1976.

———. "The Free Offer of the Gospel." In *Collected Writings of John Murray. Volume 4: Studies in Theology*, 113–32. Carlisle, PA/Edinburgh: Banner of Truth, 1982.

———. *Redemption Accomplished and Applied*. Grand Rapids, MI: Eerdmans, 1955.

Nettles, Thomas J. *By His Grace and for His Glory: A Historical, Theological, and Practical Study of the Doctrines of Grace in Baptist Life*. Grand Rapids, MI: Baker, 1986.

Nicole, Roger R. "Covenant, Universal Call, and Definite Atonement." *JETS* 38 (1995): 405–11.

———. "The Doctrine of Definite Atonement in the Heidelberg Catechism." *Gordon Review* 3 (1964): 138–45.

———. "John Calvin's View of the Extent of the Atonement." *WTJ* 47 (1985): 197–225.

———. "Moyse Amyraut (1596–1664) and the Controversy on Universal Grace, First Phase (1634–1637)." PhD diss., Harvard University, 1966.

———. "The Nature of Redemption." In his *Standing Forth: Collected Writings of Roger Nicole*, 245–82. Ross-shire, UK: Mentor, 2002.

———. "Particular Redemption." In *Our Savior God: Man, Christ, and the Atonement*. Edited by James Montgomery Boice, 165–78. Grand Rapids, MI: Baker, 1980.

Owen, John. *Of the Death of Christ, the Price He Paid, and the Purchase He Made*. In *The Works of John Owen*. Edited by W. H. Goold, 24 vols., 10:430–79. Edinburgh: Johnstone & Hunter, 1850–1855. Reprint, Edinburgh: Banner of Truth, 1967.

———. *Salus Electorum, Sanguis Jesu: Or The Death of Death in the Death of Christ*. In *The Works of John Owen*. Edited by W. H. Goold, 24 vols., 10:139–428. Edinburgh: Johnstone & Hunter, 1850–1855. Reprint, Edinburgh: Banner of Truth, 1967.

Packer, J. I. "Introductory Essay." In John Owen, *The Death of Death in the Death of Christ*, 1–25. London: Banner of Truth, 1959.

———. "The Love of God: Universal and Particular." In *The Grace of God, the Bondage of the Will. Volume 2: Historical and Theological Perspectives on Calvinism.* Edited by Thomas R. Schreiner and Bruce A. Ware. 2 vols., 413–28. Grand Rapids, MI: Baker Books, 1995.

———. "What Did the Cross Achieve? The Logic of Penal Substitution." In *Celebrating the Saving Work of God. Collected Shorter Writings of J. I. Packer. Volume 1.* 85–123. Carlisle, UK: Paternoster, 2000.

Peterson, Robert A. "To Reconcile to Himself All Things: Colossians 1:20." *Presbyterion* 36.1 (Spring 2010): 37–46.

Rainbow, Jonathan H. *The Will of God and the Cross: An Historical and Theological Study of John Calvin's Doctrine of Limited Redemption.* Allison Park, PA: Pickwick, 1990.

Rouwendal, P. L. "Calvin's Forgotten Classical Position on the Extent of the Atonement: About Sufficiency, Efficiency, and Anachronism." *WTJ* 70.2 (2008): 317–35.

Scaer, David P. "The Nature and Extent of the Atonement in Lutheran Theology." *Bulletin of the Evangelical Theological Society* 10.4 (1967): 179–87.

Schrock, David. "Jesus Saves, No Asterisk Needed: Why Preaching the Gospel as Good News Requires Definite Atonement." In *Whomever He Wills: A Surprising Display of Sovereign Mercy.* Edited by Matthew M. Barrett and Thomas J. Nettles, 77–119. Cape Coral, FL: Founders Press, 2012.

Shultz, Gary L., Jr. "A Biblical and Theological Defense of a Multi-Intentional View of the Extent of the Atonement." PhD diss., The Southern Baptist Theological Seminary, 2008.

———. "God's Purpose in the Atonement for the Nonelect." *BSac* 165 (April–June 2008): 145–63.

———. "The Reconciliation of All Things in Christ." *BSac* 167 (October–December, 2010): 442–59.

———. "Why a Genuine Universal Gospel Call Requires an Atonement That Paid for the Sins of All People." *EQ* 82.2 (2010): 111–23.

Smeaton, George M. *The Apostles' Doctrine of the Atonement; with Historical Appendix.* 1870. Reprint, Grand Rapids, MI: Zondervan, 1957.

Stewart, Kenneth J. "The Five Points of Calvinism: Retrospect and Prospect." *SBET* 26.2 (2008): 187–203.

Strehle, Stephen. "The Extent of the Atonement and the Synod of Dort." *WTJ* 51.1 (1989): 1–23.

Swanson, Andrew. "The Love of God for the Non-Elect." *Reformation Today* 51 (May–June 1976): 2–13.

Thomas, G. Michael. *The Extent of the Atonement: A Dilemma for Reformed Theology from Calvin to the Consensus.* Carlisle, UK: Paternoster, 1997.

Torrance, J. B. "The Incarnation and 'Limited Atonement.'" *EQ* 55 (1983): 82–94.

Torrance, T. F. *The Atonement: The Person and Work of Christ.* Downers Grove, IL: IVP Academic, 2009.

Trueman, Carl R. "Calvin and Calvinism." In *The Cambridge Companion to John Calvin.* Edited by Donald K. McKim, 225–44. Cambridge: Cambridge University Press, 2004.

Ussher, James. *The Judgement of the Late Arch-Bishop of Armagh, and Primate of Ireland.* London: John Crook, 1658.

Vail, William H. "The Five Points of Calvinism Historically Considered." *The New Outlook* 104 (1913): 394.

Van Buren, Paul M. *Christ in Our Place: The Substitutionary Character of Calvin's Doctrine of Reconciliation.* Edinburgh: Oliver Boyd, 1957.

Vanhoozer, Kevin J. "Atonement." In *Mapping Modern Theology: A Thematic and Historical Introduction.* Edited by Kelly M. Kapic and Bruce L. McCormack, 175–202. Grand Rapids, MI: Baker Academic, 2012.

Vos, Geerhardus. "The Biblical Doctrine of the Love of God." In *Redemptive History and Biblical Interpretation: The Shorter Writings of Geerhardus Vos.* Edited by Richard B. Gaffin, 425–57. Phillipsburg, NJ: P&R, 1980.

Warfield, B. B. "Are They Few That Be Saved?" In *Biblical and Theological Studies.* Edited by Samuel G. Craig, 334–50. Reprint, Philadelphia: P&R, 1952.

———. *The Plan of Salvation.* Grand Rapids, MI: Eerdmans, 1935.

Webster, John B. "'It Was the Will of the Lord to Bruise Him': Soteriology and the Doctrine of God." In *God of Salvation: Soteriology in Theological Perspective.* Edited by Ivor J. Davidson and Murray A. Rae, 15–34. Farnham, Surrey, UK: Ashgate, 2011.

Williams, Garry J. "A Critical Exposition of Hugo Grotius' Doctrine of the Atonement in *De satisfactione Christi.*" Doctoral thesis, University of Oxford, 1999.

———. "Karl Barth and the Doctrine of the Atonement." In *Engaging with Barth: Contemporary Evangelical Critiques.* Edited by David Gibson and Daniel Strange, 249–70. Nottingham, UK: Apollos, 2008.

Williams, Jarvis J. *For Whom Did Christ Die? The Extent of the Atonement in Paul's Theology.* Milton Keynes, UK: Paternoster, 2012.

Index of Biblical References

Index of Names

Index of Subjects

Nature of the Atonement, The (J. McLeod
Campbell), 36, 611, 612; context of, 612–13
Nestorianism, 468, 498
Niceno-Constantinopolitan Creed (381), 201
Nicomachean Ethics (Aristotle), 500
"Not All the Blood of Beasts" (Watts), 260

Of the Death of Christ (Owen), 210, 211, 218,
219; on the prisoner analogy, 211–12
Of the Death of Christ, and of Justification
(Owen), 221n63
*Of the True Intent and Extent of Christs Death,
and Satisfaction upon the Cross* (Ussher),
462
"offspring of Abraham" 396
oikonomia (Greek: economy), 334
"On the controversy among the French Divines
of the Reformed Church, concerning the gracious and saving will of God towards sinful
men" (Davenant), 424
*On the Holy Trinity and of the Godhead of
the Holy Spirit to Eustathius* (Gregory of
Nyssa), 442
On Predestination (Gottschalk of Orbais), 79
On the Trinity (Hilary of Poitiers), 69
order of decrees, 436 (table)

pactum salutis. See covenant of redemption
pāgaʿ (Hebrew [Hiphil]: to cause to meet upon,
interpose), 254n11, 262n26, 265n30
pantes (Greek: all), 296–97, 354, 354n67; in 2
Corinthians 5, 301–5, 351, 376, 379, 382
particular atonement. *See* definite atonement
pas (Greek: all), 296–97, 296n22, 300, 300n42
Passover, 231–33, 232nn15–16, 255, 525–26
pastoral ministry: central task of, 635; as a
theological calling, 608
Paul, atonement theology of, 289–91;
"doctrinal loci" texts, 290, 331, 333, 372,
372n122; important qualifications in the
interpretation of the terms "all" and "world,"
323–27; particularist texts (Christ died for
"me," for the "church," for "his people,"
for "us"), 290, 291–95, 331, 333; "perishing" texts (false teachers "obtained with
his own blood"; destroying the brother "for
whom Christ died"), 290, 321–23, 331,
333, 372; the practical relationship between
Paul's atonement theology and evangelism,
328; universalistic language of, 328–30;
universalistic texts (Christ died for "many,"

for "all," for the "world"), 290, 295–321,
331, 333, 372
Paul, soteriology of, 332–34, 372–73; on the
saving work of God as circumscribed by
God's electing grace, 333, 335, 346–49, 372;
on the saving work of God as doxological,
333, 336, 371, 372; on the saving work of
God as encompassed by union with Christ,
333, 335–36, 349–60, 372; on the saving work of God as indivisible, 333, 335,
336–45, 372; on the saving work of God as
Trinitarian, 333, 336, 360–71, 360n95, 372
Pelagianism, 130
Pentateuch, the, examples of corporate cleansing or atonement in: Aaron's censer, 240;
atonement for unintentional sins, 239–40;
the bronze snake, 241; Phinehas's action at
Baal Peor, 242–43; the water of cleansing,
240–41, 240n40
Pentateuch, the, individual atonement in,
243–44
Pious Annotations, 159
poenitentia (Latin: penal infliction), 620n52
polloi (Greek: many), 276n25, 296, 296n21,
351, 379, 395
preaching, 637–38; aim of, 635, 637; on definite atonement, 665–67; necessity of, 598;
and the use of indiscriminate, universalistic
language, 108–18, 118, 119
predestination, 335, 346–48, 372, 638, 639;
cosmic predestination, 407; double predestination, 77–80; in Reformed orthodoxy,
406–9; soteriological predestination, 407;
soteriological setting for, 416. *See also*
divine foreknowledge; election
presuppositionalism, 585–86
priesthood: and covenants, 521–23; and typology, 519–21. *See also* Jesus, as the High
Priest of the new covenant; priesthood, in
the Old Testament
priesthood, in the Old Testament: the high
priest as the representative of the covenant
people before God, 524; the high priest as
the representative mediator of the covenant
people before God, 524–28, 524–25n20; the
Levites as representatives of the firstborn
Israelites, 524n19; selection of the high
priest from among the people, 523–24. *See
also* Day of Atonement
"proof texting," 99–100, 119
providence, and the future, 102–4, 118